Encyclopedia of American Business History and Biography

Banking and Finance, 1913-1989

Edited by

Larry Schweikart
University of Dayton

A Bruccoli Clark Layman Book

 **Facts On File**
New York · Oxford

Facts On File, Inc.   Facts On File Limited
460 Park Avenue South   Collins Street
New York NY 10016   Oxford OX4 1XJ
USA   United Kingdom

Library of Congress Cataloging-in-Publication Data

Banking and finance, 1913-1989 / edited by Larry E. Schweikart.
   p.   cm. — (Encyclopedia of American business history and biography)
   "A Bruccoli Clark Layman book."
   Includes bibliographical references.
   ISBN 0-8160-2194-5
   1. Banks and banking––United States—History—20th century.
2. Finance—United States—History—20th century.   3. Bankers-
-United States—Biography.   I. Schweikart, Larry.   II. Series.
HG2481.B325   1990
332.1'0973'0904—dc20   89-29596

British and Australian CIP data available on request from Facts On File.

Facts On File books are available at special discounts when purchased in bulk quantities for businesses, associations, institutions or sales promotions. Please call our Special Sales Department in New York at 212-683-2244 (dial 800\322-8755 except in NY, AK or HI).

Printed in the United States of America

10 9 8 7 6 5 4 3 2 1

This book is printed on acid-free paper.

*To John F. Kunkel
a valued friend*

Encyclopedia of American Business History

Contents

Foreword

The Encyclopedia of American Business History and Biography chronicles America's material civilization through its business figures and businesses. It is a record of American aspirations—of success and of failure. It is a history of the impact of business on American life. The volumes have been planned to serve a cross section of users: students, teachers, scholars, researchers, and government and corporate officials. Individual volumes or groups of volumes cover a particular industry during a defined period; thus each *EABH&B* volume is freestanding, providing a history expressed through biographies and buttressed by a wide range of supporting entries. In many cases a single volume is sufficient to treat an industry, but certain industries require two or more volumes. When completed, the *EABH&B* will provide the fullest available history of American enterprise.

The editorial direction of *EABH&B* is provided by the general editor and the editorial board. The general editor appoints volume editors whose duties are to prepare, in consultation with the editorial board, the list of entries for each volume, to assign the entries to contributors, to vet the submitted entries, and to work in close cooperation with the Bruccoli Clark Layman editorial staff so as to maintain consistency of treatment. All entries are written by specialists in their fields, not by staff writers. Volume editors are experienced scholars.

The publishers and editors of *EABH&B* are convinced that timing is crucial to notable careers. Therefore, the biographical entries in each volume of the series place businesses and their leaders in the social, political, and economic contexts of their times. Supplementary background rubrics on companies, inventions, legal decisions, marketing innovations, and other topics are integrated with the biographical entries in alphabetical order.

The general editor and the volume editors determine the space to be allotted to biographies as major entries, standard entries, and short entries.

Major entries, reserved for giants of business and industry (e.g., Henry Ford, J. P. Morgan, Andrew Carnegie, James J. Hill), require approximately 10,000 words. Standard biographical entries are in the range of 3,500-5,000 words. Short entries are reserved for lesser figures who require inclusion and for significant figures about whom little information is available. When appropriate, the biographical entries stress their subjects' roles in shaping the national experience, showing how their activities influenced the way Americans lived. Unattractive or damaging aspects of character and conduct are not suppressed. All biographical entries conform to a basic format.

A significant part of each volume is devoted to concise background entries supporting and elucidating the biographies. These nonbiographical entries provide basic information about the industry or field covered in the volume. Histories of companies are necessarily brief and limited to key events. To establish a context for all entries, each volume includes an overview of the industry treated. These historical introductions are normally written by the volume editors.

We have set for ourselves large tasks and important goals. We aspire to provide a body of work that will help reduce the imbalance in the writing of American history, the study of which too often slights business. Our hope is also to stimulate interest in business leaders, enterprises, and industries that have not been given the scholarly attention they deserve. By setting high standards for accuracy, balanced treatment, original research, and clear writing, we have tried to ensure that these works will commend themselves to those who seek a full account of the development of America.

—William H. Becker
General Editor

Acknowledgments

This book was produced by Bruccoli Clark Layman, Inc. James W. Hipp is series editor for the *Encyclopedia of American Business History and Biography*. Michael D. Senecal was the in-house editor.

Production coordinator is James W. Hipp. Systems manager is Charles D. Brower. Photography editor is Susan Brennan Todd. Permissions editor is Jean W. Ross. Layout and graphics supervisor is Penney L. Haughton. Copyediting supervisor is Bill Adams. Typesetting supervisor is Kathleen M. Flanagan. Information systems analyst is George F. Dodge. Charles Lee Egleston is editorial associate. The production staff includes Rowena Betts, Anne L. M. Bowman, Polly Brown, Teresa Chaney, Patricia Coate, Marie Creed, Allison Deal, Holly L. Deal, Sarah A. Estes, Mary L. Goodwin, Cynthia Hallman, Susan C. Heath, David Marshall James, Kathy S. Merlette, Laura Garren Moore, John Myrick, Gina D. Peterman, Cathy J. Reese, Edward Scott, Laurrè Sinckler, Maxine K. Smalls, John C. Stone III, and Betsy L. Weinberg.

Walter W. Ross and Parris Boyd did the library research with the assistance of the following librarians at the Thomas Cooper Library of the University of South Carolina: Gwen Baxter, Daniel Boice, Faye Chadwell, Cathy Eckman, Gary Geer, Cathie Gottlieb, David L. Haggard, Jens Holley, Jackie Kinder, Thomas Marcil, Marcia Martin, Laurie Preston, Jean Rhyne, Carol Tobin, and Virginia Weathers.

As in the first *Banking and Finance* volume, I take great pleasure in expressing my thanks to several individuals who made this project possible. Lynne Pierson Doti, Charles Calomiris, Ed Perkins, and Ben Klebaner all read the introductory essay and offered comments. Whether or not I took their advice was a different matter, and therefore the errors that remain in the introduction are mine and mine alone. Some of the contributors again performed heroic duties, taking over where other authors could not finish or accepting entries that we both knew would be particularly difficult. Among those who aided this volume with their special efforts, I would like to thank Lynne Pierson Doti, Jim Smallwood, and Richard Timberlake. At the University of Dayton, Linda McKinley singlehandedly organized and orchestrated the assignments, contracts, and typing, and Jenny Wharton provided timely typing assistance. Once again, my wife, Dee, granted me release time from my domestic duties to write. Unlike in the first volume, which went to press some eight months ago, I cannot wax romantic about the distractions of my now two-year-old son, Adam. He has figured out how to turn on the computer, how to prompt up the commands, but not yet (thank God) how to erase. When Job was tested, the devil must have used two-year-olds. I anxiously await Adam's third birthday.

−L. S.

Introduction

The story of American banking in the twentieth century is the tale of growing financial democracy. American consumers at the end of the 1980s enjoyed more financial options and greater investment opportunities and found fewer restrictions based on race, religion, sex, or circumstances of birth than any other people in history. Except within a narrow range, state regulations and, on an international level, even national laws no longer could dictate investment or borrowing opportunities. Technology had linked Japanese lenders with car buyers in Kentucky and had tied the Wilshire Exchange to stock traders in remote Middle Eastern deserts. Once haughty Wall Street firms found themselves outflanked at every turn by open-collared financial entrepreneurs who could perceive value in a silicon chip or appreciate the promise of a small telephone company. Bond buyers no longer had to wait for Zeus-like pronouncements from the large brokers or banks on the worth of a security; instead, beginning in the early 1980s, average investors of every stripe participated in the longest peacetime economic boom in American history.

Yet the century had not started with nearly so much freedom in the world of finance. Only after much haggling and political turmoil—after placing major restrictions on banking activities, then removing them, and after separating banking from a host of other services, then reuniting them—only then had the banking and financial system of the late 1980s arrived at a relatively unfettered state. Banks in the 1980s found themselves freer than at any other time since the antebellum period, and they even had some freedoms denied to their predecessors. For the first time since A. P. Giannini tested the regulatory waters in the 1920s, the banking system verged on true interstate branch banking. One depression—but only one—came and went, and neither the collapse of the entire savings and loan (S&L) industry in the 1980s nor the 1987 stock market crash triggered bank runs similar to those in the nineteenth century. Deposit insurance, a dramatic addition of the twentieth century, paradoxically explained both the restoration of public confidence in banks in the 1930s and the incredible collapse of the S&Ls in the 1980s. Most important, perhaps, the arrival of foreign competition ended the American dominance of the world's capital markets, a position the nation had held since the end of World War I.

The creation of the Federal Reserve System in 1913, which could be considered the inauguration of the "Third Banking Era" in U.S. history, assured many Americans that the problems of the nineteenth century truly lay in the past. That century had seen the formation and rapid growth of a nationwide banking system under the regulation—or lack thereof—of two different authorities, the federal government and the states. The nineteenth century had also witnessed the end of private banks of issue and the development of a uniform national currency. But the main complaints about banking, such as the criticism that it did not provide an "elastic" money supply (one able to expand and contract to suit the seasonal needs of farmers and merchants), and the concern that banks were equipped inadequately to respond to infrequent but all-too-regular panics, still caused many to fear and curse the "Money Power." Passage of the Federal Reserve Act promised to address both those major criticisms and end once and for all the panics that seemed to appear every two decades.

The "First Banking Era" (1781-1863) witnessed the foundation of commercial banking in the United States. During that time the state governments chartered and regulated the banks. Banks issued their own money (notes), with the business of note issue constituting a far more important part of the banks' activities than taking deposits. Banks kept a reserve of gold and silver coin, called specie, to "redeem" their notes for customers who presented them. Operating on the well-established theory that only a small percentage of customers would seek to redeem their notes at any given time (assuming, of course, the absence of any suddenly damaging public information about the bank), a bank could keep as little as $5 in silver or gold for every $95 in notes it issued. That ratio, known as a reserve ratio, varied from bank to bank and with economic circumstances. In panic periods banks tried to bump their reserve ratios as high as possible to restore confidence.

Even the highest reserve ratios proved insufficient to assuage the concerns of the public in truly difficult times. Usually when one or two banks stopped paying specie, lest they run out completely (an action called "suspending" or "suspension"), the runs shifted to the more solid banks, forcing them into suspension as well. Legislatures that had granted the charters did not look favorably on suspension and often threatened the bankers with a host of retaliatory measures. Once the panic ended, however, the lawmakers' hearts softened and all was forgiven: or, at least, usually all was forgiven. Meanwhile, bankers themselves searched for ways to eliminate or ameliorate runs and panics, and they pioneered a variety of voluntary and mandatory frameworks from state to state, including the Suffolk System, the New York Safety Fund, clearinghouse associations, and free banking. All those efforts, while meeting with different degrees of success, represented attempts to substitute for a system of statewide branch banking that actually proved remarkably resilient and safe.

The period before the Civil War witnessed other interesting developments, almost all of them related to the state regulations under which the banks operated. Several states, for example, adopted free banking, under which a group could open a bank by placing on deposit with the secretary of state certain securities equal to the amount of notes issued. Should the bank fail to redeem its notes, the secretary of state could sell the securities and reimburse the noteholders. For several decades historians had accepted uncritically stories that free banking led to "wildcat banking," wherein free banks would establish branches in the frontier areas and issue far more notes there than it had specie to back. Or, as another criticism went, the wildcat bankers would collect specie while issuing notes, then abruptly take off, leaving it up to the state to reimburse the noteholders. When the state sold the bonds, it discovered their market value was less than par. Thus, the unscrupulous banker had managed to escape with a considerable amount of specie. Modern historians remain divided over the benefits of free banking but generally agree that it was far more effective than

previously thought, and, as Hugh Rockoff advises, "The system was sufficiently successful to make a careful consideration of its major characteristics worthwhile."

Other states prior to the Civil War prohibited banking altogether, or allowed only a state-owned-and-operated bank to conduct business. Some southern states cultivated impressive branch banking systems. But by and large the major form of banking in the United States on the eve of the war remained unit banking. Because of the number of unit banks in the northern states, one or two New England states had as many banks as the entire South and Far West put together. Unit bankers certainly wanted nothing to do with branching, and their cohesion on that subject made them an invincible adversary almost until 1927, when Congress passed the McFadden Act to reduce restrictions on branching.

One other important banking form existed in the antebellum period: the national bank in the form of the First and Second Banks of the United States (BUS). The First BUS (1791-1811), Alexander Hamilton's brainchild, provided unity and stability for many aspects of the government's early financial affairs. Designed as a tool to provide the government with loans and to support the value of government bonds, the first BUS soon generated animosity from those who feared that foreign stockholders, particularly the English, dominated the bank. Congress let the bank's 20-year charter expire in 1811, but the instability of the nation's finances following the War of 1812 led lawmakers to charter the Second BUS in 1816 with another 20-year charter. While the Second BUS did a credible job of handling its financial obligations to the nation, it fell victim to a personal political struggle between its president, Nicholas Biddle, and the president of the United States, Andrew Jackson. In brief, Jackson won. He vetoed an 1832 effort to recharter the bank four years early, made the veto stick, and then a year later pulled all of the federal government's deposits out of the bank, effectively killing it. With the demise of the Second BUS, no nationally chartered bank existed until 1863.

The Civil War ushered in the "Second Banking Era." It brought extensive changes to the banking system when the Republican-dominated Congress passed the National Banking Act in 1863, establishing a system in which the U.S. government routinely issued hundreds of bank charters. While neither the First nor Second BUS had faced any competition at the national level, national banks under the new system had no such monopoly privileges. They did, however, possess the privilege to issue notes. The National Currency Acts, also passed during the Civil War, taxed private bank notes out of existence. From 1863 onward, then, the nation operated with a unique "dual banking system," whereby both the federal government and the states could charter, regulate, and examine banks. That system has proved troublesome even to the present because bankers bent on unscrupulous activities could switch from national to state charters with regularity to foster confusion among the examiners and to escape unwanted regulation. More important, the national banks faced restrictions their state-chartered cousins did not, and as a result states soon made their own chartering processes easier in order to encourage more banking facilities than would have existed under the confining national banking laws. A competition of sorts developed between the two systems.

Richard Timberlake has pointed out that the National Banking and Currency Acts of 1863 and 1864, envisioned as a way to "create an institutional demand for the burgeoning volume of government securities" that the Union needed to finance the war, took on a life of their own. No southern congressmen remained to restrain the Republicans, and the government certainly had no intention of establishing a system that would benefit the South after the war. The system featured reserve cities and country banks in outlying communities. Banks in reserve cities had to hold greenbacks or specie equal to 25 percent of their deposits (in earlier years, equal to 25 percent of their national bank notes issued), while the country banks only had to hold 15 percent in reserve. The system achieved many of the goals of the numerous mechanisms that states had earlier experimented with, such as the clearinghouses, including uniform note appearance and a steady market for the notes to trade at par value. National banks had to hold government bonds as collateral for the notes, thus ensuring brisk bond sales.

Until Congress prohibited note issue by state-chartered banks, when it placed a 10 percent tax on nonnational bank note issues, state banks had little interest in joining the national system. The era of competitive money in the United States came to an end, much to the disadvantage of the South and West. At first national bank charters surpassed state

charters, which had dropped from 1,562 in 1860 to just 325 in 1870. But by 1890, nonnational banks had increased to 4,717, while national banks numbered only 3,484. By the end of the century nonnational banks outnumbered national banks almost three to one. In 1910 more than 18,000 nonnational banks existed along with more than 7,000 national banks.

Without private note issue, Treasury "greenbacks" printed during the Civil War and national bank notes provided the nation's entire currency. Congress had endowed the greenbacks, technically a fiat currency, with legal tender status, which generated considerable controversy. In a series of cases called the "Legal Tender Cases" the Supreme Court ultimately upheld the legal tender status of greenbacks. Although national bank notes technically did not also have legal tender status, most citizens assumed that when the greenbacks received the Supreme Court's blessing, so did national bank notes. In fact, however, greenbacks represented a promise on the part of the federal government to pay gold at a future date (ultimately 1879), while national bank notes were immediately convertible into gold. Since greenbacks were convertible into national bank notes, though, realistically greenbacks had the indirect backing of gold.

Not only did the nation's banks grow unevenly because of the national/nonnational problem, but sections of the country also found themselves nearly devoid of banking services. When the Union victory sealed the doom of the Confederate financial system, virtually all southern banks collapsed due to their support of the rebel government through bond purchases for war loans. Southern banks also lost huge amounts following the sudden change in the status of slaves, who served as collateral for many loans. Furthermore, the banks in the South that managed to survive the war found themselves at a severe disadvantage when it came to acquiring national bank charters. The Republican Congress certainly did not intend to grant charters to loyal Confederates, nor did Congress leap to confer charters on the freedmen. Moreover, the original National Banking Act limited total note allocation to $300 million, with Treasury Secretary Salmon P. Chase authorized to make half the allocation on the basis of population (therefore mostly in the North), and half on the basis of "existing banking capital, resources, and business" (again the North). As Timberlake points out, national banks in the South comprised only 4 percent of all national banks and received only 3 percent of national bank notes in 1870. However, national banks had to trade off profits in note issue against other profitable activities, such as lending. State banks made loans through deposit creation rather than note issue, and over the last quarter of the century deposits bypassed bank notes to become by far the largest component of the money stock. The inelasticity of note issue, caused by penalties associated with issuing national bank notes, prevented the national bank system from dominating the nation as many had predicted.

The Civil War also bred a new type of financier, the investment banker. Jay Cooke and J. P. Morgan typified the investment banker, who arranged the large capital backing for projects such as railroads, and later utilities and steel, through the underwriting of bond sales. Quite frequently that entailed forming a syndicate of several banking concerns, so large were the demands of the railroads in particular. Morgan's preeminence as an investment banker in the postbellum period grew when he guided his company and many of the railroads through the Panic of 1873. His firm provided a source of stability during the so-called Populist era as well. In addition to overseeing the reorganization of dozens of railroad lines under new structures of managerial hierarchies, Morgan assembled funding for a vast spectrum of business.

Morgan's personal role in American finance grew to the point that he almost overshadowed the government itself. During the Panic of 1893 he formed a syndicate with August Belmont & Company and the Rothschilds of London to deliver 3.5 million ounces of gold to the U.S. Treasury. Morgan almost singlehandedly prevented the nation from defaulting on its promise to exchange gold for its dollars. In 1907 another panic shook Wall Street and then spilled over to the rest of the country. Again Morgan stepped in to use his enormous wealth and influence to try to quell the money markets, lending $25 million at 10 percent interest to the New York banks (outlending the U.S. Treasury, which only deposited $19 million in those banks during the crisis). Despite Morgan's efforts, everyone recognized—especially Morgan himself—that no individual banker or even small group of banks could act as the lender of last resort any longer. The economy had simply grown too large.

Bankers had for some time studied options for reforming the American banking system that emphasized correcting the elasticity problem and reducing the dominance of the New York banks. Many bankers thought that the solution to the former problem required a central bank, but few could conceive of any type of central bank that did not give New York greater power still. The Panic of 1907 convinced almost everyone that they had to arrive at a plan soon. Congress passed as a stopgap measure the Aldrich-Vreeland Act of 1908, which authorized the secretary of the Treasury to issue emergency currency during future panics. More important, however, it created the National Monetary Commission to make recommendations to prevent future crises. That committee, too, concluded that the nation needed a central bank.

While the commission, led by Senator Nelson A. Aldrich of Rhode Island, studied the banking problem, its members met privately with many important bankers, including Frank A. Vanderlip, Paul M. Warburg, Morgan, and others. Due to deliver their report to Congress in 1911, the members had not worked out the details of their plan by late 1910. In November of that year, in a setting that some have labeled "conspiratorial," Vanderlip, Warburg, Aldrich, Henry Davison (a Morgan partner), and A. Piatt Andrew, a Harvard professor, met in secrecy on Jekyll Island, Georgia, to outline the scope, functions, management, and organization of a new financial system. But the plan, known as the Aldrich Plan, floated listlessly in Congress before it finally met defeat, largely because it promised increased centralization of power—in the government's hands, according to some, or, according to others, in the hands of the bankers.

Supporters of the Aldrich Plan quickly mounted a new offensive, with Representative Carter Glass of Virginia, chairman of the House Committee on Banking and Currency, introducing a bill to create the Federal Reserve System. Both houses of Congress quickly passed the bill, and Woodrow Wilson signed it on December 28, 1913, inaugurating the "Third Banking Era." The new system featured 12 Reserve Banks scattered throughout the country (Missouri had two!) in cities such as Minneapolis and Atlanta. It appeared that indeed New York's power had been diluted. Each Federal Reserve Bank was a corporation, which the member banks in its district "owned" through each bank's required investment of 6 percent of its paid-up capital and surplus. The member banks chose most of the Reserve Bank directors, but although those directors chose the officers, the member banks themselves did not directly vote for anyone on the central governing committee, the Federal Reserve Board. Instead, the president of the United States appointed five members of the board, and both the comptroller of the currency and the secretary of the Treasury served as ex-officio members.

The Federal Reserve System sought to contain bank runs through the rapid transfer or availability of funds from the reserve banks. There was no system of national deposit insurance, although several states, patterning themselves on the Oklahoma Deposit Guaranty Law, either had already enacted or soon passed similar laws, which proved unmitigated disasters. In a prelude to the Savings and Loan debacle of the 1980s, the collapse of the deposit insurance funds in the 1920s clearly demonstrated the dangers of making all depositors share risks with unscrupulous or ill-managed financial institutions.

Not only did the Federal Reserve System lack a deposit insurance feature, but in theory the board was to act as an apolitical body. The presence of the comptroller and the treasurer, as well as five appointees of the president, made that goal illusory. As Eugene White has shown, the New York Federal Reserve Bank quickly took the lead and dominated the policies, if not the affairs, of the system. Not only had the hope of creating an apolitical system been thwarted, but the notion that the Federal Reserve would reduce the dominance of New York by giving all banks access to loans previously available (or so critics assumed) to the "Money Trust" also went astray as smaller banks retained their state charters and became the correspondents of national banks in large cities.

The Reserve Banks exercised their powers to "regulate" the money supply through the discounting to member banks (that is, the short-term borrowing of Reserve funds). To expand credit the Reserve Banks lowered the discount rate, to contract credit they increased it. Reserve Banks discounted according to the "real bills" doctrine, a theory that held that money should represent self-liquidating, short-term loans backed by "real," tangible goods. In actuality, however, lending officers at the Reserve Banks determined the "eligibility" of bills offered for discount, thus effectively separating money from any "real" standard. That marked the system's solution to the problem of elasticity. As Timberlake ex-

plains, the authors of the Federal Reserve Act so thoroughly expected the gold standard to continue to operate that they built into the act few links between the Reserve system and gold. Consequently, discretionary discounting, increasingly based on government interventions, soon, as Timberlake put it, "divorced the results of decision-making from those who had a self-interest in maintaining the integrity of the system."

Just as the nation's most renowned and talented financial minds had contributed in one degree or another to the long process that resulted in the creation of the Federal Reserve System, so did the new system have exceptional individuals in key positions. Warburg, once called the "ablest banking mind" of a group that included Vanderlip, Henry P. Davison, and Charles Norton, played a critical role in persuading other eminent bankers to participate in the system. His efforts, along with Davison's, prevailed in persuading Benjamin Strong to serve as governor of the Federal Reserve Bank of New York. Warburg himself served as a member of the Federal Reserve Board for two years and as vice-governor for two more years and then presided over the Federal Advisory Council for two years.

Staffed with talented individuals—but often factionalized—the Federal Reserve immersed itself in managing the country's banking system. While it partially regulated the national banks that were members, it had only an indirect effect on the nonmembers, which included not only state banks but a host of other financial institutions that conducted banking business. In 1910 Congress had passed an act creating the Postal Savings System, a method by which small savers who harbored suspicions about banks could earn interest on their money. Under the act, selected post offices could received deposits and pay 2 percent interest on the accounts. Although never the serious competition to banks that bankers always complained they were, the Postal Savings Banks did offer an alternative that grew extremely attractive during the Great Depression. They faded with the coming of the Federal Deposit Insurance Corporation in 1933, and Congress abolished the program in 1967. Proposals to revive the system stirred the air in the late 1980s, however.

Another alternative banking program, coincidentally also started in 1910, the Morris Plan Banks, targeted consumer lending to working people "of good character." Whereas Postal Savings

Banks satisfied the deposit needs of low-income Americans, the Morris Plan Banks made small loans to people who had collateral or who could produce a cosigner. However, because Arthur Morris, who founded the banks, thought the risk was high, the banks charged a steep rate of interest, which usually violated normal state usury laws. They survived by having borrowers purchase with their loan an "investment certificate" upon which they technically made payments rather than directly repaying the loan itself. Morris franchised his banks, helping to start new institutions and holding a 25 percent share in them. By 1920 more than 100 Morris Plan Banks operated, although many of them gradually converted to normal commercial banking. By 1940 only 87 remained.

A third type of alternative to the commercial bank was savings and loans, building and loans (B&Ls), and mutual savings banks. Those institutions operated on the same basic principles as banks, with some exceptions. In general, they all sought to finance home construction. Mutual savings banks and mutual savings associations had the name "mutual" in their titles because the members owned the assets and all profits went into their deposit accounts. The first mutual savings bank, the Philadelphia Savings Fund Society, appeared in 1816, and by 1964 that form of bank accounted for approximately 20 percent of all savings deposits in the nation, despite the fact that many states restricted them. By 1988 only 18 states allowed mutual banking. Because they did not operate for the profit of stockholders, but for the benefit of the members who oversaw the business of the bank, mutual associations proved conservative and effective in their primary mission of financing housing construction. B&Ls, later generally superceded by S&Ls, used depositors' funds to finance long-term mortgages. In 1932, under the Federal Home Loan Bank Act, S&Ls were prohibited from making commercial loans. Somewhat in compensation, in 1966 they were permitted to pay a slightly higher interest rate to attract depositors. Since that interest rate consistently still fell well below the return on long-term mortgages, no one expected that aspect of the S&L business would prove a fatal character flaw in the 1970s and 1980s.

Whereas banking had a variety of faces in the early twentieth century, most people identified finance with New York and with one place in particular, the New York Stock Exchange (NYSE), the "largest and most important market for stock an bond trading in the United States," according to NYSE archivist Steven Wheeler. A group of traders founded the NYSE in 1817 as the New York Stock and Exchange Board, and by the end of the century 1,300 securities traded there. Trading on the exchange exceeded 3 million shares in 1901 and continued to grow through World War I, when the Liberty and Victory Loan drives convinced Americans of average means that they, too, could participate in the dealings on Wall Street. Innovative securities salesmen such as Charles E. Merrill, who went on to found Merrill, Lynch & Company, pioneered the practice of mass marketing securities. Possessed of an unmatched concern for customer education in securities, Merrill and the customers who took his advice escaped the worst consequences of the 1929 stock market crash. By the 1940s, Merrill had "democratized" securities sales and ownership to such an extent that he broke the strangle hold that a few firms and elitist attitudes had perpetuated for decades.

Because of Wall Street and the presence of the New York Federal Reserve Bank, led by its exceptional president, Benjamin Strong, in the twentieth century New York City grew more dominant than ever in American financial affairs. It replaced London as the "world's banker" during World War I, and, despite the fact that the Fed had only started to understand the tools at its command, the New York Federal Reserve Bank played an increasingly important role in determining money policy, not only for the United States but also for the European powers. The war left Germany saddled with onerous reparations payments and had eroded some of the economic base of Britain and France. With the new U.S. ascendance in world finance, New York bankers naturally found themselves wrapped up in international negotiations to determine a feasible and peaceful payment of German reparations. That, in turn, required direct involvement—foreign critics called it "meddling"—in the finances of Germany, and, to a lesser extent, Britain and France. Benjamin Strong, Seymour Parker Gilbert, Charles G. Dawes, and Owen D. Young emerged as key representatives of the American financial community during those efforts. After two years of acrimony, French occupation of the Ruhr, and general deadlock on the subject of German reparations, U.S. Secretary of State Charles Evans Hughes requested that Owen Young, a General Electric executive, serve on an expert committee chaired by Chicago banker Dawes to review the payments and work out a plan of payments that the Germans indeed could meet. The resulting Dawes Plan drastically revised the London Schedule of Payments, with its "stratospheric" level of payments, as Stephen Schucker has termed them, and required Germany to pay reparations at a low level beginning in 1924, with the amounts rising as the German economy revived.

Dawes's plan not only called for sacrifices from the Allies, who stood to receive less reparations money, at least initially, and from the American bankers, who had to divert money from more profitable domestic lending to supply the loans, but also from the Weimar Republic, which had to reorganize its banking and money system. The Germans immediately requested another commission, one headed by Young, but, as Schucker observed, "For five years . . . the Dawes Plan kept a semblance of harmony and promoted economic reconstruction in Europe." Some, such as Gilbert, the Reparations Agent called by William C. McNeil "the most powerful individual in international financial affairs" of the period, wanted to force the Germans into fiscal discipline, but he lacked the authority to control such areas as German government spending. He therefore tried to dry up the supply of American loans in New York, an attempt that in general failed. The Young Plan of 1929 revised the Dawes Plan by reducing the reparations, giving Germany all responsibility for raising her own foreign currency, and removing the Reparations Agent. Contrary to some critics' assertions that Wall Street used the reparations issue to further its own end, American involvement in German affairs clearly showed just the opposite by the time it ended: American capitalists wanted a stable German government with a sound currency and low deficits. Indeed, had the Americans had their way, Germany might have avoided its economic collapse of the early 1930s, and the corresponding rise of Nazism.

While the problems of international finance occupied some New York financiers, more mundane difficulties confronted their country counterparts, especially in the West and Midwest. First, a robbery wave swept banks in Iowa, the Dakotas, Texas, Oklahoma, and other Plains states in the 1920s. Made possible by the ease of escape provided by the automobile and the relative isolation of country towns, the surge of criminal activity posed a real crisis to small rural banks. Insurance rates in Minnesota, Iowa, and the Dakotas soared. Bankers such as George Wingfield placed shotguns behind the tellers' cages in all the banks in his chain. Arizona bankers experimented (unsuccessfully) with teller-operated tear gas guns. Gradually, however, unified action by bankers in establishing bank robber identification posters, combined with beefed-up alarm and security systems and augmented by increased police involvement and the use of police radios, brought the eruption of felonies under control. From roughly 1940 to 1960, bank robberies subsided.

As harmful as robberies were to the Midwestern banks, a far worse calamity struck in the early 1920s when farm prices fell as a result of the end of World War I. A recession struck the agricultural areas, made worse in spots by an invasion of the boll weevil, which destroyed the southern cotton crop, and horrible cold weather destroyed many of the cattle herds in Montana and Wyoming in mid decade. For farm-state banks, which faced severe difficulties as farmers defaulted on their loans, certain regulations added early in the century provided the knockout blow. Several states, beginning in 1908 with Oklahoma, established systems of mandatory or voluntary deposit insurance for all state-chartered banks. The Dakotas, Kansas, Mississippi, Nebraska, Texas, Washington, and others followed. As Charles Calomiris has shown, the mandatory laws especially, but generally all deposit guaranty laws, created an environment that fostered "moral hazard" by rewarding excessive risk taking on the part of the insured banks (as opposed to the actions of the national banks, which were not a part of any of the state deposit insurance systems). The Kansas bank guaranty fund, which had only $1.1 million in it, faced debts of $6.7 million from member banks by 1926. Oklahoma repealed its law in 1923 with outstanding obligations to depositors totaling more than $7 million. Not only did the poorly designed deposit guaranty laws prove disastrous, they delayed real reform by making legislators think, at least at first, that deposit insurance could take the place of branch banking as a safety device. The combined effect of the farm crisis and poor regulations wiped out Midwestern and farm-state banks in a "massacre," as one western bank historian called it. While still some others failed, by the time the Great Depression set in, most farm states had already seen the ranks of their financial institutions drastically thinned, with only the most solvent remaining. National totals reflected the farm state fallout: from 1919 to 1929, the number of banks dropped by more than 4,200.

The West provided the setting for another major development in banking in the Roaring Twenties, the incredible growth of branch banking in California, highlighted by the dramatic rise of the Bank of Italy (Bank of America after 1928). A. P. Giannini, a former agricultural wholesaler, founded his bank in 1904 to serve the Italian immigrants in the North Beach community of San Francisco. The bank spread its branches throughout the state, occasionally meeting competition from Joseph Sartori and his own powerful branch system, the Farmers and Merchants Bank. Giannini, truly a visionary, not only planned to create a statewide empire but also intended to find a way to cross state lines. He had purchased controlling interest in a New York bank, and sought a means to start uniting the New York and California financial networks. He ran up against state laws prohibiting branch banking. In the mid 1920s Giannini planned a two-stage approach to circumvent state antibranching laws. First, he would bring his banks into the national system, provided that Congress changed the national banking laws to permit branching, which the National Banking Act prohibited (according to successive comptrollers' interpretations). Second, he would press for changes to allow interstate banking.

Congress obliged Giannini in the quest of his first goal by passing the McFadden Act in 1927, ostensibly to staunch the flow of national banks converting to state bank charters, but specifically to bring the Bank of America's 300 branches into the national system. The relative disadvantages of national charters compared to state charters had grown so substantial that the national system experienced mass defections in the period from 1910 to 1925. Antibranching provisions had inspired some of the defections, as did the low capitalization requirements of the state banks.

While McFadden could be viewed as a victory for branching proponents, it also could be seen in a reverse light. It still maintained important restrictions against intrastate branching, and Congress never enacted laws that would allow Giannini (or anyone else) to branch across state lines. Several factors accounted for the failure. The unit bank lobby remained a strong voice in the halls of Congress,

and it adamantly refused to entertain any talk of branching for any reason. The chaos in the banking system engendered by the Great Depression led legislators to seek short-term solutions (such as deposit insurance) rather than the option of statewide or even nationwide branching. Certainly during the early years of the Depression, Giannini's own bank could hardly consider expansion: the Bank of America had received several Reconstruction Finance Corporation loans, and during the "Bank Holiday," evidence now suggests, probably was insolvent, kept open only because its closing would destroy what little confidence remained in the banking system. Finally, circumstances combined to place Henry Morgenthau, Jr., and later Marriner S. Eccles in critical positions in Franklin D. Roosevelt's New Deal presidential administration. Neither man wanted to see Giannini's empire grow. Eccles, eventually chairman of the Federal Reserve Board, who had great influence beyond the positions he held, had favored branch banking in theory, yet opposed it in practice when it came to the Bank of America.

The federal government's failure to authorize nationwide branch banking not only contributed to the collapse of the country unit banks in the 1920s, but made it difficult for some of the large chains to survive at the end of the decade. For example, the Wingfield chain in Nevada, which held more than 60 percent of all bank assets in the state, might have been saved by interstate branching, and available evidence suggests it could. Certainly the fact is worth noting that many states either repealed their antibranching legislation or modified it to permit limited branching during the Depression, an admission that they had been too restrictive in the past.

If the failure to authorize nationwide branching in the 1920s was a nonevent, no one can say the same for the merger wave and the rise of the trust companies during the same period. As elsewhere in American industry, a merger movement swept the nation's banking enterprises, leading to the formation of truly large institutions. That gave them unprecedented flexibility with investments, and helped foster the rise of trusts and holding companies. Trusts originated as nonbank enterprises, but as state laws relaxed they took on the activities of commercial banks. Trusts had less clearing activity and were less involved in correspondent banking, so they represented important competitors to banks. Trusts also often faced less regulation than national banks and thus further eroded the national bank system. Holding companies allowed banks to circumvent restrictions by placing the bank and its affiliate both under another entity, or by creating a separate entity to hold the affiliate. The Bank of Italy proved especially adept at merging banks into holding companies in the 1920s.

As larger banks developed through the merger movement, they had far more funds to invest, and the securities of the growth industries at the time—electricity, automobiles, radio—offered new fields in which the banks could put their money. Moreover, the fact that most of the large banks were in major urban areas led to a centralized securities market, explaining the close link between the mergers, the rise of trusts, and the stock market boom of the 1920s. Specifically to handle the new securities trading, banks already had started to form "security affilitates" in the early part of the century. But as the new heavy industries took off, banks expanded their underwriting activities in the bond market.

The banks' activities in the securities market have provided a target for critics. Some have argued that unsound banking practices contributed to the famous crash of October 29, 1929. They have pointed out, for example, that margin buying (buying on credit with the security standing as collateral for the balance of the loan) constituted an abuse when brokers, requiring as little as 15 percent down, extended a steadily increasing number of margin loans. Lending by brokers indeed rose from $1 billion at the beginning of the decade to $9 billion by the time of the Crash. Another abuse they have pointed to, "pyramiding," wherein holding companies owned companies that owned still other companies, proved troublesome when perfectly solvent lower-lever companies were acquired by bigger companies involved in fraud, with the best example being the utilities companies owned by Samuel Insull. The critics have argued that especially since they often occurred in combination, those practices made for a dangerous situation, one exacerbated by the continual upward climb of the stock market in the Roaring Twenties. To the critics, that posed a problem because people of ordinary means started to "play" the market as speculators, not investors. Legendary stories circulated about shoeshine boys who gave stock tips to financiers such as J. P. Morgan, Jr., and salaried salesmen could turn a $100 investment into a considerable fortune—*if* they got out of the market in time.

In the context of the banks' relationship with the securities markets, no banker received more condemnation for his activities in the bond market than National City Bank's (later Citibank) Charles E. Mitchell, the "Scapegoat of the Crash." Mitchell had succeeded the prominent Frank A. Vanderlip in the presidency of National City Bank and had pushed the bank into trust activities and securities operations. Dragged before the Senate Banking Committee's counsel, Ferdinand Pecora, Mitchell represented to all Americans the "banksters" who had manipulated the nation's financial system and brought about disaster.

Several points bear consideration when confronting traditional stories proffered by critics of the banks' role in the 1920s "boom and bust" market. First, Eugene White has shown that the banks that formed securities affiliates suffered far less during the crash and the Depression than the banks lacking such affiliates. Second, the boom in securities, particularly those related to utilities and automobiles, consisted of a natural rise in the stocks of rapidly growing new industries, not speculation. Finally, the rapid combination of the newly merged large banks, the sudden growth of trust companies, the appearance of many new, consumer-oriented industries, and marvelous advances in communication and transportation made a boom market almost inevitable. The rise of the securities markets with the new communications links helped thousands of smaller banks and millions of individual Americans directly invest in rapidly rising stocks and bonds. So somewhat naturally, banks' involvement with securities increased in the 1920s. Banking, in fact, focused the wealth of the nation at the right time on the right industries.

Critics had other bones to pick with the banks, though. In addition to the perceived ill effects of banking on the bond market through the securities affiliates and, more directly, through individuals such as Mitchell, banking suffered even greater criticisms (some of it post hoc by scholars) for its contributions to the state of the economy, both before and during the Depression. First, critics maintained that to funnel money into the bonds of large firms and foreign governments, the commercial banks had departed from the real bills doctrine. Second, critics charged that the tax cuts inspired by Secretary of the Treasury Andrew Mellon spawned a disastrous maldistribution of wealth, putting too much wealth in the hands of the upper income brackets. Finally, many scholars argue that the Federal Reserve never slowed the economy in the mid 1920s, then, when it had gotten out of control, failed to reflate the money supply.

Certainly banks made fewer commercial loans in the 1920s because of falling demand. That represented a fundamental transition in business, wherein most companies went to the securities markets for capital rather than to commercial banks. Insofar as banks loaned on anything except tangible goods, they departed from the real bills doctrine, and indeed many banks had long abandoned that view (if they ever subscribed to it at all). So in that regard, the critics were right. However, "big business" represented the fastest-growing sector of the economy, and the flow of money to that sector represented a natural development. Moreover, claims that the 1920s constituted nothing more than a "speculative bubble" are ludicrous. During the 1920s auto sales equaled those of the 1950s, radios in home use during an eight-year period increased from 60,000 to 7.5 million, total assets of the largest 200 companies doubled during the decade, industrial capital equipment increased by $100 million, and output per worker rose 43 percent from 1919 to 1929. Perhaps the most important new industry, electricity, profited from a 330 percent increase from 1899 to 1929, spurring the burst in utilities stocks. So the growth was real, and it transferred money from commercial and agricultural purposes to the industrial sector, creating a massive surge in the economy.

Closely linked to the first criticism was the second, namely that the Mellon tax cuts created a maldistribution of wealth, which led to underconsumption. That view, later espoused by historian Arthur Schlesinger, Jr., and economists such as John Maynard Keynes and Peter Temin, found contemporary champions in William Trufant Foster and Wadill Catchings, authors of *Road to Plenty* (1928). The criticism held that the tax cuts enacted along the lines requested by Secretary Mellon embodied no more than tax breaks for the wealthy in hopes that the benefits would "trickle down" to the working groups. (Hence critics frequently referred to any type of tax cut in the top brackets as "trickle down" economics.) When Mellon took office in 1921, he found tax rates for the top bracket in excess of 70 percent and that those high rates, in David Beito's words, "created a veritable cottage industry among the wealthy to find tax shelters." By

lowering the top brackets from 71 percent and 51 percent to 58 and 50 percent respectively, Mellon got exactly what he wanted: the wealthy put their money into productive, and *taxable*, enterprises rather than shelters. The percentage of total taxes paid by the wealthy rose by *15 percent* after the institution of the Mellon program until 1929, while the percentage paid by the taxpayers earning less than $5,000 fell by more than 12 percent. Mellon's cuts generated new tax revenues that reduced the federal debt by one-third and allowed the nation to lend $10 billion abroad. The reinvigorated business sector, unburdened by oppressive taxes, took off.

Most social historians appreciate the effect of the automobile on American culture and daily life, but few understand its impact on banking and credit. The automobile opened up credit markets for rural Americans who previously relied on the local bank. Suddenly—almost overnight—rural customers could shop for loans the way they shopped for shoes. Bankers no longer had captive markets. Moreover, automobiles engendered road construction, spawned a true consumer petroleum industry, and ultimately, much to consumers' dismay, required an entire support network of spare parts and mechanics. No amount of institutional change or shifts in the money supply affected lending in rural America as did the arrival of the automobile, and banks readily took advantage of it. In another respect, however, many banks missed a shining opportunity to jump into automobile financing, and institutions such as General Motors Credit Acceptance Corporation filled the void. When the opportunity came again, in the post-World War II era, banks did not make the same mistake.

Despite the freedom and competition introduced by the automobile, rural America still suffered from the worldwide overproduction of farm goods that drove agricultural prices through the floor. Banks soon reached the limit of their lending abilities, and, as a result, farmers turned their outrage toward the Federal Reserve, which they accused of contracting credit to agricultural areas. South Carolina banker David R. Coker, who served on the Richmond Fed, claimed that the Reserve Banks were "as helpful as possible" and extended as much credit as they could to agricultural areas. In fact, throughout much of the 1920s the money supply expanded (leading to charges by modern historians that Mellon had followed a program of deliberate inflation for political purposes, or that the "system" had funneled all of the money into the securities markets).

Aside from the tax cuts that generally enhanced business and which returned tax revenues *into* the Treasury at a phenomenal rate, Mellon had little to do with the expansionary monetary program followed by the Federal Reserve in the 1920s. Instead, Benjamin Strong, governor of the Federal Reserve Bank of New York, assumed the key position in formulating those policies. At the end of World War I the Fed maintained rediscount rates well below the market rates for funds "to facilitate Treasury funding of the floating debt plus unwillingness to see a decline in the price of government bonds," in the words of Anna J. Schwartz. Taken with the effect of the Mellon cuts, which consistently reduced government debt, the two positions were mutually complementary, and the Fed could have maintained the price of the bonds while the tax rates fell.

In fact, Strong came to dominate the system, despite the creation in 1923 of the Open Market Investment Committee, which superseded the Federal Reserve Banks's committee of governors in the execution of joint purchases and sales. Strong feared that a political body such as the Open Market Committee would control open market policy, but Strong himself pioneered the practices of using Federal Reserve operations to counter business slowdowns and to try to achieve price stability. He spent much of his time—when he was not too ill—in Europe trying to coordinate central bank operations. Thus, not only did the Federal Reserve have to try to balance swings in the domestic economy, but it had to do so with an eye toward reaction in the European capital markets. From that perspective, Strong remained convinced that the easing of monetary policy in 1927, which many critics blamed for fueling the stock speculation and crash, served the twofold purpose of overcoming a slowing domestic economy and strengthening European exchange rates.

Strong died in late 1928, leaving many to speculate that had he lived his talents could have prevented the more serious effects of the Great Depression. Yet the Board of Governors often refused to heed his advice, and it is improbable that, even as talented as he was, Strong could have balanced effectively all of the international and domestic political and economic developments of the late 1920s. As for policy, the Fed did attempt to reduce stock prices before the crash, to no avail. Perhaps, indeed, Strong's death, which occurred before the crash, proved timely by preserving his image untarnished.

While the stock market crash did not cause the Great Depression per se, it certainly signaled its onset. As to the exact causes of that massive recession, for the past 15 years two major theories have persisted, and thus authors even in this volume will vary in their analysis of the causes. One school of thought, the monetarist view, interprets the causes of the Depression as originating fundamentally in the monetary system. Led by Milton Friedman and Anna J. Schwartz in their *Monetary History of the United States* (1963), the monetarists maintain that the Federal Reserve made a series of critical errors in dealing with domestic and international money and banking policies from 1930 to 1933. First, they argue, the Fed failed to supply enough money to balance the inflows of gold from England. During a one-year period of contraction, they note, "the System . . . let its discounts decline by nearly twice its net purchases of government securities, and . . . let its total credit outstanding decline by almost three times the increase in gold stock." An easing of credit would have created a new round of American business expansion. As Friedman and Schwartz conclude, "the United States did not follow gold-standard rules. We did not permit the inflow of gold to expand the U.S. money stock. . . . Our money stock moved perversely, going down as the gold stock went up."

Second, the Fed failed in one of is primary missions to rescue failing banks, particularly the Bank of United States, which the New York superintendent of banks, Joseph A. Broderick, closed on December 11, 1930. The bank's liabilities to 440,000 depositors and other creditors totaled more than $188 million. Some New York City Clearing House banks attempted to forge a merger agreement, which proved unsuccessful when the different groups could not settle conflicting ownership demands. As a "lender of last resort," Friedman and Schwartz argue, the Fed had the responsibility to prevent runs from developing because it had undermined the previous method of normal constriction when people sought to convert deposits into currency. The "existence of the Reserve System prevented concerted restriction . . . by reducing the concern of stronger banks, which had in the past typically taken the lead in such a concerted move, since the System provided them with an escape mechanism in the form of discounting." However, by its existence, the Federal Reserve supported the general assumption that concerted action was unnecessary. The collapse of the Bank of United States, the largest failure in the nation to that point and the first large bank to fail in New York, set off a wave of failures that, in Friedman and Schwartz's view, differed markedly from the steady stream of Western and Midwestern small-bank failures of the 1920s. Taken together, the Fed's errors caused the money supply to fall by one-third from 1929 to 1933, with commercial deposits falling by more than 42 percent ($18 billion), and that contraction turned a cyclical recession into the Great Depression.

An earlier interpretation, made famous by Keynes in his *General Theory of Employment, Interest and Money* (1936), advanced a thesis generally called the "consumption" (or underconsumption) thesis. According to Keynes, the maldistribution of wealth and the securities boom had fostered "sumps of wealth," in which Say's Law (supply creates its own demand) no longer applies. To Keynes, the economy could reach a state of equilibrium at a level well below full employment. It could languish there virtually forever without some jolt to the system, such as a "pump priming" provided by government deficit spending. But while Keynes received most of the credit for the underconsumption thesis, the two Depression-era writers Foster and Catchings actually beat him to the punch, influencing such policymakers as Marriner Eccles with their book *The Road to Plenty*. Most recent supporters of the Keynesian interpretation include Peter Temin, whose rejoinder to Friedman and Schwartz, *Did Monetary Factors Cause the Great Depression?* (1976), obviously answered in the negative. Underconsumption caused the Depression, or at least contributed to it greatly, Temin argues.

More recent scholarship has refined and combined the two views. Neither school can claim complete victory, recent scholars argue: it depends on the particular years in question. Christie Roemer has provided powerful support for the Temin/Keynes interpretation by showing that a drastic fall in consumption did occur in 1929. By and large the Friedman and Schwartz interpretation explains much of what happened from 1930 to 1933, although new research by David Wheelock suggests that the Fed's policy did not change at all from its practices in the early 1920s. Instead, what might have been an appropriate policy in 1920 turned out to be disastrous in 1930. And an exchange in *Explo-*

rations in Economic History calls into question the effects that Friedman and Schwartz attributed to the collapse of the Bank of United States. However, the primary thesis of the monetarists—that the Fed made the Depression much worse—seems accepted by the majority of scholars. If the Friedman and Schwartz thesis is correct, then the commercial private banking system played little, if any, role in causing the Great Depression. The link between the banking system, especially the large banks, and the policymakers on the Fed and in government remains a topic of debate, however. Recent evidence by Thomas Ferguson and Gerald Epstein contends that the large banks pressured the Fed into maintaining its deflationary stance out of concern for their profits. Although some revision of the responsibility of bankers for the boom during the 1920s and the Great Depression may still occur, it is doubtful that anyone will revive the criticisms that "banksters" had engineered the Depression for their own ends.

The havoc wreaked by the Depression on banks was staggering, and it intensified the horrific carnage suffered by banks in states such as South Carolina and Wyoming in the 1920s. The number of banks in the United States that suspended from August 1931 to January 1932 exceeded 1,800, with more than $1.4 billion in deposits. Many states, searching for any expedient to revive their banks, enacted some form of branch banking law. Some states limited branches to the city of the home office or to one branch in addition to the home office. Those reforms came too late to have much of an effect in the Depression era, but they proved useful in the postwar period, when many states needed additional banking facilities to serve new populations brought in by the war. Meanwhile, the remaining banks dramatically contracted their lending, with bank loans falling by more than 44 percent from 1930 to 1932.

Responding to the crisis, in early 1932 President Herbert Hoover signed a bill creating the Reconstruction Finance Corporation (RFC), a federal lending agency to extend loans to banks not eligible for rediscount at the Federal Reserve Banks. Implied in Hoover's creation of the RFC was the premise that the Fed had not provided enough loans. In its first 11 months the RFC authorized almost $1 billion in loans, assisting 4,000 troubled banks. The RFC loans carried a relatively high rate of interest (6 percent), were for an intermediate period (6 months), and permitted the RFC to publish the names of the borrowing institutions, meaning that depositors who saw the name of their bank appear in the paper suddenly had good reason to withdraw their deposits, thus exacerbating the banks' desperate situation. Ultimately the RFC actually loaned $80 million to banks and paid depositors of 2,421 closed banks another $900 million. Under the chairmanship of Jesse Jones, who disparaged Hoover's voluntarism, the RFC took on an entirely new attitude. Under Jones the RFC increased its powers and its lending to banks and railroads, mostly through purchases of preferred stock. With the added capital, however, came increased control by the government, including, as Jones insisted, the placement of an RFC director on the board of the troubled business.

Hoover's administration also presided over the creation of the Federal Home Loan Banks, which provided short-term credit to member mortgage lending institutions, such as S&Ls, B&Ls, and thrifts. Hoover appointed a Federal Home Loan Bank Board (FHLBB) dominated by industry representatives and not subject to the regulatory provisions of the Federal Reserve System.

Individual states had already started to invoke "business holidays" to stem bank runs, with Nevada declaring the first such holiday on Halloween 1932. The public, increasingly edgy about the safety of their deposits, started to acquire gold in growing amounts. In a nine-day period ending March 3, 1933, the 12 Federal Reserve Banks lost $425 million in gold. New York ordered a bank holiday on March 4, followed by Illinois. The country's financial system bordered on chaos: at the time President Franklin D. Roosevelt took the oath of office, virtually all states had enacted state holidays or had restricted withdrawals. The Emergency Banking Act allowed Roosevelt to order a national bank holiday on March 6, 1933, in which he declared a moratorium on bank withdrawals. A few days later the holiday was extended to a total of nine days. Some states, thinking such an order unconstitutional but sympathetic to Roosevelt's goal, declared their own holidays for state-chartered banks. Roosevelt ordered the appropriate agencies, the Federal Reserve and the Office of the Comptroller of the Currency, to examine the national banks. Solvent banks were allowed to reopen on a schedule announced by Roosevelt. Of the 17,796 banks in operation in January 1933, 11,848 reopened after the holiday. Others were reorganized or liquidated. Advising the nation

during one of his "fireside chats" that the banking system had returned to solvency and safety, Roosevelt's actions ended the panic.

Or so it seemed. Recent scholarship agrees that an action Roosevelt took may have ended the bank runs and brought in bank deposits, but that action was not the bank holiday or the subsequent enaction of deposit insurance legislation. Instead, Roosevelt had taken the nation off the gold standard. Nations that remained on the gold standard experienced continued recession; those that abandoned it quickly revived. New evidence suggests that leaving the gold standard solidified the banking system and caused deposits to return.

Following Roosevelt's holiday Congress enacted sweeping banking and securities legislation, beginning with the Glass-Steagall Act (also called the Banking Act of 1933). Glass-Steagall prohibited the member banks of the Fed from affiliating with firms that issued or underwrote securities, obviously a reaction to the perceived dangers of combining commercial and investment banking the stock market crash seemingly exposed. More important in the short run, Glass-Steagall established deposit insurance through the Federal Deposit Insurance Corporation (FDIC). The FDIC insured the first $2,500 in a deposit account, with that limit raised to $5,000 in 1934 (and ultimately raised to $100,000 in 1980), which effectively insured more than 98 percent of all deposits in insured commercial banks. Insured banks paid a premium for the insurance based on their assets. In addition to the insurance itself, the FDIC furnished liquidation services that far exceeded previous processes, and, as part of its responsibilities, carried out its own examinations of member banks.

At the time, neither the insurance nor the addition of another examining body seemed a bad idea. However, both factors reappeared to trouble the banking system in the 1970s and 1980s. Part of the problem originated in yet another innocuous act, the National Housing Act of 1934, which established the Federal Savings and Loan Insurance Corporation (FSLIC), an agency that insured the deposits of federal- and state-chartered S&Ls. But the FSLIC was not a part of the FDIC, nor was it independent of Congress (as was the FDIC). An earlier act, the Home Owners' Loan Act of 1933, created federal chartering of S&Ls to allow them to compete with commercial banks. The government restricted S&Ls to mortgage lending, and beginning in 1966 allowed them to pay slightly higher interest rates on deposits than commercial banks.

Capital infusions of the commercial banks followed, encouraged by the elimination of double liability on newly issued stock. The RFC contributed to rebuilding capital structure by investing heavily in preferred stock; by 1935 it held one-third of the banking system's capital. Combined with the new insurance provisions, the expanded capital should have convinced the public that most banks were safe. Yet Congress still had concerns about the gold stock, as evidenced by the passage of the Gold Reserve Act, which nullified all of the gold obligations of the country's debt contracts. (In 1933 the president had already called in all of the monetary gold in the country from banks and individuals and deposited it in the U.S. Treasury.)

Congress also passed the Banking Act of 1935 to expand the powers of the Federal Open Market Committee (FOMC), which it reconstituted. The Federal Reserve Bank presidents had previously held the positions of primacy in the FOMC, but from 1935 on the seven members of the Board of Governors dominated. Under the new act all Fed banks had to follow as a unit whatever volume of open market operations the FOMC determined. That effectively split the Fed into two institutions: the Board of Governors and the 12 Fed Banks and branches. And, as Richard Timberlake noted, "The Board's powers to set discount rates and to alter reserve requirements became inconsequential once the FOMC had the virtually unlimited power to monetize U.S. government securities." In a significant departure from previous doctrine, the act also removed the gold standard as the fundamental base of the nation's money system: instead, government securities assumed the role. Again, Timberlake observed that "the gold standard was henceforth no more than a public relations symbol used to encourage the popular notion that gold 'backed' common money." While the act also removed the comptroller of the currency and the secretary of the Treasury from the Federal Reserve Board, the system remained sensitive to political concerns. Just how sensitive remains a matter of heated debate. Critics of monetarist and libertarian persuasions have maintained that the Fed conveniently inflated when incumbent presidents came up for reelection. Critics who approached the Fed from "populist" viewpoints, such as William Grieder in his *Secrets of the Temple* (1987), contended that the Fed held the

credit reins too tight because of its allegiance to the business interests of the country. While the monetarists and libertarians correctly pointed out that the inflationary 1970s coincided with a growing politicization of all aspects of daily life, they have minimized the difficulties of getting the board to agree on policy—a point made only too well by Grieder. They have also overlooked the fact that while the Fed may have monetized the debt for years, Congress incurred it through its votes. As for the populist critics, they forget that the Fed does not exist to propagate social justice through redistribution of wealth, even though they perhaps think that should be its purpose. Fed policies roughly coincided with the interests of business because, with the exception of the inflationary 1970s, usually business shared with the bankers the hope for a sound monetary program devoid of sharp price fluctuations, a quality that even Communist nations have come to appreciate.

Another New Deal act, the Securities and Exchange Act (1934), established the Securities and Exchange Commission (SEC), which, in Steven Wheeler's words, "ushered in comprehensive federal regulation of the securities industry." The SEC established rules to ensure correct statements in stock and bond issues and provided means for investigating infractions. Those regulatory powers generally went untested until the 1980s, when the creation of new financial instruments and the speed of securities transactions led the SEC into a broad investigation of the Drexel firm and the Chicago Board of Exchange, wherein several individuals were accused of "insider trading." When combined with the Glass-Steagall separation of investment banking from commercial banking, the Securities and Exchange Act completed a radical New Deal reorganization of the stock exchanges, commercial banking, and the nation's monetary system. It represented the most drastic overhaul of the system since the Civil War legislation.

Other peripheral New Deal legislation affected banking and credit. The Farm Credit Administration provided loans to farmers, refinancing one-fifth of the nation's farm mortgage debt in its first 18 months of existence. Farmers also benefited from the Commodity Credit Corporation, which stabilized the price of farm commodities and restored credit to farmers. Another lending agency, the Home Owners Loan Corporation, refinanced $3 billion worth of home mortgage loans between 1933 and 1936. Even Social Security, while not a lending program, affected banking by providing automatically (and by mandate) funds for retirement that individuals previously would have had to save in banks voluntarily.

Despite all of the acts and legislation, agencies, and boards, by the mid 1930s the banking system had not recovered to anywhere near where it stood in 1929. Although the FDIC and FSLIC reassured many depositors, deposit accounts rose only a fraction above the precrash levels after an entire decade of saving. In 1929 deposits totaled just more than $58 billion, but by 1939 they had only risen to $64 billion (a rate of less than 1 percent per year). Put in that light, even when allowing for deflation, to argue that deposit insurance brought all the money out from under the mattresses is difficult.

Perhaps the best indicator of business confidence—bank lending—showed that a pessimistic outlook still held American banks in thrall. RFC Chairman Jesse Jones, a Houston banker, repeatedly chided the commercial banks for their unwillingness to lend. Yet the RFC shared some of the blame. Although in theory the RFC loaned only to those businesses unable to obtain credit elsewhere, bankers knew that the RFC represented a competitor that restricted the markets of private lenders. Despite interest rates that had reached extremely low levels, banks insisted they could not find suitable borrowers. New Mexico bankers, responding to a survey sent out in 1934, reported that they had made all the loans they could, but many officers could agree with the Nebraska banker who in 1932 glumly noted that his bank had not made a loan in six months.

In reality, however, many banks found themselves caught between the new demands of safety imposed by the Fed and the FDIC (not to mention public expectations) and the credit requirements of a country whose businesses had lost much of their collateral. Examiners had become more oppressive than ever, at least to the bankers, who contended that the criticisms by regulators had caused them to curtail lending. Paul Walter, president of New Mexico's oldest bank, First National Bank of Santa Fe, reported that banks in his area were "more cautious in making advances because of criticism by bank examiners." A Montana newspaper put it more bluntly, stating that when the federal examiner left, the entire town celebrated: "If he never returns it will be plenty soon enough for a number of

people . . . who had the pleasure of doing business with this bird." Faced with the examiners' criticisms on the one hand and a collapsed economy on the other, with few real opportunities on the horizon, bankers rightfully sat on the sidelines. By 1939 banks' share of net corporate debt had fallen to only 14 percent, while a decade earlier it had exceeded 23 percent.

The Depression only reaffirmed what many people had suspected in the 1920s, namely that bank examination processes remained uneven and often unpredictable across the nation. In many states regulating agencies filled their examination and management spots with former bankers who had just "come on the market"—because their bank had failed. Political favoritism, not bank expertise, characterized appointments to positions such as bank supervisor in many states. Even experienced federal examiners who traveled a circuit often knew nothing of local conditions or customers. When they did their schedule usually allowed them no more than a single day in a national bank. The important change during the Depression was, however, that where previously people did not necessarily assume that anyone else was overseeing banks and therefore watching their money, after the creation of the FDIC and the FSLIC, most Americans entrusted the oversight and regulation functions almost entirely to federal and state authorities. By World War II consumers, borrowers, depositors, and other outsiders played a smaller role in the routine assessment of banks than at any time in the past.

Whether the nation would have extracted itself from the Great Depression without a major war continues to generate debate. Definitely, however, the war accomplished many of the goals that the New Deal had sought in vain. First, Americans willingly taxed themselves far beyond measures they previously found acceptable. Second, businesses threw themselves into a frenzy of production, unmatched in history. Third, with wartime restrictions on consumption of luxury goods, a demand for consumer goods started building in 1941 and lasted four years. Finally, bankers spearheaded wartime borrowing—$211 billion from July 1940 to July 1945—and purchased much of the debt themselves. Although Secretary of the Treasury Henry Morgenthau wanted small investors, represented by private citizens, to hold most of that debt, and although nonbank investors originally purchased 60 percent of the new debt issued during the war, banks soon acquired those bonds through repurchases.

With bonds added to the banks' reserves, a new monetary expansion ensued. That expansion greatly concerned Marriner Eccles, chairman of the Federal Reserve Board, who during the early years of the Depression had lobbied so hard for inflation. By the end of the war Eccles feared the inflation he saw building, and he opposed bond sales to banks. Eccles also advocated higher postwar taxes. Policy differences between Eccles and Harry Truman led the president to appoint another chairman in 1948, although Eccles remained on the board as assistant chairman. Perhaps Eccles's most important contribution was the one he did not make: in his capacity as chairman he could have advocated and brought to fruition interstate branch banking, an arrangement he favored in principle. Unfortunately for the nation, the reality of branch banking meant that Giannini's Bank of America would in all likelihood take best advantage of such a law, and Eccles, whether out of personal disagreements with Giannini or because the size of Bank of America concerned him, never pushed the issue.

The end of Word War II also brought renewed interest in a new world monetary order, some set of institutions that might prevent another worldwide depression that many thought had contributed to the rise of Hitler and Mussolini. In July 1944 more than 40 nations sent representatives to Bretton Woods in New Hampshire to formulate a new economic system. American policymakers, including Morgenthau and his assistant Harry Dexter White, knew that the postwar world would require the United States to play an active role as the world's banker and that the new system demanded the elimination of the types of international trade constraints that had exacerbated the Depression. John Maynard Keynes, who attended as the representative of the British Treasury, often disagreed with the American contingent, arguing for a "powerful World Bank that would issue its own currency" and which would have "real power over economic decisions for member nations." Members rejected Keynes's proposals in favor of those offered by White.

White's Bretton Woods proposals resulted in the appearance of two international organizations: the International Monetary Fund (IMF), which helped nations solve short-term international debt problems while they expanded their money supply to avoid recessions, and the International Bank for Reconstruction and Development, usually called the World Bank, which the planners initially intended to funnel money into the devastated European economies. Morgenthau took pride in the fact that, as he put it, he and Roosevelt "moved the money capital from London to Wall Street to Washington, and [the American big bankers] hated us for it." Wall Street did oppose elements of the IMF and the World Bank that threatened to relax or remove the discipline of the marketplace from borrowing countries, and for that reason bankers testified against the IMF proposal when it came up before Congress. In truth, however, the new economic order did not have a chance for success without the complete acquiescence of the large American banks. Once Congress approved the Bretton Woods agreements, American bankers simply remade the system to ensure that loans to borrowing nations included some imposed "reasonable" requirements, such as balanced budgets. Even with the ultimate support of the American banking community, the World Bank's operations came too late to extend aid to the devastated nations of Europe, for which it was intended. Eventually, it turned its attention to the less developed countries, or, as they were frequently called, the Third World.

Bretton Woods also established an open, multilateral trading system, the General Agreement on Tariffs and Trade (GATT), negotiated in four rounds from 1947 to 1956. In order to win British approval of the agreement, the United States had to lend Britain $3.75 billion. (The British expressed their anger that the United States had not loaned them $5 billion, as they had expected!) GATT represented a major step toward international free trade, breaking the cycle of economic nationalism and protectionism that had contributed to the Great Depression and the hostility that precipitated World War II.

Under the new international monetary system, which went into effect in 1946, central banks had to hold gold or a currency convertible into gold as a reserve for their own national currency. As the only currency convertible into gold, the U.S. dollar effectively served as the "world's currency." The United States held gold; other countries held dollars. That meant that U.S. dollars acted as both a reserve currency and an exchange currency. Ironically, in the United States dollars were no longer convertible into gold. No specific mechanism built into the Bretton Woods agreements required the United States to maintain the value of the dollar. The Americans agreed to convert dollars to gold at $35 an ounce, but any U.S. Administration could renege that pledge. Moreover, the British quickly discovered they could not support a convertible currency. They and the other European nations soon abandoned the Bretton Woods rules and did not allow their currencies to trade on the open market until 1957. At that time, as William McNeil shows, "the leadership of the IMF had come to fear that excessive government deficits were driving the world toward dangerous levels of inflation," and thus the IMF, an organization "set up to permit deficit spending," jawboned governments that wished to borrow from it into balancing their budgets. Of course, American financiers never intended to allow deficit financing without some quid pro quo from the borrower government, and the situation at the end of the 1950s merely confirmed their position. Meanwhile, persistent American deficits meant that the United States itself could no longer maintain the value of the dollar against gold, and in 1971 President Richard Nixon essentially terminated the Bretton Woods system by ending the convertibility of dollars into gold.

A free-floating currency market developed by March 1973. Although all currencies remained exchangeable for gold or other precious commodities at some price, most individuals and countries chose to hold dollars as the medium of exchange. Nevertheless, the currencies all exchanged against one another. No single central bank or government mandate could significantly affect the value of any national currency in the international market. The market itself set the value on a daily basis, providing a system far better than the one designed at Bretton Woods. It surpassed all previous attempts at establishing an international money standard because it needed virtually no coercion. More important, it succeeded precisely because it fostered competitive money: yen traded against francs, which traded against deutsche marks, which all traded against dollars. Foreign currencies found their own value whether the governments liked it or not, a factor that concerned the Soviet Union in the late 1980s as it scrambled to participate in the European Economic Community yet tried to keep the value of its ruble out of windows of exchange.

Domestic banking underwent an equally astounding transformation from 1945 to 1990. It began with the consumer credit revolution, again focused on the automobile, but abetted by a boom in home appliances. Unlike the 1920s, when banks eschewed consumer lending, in the late 1940s and early 1950s banks eagerly sought out consumers and especially wanted to finance auto purchases. By 1956 approximately 20 percent of the commercial bank loans in the nation took the form of consumer loans, which carried interest rates of 6 to 12 percent. Automobile loans rose from $776 million in 1940 to $1.95 billion in 1949.

Only the demand for housing matched the furious pace of auto purchases. The Federal Housing Administration (FHA), created in 1934, sought to extend government guarantees to home mortgages. After the war the Veterans Administration offered the same benefit to veterans. Together, when combined with the dramatic relocation of defense workers and military personnel to Sun Belt states after the war, the demand for housing skyrocketed. Some commercial bankers proved highly adept at making FHA loans. Walter Reed Bimson of Arizona's Valley National Bank made so many of the loans that the little southwestern institution ranked fifth nationally in FHA loan volume, originating 700 loans in a week and making $1 million worth of FHA loans in a year. Bimson and others came up with an innovative approach to mortgage lending: they offered to originate the loans, using the funds of eastern savings banks or insurance companies. Soon other Sun Belt financiers drew capital out of eastern and midwestern institutions at previously unseen rates, financing the growth of the Southern Rim, as Kirkpatrick Sale called it. Bankers from Florida to California found themselves swamped with customers and knew where to obtain the capital to retain wartime workers as permanent residents.

More important, the West and, to a lesser degree, the South learned how to attract visitors who would relocate, through a self-advertisement process called "boosterism." Many states, recognizing the unprecedented opportunity to promote their areas during the war, had lobbied to receive federal defense installations. Utah bankers under the leadership of George S. Eccles, for example, had taken active roles in persuading the War Department to locate important bases and ammunition production facilities in that state. Western cities such as San

Diego, El Paso, Phoenix, and Denver along with southern cities such as Houston, Memphis, Tampa, Atlanta, Raleigh, and Charlotte all touted their climate, scenery, and positive business environments. Bankers in those areas inevitably formed the inner circle of the booster groups. They worked out special lending programs, made specific commitments to cultural activities, and most of all spared no effort to attract new investment and industry. The resulting rise of the Sun Belt witnessed the remarkable emergence of western and southern banks as legitimate competitors of established institutions in New York and Chicago.

The shift had already started in California, where the Bank of America competed with large eastern powerhouses to establish a formidable West Coast version of Wall Street. In the 1930s and 1940s A. P. Giannini had continued to expand his empire, purchasing some 200 small banks and combining them into 46 banking companies. He then placed the 46 banks in a holding company called Transamerica Corporation until the government permitted a formal merger with Bank of America. Transamerica served as the holding company not only for all of the smaller banking companies, but for the Bank of America as well, not to mention insurance companies, tuna packers, tobacco concerns, and a metal fabricator (as well as, later, the United Artists motion picture studio and an airline). The Federal Reserve Board launched a legal action against Transamerica in 1948, charging the holding company with monopolizing western banking. Five years later Transamerica won the case, but like the gunslinger always condemned to looking over his shoulder, the company concluded that it would never have peace from the regulators, and under the threat of congressional action (which indeed eventually came to pass in the form of the Bank Holding Company Act of 1956), Transamerica decided to separate itself from the Bank of America. It still retained the 46 banks. Thus, from the seed of Giannini's Bank of Italy, two powerful bank holding companies emerged: Transamerica, with 226 branches in 11 western states by 1956, and the continually growing BankAmerica Corporation. The provisions of the Bank Holding Company Act stipulated that a bank holding company could hold one bank and other unrelated businesses, or several banks, but not both. By that time Transamerica had developed diverse business interests and chose to keep those businesses and release the banks into an-

other independent holding company that, after several permutations, emerged as First Interstate Bancorporation in 1980. Bank of America overtook Citibank as the world's largest bank in late 1977, only to lose that position in a sharp slide that saw its assets shrink from almost $120 billion in 1984 to just more than $90 billion in 1988.

Several other impressive banks arose in the West, so that by 1985 Los Angeles surpassed Chicago as the second-largest banking center in the nation. In terms of deposits, Los Angeles also gained rapidly on New York and threatened to overtake it. Along with First Interstate and the Bank of America, Wells Fargo and Security Pacific emerged as important regional financial institutions. Security Pacific, the sixth-largest bank in the United States as of 1989, had been founded by Joseph Sartori, a longtime rival of Giannini. While often overlooked, Security Pacific established itself as a strong competitor in an already noteworthy group.

Before the crash of oil prices in the 1980s, finance made up one of Kirkpatrick Sale's "Six Pillars" upon which the Southern Rim economy rested, and even the demise of much of the banking industry in Texas and Oklahoma did not completely erode the influence of western financial institutions. (Indeed, in the case of the failing Texas-based First Republic Bank, North Carolina National Bank [NCNB] arranged a merger, which left the Sun Belt-based NCNB ultimately even larger and more dynamic than ever.) The rise of NCNB also signaled the growing regional banking power of the South, with Citizens & Southern (C&S) (Atlanta), NCNB (Charlotte), Wachovia (Winston-Salem), and SunTrust (Atlanta) making up just a few of the expanding and profitable southern financial institutions. Until the energy bust, Texas also had seen its banks on a sharp ascent, as had Oklahoma and Colorado. The sudden downturn in those areas should not be misinterpreted. Banking in those states indeed had declined rapidly, but an equally rapid recovery lurked around the corner if either oil or real estate revived, and the history of the regions suggested that neither remained at low prices for long.

Banks in the West, in fact, pioneered many of the most significant changes in finance in the twentieth century. While Citibank and Chase presided over impressive innovations—the certificate of deposit and the first extensive implementation of automatic teller machines, for example—western banks dramatically altered the industry's structure, technology, and even attitudes. California banks especially exerted a major influence on the public's perception of branching. At the end of the war more than 14,000 banks conducted operations in the United States, well below the 31,000 in existence in 1921. But by 1945 more than 4,000 branches existed, and that number started to spurt with the growth of the Sun Belt, where most states permitted branching. Bank of America alone had more than 1,000 branches in 1976, and Valley National Bank in Arizona had more than 200 in the early 1980s. By 1957 the country had 8,000 branches; by 1965, 16,000; and by 1977, 32,000. Population per office increased, from a 1920 ratio of 3,400 to 1 to a 1945 ratio of 7,300 to 1, to a 1987 figure of 14,000 to 1. Deposit volume by unit banks shrank from 48 percent of all deposit dollars in 1949 to less than 25 percent in 1972.

Of course, such expansion required a sympathetic regulatory climate, and much of the change could be credited to James J. Saxon, U.S. comptroller of the currency from 1961 to 1966. As comptroller, Saxon liberalized the interpretation of branching laws and increased chartering activities. During his tenure the number of branches approved expanded by more than 2,100 (and the number approved after he left the government fell sharply). In states that did not permit branching, Saxon made it clear he intended to permit new charters to fill the void. Saxon also thought it important to loosen some of the restrictions on commercial banks, especially as those restrictions made them less competitive with other financial institutions, such as S&Ls. Indeed, in the early 1960s bankers frequently complained about "unfair competition" from S&Ls, which benefited from federally protected higher interest rates on deposits after 1966. Saxon favored removing some of the restrictions on commercial bank activities, and he liberalized lending limits and the types of loans national banks could make. But he did not permit reckless chartering. He increased the legal and examination staff of the Comptroller's Office and introduced modern management techniques. As Robert Craig West maintained, "Saxon's appointment as Comptroller had a permanent impact. The Comptroller's office has become the advocate of change in banking." West credited Saxon with an influence on succeeding comptrollers, who "have advocated expanded powers, increased competition, and many other changes consistent with Saxon's vision."

Not only did new national banks receive charters at a greatly accelerated rate, but state banks also formed in increasing numbers, most of them insured under FDIC guidelines. Between 1945 and 1961 less than 2,100 commercial banks opened, but more than three times that number opened from 1961 to 1988. As Benjamin Klebaner has observed, new banks overwhelmingly had deposit insurance, with only 761 of the banks formed since World War II lacking such coverage. Indeed, except for Texas, North Dakota, and Washington, all states required new banks to obtain FDIC insurance before state authorities would allow them to open. Again, new bank formation favored areas with growing populations: Florida, North Carolina, Virginia, Texas, Colorado (where unit banking still held sway), Arizona, and California.

California could claim leadership in structural changes, and it also provided one of the most important banking innovations of the postwar period, the bank credit card. Although as early as 1951 a New York bank had experimented with plastic credit cards, Bank of America developed the first broadbased network card, the BankAmericard (later called VISA), in 1959. Within seven years Bank of America signed up participating banks as franchisees, receiving a fee for allowing a bank to join the network. The key, however, was convincing a large merchant body to accept the card, and California proved the most appropriate spot for introduction. BankAmericard had gone national by the mid 1960s, and the concerns of Bank of America's western competitors led several of those banks to band together in the Western States Bankcard Association. Another group, formed in 1966 in New York but including banks in Pittsburgh, Milwaukee, Buffalo, Seattle, and Phoenix, appeared under the name Interbank Card Association. The two groups formed a single association of their own, with a competing card, Master Charge (later Mastercard), in 1967. Thus, both major bank credit cards in use in the world today originated, or obtained their real impetus, in California. The extent of the impact bank credit cards had on the industry could be seen in the number of cards outstanding—165 million VISAs and 145 million Mastercards as of 1987—and in the fact that more than 40 percent of American families owned at least one credit card. Both cards had international networks, and, as

VISA liked to boast in its television ads, stores and resorts in some foreign countries would accept no other card except VISA.

One major innovation for which California could not receive credit, the automatic teller machine (ATM), clearly broke in as a result of Citibank. Barclays Bank in England in 1967 had experimented with the first ATM, and some American banks had toyed with the technology. It did not take off until Citibank, under its dynamic chairman Walter Wriston (called by Milton Friedman "the most innovative banker of our time") took a significant risk by installing two ATMs at every one of its banking locations. That move proved remarkably farsighted, but at the time ATM technology remained in its infancy. Teller machines "ate" cards on many occasions, then were just as likely to disburse hundreds of dollars in cash to a thankful but undeserving customer. And no banker expressed confidence that customers really would interact with a machine! However, by the late 1970s, Wriston's gamble had paid off handsomely. For most of the 1970s, Citibank continued to edge out Bank of America as the largest bank in the world in part because of its domestic advantage that came from ATMs. In the case of ATMs, Bank of America, and indeed all of California, had completely fallen behind. Not until the late 1970s and early 1980s did Bank of America spend millions of dollars to catch up.

Neither the West Coast nor the East Coast could claim credit for the change in regulation relative to bank holding companies that resulted in a bank merger wave beginning in 1960. Chase National had joined with the Manhattan Company to form Chase Manhattan (later Chase) in 1955, marking the largest merger of that decade. The Bank Holding Company Act of 1956 and the Bank Merger Act of 1960 both sought to foster competition. Obviously, however, by the mid 1960s, with new bank formation occurring at breakneck speed and Saxon's liberalization of chartering and branching regulations resulting in an expansion of banks across the country, plenty of competition existed. Authorities generally permitted mergers unless they clearly reduced competition in a geographic market, as seen in the Supreme Court's rejection of proposed merger of Philadelphia National and Girard Trust in 1963 and the divestment proceedings against Valley National Bank's takeover of the holding company for Arizona's third-largest bank in the early

1960s. As late as 1970 the Supreme Court prohibited two New Jersey banks virtually on the same block from combining. Yet authorities also started to weigh the effect on competition against the goal of saving banks in trouble. Thus, when SeaFirst Corporation, the holding company for Seattle-First National, found itself immersed in Penn Square-related defaulting energy loans in the 1980s, the authorities allowed Bank of America to acquire it. First Interstate almost pulled off a similar merger with Bank of America when the latter bank fell on hard times in the mid 1980s, and that proposed takeover, too, had the blessings of the regulators.

By the 1970s mergers had started to reduce the number of banks: between 1977 and 1987 the number of banks declined 4 percent, from 14,399 to 13,753. Meanwhile, the share of banking assets controlled by the largest banking organizations increased, with the share controlled by the top 1 percent rising from 53 to 65 percent during the same period. Banks that converted into branches through mergers averaged less than 200 each year from 1977 to 1980, while from 1983 to 1987 they remained more than 300 each year and reached 528 in 1987. In the 1970s, Iowa, Maine, New Jersey, New York, Ohio, and Virginia all modified their laws to permit some sort of intrastate expansion through branch banking. By 1990 only four states,—Illinois, Colorado, Montana, and Wyoming,—still had unit banking. In addition, 14 states changed their laws to permitt expansion via multibank holding companies, allowing banking organizations to expand statewide by chartering separate banks under a single holding company.

The 1970s also brought changes in state laws regarding the acquisition of state-chartered banks by out-of-state banking organizations, which meant that federally chartered banks also became fair game for takeovers by out-of-staters. Concerned with the prospect of large New York or California banks moving in, state laws usually limited entry to bank organizations from nearby states. With a concept originating in New England with the New England Compact, states within regions agreed to allow regional interstate banking in the early 1980s. The Southwest, the Southeast, and New England, then, all adopted interstate banking laws for states within their regions. On its own, however, California concluded a landmark agreement with New York in which each state would allow the other's banks to compete starting in 1991. As individual states, or groups of states, gradually changed their laws, true interstate banking went on schedule for arrival in the 1990s.

Unit bank proponents had always maintained that such changes would reduce competition. Just the opposite occurred: in 1977–before the states started to allow greater interstate competition–only 154 new banks opened, but from 1982 through 1985 an average of 347 new banks per year opened. (Those numbers tailed off just slightly, to 230 per year, in 1986 and 1987, but that reflects the tumultuous banking conditions in the energy states and the spillover from the S&L crisis.) The statistics also reflect the fact that entrepreneurs saw once-in-a-lifetime opportunities to sell their banks at record profits as large regional holding companies looked for footholds in their states. Thus, from Florida to Arizona, well-run, profitable, small- to medium-sized banks brought astounding prices. Three of Arizona's top five banks all sold for more than 2.5 times book value, with one approaching 3 times book. South Carolina banks fetched similar prices as C&S, NCNB, and others looked to expand across state lines. A remarkable case of "reverse colonialism" developed, in which large eastern and midwestern institutions were gouged by wily entrepreneurs in the cotton belt, the Florida coast, and on the far western frontier. But the large holding companies could pay the price, and in the end they got what they wanted, entrance into burgeoning new markets. Large holding companies, such as SunTrust Banks in Georgia and U.S. Bancorp in Oregon, expanded; others such as Rainier Bancorporation and Oregon Bancorp found themselves gobbled up by still-larger holding companies (in those cases, Security Pacific). Even so, the regional approach succeeded in protecting quality institutions within their geographic areas, allowing them to report exceptional earnings, as in the case of First Union Bank of Charlotte, which earned 18 percent on equity in 1986. Rates of 15 percent return on equity proved quite common in some states during that halcyon period.

Technology continued to link state to state and region to region. Capital flows occurred at blinding speed, and both local banks and the large exchange markets found themselves open longer, a testament to the consumers' ability to take their business elsewhere and to the fundamental fact that the world market never closed. Between electronic funds transfers, credit cards, and computer networks, consumers had access to their accounts 24 hours a day. On a larger scale, the New York Stock Exchange had to acknowledge that even as it closed, the largest stock exchange in the world–in Tokyo–had just opened for business. Junk-bond whiz Michael Milken moved his headquarters to California in part because he could get a jump on the eastern markets by starting earlier, with the overnight news from Tokyo. By the late 1970s satellite technology allowed capital transfers to take place in seconds, crossing thousands of miles and dozens of once-sovereign borders. When the technology of banking grew irresistible, governments had to acquiesce: technology more than anything accounted for the drive to end branch banking restrictions in the late 1970s and 1980s. Money would have moved along its own path anyway, but state (and later, national) legislatures preferred some control to none.

Nothing depicted the utter frustration that institutions and even nations experienced trying to control international money flows than the developments involved in the rise of the Eurodollars and petrodollars. Originally conceived as a way for "outlaw" nations such as China to make certain that the United States did not block the exchange of dollars they earned, Europeans established banks in the 1950s that specialized in holding the dollar accounts of those countries. Those banks started to make dollar-denominated loans. The Eurodollars that ended up in the banks essentially represented a black market of finance in that virtually no controls existed over the money. Eurodollars constituted offshore currency deposits–currency held outside its country of issue, such as dollars in Paris or francs in London. Thus, no one had any reason to regulate the market. An American administration had no authority over dollars held in France, while the French did not care what people did with dollars. And when European governments did attempt to exert control, the banks simply moved their operations to offshore sites in the Caribbean or Hong Kong. By 1990 offshore money markets held almost $3 trillion and loaned approximately $300 billion a year, none of it regulated. Those markets drove dollars to their real value despite attempts by several U.S. and European governments to implement a variety of measures to maintain the value of the dollar. As American deficits appeared, then were perpetuated, Eurodollars continued to reflect the real position of the currency.

As Citibank's Walter Wriston commented, the Eurodollar system was "fathered by controls." In the early 1960s, American lending to foreigners concerned the administration, which acted in 1963 when U.S. banks loaned more than $2 billion abroad. The government taxed most foreign bonds issued in the United States and limited the amount that American corporations could send abroad to invest. Accordingly, American banks established offshore affiliates, all unregulated, that conducted the lending of Eurodollars. By the 1970s offshore American banks loaned six to seven dollars for every dollar loaned domestically, totaling $35 billion a year. The Euromarket's net size soared from $65 billion in 1970 to $160 billion in 1973. As Jeffery Frieden noted, "the World's international bankers were lending more in two years than they had in the previous century," all due to the Euromarket. Citibank's Julien-Pierre Koszul called the offshore Euromarket "a marvelous platform from which it is easy to rebound, in any direction, to any country, into any currency–and with anonymity." The Euromarket also benefited from the reaction to attempts at domestic controls. Wriston's comment also could have applied to the system of interest controls in the United States, which made deposits in this country less profitable than offshore or in Europe, where no interest ceilings existed.

The rise of the Eurodollar took place over time and without any sudden shocks. A much different experience awaited the American banking system–and the world's system as well–in the 1970s when the Organization of Petroleum Exporting Countries (OPEC) unexpectedly boosted the price of oil. American banks, first whipsawed by inflation (which contributed mightily to the inversion of the yield curves at the S&Ls), responded by pushing interest rates to the point that the domestic economy slumped. The nation teetered on the brink of hyperinflation, with the inflation rate reaching 12 percent at one point. A second, seemingly more benign, shock followed. As American and European currencies flooded into Arab states in return for oil, the countries in the Middle East grew phenomenally wealthy. (In the 1970s Arab countries exported oil worth $1,207.3 billion). At one time or another, Saudi Arabia, Kuwait, Abu Dhabi, and Bahrain all topped or stood near the top of the world's per capita income ladder. But the Koran prohibits most types of banking, and the Arab members of OPEC in particular found themselves awash in dollars. For a brief time the Arabs held one-half of all the world's liquidity, almost $80 billion in cash.

Those Arab nations had no wish to aid the underdeveloped countries, and the vast majority of the oil dollars went directly into weapons purchases. Nevertheless, the World Bank, with former U.S. Secretary of Defense Robert McNamara as its president, harangued the developed nations for giving too little in aid but almost completely excused the Arab world. But just as the money system forced the dollar to its real value, the system transferred money where it was needed, or, at least, where profits for banks seemingly existed. The Arab oil money, by then called "petrodollars," went into American and European banks as deposits–more than $150 billion from 1974 to 1980 worked its way into the Euromarkets. With the U.S. economy sagging as a result of the oil-induced recession, American banks had no domestic outlets for lending. Plenty of willing borrowers, however, awaited in Latin America, including at least a few countries who had some likelihood of repaying the debts because of their own oil reserves, specifically Venezuela and Mexico. Once the lending boom began with the petrodollars, it spread. Soon, BankAmerica, Citibank, Chase, Manufacturers Hanover, and even Valley National Bank and First Republic Bank expanded their lending list to include Brazil, Chile, and dozens of less developed countries in Latin and Central America. Suddenly Arab liquidity vanished into the black hole of the LDCs, which sucked up $200 billion in offshore loans in the 1970s. For a short time many American bankers expressed great concern that the Arabs could use the "money weapon" and immobilize the banking system through massive withdrawals. But Wriston calmly observed that when a nation took its money out of Citibank and put it in *Credit Suisse*, Citibank merely credited *Credit Suisse* and debited Citibank. Its balance sheet stayed the same. Or, as he wryly noted, "There isn't any way money can leave the system. It's a closed circuit."

A more serious problem developed with the LDC borrowers, however. When oil prices finally fell, Mexico and Venezuela had no way to repay their debts. A "debt crisis" ensued. It is useful to understand that "the United States" did not loan money to "Mexico." Rather, individual American banks loaned money to individual Mexican companies in large packages that might tie several hundred loans together, American investors purchased foreign treasury notes, or American bankers, if they chose, could indeed make direct loans to foreign governments. In the United States, nine large commercial banks—Citibank, Chase, Chemical, Manufacturers Hanover, Morgan Guaranty, and Bankers Trust, all New York banks, plus Bank of America and Security Pacific in California and First Chicago—joined five leading investment banks—First Boston, Morgan Stanley, Salomon Brothers, Merrill Lynch, and Goldman Sachs—in providing the vast bulk of lending abroad. Mexico (or Mexican companies), in the 1982-1983 crisis, owed some $28 billion to more than 1,400 foreign banks, including many American institutions. So President Ronald Reagan was correct when he argued that the debt crisis was a matter between the banks and the debtor countries, except for that recurring problem, deposit insurance. Without deposit insurance, the portending default by the Third World threatened only the profits of the banks. Faced with that reality, the Reagan administration in 1982-1983 intervened to help restructure the debts of Brazil, Mexico, and Argentina. (In the Mexico rescheduling, representatives of five large U.S. banks served on a committee to negotiate with the Mexican government; those five banks acted as liasons to ten middle-sized U.S. banks, which in turn dealt with smaller banks, and so on). Only the deposit insurance feature forced the intervention, and the banks quickly implemented their own recovery measures. For a few years the banks restructured the debts, mostly allowing the borrowers to pay only the interest. Stockholders, however, realized that most of the debts would never be paid. So did management, with the exception of Wriston, who emphatically argued that the debts would eventually be settled. Shortly after Wriston retired in 1984, Citibank set aside massive loan loss reserves, a grim admission that the bank considered the debts irrecoverable. Chase followed suit. The only major bank that tried to ignore its LDC loans, BankAmerica, almost failed.

BankAmerica, after passing Citibank to take the position as the world's largest bank, had refused to deal with its problem loans. When in 1981 Sam Armacost replaced "Tom" Clausen as chairman of BankAmerica when Clausen replaced Robert McNamara as head of the World Bank, BankAmerica already had several deeply entrenched problems. Armacost staunchly maintained that the losses that greeted the bank each quarter were "temporary" until a directors' revolt, led, ironically, by

McNamara, who had been asked to serve on the BankAmerica board when he left his World Bank position, demanded action. Supported by federal regulators, who thought the bank's loan loss reserves insufficient, BankAmerica finally started to admit the size of its problem loans (almost $5 billion in 1987, of which 80 percent were foreign). It also unloaded Armacost, and, in a controversial move, brought back Clausen. Observers continue to debate whether Clausen indeed worked a miracle or whether the bank still has serious problems, but by mid 1989 BankAmerica had pulled itself from the brink. It recovered from a $1.8 billion loss from 1985 to 1987 to a $726 million profit in 1988 and a $1.103 million first-quarter profit in 1989.

American banks in the 1980s pulled back from many of the types of foreign loans they had made in the previous decade. Their action went almost unnoticed in the widely publicized and highly politicized debate over trade deficits. By the mid 1980s the United States showed a trade deficit of approximately $130 billion, much of it to Japan. Some insiders admitted that the publicly stated figure resulted from double counting of some Japanese exports and from different accounting procedures on opposite sides of the Pacific. Those experts estimated that a more accurate system would leave the United States with a deficit more in the $100 billion range. Other critics noted that the book value of U.S. investments abroad reflect older (lower) values and that, when measured in current values, much of the deficit disappears. Even most experts in foreign trade, however, frequently ignored a more glaring fact: in the 1970s and early 1980s (when the U.S. trade balance was in surplus) the large banks had roughly $100 billion in foreign (mostly LDC) loans on their books. Those loans appeared on the asset side of the national wealth ledger, whether they were ultimately recoverable or not. The loans that the banks wrote off in the late 1980s were the same loans that generated the "surplus" in the 1970s and early 1980s. The fact was that the United States had been a "debtor nation" for most of the years since 1970, but the false values represented by (irrecoverable) LDC loans made the foreign trade ledgers appear "in balance" or "in surplus." Nothing really changed between 1970 and 1990 except the banks' admission of the uncollectible nature of the loans; so, apparently, the "trade deficit" has no real effect on the economy. The economy stagnated with a "surplus" (actually a false data entry) throughout much of the 1970s, and boomed with a "deficit" (actually a more accurate data entry). The reader should wonder which set of terms more correctly explained economic reality.

Even with all those foreign loans, the fall in domestic oil prices paradoxically caused the greatest American bank catastrophes since the Great Depression. A small, storefront Oklahoma City bank, Penn Square National, had soared into the world of high finance during the 1970s by packaging energy loans and selling them to larger banks in vehicles called "participations." Penn Square grew from a $35 million bank to a $100 million bank in a five-year period, but its participations reached $2.1 billion by 1982. When oil prices fell, the FDIC closed the bank, but the FDIC paid off its depositors and holders of uninsured funds. More than Penn Square itself was involved, however. The banks holding the participating loans also found themselves in serious trouble. Two banks in particular had extensive exposure, including Continental Illinois, with $1.3 billion, and Seattle-First National, with $375 million. Losses from those loans led to the takeover of Seattle-First by BankAmerica. Continental Illinois found itself weakened to the point that a severe run developed in May 1984, and within two months half of its deposits had flowed out of the bank. Regulators determined they had to bail it out, and the FDIC supervised a program of lending to Continental Illinois wherein it bought $4.5 billion worth of the bank's bonds. The Continental Illinois rescue represented the largest bank bailout in American history.

More than 256 banks in energy belt states failed from 1985 to 1987. Unlike the failures in the 1930s, those casualties constituted a group that by and large had taken a reasonable risk that had not paid off. (Their risk seemed especially reasonable if one consulted virtually any media prediction or stock market prognosticator in the early 1980s: the "oil crisis" was permanent, they glumly agreed, meaning permanent higher oil prices). A different sort of disaster had overtaken the nation's S&Ls in the 1980s. For decades S&Ls borrowed from depositors short-term funds at one rate and loaned on long-term home mortgages at a much higher rate. Once federal authorities deregulated interest rates, the S&Ls saw that their short-term funds cost far more than they received from the long-term loans that they could not renegotiate. The Garn-St Germain Act of 1982 expanded the S&Ls' power to pursue in-

vestments in the realm of commercial banking. To offset the interest rate mismatch, the government allowed the S&Ls to offer adjustable rate mortgages. Yet even if an S&L immediately loaned to its full extent on adjustable rate mortgages, it still faced years of mounting losses while it retired its existing long-term mortgages. S&Ls moved into increasingly risky loans, and more than a few swindlers saw S&Ls as perfect vehicles for their flimflams. Numerous books, including *Inside Job* (1989), by Steven Pizzo and others, Paul Zane Pilzer's *Other People's Money* (1989), and James Ring Adams's *The Big Fix* (1990), have documented the many con men who acquired S&Ls as fronts for land operations. One especially preferred scheme involved land flips, wherein swindlers sold a piece of land among themselves (or to their friends in other S&Ls), inflating the price with each exchange. Eventually they convinced someone outside the pool that the price was only going to continue to increase, at which time they unloaded the virtually worthless land. The S&L owner financed each "flip" until the last with S&L funds. When the land market crashed, however, most of the flips never got into the hands of the outsiders, and legitimate S&L investors had millions of dollars of loans on their books backing land whose value came to only a fraction of what the borrower had received. S&Ls also ventured into junk bonds, a low-grade but potentially high-yield investment instrument. When many of those loans failed, so did the S&Ls.

Several specific elements had combined to produce the S&L disaster. Not only had the interest rate mismatch affected S&Ls' profits, but deregulation had left them particularly uncompetitive. Some critics charged that the Reagan administration reduced the number and effectiveness of examiners. On the whole, though, the S&L proved as much the Democrats' problem as the Republicans': numerous prominent Democrats, including Speaker of the House Jim Wright and Democratic House whip Tony Coelho, had to resign after press disclosures of their unethical (and possibly illegal) ties to Texas and California S&Ls. When the California-based Lincoln Savings and Loan collapsed, evidence surfaced that five U.S. senators (four Democrats and one Republican) had met privately with the chairman of the Federal Home Loan Bank Board to persuade him to drop, or at the very least ameliorate the results of, an investigation of Lincoln. All five had received substantial political contributions from Lincoln's chairman/owner Charles Keating.

Another remnant of the New Deal surfaced to plague the financial system in the S&L debacle. Deposit insurance had produced a "moral hazard": with the S&Ls' depositors insured, it paid for S&L managers to take exceptional risks to get out of the holes in which they found themselves. Like gamblers betting double or nothing, convinced that the next hand would save them, S&Ls managers continued to search out risky loans. But unlike gamblers, the S&Ls knew they were playing on taxpayers' money, because the FSLIC stood behind them. Although no immediate depositor worries seemed apparent in the banking system, in the late 1980s academics and regulators alike started to agree on the need to alter the deposit insurance system drastically. Meanwhile, the S&Ls paid a heavy price. Where 6,000 S&Ls did business in 1960, fewer than 3,000 remained in 1989.

By 1989 the FSLIC had to fold, saddled with more than $100 billion in losses and no end in sight. That year, Congress, in a bailout 50 times larger than the New York City bailout and 80 times larger than the Chrysler "rescue" (even though those were technically "bond guarantees"), earmarked approximately $115 billion to liquidate or reorganize insolvent S&Ls. It separated FSLIC from the Federal Home Loan Bank Board and reorganized it as the SAIF (Savings Association Insurance Fund) under the administration of the FDIC, which also had the responsibility of administering a new Bank Insurance Fund. The "full faith and credit" of the federal government stood behind each fund. But even SAIF proved not so safe. As losses kept mounting, estimates of the final bill for the S&L cleanup ranged from $257 to $400 billion. A new financing entity, the Resolution Funding Corporation (REFCORP), also called Resolution Trust Corporation (RTC), planned to enter operation in 1996 to cover the FSLIC's obligations. But those obligations grew even as RTC remained on the drawing board. The Bush administration twice revised its estimate upward since RTC originated, but it also mandated new rules raising the capital core of the S&Ls and established a new minimum tangible-capital-to-assets ratio.

Some critics wanted to blame the S&L disaster on junk bonds, and certainly some S&Ls, particularly Keating's, had invested heavily in those securities. The criticism did not hold water. Junk

bonds had arrived on the financial scene in the 1970s almost totally through the efforts of one man, Michael Milken. A trader at Drexel Burnham Lambert, Milken recognized that a need existed for below-grade securities (bonds not rated "investment grade" by the major investment banking houses). Hundreds, if not thousands, of excellent companies, epitomized by the MCI long-distance telephone firm, failed to qualify for bonds of investment grade. On the other hand, several companies received AAA ratings and went bankrupt within months. To Milken that inequity cried out for market justice. He delivered it in the form of junk bonds, high-yield and high-risk security instruments that allowed virtually any company to raise capital on the bond market. Junk bonds proved an astounding success—and a shocking development to the Wall Street firms that resented the upstart Drexel telling customers that companies no longer needed the blessings of the elite investment banks. Milken's exploits reached fabled proportions: he seemed able to raise $1 billion on the securities markets with a few telephone calls, and he originated an exchange meeting in Beverly Hills known as the "Predators' Ball."

Milken's rise engendered tremendous hostility from mainline Wall Street. Most of the traditional firms, including Merrill Lynch, which half a decade earlier had itself stood as an "outsider" with "radical" notions of securities marketing, considered Milken and Drexel impertinent and irresponsible. The five elite houses—First Boston, Morgan Stanley, Salomon Brothers, Merrill Lynch, and Goldman Sachs—handled two-thirds of all U.S. bond underwriting. They wanted no upstart competitors in their neatly divided realm. As for junk bonds, the Street declared them anathema.

Eventually, Milken and Drexel and other securities traders came under investigation by the Securities and Exchange Commission and other U.S. regulatory agencies. Several traders, including Ivan Boesky and Milken, were indicted, paid stratospheric fines, or served time in prison. But just as the indiscretions and even criminal activities of some individuals who participated in the S&L disaster did not invalidate the original concept and benefits of the S&Ls themselves, neither did the troubles of Milken and the others mean that junk bonds did not serve a useful purpose. In fact, junk bonds continued the unceasing and increasingly rapid democratization of all banking and financial institutions and markets. The junk bond provided the perfect tool for aspiring entrepreneurs who needed quick access to capital in order to take advantage of revolutionary technology or of split-second market openings for their products.

Indeed, the junk bond coincided with the end of the era of managerial hierarchies. Large management-oriented industries, so successful from 1880 to 1970, had become dinosaurs, immobile and slow to react to new competitive threats. The investment banks that provided their capital in many ways came to resemble them. Infatuated with autos, steel, and utilities, the traditional investment bankers tended toward a stifling conservatism. But the Japanese posed a serious threat to American business by adopting different management methods. While the United States made much political hay out of the Japanese government's support of domestic industries, in fact Japan surpassed the United States in several industrial areas by creating more competitors, not fewer. During its rise to its position as number two behind the United States in the international economy, Japan created 53 integrated steel firms, 50 motorbike companies, 12 auto companies, 280 robotics firms, and 20 copier manufacturers. The pressing need to compete required more entrepreneurs, not a few sclerotic giants. Junk bonds fed American entrepreneurs at the very time their presence was most needed, eroding Byzantine investment rating services. They offered millions of American investors new and challenging opportunities to participate in cutting-edge businesses.

Consequently, by 1990 three separate streams of democratizing forces converged on banking and finance in the United States: the state and national deregulation of laws against branching and holding companies; the dramatic technological breakthroughs that tied the world together in a complex cash nexus still revolving around the U.S. dollar; and the creation of new securities instruments that responded more quickly and individually to the capital needs of a new wave of entrepreneurs. Those forces spread a democratic blanket over banking and finance unseen in history, and it extended well beyond America's own borders. The implications of the new financial democracy did not go unnoticed by the dean of American bankers, Walter Wriston, in a 1988 essay in *Foreign Affairs* called "Technology and Sovereignty." Wriston argued that the new information revolution has made sovereignty over a nation's own economy an obsolete concept:

Today, information about all countries' diplomatic, fiscal and monetary policies is instantly transmitted to more than two hundred thousand screens in hundreds of trading rooms in dozens of countries. As the screens light up with the latest statement of the president ... traders judge the effect of the new policies on the relative values of the country's currency and act accordingly.... The whole world is linked electronically, with no place to hide.... Money and ideas move across borders in a manner and at a speed never before seen.... Since global financial markets are a kind of free speech, many complain about what the markets reveal about their country's policies.

Nowhere have the complaints been more shrill than in the United States, especially where it concerned Japanese competition. And nowhere did the new Japanese power seem more visible than in California. The logos of Japanese banks that acquired California banks graced the Los Angeles skyline, and five of the twelve largest Japanese banks established their U.S. retail banking subsidiaries in Los Angeles, not New York. American bankers legitimately complained that often their foreign competitors faced less regulation in America than did domestic banks. Whatever the cause, the effect was stunning. Obviously the United States benefited from the tremendous expansion in Asian trade. Los Angeles' international trade volume between 1972 and 1982 soared 500 percent, and Long Beach became the nation's single largest port in terms of dollar volume of cargo handled. But other signs seemed less benign. Japanese banks already controlled more than 13 percent of the area's banking market, and a First Interstate Bank official estimated that the Japanese banks would hold 30 percent of the market within 20 years.

Still other signs caused concern among American bankers. Where once Citibank and BankAmerica battled for the position of largest bank in the world, by 1990 the world's seven largest banks and 16 of the top 25 are Japanese. Four of the top five banks are located in Tokyo, with Dia-Ichi Kangyo holding the top spot as of 1990. The equity value of Japan's largest banks averaged $50 billion to $80 billion, while the equity value of the largest banks in the United States averaged $10 billion. Even in securities, Wall Street has been surpassed by the Tokyo Exchange, with the largest securities company in the world, Nomura, headquartered there.

The rapid rise of Japanese banks stemmed from the constricting consumer market in Japan. Consumers there have far fewer consumer items available, and most cannot hope to ever own a home of the type an American insurance salesman might have, so they save. Import taxes reinforce the saving habit. New studies also suggest a strange collusion between large industry and the banks to deemphasize consumerism in Japan to promote savings. Consequently, Japanese banks bulged with deposits, which they employed in profitable ways.

The resulting tenfold rise in overseas investment produced a "capital flight from Japan [and] a capital surplus for the United States," as George Gilder noted. America accounted for 44 percent of Japanese overseas investment as of 1985, and between 1984 and 1988 Japanese banks accounted for more than one-half of the measured growth in international banking activity. Japan's insurance companies alone held $31 billion in foreign securities, while Sumitomo, the most aggressive bank to invest in foreign holdings, increased its proportion of revenue from foreign operations to 22 percent in 1988 and expected it to continue to rise to at least 40 percent in the next few years. Hiroshi Takeuchi, chief economist of the Long Term Credit Bank, predicted, "Japan is the next America." To some Americans, especially bankers, that seemed a grim warning indeed.

Alarms sounded, and "exchange rate mercantilists," seeing the Japanese investment as only a threat, sought ways to control capital flows as a means to address the aforementioned illusory trade deficit. Instead, the capital flow "reflected confidence in the leadership of the United States in the global quantum economy." Ultimately, Japanese investment in the United States illustrated exactly what Wriston meant when he said "money goes where it's wanted and only stays where it's well treated." In the 1980s, when France announced it planned to enact new socialist programs, one-third of its foreign exchange flowed out of the country in a single week. Capital searches out stability, profitability, and freedom, which is why Japanese capital flowed to American shores in the same decade. Moreover, to view capital flows the same way one views trade in physical goods involves a misunderstanding of the fact that capital only represents perceived value. Otherwise, a peso would equal a dollar. Thus, as Japanese capital flowed into the United States, the assets it represented showed up on Japanese balance sheets. If the value of investment in America fell, so would the asset side of the Japanese banks. Thus, foreign countries' investment in the United States in many ways represented not only a risk but a commitment. Ultimately, where else in the world are countries going to put their money? Brazil? Lebanon? So the free movement of capital to America underscored the tremendous faith that foreigners have in the American economy and emphasized the inability of sovereign states to control something as elusive as money.

At the same time, "the new technologies . . . [have] completely transform[ed] the balance of power between the entrepreneur and the state," in Gilder's words. By 1990 the American banking network increasingly needed the state for only the most minimal of regulatory and infrastructure support. Banks moved to the point that they became passive agents of transmission, carrying economic and political pulses from market to market. Banking, having long abandoned the gold standard, has come to the point where it relies on two premises for its activity: money moves faster than goods, and the knowledge of value moves faster than its vessel. As the first nation in the twentieth century (other than Hong Kong) to liberalize and unshackle its financial and banking markets, the United States stood poised to reap the gains of the "decline of geography." Despite the impressive size of the competitors in the Far East, bankers appear to have grasped the appropriate operating principles for twenty-first-century success. Strategies and processes that favor people, including immigrants, stand to gain the most in the Information Age . As the most democratized banking system in the world, the American financial industry has already placed itself in a position to dominate that age.

–Larry Schweikart
University of Dayton

Banks in the United States, 1910-1990

Year	Number	Assets (in $ billions)
1910	25,151	22
1920	30,909	53
1930	24,273	74
1940	15,076	79
1950	14,676	179
1960	14,019	282
1970	14,187	611
1980	14,689*	1,673
1989	12,912**	3,205**
1990	13,343 (July)***	3,246 (April)**

Sources: U.S. Bureau of the Census, *Historical Statistics of the United States: Colonial Times to 1970*, 2 volumes (White Plains, N.Y.: Kraus International Publications, 1989), II: 1019; *Federal Reserve Bulletin* (December 1989): A-17, A-73, A-77; (July 1990): A-18.

*   includes domestically chartered commercial banks, branches and agencies of foreign banks, Edge Act and agreement corporations, and New York State foreign investment corporations

**   includes all commercial banks

***   includes FDIC insured banks only

Encyclopedia of American Business History and Biography

Banking and Finance, 1913-1989

Agricultural Lending by the Federal Government

by James Smallwood

University of Texas at Tyler

Soon after the turn of the twentieth century, as the Progressive movement swept the United States, the federal government began devoting more attention to the agricultural community. The Populist movement of the 1890s had advocated many of the reforms that became law. President Woodrow Wilson presided over the government when Congress implemented the Federal Farm Loan Act in 1916. That reform established 12 Federal Land Banks, which paralleled the 12 regional banks of the Federal Reserve System, created in 1913. The land banks offered farmers long-term loans (up to $100,000 financed for a maximum of 45 years) at low interest rates. That cheap credit, long advocated by rural leaders, helped many farmers modernize.

Under the program farmers received loan amounts of up to 50 percent of the value of their land and of up to 20 percent of the value of their permanent improvements. They used the money to finance the purchase of land, livestock, and equipment and to conduct regular farm operations.

The Federal Farm Loan Act also provided for Joint Stock Land Banks. Incorporated independently and financed privately, those banks could go beyond the $100,000 limit of the publicly owned system.

The Wilson government's Warehouse Act of 1916 also opened more avenues of easy credit to farmers. The act allowed the farmers to deposit their goods in storehouses and to receive government script in return—script that could be used as collateral for bank loans.

The Smith-Lever Act of 1914 also assisted farmers. The federal government agreed to offer matching funds to state governments if they would support agricultural extension efforts provided by state demonstration agents. Additionally, the Smith-Hughes Act of 1917 offered to match state funds for the teaching of agriculture and home economics in high schools. The Federal Highway Act of 1916 allowed states to obtain federal matching funds for building rural post roads.

Although conservative politics dominated the decade of the 1920s, Congress nevertheless passed more legislation designed to help beleaguered farmers. The Agricultural Credits Act of 1923 established 12 Federal Intermediate Credit Banks. Although they did not deal directly with farmers, the banks did serve as banks for bankers—rediscounting agricultural paper for periods of six months to three years.

In the latter 1920s, Congress tried to give farmers yet more aid. But President Calvin Coolidge twice vetoed the McNary-Haugen bill, passed by Congress in 1927 and 1928. The bill would have placed a high tariff on agricultural goods imported from other countries and allowed the federal government to buy surplus farm products and sell them internationally at market prices. For that protection agriculturalists would have paid only a small tax, designed to recoup any losses incurred by the government. But Coolidge feared farm overproduction and retaliation by America's trading partners.

As one phase of the New Deal attack on the Great Depression, Congress passed the Agricultural Adjustment Act in 1933. The Agricultural Adjustment Administration paid farmers subsidies to decrease their production, and prices for agricultural goods rose. Moreover, after the harvest of 1933, the Agricultural Adjustment Administration established the Commodity Credit Corporation, an agency that accepted crops as security for loans. Although the Supreme Court later declared the original act unconstitutional, the New Dealers simply revised the law until it could withstand the court's scrutiny. Further, the Farm Credit Act of 1933 allowed farmers to refinance their mortgages for a longer payback period, thus lowering the annual payments farmers owed their bankers.

President Franklin D. Roosevelt signing the Agricultural Adjustment Act, May 13, 1933
(courtesy of International News)

The Bankhead-Jones Farm Tenancy Act of 1937 created the Farm Security Administration (FSA), an agency that allowed tenants and sharecroppers to secure loans to buy the land they worked. The FSA had only limited success because of its low annual budgets.

Since the New Deal era the federal government's relationship to the country's agriculturalists has been refined but seldom enlarged. During World War II the federal government supported farmers at 110 percent parity to encourage maximum production. In the Agricultural Act of 1949 the administration of Harry Truman promised 90 percent parity through 1950 on such basic commodities as cotton, wheat, corn, tobacco, rice, and peanuts; not less than 80 percent parity in 1951; and from 75 to 90 percent parity thereafter.

Further action came in the Republican administration of President Dwight D. Eisenhower. Farmers benefited from the Agricultural Act of 1954, which established flexible price supports, authorized commodity "set-asides," and provided new support payments for wool growers. Also, because agricultural surpluses continued to lower prices and reduce farm income, Congress established the Federal Soil Bank program in 1956. The program increased direct subsidies to farmers who withheld land from production and converted it into pasture or forest.

In the most recent era, from the 1960s to the 1990s, few new farm programs have been sponsored by the federal government; rather, government has emphasized the reform of existing programs. In 1962, for example, President John F. Kennedy called for lower price supports and a comprehensive, long-range program to replace what he called "the present patchwork of shortrun emergency measures," but Congress defeated his effort while continuing to spend approximately $5 billion a year on subsidies. Those subsidies continued to rise in absolute dollar amounts from the 1970s to the 1990s.

References:

Murray R. Benedict, *Farm Policies of the United States, 1790-1950* (New York: Twentieth Century Fund, 1953);

William H. Clark, *Farms and Farmers* (Freeport, N.Y.: Farrar, Straus & Giroux, 1970);

Wayne D. Rasmussen, ed., *Readings in the History of American Agriculture* (Urbana: University of Illinois Press, 1960);

Paul Studenski and Herman F. Krooss, *Financial History of the United States* (New York: McGraw-Hill, 1963);

Herman Van Der Wee, *The Search for Prosperity: The World Economy, 1945-1980* (Los Angeles: University of California Press, 1986).

American Bankers Association

by Benjamin J. Klebaner

City College, CUNY

At the 40th annual convention of the American Bankers Association (ABA), held in October 1914, association president Arthur Reynolds congratulated the membership for overseeing the "wonderful growth and progress" of an organization "recognized as one of the most important . . . voluntary organizations of the present time." Membership had risen from around 1,600 in the first decade to more than 14,300 banking institutions in 1913. Such progress would continue: in 1920 the ABA boasted some 22,300 members; 70 percent of all banks claimed membership in 1929, 80 percent in 1939. By 1932 ABA banks held 90 percent of total bank assets in the United States; by 1989 that figure had increased to 95 percent.

Beginning in 1896 the ABA formed several special sections to accommodate an increasingly diverse membership. The creation of a Trust Company Section in that year was followed by a Savings Bank Section in 1902, which grew to include all member banks with savings and mortgage departments by 1940. A Clearinghouse Section formed in 1906 became the ABA Commission on Banking Practices and Clearinghouse Functions. Beginning in 1900 the association offered an educational service through its sponsorship of the Institute of Bank Clerks. Members renamed the institute the American Institute of Banking (AIB) in 1908 and made it another ABA section. The AIB emerged as the largest industry-sponsored employee-education program in the world. In 1932 Nathaniel Feffer of the American Association for Adult Education characterized the program as more successful than that in any other industry. As of 1989 the AIB contained more than 600 local chapters. In 1910 the ABA continued its expansion, converting its Organization of Secretaries of State Bankers' Associations (sponsored beginning in 1902) into the ABA State Association Section.

Arthur Reynolds, president of the American Bankers Association in 1913 and 1914

In July 1908 the ABA began publishing a monthly journal, known as *Banking* until July 1910, when the title changed to *Journal of the American Bankers Association*. In its early years the journal focused on association activities, then it started to include more general banking information. In 1979 the journal's title changed again, to *ABA Banking Journal*. In 1980 the association started an *ABA Bankers Weekly* oriented more toward current financial issues. In addition, the modern ABA has published ten specialized journals and has available some 400 technical publications.

By 1912 national banks no longer constituted a majority in the ABA. To deal with the special concerns of those institutions, the association formed a National Bank Section in 1915. That section represented the nationals' interests before the U.S. Office of the Comptroller of the Currency, the national-government agency that supervised and regulated the national banks. The Federal Reserve Board, formed by an act of Congress in 1913, employed the National Bank Section as a liaison body. A State Bank Section formed in 1916 promoted uniformity in state banking laws through its proposal of a model bank code. The state section also pushed for nonpolitical appointments of state bank commissioners and sought to improve financial efficiency by making quinquennial surveys of all state banking departments. The national and state sections existed as separate entities until 1971.

Several ABA committees (later known as commissions) have engaged in a wide range of functional activities involving banking. The Agriculture Committee formed in 1911, the Public Relations Committee formed in 1914, and the Commerce and Marine Committee formed in 1918. To deal with problems of world trade, the association formed an Economic Policy Committee in 1920, including economists as well as bankers. The Public Relations Committee, formed in 1921, sought to enlighten the public on the role of banks in the economy. In 1943 the ABA created two commissions, one on Country Bank Operations to assist the thousands of small rural banks comprising the majority of ABA members, and another on Credit Policy to fight the expansion of federal lending activities. A Postwar Small Business Commission set up in 1944 assured the public that "American banking will see that small business lives and is given the opportunity to grow and prosper."

The ABA began to offer general advice on internal banking operations in 1928. That service developed into the organizations's central activity over the ensuing 25 years. A Bank Management Commission, set up in 1930, served as the ABA's "fact-finding, clinical research laboratory of banking practices." Its role narrowed in 1937 to focus on bank operational activities, as newly created departments dealt with such matters as personal loans and personnel issues. In mid November 1963 the association sponsored the first annual National Auto-

mation Conference, only a few years after banks installed their earliest computers.

Over the years several peripheral organizations have become part of the ABA. The Bankers Association for Consumer Credit, organized in 1939, became part of the ABA Consumer Credit Department in 1940, marking the ABA's recognition that consumer credit was an "economically important" part of serving the "reasonable credit requirements" of a bank's territory. The Bank Marketing Association became an ABA affiliate in 1972, as bankers increasingly recognized the importance of the retail market to their industry. Also in 1972 the ABA absorbed the Foundation for Full Service Banks, founded in 1958 by the Reserve City Bankers Association. In 1970 the foundation instituted a national advertising program on behalf of the commercial banking industry on network television.

When the Federal Reserve System became a reality in 1913, the ABA advocated changes to ease membership requirements in order to make the system more attractive to state banks. A Federal Reserve Membership Campaign Committee, formed in September 1917, urged nonmember banks to join. ABA president Charles A. Hinsch hailed the Fed as "the salvation of the country" at the 1918 convention. In a review of the operation of the system undertaken at the 1925 convention, the ABA applauded the Fed's success in an "exceptionally difficult" period and advocated renewal of the Fed's charter to assure its permanence.

The Federal Reserve's early campaign for universal check clearance at par value met powerful resistance from nonmember banks with the support of the ABA. The Fed abandoned its attempt to force universal par clearance in 1923, and the number of nonpar banks that levied exchange charges increased. The issue remained alive as late as the 1967 ABA convention, which exhorted bankers in the 13 states where nonpar clearance still survived to "promote a smooth transition to par clearance." Not until 1980, however, did all banks remit at par. Earlier, in an important step that facilitated the movement of checks from bank to bank, the ABA decided in 1958 to promote national standardization of magnetic ink code recognition to enable machine reading of checks.

Among recurring issues at ABA conventions, none engendered more bitter controversy than branch banking, which members first discussed in 1898. The 1922 convention formally proclaimed its opposition to branching "in any form." Several years of acute controversy preceded the 1927 passage of the McFadden Act, which allowed some branching in the national bank system. The 1930 convention, while reaffirming its support of unit banking, accepted community-wide branch banking in metropolitan areas and country-wide branching in rural districts "where economically justified." That proved too much for many in the ABA, and association opponents of branching organized the Independent Bankers Association that same year.

With regard to bank chartering policies, the 1927 convention claimed that the excessive number of banks supplied the major cause of the wave of bank failures marking the 1920s and proposed limiting new bank charters to reflect the needs of communities. In 1928 the ABA urged that states set a $25,000 minimum capital requirement for new banks. The 1963 centennial of the passage of the National Banking Act served as the occasion for an ABA public relations program reaffirming the association's stand in favor of the preservation of the dual banking system, which offered banks options in chartering and supervision. In March 1989 ABA president Thomas P. Rideout cautioned the U.S. House Banking Committee against curtailing the traditional authority of states to charter banks and determine the scope of their activities.

The ABA denounced the effort of the New Deal Congress to inaugurate a system of deposit insurance, claiming that such a system was "unsound in principle and unworkable in practice." The 1933 convention strenuously but vainly urged postponement of the result of the congressional effort, the new Federal Deposit Insurance Corporation (FDIC). In 1989 the ABA fought successfully against merging the bankrupt Federal Savings and Loan Insurance Corporation with the FDIC.

Federal lending programs, however, never met with the same uniform opposition. The ABA did not fight the 1916 act that set up 12 Federal Land Banks or the 1923 act establishing Federal Intermediate Credit Banks and expressed little opposition to the Federal Home Loan Bank Act of 1932. It accepted the agricultural lending agencies established in the 1930s as relief measures as well as the Depression-era system of federal mortgage insurance. However, in 1930 the ABA voiced disapproval of government-subsidized loans and unfair competition with chartered banks. As the economy recovered from the Depression, the ABA reiterated its longstanding opposition to direct or indirect federal lending that subsidized losses. The 1947 ABA convention summarized the association's stand against further extension of governmental or semigovernmental loan guarantees and urged "a drastic reduction of government's wartime or emergency powers." Private credit agencies stood in a position to supply business with "the credit it requires and should have."

Unequal tax treatment for banks vis-à-vis thrift institutions has long generated protest from the ABA. The 1958 convention resolved to seek "the elimination of inequity in the taxation of financial institutions," and 48 percent of ABA members voted to exclude mutuals from membership. By 1961 only 38 percent of mutual savings banks remained ABA members. The 1963 convention applauded the passage of the Revenue Act of 1962 as "a step toward the achievement of equitable tax measures" relating to banks.

For decades the ABA has pushed for the enlargement of the range of services banks are allowed to offer and for less burdensome regulation and reporting requirements. The Continental Illinois National Bank crisis of 1984 set back efforts at deregulation. Critics blamed antiquated laws and costly regulations for America's decline in world financial markets. The ABA expressed great concern with "leveling the playing field" for regulated and restricted banks in their contest with unregulated institutions for slices of the financial pie.

In addition to its concern about the law and regulation, the ABA has had to adapt to changing perceptions about the relationship between gold and currency. Consistent with the association's historic position, the 1922 convention affirmed that "a sound currency system based upon the gold standard is absolutely essential . . . for the maintenance of civilized life." In February 1965 the ABA changed its position, reluctantly accepting the elimination of the 25 percent gold certificate requirement for Federal Reserve Bank deposit liabilities while holding fast to the gold cover for Federal Reserve notes. Three years later the ABA viewed the latter as a threat to the "continued efficient operation of the international monetary system—based upon gold and the dollar." Hence, the ABA was willing to accept a relaxation or removal of that statutory requirement. In 1968 the convention labeled the possibility of an American gold embargo or a devaluation of the dollar as representing "a breakdown in the international monetary system," but both occurred during the presidential administration of Richard M. Nixon in 1971.

ABA conventions have been held annually since the association's inception in 1875, except for three years when war-related transportation and hotel shortages precluded large numbers from gathering. It kept its headquarters in the Wall Street area until May 1923, when they were relocated in midtown Manhattan. A Washington, D.C., office opened in July 1919 initially served as headquarters of the National Bank Division. In 1971 operations were consolidated in the capital. At the 1967 convention ABA president Jack T. Conn boasted that the ABA carried on more meaningful activities than any other trade association. With a staff of 450 as of 1989, the ABA engages in trade and professional functions, keeps close watch over legislation relat-

ing to banking and finance, and offers research and educational programs. The 1980s saw the association respond vigorously to bankers' needs for management tools to enable them to survive in the marketplace. The modern ABA continually faces the challenge of serving a rapidly evolving financial services industry under pressure from foreign institutions, nonbank rivals, and societal forces.

References:

American Bankers Association, *Proceedings of the . . . Annual Convention* (American Bankers Association, 1875-);

Richard Hill, *Fifty Years of Banker Education* (New York: American Institute of Banking, 1950);

Wilbert M. Schneider, *The American Bankers Association: Its Past and Present* (Washington, D.C.: Public Affairs Press, 1956).

Samuel Henry Armacost

(March 29, 1939 -)

by Scott W. Fischer

University of Virginia

CAREER: Credit trainee (1961-1962), assistant vice-president in corporate finance (1964-1968), assistant vice-president (1968-1969), vice-president, London (1969-1971), participant in an exchange program with the Office of Monetary Affairs, U.S. State Department (1971-1972), branch manager, London (1972-1974), senior vice-president, Chicago corporate lending office (1974-1975), senior vice-president, Corporate Service Center, San Francisco (1975-1977), executive vice-president, Europe, Mideast, and Africa Division (1977-1979), head cashier (1979-1981), president and chief executive officer, BankAmerica Corporation (1981-1986); managing partner (1986-1987), managing director, Merrill Lynch Capital Markets (1988-).

Samuel Henry Armacost, beleaguered president and chief executive officer (CEO) of BankAmerica Corporation during the early 1980s, was born in Newport News, Virginia, on March 29, 1939, the son of George Henry and Verda Gay (Hayden) Armacost. His parents met while pursu-

ing doctorates in education at Columbia University. The Armacosts later moved to Virginia, where both taught school. George Armacost became a professor and later dean of men at the College of William and Mary in Williamsburg, Virginia. When Sam was six the family moved to the southwest Los Angeles suburb of Redlands, California, when the University of Redlands, a respected liberal arts college, offered George Armacost its presidency.

George and Verda Armacost raised three boys and one girl. Peter, the oldest, followed in his father's footsteps and became president of Eckerd College in St. Petersburg, Florida; he also was a Wilson and a Danforth Fellow. Michael, the second son, was a Fulbright Fellow and a White House Fellow during the Nixon administration. He served as ambassador to the Philippines in 1983 and later as undersecretary of state for political affairs in the Reagan administration. Both the elder sons graduated Phi Beta Kappa. Mary, the Armacost daughter, served as a leader in a Baptist church in Denver, Colorado, which ordained her as a minister in 1985.

Samuel Henry Armacost

Sam Armacost was the youngest child. As a youth he was active in swimming and water polo and served as a summer lifeguard in a local municipal pool. Popular as a student, his senior class elected him its president. Armacost attended Denison University in Granville, Ohio, but did not perform academically as well as his brothers. He played lacrosse and joined Beta Theta Phi, which even its own members labeled a "jock house." George Armacost considered taking his son out of school during his freshman year because of low grades. Armacost changed his major from premed to economics during his sophomore year, and his academic record improved, but he did not make Phi Beta Kappa. He graduated in 1961 and married Mary Jane Levan, his college sweetheart, after she completed her degree a year later.

Immediately after graduation Armacost joined BankAmerica (then known as Bank of America) in San Francisco as a credit trainee, but he left a year later to pursue a master's degree in business administration at nearby Stanford University. After finishing his M.B.A. in 1964 he returned to BankAmerica as an assistant vice-president in corporate fi-

nance, quickly earning a reputation for his sales ability.

In 1968 Armacost became an assistant vice-president and worked with BankAmerica executive vice-president Tom Clausen on one of the most important international transactions the organization ever conducted, a project that raised $250 million for an open-pit copper mine on the island of Bougainville in the South Pacific. The loan involved the Kaiser Aluminum and Chemical Corporation in the United States and the Australian subsidiary of the Rio Tinto Zinc (RTZ) Corporation, a British mining company; the extremely complex transaction involved several subsidiaries of RTZ and various banks in Australia, England, and the United States. The paperwork alone took nine months to complete. Although Clausen received most of the public credit for the venture, his assistant earned new status within the industry. The rank and file at BankAmerica credited Armacost for the deal.

Until he assumed the presidency of BankAmerica in 1981, Armacost never spent more than two years at a given job, a factor that critics later faulted as an inadequacy. After his 1968 triumph, in 1969 the bank made him a vice-president and transferred him to its London branch, where he helped create a multinational lending unit aimed at the world's largest corporations. In 1971 he became BankAmerica's first participant in an executive exchange program with the federal government, serving for a year in the U.S. State Department's Office of Monetary Affairs in Washington, D.C. Armacost returned to the London branch in 1972, this time as branch manager. BankAmerica promoted him to senior vice-president in 1974 and transferred him to Chicago to lead the bank's first corporate lending office outside California. Less than two years later he returned to San Francisco to head the main Corporate Service Center and to serve as the liaison between BankAmerica CEO Tom Clausen and the international division.

Armacost returned to London for a third time in 1977, this time as executive vice-president in charge of the Europe, Mideast, and Africa Division, the most profitable of BankAmerica's three international divisions; operation chiefs in more than 80 countries reported directly to him. Armacost took immediate action to improve the division's management systems, which had failed to keep pace with rapid expansion. He hired specialists to improve the computer and personnel systems.

Although Armacost was successful at that position, observers noted a reluctance to make tough decisions about personnel, a trait that contributed to his downfall. He delayed a decision whether to pull out of a consortium bank in Africa or even cease all African operations; his successor had to decide that issue. On several occasions he showed poor judgment in predicting the financial markets; he also failed to avoid potentially troublesome loans. Despite those traits, Armacost won almost universal praise for his communications and sales abilities; he had earned a reputation as a "boy wonder."

In November 1979 Clausen, BankAmerica CEO, reassigned Armacost to San Francisco in a reshuffle of the bank's top executives, making Armacost head cashier, a position that involved oversight of the bank's finances. Clausen contended that the reshuffle gave the executives experience in new areas, but critics later questioned the decision because the shifts occurred during a period of high uncertainty in the banking industry. Federal Reserve chief Paul Volcker had initiated a tight money policy to control inflation, and Volcker and President Jimmy Carter had slapped credit restraints on the banking industry. Congress was debating a massive deregulation bill, the most sweeping banking revision since the Great Depression of the 1930s. The final bill, known as the Depository Institutions Deregulation and Monetary Control Act of 1980, eliminated Regulation Q, which had prohibited banks and savings and loans from paying interest on checking accounts. Deregulation thus posed a threat to BankAmerica, whose main source of profits traditionally had been inexpensive consumer deposits.

As head cashier Armacost chaired the money and loan policy committee, which decided the loans the bank made. In an attempt to make up for losses in 1979 the committee assumed that interest rates would fall and voted to make more mortgages. During committee debates Armacost abdicated his role as leader and accepted the majority consensus; he did not even vote. The committee's action, however, backfired. According to BankAmerica studies the bank lost $500 million in 1980 as interest rates soared: ultimately the rise in interest rates cost the bank $3.5 billion.

By the spring of 1980 the rise in interest rates triggered a slowdown in earnings that threatened to end ten years of increasing profits. In response, Armacost ordered BankAmerica's five divisions either to increase revenues or lower costs by 5 percent. Focusing on short-term methods to raise profits, he increased the quarterly percentage rate that determined the reserve set aside to cover against possible loan losses, but the rate remained too low to compensate for the growth in outstanding loans. That increased BankAmerica's short-term profits by $12.5 million, but it happened when the number of problem loans on the books and actual losses were increasing.

Armacost, apparently with Clausen's consent, instituted a questionable accounting procedure to determine the value on the bank's venture capital investments. He also initiated several moves that, although legal, overstated the bank's long-term financial condition. One reversed the Europe, Mideast, and Africa Division's decision to create a $5 million reserve against possible losses, and in another, the bank repurchased $200 million in outstanding debt. The actions generated an additional $85 million in short-term profit, suggesting that BankAmerica had actually increased its profits in 1980, a year in which most observers expected losses arising from deregulation and tight money.

As head cashier Armacost served as heir apparent to CEO Tom Clausen. During the waning months of the Carter administration, Clausen was appointed president of the World Bank, and consequently Sam Armacost, at age forty-one, became president and chief executive officer of BankAmerica on April 22, 1981. Clausen left just in time, for BankAmerica's condition progressively worsened during the ensuing five years.

Armacost did have a few successes during his early tenure as BankAmerica CEO. In a move to shore up BankAmerica's California operations, Armacost initiated a massive program to install automatic teller machines (ATMs) in most California branch offices. He ordered the installation of more than one machine a day during 1981. Clausen had opposed such modernization as a passing fad; accordingly, BankAmerica ranked near the bottom of major banks in installing ATMs. Under Armacost, BankAmerica bypassed New York's Citibank and advanced to the number one position in the ATM race. Armacost also reversed Clausen's policy of booking all earnings from loans up front. Instead, he ordered earnings to be spread out over the full term.

On November 22, 1981, BankAmerica announced it had purchased the discount brokerage house Charles Schwab & Company for $53 million. In exchange Armacost agreed to nominate founder Charles Schwab to BankAmerica's board of directors. The acquisition challenged a portion of the 1933 Glass-Steagall Act, the antidepression statute separating the commercial banking business from the securities industry. Although the securities industry ultimately challenged the purchase, the Supreme Court in 1983 upheld lower court rulings approving the sale. Although the purchase cost less than the installation of the ATMs, the program gained notoriety for Armacost as an aggressive leadership move.

In 1983 Armacost completed another deal that brought him recognition. BankAmerica purchased SeaFirst Corporation, the parent body of Seattle-First National Bank, the major bank in Washington State that bordered on failure because of poor loans in the oil and gas industry. Except for that area, Seafirst had a solid consumer business similar to that of BankAmerica's in California. At that time federal law only permitted the purchase of out-of-state banks if the target bank were failing. BankAmerica purchased Seafirst for $125 million in cash and the equivalent amount in a special preferred stock. That proved a good long-term deal for BankAmerica, which could buy back the preferred shares in 1990 at a price determined by Seafirst's losses. By 1987 the value of the preferred shares had dropped from $25 to $2, which allowed BankAmerica to complete the purchase for $9 million.

Despite those bright spots, Armacost's troubles mounted right after he took office. He tried to pilot the bank to greater profitability with the same techniques he utilized throughout his career. Although BankAmerica earned a $646 million profit during Clausen's last year as CEO, it posted a 19 percent drop in earnings during the first quarter of 1981. Two months after the Schwab deal was announced, BankAmerica announced that profits had dropped 31 percent during Armacost's first year in charge. As the world economy worsened during the early 1980s, many loans made during Clausen's tenure in agriculture, energy, shipping, and commercial real estate became unstable. Although profits dropped further during 1982 and 1983, Armacost could not solve disputes between his top executives and relocated personnel instead of firing them.

From 1981 to 1984 actual losses increased from $345 million to more than $1 billion.

Armacost assured everyone, including himself, that BankAmerica would prevail in time. He blamed Clausen for his predicament, but one retired BankAmerica officer stated, "It was OK the first year or so, but after that people got tried of hearing how the bank's problems were Clausen's fault." In 1984 Armacost continually told his directors that the worst of the bank's problems had passed. A year earlier he began a massive reconfiguration of the bank's California delivery system, which called for the closing of 125 to 130 branches by the end of 1984. In order to show additional progress Armacost resorted to a familiar tactic he had used under Clausen—lowering the loan-reserve percentage against possible losses. In the short run profits rose, but the move ultimately may have increased losses. The bank used 90 percent of the loss reserve to cover loan write-offs in 1984, and the U.S. Office of the Comptroller of the Currency pressured the bank to raise the rate. The Comptroller's Office stressed that BankAmerica's loan reserve, as a percentage of total problem loans, was the lowest among the 15 largest commercial banks in the United States.

Armacost's severest critics assert that, instead of immediately cutting expenses, he chose first to study the reasons for the bank's problems; that, however, led to additional layers of staff instead of cutbacks. One former bank official told the *San Francisco Examiner*, "It got so bad that when you'd go through the BankAmerica directory—which is twice as thick as the San Francisco white pages—you'd have trouble finding the operations people amid all the administrative staff listed." Armacost also was secretive to his board. In one incident he kept details from BankAmerica's board of directors when the bank lost $27 million in a mortgage scheme in which a branch office had, in effect, assured collateral. During that period Armacost refused to fire the senior executives who had made a series of errors in which the bank unintentionally paid funds to or sent bills to the wrong customers and instigated a problematic computer conversion that involved switching to new accounting and bookkeeping systems.

After four years on the job Armacost finally announced a revised long-term plan to the senior management and the board of directors in 1984. Because of its shortage of capital BankAmerica would no longer be all things to all people. The bank curtailed expansion and overseas small-business and retail lending; instead, it concentrated on serving consumers and small businesses in the western United States. The bank sought only large corporate customers conducting enough business to generate a clear profit.

After the failure of Continental Illinois Bank in Chicago in 1984, the Comptroller's Office audited major banks more carefully. The comptroller's report on BankAmerica proved extremely unflattering. It contended that the bank's amount of bad loans had grown too fast, that the loan-loss reserve was insufficient, and that most of the bank's computers and information-gathering systems were outdated. Armacost had kept the reserve down in 1984 and held it to $500 million in 1985. He viewed the report as a personal affront and challenged the bank examiners on almost every point. However, in November 1984 BankAmerica signed an agreement with the Comptroller's Office to raise its primary capital (a combination of equity capital loan-loss reserve, and debt that can be converted into equity) to 6 percent by 1986. Earnings rose 13 percent during the first quarter of 1985, but the comptroller's office initiated a new audit of BankAmerica in March. That report ordered the bank to add at least $527 millon in loan-loss reserves. BankAmerica complied with the minimum figure, which contributed to a $338 million loss for the second quarter of 1985.

Armacost scrambled for further ways to cut costs and raise cash. In late 1985 he and other BankAmerica officers started soliciting business by calling potential customers at their homes when several large corporate customers deposited their funds elsewhere. Instead of cutting dividends to stockholders, Armacost also sold assets such as BankAmerica's San Francisco headquarters building, which brought in $600 million. Shortly thereafter, the corporation also sold its interest in the ARCO Plaza headquarters complex in Los Angeles. (ARCO sold its share of the headquarters, too, indicating the lucrative price offered.)

Armacost demonstrated his willingness to sell just about any BankAmerica subsidiary except for SeaFirst and Charles Schwab & Company, the units purchased during his tenure. Despite Armacost's sale of the FinanceAmerica subsidiary (a consumer finance company with 250 offices in 42 states) to Chrysler Corporation for $405 million, Bank-

America still lost $577 million during the first half of 1986. In that action, Armacost, supported by a solid majority of the BankAmerica board, flouted the Comptroller's Office and the Federal Reserve, both of which had recently announced their opposition to a banking company selling its assets in order to pay dividends. In January 1986, however, BankAmerica finally eliminated its quarterly dividend. By the end of 1985 the Comptroller's Office and the Federal Reserve agreed that BankAmerica needed a replacement of its top management, especially Armacost.

On January 31, 1986, Sanford Weill, Wall Street leveraged-buyout specialist and former chief of Shearson-Lehman, offered to replace Armacost as BankAmerica's CEO, promising to raise $1 billion in new capital. Although the board rejected the offer, when news of a second Weill offer leaked to the media, BankAmerica stock rose by $3 a share. In response to those threats to his tenure, Armacost ordered BankAmerica's strategic planning department to prepare a five-year plan containing promising projections of the results of Armacost's plans for the bank that some company members labeled "Project SSJ," for "Save Sam's Job." It promised a target of $1 million in profit before taxes and a stock price of $40 in 1990. Armacost also obtained backing from three of the country's largest investment banks, Soloman Brothers, Merrill Lynch, and First Boston, to help raise capital for BankAmerica. After hearing the plan, including Armacost's optimistic forecasts that the bank would net $415 million in 1986, the BankAmerica board again rejected Weill's overtures.

Although earnings rose somewhat during early 1986, BankAmerica's financial condition worsened as the year progressed. Despite his rosy pronouncement three months earlier, in July Armacost reluctantly announced second quarter losses of $640 million. At that point a faction of BankAmerica board members including Charles Schwab, Robert MacNamara, and former Bank-America president Rudolph Peterson gained additional support for Armacost's removal. Speculation on his removal increased when Schwab resigned from the board in August. The following month the board informally polled its members on the issue of whether Armacost should be fired; his opponents lost by one vote because they had not yet considered a replacement.

During September 1986 worldwide rumors spread of the imminent collapse of BankAmerica and a possible bailout by the Federal Reserve. Armacost responded by asking the Securities and Exchange Commission, the New York Stock Exchange, the Chicago Board of Options Exchange, and banking authorities in London and Tokyo to investigate the source of the rumors. He stated, "We are extremely angry at the parties responsible for spreading these rumors, which have the potential of harming thousands of shareholders and placing the integrity of the market at risk." Although the level of consumer deposits in California had eroded as early as 1984, the pace quickened with news of the rumors. On September 24 Armacost, in an attempt to reassure investors and depositors of the bank's soundness, personally appeared in a one-minute radio commercial carried across California. Despite that move, the rumors convinced more directors that Armacost should be replaced and ultimately cost BankAmerica at least $2 billion in deposits and a sharp decline in the value of its stock.

The last straw occurred on October 3, 1986, when First Interstate Bancorp, a former BankAmerica affiliate spun off during the 1950s, informed its former parent organization of a hostile takeover bid. A year earlier, First Interstate had attempted a friendly merger with BankAmerica, which would have made First Interstate's CEO, Joseph Pinola, chairman and CEO of the merged bank. BankAmerica's board readily rejected the proposal. In February 1985 another First Interstate proposal almost won approval, but the board rejected it for several reasons, one of which was Pinola's refusal to guarantee that Armacost would succeed him after he reached retirement age in five years. The third attempt proved more threatening, and a few days later the investment firm of Drexel Burnham Lambert proposed its own unsolicited takeover bid.

BankAmerica's board needed a way to counter the takeover attempts and calm remaining depositors. At a meeting on October 6, 1986, the directors decided to ask for Armacost's resignation, and Armacost complied on October 11. He stated, "External perceptions about the bank have been so eroded by rumor and speculation that a change in management is necessary to restore confidence in this organization. The best interests of our shareholders, customers, and employees have always been my principal concern, and if stepping aside serves that purpose, I do so willingly." By that point, Bank-America had slipped from the largest to the third largest bank in the United States, far behind Citibank and Chase Manhattan Bank. Bank-America's board replaced Armacost with his predecessor, Tom Clausen, who had not been renominated for a second term at the World Bank.

Many critics thought that Armacost, despite his mistakes, had suffered the brunt of Clausen's policies. During Armacost's last year as president BankAmerica's basic banking business lost more than $1 billion, and the value of its stock fell from $25 a share to $9.50. During his tenure the corporation wrote off $4.1 billion in loans, while another $4.6 billion in bad debts was left on the books. In an interview given after his departure Armacost admitted, "I made some mistakes as president. If I had it to do over again, I would come in on the first day and declare a major crisis." Although much of BankAmerica's problems were caused by Armacost's inaction, critics were sharp to point out that Clausen's emphasis on short-term profits had merely delayed problems, and that they were compounded by the fact that Armacost was not experienced enough to deal with the new conditions entailed by deregulation. He had simply risen too fast and had not gained enough experience in any one position.

In what observers labeled a "golden parachute," BankAmerica paid Armacost an amount equal to three years of salary as severance pay and made him eligible for options on BankAmerica stock worth $1.7 million. Facing a search for a new job, Armacost expressed an interest in a position that would "build on his experience" but which did not necessarily have to involve management. He also wished to remain in the San Francisco area. Shortly after his departure from BankAmerica, Merrill Lynch Capital Markets approached Armacost. His extensive contacts in the Bay area would help the firm increase its presence there, Merrill Lynch thought. After taking a long vacation Armacost became a managing partner in Merrill Lynch's San Francisco office, concentrating on large corporations and industry. He found himself in a significantly less prestigious position, in charge of a staff of 25 and five steps removed from the highest leadership positions in the company. In 1988 Merrill Lynch promoted him to managing director.

Publications:

"The Fettering of American Banking," *Euromoney* (October 1981): 64;

"The Problem Behind the Problem with the Economy,"
Public Relations Journal, 39 (January 1983): 19-20;
"The Road To Renewal," *Vital Speeches of the Day*, Sep-
tember 15, 1983, pp. 729-733.

Reference:
Gary Hector, *Breaking the Bank: The Decline of
BankAmerica* (Boston: Little, Brown, 1988).

Automatic Teller Machines

by James Smallwood

University of Texas at Tyler

Electronic funds transfers and automatic teller machines (ATMs) are still in their infancy. First used
by Lloyd's Bank in England in 1965, American
ATMs have seen use since 1967 when pioneer bankers in Columbus, Ohio, and Atlanta, Georgia, installed them. ATMs now vary from inexpensive and
relatively small, unsophisticated cash disbursement
machines to fully automated banking terminals,
where many routine consumer-oriented transactions
can be implemented without the aid of a bank employee. Using a plastic card with an embedded magnetic strip, consumers activate a terminal that
"reads" the personal account number on the strip.
By manipulating a keyboard, the customer can complete many simple banking transactions. ATMs
allow customers 24-hour access to their accounts
and thereby allow maximum convenience. Although
such machines may well relieve bank employees
from onerous tasks, ATMs remain expensive due to
such factors as the need to provide security for the
currency in the machines, the cost of equipment
and repairs, and the cost of "downtime."

When first introduced, ATMs functioned
within the regulatory policies established by the
comptroller of the currency and the Federal Home
Loan Bank Board, which allowed the machines to
be installed without being defined as branch banks
in conflict with branch banking laws. However,
court decisions, seven by 1978, ruled that ATMs indeed constituted branches for national banks. For
many institutions the costs of the application process for branch banking made terminals economically unfeasible for a time. Subsequent congressional legislation, however, allowed ATMs to operate
even in the face of the branch banking prohibition
in some states.

From the late 1960s to the 1990s most major
banks installed ATMs even though they were still ex-

pensive. One leader was the Chemical Bank of New
York City, which installed its first ATM in 1969.
The Chase Manhattan soon followed, as did
Citibank, the latter placing two machines in each of
its retail service areas.

Nationwide, by mid 1979, 11,000 banks had
installed ATMs. Even California, which generally
lagged behind, had made a beginning. Wells Fargo
had 19 ATMs in place by mid year, Crocker had
45, City National in Beverly Hills had 48, and
United California Bank had 22. Bank of America,
however, still trailed with only five ATMs.

That many conservative bankers in California
and other states were at first leery of ATMs was un-
derstandable. When first introduced, the ATMs' cost-
effectiveness represented an unknown. However, by
the late 1970s, improved technology allowed ATM
costs to come down drastically; although expenses
remained relatively high, more executives were willing to take the risk as costs declined. Customer resistance represented another factor in the ATM puzzle.
Many traditional customers only ever so slowly
used the new automated tellers. Gradually, however, most consumers came to appreciate the convenience of the new "always open" machines. Further, ATMs proved helpful in overcoming the nation's banks' major problems, which one executive
summarized as "people, paper, and premises." In
the 1970s more and more bankers feared becoming
awash in a turbulent sea of checks. By 1979 California's Bank of America processed 10 million paper
items every night. Such strains on the system led
the Californians in 1972 to establish the California
Automated Clearing House Association, which in
turn led to the founding of NACHA (National Automated Clearing House Association).

By 1990 ATMs no longer represented the
"wave of the future." Rather, 82,000 of them oper-

ated on a daily basis, representing continuing convenience to customers and continuing aid to executives facing their "people, paper, and premises" problems.

References:

William H. Baughn and Charles E. Walker, *The Bankers' Handbook* (Homewood, Ill.: Dow Jones-Irwin, 1978);

Bill Orr, "California a Foot Dragger in ATMs," *ABA Banking Journal*, 71 (September 1979): 139-144;

James Smallwood, *An Oklahoma Adventure: Of Banks and Bankers* (Norman: University of Oklahoma Press, 1979);

Herman Van Der Wee, *The Search for Prosperity: The World Economy, 1945-1986* (Los Angeles: University of California Press, 1986);

John Wilson, *The Chase: The Chase Manhattan Bank, N.A., 1945-1985* (Cambridge, Mass.: Harvard Business School Press, 1989).

BankAmerica

by Michael F. Konig

Westfield State College

Shortly after World War II the Bank of Italy, which had been renamed the Bank of America National Trust and Savings Association in 1930, became the largest bank in the world. With 538 branches in 317 California cities and towns in 1954, the bank possessed more than $8 billion in resources. Despite that enormous financial power, the Bank of America functioned in many respects similarly to the original Bank of Italy founded by A. P. Giannini in 1904 in San Francisco. The bank always served persons of moderate means or people who had never used a bank. As Giannini put it, the Bank of Italy began as and remained a financial institution for "the little fellow."

Giannini also organized the Bank of Italy because San Francisco banks tended to ignore the North Beach Italian colony of the city. Many of the Bank of Italy's early patrons were immigrants, unsophisticated in the ways of financial affairs. Giannini served that clientele so ably that he opened branches of the bank throughout San Francisco and eventually Los Angeles, at a time when branch banking constituted a controversial issue. State and federal regulatory agencies only gradually modified their positions in favor of branch banks, in effect following the lead of Giannini and the Bank of Italy.

The earthquake and fire of 1906 devastated San Francisco and left the city's financial district in ruins. Among San Francisco banks the Bank of Italy resumed operations most quickly after the disaster. Giannini's fortitude in dealing with the crisis and then the Panic of 1907 contributed to the rise

Optimistic Bank of America advertisement, 1932

of the Bank of Italy's reputation. The bank not only made its branch functions available to California's urban residents but also to the state's agricultural entrepreneurs. Giannini established a policy of accepting farm mortgages at interest rates well below the norm, reflecting the desire of the bank's founder to protect the small borrower as well as his desire to expand his operation. As Marquis James and Bessie R. James put it, "It was the first bank to move on a large scale into lending fields that had once been bonanzas for loan sharks." Giannini also initiated the practice of advertising in order to attract the legions of small borrowers he sought to serve. Giannini died in 1949, but by 1936 he had already relinquished control of the Bank of America to his son Lawrence Mario Giannini. The younger Giannini initiated broad developments in installment banking after he became president. Under Mario Giannini the institution grew faster than ever.

By 1970 the Bank of America possessed more than $25 billion in deposits. It served more than 2.5 million customers and had diversified into new fields such as international lending. At the same time the Bank of America's California branch system dominated banking in that state, and the bank's new World Headquarters Tower, which stood as the tallest building in the western United States, reflected its preeminent position. During the 1970s the bank jostled with Citibank for the position of the world's largest bank, edging out its New York rival in the latter part of the decade.

Yet certain changes had occurred within the institution's management structure and style that had begun to transform the bank into an entity much different than that envisioned by A. P. Giannini. The Bank of America now lent heavily to large corporations and also initiated the issuance of the bank credit card. By 1970 the BankAmericard system had 29.5 million cardholders and proved so successful that it became a separate company, VISA, within the Bank of America corporate structure.

The 1969 selection of a new chief executive, Alden Winship "Tom" Clausen, reflected the change in management style. While Giannini had always refused a private office, Clausen received a large and rather isolated suite in the new World Headquarters Tower. During Clausen's tenure, from 1970 to 1981, Bank of America, or BankAmerica, as it became known, quadrupled its profits and became a powerful force in international lending. But Clausen did not always provide the institution with leadership that focused on the bank's long-term interests. According to one account, the bank expanded its international lending program beyond a reasonable level and sought corporate customers while ignoring its own dwindling profits. In essence, the Bank of America, along with its new management, became "infatuated by its success."

The 1970s and the 1980s presented challenges that the Bank of America often could not meet. Slow economic growth, oil embargoes, steadily rising inflation, and high unemployment severely eroded the economic power of the United States within the world financial community. Those events eventually translated into a serious decline in the bank's profits from corporate and international lending. The federal deregulation of the banking business and the Bank of America's inability to respond to the new conditions created by that action led to a severe decline in the reliable core of small depositors that had always constituted the backbone of the institution.

Perhaps the most difficult situation for the Bank of America during the Clausen years arose from the institution's lending policies toward Latin America, especially Mexico. Bad loans to that nation, which had staked its economic future on domestic oil production, had to be written off. By 1986 Bank of America no longer stood as a supremely powerful force within the nation's banking community. Institutions such as Citibank, Bankers Trust, and even Chase Manhattan exercised more influence and leadership over national financial affairs, and foreign competition, especially Japanese banks, permanently knocked Bank of America out of the world's top ten banks.

While Bank of America substantially decreased its write-offs of bad loans, its overall present strength is difficult to determine. Some analysts predict that Bank of America will be acquired by another company. Others envision the institution being broken up and sold in pieces. Still another alternative involves federal regulation, which could force the bank to shrink. That has already been occurring, with deposit totals dwindling from $120 billion in 1985 to $93 billion by 1988. But even as Gary Hector stated in his excellent portrayal, *Breaking the Bank: The Decline of BankAmerica*, that the institution would most probably "end up as a relatively small player by world standards, a California bank with a solid customer business," it suddenly revived. By 1990, the bank again was profitable, and its loan losses continued to decrease. Its net income rose from $726 million in 1988 to $1.1 billion in 1989, and it showed a total first and second quarter profit of $545 million in 1990. Second quarter 1990 profits were higher than any other banking company in the United States. Third-world debt loan losses remained high, but the bank had started to expand on an absolute basis again. Net branch openings increased. Bank of America added 67 branches of the former Western Savings and Loan in Arizona (sold by the Resolution Trust Corporation) and 14 branches of a Nevada savings and loan, also acquired through Resolution Trust, by mid 1990.

References:

Gary Hector, *Breaking the Bank: The Decline of BankAmerica* (Boston: Little, Brown, 1988);

Marquis James and Bessie R. James, *Biography of a Bank: The Story of Bank of America N.T. & S.A.* (New York: Harper, 1954).

Bank Holding Company Act of 1956

by Lynne Pierson Doti

Chapman College

Commercial banks may exist as independent corporations or as holding company subsidiaries. A bank holding company may own one bank and perhaps other businesses, or it may hold more than one bank. Bankers have used holding companies to provide flexibility denied by law. For example, bankers have formed multibank holding companies to create or purchase new bank offices in neighboring communities, circumventing laws against branching. For many years, holding companies also allowed bank owners to engage in business activities denied to banks.

The Bank Holding Company Act of 1956 substantially lessened that advantage of bank holding companies. Passed after Transamerica Corporation's victory over federal prosecution for monopoly, the act forced holding companies to choose between banking and other businesses. The act also restricted multibank holding companies from engaging in unrelated activities and also from acquiring banks in more than one state (although existing arrangements were allowed to stand in the latter requirement).

While the Bank Holding Company Act of 1956 limited the activities of multibank holding companies, the one-bank holding companies remained unrestrained, and those companies proliferated in the 1960s. By 1970 one-bank holding companies had interests in approximately 100 different non-banking activities. Concerned that problems in other industries could infect the banks, Congress in 1970 brought one-bank holding companies under the provisions of the 1956 act and also gave the Federal Reserve Board of Governors the power to regulate the activities of all bank holding companies.

The Federal Reserve Board has granted bank holding companies the right to engage in activities closely related to banking, which by the 1980s included 21 different types of business. But it has denied to the banks all underwriting services, management consultation, travel agency operation, and real estate development—activities once common in banking organizations.

Reference:

George Kaufman, *The U.S. Financial System* (Englewood Cliffs, N.J.: Prentice-Hall, 1986).

Banking Act of 1935

by Richard H. Timberlake

University of Georgia

The Banking Act of 1935 was the capstone to a series of acts the U.S. Congress passed between 1932 and 1935 that had significant effects on the American monetary and banking system. The first of those acts established the Reconstruction Finance Corporation (RFC) in 1932. When he signed the RFC bill into law, President Herbert Hoover directed the new government corporation to "extend loans to banks not now eligible for rediscount at Federal Reserve Banks." Hoover's charge to the RFC emphasized official disappointment over the failure of the Federal Reserve Banks to make such loans and thereby prevent the economic contraction that began in 1929.

Subsequent to the RFC Act came an abundance of other economic legislation: the Glass-Steagall Act of 1932 allowed the Fed Banks to collateralize their monetary base materials with U.S. government securities. The original Federal Reserve Act allowed only gold or eligible bank paper to serve as collateral for loans from the Fed Banks. The Emergency Banking Act of 1933 gave new president Franklin D. Roosevelt the authority to close the nation's banks as for a "holiday" in order to stop the internal drain of their reserves into hand-to-hand currency. The subsequent Thomas Amendment, or "Inflation Bill," gave the president authority to reduce by 60 percent the gold content of gold currency of any monetary denomination. (The president devalued the gold dollar by 59.06 percent.) The Banking Act of 1933 separated investment banking from commercial banking and prohibited banks from paying interest on demand deposits. It also gave the Federal Reserve Board the authority to impose a ceiling on the rate of interest banks paid on time deposits. While giving the president the power to revalue gold by the Gold Reserve Act of 1933, Congress also gave him the power to call in all the monetary gold in the country from banks, individuals, and businesses and to deposit

that gold in the U.S. Treasury to the credit of the government. The same act also nullified gold obligations in the debt contracts of the U.S. government. The Silver Purchase Act of 1934, by which the Treasury bought silver for $.50 per ounce and spent it into existence at $1.29 per ounce, was the final monetary legislation before passage of the Banking Act of 1935.

The consensus of the 74th Congress, which convened in 1935, was that excessive speculation and stock gambling, aided and abetted by the loose credit policies of the Federal Reserve Banks, caused the crash and contraction. The apparent inability of the Fed to reverse the slide, Congress felt, signified that the entire Federal Reserve System needed restructuring and additional discretionary powers.

The Fed Banks served as the original policy-making units in the system. The original Federal Reserve Act limited their power to setting the discount rate they charged member banks for borrowing. The Federal Reserve Act (as amended in 1917) severely limited Fed Bank purchases and sales of U.S. government securities and maintained the autonomous status of each bank in its own region. The Fed Bank presidents acted as the major power factors in the system, but it was a system of strictly limited ends and means for effecting policy.

The Federal Reserve Board, in contrast to the 12 Fed Banks, originally acted only as a watchdog committee that did little more than provide oversight and interpretation of Federal Reserve law. The president of the United States appointed the seven members of the board. Their terms ran for 14 years and were staggered, so that a vacancy occurred once every two years.

Over the first two decades of the Fed's existence the board and the banks engaged in numerous turf skirmishes. Each element sought power and influence, especially to escape the constraints of the gold standard that remained by law the domi-

President Franklin D. Roosevelt signing the Banking Act of 1935, August 23, 1935. Federal Reserve chairman Marriner S. Eccles looks on from the far right (courtesy of the Federal Reserve Board).

nant institution guiding the monetary system. During that time a voluntary group of Reserve Bank presidents under the leadership of Benjamin Strong, president of the Fed Bank of New York, organized the Open Market Investment Committee. That committee operated sporadically for ten years as an open market policy-making unit for those Reserve Banks that wanted to participate.

The Banking Act of 1935 took shape under the guidance of the administration's unofficial monetary policy committee consisting of Marriner S. Eccles, whom President Roosevelt had appointed chairman of the Fed Board in 1934; Henry Morgenthau, Jr., secretary of the treasury and the administration's chief adviser on monetary affairs; and Professor Lauchlin Currie, an economist at Harvard University. The congressional counterpart to the administration's spokesmen included Henry Steagall of Alabama in the House of Representatives and Carter Glass of Virginia in the Senate. Those two men figured prominently in all banking legislation of the period. Glass, however, had joined the conservative opposition to the administration's expansive monetary policies, while Steagall led the group favoring enhanced powers for the Fed.

The proper focus of control for the system, Steagall argued, was the Board of Governors. "We all know," he asserted in a classic statement of men-versus-law doctrine, "that it does not matter so much what we write into the law as it does who administers the law." The rule of men, he felt, would function more expediently if the board rather than the banks controlled credit and monetary policies.

The administration primarily concerned itself with how to finance the ongoing fiscal deficits that accompanied the dearth of tax revenues resulting from the Depression. In addition, expansive fiscal policy as an antidote for reduced business activity added a supporting argument that Eccles and others offered to complement the practical fiscal anxieties of the administration.

The act as finally passed strengthened the Federal Open Market Committee (FOMC), giving it the form is has had ever since. Where it had been (unofficially) composed of Fed Bank presidents, power now rested with the seven members of the Board of

Governors. Five Fed Bank presidents made up the rest of the committee. (The president of the New York Fed became a permanent member; the other 11 Fed Bank presidents took turns filling the remaining four positions.)

The Banking Act of 1935 greatly extended the powers of the FOMC. Open market operations in government securities became the dominant instrument of policy. The act committed all the Fed Banks as a unit to whatever volume of open market operations the FOMC determined. The act also vested the board with the authority to set discount rates as well as to fix commercial member-bank reserve requirements within the percentage ranges 7 to 14, 10 to 20, and 13 to 26, depending on the size of the city in which the bank operated. The act relegated the Fed Banks to no more than administrators of the commercial banks and managers of the money stocks in their districts. They continued to supervise reserve requirements, the entry and exit of banks, and other legal matters. But so far as policies were concerned, the Fed Banks after 1935 only provided convenient vehicles for accounting the monetary changes the FOMC initiated.

The board's powers to set discount rates and to alter reserve requirements became inconsequential once the FOMC had the virtually unlimited power to monetize U.S. government securities. The Fed Banks still faced a gold reserve requirement against their demand obligations—Federal Reserve notes and member bank reserve accounts—but that constraint was practically inoperative because of the Fed's large gold reserve. When the consolidated balance sheet of the 12 Fed Banks reached a point where the gold requirement might have inhibited the Fed's open market policies, Congress conveniently removed the requirement (in 1966 and 1968). Thus, the Fed's gold certificate account served only as a constraint when it posed no threat of constraining.

The Banking Act of 1935 changed the character of the banking and monetary system more than the Federal Reserve Act did when it put the original Federal Reserve institution in place. No longer did the commercial banking system initiate policy. That was done by the Fed Board and the FOMC. No more did a gold standard determine the fundamental base of the monetary and banking system. Even though the Fed Banks continued to show large quantities of gold in their balance sheets, U.S. government securities became the Fed's means for creating money. The gold standard henceforth constituted no more than a public relations symbol used to encourage the popular notion that gold "backed" common money. The secretary of the treasury and the comptroller of the currency no longer served on the Fed Board. But their removal coincided with the greater influence the secretary of the treasury wielded from behind the throne of the board's chairman. The administration's fiscal concerns and the political pressures from congressmen and bureaucrats found fertile ground on Federal Reserve soil that had originally been sanctified as "independent."

In effect, the Banking Act of 1935 split the Fed into two institutions. The 12 regional Federal Reserve Banks and branches acted as one institution. They were made overseers and administrators of the banking and credit system with almost no policy-making powers. The Board of Governors of the Federal Reserve System (as it was renamed) acted as the other institution. The board and its staff, formerly housed in the Treasury building, received its own beautiful new building in Washington together with almost unlimited technical powers for effecting monetary policy. It thereafter faced only one principal constraint: the informal political necessity of accommodating the economic programs of the Executive Branch.

References:

Benjamin M. Anderson, *Economics and the Public Welfare* (New York: Van Nostrand, 1949);

Board of Governors of the Federal Reserve System, *The Federal Reserve Act* (Washington, D.C.: Government Printing Office, 1983);

Marriner S. Eccles, *Beckoning Frontiers: Public and Personal Recollections*, edited by Sidney Hyman (New York: Knopf, 1951);

Milton Friedman and Anna J. Schwartz, *A Monetary History of the United States, 1867-1960* (Princeton: Princeton University Press, 1963).

Banking Journals: *Bankers Magazine* and *American Banker*

Publication of *The Bankers' Magazine and State Financial Register*, "devoted to the dissemination of bank statistics . . . [and] sound principles of banking and currency," began in July 1846. The first issue, some 60 pages long, included editorials by a variety of contributors, some named and some anonymous, as well as pieces by the editors. It contained reports and statistics related to commerce, "legal miscellany," and an update on the developments related to banking in foreign countries. It also carried congressional debates and news items related to state finance. Published by J. Smith Homans in Baltimore, who in 1889 added the *Banking Law Journal* to his operation, the magazine continued under his control until Theodore Lamont Cross of Boston purchased it in 1890. Beginning in 1906 the magazine opened a banking publicity section to discuss advertisements analytically. That development emphasized the growing importance of advertising to banks.

Bankers Magazine continued in its general approach to bank-related issues until World War II, when a 20-year hiatus interrupted publication. In 1964, Theodore Cross inherited the rights to the magazine and resumed publication. Cross formed Warren Gorham & Lamont as a closely held partnership, and the partnership also purchased other interests in business. By 1968 the company expanded with additional reports on business law, banking law, and real estate, including the *Mortgage and Real Estate Executive Report* and the *Uniform and Commercial Code Law Letter*. A public corporation, also controlled by the Cross family, published books on banking and lending, such as the *Truth in Lending Manual* by Ralph Clontz, and several checklists, all designed for frequent and profitable updating. In 1980 the International Thomson Organization acquired Warren Gorham & Lamont and injected more resources into the publications, which by then covered most aspects of accounting, banking, finance, real estate, and taxation.

Bankers Magazine arguing against "centralized banking" two months before Congress passed the Federal Reserve Act

Most of the *Bankers Magazine* articles published from 1964 to the 1980s, written by bankers, regulators, lawyers, or consultants, involved changes in bank law, administration, competing institutions, and merger trends. The journal also carried interviews with prominent bankers and added a book review section. Slick and professional, *Bankers Magazine* had as its mission "to aid in the strategic goal of helping bank executives plan for and manage change." Published six times a year beginning in 1978—previously it was published quarterly or bimonthly—the subscription-oriented journal ran very few ads, relying instead on circulation revenue.

American Banker started in 1839 as *Thompson's Bank Note Reporter*. The magazine's founder, John Thompson, later founded New York's First National Bank. The *Reporter* carried the latest note and bond discounting quotations as well as general financial news. It proved reliable in conveying important financial information on a weekly basis. In 1887 the title of the journal changed to *American Banker*, and the format shifted to make it similar to that of *Bankers Magazine*. The International Thomson Organization added also ultimately added *American Banker* to its list of publications.

Reference:
Benjamin J. Klebaner, *American Commercial Banking: A History* (Boston: Twayne, 1990).

—Editor

Bank Merger Act of 1960

The Bank Merger Act of 1960 made bank mergers subject to the approval of various central authorities. The Office of the Comptroller of the Currency gives approval for national-bank mergers, the Board of Governors of the Federal Reserve System gives approval for mergers in which the resulting bank is a state member bank of the Federal Reserve, and the Federal Deposit Insurance Corporation (FDIC) gives approval for mergers in which the resulting bank is FDIC-insured but not a member of the Federal Reserve System. A subsequent act of 1966 strengthened FDIC control over independent bank mergers.

—Editor

Bank of United States

by Anna J. Schwartz

National Bureau of Economic Research

The Bank of United States was chartered on June 23, 1913, by the superintendent of banks of the State of New York as a commercial bank with a capital of $100,000 and a surplus of $50,000. It opened for business on July 1, 1913, in a building at 81 Delancey Street on the Lower East Side. Joseph S. Marcus, a Jewish emigrant from Russia, founded the bank. He was first a garment worker and then for 25 years a clothing manufacturer. In 1906 he founded a predecessor bank of which he became president, gaining a reputation for shrewdness and honesty. Because he quarreled in 1912 and 1913 with the vice-president, the latter resigned and formed a rival bank. Marcus in turn also re-signed and proceeded to organize the Bank of United States. Ten years later it had three branches in addition to its head office and assets of $45.8 million. When Marcus died on July 3, 1927, the bank had six branches and a capital of $6 million. His son, Bernard Marcus, who had started to work at the bank as cashier when it first opened and then rose to vice-president, succeeded him.

Bernard Marcus embarked on a sequence of mergers with other banks that by May 1929 enlarged its capital to $25 million and increased the number of its branches tenfold. He also established a security and investment affiliate, the Bankus Corporation, which invested in New York real estate,

The Bank of United States fails, December 11, 1930 (UPI/Bettmann Newsphotos)

and two other affiliates. To enable the affiliates to buy the properties on which the bank originally held mortgages but had subsequently acquired, it made short-term loans to them. Then, in order to conceal the affiliates' loans and the bank's real estate assets from bank examiners, Marcus and his associates concocted an elaborate scheme involving transfers of book entries from the affiliates to two dummy corporations and three safe-deposit companies the bank owned. In effect the affiliates' debt was repaid by the bank's lending an equal amount to the other subsidiaries.

On December 11, 1930, when Joseph A. Broderick, the superintendent of banks, closed the bank, it controlled 59 branches scattered over the city, many subsidiary corporations, and an indemnity and insurance company in addition to the three affiliates and three safe-deposit companies. It was the largest bank that up to that time had been permitted to fail, its liabilities to 440,000 depositors and other creditors at closing amounting to $188.5 million.

The failure of the Bank of United States raises two questions that since its demise have aroused continuing controversy and account for its inclusion in

an encyclopedia of business history. The questions are: When the bank was closed, was it a solvent bank that should have been saved or an insolvent bank that should have been allowed to fail? Of greater importance, what effect did the failure have on monetary and economic developments in the country as a whole?

Opinions have differed regarding the solvency of the Bank of United States at the time of its failure. Broderick deemed it solvent. The chief ground for declaring the bank insolvent was its large portfolio of real estate, which it had acquired after extending loans to the builders to construct apartment houses on prime locations on Central Park West in New York City—their names, the Beresford, the San Remo Towers, and others, 60 years after their construction, still represent distinguished residential property—and prime commercial sites in Wall Street and the garment center. In the disturbed conditions of 1930 the outlook for real estate in New York City and elsewhere in the United States was far from sanguine.

American banking legislation regarded lending on the security of real estate as an unacceptable activity of banks. In the 1920s a boom in real estate comparable to that in the stock market led to an increase in real estate loans in bank portfolios. In August 1929 the bank's examiners criticized its real estate holdings and building ventures as frozen assets. One may question whether the examiners were equipped to value accurately properties that to this day stand for quality. Broderick concluded that none of the other New York City banks knew anything about real estate because they never had shown any interest in the field.

One fact argued for the solvency of the bank: it ultimately paid off 83.5 percent of its adjusted liabilities despite its having to liquidate a large fraction of its assets during the extraordinarily difficult financial conditions that prevailed during the next two years. However, to the extent that stockholders, under the double liability clause of the state banking law, actually paid the receiver the par value of their stock, the payout to depositors may not have come exclusively from the liquidation of the bank's assets.

A second fact is that until the day the bank closed, New York City Clearing House banks had tried to arrange a merger of the bank with three other New York City banks, with J. H. Case, the Federal Reserve agent at the New York Federal Reserve Bank, to serve as chairman. Those banks had a majority of stockholders and directors of Jewish origin and of similar social and financial background as most of the stockholders and directors of the Bank of United States. The Clearing House banks offered to contribute $30 million of capital to the new institution, although the president of the Clearing House Association opposed a takeover by the Clearing House banks themselves. He attributed the merger's unsuccess to conflicting demands by each of the three groups of stockholders for a larger share of the new institution than the others wished to accord.

Even after the closing, various sources expressed interest in taking over the bank on a liquidating basis and placing immediately at the disposal of depositors 50 percent of their claims. One interested institution abandoned its proposal because it feared it would be affected by the agitation arising out of the closing of the bank. Another interested party was Herbert Satterlee, J. P. Morgan's son-in-law. He hired an accounting firm of worldwide reputation to investigate and appraise the assets of the bank. It reported a basis of values upon which to accomplish reorganization. Unfortunately, by September 1931 the deterioration of the economy undermined such an outcome. In the end, the state appointed National City Bank as liquidator.

Observers have alleged that anti-Semitism accounted for the decision of the New York Clearing House banks to let the Bank of United States fail. Mainstream bankers tended to regard Bernard Marcus and the executives of other Jewish-owned banks as not members in good standing of the banking fraternity—a not uncommon attitude before World War II. Although prejudice probably played a role in the decision to close the bank, Bernard Marcus's proclivities as a high roller also contributed to the decision. In March 1931 he and two other executives of the bank were tried and convicted by a jury of violating banking laws by the maneuvers they engaged in to give the appearance that the affiliates had paid off their loans from the bank.

The failure of the bank aroused strong feelings not only against its management but also against Broderick, whom a New York grand jury indicted for alleged neglect of duty in failing to close the bank before he did. The first proceedings ended in a mistrial in February 1932. A second trial acquitted him on May 28.

On the question of whether regulators should have allowed the bank to fail, again opinions have differed. The Bank of United States was a state bank member of the Federal Reserve System. On the day before it was closed, it borrowed $19 million from the New York Reserve Bank. Technically it could not have been regarded as insolvent on that day, since the discount window was not open to an insolvent bank.

The New York Reserve Bank reported that large withdrawals of deposits from several other New York City banks doing business with customers generally similar to those of the Bank of United States in the same parts of the city followed the closing of the bank. Withdrawals of currency over and above usual seasonal drains occurred also in the country as a whole. In a fractional reserve banking system, drains of currency from banks reduce their reserves and, unless adequate additional amounts of currency and reserves are provided, result in a multiple contraction of deposits that reduces the stock of money. The banking difficulties at the end of 1930 and the series of liquidity crises that followed prolonged and deepened the business cycle contraction that had begun in August 1929 and did not terminate until the banking holiday of March 1933.

Whether the Bank of United States played a key role in the U.S. banking panic of 1930 or whether, as some have contended, a more important role was played by the failure in November 1930 of a firm that controlled the largest chain of banks in the South with assets in excess of $200 million and also the largest insurance group in the region with assets totalling $230 million (Caldwell and Company of Nashville, Tennessee), what is not in dispute is that the banking panic late in that year changed the monetary character of the business cycle contraction then under way.

References:

Harold van B. Cleveland and Thomas F. Huertas, *Citibank, 1812-1970* (Cambridge, Mass.: Harvard University Press, 1985);

Milton Friedman and Anna J. Schwartz, "The Failure of the Bank of United States: A Reappraisal: A Reply," *Explorations in Economic History*, 23 (April 1986): 199-204;

Friedman and Schwartz, *A Monetary History of the United States, 1867-1960* (Princeton: Princeton University Press, 1963);

Joseph L. Lucia, "The Failure of the Bank of United States: A Reappraisal," *Explorations in Economic History*, 22 (October 1985): 402-416;

State of New York, *Annual Report of the Superintendent of Banks* (December 1931);

Peter Temin, *Did Monetary Forces Cause the Great Depression?* (New York: Norton, 1976);

M. R. Werner, *Little Napoleons and Dummy Directors* (New York: Harper, 1932);

Elmus Wicker, "A Reconsideration of the Causes of the Banking Panic of 1930," *Journal of Economic History*, 40 (September 1980): 571-583.

Walter Reed Bimson

(April 25, 1892 - April 28, 1980)

by Larry Schweikart

University of Dayton

CAREER: Various positions, Berthoud National Bank, Boulder, Colorado (1912-1916); U.S. Navy (1917-1920); various positions, Harris Trust and Savings Bank, Chicago, Illinois (1920-1933); president (1933-1953), chairman (1953-1970), chairman emeritus, Valley National Bank, Phoenix, Arizona (1970-1980).

Termed a "banker extraordinaire" by observers of Arizona banking, Walter Reed Bimson set a pattern for lending and growth at Valley National Bank, the state's largest financial institution from the mid 1930s to the 1970s, leaving a legacy that remains with the bank even to the present. Born on April 25, 1892, in Berthoud, Colorado, in humble surroundings, Bimson was the son of blacksmith Alfred G. Bimson and Margaret Bimson. He grew up in Berthoud and attended the University of Colorado in Boulder, but he had to leave the university for financial reasons before he graduated. Beginning in 1912 he worked as a janitor for $40 a month at the Berthoud National Bank (in which his father had purchased an interest), advancing to the position of assistant cashier. By 1916 he had ac-

cumulated enough money to return to university studies. He enrolled in the University of Chicago, taking economics and finance courses, but World War I intervened, again before he could graduate. He enlisted in the U.S. Navy in 1917 and assumed an assignment at the Sixth Division's Bureau of Navigation. From there he received an appointment to Naval Officers Training School in Great Lakes, Illinois. Bimson had extensive training in firearms as a young man and while an enlisted man in the Navy won a shooting competition.

At war's end Bimson remained in the Chicago area, accepting a position at the Harris Trust and Savings Bank in 1920. His responsibilities at the bank grew, and although he eventually was promoted to the rank of vice-president, he saw a need to take additional economics and finance courses. From 1928 to 1929 he completed graduate courses in finance and economics at Harvard University. Back at Harris, Bimson developed one of the keys to his banking philosophy, namely, the advantage in making large numbers of small loans. He was especially interested in lending in "the Loop" area, although Harris Trust had little previous interest in that part of

Walter Reed Bimson

the city. The area supported numerous small business and wage earners who commuted from the suburbs, and no downtown bank served them. Their own suburban banks were closed when they returned home at night. Even though the Depression loomed, Bimson envisioned building a business based on those "little people." By establishing links to small depositors, Bimson thought Harris could become the city's largest bank. He prepared a detailed report to the upper management, but it was rejected as "chicken feed." Still, Bimson remained committed to a "wholesale banking" approach similar in concept to that of Bank of Italy founder A. P. Giannini. Later he summed it up by saying that "if people had money, we wanted to take care of it for them, and if they needed money we wanted to lend it to them."

Harris, a conservatively run institution, had fewer problems than most banks during the Depression. But Harris management agreed that Bimson should learn about European remedies for the economic downturn by investigating finance and banking there. The bank sent him on a tour of European countries for several months in 1930 and 1931 to study their systems, and in a report he

warned that if American banks that had money to lend did not combat the Depression, the government would step in. He feared a government takeover of the private banking system in the manner of crisis-ridden Europe and admonished banks to expand consumer credit. The report's predictions already were being manifested in the Hoover administration's Reconstruction Finance Corporation and Federal Farm Board.

Nevertheless, when Bimson got back to the States, he found himself a part of the government structure he disparaged when he was made a member of an Illinois state committee on unemployment relief. While serving on the committee he experienced firsthand cases of human tragedy caused by the Depression. He also received an offer to take over the presidency of the Valley National Bank in Phoenix, Arizona.

As a part of Harris's business department, Bimson had frequently traveled to the Southwest. Arizona especially captivated him as he crossed its deserts to negotiate loans with local farmers. In the course of those trips Bimson met Dr. Louis D. Ricketts and other principal officers of the growing Phoenix-based bank. As the Depression deepened, Valley National found itself nearly insolvent due to its agricultural loans. Ricketts had pledged his considerable mining fortune to keep the bank afloat and had saved it. But the bank clearly was on a downward spiral and needed new leadership.

Bimson took over at Valley National Bank on New Year's Day 1933 and implemented a new—indeed radical—banking philosophy. He ordered the staff to "make loans" and instructed his officers to make a large number of small loans rather than a small number of large loans. Lending bolstered the confidence of depositors, and the bank's deposits soared by $200,000 in Bimson's first ten days as president. Less than 1 percent of the new borrowers defaulted. An "old-fashioned" banker in some ways, Bimson believed in personal honor and once concluded a $280,000 loan to a cattleman on "a handshake and a smile."

Yet in many ways Bimson had radical thoughts about banking, and he stopped at little to implement his programs. Convinced that rural Arizona towns needed new branches, which the Federal Reserve Board prohibited in 1933, he simply instituted "money-changing offices" in conjunction with local businessmen. He resisted pressure to close those "bootleg banks" until the Federal Reserve Board again permitted new branches to be opened. When Bimson learned that California governor James Rolph had ordered a banking holiday, he persuaded Arizona governor Benjamin B. Moeur to do the same out of concern that the frozen assets of Arizona banks in California would cause a run in Arizona.

Under Bimson, Valley National Bank was the first to offer Federal Deposit Insurance for its customers' accounts, and, although he repeatedly expressed his misgivings about working with the federal government, Bimson quickly learned how to take advantage of virtually all federal programs. His most noteworthy success was in pioneering Arizona banks' involvement in the Federal Housing Administration (FHA) program, by which the U.S. government guaranteed home loans beginning in 1934. Bimson immediately realized the significance of the program and dispatched employees in a door-to-door campaign to sell the loans. The bank even went to the extent of ordering house plans from architects, obtaining cost estimates from building contractors, then offering the houses—plans, estimates, loans—to the public. By 1935 Valley National ranked fifth in the nation for dollar volume of FHA loans. Carl Bimson, Walter's brother, who also joined the bank in 1933, recalled that "we had built homes 'like mad' all during the war" and that commercial building, prohibited throughout the war years, "exploded" after the restrictions were lifted. The bank, like others, obviously profited from the influx of new residents—ex-servicemen, new defense industry employees, retirees attracted to the Arizona sunshine—but it exceeded the growth rates of other Arizona banks. Not only were other banks still tied to conservative policies and still others committed to lending in agriculture and mining, but Valley National Bank also had a built-in advantage in that many competitors already had sizable loan portfolios that were "locked in" so that they could not make new home loans. Moreover, Valley National Bank's chief local competition in the home loan market, Western Savings and Loan, would not lend at the 5 1/2 percent rate set by the government on FHA-insured loans.

Indeed, Bimson had appreciated the importance of the FHA program from the outset, and had dispatched his brother Carl to testify before Congress in favor of the National Housing Act creating the FHA. Carl recognized that Title I of the act could be applied to appliances inside or attached to homes, and the bank found another huge outlet for its loans. Equally important, the Title I loans—up to $2,500—were unsecured, and that drew people who had never done business with banks previously. Soon, Valley National loan officers made 700 Title I loans a week. In the first year of the FHA program, the bank made $1 million worth of home loans in the two major Arizona cities—Tucson and Phoenix—alone, and Arizona exceeded its loan quota of $3 million. The success of Valley National led the federal government to take a hard look at the Bimson brothers' abilities, and it soon requested that Carl serve as a national "salesman" for the FHA program. The bank "loaned" Carl to the government for that purpose, and he toured the country touting the advantages of the new program at auditoriums, parties, and club luncheons.

Under the Bimsons' leadership, from 1934 to 1945 Valley National Bank made 198,000 loans and frequently threatened to exceed its loans-to-reserves ratio. That was especially true in the case of FHA loans, for which demand remained high. As a result, the bank looked for ways to continue to sell and originate those loans with outside cash. It offered eastern insurance companies FHA loans at a 2 percent discount but received no offers. Ultimately, A. P. Giannini's Transamerica Corporation purchased $1 million of the FHA loans from Valley National. (Ironically, also under Bimson's watch Valley National lost its edge in home loans and construction loans to the aggressive Phoenix-based A. B. Robbs Trust Company, which in the late 1950s became the 11th largest mortgage lending institution in the United States. Robbs Trust Company succeeded in doing what Valley National could not: sell loans to eastern investors.) Valley National also established Arizona's first automobile loan department in the 1930s, and it created special installment loan departments to the extent that Carl Bimson, visiting a customer's home, boasted that the bank had financed everything in the house but the baby. Other bankers thought Walter Bimson's reflationary somewhat eccentric. One even termed Bimson's lending programs "immoral," to which Bimson exploded, "Immoral! [Is it] immoral to help an enterprising individual equip and start a business on his own? Immoral to enable a teacher to go to summer school so she can earn more pay and teach better? . . . Nonsense!" Under Bimson, Valley National looked for any lending opportunity it could find.

During World War II, Walter Bimson took advantage of the opportunity to impress upon the thousands of servicemen and women brought to Arizona's air bases, training facilities, and defense-related plants the virtues of living in Arizona. He intended to attract them back to the Southwest after the war. To do that, he and Carl designed a special loan for aviators known as the "300 Club," by which cadets were made eligible for an "instant credit" line of $300 upon graduation, to pay their way home for leave and to have spending money once they got there, with repayment to come automatically out of the airmen's checks. Nearly 14,000 GIs took advantage of that program. Overdrafts were rare, and the bank found itself "out" only a minimal amount, most of that due to death in action. After the war, to facilitate veterans' relocation to Arizona, Bimson set up a "GI Bank," a division of Valley National that loaned more than $17 million to servicemen who became new Arizona residents.

Bimson realized that Valley National's growth depended on the continued growth of Arizona, especially the Phoenix and Tucson metropolitan areas. Although the bank did not ignore mining or agriculture, its main areas of concern under Bimson's predecessor, Ricketts, Bimson believed Arizona''s future depended on business, "clean industries," defense, tourism, recreation, and consumers. To attract visitors—and ultimately residents—Bimson suggested to longtime employee Herb Leggett that he oversee production of a nationally distributed publication to review the state's growth in a statistical fashion. (Arizona already benefited from the popular and photographically beautiful *Arizona Highways* magazine, which displayed the state's warm deserts, colorful vegetation, and picturesque mountains to readers in the Midwest and East, who frequently read it in the midst of winter snowstorms!) Leggett's creation, called *Arizona Progress*, measured housing starts, population, industrial production, agricultural output, and so on. The bank sent the pamphlet, published on a regular basis, to all major banks around the country. Virtually every person considering moving to Arizona could pick up *Arizona Progress* at his local bank. It became the single best piece of business promotional material in the state's history, and it inspired several banks to imitation. Bimson appreciated advertising in all its forms and also commissioned the first bank history written in Arizona, *Financing the*

Valley National Bank Center, Phoenix, Arizona (courtesy of Valley National Bank)

Frontier (1950), by Arizona State University journalism professor Ernest J. Hopkins. (Bimson canceled a subsequent volume by Hopkins, slated to bring the story up to the early 1960s, because he thought it overemphasized his achievements.) Furthermore, in the 1960s Valley National paid the salary of one of its executives, Patrick Downey, while he was "on loan" to the Phoenix Chamber of Commerce to travel across the nation as a representative of the Phoenix Thunderbirds, a booster group. Downey and the Thunderbirds proved an important arm of the Chamber of Commerce in luring new industries to Phoenix. Because of the efforts of Leggett, Downey, and the Bimsons, Arizona bankers developed a reputation as active community boosters. Valley National profited from those efforts, which brought in important businesses such as Motorola Corporation. That communications company received its first loan from Valley National.

Bimson's abilities had long been known to the federal government, which requested that he assist in drafting the Small Business Act. By the time it was completed insiders called it the "Bimson Plan." Several years later the Eisenhower administration appointed Bimson to a survey team for the Bureau of Indian Affairs. His fame had spread so much that *American Magazine* did a feature article on him by Keith Monroe that was reprinted in *Reader's Digest*. There the full range of Bimson's community activities became public: he had helped found the Thunderbird Graduate School of International Management and the Society for Applied Solar Energy as well as the Arizona Town Hall.

A frustrated artist, Bimson developed a reputation as an art connoisseur. He collected paintings and sculpture of western artists, amassing a huge inventory in Valley National Bank buildings. He emphasized collecting the work of little-known artists, arguing that it was the unknown who needed the financial support. At first he furnished art for the buildings gratis, but soon the cost grew too great. Although he continued to leave his personal collection in Valley National offices, the bank decided to purchase some of the art itself. Among the pieces Bimson acquired was a famous Russell stagecoach painting, as well as the "Horsemen of the West" series that was featured in *Arizona Highways,* which Bimson purchased intact from the Scribner Publishing Company. He also headed the effort to organize the Phoenix Art Museum, thereby helping to develop western art as a legitimate form. His interest in art ranged to architecture: all of the branches of Valley National employed operating specialists whose sole concern was the functional flow of the banks' interiors. Disgusted with the "grocery store" facilities that most banks used as their headquarters, Bimson took a personal interest in the design and construction of Phoenix's Valley National Bank building–as of 1989 still the tallest structure in the city's skyline. He insisted that the bank occupy an entire city block and not be surrounded by any other structure. He wanted the headquarters to be visible from all sides. (Even the headquarters proved a controversial enterprise: many urged Bimson to take the bank's central office to the North Central Avenue area, Phoenix's new hub. But he committed the bank to the downtown section, contributing to the revitalization of central Phoenix.) Bimson especially wanted Frank Lloyd Wright to design a prominent building in Arizona. At one time he solicited a design from Wright for a bank office building, but according to Carl Bimson, "the plans were discarded because the design, and the materials [needed] were so advanced and radical by Arizona builders' standards that . . . we could not get a builder to bid on it." But Bimson played a key role in getting a

Wright design for Arizona State University's Grady Gammage auditorium, so much so that he guaranteed the architectural fees to Wright to draw plans even before the state legislature appropriated the money for the auditorium's completion.

Bimson also worked to revise Arizona's tax codes in the 1930s, charging that heavy bank taxation endangered the entire state banking system. He succeeded in getting the Arizona codes revised. In other public service, he served on the state Board of Regents and encouraged the improvement of science, engineering, and business courses in Arizona colleges and universities.

Bimson's most significant role, however, was in leading Valley National Bank into the position of the most dominant bank in Arizona. He accomplished that despite losing much of the residential lending market to the Robbs Trust Company in the 1950s. In addition to the tremendous growth the bank had experienced through wartime lending programs, Valley National actively acquired other banks in the 1950s. First, it used the employee profit sharing plan to purchase the bank's own outstanding stock. Then, the third-largest bank in the state, Frank C. Brophy's Bank of Douglas, came up for sale. Although Bimson was reluctant to merge it with Valley National, he created a holding company, Arizona Bancorporation, to acquire the Bank of Douglas. That acquisition put Valley National in possible violation of the Bank Holding Company Act of 1956. Under that law a bank holding company had to forfeit control of any bank it held, directly or indirectly owned, or of which it held 25 percent of the shares within two years of the passage of the act. Valley National Bank simply unloaded some of its voting shares, merged other institutions, and came within the allowances of the law. Shortly thereafter the bank began a powerful drive to open branches throughout the state. It controlled more than 200 branches by the late 1970s, and branch managers received considerable autonomy. The branches also generated a considerable amount of new loans. By 1956 Valley National Bank had $28 billion in 21 million installment loan accounts.

The tremendous concentration of assets caused by Bimson's multiple mergers and consolidations brought increased federal scrutiny. When Valley National Bank's assets, including those of the Bank of Douglas (which it controlled), were added to those of the state's second largest bank, First National Bank and its held companies, those two institutions controlled 93 percent of the states' bank assets. Not surprisingly, government investigators arrived in 1956, and the Federal Reserve Board of Governors soon concluded that Valley National Bank's control of the Bank of Douglas constituted a reduction in competition in the state. Still, no immediate action followed. Not until 1962 did the Department of Justice bring antitrust charges against the bank. The case dragged on until the bank relinquished control of the holding company in 1966. By then it had its branch program well in place, although, perhaps not coincidentally, several smaller specialized competitors were founded during the period 1962 to 1970 when Valley National was still enmeshed in its case.

When Bimson took over as Valley National's chairman of the board in 1953, the bank ranked 70th in the nation with $300 million in deposits. Seventeen years later, when he retired, it ranked 34th and held $2 billion in deposits. Much of the bank's continued success was due to the Walter's brother. Carl Bimson had taken over as president of the bank when Walter became chairman, and he held the position until 1963. From 1960 to 1962 he was also president of the American Bankers Association, the first time an Arizona banker ever held that post. Carl also chaired numerous national banking committees and served as a member of the U.S. Chamber of Commerce Finance Committee. Of course, Walter garnered more than his share of credentials: he served on the same committee as Carl for the chamber and was a director on the Council of Profit Sharing Industries from 1963 to 1968.

With both Bimsons out of executive positions in 1965, the bank drifted into a lethargic period. The board requested that Walter return to more active management, and he stayed on as chairman of the executive committee. But his influence soon fell as a shadow over younger bankers. Although the bank retained its dominant position in the 1960s, a host of aggressive new banks took some of its market share. Walter Bimson's son, Earl, was promoted to the presidency in 1967 and remained as president until 1972, but Valley National, although growing, had settled into a much slower rate since Walter Bimson had left active management. By 1970 both Walter and Carl had retired from their board positions. After five years of failing health, Walter Bimson died on April 28, 1980.

Bimson had two sons by his first wife, Florence, whom he married in 1919 and divorced in 1935. His son Earl, although an excellent specialist and mid-level manager, never dominated Valley National the way his father had. Ironically, Walter's other son, Lloyd, developed a reputation as a talent with the Arizona Bank (formerly the Bank of Douglas). Lloyd died of cancer at the peak of his career. As of 1989 Carl continued to work in his office every day.

Walter Bimson came along at a critical time in Arizona banking history. He is remembered by virtually all living Arizona bankers with respect and is by far the most important figure in Arizona banking history.

References:

Don Dedera, "Walter Reed Bimson: Arizona's Indispensable Man, Compleat Banker," *Arizona Highways*, 49 (April 1973): 1, 21-29;

Ernest J. Hopkins, *Financing the Frontier* (Phoenix: Arizona Printers, 1950);

Keith Monroe, "Bank Knight in Arizona," *American Magazine*, 140 (November 1945): 24-25, 116-122;

Larry Schweikart, *A History of Banking in Arizona* (Tucson: University of Arizona Press, 1982).

Ivan F. Boesky

(March 6, 1937 -   )

by Peter De Trolio III

University of Dayton

CAREER: Clerk, Federal District Court Judge Theodore Levin (1964-1965); tax accountant, Touche, Ross & Company (1965-1966); securities analyst, L. R. Rothschild Company (1966-1967); securities analyst, First Manhattan Company (1968-1970); securities analyst, Kalb, Voorhis (1970-1972); partner, Edwards & Hanley (1972-1975); managing partner, Ivan F. Boesky & Company (1975-1981); managing partner, Ivan F. Boesky Corporation (1981-1986).

At the height of his power Ivan Boesky used a 160-line telephone and worked 20-hour days. He had amassed a fortune that rivaled the best of the nineteenth-century financial giants. To some he embodied the Horatio Alger myth; to others he appeared an invincible financial seer. But it all came tumbling down.

Boesky was born on March 6, 1937, the son of a Russian immigrant milkman turned restaurateur in Detroit, Michigan. Industrious as a youth, at age thirteen he purchased a 1937 panel truck and sold ice cream from it, earning about $150 a year. He started a lackluster academic career at Cranbrook Prep School, but he remained there only until the end of his sophomore year. After completing high school at the local public facility, he was admitted to Wayne State University. From there he transferred to the University of Michigan, where he stayed for two semesters. Then he left Michigan to attend Eastern Michigan College. He never graduated. In 1959 he enrolled in the Detroit College of Law, an institution that did not require an undergraduate degree for admission. He dropped out of law school twice but finally graduated in 1964. Meanwhile he met Selma Silberstein, the daughter of the owner of the Beverly Hills Hotel. Boesky and Selma Silberstein married in 1962.

After graduation Boesky accepted a clerkship with Federal District Court Judge Theodore Levin. When he completed the clerkship in 1965 he took a position as a tax accountant with Touche, Ross & Company. Unhappy in that position, a year later he moved to a securities analyst position with the L. R. Rothschild Company. At about that time he learned about a type of stock trading known as arbitrage, where a trader simultaneously purchases stock in one market and sells it in another, at, he hopes, a higher price. At the time only a few small firms handled arbitrage trading. They were a tightly knit group that did it only on a small scale; as Connie Bruck observed, on Wall Street most considered arbitrage a "dirty business." Boesky wanted to work in the arbitrage department at Rothschild, but his superiors refused to let him. Consequently, he left Rothschild in 1967 for the First Manhattan Company, where he worked from 1968 to 1970. From there he went to the firm of Kalb, Voorhis, where he remained until 1972.

From Kalb, Voorhis Boesky went to the brokerage firm of Edwards & Hanley to run the arbitrage department. While he worked in that position the New York Stock Exchange fined him $10,000 for selling stocks short in excess of the firm's ability to deliver. Still, Boesky started making arbitrage a new kind of business while at Edwards. Contrary to tradition, he refused to share information with other arbitrage traders for fear of compromising his own position. But Edwards was too small to realize Boesky's plans. In 1975 that firm folded, and Boesky set out on his own.

With a loan of $700,000 from his in-laws, Boesky set up Ivan F. Boesky & Company, the first Wall Street limited partnership devoted solely to arbitrage trading. He also structured his business in a new way. Previously arbitrage traders acted as "back scratchers" for their clients. They wanted to keep arbitrage "behind the scenes" and thus con-

Ivan F. Boesky (photograph by Steven Borns)

tented themselves with modest profits. Boesky wanted to expand. He broke with tradition to advertise his services in the *Wall Street Journal* to drum up business, which in an era of increasing mergers was not difficult to find. He arranged his transactions so that he received 55 percent on all profitable deals but suffered only 5 percent on deals that incurred losses.

Initially Boesky met with great success. He parlayed the original $700,000 capitalization into $94 million by 1979. In 1980 he got himself into financial trouble when a bid to corner the silver market by Texas investors and oilmen the Hunt brothers failed. Wall Street thought he was finished. In early 1981 he dissolved his partnership.

Boesky was able to come back quickly. In May 1981 he opened another brokerage firm, the Ivan F. Boesky Corporation, but by 1982 problems had appeared. He banked on a merger between Gulf Oil Corporation and Cities Services Corporation, purchasing 2 million shares of Cities, but when Gulf withdrew its merger offer Boesky's $70 million investment was frozen. When the dust settled he had lost about $20 million. He managed to re-

cover from that loss, however, by making $60 million in the Getty-Texaco oil company merger later that year. The corporation reported a $12.4 million profit for 1982.

In 1983 Boesky hit his peak. He made several successful deals in the steel and oil markets, invested heavily in real estate and in other securities firms, and enjoyed his 200-acre estate outside of New York City. He slept only about four hours a day, even working in his limousine on the way into the city. Meanwhile rumors circulated that he was receiving inside information to help him make the successful deals.

The house of cards began to tumble in 1984. Boesky made a considerable amount on a deal involving the Holiday Inn hotel chain, but then lost $40 million in an oil deal. He reorganized his corporation in 1985 and in October began collecting investors in an effort to raise $1 billion, which he used to make $15 million on a deal involving the CBS Corporation. Still, he made enough bad deals so that he mustered only a 7.7 percent return on his investors' money for the year.

The pressure to succeed compromised Boesky's success. Dennis Levine, an employee of Boesky's investment banker, Drexel Burnham Lambert, had been feeding Boesky inside information on stock purchases since February 1985. Levine's tips garnered Boesky $50 million in illegal profits in the final quarter of 1985. In May 1986 the Securities and Exchange Commission (SEC) arrested Levine for insider trading violations. The Drexel employee cooperated with the government and identified Boesky as a violator. As soon as Boesky learned that Levine had named him, he went to the SEC to work out a deal. (Some argued that the SEC intended to use Boesky to build its case against "junk bond" dealer Michael Milken.) The SEC allowed him to sell $1.3 million in stock to reduce his liability before his arrest. He also wore a "wire" to record compromising conversations with others. On November 14, 1986, Boesky was arrested, and he pleaded guilty at his trial. He received a then-record fine of $100 million and a prison sentence of three years and was barred for life from trading on the New York Stock Exchange.

Although his fines were large, experts estimated that Boesky had a huge fortune awaiting him on the outside. He still owned the 200-acre estate, and his wife netted $70 million from the sale of her late father's hotel. Boesky was released from prison in April 1990, fit and healthy after a behind-bars exercise and weight-lifting program.

Reference:
Connie Bruck, *The Predators' Ball* (New York: Penguin, 1989).

Branch Banking, Interstate Banking, and Franchising

Some pockets of interstate banking existed prior to 1980. Both of the federally chartered Banks of the United States (1791-1811, 1816-1836) established branches in several states. In the antebellum South a few banks maintained out-of-state "agencies," but those agencies usually did not emit notes. In 1853 George Smith, a Scottish banker who operated in Illinois and Wisconsin, purchased the Bank of Atlanta to emit its notes through his offices in Chicago. In that money-starved city Smith's Atlanta bank notes on occasion made up almost all of the circulating medium. After the Civil War, the Bank of California maintained a branch in Nevada that authorities permitted it to keep until the bank suspended operations in 1875. In the 1930s and 1940s A. P. Giannini attempted to create an interstate branch system of his Bank of Italy, but federal officials, especially Treasury Secretary Henry Morgenthau and Federal Reserve chairman Marriner Eccles, blocked Giannini's efforts.

Virtually no other interstate banking initiatives occurred until the late 1970s, when large banks and other companies started to take advantage of "nonbank bank" clauses in state laws. Those clauses usually restricted institutions from performing *all* banking functions, but not *some*. As a result, organizations such as Merrill Lynch and Sears established offices (usually in prime Sun Belt locations) that *either* made loans *or* accepted deposits—usually the former—but not both. The companies intended those quasi-banking offices to serve as a "foot in the door" if interstate banking won the federal approval they anticipated.

In the early 1980s a deregulatory mood that filtered down from President Ronald Reagan and up from academia (where since the early 1970s economists and historians had identified harmful effects of bank regulation) exerted an unprecedented effect on the financial services industry. Bank regulators started to adopt a more lenient interpretation of the 1927 McFadden Act regulating branch banking. One of the first successful challenges to the McFadden Act came when Citibank of New York realized that state usury laws varied and that a credit card issued in South Dakota could carry higher interest than one issued in New York. Citibank negotiated with the governor and legislators in South Dakota, who revised that state's laws to allow Citibank to locate a credit card operation there. In return Citibank brought jobs and tax revenues to the state.

Intended to allow national banks to compete better with state banks, the McFadden Act allowed national banks to branch only if state laws permitted branching. Bankers in several regions of the country therefore started to lobby for changes in state laws to permit reciprocal state banking agreements. Regional "compact" arrangements started to appear, first in New England, whereby a group of states allowed their banks to invest in each other. In each case, regions sought to permit other banks in the region to merge or establish branches across state lines but to exclude large banks outside the region. A highly successful southeastern compact agreement allowed banks in North Carolina and Georgia (North Carolina National Bank Corporation and Citizens & Southern National Bank Corporation) to expand their operations greatly. In the Southwest, Arizona simply permitted New York banks to purchase local institutions.

In 1980 Joseph Pinola of California's Western Bancorporation formed a network of the 21 banks in 11 states held by the company that brought the banks together under a common name, First Inter-

state. That action, which changed the name of the holding company to First Interstate Bancorporation, prepared the organization for the anticipated dawn of federally sanctioned interstate branch banking. In a unique "franchising" arrangement, First Interstate even licensed banks not owned by the holding company to use the organization's logo, its automatic teller system, and a pool of loan funds.

The change in federal law that Pinola and others have anticipated has not come as of 1990. Still, the move toward greater integration in banking continues. The California and New York legislatures have passed laws admitting each other's banks beginning in 1991. Thus, while not technically legalized nationally, interstate branching is rapidly becoming a reality.

See also:

BankAmerica, Citizens & Southern Corporation, First Interstate Bancorporation, A. P. Giannini, McFadden Act of 1927, NCNB Corporation, Joseph J. Pinola, Transamerica Corporation.

—Editor

Bretton Woods Conference, the International Monetary Fund, and the World Bank

by William C. McNeil

Barnard College, Columbia University

In July 1944 representatives from more than 40 nations met at the mountain resort of Bretton Woods, New Hampshire, to formulate a new international economic system. The agreements reached there and put into effect during the next two years formed the basic structures of the Western monetary and trade system for the next generation.

The planning that led to Bretton Woods began soon after the United States entered World War II. American policymakers concluded that the failures of the international economic system in the 1920s and 1930s had been instrumental in bringing on the war. Following the analysis of Secretary of State

Cordell Hull, American officials believed that the failure of American economic policies in the 1920s had helped cause the Great Depression. The Depression, they thought, had set the stage for the rise of fascism. Fascist governments had tried to divide the world into autarchic economic spheres, and that, according to the American analysis, ultimately caused the war. Reversing those failures after the war required active American participation in the world economy and the creation of an open, multilateral economic system that promoted economic growth and worldwide economic integration.

In addition to their vision of reform in world

*Henry Morgenthau, Jr., and John Maynard
Keynes at Bretton Woods, July 1944
(Alfred Eisenstaedt–pix)*

trade, policy planners also looked for a way to escape from one of the fundamental traps that had befallen politicians during the interwar years. In the course of the twentieth century, western capitalist nations had increasingly depended on their national governments to provide relief from the booms and busts of the business cycle. Government spending on construction, welfare, housing, health, unemployment relief, and the military all made the government a major force in national economic stabilization. But under the gold standard, which remained the ideal (even if not the reality), government spending could overstimulate a nation's economy and induce a balance of payments crisis. As a nation's economy expanded, its imports grew, and inflation made its exports less attractive on the world market. The resulting trade deficit could, and often did, create such a large balance of payments deficit that governments had to sacrifice their domestic political needs to the international monetary system. As the world learned the lessons of the Great Depression, policymakers searched for a way to

structure the international monetary system so that it would permit domestic Keynesian economic expansion without creating a monetary crisis.

Secretary of the Treasury Henry M. Morgenthau, Jr., and his assistant Harry Dexter White took the lead in formulating an American response to those problems. They believed that a satisfactory system would have to include active participation of both the United Kingdom and the Soviet Union. It also had to ensure successful reconstruction of the European economies from the destruction of the war.

To meet the challenge the Treasury formulated a series of reforms and then called an international conference to debate, amend, and institutionalize the new system. A brief preliminary conference at the Claridge Hotel in Atlantic City, New Jersey, allowed America's major allies to offer some modifications to the plans drawn up by White. But at Atlantic City and later at Bretton Woods, important divisions opened up between the Americans and Britain's chief negotiator, John Maynard Keynes.

Keynes by that time had become the most influential economic thinker in the western world. Harry Dexter White had hoped to create a system that gave nations the flexibility to pursue Keynesian fiscal and monetary policies. In addition Keynes wanted to create a new international economic agency with real power over worldwide investment and consumption decisions. He wanted to create a powerful World Bank that would issue its own currency, which Keynes called "Bancor." The new currency would take the place of gold and dollars as the basic reserve unit of all national banks, and the issue and control of Bancor would give the World Bank real power over economic decisions of member nations.

Keynes also foresaw that in the postwar world some nations, most prominently the United States, would run persistent and large trade surpluses since the rest of the world would depend on American factories, which had survived the war unharmed. Other nations, mostly in Europe, would run large trade deficits since the war severely damaged their productive capacity. Under the American proposals the pressure to adjust currency rates and fiscal policies to achieve a trade balance rested almost entirely on the deficit countries. That meant they would have to devalue their currencies or cut government spending and risk high unemployment to achieve a balance in international accounts.

Keynes wanted to force the surplus countries to share some of the costs of adjustment through stimulation of their economies or raising their exchange rates. He also called for greater flexibility in exchange rates than the Americans were willing to accept. At Bretton Woods, White's plan, not Keynes's, triumphed.

The proposals put forth by the United States and adopted by the nations meeting at Bretton Woods called for the creation of two new international organizations. The International Monetary Fund (IMF) was given the task of helping nations solve their short-term international debt problems while they employed expansionary monetary and fiscal problems to ease the burden of a recession. The fund would be run by a Board of Governors selected by the five largest subscribers. The governors were granted weighted voting power based on their nations' contribution to the IMF. That gave the United States effective control of the organization.

Each nation that joined the IMF received a quota on which it could draw to cover short-term trade or monetary deficits. Since a large quota gave a nation more flexibility in dealing with its international payments balance, each nation sought the largest possible quota. In order to entice the Soviet Union to join the fund, American negotiators granted the Soviets a much larger quota than its share of world trade justified.

While the IMF in theory helped solve short-term trade problems, the planners also wanted to create an organization to provide long-term capital investment in poorer countries. To that end they created the International Bank for Reconstruction and Development. The founders intended the organization, known as the World Bank, to funnel money into the war-torn European economies. Once it accomplished that task, the World Bank was to help less industrially developed nations find the investment funds needed to industrialize. Each nation that joined the World Bank put up a subscription that the bank could call on if it needed to cover defaulted loans. Since the United States was virtually the only nation in the world with excess capital supplies, it had to make the largest commitment, and other nations negotiated to keep their subscriptions to a minimum.

Planners intended the World Bank to make some loans and to guarantee a larger volume of private bank loans. In that way it set a fair price for international loans and ensured that loans went for

sound, productive purposes. Planners wanted to prevent the extravagant loans of the 1920s, which had netted New York banks large profits as they sold foreign bonds to thousands of small investors who lost money when the bonds went into default during the Depression. American bankers largely opposed the Bretton Woods system because they believed the World Bank would take power away from the marketplace and that the IMF threatened to stimulate inflationary fiscal and monetary policies.

At Bretton Woods, American and British negotiators shared the belief that reform of the international monetary system was vital. Yet the British found many of the American demands disturbing. Most troubling for British politicians, the Americans insisted on the elimination of bilateral trade agreements. The Americans equated closed trading agreements with fascist economics and called for an open, multilateral system. To British conservatives, that amounted to a call for the end of the British Empire, which was a closed trading and monetary system tied together by the pound sterling. British labor leaders also feared that the American plan would hurt the relatively expensive, inefficient British worker.

To win British support the United States eventually tied a large loan for Britain to the approval of the Bretton Woods agreements. The British had expected a $5 billion grant from the United States. They expressed anger and disappointment at being forced to accept a $3.75 billion loan instead. But the administration in Washington thought that this was all it could realistically get from Congress. Historians today tend to emphasize that the very low interest rate (2 percent with no repayment for 5 years) and protective clauses combined with the waiver of repayment of $26 billion in lend lease and other aid made a package of American assistance that many considered very generous.

In return the British agreed to return the pound sterling to gold convertibility within one year. The British attempted to honor that commitment in the summer of 1947. But a run on the pound forced the government to suspend free trade in sterling for more than a decade.

The new monetary system was to be based on national banks holding gold or a currency convertible into gold as reserves for their own national currencies. Since the U.S. dollar offered the only convertible currency, the system effectively became one in which the United States held gold as its reserve and the rest of the world held dollars.

The Bretton Woods system went into effect in early 1946 when the World Bank and International Monetary Fund held organizing sessions and their first formal meetings. Yet, in reality, the system did not evolve as anticipated by American officials. When the British discovered that they could not afford to support a convertible currency, that signaled the inability of all European states to follow the rules set up at Bretton Woods. Not until 1958, when their economies and exports had enjoyed long recoveries, did the Europeans allow their currencies to be sold on the open market. The Soviet Union refused even to ratify the agreements as they became entangled in the emerging of the Cold War of the late 1940s.

Even the American hope that the IMF and the World Bank would help promote world economic recovery and trade met with disappointment. The open exchange and trading systems envisioned at Bretton Woods could only function in a world economy in which the major nations operated at near equilibrium. American strength and European and Japanese weakness in the early postwar years made that impossible. Instead, the American government had to shoulder the responsibility of providing foreign aid to promote economic growth. The Marshall Plan of 1947 signaled the failure of Bretton Woods in that sphere.

By the mid 1950s the conditions for stability had finally developed. European growth made the European nations ready and able to accept freer world trade and convertible currencies. By 1958 most European currencies were freely convertible into gold and dollars. The Bretton Woods system was becoming a reality. But by an ironic twist of fate the leadership of the IMF had come to fear that excessive government deficits were driving the world toward dangerous levels of inflation. As a result, the organization that had been set up to permit deficit spending exercised its growing power to induce governments that wished to borrow from it to balance their budgets. That policy came to be bitterly resented by less-developed countries in the 1970s and 1980s.

The formal Bretton Woods system had only a brief life. It went into effect with the European return to convertibility in 1958 but was being undermined by the late 1960s. Perpetual American fiscal deficits had dissolved the American trade surplus by the end of the 1960s. The modest countercyclical Keynesian deficits envisioned at Bretton Woods now formed the unremitting basis of American economic and political management.

By 1971 the United States could no longer pursue its domestic policy of economic expansion while maintaining the value of the dollar. On August 15, 1971, President Richard M. Nixon brought the formal Bretton Woods system to an end when he ended the convertibility of the dollar into gold.

Analysts who emphasize the revolutionary impact of the closing of the gold window in 1971 may have overreacted to that dramatic change. The IMF and the World Bank have continued as important actors in the international financial system. But their impact has been far greater on third world nations than on the western, industrial nations they were created to help. Despite the floating world currencies that emerged after 1971, the international monetary system has largely remained dominated by the cooperative efforts of the finance ministers of the major trading states.

While the formal Bretton Woods system with its stable exchange rates has ended, the core intentions of the system remain. As of 1989, nations have considerable flexibility to pursue domestic economic stimulation without immediate restraint from crushing trade deficits. Yet even under the modified Bretton Wood system, long-term deficits still place policy makers under mounting international monetary pressure to moderate their deficit policies.

References:

Margaret Garritsen de Vries, *Balance of Payments Adjustment, 1945 to 1986: The IMF Experience* (Washington, D.C.: International Monetary Fund, 1987);

Alfred E. Eckes, Jr., *A Search for Solvency: Bretton Woods and the International Monetary System, 1941-1971* (Austin & London: University of Texas Press, 1975);

Richard Gardner, *Sterling-Dollar Diplomacy: The Origins and the Prospects of Our International Economic Order*, revised edition (New York: McGraw-Hill, 1969);

Robert M. Hathaway, *Ambiguous Partnership: Britain and America, 1944-1947* (New York: Columbia University Press, 1981);

John Ruggie, "International Regimes, Transactions, and Change: Embedded Liberalism in the Postwar Economic Order," *International Organization*, 36 (Spring 1982): 379-415;

Armand Van Dormel, *Bretton Woods: Birth of a Monetary System* (New York: Holmes & Meier, 1978).

Arthur F. Burns

(April 27, 1904 - June 26, 1987)

by Rebecca Strand Johnson

Loyola University of Chicago

CAREER: Instructor in economics, Rutgers University (1927-1930); research associate (1930-1948); director, National Bureau of Economic Research (1948-1953, 1956-1961); professor of economics (1934-1969), professor emeritus, Columbia University (1969-1987); chairman, Council of Economic Advisers (1953-1956); member, Advisory Committee on Labor-Management Policy (1961-1969); counsellor to the president, Cabinet Committee on Economic Policy (1969); chairman, Board of Governors, Federal Reserve System (1969-1978); U.S. ambassador to the Federal Republic of Germany (1981-1986).

Since the time of Adam Smith every generation has hosted one or two economists whose opinions have helped shape a society's economic perspectives. From the 1950s through the 1980s Arthur F. Burns was one of those economists in the United States. Burns produced authoritative work on business cycles and enjoyed a long and prestigious teaching career at Columbia University. His advisory role in three presidential administrations (Eisenhower, Kennedy/Johnson, Nixon/Ford) and his chairmanship of the Federal Reserve Board carried his economic views, especially those concerned with curbing inflation, into international recognition.

Burns was born Arthur Frank Burnseig on April 27, 1904, in what was then Austro-Hungarian Galicia, now a part of the Ukrainian Soviet Socialist Republic. An only child, he and his Jewish parents Nathan and Sarah (Juran) immigrated to the United States when he was still young. The family settled in Bayonne, New Jersey, and there Burns, his name shortened by a teacher, received his first years of education in the local schools. He was a good student. By age six he had completed a German translation of the Talmud, and although in later years he felt obliged to learn

his father's trade, housepainting, his family recognized his academic potential and steered him in that direction.

Outstanding grades and talent as a debater in high school earned him a scholarship to a local college, but Burns, searching for a more prestigious affiliation, so impressed the dean of students at Columbia University that the dean allowed him admittance on a scholarship in September 1921. Burns worked as a waiter, shoe salesman, housepainter, postal clerk, and seaman to earn his room and board and also contributed articles to the business section of the *New York Herald-Tribune*.

Fascinated by many career possibilities, Burns contemplated a future either in law, architecture, or dramatic criticism when he registered for a Columbia economics course taught by Wesley C. Mitchell, the first economist to popularize the idea of the "business cycle" among businessmen and politicians. In 1920 Mitchell had founded the National Bureau of Economic Research (NBER), a nonprofit statistical research organization initially intended to compile data solely on the distribution of national income. The NBER soon widened its scope to include research on domestic and international economic relationships and in the process developed many of the statistical conventions of modern economic study. Mitchell's enthusiasm and his emphasis on quantification impressed Burns, the former because it made students feel they too could help develop the science and the latter because it related economic thinking to underlying social and political contexts. Burns came to believe that Mitchell had discovered a theoretical basis for economic study, and with that realization he decided to pursue the field in a teaching career. After election to Phi Beta Kappa, he graduated from Columbia in 1925 with both the A.B. and A.M. degrees in economics.

In the fall of 1925 Burns began work on a Ph.D. at Columbia and during the 1926-1927

Arthur F. Burns (Wide World Photos)

school year also lectured in Columbia's extension program. Beginning in fall 1927 he served as an instructor in economics at Rutgers University and worked on his dissertation. He accepted a position as a research associate at the NBER in 1930, the same year he married Helen Bernstein. The couple would have two sons, David and Joseph. In 1934 Burns received the Ph.D. and saw his dissertation published as *Production Trends in the United States Since 1870.* Armed with his doctorate, he took a position as professor of economics at Columbia to go along with his NBER associateship under Mitchell.

Over the years the relationship between Burns and Mitchell had developed from one of teacher-student into one of collaboration. The collaboration culminated in 1946 with the publication of a jointly authored volume, Mitchell's definitive work, *Measuring Business Cycles.* Central to the pair's characterization of business cycles was the idea that economic peaks and valleys could be predicted by studying changes in "leading indicators" such as construction starts and stock prices. The job of the economist was to compile data on such relevant indicators and recommend governmental policy to lessen the virulence of downturns. Through careful governmental management, Burns came to believe,

a government could prevent a period of economic expansion from collapsing.

Burns's interest in the role of government in economic management soon led him to the work of British economist John Maynard Keynes. He became a close student of Keynesian maxims relating to the business cycle but opposed the Keynesian solution to the problem of the downturn: public spending to provoke growth. Instead, Burns believed in fiscal stimulation through tax reduction. The Keynesians, in Burns's view, took a "sky's the limit" approach to the problem without fully appreciating the limitations inherent in governmental action. In 1946, the same year of the publication of the definitive Mitchell-Burns collaboration, Burns also came out against the Keynesians in a monograph published by the NBER entitled *Economic Research and the Keynesian Thinking of Our Times.*

Upon Mitchell's death in 1948 Burns succeeded his former instructor as director of the NBER, and he continued in that capacity until 1953. His studies published by the NBER, which contained healthy doses of policy recommendation, won him national attention and the confidence of Republican presidential nominee Dwight D. Eisenhower, who, upon succeeding Harry Truman as president, named Burns chairman of the Council

Burns during his tenure as chairman of the Federal Reserve Board (AP/Wide World Photos)

of Economic Advisers. Republicans worried over the appointment: despite Burns's seeming economic conservatism he had remained a Democrat throughout his academic years, and his tweed suit and professorial manner reminded party stalwarts of the New Dealers they had worked so hard to oust.

As chairman of the Council of Economic Advisers, Burns correctly predicted that the Federal Reserve Board's tight money policy would bring on a recession and recommended tax reduction and easier credit. Passage of the tax cut recommended by the chairman helped cause a record breaking boom in 1955. Burns also helped establish a framework for the administration's policies on spending, successfully persuading Eisenhower of the necessity for a liberal program of unemployment insurance. But he

felt constrained by the fast pace and consuming work of government service and left his position as chair of the council in 1956 to return to Columbia and the NBER.

Back in private life, Burns continued to influence public policy, unofficially advising the Eisenhower administration when asked. Always he urged the president to recommend tax cuts to further stabilize the economy. Later, he warned vice-president Richard M. Nixon, the 1960 Republican presidential nominee, that the ongoing recession of the election year would continue if the government did not immediately act. But the budget already suffered from deficit, and the administration did not take Burns's advice. Nixon lost the election, probably (as is traditional in American politics) in part because of the unfortunate economic situation.

The new president, Democrat John F. Kennedy, anxiously sought Burns's advice and nominated him as a member of the Advisory Committee on Labor-Management Policy. Always concerned with the problem of unemployment, Burns recommended the establishment of training programs for unskilled workers, technical assistance for small companies, and tax cuts to increase private investment. At the same time he disputed the idea held by many in the Kennedy administration that budgetary deficits were secondary to the problem of maintaining economic growth and maximum employment. Consistent with his later view that the European welfare systems created economic stagnation in those countries, he often stated that the best a government could do was to implement policies that created confidence in its nation's economic future and helped people employ their own funds to create growth.

The threat of inflation inspired Burns's warnings about government overspending. To Burns the problem of rising prices hurt the disadvantaged more than anyone else. He consistently recommended ways to boost the economy by creating investment capital. In suggesting a major rewriting of the tax code in 1963, Burns told the congressional Joint Economic Committee that tax breaks to upper-income individuals and corporations, aimed at freeing up investment capital, would lessen inflation while promoting growth: "The average dollar spent by private citizens is more productive of wealth and, therefore, more productive of growth than the average dollar spent by government."

As he devoted more and more of his time to Washington politics during the Kennedy and Lyndon B. Johnson administrations, Burns gradually loosened his ties to the National Bureau of Economic Research. He served briefly as chairman and then honorary chairman of the NBER in 1967 and 1968, then, with the election of Nixon as president in the latter year, left the bureau for good to take on another advisory role, this time as counselor to the president.

Nixon asked Burns to act as a generalist with the aim of dealing with a broad province of legislative and executive policy matters. He sat at meetings of what was known as the "economic quadriad," composed of Secretary of the Treasury David M. Kennedy; Federal Reserve chairman William McChesney Martin, Jr., Budget Director Robert P. Mayo, and Council of Economic Advisers chairman Paul W. McCracken. In addition to those duties, Burns sat in on Cabinet meetings and won infamy for expressing his views on domestic issues not related to financial policy. He spoke for an expansion of the food stamp program and for better control of the program's resources, for higher minimum welfare payments and tougher work requirements for welfare recipients, and for a revision of the tax code to eliminate income taxes for those living below the poverty level.

Although Burns had an opinion about almost every aspect of executive branch business, he nevertheless excelled in his own staff position. He questioned every proposal he thought needed more study and challenged many an agency chief. He brought broad knowledge and experience to the job. In the opinion of many, Burns quickly emerged as the most outstanding member of the Nixon Cabinet.

He remained only a few months at the post, leaving when Nixon appointed him chairman of the Board of Governors of the Federal Reserve System to replace outgoing chairman William McChesney Martin. The appointment stirred simultaneous feelings of confidence and anxiety in the hearts of bankers and financial men. Never before had a professional economist with no experience in the practical world of finance reached the highest echelon of the financial world. The Fed chairmanship possessed great actual and symbolic power, and the possibility existed that Burns might work against the system rather than for it. But he won praise from congressmen and from many of the bankers, and gener-

ally the opinion that Burns would usher in an era of stability at the Fed prevailed. Democratic senator William Proxmire, chairman of the congressional Joint Economic Committee, called the appointment "probably the best Nixon has made."

Of course, controversy also followed Burns into the chairmanship of the Fed. Despite the inconsistency of Fed policy under Martin, the former chairman had come to represent a nearly permanent fixture in Washington. His departure opened the door to a period of transition. Burns spent his first year at the Fed trying to neutralize what he thought had been gigantic errors in financial policy undertaken in the late 1960s. By the end of his first year the critics were silent. After a harrowing year in which the nation's securities industry had nearly collapsed and a major railroad, the Penn Central, had declared bankruptcy, the Federal Reserve Board entered 1971 with interest rates plunging and an increase in money stocks in both banks and mortgage brokerage houses. Monetarist economists led by Milton Friedman, professor at the University of Chicago and a former student of Burns's, cheered the chairman's effort to better manage the money supply.

Still, critics expressed concern over Burns's friendship with the president, which they thought threatened the traditional independence of the Fed. That never turned out to be a problem. Nixon, for his part, argued openly with Burns when the chairman refused to expand the money supply in time for the 1972 election. Burns continued to exert his independence after the election, suggesting (after Nixon's August 1974 resignation) to new president Gerald R. Ford that Ford allow the federal government to act as an "employer of last resort" to reduce unacceptable employment levels. Said Burns of his position at the Fed, "I see this job as a judicial, a quasi-judicial function."

When in 1973 the Fed realized that the money supply had grown faster than projected, it made policy changes to raise interest rates sharply. Later, because the money supply was so large (averaging an annual increase of almost 7 percent between 1970 and 1973), economists blamed the Fed for implementing corrective measures too late and aggravating the recession and double-digit inflation of 1974-1975. In time, Burns's monetary policies and his strenuous advocacy of price controls, which rendered an international monetary standard redundant, perturbed critics to the point that Burns attracted blame for destroying America's money supply. Burns repeatedly blamed deficit spending during the Vietnam War as the cause of the subsequent inflation.

On the heels of the recession and the attacks on Burns, President Jimmy Carter entered the White House in 1977. Having established himself as a leading voice of opposition to the president on issues that normally lay beyond the concerns of the Fed, Burns faced replacement at the end of his term. The Carter administration, advised from all sides to retain Burns to signal the intent to maintain stability in finance, still chose not to tolerate his conservatism. Hoping for an era of easier money and faster growth, Carter did not renew Burns's appointment in 1978. Burns spent three years in semiretirement alternating between his Maryland home and his Vermont farm. In 1981 new president Ronald Reagan, informed of Burns's close relationship with officials in the government of the Federal Republic of Germany, asked the economist to fill another role in public service, as ambassador. Burns accepted and from 1981 to 1985 enjoyed a mutually friendly relationship with the German government. As ambassador Burns worked as independently as he had with the Fed, both charming and annoying the Germans with his candid lectures and matter-of-fact ways. His strong commitment and his unwavering American patriotism made his tenure as ambassador highly successful.

On June 26, 1987, Burns died from complications following triple-bypass surgery. In a career that spanned more than 60 years of American economic and political history he produced many books and articles and won such prestigious awards as the Alexander Hamilton Medal from Columbia University, the Jefferson Award from the American Institute for Public Service, and the Grand Cross Order of Merit from the Federal Republic of Germany. His belief that economic issues girded all of social development made him an influential political figure and one of the outstanding scholars of the twentieth century.

Selected Publications:

Production Trends in the United States Since 1870 (New York: National Bureau of Economic Research, 1934);

Economic Research and the Keynesian Thinking of Our Times (New York: National Bureau of Economic Research, 1946);

Measuring Business Cycles, by Burns and Wesley C. Mitchell (New York: National Bureau of Economic Research, 1946);

Wesley Mitchell and the National Bureau (New York: National Bureau of Economic Research, 1949);

Looking Forward (New York: National Bureau of Economic Research, 1950);

New Facts on Business Cycles (New York: National Bureau of Economic Research, 1950);

The Instability of Consumer Spending (New York: National Bureau of Economic Research, 1952);

Wesley Clair Mitchell: The Economic Scientist, edited by Burns (New York: National Bureau of Economic Research, 1952);

Business Cycle Research and the Needs of Our Times (New York: National Bureau of Economic Research, 1953);

The Frontiers of Economic Knowledge: Essays (Princeton: Princeton University Press, 1953);

Prosperity Without Inflation (New York: Fordham University Press, 1957);

The Management of Prosperity (New York: Columbia University Press, 1966);

Full Employment: Guideposts and Economic Stability, by Burns and Paul F. Samuelson (Washington, D.C.: American Enterprise Institute, 1967);

The Business Cycle in a Changing World (New York: National Bureau of Economic Research, 1969);

Reflections of an Economic Policy Maker: Speeches and Congressional Statements, 1969-1978 (Washington, D.C.: American Enterprise Institute, 1978);

The Reagan Economic Program (Washington, D.C.: American Enterprise Institute, 1981);

Regaining a Stable Price Level (Washington, D.C.: American Enterprise Institute, 1981);

The United States and Germany (New York: Council on Foreign Relations, 1986).

References:

"After Burns: The Fed Will Lean to the Left," *Business Week,* no. 2510 (November 21, 1977): 108-116;

Richard O. Bartel, "An Economist's Perspective Over 50 Years," *Challenge,* 27 (January-February 1985): 17-25;

"High Marks for the Fed's Freshman Boss," *Business Week,* no. 2161 (January 30, 1971): 38-39;

"Interview with Arthur Burns: Economic Analysis and Reminiscences," *Business Week,* no. 2549 (August 1978): 93-108;

"Replacing a Monetary Legend," *Economist,* 233 (October 25, 1969): 42-45;

Helmut Schmidt, "Arthur F. Burns: Ambassador and Friend to the Germans," *Challenge,* 28 (September-October 1985): 53-55;

Lawrence Walkin, "A Practical Politician at the Fed," *Fortune,* 83 (May 1971): 148-151, 254, 259-260, 262-264;

William Wolman, "Piling Up Economic Evidence," *Business Week,* no. 1664 (July 22, 1961): 58.

J. Willis Cantey

(March 3, 1917 - October 15, 1986)

by Olin S. Pugh

University of South Carolina

CAREER: President (1945-1958), chairman of the board, Columbia Outdoor Advertising Company (1958-1986); assistant to the president (1958-1960), president (1960-1971), chairman of the board, Citizens & Southern National Bank of South Carolina (1971-1974); president, Citizens & Southern Corporation (1969-1974).

James Willis Cantey entered banking in 1958 after a successful career in advertising. He became a charismatic leader of his bank, Citizens & Southern (C&S) National Bank of South Carolina and the banking profession as a whole. Cantey carried forth a rapid expansion program at C&S through acquisitions and de novo entry. He also served on several major corporate boards in the Carolinas, on the board of the Charlotte Federal Reserve Bank for six years, and as a civilian aide in South Carolina to the secretary of the Army from 1981 to 1985.

Born on March 3, 1917, in Columbia, South Carolina, Cantey was the son of J. M. and Elizabeth Cantey. He graduated from the University of South Carolina in 1938. In 1941 he married Nancy Moorer; the couple had three sons. Cantey served as a lieutenant in the National Guard when his unit mobilized in 1940. His distinguished military service left him the recipient of three Silver Stars, the Legion of Merit, the French Croix de Guerre, and the Purple Heart. He retired from the U.S. Army Reserve in 1955 as a colonel. Cantey kept a close association with both the University of South Carolina and the U.S. Army throughout his life.

Cantey enjoyed a successful career as president of Columbia Outdoor Advertising Company from 1945 to 1958, and that led to the development of a real estate interest. Then he joined the Citizens & Southern National Bank as assistant to the president. He became president of C&S in 1960

J. Willis Cantey (portrait by Del Priore; courtesy of the University of South Carolina)

and chairman in 1971. When Cantey joined the bank it operated in four cities; by 1974 C&S served 25 cities with 76 branches. The bank's assets increased fivefold during his years as president.

Cantey saw the need for C&S to expand throughout South Carolina as the state grew to become a diversified industrial area. He negotiated seven bank acquisitions and planned de novo entries into markets throughout the state. The establishment of a one-bank holding company with subsidiary corporations contributed to the expansionary movement. Cantey's interpersonal skills operating from the base of a profitable organization facilitated the expansion. His vigorous leadership made C&S a major banking competitor statewide.

Cantey's pleasant personality and his ability to deal with people made him very popular both within and without the Citizens & Southern National Bank of South Carolina. Cantey's associates saw him more as a dynamic leader than as a traditional banker. His positive approach to life and his good sense of humor often masked his seriousness of purpose in business and life.

Cantey served as a member and chairman of the South Carolina State Ports Authority for nine years, as a member of the Banking and Monetary Committee of the U.S. Chamber of Commerce, and as a director of the Federal Reserve Bank of Richmond in Charlotte from 1967 to 1972. He was president of the South Carolina Bankers Association from 1966 to 1967, a founding member of the Board of Trustees of the University of South Carolina Business Partnership Foundation, and a recipient of the Distinguished Alumnus Award and an honorary doctor of laws degree from the University of South Carolina. After his death on October 15, 1986, the College of Business Administration at the university created a chaired professorship designated the J. Willis Cantey Professor of International Business and Economics.

Cantey also served on the boards of the Liberty Life Insurance Company, the State-Record Company, Carolina Freight Carriers, and Standard Savings and Loan Corporation. His work in the commu-

nity was equally strong. As a college student he was a boxer and played varsity basketball for three years. He was a strong believer in teamwork, and he continued to make valuable contributions to his state and community throughout his life. Cantey's associates hold that much of his success as a leader was due to his spontaneous wit, a generous nature, and a concern for others. His wit was renowned throughout the region as a result of his ability to relate a good story and his seemingly endless stock of stories and incidents to use with any group.

Within his bank, Cantey was noted for having the ability to select talented people and to help them develop in their careers. In the process C&S grew rapidly while maintaining a high level of profitability. Cantey's understanding of what constituted effective advertising enabled him to establish promotion campaigns that attracted much attention. Also, the innovative and aggressive applications of computer technology in the ATM field earned the bank several national awards. Altogether, Cantey led C&S in the development of a reputation for friendliness, growth and effectiveness.

Reference:

John G. Sproat and Larry Schweikart, *Making Change: South Carolina Banking in the Twentieth Century* (Columbia: South Carolina Bankers Association, 1990).

Central Banks

Modern Americans associate the term "central bank" with an institution that engages in deliberate, planned, and discretionary management of the money supply. A central bank is usually a relatively large, nationally created and chartered institution empowered to create money (that is, issue bank notes). It not only holds the reserves of other domestic banks but also holds international monetary reserves, and thus it serves as a focal point for international financial exchanges. As one of its primary responsibilities, a central bank handles government financial transactions and usually holds government deposits. Part of its obligation to government involves making loans to the government,

presumably on a basis no other bank could or would.

American concepts of central banks derive in great measure from the colonists' experiences with the Bank of England (created in 1694), although the Swedish Riksbank predated it by almost 30 years. To Americans in the early Republic, discussions of a central bank concentrated on the control of the country's gold reserves and on the questions of loans and note issue. The control over large gold and silver (specie) reserves allowed the central bank to operate as a "lender of last resort"—essentially to make loans to commercial banks in distress when no other bank could. That position, however, eventually entailed some regulatory functions, for, faced with limited resources, in a crisis the central bank had to determine who was deserving of its assistance. In normal times the bank had to pursue policies that would, if at all possible, prevent distress in the commercial banking sector. Ultimately such policies took on the aura of "political" decisions, and therefore the banks, especially in the United States, fell victim to considerable criticism, for policy decisions always favored some groups or sectors of the economy over others. For that reason central banks have always been the source of much hostility in the United States.

Central banking in the United States originated with the First Bank of the United States (BUS). Historians and economists still dispute whether either the First or Second BUS had true central banking powers or if either used what powers they had. Scholarly opinion seems to have arrived at the consensus that neither bank, despite the relatively large size of each at the time of creation (1791 and 1816, respectively), attempted to wield central banking powers to any great extent. Although both had a large number of notes in circulation compared to any other bank, historians doubt that either controlled the money supply. Nevertheless, the public frequently believed that both banks could influence the economy in a significant way. Both banks, for example, issued notes acceptable for payment to the government, but BUS notes never carried "legal tender" status, meaning that no one was obliged to accept them in payment for goods or services. The First BUS failed to receive a recharter in 1811, and people blamed the financial disruptions that occurred during the subsequent five years in part on the absence of a national bank. Congress saw a new BUS as a means to bolster the sale of government bonds and thus help finance the debt from the War of 1812. Therefore Congress chartered the Second BUS, modeled along the same lines as the first, in 1816. It had a 20-year charter and like the first was authorized to do something no other bank could: establish branches in the states. Nevertheless, both were commercial banks first and foremost and conducted their operations as such.

With the expiration of the national charter for the Second BUS in 1836 (or its virtual emasculation in 1833 when President Andrew Jackson ordered federal deposits withdrawn), the United States no longer had a central bank of any type. The Trea-

sury Department conducted some central banking activities, but no mechanism of centralized control of the money supply existed again until the creation of the Federal Reserve System in 1913. Unlike the First or Second BUS, the Federal Reserve Banks did not engage in commercial banking but instead acted as "banker's banks." They held the reserve deposits of the member banks and made loans to them from the pool of deposits (called "discounting" commercial paper). As envisioned, the Federal Reserve System, or, colloquially, the Fed, proposed to provide central banking functions and an elastic money supply and was empowered to regulate banks in a limited sense through the management of the member banks' reserves or by the interest rate it charged on its loans to member banks (called the "discount rate"). In addition, the Federal Reserve Banks examined member banks.

Unlike other central banks, the Federal Reserve featured 12 district Reserve Banks, which were located in cities across the country and at first remained highly independent of each other. Despite the forces that had succeeded in establishing the central bank, enough opposition remained against concentrating the power of money in the United States (especially in New York City) that Congress sought to distribute the representation and benefits of the bank throughout the country, with the South and West heavily represented among Reserve cities. Each Reserve Bank had jurisdiction over all commercial banks in its district, and although only national banks were required to become members, the founders envisioned state banks joining. That did not become reality in the early years of the system.

With the creation of the Federal Reserve System the forces that had lobbied for a central bank saw their vision come to fruition. The member banks selected each Reserve Bank's nine-member board of directors. A seven-member Board of Governors in Washington supervised the overall system, but at first the New York Federal Reserve Bank effectively made policy with its actions. Originally, the secretary of the Treasury and the comptroller of the currency automatically served on the Board of Governors, with the president choosing the remaining five members. Thus the system had the potential to be highly politicized. The predominance of the New York Bank's power prevented such a politicization from having much of an effect, however.

The Federal Reserve issued a new type of paper currency, called Federal Reserve notes, which eventually replaced all national bank notes, gold certificates, and silver certificates. Because the new currency was based on collateral and reserve requirements, the issue of notes remained tied to gold until the 1930s, when the United States abandoned the gold standard. Through its power to issue money, the Fed had one important tool to combat any panic that might arise. Its rediscount feature comprised the Fed's second important tool. In the rediscount process, the Fed stood ready to buy its customers' promissory notes from member banks. Those notes represented short-term, self-liquidating debts that, in turn, represented "real" transactions in commercial exchange backed by "real goods." Hence, the Fed's rediscount process complied with the "real bills" doctrine. The Fed charged an interest rate—a rediscount rate that it raised or lowered in purchasing the promissory notes. Member banks, contrary to the intention of the Fed's founders, often borrowed to bolster their own reserves in order to increase lending. Finally, member banks were expected to clear checks at par to facilitate a national interregional payments system. But small member banks, which had charged an exchange fee on check clearings, lost substantial revenue with the process and harbored no good-will toward the Fed for imposing itself on them.

How successful has the Fed been in meeting its goals? Most observers tend to rate Fed actions differently for different periods: during the period 1913 to 1933 many, if not most, scholars find the Fed's actions as ranging from barely adequate to completely inept; from 1933 to 1970, adequate to commendable; from 1970 to 1983, poor; and in the recession of 1983, too restrictive.

During the first period Fed officials not only had to get used to their newly available tools but to support the monetary policy during a war. The Fed made low-interest loans during World War I to banks that provided government securities as collateral. After the war the bank loans and deposits contributed to a rise in consumer prices. A drop in gold reserves prompted the Fed to raise rediscount rates, forcing a contraction in 1920-1921. Agricultural prices fell sharply. Many critics blamed the Fed's tight credit policies for the agricultural problems, but in fact the end of the war and the subsequent return to farming by millions of Europeans provided the necessary cause. Even so, American agriculture remained depressed for the remainder of the decade, and hundreds of farm-related banks failed.

A congressional investigation into the Fed's role in the agricultural collapse of 1920-1921 failed to reveal any obvious villains. Fed officials blamed the gold standard. Soon thereafter, however, the Fed discovered "open market" operations, by which it purchased or sold government securities through the Federal Reserve banks as a means of expanding or contracting the money supply. Consequently, in 1923 the Fed formed the Open-Market Investment Committee (changed to Federal Open Market Committee in 1933). Yet critics maintain that the Fed failed in exactly the type of open market operations it had started to undertake in the economic debacle of 1929-1933, when more than 9,000 banks failed and when the money supply fell by more than one-third.

Despite the shocking wave of bank failures across the country, Federal Reserve credit remained virtually unchanged from 1929 to early 1932 ($1.6 billion in open market securities and loans). Other major errors made by the Fed included its repeated statements that credit was "easy" even though the interest rates on private bonds continued to fall, thus eroding the value of those bonds held by banks as assets. In 1931, ostensibly to offset gold outflows, the Fed actually *raised* the rediscount rate. Congress apparently thought that the Fed had failed in its central task of providing and expanding money supply, because in 1932 it chartered the Reconstruction Finance Corporation to provide emergency loans to distressed borrowers—exactly what the Fed should have done. And, as Milton Friedman and Anna J. Schwartz contend, the Fed refused (or was unable) to bail out the Bank of United States, which spurred a new wave of bank failures, failures that differed markedly from the previous failures in the 1920s. While Friedman and Schwartz remain among the most cited of the Fed's critics, numerous other scholars have supported their work or revised it in such a way that the Fed still remained culpable. Most observers concede that the Fed could have either prevented the Great Depression or greatly ameliorated its effects through open market purchases of securities beginning in 1930.

Several New Deal programs focused on Fed policies and powers, including the creation of the Federal Deposit Insurance Corporation, which essentially admitted that the Federal Reserve System itself was incapable of generating sufficient depositor confidence to revive the banking system. Ironically, recent research discredits the Roosevelt "fireside chats" and the role of deposit insurance in accounting for the inflow of deposits back to banks in 1933, and the extremely low level of deposit growth during the decade somewhat dispels the myth that people ran back to the banks with their money after the advent of deposit insurance.

Congress had not finished, however. In 1935 it abolished the entire existing Federal Reserve Board, replacing it with a new agency called the Board of Governors. The secretary of the Treasury and the comptroller did not serve on the new governing body. The Federal Open Market Committee, consisting of the seven governors and five of the presidents of the twelve Reserve Banks, received statutory recognition in 1933 and 1935. It soon dominated the Fed's affairs. Also in 1935 the Fed received the power to vary the legal reserve requirements, a power it promptly used to increase the requirements and initiate the "Roosevelt recession."

During World War II, the Fed played an important role in financing the wartime deficits by supporting the prices of government securities at low interest rates. Reserve holdings of government securities rose by a factor of 12 between 1941 and 1945. Nevertheless, the Fed could not do that and simultaneously hold down prices, even with the aid of price controls. Postwar prices shot up 63 percent higher than their 1941 levels. Most of the difficulties between 1945 and 1951 came from the Fed's commitment to support the price of government securities. Once the Treasury set prices in line with market rates, the Fed could start to use its open market operations as it wished. For the remainder of the decade the Fed used its powers to offset unexpected changes in bank reserves and to attempt to stabilize the economy. The Fed restrained the growth of "high-powered money" that its open market purchases created in currency or bank reserve deposits. "High-powered money" received its name because each dollar supported several dollars of bank deposit liabilities.

In the 1960s the Fed increasingly relied on professional economists and on market indicators, such as short-term interest rates or the reserve positions of the commercial banks, to aid in making policy. High-powered money increased in the 1960s, mainly because of the financing of the Vietnam War. Critics maintained that the Fed could not do both simultaneously, that is, support government fis-

cal policy and adhere to the direction of market indicators. Many argued that the policies in the 1960s revealed themselves in the inflation of the 1970s. Inflation bordered on hyperinflation, at times running at 10 to 12 percent. The Fed seemed incapable or unwilling to slow down the expansion of the money supply, leading to charges (again, with Milton Friedman among the most vocal) that the Fed had become a policy arm of the administration. Friedman increasingly argued for fixed rates of monetary expansion (or contraction) based on specific indicators.

The appearance of stagflation, which combined both inflation and a stagnant economy, disproved the Phillips Curve and broke the once widely accepted link between monetary expansion and unemployment. With that link broken, it became possible to pursue both lower inflation and lower unemployment simultaneously. Several monetarists also came to serve on the Board of Governors in the late 1970s and early 1980s, somewhat splitting the board.

The most recent Fed policy snafus occurred in the 1980s. Ronald Reagan had campaigned on a platform of supply-side tax cuts to restore productivity. However, Paul Volcker, chairman of the Federal Reserve Board, was committed to squeezing out inflation. In early 1981 the administration asked the Fed to reduce the growth rate of the money supply by 50 percent over four to six years. But Volcker feared (and predicted) inflation resulting from the tax cuts. So the Fed "collapsed the growth of the money supply, and delivered 75 percent of the multiyear reduction in 1981," according to one Treasury official. By 1982 inflation reached the low rate that the administration predicted for 1986, which caused "the most severe recession in the postwar era," according to economist Paul Craig Roberts, and brought about "a totally unexpected collapse in the growth of nominal GNP," which in turn produced the budget deficits. (Because revenues were predicted in the past and government expenditures already set in the budget, even the positive effects of the tax cuts could not offset the monetary policy). Worse, the Reagan tax cuts—which Congress phased in over a three-year period, thus postponing until the third year the benefits the cuts engendered— lowered government revenue until the third installment took effect. A policy war developed between supply siders in Congress and the administration and monetarists in the Fed. As a result of the tight money policy, a recession occurred until the final increment of the tax cuts took effect. The Fed should have expanded the money supply gradually to keep up with the phased-in tax cut effects; instead, it forced a virtual contraction. Critics charged that the deficits led to higher interest rates, but in fact high interest rates preceded the large deficits. The Federal Funds rate, an overnight rate set by the Fed, actually exceeded the rate on long-term AAA corporate bonds from October 1980 to October 1981 and from March 1982 to June 1982, the pit of recession. Nevertheless, the combined effect of the tight money policies and the revival of investment and productivity brought about by the lower interest rates and the final increment of the tax cut led to a revival that even critics found impressive. Inflation sank to almost zero at one point, and remained at 4 percent–usually much less–into the 1990s. Employment, caused by the investment generated by the tax cuts, soared. More than 15 million new jobs were created in a decade when Europe had zero net new job growth. From 1983 to the present the economy has witnessed the longest peacetime boom in American history.

The Fed-induced recession in 1982-1983 showed that, contrary to critics, the Fed remained completely independent of administrative influence.

But it was by no means removed from the effects of politics. In fact, critics often argued that Volcker, in his efforts to maintain his independent image, effectively undercut the administration's policies. The recession also showed the danger of having two independent entities within government that play a crucial role in the nation's monetary policy act without coordination. It gave new reason to reconsider the link between fiscal and monetary policies.

With the rapid integration of the world's financial markets, central banks will still have a role in setting policies, but the effects of those policies will be apparent much more quickly than at any time in the past, meaning that the power of central banks to act on impulse or out of political duress will generate an immediate response that few nations, including the United States, can long ignore.

See also:

Banking Act of 1935, Marriner S. Eccles, Glass-Steagall Act, William McChesney Martin, G. William Miller, John Pierpont Morgan, Jr., Henry Morgenthau, Jr., Wright Patman, William Proxmire, Henry S. Reuss, Benjamin Strong, Paul Volcker.

–Editor

Certificates of Deposit (*see* **Money Instruments**)

Chase Manhattan Bank

by Alec B. Kirby

George Washington University

In the twentieth century and particularly after World War II, Chase Manhattan Bank transformed itself from a largely domestic concern serving large financial institutions into a broad-based international corporation with assets approaching $100 billion. Chase traces its roots to 1877, when John Thompson, an experienced New York banker and the publisher of *Thompson's Bank Note Reporter*, established the Chase National Bank. But the future policies of the bank were established by Henry

White Cannon, who succeeded Thompson as bank president in 1887. Cannon's program centered on extending financial services to other banks. By 1900 Chase boasted deposits of $43 million, 70 percent of which flowed from other banks. Cannon's leadership came naturally from his prior experience as comptroller of the currency under President Chester Arthur. In 1904 another former comptroller, A. Barton Hepburn, assumed the bank's presidency and continued Cannon's institutional approach. Buoyed

Willard C. Butcher, chairman and chief executive officer of Chase Manhattan Corporation from 1981 to 1990 (photograph by Jacques Lowe; courtesy of Chase Manhattan Corporation)

by an expanding national economy and an increasingly solid reputation, by 1914 Chase deposits totaled $135 million, two-thirds of which came from other banks. Hepburn also cautiously expanded Chase operations to include financial services for commercial and industrial firms. That proved a fortunate policy, since most of Chase's bank deposits were lost to the Federal Reserve after 1914. Albert Wiggin, who joined the bank as vice-president in 1904, directed Chase's diversification. After assuming the presidency in 1911 he increased Chase's relationship with major corporations. He himself served as a director of 50 companies during his career.

Chase continued its explosive growth after World War I and especially during the 1920s. Much of the bank's growth in that period reflected the changing nature of the U.S. economy. Large profits allowed corporations to finance expansion with retained earnings and corporate securities; hence, loans to commerce and industry increased little over the decade. Chase, which had accumulated worldwide contacts during and after the war, superseded the role of older, established investment houses in underwriting and distributing those securities. A Chase affiliate, the Chase Securities Corporation, founded in 1917, accomplished that role for the bank. Capital funds from the astonishingly successful affiliate leaped from $2.5 million to $20.5 million in 1926, at which point it sold securities it underwrote to people as well as to institutions, with an issue of bonds by the Argentine government being the first offering publicly advertised by the firm. By 1929 Chase Securities operated offices throughout the United States and in principal European capitals. Expansion continued through the early 1930s, yet the deepening depression limited new security issues. In 1933, shortly before Congress enacted the Glass-Steagall Act separating commercial from investment banking, Chase liquidated its affiliate. That liquidation marked a hiatus in Chase's effort to internationalize its operations.

The development of the Chase Bank also reflected the state of the U.S. economy in the 1920s insofar as much of its growth came through acquisitions and mergers. Through the decade, five banks merged with Chase. In 1929 the bank also acquired ownership of American Express, although Chase later sold that company as part of the liquidation of Chase Securities. A more permanent expansion took place in 1930 with the merger of the Equitable Trust Company of New York.

Financially the Chase Bank weathered the Great Depression well, and it also rescued many banks that faltered during the banking panic that reached its climax in March 1933. However, the reputation of the bank was damaged by revelations of the Pecora Committee, named after the counsel to the Senate Banking and Currency Committee. The committee revealed that Albert Wiggin, then retired, had directed companies that had realized a profit of $10 million by dealing in Chase stock. A substantial part of that profit came from selling the stock short while the market collapsed in late 1929, with some of those sales going to a group sponsored by Chase affiliates in an effort to support the market.

Fortunately for Chase, Winthrop Aldrich assumed the presidency of the bank in the early 1930s. Aldrich gained a favorable reputation for his professional competence and vigorous activities on the civilian front during World War II. His delegation-based management style freed him to serve as Chase's ambassador to business, government, and the national and international public. The role of worldwide ambassador had become imperative for a Chase president by 1953, when Aldrich retired. The succession of John J. McCloy to the Chase presidency assured the continuation of such efforts. McCloy had served as a special assistant to Secretary of War Henry Stimson before becoming assistant secretary of war and later president of the World Bank and U.S. high commissioner in Germany.

By the time of McCloy's succession to the presidency, Chase ranked third in assets among American banks. But deposits lagged, and McCloy continued Aldrich's efforts to effect a merger to bolster Chase. McCloy focused on the Bank of the Manhattan Company, the second-oldest banking institution in the United States. The two companies consummated the merger in 1955, creating a mammoth institution with total resources of about $7.6 billion, second in size only to the Bank of America.

The merger with Manhattan stood as the most important single event in Chase's history. It moved the bank into the retail business within New York City and laid the foundation for expansion into the suburbs and upstate. With its bolstered financial condition came the impetus behind a vigorous expansion into foreign branches beginning in the 1950s.

By the mid 1980s Chase's assets stood at $88 billion. More than two-thirds represented loans, mostly to commerce and industry worldwide. The bank also made sizable loans in real estate, to individuals, and to foreign governments. Foreign credits constituted about half the total. Chase was also competitive in savings, with deposits totaling more than $10 billion. Despite a continuing deep involvement in third-world loans, Chase Manhattan remains in a firm financial condition, and has ranked in the top five American banks—usually third—for several decades.

References:

William Hoffman, *David* (New York: Lyle Stuart, 1971);
John Donald Wilson, *The Chase: The Chase Manhattan Bank, N.A., 1945-1985* (Boston: Harvard Business School Press, 1986).

Citibank

by Alec B. Kirby

George Washington University

Citibank traces its origins to 1812, when it was established as the City Bank of New York. By the end of the 1800s, after transforming itself into National City Bank of New York in 1865, it had emerged as one of the largest banks in the United States. In 1956 National City Bank became First National City Bank, and in 1977 it took the name Citibank, after its parent holding company, Citicorp, incorporated in the state of Delaware.

Citibank entered the twentieth century guided by James Stillman, president of the firm from 1891 to 1908. Stillman inherited the 12th largest commercial bank in New York. Under his direction, Citibank abandoned its narrow field of operations and branched out into investment banking, becoming involved in railroads, trust companies, insurance, and other concerns while acquiring 11 correspondent banks. Known as a "big business bank," Citibank involved itself in every stage of the process of underwriting corporate securities. That diversification proceeded apace under Stillman's successor, Frank Vanderlip, and was tacitly encouraged by the Federal Reserve Act of 1913, in which Congress refused to outlaw investment banking by commercial banks. By 1916 the number of corporate accounts at Citibank had increased by nearly 100 percent. The firm had attained an enviable position before the U.S. entry into World War I, as companies sought to build up their inventories to secure themselves against rising prices of raw materials and the dangers of ocean transport. That effort required the issuance of new securities to raise capital, an effort from which Citibank profited.

In an effort to increase foreign trade, the Federal Reserve Act also allowed banks to acquire foreign branches. Citibank opened the first foreign

*Park Avenue headquarters of Citibank
(courtesy of Citibank)*

its surged from $900,000 in 1923 to $22.8 million in 1929.

Citibank's profits and investment-based strategy fell victim to the Great Depression. From 1929 to 1932 the bank's total resources declined by 27 percent to $1.6 billion. Deposits dropped by 21 percent and loans by 50 percent. Citibank's 1929 profit of $22.8 million fell to a $12.6 million loss by 1932. The bank found its strategy of underwriting corporate securities prohibited by the Glass-Steagall Act of 1933, which required the separation of commercial and investment banking. A third casualty of the Depression was Charles Mitchell, who resigned in February 1933 after being accused of unsound management.

The new Citibank president, James Perkins, led a Citibank recovery through the 1930s. Focusing on commercial banking, the firm competed vigorously for deposits and renewed its commitment to foreign banking. From 1933 to 1939 deposits grew 10 percent annually and assets grew at a rate of 7 percent. By the end of the decade Citibank stood as the second largest U.S. bank, behind only Chase. The recovering foreign branches, however, suffered a setback during World War II, as enemy troops occupied most of Citibank's branches in Europe and the Far East. Briefly the firm became little more than a domestic repository. Yet the experience and contacts Citibank had made left it poised to capitalize on foreign banking after 1950. Under the direction of Walter Wriston, who took command of the Overseas Division in 1959, Citibank established a branch in every significant country in the world. Meanwhile, the firm established corporate customers at home, loaning corporations funds and offering improved corporate services such as trust administration and financial planning. By 1967, when Walter Wriston became the bank's president, Citibank was more deeply involved in the corporate market than Chase Manhattan or Morgan Guaranty, Citibank's closest competitors. In a daring move, Wriston also led Citibank into the installation of Automatic Teller Machines (ATMs). Decreeing that the bank place two ATMs in every banking office—at a cost of millions—Wriston ensured Citibank's position for years as the number one U.S. bank.

Citibank continued its growth through the 1970s and 1980s, although it did not escape controversy. Early in the 1970s, Stanley Sporkin, the director of the Securities and Exchange Commission's

branch of a nationally chartered U.S. bank in Buenos Aires, Argentina, in November 1914. The explosive growth that Citibank enjoyed during the World War I era was thus international in nature. However, the recession of 1920-1921 dealt a severe blow to the bank, and in May 1921 Stillman resigned in favor of Charles Mitchell. Mitchell established the firm's finances and continued to expand Citibank into a wholesale commercial and investment bank serving large corporations and correspondent banks. After an inauspicious beginning, Citibank experienced a boom in the 1920s, and prof-

Division of Enforcement, accused the firm of manipulating foreign currency transactions to evade foreign taxes. Several of Citibank's officers received fines. The bank also had to pay a total of $11.9 million in back taxes and penalties in four countries. Yet the firm remained on a solid international footing, ranking as the number one foreign exchange dealer. A 1983 study by an independent investment firm estimated the total volume of Citibank's trading in the foreign exchange market to be $62.5 tril-

lion. The bank's assets made up approximately 4 percent of the total of all U.S. banks. As the 1980s came to an end, Citibank had every reason to expect continued growth.

References:
Harold Van B. Cleveland, *Citibank: 1812-1970* (Cambridge, Mass.: Harvard University Press, 1985);

Robert A. Hutchinson, *Off the Books* (New York: Morrow, 1986).

Citizens & Southern Corporation

by John Landry

Brown University

Citizens & Southern (C&S) Corporation, a holding company for financial services based in Atlanta, evolved from the Citizens Bank of Savannah, incorporated in Georgia in 1887. By a series of mergers and acquisitions of other banks, including several outside Georgia, it became a regional banking company, with more than $21 billion in assets in 1989.

Five weeks after its September incorporation, Citizens Bank of Savannah convinced stockholders of the Citizens Mutual Loan Company, also of Savannah, to merge. The merger provided the new bank with $200,000 in capital, and it opened for business on January 2, 1888.

Growing with the busy port of Savannah, the bank increased its capital to $500,000 by 1890. A year later, Mills B. Lane joined the bank as executive vice-president. Lane's expansionary drive helped to increase the customer base and deposits of the young bank, and he went on to serve as its president from 1901 to 1939. His son, Mills B. Lane, Jr., president from 1946 to 1971, continued his father's attempts to increase the bank's holdings.

By 1906, Lane, Sr., had built Citizens into the second largest bank in Georgia. That year he arranged for a merger with the largest bank, crosstown rival Southern Bank of the State of Georgia. The new bank was called Citizens & Southern Bank, with Lane at the helm.

In the next 20 years C&S acquired or opened branches in all parts of Georgia, including one in Atlanta in 1919. In 1927 the state legislature forbade

Hugh M. Chapman, president and chief operating officer of C&S Corporation and chairman of C&S South Carolina Corporation from 1986 (photograph by Gittings; courtesy of C&S Corporation)

branch banking. C&S managers, in response,

formed the Citizens & Southern Holding Company and had that company own all of the shares of its now legally separate banks. They also acquired a national charter for the base C&S bank in Savannah, and, in an unusual arrangement, had that bank own the shares of the holding company. C&S bought four more banks in the next two years, but then did not expand again until the 1960s.

Outside of the state, the holding company in 1928 purchased the Atlantic Savings Bank (begun as Germania Savings in 1874) and the Atlantic National Bank (begun as Germania National in 1916), both of Charleston, South Carolina. Those two banks were combined in 1934 and named the Citizens & Southern Bank of South Carolina. Under Hugh C. Lane, another son of Mills B. Lane, Sr., the bank convinced the parent holding company to let it go. C&S of South Carolina became independent in 1940 and remained so until 1986, when it merged back with what had become C&S Georgia Corporation.

While acquiring more Georgia banks in the 1960s, C&S purchased Joel Hurt Factors, a trading company, and established offices for international banking in New Orleans and Miami. C&S had already opened a service center for corporate clients in New York in 1956, and offices in Los Angeles and New York followed. Along with the booming Atlanta economy, C&S, now based in that metropolis, grew rapidly into the early 1970s.

Over the years C&S innovated in several customer services. In 1951, it introduced drive-in banking, the first bank in the nation to do so, and in 1971 it was among the first to allow instant cash withdrawals from automated teller machines.

The recession of 1974-1975 hit Atlanta severely. Lane, Jr.'s, practice of employing managerial recruits as credit analysts, with little supervision from the credit audit committee that was deemphasized in the late 1960s, caught up with him. After years of aggressive lending, C&S was caught with a large portfolio of real estate loans of low quality and with a large proportion of fixed rate assets. It was forced to post a net loss of $7.8 million in 1977, its first loss ever. Strict controls on lending imposed by its new president, Bennett Brown, along with continued strength from banking subsidiaries outside of Atlanta, allowed C&S to resume paying dividends in 1979. Bennett's reforms included inverting the company's structure, so that the holding company, C&S Georgia Corporation, held C&S National Bank as well as the smaller banks.

The company grew rapidly again in the mid 1980s, this time by acquiring out-of-state banks as well. (With the advent of liberal branching laws, C&S also gradually merged back all the banks in the holding company that had been legally separate.) The first was the $4 billion Landmark Banking Corporation of Florida, purchased in 1985 under new reciprocal interstate banking laws. The next year, as mentioned, C&S acquired C&S of South Carolina, which by then held $3 billion in assets.

The out-of-state acquisitions brought a corresponding change in name. The new holding company became simply C&S Corporation, and it held the following subsidiaries: C&S Georgia Corporation, C&S Florida Corporation, C&S South Carolina Corporation, C&S Trust Company, and C&S Investment Advisers, Incorporated.

In 1989, C&S announced a merger with Sovran Financial Corporation, a large banking company based in Norfolk, Virginia, with extensive holdings in the Washington metropolitan area. C&S Sovran Corporation, the name proposed for the new company, would be the largest regional banking company in the country, but as of June 1990 concerns under the Community Reinvestment Act had delayed the merger.

References:

Sanford Rose, "The Day the Profits Stopped at Citizens and Southern," *Fortune*, 97 (June 5, 1978): 104-106;

John G. Sproat and Larry Schweikart, *Making Change: South Carolina Banking in the Twentieth Century* (Columbia: South Carolina Bankers Association, 1990).

Tom Clausen

(February 17, 1923 -   )

by Scott W. Fischer

University of Virginia

CAREER: Cash counter, lending officer, head of corporate finance (1949-1961), vice-president (1961-1965), senior vice-president (1965-1968), executive vice-president (1968-1969), vice-chairman of the board (1969), president and chief executive officer, BankAmerica Corporation (1970-1981, 1986-   ); president, International Bank for Reconstruction and Development [World Bank] (1981-1986).

Alden Winship "Tom" Clausen, head of BankAmerica Corporation during its boom of the 1970s and renaissance of the late 1980s and World Bank president in the early 1980s, was born on February 17, 1923, the son of Morton and Elsie (Kroll) Clausen. He spent his youth in the small Mississippi River town of Hamilton, Illinois, where his father published and edited the local weekly newspaper. Clausen and his sister Jocelyn grew up in a staunch Presbyterian and conservative Republican family that survived the Great Depression with few problems. Both children attended the local public schools. In high school Clausen played flute in the band, edited the school newspaper, and was class valedictorian. In a school theater production he played a character named "Tom" and that experience tagged him with an enduring nickname.

Clausen graduated from high school in 1940 and entered Carthage College in Kenosha, Wisconsin, where he helped finance his education by working as a linotype operator in nearby print shops. Upon completion of his B.A. in 1944 he entered the Army Air Corps and served as a flying meteorological officer based in the Azores. After his discharge in 1946 he used his G.I. Bill funds to enter law school at the University of Minnesota in Duluth; he completed his LL.B degree and passed the Minnesota state bar exam in 1949.

Although Clausen had intended to practice law in Minnesota, he instead followed Mary Marga-

Tom Clausen

ret "Peggy" Crassweller, the sister of one of his law school classmates, to Los Angeles, where she had found a teaching position. He hoped to marry her and return to Minnesota; however, she had other ideas. Until she accepted his proposal, Clausen remained in Los Angeles and studied for the California bar. On the advice of a friend in the legal department at BankAmerica (then known as Bank of America) in Los Angeles, Clausen took a part-time job as a cash counter at the bank's main Los Angeles branch. Peggy Crassweller finally married Clausen on February 11, 1950. The couple had two sons, Mark Winship and Eric David.

BankAmerica offered Clausen a $225-a-month full-time position in a recently established executive training program after he passed the California bar. He decided that banking might be more interesting than law and accepted the position—an easy choice since he had not received any law offers. In a 1978 interview Clausen stated, "Once I decided to stay with the company, I set out to be the very best at whatever I was doing." He earned a reputation for working long hours and being concerned with details, especially after he worked overtime on the day of his wedding to correct a $10 bookkeeping error; years later he could still cite the amount of his first major loan loss: $645,312.13. Colleagues also noted that he enjoyed decision making. After beginning in the loan department, where he specialized in start-up high-technology firms such as Memorex and Teledyne, he moved up to head the branch's corporate finance department.

In 1961 Clausen was appointed a vice-president in charge of financial relationships in electronics; two years later BankAmerica's president and chief executive officer Rudolph Peterson promoted him and transferred him to the bank's San Francisco headquarters to lead a reorganized corporate finance group. Clausen became senior vice-president in 1965, and a year later the bank sent him to Harvard University's Graduate School of Business to attend its advanced management program. He was promoted in 1968 to executive vice-president and became a member of the managing committee, the bank's top policy unit. In that position Clausen responded to the complaints of local lending officers that they were hindered by bureaucratic procedures for setting up regional offices throughout California and delegating more decision making to them. The following year Peterson put him in charge of the bank's lending activities worldwide.

Clausen quickly received credit for arranging one of the bank's most important international deals, a project that raised $250 million for an open-pit copper mine on the island of Bougainville in the South Pacific by the Australian subsidiary of the British mining concern Rio Tinto Zinc (RTZ) Corporation. The transaction was complex because it involved the legal systems of the United States, Australia, and England, banks in those countries, and several subsidiaries of RTZ. The paperwork alone took nine months to complete. Although Clausen received most of the credit, the rank and file in the company also gave much acclaim to Samuel Armacost, a young executive and recent graduate of Stanford University's M.B.A. program, for his involvement in the project. Armacost eventually became Clausen's protégé and successor at BankAmerica.

After the RTZ deal Clausen became vice-chairman of the BankAmerica board in May 1969. Shortly afterward BankAmerica CEO Rudolph Peterson announced his retirement, effective in 1970; the board selected Clausen as successor despite his relative youth and lack of notability. Clausen became president and chief executive officer of BankAmerica on New Year's Day 1970, at the age of forty-seven. The corporation's assets quadrupled in ten years as Clausen expanded its worldwide activities, including lending to giant corporations and foreign governments, especially in the third world. Eventually, international business rivaled in importance BankAmerica's original retail consumer business in California.

During his first five years as CEO, Clausen emphasized profit making in all units of the bank and instituted tight controls in a "building block" cost allocation system that measured return on assets according to operating function and geographical region. He once stated, "People around here used to be concerned about size and volume. Ask a loan officer, 'how's business?' and you'd immediately hear how many loans he'd made. I've tried to leave my stamp by making everyone aware of profit." Each individual branch became a separate profit center where local managers made pricing decisions based on the marginal cost of funds. Branch managers also gradually received broader authority over promotions and salaries.

Similarly, when rivals withdrew from many markets after suffering losses on real estate investments triggered by the 1974 Arab oil embargo and the resulting economic slump, Clausen tried to take advantage of the situation by decentralizing credit authority and raising the lending limits of BankAmerica's loan officers. Author Gary Hector criticized that effort because Clausen depended on a very inexperienced and underpaid lending staff and did not implement adequate controls to measure its performance. Many of the loans made in that period haunted Clausen's successor, Samuel Armacost, but during Clausen's tenure BankAmerica made more money than any bank in history.

Clausen's second major effect and his main priority during his second five years was to continue his decentralization plan. He divided Bank-America's multinational operations into four major units operating in Caracas, London, Los Angeles, and Tokyo. By 1980 BankAmerica had expanded to 1,100 offices in California and more than 500 international offices in more than 100 countries. Despite the seeming emphasis on decentralization, Hector asserted that Clausen actually centralized decision making and intervened in the most minute details of field office operations. Junior executives watched Clausen's travel schedule; their bosses frequently delayed decisions during Clausen's absences, fearing that he would overrule them once he returned. Clausen even sat on a committee that reviewed the salary increases of every bank employee who earned $20,000 or more. As inflation worsened in the late 1970s, Clausen occasionally made announcements such as, "No one we're going to review today will get a raise of more than 9 percent."

Clausen was obsessed with competing with BankAmerica's largest rival, the New York-based Citibank and its holding company Citicorp, to earn the prestige of being the most profitable banking institution in the United States. Citibank had passed BankAmerica in the race in 1971, but BankAmerica recaptured the position by the end of 1977. Part of that gap was a result of the depression in profits caused by Citicorp's multimillion-dollar decision to install two automatic teller machines (ATMs) in every retail office. Most observers at the time questioned the program because of doubts that it would ever pay for itself; BankAmerica decided to wait until the cost of the machines dropped. During the 1980s however, BankAmerica found itself scrambling to catch up as ATMs became the rage in the industry. The other reason for the gain on Citicorp was Clausen's emphasis on short-term profits, especially inflated profits caused by the economic conditions of the late 1970s, at the expense of innovation. Despite decentralization, BankAmerica had not modernized its branch system in California or its computer and data retrieval systems and had not reorganized its check and loan processing procedures.

BankAmerica executives and employees noted Clausen's gruff personality and a mastery for detail that included a prodigious memory for numbers and statistics. He did his homework before meetings and often verbally attacked employees who

could not answer his questions. He seemed to enjoy catching people unprepared; a typical rebuke ran, "How come I know that and you don't? You're the expert, I'm the chief executive. You should know those things. How can you manage those things if you don't?" Clausen also frequently worked late hours and took home large quantities of work. He once stated, "All my life it's been difficult for me to say 'Hello' or 'good morning,' until ten o'clock coffee"; accordingly, colleagues and subordinates avoided him early in the morning.

In 1980 a critical change occurred at Bank-America. When profits shrank early in the year, Clausen ordered every unit to increase revenues or lower costs—since his ten-year string of continually rising earnings was threatened. By then Samuel Armacost had risen to the position of head cashier, BankAmerica's chief financial officer. In a series of legal but questionable accounting and procedural moves Armacost added $85 million to the bank's 1980 profits; however, they had drastic long-term effects. Under Clausen, BankAmerica managers booked up front all earnings to be made over the full term of the loan; that also exaggerated profits.

Although BankAmerica's profits rose during Clausen's last year, most of the rise was due to his emphasis on the short term. During his last five years in office net income growth averaged 18.7 percent a year; no other mortgage bank even came close to that figure. In October 1980 the Boston Consulting Group, one of the nation's leading management consulting firms, completed a one-year study of the strategy of BankAmerica's corporate planning staff. That report, a ringing indictment of Clausen's last five years in office, concluded that while BankAmerica's California lending operation was three times more profitable than the next closest division, Clausen had milked the division for profits instead of expanding it. The report criticized Clausen for not investing where profits were highest and investing without clear targets. Others interpreted the findings as evidence of weak management.

After the 1976 election Democratic president-elect Jimmy Carter briefly considered nominating Clausen, a conservative Republican, as secretary of the Treasury, but Clausen withdrew from contention, saying, "I know how to get things done in the corporate world, but I'm not so sure about Washington." Carter's eventual ambassador to the United Nations, Andrew Young, had suggested Clausen's name after Clausen had urged more aid for developing countries at a meeting of the International Monetary Fund in 1973. In June 1980 Robert S. MacNamara informed President Carter of his plans to retire as president of the International Bank for Reconstruction and Development (World Bank) on his sixty-fifth birthday in 1981. Both Carter and MacNamara hoped to prevent a move by other World Bank member nations to name a non-American to the post. After consulting with Republican presidential nominee Ronald Reagan, Carter appointed Clausen to replace MacNamara on October 31, 1980. Although he left BankAmerica in April 1981, Clausen did not assume his new position until July 1, 1981. In the meantime he started a comprehensive review of international business affairs and financial problems and took an extended trip to consult with various world political, financial, and business leaders.

During his last months at BankAmerica Clausen scrambled for ways to cut costs. When one executive defended an investment as good long-term venture, Clausen retorted, "You're talking about tomorrow, I'm talking about this afternoon." Profits dropped 19 percent during Clausen's last year, the bank's first decline in 14 years, and the officers had no more accounting moves or stored reserves left to raise profits. Despite his private worries about the bank's financial future, Clausen did not let on about them at his last annual meeting or in the 1980 annual report.

Clausen's style of leadership at the World Bank was more relaxed and decentralized than that of his predecessor. In September 1981 he delivered his first address to the bank's board of directors and underscored the importance of the bank's role in the development of agriculture and energy and the region of Africa. Ultimately, the World Bank prepared a program for sub-Saharan Africa that observers called propitious and well developed; however, critics charged that efforts to meet the urgent African situation came at the expense of other needs.

The bank faced several unforeseen challenges during Clausen's tenure, including restructuring the debts of middle-income countries and addressing excessive indebtedness by several major borrowing countries. During the 1980s economic malaise prevented growth in the private sector in many less developed countries, much of which was attributable to socialist governmental policies that impeded—or completely killed—growth. Under Clausen the World Bank shifted its emphasis from tackling poverty to encouraging growth by deregulating business and agriculture, emphasizing fiscal prudence and competitive exchange rates, and privatizing public companies.

The bank wasted much of its funding on projects whose success was prevented because of faulty policies of borrowers; in response, loans stipulating policy changes rose from $400 million in 1980 to $4.4 billion in 1987. Clausen stressed the need for a better balance between the public and private sectors, increased infrastructure investments, and policy changes to make enterprises more efficient. He also expanded the International Finance Corporation, the World Bank affiliate that promotes private investment in developing countries, and sought new means to finance World Bank lending and to increase cofinancing with private banks. He stated, "I want to focus especially on what I believe can be a new era of partnership between The World Bank and international commercial banks for helping the economies of developing countries. . . . The World Bank's project lending is a strong complement to the lending that commercial banks do." In 1983 Clausen announced a new cofinancing mechanism known as B-loans, whereby the World Bank and other banks participate on an equal footing, with one syndicated loan.

Clausen stressed the benefit of private assistance and participation of nongovernmental organizations in population control programs in less developed countries. At the 1984 International Population Conference he announced the bank's plan to implement double lending for population and health programs. The bank considered programs effective when they offered a variety of family planning methods, provisions of basic health care, and means of delivering services, especially through outreach programs in individual communities.

Despite Clausen's reputation as a conservative Republican he frequently clashed with the Reagan administration. He supported the president's efforts to reduce the size of government but disagreed that the World Bank should be affected by budget cuts. Clausen followed MacNamara by stressing the desperate needs of developing countries and the ability of the developed world to help alleviate them. He viewed his role as a salesman who must convince the "have" nations that it was in their interest to help the "have-nots": "If we can help the Third World countries expand their economies, ours will also expand, and there will be more jobs in the United States." He cautioned that if the United States did not provide funding, the economy could respond negatively: "Where people are desperate, you have revolutions. It's in our own evident self-interest to see that they are not forced into that. You must keep the patient alive, because otherwise you can't effect the cure."

Clausen's stance conflicted with that of conservative members of Congress and the Reagan administration such as Representative Jack Kemp and Undersecretary for Monetary Affairs Beryl Sprinkel, who viewed World Bank programs as socialistic or redistributionist. Clausen ignored Treasury officials over certain nominations to World Bank affiliates and its salary levels. In particular Treasury Secretary Donald Regan fought with Clausen, especially over Clausen's effort to increase funding for the World Bank soft-loan affiliate, the International Development Association, which grants interest-free loans to the world's poorest nations. Regan publicly pushed Clausen to further tighten World Bank loan requirements to middle-income developing countries that he wanted "graduated" into the private market.

Relations with the Reagan administration thawed somewhat when James Baker, who was more supportive of the bank, became treasury secretary in 1985. Clausen was an outspoken proponent of the so-called Baker Plan to help alleviate the international debt crisis, part of which included a proposal to disburse an additional $9 billion over three years from the World Bank and the Inter-American Development Bank and encourage developing countries to adopt more market-oriented policies. Despite the improvement in relations and Clausen's willingness to stay, Reagan refused to renominate him when his term expired in 1986. That refusal broke a tradition of longevity in the World Bank's leadership—MacNamara held the position for 13 years.

Under Clausen's leadership, the World Bank made a record $1.2 billion in profit in fiscal 1986, a year in which it made $16.3 billion in loans to developing countries. During his tenure Clausen had presided over a systematic and thorough appraisal of the future role of the World Bank, which the bank combined into a new agenda when his term ended in June 1986. Clausen, however, left his successor the task of making the requisite procedural and organizational changes. Similarly, the bank had

not developed as of mid 1987 a strategy to deal with the international debt problem. *Business Week* criticized Clausen by stating that the bank "drifted aimlessly while Clausen bickered with the Reagan administration. As a result, despite $11 billion in annual lending, the Bank sat on the sidelines while the International Monetary Fund assumed leadership in handling the worsening debt crisis." Clausen saw the bank's need to combine its analyses and recommendations on individual projects into a unified development policy; however, he rarely involved himself personally in policy discussions with individual countries.

Clausen's tenure at the World Bank proved a temporary personal interlude away from the developing saga at BankAmerica. While Clausen managed the World Bank, BankAmerica's financial condition worsened under the leadership of Armacost. During the two years preceding his departure, Clausen, with Armacost as his head financial officer, expected interest rates to fall and dramatically expanded BankAmerica's home mortgage loan portfolio. That strategy backfired when deregulation and recession rocked the banking industry during the early 1980s. Interest rates soared, leaving the bank with low-yield mortgages while paying high interest rates on consumer deposits. As a result Armacost faced problems that many saw him incapable of solving.

Ironically, the third-world debt problem that had plagued Clausen and the World Bank also threatened BankAmerica. Many loans incurred by BankAmerica under Clausen's leadership, including those to developing third-world countries and in real estate, shipping, and energy concerns, went bad. Armacost's defenders quickly pointed out that, besides the bad loans, Armacost had inherited several other problems from Clausen. BankAmerica had invested little in basic management systems and new computer technology.

Armacost unsuccessfully struggled for six years to improve BankAmerica's health, but conditions continued to deteriorate. After six years of declining earnings and mounting losses, the corporation's board of directors ignored critics who blamed Clausen for most of the bank's problems. On October 6, 1986, the board invited Clausen, who was only 16 months away from the standard retirement age of sixty-five, to return as president and CEO of BankAmerica.

Newspaper reports stated that Clausen thought the bank's management had tried to blame him for its current problems. When asked about his previous tenure, he responded, "I'm not going to conduct a post-mortem on my performance, except to say that if I had known that deregulation would pass so soon, it would have changed my thinking." He also admitted focusing too much on the short term. Responding to queries about when BankAmerica might return to profitability, he asserted, "If I don't do it fast enough, I may not be here very long."

October 12, 1986, marked Clausen's first full day in his old position. At that point his main challenge was the hostile takeover bid by former BankAmerica subsidiary First Interstate Bank in Los Angeles—the last straw that had led the board to demand Armacost's resignation. Two weeks later, First Interstate raised its bid by $600 million to $3.4 billion, a price much higher than the market value of BankAmerica stock. Clausen stalled with the unorthodox move of asking First Interstate to table its offer until the new management could examine the bank's condition. The takeover fight lasted several months, but BankAmerica's board finally rejected the offer in January 1987.

Clausen's main problem was the fact that BankAmerica's income was shrinking faster than its expenses. The day after his first press conference in October 1986, BankAmerica announced a $23 million loss that would have been bigger had the bank not sold its Los Angeles headquarters and other assets, bringing in $169 million. First, Clausen continued a restructuring begun under Armacost. He also almost completely changed the corporation's top management and hired top executives away from Wells Fargo & Company, BankAmerica's San Francisco rival noted for its high profits and tough cost control procedures. Clausen reduced BankAmerica's work force by 25,000 employees and concentrated more on consumer banking and operations in California. He even removed half of the computer systems managers recruited during Armacost's last three years.

Unable to raise money on the stock market because of depressed prices, the bank sold discount stock to its shareholders and debt and preferred stock to Japanese companies. In order to raise capital the bank scaled back its worldwide operations and sold off assets such as its highly profitable Italian bank, an action begun under Armacost, and its

Charles Schwab & Company discount brokerage, which Armacost had purchased from founder Charles Schwab in 1981. The Schwab deal effectively ended further First Interstate takeover efforts; First Interstate CEO Joseph Pinola, who had once worked under Clausen at BankAmerica, stated, "As profitable and strategic BankAmerica Corporation assets are sold, the remaining Latin American debt and other [less-developed country] debt, together with other substantial nonperforming assets, become an increasing large part of the smaller banking company. Further, the capital raised through the sale of these assets is required to support the balance sheet and thus not available for asset growth."

Promising profits by the end of 1987, Clausen announced his two major objectives for the bank's future at a stockholders' meeting in late May 1987: "We will be the dominant provider of premier retail and wholesale banking services in the United States, and we will be a preeminent wholesale bank offering a wide range of financial services in the United States and world markets. . . . Our conscious goal is to be a smaller company, a much more focused company, and most important, to become once again a very profitable company." Although BankAmerica's financial condition eventually improved, it did not occur, as Clausen had predicted, during 1987, a year which turned out to be one of worst years for the banking industry since the Great Depression.

Less than two weeks after promising profitability, Clausen announced second quarter losses of more than $1 billion—BankAmerica's largest loss ever, and twice as bad as the worst during Armacost's tenure. During 1987 the value of BankAmerica's stock declined by $1.1 billion—half of its value. Many banking observers criticized Clausen when he stated that BankAmerica's reserves for Latin American loans were adequate in a period when most major American banks, led by Citicorp, had established large special reserve funds. When Clausen did establish a similar special reserve fund, he utilized a dubious method to determine its level that critics labeled as double counting; he also used a reserve counting method that listed loans already written off by the bank. Ironically, during the last year of Clausen's first stint as president in 1980, BankAmerica and rival Citicorp were roughly equal in assets and stock value; in 1987 Citibank had nearly twice the assets as BankAmerica and four times the stock value.

Clausen's program ultimately caused moderate improvements in BankAmerica's condition. Despite the massive losses in 1987 the quality of its loan portfolio improved, especially in the problem areas of real estate and agriculture. Profits rose quarter by quarter in 1988, and loan losses dramatically reduced. At the end of 1988 *American Banker* ran the headlines, "BankAmerica Off Critical List." In fact, by 1989, BankAmerica had met several capital requirements mandated by the Federal Reserve for 1992. On February 6, 1989, Clausen announced that BankAmerica had issued its first quarterly stock dividend since 1985, although the dividends were 15 cents a share compared with 20 cents in 1985 and 38 cents in 1984. Some critics considered that move slightly premature, but they recognized the bank's need to soothe its stockholders.

Most analysts in 1989 agreed with Donald Crowley of the major credit rating firm of Keefe, Bruyette & Woods, who applauded BankAmerica's "phenomenal comeback" and labeled the bank as "one of the most undervalued major banks." Crowley stated, "Today, advances are being made on all fronts: profitability, credit quality, capital adequacy, and expense control." Crowley's report cited a decline in expenses as a percentage of average earnings assets and an improvement in non-performing asset ratios, particularly in domestic non-performing assets.

In the first quarter of 1989 Clausen reported a sharply higher net income, most of which was due to the attraction of new business, consumer loans, and mortgages. In April 1989 BankAmerica announced that instead of selling off assets it was purchasing them; within a one-week period the bank announced the purchase of First Development Corporation in Nevada and American Savings Financial Corporation in Washington State.

Despite the rosy news, billions of dollars in foreign loans still threatened BankAmerica's future. In 1989 BankAmerica had $8 billion outstanding in non-trade-related loans to less developed countries; it had reserves to cover only 33 percent of its loans to developing countries, although some analysts recommended a 50 percent figure and many other U.S. banks, including First Interstate, had sold off foreign loans at 50 cents on the dollar. BankAmerica also slipped to the third largest banking company in the United States, behind old rival Citicorp and Chase Manhattan Bank. Any forced large-scale rise in the reserve would again eat into capital. Despite those factors, Clausen stated in 1989, "We've come a long way." Although he noted that modest cutbacks might still be necessary, he was confident that he had returned BankAmerica to financial health.

Selected Publications:

"The International Corporation: An Executive's View," *Annals of the American Academy of Political and Social Science*, no. 403 (September 1972);

"Private-public Partnership for Development of Poorer Nations," *American Banker*, June 11, 1982, p. 4;

"Population Growth and Economic and Social Development" (Washington, D.C.: World Bank, 1984);

World Development Report 1984 (New York: Oxford University Press, 1984);

"The Economic Situation in Developing Countries: Sub-Sahara Africa and the Third World Debt," *Vital Speeches of the Day*, January 15, 1985, p. 213;

"In Search of Stability: United States, Japan and West German Cooperation," *Vital Speeches of the Day*, January 15, 1988, p. 209.

References:

Teresa Hayter and Catherine Watson, *Aid* (London: Pluto, 1985);

Gary Hector, *Breaking the Bank: The Decline of BankAmerica* (Boston: Little, Brown, 1988).

Commercial Banks and Investment Banks

All early American banks owed their existence to the daily operations they conducted on behalf of merchants, including lending, exchanging drafts for specie (gold or silver coin) or other drafts of local merchants' accounts, and issuing notes against a specie reserve. Thus they were viewed as "commercial banks," meaning they facilitated commerce. Most of their operations involved short-term loans (usually outstanding for no more than six months) that were secured by the goods themselves as collateral. Those loans came to be referred to as "short-term, self-liquidating paper." Few banks prior to the Civil War had the resources to back large-scale projects, and none had the resources to finance more than minor business development. Even when a bank undertook a large-scale project it acted as an adjunct of a business, such as a railroad company, which sold its own bonds to finance its construction. The bank merely facilitated the bond sales and usually did not underwrite the railroad's construction. Since traditionally commercial banks concentrated on providing banking services for businesses rather than individuals, their assets consisted of the short-term, self-liquidating loans to businesses. Even when they made loans on real estate, they tended to use the real estate as collateral on a business loan. On the liabilities side, banks focused on short-term liabilities, such as checking accounts (known as demand deposits) for businesses.

For those projects too large for individual commercial banks to finance, such as railroad construction, a new institution emerged called the investment bank. Investment banks provided capital by helping businesses create and sell securities, although investment banks also advanced some funds to the businesses during the sales period, a procedure called "underwriting." While commercial banks also engaged in underwriting before 1933, investment banks existed specifically for that purpose. The securities created and sold by the investment banks could take the form of stocks or bonds. Bonds represented a loan made to the company with a guaranteed interest payable at a speci-

fied time. Stock represented a share of ownership in the company, and thus stockholders had a lower priority on the claims of the company's assets than bondholders if the company went into liquidation. On the other hand, as part owners, stockholders could control the company through their voting rights.

Jay Cooke gave investment banking a great deal of respectability when he managed the sales of U.S. government bonds to finance the Union victory in the Civil War. But the most famous of the investment bankers, J. P. Morgan, made his fortune by financing railroad reorganizations. Eventually his firm's wealth made it, for all practical purposes, the "lender of last resort" for most commercial banks during panics. Most of the investment bankers at one time or another had specialized in railroads, with Daniel Drew being among the earliest and most infamous, although as they grew more comfortable in investment banking activities, they involved themselves in other businesses. Frequently the size of a railroad reorganization dwarfed the resources of a single investment bank, even Morgan's or Kuhn, Loeb & Company. At those times, the financiers formed syndicates in which they shared the risk—and the profits—with other houses. Often, syndicates involved firms overseas, and foreign bankers proved reliable outlets for bond sales.

By 1900, although no laws prohibited commercial banks from engaging in investment banking, or vice versa, each type of bank remained relatively confined to its own specialty, except for some of the largest New York and Chicago commercial banks.

After World War I, businesses increasingly raised money through securities issues. Advances in communications and transportation gave large city banks a larger pool of funds than ever before from which to lend, and they steadily shifted their lending activities from commercial lending to securities activity. The larger banks had developed for the purpose security affiliates to underwrite and trade in securities. With the appearance of the Great Bull Market in the 1920s, those securities affiliates led the way in linking commercial banks to investment banking.

Following the stock market crash in 1929 and the ensuing Depression, many lawmakers came to believe that the activities of commercial banks trading in securities had played a major role in the boom and bust. As a result, the Glass-Steagall Act separated commercial and investment banking in 1933. Banks had to choose one or the other. By the 1990s, however, such a separation no longer seemed appropriate, as banks had started to engage in a wide variety of financial activities. Accordingly, regulators started to discuss more seriously the possibility of removing the barriers that separated investment and commercial banking.

See also:

Carter Glass, Glass-Steagall Act, Charles E. Merrill, Charles F. Mitchell, Michael Milken, New York Stock Exchange, Trust Companies and Trust Departments.

—Editor

Commodities Financing

by Jeffrey Williams

Stanford University

Financing of commodities before the 1940s principally concerned wheat and cotton, both highly storable products shipped in large amounts and long distances. Fresh fruits, vegetables, and meat by their nature could not tie up capital for very long. Although corn and oats carried until the next harvest represented sizable investments, kept on farm as feed they did not require the complicated financial arrangements of those crops moving through marketing channels.

Rarely did farmers retain title to their wheat or cotton beyond the local assembly point. Moreover, most were in a hurry for cash. Thus, the collective problem for the banking system was to get funds for immediate purchases into the hands of country elevators, in the case of wheat, and country-store owners and interior buyers, in the case of cotton. How those country elevators and interior buyers obtained their financing depended on whether they kept the commodity in storage locally or shipped it forthwith to a terminal market, and if shipped whether they arranged the sale themselves (a "direct" sale) or on consignment.

The majority of wheat and cotton went to terminal markets on consignment. In the grain trade the agents making those sales were called commission merchants and in the cotton trade, factors. Both groups were as much financial intermediaries as brokers, giving "advances" to the country-based owners before the final sale, indeed, before the arrival of the shipment. A country elevator, as it started a carload of grain on its way, would "draw" on its commission merchant for typically 80 percent of the shipment's value, in effect writing a check against the commission merchant's account. The country elevator would cash that sight draft at its local bank and with the money set about buying more wheat from farmers. Meanwhile, the local bank would send the check to its correspondent bank in the terminal market, where it eventually would be presented against the commission merchant's account at his bank.

Of course, the ultimate source of funds was a bank (or sometimes a warehouse) in the terminal market, because the commission merchant, too, required funds with which to make advances. Thus, the system in practice meant that big-city banks financed much of the country trade in commodities. The loans between banks and commission merchants or factors were secured by bills of lading, or, once the shipment had arrived, by warehouse receipts. Commission merchants typically charged for advances at the rate of 1 percent or 1.5 percent per annum above their own cost of funds. In some regions of the country the main competition for consignments was through the financing facilities offered.

In contrast, if the country elevator or interior buyer made a direct sale, the source of financing was probably a local bank. A direct sale, arranged

Agents purchasing agricultural products at a commodity exchange, circa 1960 (photograph by Dick Hanley; courtesy of Merrill Lynch & Company)

at the time of shipment, was usually "to arrive on track," that is, for delivery in 30 days or so at the terminal market. The buyer would pay at delivery. With the shipment already sold, and hence not in danger of falling in value while in transit, local banks offered much better terms.

Likewise, banks often lent at a lower interest rate and extended more credit if a commodity dealer routinely "hedged," that is, sold a contract for future delivery against his inventory. The more sophisticated the dealers and banks, the more likely those concerned with a particular commodity used futures. Organized futures markets for wheat and cotton date from at least the 1870s. Whether or not dealers who "hedge" are buying price insurance from speculators—there is much controversy about the best description of the contribution of futures markets—their net position is much less risky. Speculators did not, in any case, provide financing to dealers.

Over the past 60 years shipments on consignment have shrunk in favor of direct marketing. As grading became more reliable, the sample-oriented

trading of commission merchants and factors has become expensive relative to the straightforward sale of, say, No. 2 wheat. Also, some regions, especially the Upper Plains states, shipped on consignment in large part because the local banking infrastructure was so underdeveloped. That was no longer a problem as of 1989. Actually, direct marketing by then came under pressure from large integrated firms, which buy locally and process far away without a change in ownership. Those firms raise funds as a corporate entity, not in connection with each carload.

Another trend over the past 60 years has been the growth in involvement of the U.S. government in agriculture in general and commodity financing in particular. The Commodity Credit Corporation, established in 1933, has often served as the principal owner of wheat and cotton in commercial channels.

Reference:
Federal Trade Commission, *Report on the Grain Trade,* 7 volumes (Washington, D.C.: U.S. Government Printing Office, 1920-1926).

Community Reinvestment Act of 1977

Concerned with charges that banks had engaged in "red lining" (refusing to lend to individuals or businesses located in depressed areas or areas of high minority concentration), in 1977 Congress passed the Community Reinvestment Act, as Title VIII of the Housing and Community Development Act of 1977. The act required the Federal Deposit Insurance Corporation (FDIC) to take into account a bank's record of meeting the credit needs of the community it served, including low- and moderate-income neighborhoods, when the FDIC considered a bank's application for deposit insurance, branch establishment or relocation, or a merger or acquisition.

—Editor

Computerization in Clearinghouse Operations: The New York Clearing House Association

by Richard H. Timberlake

University of Georgia

The New York Clearing House Association was the first organization of its kind and the prototype for all subsequent clearinghouse organizations in the United States. Its historical development, therefore, serves as a model for the behavior and characteristics of clearinghouses in general.

Prompted by the desire to see banks quickly settle demand obligations among themselves, officers of 52 New York City banks organized the New York Clearing House Association (NYCHA) in 1853. Providing a central location to clear interbank obligations added greatly to the efficiency of the payments system. Certificates issued to the banks by the NYCHA upon deposit of funds in the clearinghouse provided the primary medium of interbank exchange. The clearinghouse certificates acted virtually as a "members only" currency, and before the advent of the Federal Reserve System the NYCHA issued additional clearinghouse loan certificates based on interest-bearing collateral securities that member banks pledged for the loans.

Beginning in the 1970s the NYCHA pioneered in the development of local and national electronically automated clearing systems. The association's automated system is known as the New York Automated Clearing House (NYACH). Computers have largely replaced checks and other paper items in the clearing process. The computers sort electronic entries from financial institutions and government agencies and send the entries to the recipient financial institutions to be entered as credits and debits in the proper customer accounts. The NYACH computers then determine the net due-to and due-from each financial institution and send the results to the Federal Reserve Banks for daily settlement in the accounts that all financial institutions keep with the Fed. Approximately thirty other clearinghouses are electronically linked to the NYACH to provide a national clearing system.

The passage of the Depository Institutions Monetary Control Act of 1980 gave a boost to the private clearing system by requiring the Fed Banks to price their clearing services, which they had provided free of charge. Since that time the NYACH has again become the center of the national clearing system. As a private enterprise it has the profit incentive to make the payments system work efficiently.

In 1970, before the domestic automated system was in place, the NYCHA instituted the Clearinghouse Interbank Payments System (CHIPS) to transfer international transactions based on U.S. dollars. It handles more than 90 percent of the world's dollar transactions—often more than $400 billion per day. CHIPS is tied in with the Fed Bank of New York and with foreign computerized clearing systems.

Automated electronic clearing systems clear more than demand deposits. The NYACH also transfers loan payments, pension payments, insurance premiums, and direct payroll deposits. Technological advances promise continual increases in the economy of the system. In ancient times money replaced the barter system. Likewise, electronic clearing has replaced the manual process of check clearing.

Consumer Protection Act

In addition to the protections supplied in the Truth in Lending Act (1969), the Consumer Protection Act also protected consumers against circulation by creditors of inaccurate or obsolete information and required reporting agencies to adopt fair and equitable procedures for compiling information on consumers. The act required creditors to inform borrowers when information from a credit report or from a third party contributed to the denial of a loan or an increase in the cost of credit. Title VII of the act prohibited discrimination based on race, color, or religion in the extension of credit. Creditors were also prohibited from using harassing or deceptive debt collection techniques.

The Fair Credit Billing Act of 1974 added to the protections extended under the Consumer Protection Act. It prohibited banks from debiting a customer's checking or savings account to pay a credit card bill without a court order. It also required creditors to take prompt action to correct billing errors.

—Editor

Correspondent Banks

Banks have traditionally maintained accounts with other banks, called "correspondents," to facilitate clearances. Isolated country banks that received out-of-town or out-of-state notes needed correspondents in the areas from which those notes were drawn to assist with collections in distant towns. The country bank, upon receipt of an instrument drawn from an out-of-town bank, simply sent it to its correspondent in the appropriate city, and the correspondent arranged for collection. The country correspondent performed the same service for city banks, but obviously the balances kept by the country banks in the city banks far exceeded those which the city banks kept in their country correspondents. Consequently, country banks maintained balances in city banks from which the city banks could either credit or debit. Those processes encouraged the use of checks for clearing. City banks routinely levied charges for out-of-town clearing but paid a small interest (2 percent) on the balances.

Not only did the city banks with country correspondents profit from having larger balances, they also counted checks in transit or in the process of collection as part of their reserves even while they were still in the mail. The enhanced deposit pool added to the investment funds available to the city banks. That led to a process of "pyramiding" of bankers' balances in New York City. Banks there used the balances to invest in the stock market. Since the nation lacked a well-developed branch system, the predominance of unit banks resulted in an even more exaggerated need to delay payments between banks in different regions. Since no interstate branching system existed, correspondent banking contributed to the transfer and allocation of funds throughout the country. In times of panic, however, a run on New York banks could send shock waves throughout the entire nation; conversely, any sudden demand by country banks to convert their balances to cash made the New York banks vulnerable, as in the situation that occurred in 1907. By 1912 eight banks in New York held almost 60 percent of that city's total interbank balances.

The federal government expected the Federal Reserve Banks to take over two primary functions of city correspondents: the extension of short-term loans to the country banks and the provision of a national clearing system. Beginning in 1914 banks transferred their correspondent balances to the Federal Reserve Banks over a four-year period. The Reserve Banks paid no interest on those balances, but to entice banks to join the system the government reduced the required reserve to a smaller amount than that required by the National Banking Act of 1863. Because member banks of the Federal Reserve System only had to transfer their legal reserves to the Federal Reserve Banks, they remained free to hold correspondent balances in excess.

Thus, as Eugene White has noted, "the Federal Reserve's clearing system failed to dislodge the correspondent banks from their position of eminence in the banking system."

The Federal Reserve System also hoped to attract new member banks by giving them the privilege of borrowing from the Fed at an interest rate known in advance and uniform for all borrowers—the rediscount rate. The Fed fixed the rate "with a view of accommodating commerce and business" and sought to relate rediscounts to the volume of goods bought and sold. Banks did not flock to join, however, because they still could have access to the Federal Reserve's lending powers (the "discount window") by borrowing from member banks. Most correspondents simply maintained their existing relationships with banks in New York, who could borrow from the Fed.

References:

Benjamin J. Klebaner, *American Commercial Banking: A History* (Boston: Twayne, 1990);

Eugene White, *The Regulation and Reform of the American Banking System, 1900-1929* (Princeton: Princeton University Press, 1983).

                                                                                    —Editor

Credit Cards: VISA, Mastercard

by James Smallwood

University of Texas at Tyler

A new type of banking service emerged in the post World War II era. In 1950 Diners Club pioneered a charge card for meals, and in 1951 Franklin National Bank of Long Island issued a charge card for use in local department stores. Those cards and others like them, including the American Express card, required payment in full at the end of each monthly period. The comprehensive bank-issued credit card did not come into widespread use until the end of the 1950s, however.

California's Bank of America pioneered the first true domestic credit card that extended beyond a merely local use when it introduced the BankAmericard in 1959. The bank had several purposes in mind when it started the card: it wanted

to offer customers a widely recognized method of purchasing goods and services using a pre-negotiated line of credit, and the card advertised the name of the prestigious bank. The BankAmericard grew so popular in California that Bank of America executives realized that the bank could market the program nationally through its network of correspondent banks. In 1966 Bank of America created the Bank of America Service Corporation to select and administer BankAmericard franchisees. That service corporation licensed banks that paid a stipulated fee ($25,000 plus .5 percent of volume) to join the program and work within the system's uniform operating procedures. Under the BankAmericard system, licensed banks could interchange (process sales drafts cooperatively).

The BankAmericard program expanded so rapidly that it surpassed all goals originally envisioned by its creators. But that rapid expansion created problems of administration and coordination, problems that became severe by 1968. Consequently, franchisees named committees to study problems that had emerged in such areas as fraud control, authorizations, and draft exchange. In 1970 the franchisees established National BankAmericard, Incorporated (NBI), to deal with the problems and administer the system. NBI replaced the Bank of America Service Corporation as the governing body for the licensees. In effect the licensees purchased the right to coordinate the domestic BankAmericard program, and the Bank of America—relinquishing its dominant position—became a member of NBI.

Bank of America remained the owner of the name BankAmericard and the card's blue, white, and gold design. To achieve uniformity, in 1977 licensees adopted the name "VISA" for all licensed cards, and NBI changed its name to VISA U.S.A. Structured as an independent nonstock corporation, VISA U.S.A. continues to administer, promote, and develop the VISA credit card system, which had accepted international licensees almost as soon as Bank of America first organized it.

In 1972 the international members of the BankAmericard system started studying the possibility of creating a multinational membership corporation to administer the card program worldwide. That study culminated in 1974 with the incorporation of IBANCO, which changed its name to VISA International Service Corporation in 1977.

While Bank of America was pioneering the BankAmericard system, a group of New York bankers led by First National City Bank launched the program that began the competing Master Charge system. In 1966, 14 New York banks formed Interbank Card, Incorporated, to administer a system of credit card licensing. That company soon changed its name to Interbank Card Association (ICA). By the end of the year banks in Buffalo, Pittsburgh, Milwaukee, Seattle, and Phoenix had joined the system.

Also in 1966 four large California banks organized the Western States Bankcard Association (WSBA), using the name "Master Charge" as the name of their card. Executives of ICA and WSBA quickly recognized the commonality of their goals;

leaders of both groups wanted to establish a national system to compete with the BankAmericard system. In 1967 the two organizations merged: ICA became the national governing body, and WSBA became a processing member association. Executives retained the name Master Charge, which appeared on a majority of the cards issued by ICA. Like VISA, Master Charge quickly went international. In its organization, ICA was similar to VISA U.S.A., but it did include international members on its board of directors.

ICA differed from VISA U.S.A. in other ways potential licensees found attractive. It was more loosely organized and gave individual bankers more leeway in setting credit standards, bookkeeping procedures, and operating policies. Further, ICA charged lower licensing fees ($2.50 per $1 million in bank assets and a small pro rata to cover expenses). Citibank's Edward Gottlieb summarized ICA's appeal: "The BankAmericard did not offer us the kind of independence that Interbank does."

Despite their competition or perhaps because of it, the VISA and Master Charge programs became practically overnight successes. Consumer costs remained low through the 1960s. By 1968 consumers held 17 million of the cards. Comparatively, only 3 million used American Express, and only 2 million used Diners Club because those programs cost both customers and retailers more.

Both the VISA and Master Charge programs continued to grow during the 1970s, expanding the types of cards and credit lines offered. In 1979, two years after the similar shift at VISA, ICA changed the name of its cards to "Mastercard." Over the years the companies grew more similar to each other, so that in many areas of the United States banks started to offer both the VISA and the Mastercard to their customers. In the 1980s the banks instituted aggressive postal marketing programs, offering often-unsolicited lines of credit to millions of consumers. By 1984 more than 54 percent of American families held at least one credit card, and almost 3,000 banks offered their own cards independently of the two large issuers, which counted thousands more banks as their agents. As of 1987, VISA, which had fallen behind and then overtaken Mastercard, had 165 million credit cards outstanding, compared to 145 million Mastercards.

Credit programs such as VISA and Mastercard proved great boons to consumers around the world. Access to revolving credit within set limits enabled customers to manage their financial affairs more creatively and to make purchases that might otherwise have been postponed because of the unavailability of "traditional" credit. Of course, in the 1980s a new kind of insolvency emerged along with the explosion in plastic: some credit card users accumulated so much debt on so many cards that they were unable to pay more than the interest without help. Still, the card systems—new international financial giants—play a key role in the modern world economy.

References:

William H. Baughn and Charles E. Walker, eds., *The Bank-ers' Handbook* (Homewood, Ill.: Dow Jones-Irwin, 1978);

Gary Hector, *Breaking the Bank: The Decline of BankAmerica* (Boston: Little, Brown, 1988);

"Here Come the Bank Cards," *Forbes*, 103 (February 15, 1969): 39-40;

Benjamin J. Klebaner, *American Commercial Banking: A History* (Boston: Twayne, 1990);

James Smallwood, *An Oklahoma Adventure: Of Banks and Bankers* (Norman: University of Oklahoma Press, 1979);

Paul Studenski and Herman F. Krooss, *Financial History of the United States* (New York: McGraw-Hill, 1963);

John R. Wilson, *The Chase: The Chase Manhattan Bank, N.A. 1945-1985* (Cambridge, Mass.: Harvard Business School Press, 1989).

Charles G. Dawes

(August 27, 1865 - April 23, 1951)

by Stephen A. Schuker

Brandeis University

CAREER: Attorney and utility executive, Lincoln, Nebraska, and Evanston, Illinois (1887-1896); U.S. comptroller of the currency (1898-1901); founder and president (1902-1921), chairman (1921-1925, 1932-1951), honorary chairman, City National Bank and Trust Company [Central Trust Company of Illinois to 19?, Central Republic Bank and Trust Company to 1932] (1930-1931); chairman, General Purchasing Board, American Expeditionary Force (1917-1919); member, Military Board of Allied Supply (1918-1919); member, U.S. Liquidation Commission (1918-1919); director, U.S. Bureau of the Budget (1921-1922); chairman, First Committee of Experts, Reparations Commission (1924); vice-president of the United States (1925-1929); U.S. ambassador to Great Britain (1929-1932); chairman, Reconstruction Finance Corporation (1932).

Charles Gates Dawes, one of the most colorful and outspoken public figures of his era, had a long and varied career as a lawyer and principal in gas and light companies, as a founder of a leading Chicago bank, as a political kingmaker and sometime Republican politician, and as a public servant who distinguished himself in numerous positions over 35 years, including one term as vice-president of the United States.

The eldest of six children, Dawes was born into a prominent family in Marietta, Ohio, on August 27, 1865. His father, Brigadier General Rufus R. Dawes, had distinguished himself on Civil War battlefields from Antietam to Gettysburg as commander of the Sixth Wisconsin "Iron Brigade"; he later served one term in Congress and, despite reverses in the Panic of 1873, made a relatively successful business career as an iron manufacturer, oil-and-gas wildcatter, and operator of a wholesale lumberyard. Dawes's mother, born Mary Beman Gates, was the daughter of a leading Marietta banker. Both families came from old New England stock. The paternal line can be traced to 1635, when the first Dawes migrated from England to the Massachusetts Bay Colony. One great-great-grandfather, William Dawes, had ridden with Paul Revere in 1775; another, Manasseh Cutler, had helped to write the Northwest Ordinance for the governance of the area that included Ohio in 1787.

Charles Gates Dawes came of the fourth generation that resided in Marietta. The family enjoyed an intimate and fulfilled domestic life. During his adult business career, Charles Dawes worked closely with his younger brothers Rufus, Beman, and Henry. He also cultivated an unusual talent for making and sustaining warm friendships outside

Charles G. Dawes (courtesy of Moffett Studios)

the family circle. Although he became one of Chicago's leading bankers and later won national acclaim for his organization of supply services for the American Expeditionary Force (AEF) in World War I, his rationalization of the federal budget process, his contributions to solving the German reparations problem, and his stewardship of the Reconstruction Finance Corporation during the Great Depression, Dawes never developed more than a modest command of the technical intricacies of finance. His successes stemmed rather from his ability to lead and to inspire loyalty, his genius as a facilitator and a patron of talented subordinates, his unflagging energy, his high character, and his ebullient personality.

Dawes graduated fourth in his class from Marietta College in 1884 and qualified for an A.M. degree there in 1887. He received an LL.B. degree from Cincinnati Law School in 1886, where, by the sort of coincidence that occurred repeatedly throughout his life, he was a student of future president William Howard Taft. The slowly growing town of Marietta offered limited opportunities for young lawyers. In April 1887, therefore, Dawes struck out for

Lincoln, the capital of Nebraska, which had undergone an agricultural and real estate boom. He quickly made a name for himself as counsel for the Lincoln Board of Trade, which engaged in a fight over discriminatory freight rates on the local railroad. Dawes successfully prosecuted several railroad cases against the Burlington, the Union Pacific, and the Missouri Pacific on behalf of local Nebraska industries that objected to the preferential rates accorded long-haul customers.

A reed-thin, 125-pound bundle of kinetic energy, still in his early twenties, Dawes savored his reputation as an "anti-monopoly agitator." Meanwhile, he solidified his personal life in 1889 with an emotionally satisfying and financially advantageous marriage to Caro Blymyer, the daughter of a leading Cincinnati manufacturer. The couple had two children, Rufus Fearing and Carolyn, and later adopted two more. In his early Lincoln years Dawes also made a pair of lifelong friendships that would affect his subsequent career. The first was with Second Lieutenant John J. Pershing, then enduring a purgatory as professor of military science at the University of Nebraska, who a generation later would call on Dawes to organize supply services for the American army in France. The second was with his neighbor William Jennings Bryan, with whom Dawes fiercely debated the merits of the gold standard at the Lincoln Round Table. Dawes argued for a stable gold currency and against a bimetallic standard, although he favored certain innovations, such as a government guarantee of bank deposits. Reflecting on the Panic of 1893, Dawes codified his hard-money views in a notable first book, *The Banking System of the United States and Its Relation to the Money and Business of the Country* (1894), which helped bring him to the attention of Major William McKinley, then governor of Ohio and an aspirant for the presidency.

As his law earnings grew, Dawes branched out into real estate and the packing business and also became a director of the local American Exchange Bank. Through prudent management he survived the Panic of 1893 with his fortune more or less intact, but Lincoln as a whole entered a prolonged depression, exacerbated by a Great Plains drought that arrived the next year. Dawes decided to seek greener pastures. He purchased the LaCrosse Gas Light and Coke Company of LaCrosse, Wisconsin, the Northwestern Gas Light and Coke Company in Evanston, Illinois, and three other midwestern gas plants. In 1895 he relocated the base of his operations to Chicago, where he remained for the rest of his life.

Dawes shortly agreed to organize William McKinley's campaign for the 1896 presidential nomination in the state of Illinois. Illinois figured as a crucial state in McKinley's strategy. It ranked third in population in the country and would select convention delegates earlier than any other big state. Despite opposition by the local Republican machine, Dawes won the battle for McKinley at the state convention, helped shape the gold-standard plank at the national convention in St. Louis, and went on to work under Mark Hanna as finance chairman in the general election campaign. Some months after his election, McKinley appointed the thirty-one-year-old Dawes U.S. comptroller of the currency. Dawes served in that capacity from January 1898 to October 1901. In the era before creation of the Federal Reserve Board, this was a key position for influencing national monetary affairs. Dawes made the most of it. From his office in the Treasury Department he supervised the national banking system and dealt authoritatively with bank failures.

Dawes solidified a warm personal friendship both with McKinley and Secretary of the Treasury George Cortelyou, and he served as a sounding board for the president on a wide range of foreign and domestic issues. Always sensitive to political currents, Dawes counseled Senator Mark Hanna and others in the president's entourage not to try to block Theodore Roosevelt's nomination for vice-president in 1900. Although the Rough Rider came from another wing of the party, Dawes got along with him fairly well. In October 1901, shortly after McKinley's assassination and Roosevelt's elevation to the presidency, Dawes nevertheless resigned as comptroller in order to run for the Senate from Illinois. Having beaten the Illinois Republican machine on McKinley's behalf in 1896 and 1900, Dawes could not do as well for himself. His campaign for elective office failed. Never a man inclined to brood, he immediately turned back to business.

With the backing of influential friends such as Charles M. Schwab of U.S. Steel and George Perkins of J. P. Morgan & Company, Dawes organized the Central Trust Company of Illinois in July 1902. The "Dawes Bank," as the Central Trust and its successor institutions would be known for the next half century, billed itself as a "big bank for small people" and found a profitable niche in the Chicago financial community. The Central Trust Company (in later incarnations the Central Republic Bank and Trust Company and the City National Bank and Trust Company) served as the focal point for Dawes's business career until his death in 1951. He remained active as president until 1921 and stayed on as chairman or honorary chairman in between periods of public service until the age of eighty-five. While the bank engaged largely in traditional deposit and trust business, Dawes personally did a certain amount of merger and acquisition work in the first decade of the century, and the contacts he gained brought him a widening acquaintanceship among the top corporate executives and financiers of the nation. In 1908 he made the select list of the 100 men Robert M. La Follette, the radical senator, accused of "running" the country.

Dawes's merger and acquisition work turned him into a strong critic of existing antitrust legislation. The Sherman Antitrust Act, he came to feel, encouraged the formation of giant horizontally integrated corporations precisely because it forbade the simpler form of trade agreements. The "muckrakers," in his view, had a one-sided and superficial conception of optimal industrial structure. Dawes's convictions in that regard set him on a collision course with President Roosevelt, who sought political popularity by some highly publicized criminal prosecutions under the Sherman Act. In 1905-1906, Dawes intervened with Roosevelt on behalf of the Chicago meatpackers, whom the Justice Department had accused of actions in restraint of trade on the basis of information the packers had voluntarily and confidentially supplied to the Department of Commerce. After hearing Dawes out, Roosevelt appeared to agree not to indict the packers for actions preceding an injunction under the Sherman Act. Subsequently he changed his mind and brought an indictment anyway. Although the federal courts ultimately dismissed the indictment as procedurally improper, Dawes felt betrayed by the president. Their relations never recovered. Not surprisingly, Dawes supported his old law school teacher William Howard Taft against Roosevelt's Bull Moose party when the Republicans split in 1912.

Although he spent most of his life concerned with business or the public arena, Dawes was far from being an aesthetic philistine. A gifted amateur musician, he also became a patron and fund-raiser for the Chicago Opera. He composed a dozen popular musical songs, including "Melody in A Major,"

Dawes (second from left) with representatives of the Italian, French, British, and Belgian armies at a December 1918 meeting of the Military Board of Allied Supply in France (Signal Corps, American Expeditionary Force)

which became a hit gramophone record in 1911 and was revived 40 years later under the name "It's All in the Game." After he bought a grand house in Evanston in 1909, Dawes built a library of 10,000 volumes and became something of a bibliophile. In keeping with the custom of voluntarism so prominent in the Progressive era, he also devoted a considerable amount of time to public benefaction, and he increased his charitable commitments after the tragic death of his eldest son, who drowned in 1912. In honor of his son, Dawes opened three large hotels for the indigent and unemployed in Chicago and in Boston. The hotels continued to perform useful service even after the institutionalization of charity under the New Deal. Dawes took great satisfaction in their operation.

When the United States declared war on Germany in 1917 Dawes, then age fifty-one, hastened to enlist. His old friend, General John J. Pershing, headed the American Expeditionary Force, and the general arranged a commission for Dawes in the Army Corps of Engineers. In August 1917, Dawes's regiment figured among the first American units to land in France. While Dawes initially hoped for assignment to the front, Pershing shortly drafted him

to head the General Purchasing Board, which coordinated procurement of all supplies for the U.S. Army in Europe. Setting to work with characteristic brashness and energy, Dawes acquired the maximum amount of food, coal, civilian labor, rolling stock, horses, mules, and a myriad of other supplies in the European theater so that scarce Atlantic shipping could be reserved for the transport of troops. When France, Britain, and the United States agreed to form a unified military command under Marshal Foch in the spring of 1918, Dawes immediately proposed a comparable command of the three major powers to handle logistics. Largely owing to Dawes's persuasiveness with Georges Clemenceau and Lloyd George, a Military Board of Allied Supply took shape in May 1918.

With his impatience for red tape, calculated use of profanity, and ubiquitous black cigars, Dawes cut a rather unmilitary figure. Yet he invariably accomplished the job at hand. Dawes could move mountains, logistically speaking, in part because he encouraged a "can-do" spirit among his staff. As General Jean-Marie Payot, the French representative on the Military Board of Allied Supply, ruefully observed: "Both Dawes and I work sixteen hours a day. But Dawes spends all his time fighting the Germans. I work four hours fighting the Germans and twelve hours fighting my own people." Members of the U.S. high command attributed the cooperative spirit prevailing in American ranks as much to Dawes's unique brand of leadership as to any particular national characteristics. General James G. Harbord, the AEF chief of staff, described Dawes at this time as "generous, high-minded, straightforward, courageous . . . outspoken and apparently impulsive . . . a winning personality." Accordingly, no one tried to make Dawes fit into a preformed military mold. While Dawes himself claimed that he was "learning to flop up my hand in receiving salutes," for example, General Pershing despaired of inculcating army habits in his old Nebraska friend. Still, he valued Dawes's services immensely, and arranged his promotion to brigadier general in October 1918.

When the Armistice came the following month, the United States had $1.5 billion of war supplies dispersed all over France. With transportation still scarce, it made no sense to take war materiel home. Dawes became the military member of a U.S. Liquidation Commission appointed by the War Department to inventory the accumulated stockpile and to figure out how to dispose of it. At the same time, he wore a double hat as a member of the AEF's own Advisory Settlement Board. Although Dawes never learned more than a few words of French, he had become highly popular in the host country, and he made a decisive contribution to the Liquidation Commission's work. In July 1919 the War Department sold the stocks for $400 million to the French government. As it turned out, the French never turned over most of the money. In 1926 the World War Foreign Debt Commission agreed to roll the obligation into the general French war debt, and, when the French defaulted seven years later, the stocks debt too remained unpaid. But that unhappy denouement lay far in the future. Dawes embarked from Brest for New York in August 1919, taking satisfaction in a job well done.

Paradoxically, Dawes became a household name to the average American less because of his work in France than because of his electrifying congressional testimony in defense of it. In February 1921 the House Committee on War Expenditures conducted a fishing expedition into the logistic supply of the AEF with a view to embarrassing the outgoing Wilson administration. For seven hours

Dawes replied to the insinuation that he had paid excessive prices with an uncompromising defense of the effort overseas. "There was nothing pink-tea about the way we handled it," Dawes roared in the stentorian manner that his coworkers in France had come to know so well. "When Congress declared war, did it expect us to beat Germany at twenty per cent discount? . . . Men were standing at the front to be shot at. We had to get them food and ammunition. We didn't stop to dicker. Why, man alive! We had a war to win!" Dawes's graphic account of how he had done his job, even in one case by hiring professional smugglers to lead horses over the Pyrenees, generated headlines all over the country. With an instinctive sense for public relations, he knew how to spice up his language in order to make good newspaper copy. When one carper after the event complained about excessive prices for mules, Dawes literally jumped from the witness table. "Helen Maria! I would have paid horse prices for sheep, if the sheep could have pulled artillery to the front!" "Helen Maria" had served as a very mild expletive on the Nebraska frontier in the 1890s, but the wire services garbled the story. From then on, "Hell 'n' Maria" Dawes became a familiar icon of American popular culture.

Dawes took little part in the presidential campaign of 1920, and his ringing defense of the Versailles Treaty put him at odds with isolationists in the Republican party. But his connections with the Ohio political establishment, dating back to the McKinley and Hanna years, remained intact. Shortly after the election President Harding called Dawes to Marion and asked him to become secretary of the Treasury. Harding sought to reverse the gargantuan expansion of the federal bureaucracy that had taken place during the war and to promote economy and efficiency. He had read a popular article by Dawes entitled "How a President Can Save a Billion Dollars." He asked Dawes to show him how to do it. Dawes persuaded Harding that he could perform the task better as the director of a nonpartisan Bureau of the Budget than as Treasury secretary. Congress passed the requisite enabling legislation in June 1921, and Dawes came to Washington to serve for one year. Within that span of time he established the Bureau of the Budget as a functioning institution, eliminated redundant procurement by competing agencies, and slashed government expenditures by one-third, thus achieving a budget in comfortable surplus for the first time since the outbreak of war. After resigning he wrote a book, *The First Year of the Budget of the United States* (1923), explaining how he had done it. Although the details held more interest for accounting specialists than the general public, the institutional framework established by Dawes remained in place until 1933, when Franklin Roosevelt decided that he had higher priorities than economy in government.

Dawes had scarcely returned to his desk at the Central Trust Company when another challenge beckoned. To good-government conservatives such as Dawes, Chicago and the state of Illinois appeared threatened by incipient social breakdown. In April 1923 Dawes formed an organization called "Minute Men of the Constitution" to uphold law and order and to change the political climate. The group sought to rally middle-class citizens generally and veterans in particular against the Chicago racketeers and the corrupt politicians at City Hall and in Springfield who allowed them to operate, against the inroads of the Ku Klux Klan downstate, and against the perceived excesses of organized labor. Dawes lashed out, with calculated indiscretion, at "the wide disrespect for law, the cowardice of political leaders in evading issues involving good government when they tend to antagonize organized minorities, and the arrogance and lawlessness of certain unworthy leaders of special groups." Opponents accused the Minute Men of advocating the closed shop. Dawes denied it but gave no quarter to the dominant labor leaders in Chicago. With characteristic hyperbole, he stated, "Union labor is, in the great majority, patriotic. In Chicago, it is suffering under a leadership in part composed of gunmen and criminals, who impose a slavery through intimidation upon their membership to which only the autocracy of Lenin and Trotsky can be compared."

Forces backed by the Minute Men won the Chicago mayoral election of 1924, but the social problems they identified did not prove soluble through social uplift. Relations among the diverse ethnic groups in Chicago remained uneasy, and the bootleggers continued to thrive. Dawes, meanwhile, had moved on to a new undertaking, as chairman of the First Committee of Experts set up by the Reparation Commission in December 1923 to investigate German reparations.

Statesmen at the Paris Peace Conference of 1919 had failed to agree on how much Germany should pay for the damage it had caused during the war. The peace treaty therefore charged an interallied Reparation Commission with assessing Allied losses and determining how much Germany owed toward the costs of reconstruction. Reparations quickly became the central problem of diplomacy in the years after the war. It took on a larger meaning as the fulcrum of the Franco-German struggle for economic dominance in Europe. After much wrangling, the Allies forced Germany in May 1921 to accept the so-called London Schedule of Payments. That schedule set Germany's theoretical liability at $33 billion and its practical obligations for the foreseeable future at $12.5 billion. The requisite annual payments came to approximately 5.4 percent of German national income at the time. That was a high but not impossible sum. A succession of weak and nationalistic governments in Berlin resisted payment, however, and allowed inflation to escalate into hyperinflation rather than impose the taxation that would make a reparations transfer feasible. French and Belgian troops occupied the Ruhr in January 1923 in order to enforce payment, but the military effort shortly led to crippling financial and currency problems in France. By the fall of 1923 all the major European powers appeared ready for a new approach. Secretary of State Charles Evans Hughes had proposed in December 1922 that an independent committee of businessmen investigate the problem from the point of view of German capacity to pay. He now revived the proposal and (since the U.S. government pretended not to be officially involved) suggested that the Reparation Commission invite Dawes to serve as chairman of the principal investigatory committee.

Dawes was a logical choice for the job. President Harding, before his death in August 1923, had often spoken of Dawes as a possible White House successor. The exuberant Dawes and the taciturn President Coolidge stood at opposite poles in temperament, but Coolidge nevertheless understood Dawes's political utility. As a midwestern banker, Dawes was not identified in the public mind with Wall Street or the Eastern internationalist establishment, yet he had supported the Versailles Treaty and stood high in the esteem of Wilsonians. He boasted a strong friendship with Herbert Hoover going back to the war and thus could bridge the rivalry between the State and Commerce departments. He had spoken in favor of the Ruhr occupation and remained highly popular in France. Above all, he knew how to get a committee of prima donnas to work together harmoniously.

Dawes and Owen D. Young (third and fourth from left) on their way to the Paris meetings of the Reparations Commission to discuss rescheduling the German war debt, aboard ship, January 1924

Dawes knew next to nothing about international finance, but that did not prove a serious disqualification. Owen D. Young, chairman of the General Electric Company and the second American delegate, provided the day-to-day leadership on the main subcommittees, and an able staff of professors and State and Commerce officials, headed by Rufus C. Dawes, brother of the general, advised on technical economic matters. President Coolidge offered only delphic advice to the department delegation: "Just remember that you are Americans!" He also counseled Dawes that, since he was going to Paris, he should take his wife along. The warning was hardly necessary for a man as uxorious as Dawes.

The official charge of the Expert Committee was to consider means to balance the German budget and to stabilize the German currency after the end of the great hyperinflation. Although the committee had no mandate to revise the total sum owed in reparations by Germany, in practice it had sufficient latitude to propose a new schedule of annual payments that would last until political circumstances made a comprehensive settlement possible. Dawes went to Europe resolved to keep an open

mind about the best manner to proceed. He sought to fashion a commonsense political compromise and then to use his public relations skills to sell it to the world. He set little store in the theoretical arguments of economists about capacity to pay or the ways to solve the transfer problem. Economists, he wrote when the committee began its inquiry, enjoyed "a general range of possible asininity, wider and more unchallenged than any others." As a result he paid little attention to the technical staff and a great deal to the personal dynamics among fellow committee members. "When it is over," he reminded his colleagues, "we shall get either garbage or garlands. I'll run the risk of the garbage."

After three months of intensive work in Paris and Berlin, the Dawes Committee published its report in April 1924. The committee proposed a new schedule of reparations annuities that would increase gradually to $625 million (as it turned out, 3.1 percent of German national income) in 1929. It sought to depoliticize the ticklish issue of transferring marks into foreign currencies by setting up an Allied-dominated Transfer Committee to handle the matter. It laid down guidelines for a new German central bank and for the eventual alignment of the Deutschemark on the gold-based American dollar. It called for a foreign loan to get the plan started and an agent-general to oversee its operation. The American public waxed enthusiastic, and, despite private reservations, the major European parties to the reparation dispute also accepted the plan in principle. The Wall Street bankers who would have to make the loan denigrated the report privately as "a skillful performance in carrying water on both shoulders" and complained that Dawes and his colleagues had evaded difficulties rather than solved them. But they too went along in the end. In the summer of 1924 the Allies and the Germans held a conference in London and worked out a broad-based political settlement to put the plan into operation. The Reparations Commission lost its power to enforce sanctions; the French agreed to evacuate the Ruhr and eventually the Rhineland as well. The settlement established the preconditions for American loans to pour into Europe and for currency stabilization across the Continent. The Germans intended from the start to demand another inquiry before the partial moratorium expired, and in 1929 Owen D. Young headed a new committee to revise reparations again. For five years, however, the Dawes Plan kept a semblance of harmony and promoted economic reconstruction in Europe.

In 1925 Dawes shared the Nobel Peace Prize for his efforts. Sir Josiah Stamp, the British delegate who had done most of the sophisticated statistical work on the plan, later paid fulsome tribute to Dawes's contributions. Dawes, he wrote, "kept the contacts with the outside world during our proceedings" and, by not entering into detailed contention, stood as a "final court of judgment in case of dispute." Committee members learned, he added, that "underneath the 'Hell and Maria'-ness of a rather mythical violence was a singularly generous nature, punctuating faith in himself with strange essential humilities and almost extravagant appreciations of the qualities and work of others." As invariably happened wherever Dawes lent a hand, a web of friendships developed that endured until the end of the committee members' lives.

Fresh from his triumph in Paris, Dawes labored to secure the 1924 Republican vice-presidential nomination for his friend, former governor Frank Lowden of Illinois. But when Lowden at the last minute declined to run, the convention stampeded to Dawes. "The vice-presidential

Dawes, as U.S. ambassador to Great Britain from 1929 to 1932, with President Herbert Hoover (courtesy of Kaufman & Fabry)

candidate," wrote William Jennings Bryan in the press, "is a more vigorous personality than the president." While Coolidge stayed home in the White House, Dawes stumped the country against Democrat John W. Davis and Progressive Robert M. La Follette. He amplified the familiar themes he had earlier sounded at the local level on behalf of the Minute Men of the Constitution. He stood for internationalism in foreign affairs, economy in government, repudiation of the Ku Klux Klan on the right, and resistance to "minority group acts of lawlessness" on the left. The issue, he reiterated with a flourish, "is whether you stand on the rock of common sense with Calvin Coolidge or upon the sinking sands of socialism with Robert M. La Follette." The Republican ticket won handily, sweeping the country outside the South.

Before World War II, the vice-president presided over the Senate but by custom took no active part in policymaking. Dawes considered it constitutionally correct to stay away from cabinet meetings, but he did not have the temperament to remain a cipher. In his inaugural speech before the Senate, he denounced legislative time wasting and demanded abrogation of the rules that allowed filibustering. This, however, foreshadowed one fight that Dawes was not destined to win. During his term he nonetheless took a modest role in shaping legislation in areas he deemed of special interest, including banking reform, naval appropriations, and farm relief. He also helped to secure ratification of the Kellogg-Briand peace pact. His friends launched a modest boomlet to promote him for president in 1928, but the effort did not succeed. The eastern wing of the party nourished reservations. True to his midwestern loyalties, Dawes had facilitated Senate passage of the irresponsible McNary-Haugen bill for dumping farm surpluses overseas and thus embarrassed President Coolidge by forcing him to veto it. In any case, Dawes had admired Herbert Hoover as a man of "courage and character" ever since their common service in France, and he would take no part in the stop-Hoover movement that enjoyed discreet sympathy on Wall Street and elsewhere.

After leaving office in March 1929, Dawes briefly headed a commission charged with introducing a budgetary control system in the Dominican Republic. Thereafter he intended to return to his bank in the "Windy City" and to assist his younger brother Rufus in planning for the Chicago World's Fair. Hoover, however, immediately drafted him to serve as ambassador to Great Britain, and Dawes served in that post from May 1929 to February 1932. He presided over the embassy during a crucial period in Anglo-American relations. The two nations had disagreed bitterly about cruiser size and armaments during the naval negotiations of 1927, and financial rivalry between New York and the London City also ran very deep. But the Labour government of J. Ramsay MacDonald wished to improve relations, and the pacifistic Hoover stood prepared to make major concessions of his own in order to extend the Washington Conference model for naval disarmament. Dawes left most of the technical detail at the Five Power Naval Arms Limitation Conference of 1930 to the State Department specialist Hugh Gibson; yet offstage he worked hard to nurture a general understanding with MacDonald and the Japanese ambassador, Tsuneo Matsudaira. Although the three principal powers failed to agree on an explicit "yardstick" for comparing smaller naval vessels, they eventually fudged their differences. They reached a compromise of sorts on total tonnage that held for the next few years, even though the French and Italians declined to go along.

Dawes played a rather greater role in reestablishing diplomatic relations between Britain and the United States on a friendlier basis. He also provided his good offices to keep discussion going between the embarrassed Matsudaira and the Chinese representative to the League of Nations Council when the Japanese army invaded Manchuria in September 1931. Dawes had a ringside seat in London during the negotiations for implementing the Young Plan on reparations and the establishment of the Bank for International Settlements in 1930. And he reported to Washington on the British decision to abandon the gold-exchange standard in September 1931 and in effect to embark on competitive currency depreciation with the United States.

Dawes had early sensed that the stock market crash of October 1929 would progress to a serious depression. He noted in his diary that history afforded few examples of overexpanded credit leading to orderly liquidation. Having survived the depression of 1893 with his fortune intact, he had learned the personal lesson, as he put it, that "ninety-day notes become due." Yet his dispatches on the European financial crisis of 1931 suggest that he remained more a bystander than a participant. Secretary of the Treasury Andrew Mellon came personally to London in 1931 to handle the difficult negotiations about implementing the Hoover moratorium on reparations and war debts. The Federal Reserve Bank of New York and J. P. Morgan & Company rather than the embassy coordinated the American attempts to bolster sterling a few weeks thereafter. Given his intimate ties with MacDonald and his visceral conviction that reason and good will could smooth over the rough spots in Anglo-American relations, Dawes navigated uncertainly in the new era in which the British Treasury sought financial salvation through a beggar-thy-neighbor policy directed largely against the United States.

As the American banking crisis became more severe in the winter of 1932, President Hoover called Dawes home to chair the Reconstruction Finance Corporation. The RFC lent money to banks, trust companies, mortgage institutions, and railroads that seemed in danger of failing and thereby deepening the downward spiral of output and employment. Dawes and his fellow director, Jesse H. Jones, worked 16 hours a day seven days a week and made more than 4,000 loans during the spring of 1932.

Dawes resigned in June 1932 to deal with a crisis back home in Chicago. The "Dawes Bank," as a result of a merger now called the Central Republic Bank and Trust Company, had encountered severe liquidity problems. Dawes had not taken an active role in the bank since 1921, but he demanded to be reelected chairman and immediately took hold. After studying the books he concluded that the bank remained basically solvent but that it should close to avoid a run and a liquidation under panic conditions. He was prevailed upon to change his mind only by dint of heavy pressure from other Chicago banks. Melvin Traylor of the First National Bank, Chicago's premier institution, called on Jesse H. Jones of the RFC and argued that, if the Dawes Bank closed its doors, other Chicago banks would have to follow suit. Having confirmed that the Central Republic was illiquid but not insolvent, Jones consulted the president, who ordered him to pump in $90 million to save the institution. A national wave of bank closures was thus postponed until March 1933. As the 1932 election campaign heated up, Dawes took a certain amount of criticism for having secured a loan from a government agency on which he had lately served. But the loan involved no "influence-peddling," and Dawes had accepted it reluctantly and only upon the appeal of his fellow bankers and public officials.

Dawes never again served in a major public capacity. He lived on quietly in Evanston until his death on April 23, 1951. He rode downtown daily to his office at the renamed City National Bank and Trust Company, served on local civic committees, and commented with his usual indiscretion about matters of public concern. As a quintessential proponent of the voluntarist tradition, he had little use for the New Deal. He had never studied economics in a systematic way, and Keynesian notions of macroeconomic management held no appeal for him. He saw his contributions to economy in government permanently undone, his labors for closer Anglo-American relations temporarily undermined. By a strange political transmutation, he became something of an isolationist himself in the late 1930s. With old friends such as Pershing and Hoover, he took pleasure in "viewing with alarm." To the end, he represented the tradition of voluntarist commitment to the public good, unstinting personal sacrifice, and freedom through limited government that Hoover had celebrated a generation before in

his programmatic work, *American Individualism* (1922).

Publications:

The Banking System of the United States and Its Relation to the Money and Business of the Country (Chicago: Rand-McNally, 1894);

Essays and Speeches, with extracts from the journal of Rufus Fearing Dawes, and an address upon the Army of the Potomac by General R. R. Dawes (Boston & New York: Houghton Mifflin, 1915);

A Journal of the Great War, 2 volumes (Boston & New York: Houghton Mifflin, 1921);

The First Year of the Budget of the United States (New York & London: Harper, 1923);

Notes as Vice President, 1928-1929 (Boston: Little, Brown, 1935);

How Long Prosperity? (Chicago: Marquis, 1937);

Journal as Ambassador to Great Britain (New York: Macmillan, 1939);

A Journal of Reparations (London: Macmillan, 1939);

A Journal of the McKinley Years, edited, with a foreword, by Bascom N. Timmons (Chicago: Lakeside, 1950).

References:

Carl Williams Ackerman, *Dawes—the Doer!* (New York: Era, 1924);

Allied Powers, Reparation Commission, *Rapport du premier Comité d'experts. Report of the First Committee of Experts* (Paris, 1924);

Martin L. Goslin, *Charles Gates Dawes, 1865-1931* (Evanston, Ill., 1951);

Paul Roscoe Leach, *That Man Dawes* (Chicago: Reilly & Lee, 1930);

Melvyn P. Leffler, *The Elusive Quest: America's Pursuit of European Stability and French Security, 1919-1933* (Chapel Hill: University of North Carolina Press, 1979);

Werner Link, *Die amerikanische Stabilisierungspolitik in Deutschland 1921-32* (Düsseldorf: Droste Verlag, 1970);

Arthur MacDonald, *Charles G. Dawes, étude de politique scientifique* (Paris, 1924);

James Stuart Olson, *Herbert Hoover and the Reconstruction Finance Corporation, 1931-1933* (Ames: Iowa State University Press, 1977);

Stephen A. Schuker, *The End of French Predominance in Europe: The Financial Crisis of 1924 and the Adoption of the Dawes Plan* (Chapel Hill: University of North Carolina Press, 1976);

Donald Smythe, *Pershing: General of the Armies* (Bloomington: Indiana University Press, 1986);

Bascom M. Timmons, *Portrait of an American: Charles G. Dawes* (New York: Holt, 1953).

Archives:

An extensive collection of Charles G. Dawes Papers is located in the Northwestern University Library, Evanston, Illinois.

Deflation (*see* **Interest, Inflation, and Deflation**)

Depository Institutions Deregulation and Monetary Control Act of 1980

by Richard H. Timberlake

University of Georgia

The Depository Institutions Deregulation and Monetary Control Act (DIDMCA) of 1980 was hailed by Wisconsin senator William Proxmire, one of its sponsors, as the "most significant banking legislation since [the passage of the Federal Reserve Act in] 1913." More accurately, it was the most significant banking legislation since the Banking Act of 1935, because the 1935 act was at least as momentous as the 1913 original. The three acts together reflect a general consensus regarding the monetary and banking system that has existed for most of the twentieth century. The original Federal Reserve Act left the gold standard as the dominant money-determining institution; the act of 1935 gave a restructured Federal Reserve System, particularly the Federal Open Market Committee (FOMC), virtually unlimited control over the monetary system. It left the gold standard in the picture only as a functionless piece of window dressing. The DIDMCA extended Fed control over the monetary system even further and at the same time deregulated private financial institutions.

The DIDMCA has in total eight titles, which deal with truth-in-lending simplification, state usury laws, amendments to the national banking laws, and other matters. The first two titles contain the principal substance of the act as well as its contradictory implications: Title I greatly extends the Fed's powers and regulatory scope, while Title II significantly relaxes restrictions on economic activity for the rest of the banking and financial system.

Most of Congress's legislative energy was spent on Title II, the section of the act that provided for limited deregulation of the financial industry. Title II allows nonbank institutions to issue demand deposits and permits banks to pay interest on their demand obligations. All institutions could thereafter compete for depositors on a "level playing field." Title II also provided for the phasing out of Fed ceilings on interest rates paid on time deposits. The overwhelming vote by which Congress passed the act in late March 1980 reflected the common sense of the provisions.

The rest of the DIDMCA, except for Title I, is relatively unimportant. Title IV extended the range of financial activity accessible to other thrift institutions, particularly savings and loan associations and mutual savings banks. Title V "preempted" state government control over mortgage usury laws. Title VI aimed to increase consumer understanding and creditor compliance with the Truth in Lending Act. Title VII amended the administration of the national banking laws, particularly with respect to the Bank Holding Company Act, and Title VIII called for simplification of financial regulation. Title IX restricted foreign takeovers of any domestic financial institution. "Takeover" meant the acquisition of 5 percent or more of an institution's assets.

The substance of Title I of the DIDMCA is momentous. Far from any "deregulation" as implied in the label of the act, Title I greatly enlarged the powers of the Fed Board and the FOMC. First, it extended the board's control over reserve requirements to all banks—member banks of the Federal Reserve System and nonmembers alike, plus all other financial institutions that issue checkable deposits and are eligible for federal deposit insurance. That section also altered the board's control over reserve requirements to a range between 8 and 14 percent (with an initial setting of 12 percent), and it specified that the first $25 million of deposits required only a 3 percent reserve. From this time on, Title I stipulated, reserve requirements were to be set uniformly over the financial system without regard to a bank's volume of deposits or location. Prior to DIDMCA, reserve requirements were graduated against a bank's deposits much in the fashion of a "progressive" tax on income. The allowable range had been 7 to 16.25 percent.

Since the passage of the DIDMCA in 1980 reserve requirements have remained at 12 percent, and requirements against time deposits have remained constant at 3 percent. The obvious reluctance to use reserve requirements as a tool of policy reflects the undesirability of that means for manipulating money stocks.

Title I also provided for an eight-year phase-in of the reserve requirement changes. Since nonmember banks and other financial institutions were subjected to reserve requirements, they also became eligible for Fed discounting privileges. By the same token, the DIDMCA required all those institutions to report their balance sheet positions to the board on a regular basis.

Title I also ordered the board to publish a set of pricing principles and fees for the services Fed Banks render to banks and other financial institutions. Such services include check-clearing and collection, wire transfers of money, and securities safekeeping. Pricing of Fed Bank services is recognition that such activities require real resources and that their costs should be borne by the institutions that derive benefits from them. It also disavows the 100-year-old prejudice that the costs of many payments services, such as check-clearing, should be free.

The most important part of Title I (and of the entire DIDMCA) was the section innocently labeled "Miscellaneous Amendments." A significant paragraph that received almost no publicity expanded the "eligible collateral" for Federal Reserve notes to include "obligations of, or fully guaranteed as to principal and interest by, a foreign government or agency of a foreign government, as well as any other assets that may be purchased by [Federal] Reserve Banks."

That provision in large measure encapsulates the evolution of the Federal Reserve System. Prior to the DIDMCA, the FOMC already had unlimited power to alter the stock of Federal Reserve notes by purchasing and thereby monetizing U.S. government securities. The securities served as collateral, dollar-for-dollar, for the notes issued. Therefore,

the Fed could never "run out" of sufficient collateral for its note issues even in a technical sense. Since Federal Reserve notes are full legal tender for all debts public and private, the provision requiring "eligible" collateral to support the notes serves only as a gesture that conforms to an obsolete provision in the original Federal Reserve Act. Anything that is legal tender needs no collateral support. So what was the necessity for a new provision that gave the FOMC power to monetize any securities of foreign governments or any other "assets" that the FOMC might designate for purchase?

When the DIDMCA bill went through Congress in 1979, Federal Reserve spokesmen, including Paul Volcker, chairman of the Reserve Board, and two former chairmen, Arthur E. Burns and G. William Miller, initiated and lobbied for the Fed to have that power. Their arguments for the benefit of their monetarily unsophisticated congressional legislators inverted the routine monetary procedures of Fed money creation. They implied that the upcoming reductions in reserve requirements for financial institutions might denude the Fed Banks of so much government security collateral that the banks would find themselves short. Such a development was technically impossible. In any case, actual experience since passage of the DIDMCA has shown no shortage of collateral for Federal Reserve notes. The Fed Banks' consolidated balance sheet never at any time since 1980 has shown less than an excess of $9 billion in conventional collateral (gold certificates, commercial member-bank loans at Fed Banks, and U.S. government securities) over the outstanding volume of Federal Reserve notes.

The only possible reason for Fed officials to have cultivated this fictional "need" for their money-creating activities was to extend the Fed's hegemony to the international sphere. With this new power the Fed can intervene in any foreign securities environment and, by monetizing some of a bankrupt government's "non-performing" debt, owed, say, to large commercial banks in the United States, furnish the means (the money) that keeps the government in office. By acquiring this power the Fed has become a monetary surrogate of the U.S. Department of State.

As if to provide an elegy for the original concept of the Federal Reserve System—a lender of last resort for commercial banks and the provider of an elastic currency—the final paragraph under "Miscellaneous Amendments" states that the "penalty rate on Federal Reserve advances to depository institutions secured by 'ineligible' paper is repealed." Since nothing could be more "ineligible" than the securities of a bankrupt third-world government, the question of the quality of the collateral offered by member banks seeking Fed accommodation has paled to insignificance.

Congress passed the DIDMCA in March 1980 with virtually no dissenting votes. No congressman seemed to understand the extent of the powers that Title I bestowed on the officials of the Federal Reserve System. Everyone, however, appreciated and accepted the act's beneficial aspects in extending deregulation throughout the financial system. However, the term "deregulation" applied only to financial institutions as private business enterprises; the term "control" referred to the powers of the Federal Reserve System.

The Garn-St Germain Act of 1982 amended the DIDMCA of 1980 by reducing the required reserve ratio on the first $2 million of reserve liabilities from 3 percent to zero percent. It also authorized the creation of money market depository accounts (MMDAs) to be competitive with money market mutual funds (MMMFs). That latter change allowed banks to issue accounts based on money market securities and thereby compete with MMMFs that had innovated limited checking accounts on such asset holdings. Essentially, the act simply extended financial deregulation somewhat further than the DIDMCA of 1980.

References:

Charles R. McNeill, "The Depository Institutions Deregulation and Monetary Control Act of 1980," *Federal Reserve Bulletin*, 66 (June 1980): 444-453;
Richard H. Timberlake, Jr., "Legislative Construction of the Monetary Control Act of 1980," *American Economic Review*, 75 (May 1985): 97-102.

Deposits, Reserves, and Fractional Reserve Banking

Deposits made up those funds brought by individuals or businesses to a bank or financial intermediary for safekeeping. To induce the customer to part with his money for a period of time, banks often paid interest—a fee—to the depositor.

Once deposits came into a bank, they added to the institution's reserves; that is, the pool of money it held back (refrained from lending) in order to meet the daily demands of depositors wishing to withdraw their money or, in antebellum times, convert their notes into gold or silver (specie). No bank ever maintained $100 on reserve for every $100 worth of deposits—it would go out of business. Instead, banks operated on the principle of "fractional reserve banking," in which they loaned out all but a portion of their deposits and kept only a small reserve. The money they loaned might itself be put on deposit at another bank, with the process repeating itself. Economists have termed that process the "money multiplier" and have discovered that $1 in deposits generates $2.70 after the money multiplier has taken effect.

The ratio of reserves to outstanding notes or deposits constituted the "reserve ratio." It varied according to the financial tenor of the times. Usually in antebellum times a ratio of 8 to 15 percent proved sufficient, and generally the healthier the bank, the lower a reserve ratio it could carry, because customers knew their money was safe. In panic times bankers had to bolster their reserves, but even then, sometimes they could not meet the demand by customers for their money or to convert the banks' notes into specie. At those times the banks "suspended" and essentially refused to pay in specie or allow depositors to withdraw money (although they still welcomed new deposits).

After the National Banking Acts of 1863 and 1864, private note issue disappeared. The process of suspending disappeared as well, as banks no longer had to hold gold to back their own note issues but rather had to hold sufficient reserves to exchange for deposits. Failure to maintain enough reserves to cover deposits meant that the bank would simply go insolvent. Bankers and regulators thus shifted their strategy to build flexibility into the system. The Treasury attempted to maintain a substantial gold reserve for redeeming its currency, including, in earlier periods, contracting with J. P. Morgan to furnish gold in the Panic of 1893. Bankers sought ways of expanding the bank reserves in panic times by issuing clearinghouse loan certificates and, later, emergency currency.

The creation of the Federal Reserve System in 1913 aimed at providing an even more flexible system by furnishing an "elastic" currency through the Federal Reserve Banks. Because the Federal Reserve Act established legal reserves for all the members, which the 12 district banks held, it had a pool of reserves for an emergency. The Federal Reserve issued a new currency and provided loans to member banks. It therefore became the lender of last resort, wherein it bought the banks' promissory notes (representing short-term self-liquidating debts). Banks in that manner could and did add to their reserves, which they could then lend out as described in the economic multiplier above.

Although in 1933 the government abolished private gold holdings, gold still nominally "backed" Federal Reserve liabilities until 1963. Perhaps more important, the creation of the Federal Deposit Insurance Corporation (FDIC) effectively meant that small deposits in insured banks were safe. Follow-

ing several bailouts in the 1970s and 1980s, capped by the Continental Illinois bailout in 1984, the government made it clear that every large depositor whose deposits exceeded the insured limit of FDIC protection would nevertheless be covered. The Savings and Loan collapse in the late 1980s, in essence, took that protection a step further, making the government—not the Federal Savings and Loan Insurance Corporation (FSLIC)—the ultimate source of depositor protection. Since its creation, many critics had argued that the FDIC (and FSLIC) really were only as good as the taxpayers' will to keep them solvent.

While the FSLIC insolvency did not immediately threaten the FDIC, it did serve as a reminder that the taxpayer remained the ultimate guarantor of bank and savings and loan deposits in the United States, regardless of the cause of a bank's or S&L's failure. Thus, in the early 1990s, increasing discussions about restructuring deposit insurance or removing it altogether had surfaced.

See also:

Banking Act of 1935, Glass-Steagall Act, Penn Square-Continental Illinois Bank Failures, Savings and Loan Crisis.

—Editor

C. Douglas Dillon

(August 21, 1909 -   )

by John Landry

Brown University

CAREER: Director (1938-1953, 1971-1981), vice-president (1938-1946), chairman, Dillon, Read & Company (1946-1953, 1965-1981); U.S. Navy (1941-1945); president, United States and Foreign Securities Corporation (1946-1953); president and chairman, United States and International Securities Corporation (1946-1953); U.S. ambassador to France (1953-1957); U.S. deputy undersecretary of state for economic affairs (1957-1958); U.S. undersecretary of state for economic affairs (1958-1959); U.S. undersecretary of state (1959-1961); U.S. secretary of the Treasury (1961-1965).

Clarence Douglas Dillon, a leading investment

banker, and U.S. secretary of the Treasury from 1961 to 1965, was born on August 21, 1909, in Geneva, Switzerland, the son of Clarence Dillon and Anne Douglass Dillon. His father served as senior partner of the New York investment house Dillon, Read & Company (formerly Wm A. Read & Company) from 1920 until his death in 1979. C. Douglas Dillon received a prep school education at Groton and graduated from Harvard in 1931. After graduation he took a job on the New York Stock Exchange and worked for his father's company. Also in 1931 he married Phyllis Ellsworth, and the couple had two daughters. In 1938 he gained promo-

C. Douglas Dillon

tion to vice-president and director of the firm and then rose to the position of chairman of the board in 1946, serving until 1953. During World War II he served in the U.S. Navy, rising to the rank of lieutenant commander. He won the Legion of Merit and the Air Medal for withstanding kamikaze attacks in the Lingayen Gulf in the Phillipines and for flying a dozen combat missions.

As Dillon assumed the chairmanship of Dillon, Read in 1946, he also took the positions of president and chairman of United States and Foreign Securities Corporation and its subsidiary, United States and International Securities Corporation. He left all those offices in 1953 to enter public service, when President Dwight D. Eisenhower appointed him U.S. ambassador to France.

Dillon gave distinguished service as U.S. French ambassador until 1957, when he returned to the states to oversee the reorganization of the economic functions of the Department of State, taking the position of U.S. deputy undersecretary of state for economic affairs. He won promotion to undersecretary of state for economic affairs in 1958 and to un-

dersecretary of state in 1959. In those offices Dillon assumed authority over the federal government's International Cooperation Administration and began to coordinate U.S. foreign aid policy with the aims of foreign policy in general. The establishment in 1959 of the Inter-American Development Bank, designed to promote the economic development of the Latin American countries, brought one aspect of the State Department foreign aid coordination policy to fruition. As undersecretary of state Dillon also promoted the establishment of the Organization for Economic Cooperation and Development (OECD), combining the nations of the European Common Market and the European Free Trade Association. During Dillon's tenure at the State Department the OECD sought to reduce European and European-American trade barriers, to attract greater public capital investment among European nations, and, most important, to coordinate monetary policies among member nations with the aim of stemming the outflow of U.S. gold that was the result of the American trade deficit.

A lifelong Republican and a supporter of Richard M. Nixon in the 1960 presidential race, Dillon took the position of secretary of the Treasury in the administration of President John F. Kennedy, who desired a counterweight to the fiscal expansionism of other cabinet members. Kennedy, only a narrow victor in the presidential election, also wanted Dillon to shield him from criticism from Republicans and businessmen. Dillon had also impressed Kennedy with his competence in his jobs in the State Department and his lack of dogmatism.

The first problem Dillon tackled as secretary of the Treasury was recession. Prompt antirecessionary action—deficit spending, supported by the secretary despite his ideological opposition—brought the economy into recovery in 1962. Next, Dillon and the Treasury, at the president's direction, wrote tax reform and reduction legislation, designed to increase the profitability of investment, that passed Congress in 1963. In international finance, Treasury Secretary Dillon continued the association of the federal government with the OECD, with the result that the trade deficit fell from $3.9 billion in 1960 to $2.2 billion in 1962. Gold outflow dropped from $2.2 billion in 1960 to $.9 billion two years later.

Dillon left the government in 1965 to return to the chairmanship of Dillon, Read and the presidency and chairmanship of the United States and Foreign Securities Corporation. He retired from active duty in 1981.

Aside from his business and governmental service, Dillon has actively served several civic organizations, including as chairman of the Board of Trustees of the Metropolitan Museum of Art and as a trustee for several other arts organizations. He has also served as chairman of the Board of Overseers of Harvard University and as chairman of the Brookings Institution.

James Stuart Douglas

(June 19, 1868 - January 2, 1949)

by Thomas G. Smith

Nichols College

CAREER: Assayer, Copper Queen Consolidated Mining Company, Bisbee, Arizona (1891-1892); assayer, timekeeper, bookkeeper, superintendent, Commercial Mining Company, Prescott, Arizona (1892-1900); superintendent, Picacho Mine Company and Moctezuma Copper Company, Nacozari, Mexico (1900-1909); vice-president and director, Bank of Bisbee (1900-1934); founder, Douglas Investment Company (1903); president and director, Bank of Douglas (1902-1934); president, United Verde Extension Mining Company (1912-1937).

James Stuart Douglas, leading Arizona mine owner and banker in the first three decades of the twentieth century and cofounder of the Bank of Bisbee and the Bank of Douglas, was born in Megantic Township, Quebec, on June 19, 1868, the first son of James and Naomi Douglas. His father, James Douglas, a metallurgist, mining engineer, and mining executive, led the industrial development of the American Southwest as president of Arizona's Copper Queen Consolidated Mining Company and then its parent firm, Phelps Dodge Company, from 1885 to 1916. James Stuart Douglas worked his way up in the mining business and achieved independent success in that industry, especially as president of the United Verde Extension Mining Company from 1912 to 1937, as well as in finance.

Moving with his family (James Douglas worked chiefly as a mining consultant during much of Douglas's childhood), Douglas, strong-willed as a boy, got his education in public schools in Quebec, Phoenixville, Pennsylvania, and Tarrytown, New York, before striking out on his own to home-

James Stuart Douglas

stead in Manitoba, Canada, when he was seventeen. In 1890, five years later, he moved to Sulphur Springs Valley, Arizona, to find relief from severe asthma and to raise strawberries. The next year he moved to Bisbee, Arizona, home of the Copper Queen mine, at his father's request to work as an assayer. Late in 1891 he married Josephine Leah Williams, daughter of Lewis Williams, a founder of the town of Bisbee in 1880 and superintendent of the

Copper Queen smelter until his retirement in 1901. The couple would have two children, Lewis and James.

Douglas remained at Copper Queen Consolidated Mining Company only until 1892, when he moved to the Senator Mine of Commercial Mining Company of Prescott, also an affiliate of Phelps Dodge. He also worked as superintendent of the company's Big Bug smelter. In 1900 he took his family to Nacozari, Mexico, site of the newest Phelps Dodge operation, to serve as mining superintendent for the Picacho Mine Company and the Moctezuma Copper Company.

Independent-minded and aggressive, Douglas disliked working for Phelps Dodge subsidiaries, even though his father ran them, and worked to establish his independence, albeit with the elder Douglas's advice. Before he went to Mexico he began investing in mines, utilities, real estate, and banks. As early as 1899 he set his sights on acquiring potentially lucrative claims surrounding the United Verde Mine in Jerome. After a visit to Jerome that year Douglas wrote his father, "I think we have a prospect there that may make a mine. It is undoubtedly a very good showing & the marvel of it is that it could have been there all these years. . . undiscovered until now." In what turned out to be a great understatement, he continued, "I may be wrong but it wouldn't shock me much if I made some money out of the scheme." In 1912 he and George Tener organized the United Verde Extension (UVX) Mining Company to take advantage of the site, securing capital enough also to purchase the original United Verde Mine. After a long and expensive search the company discovered copper ore in 1914, and by late 1916 UVX produced $700,000 worth of copper per month. As president and the major stockholder of the company, Douglas reaped a huge personal fortune.

In the late 1890s Douglas's father, still president of Copper Queen Consolidated, persuaded Phelps Dodge officials to construct a smelter located on the Mexican border halfway between Bisbee and Nacozari. The town that grew up along with the smelter was named Douglas in his honor. James Stuart Douglas led in the movement to create the town, and in 1903 he and William Brophy, general manager of the Copper Queen company store in Bisbee, founded the Douglas Investment Company there to sell electricity, telephone service, ice, and real estate. Within a decade the town boasted a

population of more than 6,000 and the company was earning handsome profits.

Douglas also pioneered in the development of Arizona's banking industry with Brophy. At the turn of the century the territory claimed only a few small banks, in towns such as Phoenix, Tucson, Flagstaff, Solomonville, Tombstone, and Prescott. Some of those, to use Douglas's phrase, were in "weak hands." Meanwhile Arizona farmers and ranchers and the growing mining and industrial contingents living in new towns such as Bisbee and Douglas lacked service. Douglas met with his father in New York to discuss the possibility of forming a bank in Bisbee, after Brophy apparently originated the idea. After receiving his father's counsel and endorsement (and therefore the approval of Phelps Dodge), he worked with Brophy on the financial arrangements. Douglas, Brophy, Mike Cunningham (a Copper Queen store employee), and Ben Williams (Douglas's uncle and a supervisor at Copper Queen) capitalized the Bank of Bisbee at $50,000. "A bank in Bisbee is the latest," he wrote Williams. "I have written Billy [Brophy] & will be governed largely by his advice. Have talked to my father & he thinks well of it." Copper Queen officials encouraged their employees to make deposits in the bank, and Douglas, who served as vice-president and a director (with Brophy as president), expected it to become "the prettiest money maker in the deck."

Finding a suitable site for the Bank of Bisbee proved difficult. The elder Douglas proposed locating in the Copper Queen Consolidated office building, but the son balked. "I do not think we want to get quite so close to the Co.," he wrote Brophy. "For instance they might feel that they had the right to shape our policy in any way. . . . I think we should keep ourselves in an independent position." Eventually the group found a site on Main Street in the town, and the bank prospered. In its first month it gained $85,000 in deposits and $580 in profit. Douglas saw to it that the bank remained open late on Fridays when the miners got paid, to win the employees' wages before the saloons could. After only a few months of operation he reported to his father that the bank was doing "very nicely. Our gross receipts for the last three months have been somewhere about $900 per month. . . . Our loans as yet have grown to only about $30,000, but I think so far they are all first class."

After meeting success in the Bisbee bank venture, Douglas, Brophy, and associates moved on to

The Bank of Douglas, one of two banks founded by James Stuart Douglas, circa 1902
(courtesy of the Arizona Bank)

the town of Douglas, where they founded the Bank of Douglas in 1902. Douglas served as president and a director of that bank (with Brophy as vice-president) from the time of its inception. Like its sister bank it was immediately successful, within a decade holding deposits of nearly $1 million and netting $40,000 annually in profits.

During the first two decades of the twentieth century Arizona's economy experienced a series of severe disruptions resulting from the Panic of 1907 and from the territory's transition to statehood, a status it achieved in 1912. While many banks failed during those years, the Douglas-Brophy organizations thrived under the support of the region's flourishing copper industry. The Bank of Bisbee grew to second largest in the territory by 1910, and the previous year Douglas estimated his 151 shares of Bisbee stock to be worth more than $60,000. At the same time he valued his 98 shares of Douglas stock at nearly $30,000.

While many Arizona bankers retrenched, Douglas and Brophy expanded. By 1910 they established banks at Naco and Lowell and obtained controlling interests in the Phoenix National Bank and the Phoenix Savings & Trust Company. When the Federal Reserve Act passed the U.S. Congress in 1913, the first year of the Woodrow Wilson presidential administration, the Douglas-Brophy banks refused to join because Douglas opposed federal restriction of private enterprise. Meanwhile he planned to open a bank in Jerome, but World War I intervened.

Like most bankers Douglas strongly supported the government's Liberty Loan drives during the war. He also directed his banks to back the military effort further by increasing their investments in U.S. Treasury bonds. He and Brophy also volunteered their management skills. Both served in Paris in the distribution system of the Red Cross. While in France, Douglas met and befriended Premier George Clemenceau; the pair remained close after the war. When he returned to the States in 1918, Douglas founded a smelting town outside Jerome and named it after his new French friend. In 1921 he and Brophy established a bank there and placed a large bust of Clemenceau outside the building. Much later, when an aging Clemenceau could no longer afford to maintain his Paris home, Douglas purchased it anonymously and charged the Frenchman only nominal rent. After Clemenceau's death Douglas donated the home to the people of France.

In 1922 William Brophy drowned after he was swept from a fishing boat off the coast of Mexico. His son Frank inherited his interests, but, perhaps because of his youth, Douglas never took him seriously as a partner. Their relationship became strained and at times acrimonious. "This association proved to be one of the most difficult, though most interesting, experiences of my banking and financial career," Frank Brophy later wrote.

Heavy state taxes, overexpansion during the war years, and declining copper and farm prices caused many bank failures in Arizona in the 1920s. By the end of the decade 31 of 60 state banks had folded. Douglas-Brophy banks continued to prosper, although net earnings declined slightly. Early in 1929 Douglas sought to purchase Frank Brophy's interest in the Douglas-Brophy banks. He offered $200 and $225 per share respectively for Brophy's stock in the Bank of Bisbee and the Bank of Douglas. "I am afraid that you may think my ideas of values are low," he wrote Brophy, "but I cannot help but feel that at this time the above figures are about what the stuff is worth." But Brophy refused to consider an offer of less than $425 per share, and Douglas backed off. The following year Douglas wanted to attract an advantageous candidate to a directorship in the Douglas bank through an offer of 20 Bank of Douglas shares—10 from Douglas and 10 from Brophy—at $250 per. That time Brophy refused to sell for anything less than $450, incensing his senior partner. Douglas also thought that Brophy was "turning against your old friends" when Brophy refused to support a proposed state law calling for equal assessment of property values because he thought it would raise the tax on farm and ranch lands without a corresponding reduction in the tax on the property of the mines and banks. To the dismay of Douglas, the bill failed.

The hard times of the Great Depression stretched Douglas's relationship with Brophy to the breaking point and ultimately forced Douglas out of banking. By the late 1930s, through extensive behind-the-scenes maneuvering, Brophy had acquired control of all Douglas-Brophy banking interests. The Arizona economy hit bottom in the period from 1930 to 1932. Copper production dropped from $156 million in 1929 to $15 million three years later. Both Douglas and Brophy realized that, at least temporarily, for banks "the bonanza days are a thing of the past."

During the course of the Depression Douglas and Brophy disagreed vigorously over various aspects of bank policy. Douglas pointed out that "safety first for banks should be a motto for the future, even more than it has been in the past." To Brophy there was "a difference between conservative management and highly intelligent management." Declining profits prompted Douglas to cut the salaries of bank employees by 10 percent, reduce the dividend rate, and lower the interest rate on savings accounts. Brophy opposed those measures and spoke out against them at a directors' meeting. Douglas urged him not "to bother your head on such subjects. I read over one page of the minutes of the Bank of Douglas, and your recommendations were rotten."

In 1932, the worst year of the Depression, nearly 5,000 banks closed nationwide. In Arizona, Douglas voluntarily closed the banks at Lowell and Naco. Due to shrinking profits he eliminated savings accounts at the Bank of Douglas. He also recommended, over Brophy's strenuous opposition, the sale of all government bonds because of declining values. Finally, he accused Mike Cunningham, who then presided over the Bank of Bisbee, of mismanagement. Cunningham, he claimed, issued too many loans without sufficient security. He particularly criticized a loan made to Cunningham's son. He gave the bank president 30 days to "wake up" or else he would be fired.

Disgusted with "one man banks," Brophy proposed an end to the partnership. "From my point of view it is most undesirable for individuals to be associated in business when there is apt to be a continued strong difference of opinion." Douglas accused Brophy of "childish peevishness" and urged him "to forget the subject." For the moment Brophy agreed.

Meanwhile the banking crisis worsened. To prevent runs and closings, several states in late 1932 and early 1933 declared bank holidays. At the suggestion of Walter Bimson, president of the Valley National Bank, Arizona governor Benjamin B. Moeur proclaimed a state banking moratorium on March 2, 1933. Considering the proclamation "advisory," some bankers, including Douglas, refused to close. The governor made it clear the next day that the order was mandatory, but the Banks of Clemenceau, Bisbee, and Douglas remained open. When Moeur warned that he would instruct the National Guard to enforce the proclamation, Douglas finally relented.

Even though his son, Lewis, had been appointed U.S. director of the budget, Douglas fiercely criticized the New Deal of President Franklin D. Roosevelt. Brophy, on the other hand, initially supported Roosevelt's policies, although that attitude soon changed. Besides the bank holiday, Douglas denounced currency tinkering, abandoning the gold standard, and deficit spending. He also denounced the National Industrial Recovery Act (NIRA), which his son helped to write. The NIRA called for voluntary codes for numerous industries, including copper. Douglas was consulted concerning the copper code, but his advice went unheeded. The codes set guidelines for prices, wages, and production. They also recognized labor's right to unionize. Cooperating industries received a "blue eagle" decal for display. "The Code cannot be signed honorably by anybody and the U.V.X. won't sign it," Douglas wrote his son. The NRA blue eagle symbol was an "outrage" because it resembled the Prussian eagle. Roosevelt's "drift toward socialism" and high state taxes eventually convinced Douglas to liquify his business interests and leave the country. (Douglas saw many links between the Depression and Germany; he called the Depression a "German Plot," according to Brophy.)

In typical autocratic fashion Douglas closed the Bank of Clemenceau in late 1933. Two robberies totalling $6,900 had resulted in the cancellation of the bank's holdup insurance. Douglas also attributed the closing to "excessive" taxation and the depressed copper industry.

Against the advice of Brophy, Douglas suspended dividend payments at the Banks of Bisbee and Douglas and sold most of the holdings in government bonds. He also deposited nearly $500,000 in funds in the Bank of Montreal because he considered American banks unsafe. His actions once again provoked Brophy. Douglas expressed displeasure at his partner's "persistent obstinacy" and his reluctance to "consider the advice of your elders." For his part, Brophy contended that "being a partner of his in a bank is about as comfortable as flying in a high speed Lockheed with a drunk pilot."

In late December 1933 Douglas stunned Brophy by proposing the liquidation of the Bank of Bisbee. Brophy offered to purchase Douglas's stock.

Fearful that Brophy might acquire the bank only to sell it to a third party, Douglas balked. Brophy made assurances that he would not transfer the bank, but he could not win over Douglas. Brophy next asked Douglas to consider the economic impact on the employees and the community. "Sure the employees have to be considered," Douglas wrote, "but what is best & wise for us to do is almost certain to be best for them."

At a mid-January meeting in Bisbee, Douglas offered Brophy an opportunity to save the Bank of Bisbee. He presented Brophy with an option: agree to the liquidation or swap even up his shares in the Bank of Douglas for Douglas's shares in the Bank of Bisbee. Douglas gave his partner a day to think it over. Brophy agreed to choose one of the options. A few days later he rejected the stock swap and resigned from the boards of both banks.

Seeking Brophy's cooperation on liquidation, Douglas made another proposal in late January 1934. Brophy would write Mike Cunningham supporting Douglas's decision to close the Bank of Bisbee. In return, he could have a three-month option on his partner's Bank of Douglas stock for $90 per share. Surprised by the exceedingly low sale price, Brophy declared: "I don't think you want to do that. Hell, I wouldn't think of offering you my stock on that basis." Douglas persisted and the two men reached a verbal agreement.

On February 1, 1934, Douglas publicly announced the liquidation of the Bank of Bisbee. The institution was closing, he explained, because of heavy state taxes. A few days later Douglas backed away from his stock-option offer. Brophy sought to seal the verbal agreement with a check, but Douglas returned it. At a meeting with Douglas an incensed Brophy explained that he had gone along with liquidation so Douglas should have kept his part of the bargain. Douglas, however, "just walked away." Brophy then severed his relationship with Douglas. "I . . . leave you in full control of our mutual investments," he wrote, "but you are likewise going to have to accept full responsibility for them." As for the stock option deal, Brophy asked Douglas to "not bring the matter up again because it . . . will probably only tend to make an extremely unpleasant situation more so."

Regarding Douglas as "a double-crosser and welcher," Brophy worked on a plan to take over the Bank of Douglas. In the summer of 1934, while Douglas vacationed in Europe, Brophy acquired enough stock to gain control. On August 10 the board named Brophy president. Brophy soon purchased the Bisbee bank building and opened it as a branch of the Bank of Douglas. Within two decades the Bank of Douglas had 16 branches with total assets of nearly $75 million.

Outraged by Brophy's action and the meddlesome economic policies of the New Deal, Douglas sold his business interests, renounced his citizenship, and moved to Montreal, Canada, in 1938. A decade later he returned to Arizona to visit old friends. While touring the town of Jerome with his former secretary, Sam Applewhite, he came across newspaper advertisements issued by the Bank of Douglas. Those advertisements credited William Brophy as the founder of the bank. Angered, Douglas "wanted to SOS Frank Brophy and straighten him out." He did contact Brophy, and the two antagonists patched up their differences. The following year, on January 2, Douglas died. Having given away most of his fortune, he left his two sons slightly less than $1 million apiece, but his legacy also included much of the industrial and financial accomplishment of modern Arizona.

Publication:

"Facts About the Verde and Copper, but Not 'Roman-

tic,' " *Mining and Metallurgy* (June 1935): 258-259.

References:

Frank Brophy, "The Reluctant Banker: From the Reminiscences of Frank Cullen Brophy," *Journal of Arizona History*, 15 (Summer 1974): 159-184;

Robert Paul Browder and Thomas G. Smith, *Independent: A Biography of Lewis W. Douglas* (New York: Knopf, 1986);

William H. Jervey, Jr., "When the Banks Closed: Arizona's Bank Holiday of 1933," *Arizona and the West*, 10 (Summer 1968): 127-152;

Larry Schweikart, "Brophy versus Douglas: A Case Study in Frontier Corporate Control," *Journal of the West*, 23 (April 1984): 49-55;

Schweikart, "Collusion or Competition: Another Look at Banking During Arizona's Boom Years," *Journal of Arizona History*, 28 (Summer 1987): 189-200;

Schweikart, *A History of Banking of Arizona* (Tucson: University of Arizona Press, 1982).

Archives:

The papers of James Stuart Douglas, including an unpublished biography by Douglas Martin entitled "The Douglas Family of Arizona," are located in the Special Collections Division of the University of Arizona Library, Tucson. The papers of William and Frank Brophy are at the Arizona Historical Society in Tucson.

Lewis Williams Douglas

(July 2, 1894 - March 7, 1974)

by Thomas G. Smith

Nichols College

CAREER: U.S. Army (1917-1920); instructor in history, Amherst College (1920-1921); instructor in chemistry, Hackley School (1921); mine company official, Bisbee, Arizona (1921-1923); state representative, Arizona (1923-1925); U.S. representative, Arizona (1927-1933); federal budget director (1933-1934); vice-president, American Cyanamid Company (1934-1937); principal and vice-chancellor, McGill University (1937-1939); president (1940-1947), chairman, Mutual of New York Life Insurance Company (1950-1959); deputy administrator, U.S. War Shipping Administration (1942-1944); special economic adviser to General Lucius Clay, U.S. Army, Germany (1945); U.S. ambassador to Great Britain (1947-1950); chairman, Southern Arizona Bank & Trust Company (1951-1965).

Lewis Williams Douglas, prominent American politician and public official from the 1920s to 1950, grandson of metallurgist, mining engineer, and copper mine executive James Douglas and son of mine executive and financier James Stuart Douglas, and an important Arizona banker in the post-World War II era, was born in Bisbee, Arizona, on July 2, 1894, when his father was working as an assayer and superintendent for one of the mines of Arizona's Phelps Dodge Company. The eldest surviving son of James Stuart Douglas and his wife, Josephine, Douglas enjoyed a childhood of comfort and good fortune and attended the Hackley School in Tarrytown, New York, and Amherst College in Massachusetts. Before that, in 1900 the family moved to Nacozari, Sonora, Mex-

Lewis Williams Douglas

ico, where James Stuart Douglas assumed the superintendent's position at a series of Phelps Dodge concerns. James Stuart Douglas and family remained in Mexico until 1909. During that period Lewis Douglas often visited his grandparents James and Naomi Douglas and so fell under the influence of the grandfather, who projected an image considerably more humane and serene than that of Lewis's father and won a reputation for fairness and geniality in his business dealings. But Lewis Douglas admired both men, especially his strong-willed father's independent-mindedness and firmness. He sought his father's advice throughout his political and business career, and the older man often praised the son for standing up to him. He also taught Lewis fly-fishing, a lifelong passion for both.

After graduating with a B.A. cum laude in economics from Amherst in 1916, Lewis Douglas performed a year of graduate work in metallurgy and geology at the Massachusetts Institute of Technology before enlisting in the U.S. Army and fighting on the Western Front in World War I. He rose to the rank of first lieutenant and was decorated for heroism at Epinonville, France, and Lys-Escault, Belgium. Upon return to the states in 1920 he taught

history at Amherst, moving on to teach chemistry at Hackley School (his father's prep school too), in 1921, the year he also married Peggy Zinsser. Later that year the couple returned to Arizona and the mining industry. Lewis and Peggy Douglas would have three children–James Stuart II, Lewis Williams, Jr., and Sharman–but for Lewis the mining career would wait.

Two years after returning to Arizona, Douglas entered politics and won election to the state legislature. He served one two-year term, attracting local praise in 1923 for his advocacy of amendments favoring Arizona interests in the Colorado River Compact for regional development and then ran as a Democrat for U.S. representative in the 1926 election. He won that election, then won reelection in 1928, 1930, and 1932. In the House he unsuccessfully opposed passage of the 1928 Swing-Johnson bill enacting the Colorado River Compact and the construction of the Boulder Dam. After the beginning of the Depression he often privately agreed with President Herbert Hoover but voted against the president on major issues, breaking pattern only to argue in support of a modest tariff protection bill for his home state's mining industry that passed in 1932 and to support the creation of the Reconstruction Finance Corporation. In 1933 new president Roosevelt appointed the thirty-nine-year-old Douglas federal budget director.

During his two years in the White House as budget director Douglas proved a careful custodian of the public purse. He was a budget balancer: one who believed that balanced budgets and minimized federal expenditures boosted business confidence and invigorated investing. Roosevelt campaigned for the presidency with that conservative view and attempted to hold to it in the beginning of his term. During the period of the early New Deal, Roosevelt praised Douglas as "the find of the administration" and remarked that in due time he "would be a good Democratic candidate for President."

A member of the select group known as the "Bedside Cabinet," Douglas met with Roosevelt nearly every morning, and for a while he exerted some policy influence. He drafted the Economy Act of March 20, 1933, that sought to balance the budget by chopping veterans' pensions and federal salaries by a total of $500 million. With the Independent Offices Act of June 16, 1933, Douglas achieved additional savings through a program of bureaucratic streamlining, a time-honored federal tradi-

Douglas (right) campaigning with Arizona adjutant-general Colonel Oscar F. Temple, Arizona governor G. W. P. Hunt, and presidential candidate Franklin D. Roosevelt at a ranch near Williams, Arizona, 1932 (courtesy of the Arizona Historical Society)

tion in times of economic stress. His inclusion in the White House inner circle both thrilled and humbled him. "It seems queer," he wrote his father early in 1933, "to be writing a Presidential message to Congress on the budget," and to have unlimited access to the president. "How strange for an insignificant young man from Arizona to be in such a position." At the same time, however, Douglas demonstrated strong resolve in matters of policy and expressed a fear that he might be required to leave the administration if Roosevelt followed his more liberal advisers and departed from fiscal conservatism.

In the end that fear was realized. Despite his efforts, in the long run Douglas failed to discourage Roosevelt from experimenting with unorthodoxy in economic policy. "I never know when some new and foolish idea is going to be sprung," he complained in another letter to his father. When Roosevelt abandoned the gold standard in April 1933, Douglas remarked, "Well, this is the end of Western Civilization." He called a currency inflation amendment to the proposed Agricultural Adjustment bill an "insane proposal." He regarded national industrial planning, embodied in the National Industrial Recovery Act creating the National Recovery Admin-

istration in June, as a step toward socialism. As an advocate of currency stabilization, lower tariffs, and international economic cooperation, he grew disillusioned when the president snubbed the World Monetary and Economic Conference held in London in July.

Douglas's disillusionment turned to despondence when Roosevelt and Congress initiated a policy of deficit spending. Although the president's support for economy in government and a balanced budget appeared genuine, he willingly and repeatedly postponed an answer to the deficit question in order to finance relief and recovery measures. Douglas believed that the government could best relieve economic distress through direct assistance, not through massive public works he thought were inefficient and expensive. Large scale deficit spending, Douglas continued to warn, would create huge budget gaps, jeopardize the nation's credit, and bring runaway inflation.

Throughout 1933 and 1934 the articulate and outspoken Douglas pressed for restraint and equilibrium. After one cabinet meeting, secretary of the interior Harold Ickes confided in his diary that in disagreeing with the president, Douglas "went a little too far both in the substance of what he said and the manner of its expression." The budget director's steadfast views occasionally caused Roosevelt to lose his patience. "Lew, you are obsessed on this subject," he once snapped. "Perhaps I am, Mr. President, but . . . it is a conviction and a deep one that we cannot spend ourselves into prosperity." On another occasion Roosevelt expressed displeasure with Douglas's practice of submitting memoranda detailing his opposition to federal extravagance. "He makes a written record of everything," Roosevelt complained. "If things go wrong he wants to be in a position so he can show that on such and such a date he advised the President not to do thus and so. Of course, he makes a very good watchdog of the Treasury but I don't like it."

Unable to check the administration's "mad and reckless" expenditures, Douglas decided to resign as budget director in the summer of 1934. When he met with the president at Hyde Park on August 30, Roosevelt initially refused to accept the resignation. "Your job has been . . . an unpleasant one. Your job is to sit on the lid. When you have come in and criticized after you have gone out I have always said, 'There goes dear old Lew doing his job better than anyone could do it.' I should be the one to criticize you for criticizing but I never have." The two-hour meeting ended when Douglas agreed to sleep on the decision. The next day, however, he telephoned Roosevelt to say that he would not reverse his decision. The president, hurt by the resignation, eventually sent a warm expression of gratitude. "I do not need to tell you that in spite of the wide divergence of views that developed, our personal friendship continues, and of course I shall always feel grateful for the unselfish valuable contribution you made during those early troubled days when we were getting things back on their feet again." In acknowledging the president's letter, Douglas could not resist a final word of economic caution. "I hope, and hope most fervently, that you will evidence a real determination to bring the budget into actual balance, for upon this, I think, hangs not only your place in history but conceivably the immediate fate of Western Civilization. Yours, as ever doubtful but so sincerely wishful of success."

After leaving public service Douglas served as vice-president of American Cyanamid Company, then in 1937 he became the first American to serve as principal of McGill University in Montreal.

Three years later he resigned from McGill to become president of Mutual of New York (MONY) Life Insurance Company. He remained with MONY until 1959, during his last nine years as chairman of the board of directors.

As a private citizen during the 1930s Douglas stood as a hard-hitting critic of the New Deal. In speeches, articles, and a book he assailed government policies that he believed would lead to socialism. In the presidential election of 1936 he bolted the Democratic party to support the Republican nominee, Alf Landon. "It made no difference to me how bad Mr. Landon might be," he wrote a friend. "I was going to vote against Mr. Roosevelt as a matter of protest." During the presidential campaign of 1940 he denounced Roosevelt for attempting to violate the two-term tradition and formed an organization called Democrats for Willkie to support the Republican candidate. His assaults on the New Deal subsided with the outbreak of war in Europe. An internationalist, he staunchly advocated all-out aid to the Allies. He was an early member of the Committee to Defend America by Aiding the Allies and served as chairman of that organization's policy board.

Soon after the United States entered World War II, Roosevelt invited Douglas to return to public service. W. Averell Harriman, Lend-Lease administrator to England, wanted Douglas to serve as his assistant and the president reluctantly agreed. Harriman described the reconciliation of the two friends as "touching," and before Douglas assumed his position with Harriman, Roosevelt asked him to join the War Shipping Administration headed by U.S. admiral Emory Land. Roosevelt had good reason. The loading and routing of allied merchant shipping was poorly organized. Moreover, merchant shipping losses in the spring of 1942 rose to more than 800,000 tons monthly. Named deputy administrator in May 1942, Douglas used his managerial and diplomatic skills to organize and direct merchant shipping operations. Although Land remained titular head, Douglas actually ran the agency. He had insisted upon having a free hand before taking the position. He pointed out to Roosevelt that with the shortage of ships he would be pressed from all sides: "General Marshall will be on my neck for shipping. Admiral King will be on my neck for shipping . . . the War Production Board will be on my neck for shipping. . . . The British will; the Russians will. . . . Mr. President, I have got to allocate these

Ambassador Douglas with U.S. secretary of state George Marshall and British foreign secretary Ernest Bevin at 10 Downing Street during a meeting of the Council of Foreign Ministers, 1947 (courtesy of the New York Times)

ships and I must have your support. . . . If I don't have your support, Sir, I can't do it nor can anybody else." In reply, the president said, "Lew, I'll give you my word that I will never allocate any ships to anybody and I will never fail to back you up." Recalling Roosevelt's promise years later, Douglas wrote, "He could not have been more loyal or more true to the commitment he gave me. . . . He kept it meticulously." During that same meeting Douglas relied on humor to heal old wounds. "You know that you and I disagreed once on the budget, but this, Sir, is a budget that has to be balanced." "Why do you say that, Lew?," Roosevelt inquired. "Because, Sir, you can't print ships." With that response, Roosevelt tossed his head back and roared with laughter. Working closely with presidential adviser Harry Hopkins, Douglas effectively directed the allocation of merchant shipping until ill health forced him to resign in June 1944.

Douglas resumed his public service career in the Harry S Truman administration. After VE Day he served in Germany as a special economic adviser to General Lucius Clay, military governor of the American zone of occupation in Germany. He resigned that post after only two months because he opposed JCS 1067, the proposal for American economic policy in occupied Germany. "Economic idiots," he concluded, assembled that proposal, because it would strip Germany of its industrial base and transform it into an agricultural nation, hurting the whole continent. Douglas expressed his concerns to Truman, who remained noncommittal although impressed with Douglas.

In March 1946 Truman asked Douglas to become the first president of the International Bank for Reconstruction and Development. The World Bank, as it came to be known, was created in July 1944 by the United Nations Monetary and Finan-

Douglas (right) and banker John J. McCloy wearing their wives' hats to protect them from the sun during the dedication ceremony for the George C. Marshall Research Library in Lexington, Virginia, May 23, 1964 (George C. Marshall Research Library/Andre Studio/University of Arizona Special Collections)

cial Conference at Bretton Woods, New Hampshire. Since most of the bank's funding came from the United States, participants at Bretton Woods agreed to locate the bank in Washington, D.C., and head it with an American. The position attracted Douglas (at a salary of $30,000 tax free), but he declined it. The authority of the World Bank president remained ill-defined, the institution probably would have little independence from political interference, and loans might degenerate into a means of "deceiving people into the belief that production and distribution are not the basic remedies" for economic recovery. Douglas also felt a sense of obligation to Mutual Life. Declining the World Bank presidency, Douglas recalled, constituted "the most difficult decision I think I ever made in the life." His decision was all the more difficult because it nearly ruptured his relationship with his hot-tempered father. James Stuart Douglas saw the post as a chance for his banks to provide financial help to Britain and

France. When Douglas turned down the position, his father threatened to disinherit him. Hurt and dismayed, Douglas informed his father that he would have to alter his future plans. "I had hoped to enter public life again. . . . All of this must now change." His father's response hardly reassured him. "Yes, I knew well that my letter . . . would be very disturbing. You must not be miserable. Ask for God's help." Fortunately the crisis passed and Douglas saved his inheritance when Truman offered him a more prestigious position the following year.

In March 1947 Truman appointed Douglas ambassador to Great Britain, a position he filled with distinction for nearly four years. In his letter of appointment the president wrote that "At no time in our history has it been more essential that the man who speaks for us in London should combine outstanding ability with those qualities which represent all that is best in our American life and tradition." As ambassador Douglas enjoyed a close relationship with Secretary of State George Marshall and helped shape American foreign policy during the early Cold War period. Like most policymakers he believed that an expansive Soviet Union might insinuate itself upon the war-torn nations of Europe. The United States should use military, economic, and diplomatic means to contain the Soviet threat to Western Europe. His reports from London detailed the economic crisis and cautioned that the continent might fall to communism unless the United States supplied financial aid. When the European Recovery Program, or Marshall Plan, was announced in the summer of 1947, Douglas served as one of its most enthusiastic and articulate champions. In London and Paris he worked closely with Western European leaders to formulate a plan for economic cooperation, a precondition for U.S. assistance. Undersecretary of State Robert Lovett called him the "friendly oil which lubricated the whole affair over there." Because of his intimate understanding of European economic conditions, congressional experience, close relationships on Capitol Hill, and eloquence, Douglas served as a principal spokesman for the Marshall Plan in hearings before the House and Senate Foreign Relations committees. When Congress passed the $13 billion program in April 1948, Marshall congratulated Douglas for his "leading part in passage of ERP." British foreign secretary Ernest Bevin wrote, "I wish I could find words adequate to express the depth of my feeling and the gratitude which I feel towards you for what you have done in connection with the European Recovery Programme."

American policymakers also responded to their perceptions of the Soviet military threat. In the spring of 1948, Ambassador Douglas presided over secret Anglo-American-Canadian discussions at the Pentagon that resulted in the creation of the North Atlantic Treaty Organization (NATO).

Throughout his diplomatic career Douglas considered the economic reconstruction of western Germany as the cornerstone to European prosperity and security. In 1948 he served as a representative to the London Conference on Germany. At that meeting, the Americans, French, and British reformed the area's currency and combined their areas of occupation into what became West Germany. In retaliation the Soviet Union imposed the Berlin Blockade.

Douglas supported the decision to sustain Berlin by means of an airlift. His principal role in London during the crisis was to confer with the leaders of Western Europe and formulate a common response. For three months he worked continuously with the British and French, smoothing out differences and drafting similar diplomatic messages and initiatives to the Kremlin. Marshall acknowledged his contributions when he wrote, "I don't know what we would do without you. Literally, you have rendered a very great service to your country."

In the summer of 1948 Douglas also participated in discussions concerning the Palestinian crisis. He preferred partitioning the British Mandate into two states: one Jewish, one Arab. He opposed transforming the entire disputed area into a Jewish state because it would offend the British, anger Arabs, and create political turbulence that might allow Soviet penetration into the region. Privately, he criticized Truman's recognition of Israel as a "shocking performance" designed to win the votes of Jewish-Americans in the election of 1948. "What an unholy mess we have made of it, solely because of political considerations at home." Perhaps for that reason he refused a request from the chairman of the Democratic National Committee to make a substantial contribution to Truman's campaign for reelection. Douglas voted for the Republican nominee, Thomas Dewey.

Douglas's influence waned after 1948 for two reasons. First, Dean Acheson succeeded George Marshall as secretary of state and he was less inclined to seek the ambassador's counsel. Second, in April 1949 Douglas suffered an eye injury that damaged his health and sapped his energy. While fishing on the River Test in England, a gust of wind whipped a salmon fly into his eye. He was rushed to the hospital but eventually lost sight in that eye. Douglas was cheered by letters of condolence. One visitor, former British prime minister Winston Churchill, patted his leg and said: "My dear Lew, you must not let this disturb you. You must remember that Admiral Nelson had only one eye." Eventually, Douglas took to wearing a black patch, which became a distinguishing mark. In fact, he became the inspiration for the Hathaway Shirt advertising campaign that featured a male model sporting an eye patch. The injury, which caused considerable pain and discomfort, forced his resignation from the ambassadorship in December 1950.

Friendly, charming, and humble, Douglas was an extremely popular diplomat. Although a conservative, he had won the confidence of the British Labour government and enjoyed a warm rapport with

*Douglas (left) with Frank Brophy in Bisbee, Arizona, where their fathers started a bank in 1900
(Balte Wilcox Studio/University of Arizona Special Collections)*

British foreign secretary Bevin. He also was a close friend of the Conservative leader, Churchill. Douglas's wife, Peggy, and daughter, Sharman, were also very popular with the British and American public. Sharman, one of Princess Margaret's closest friends, was honored by Harvard University's Hasty Pudding Club as its "Woman of the Year" in 1949. The Bevins honored the Douglases before their departure at a formal dinner at the ministerial residence. Churchill also honored the couple at a private affair at his residence. There, in a touching gesture, Churchill revealed a painting he had completed and remarked: "My dear Lew, I do not give my children away lightly, but I want you and Peggy to have that."

Douglas's service as ambassador won praise in both England and America. A British newspaper predicted that he "may well go down to History as the most revered United States Ambassador London has ever had. . . . He has walked with Kings and not lost the common touch." Truman lauded his "wise counsel" and pointed out that the ambassador-

ship "rounds out a career of singular versatility and usefulness." But a new career loomed.

Douglas's experience in banking began as a youth in Arizona. In the summers he and his close friend Frank Brophy worked at their fathers' bank in Bisbee. Both also held shares in that bank. Douglas did not become a bank officer until 1949, when he acquired the controlling interest in the Southern Arizona Bank & Trust (SAB) in Tucson.

Southern Arizona Bank & Trust was founded in Tucson in 1903 by Nathaniel Plumer and Fred Steward. During its first three decades the institution grew gradually and became one of the largest banks in the state. With total assets of $10 million in 1940, it ranked behind the Valley Bank ($45 million) and the First National Bank ($18 million). After World War II the bank continued to expand under its president and principal stockholder Hubert d'Autremont.

Prior to his appointment as U.S. British ambassador, Douglas approached d'Autremont about acquiring some stock in SAB. When d'Autremont died in 1947, his widow, Helen, informed Douglas that she would sell the family's controlling interest in the bank so long as it remained under local control. Douglas agreed, but with one reservation. At some point in the future stockholders and depositors might find it necessary or advantageous to have another institution acquire the bank. The parties did not make that condition public when they announced the deal.

The d'Autremont family possessed 1,050 of 2,500 outstanding shares of SAB stock. Using money from his inheritance, Douglas obtained 800 shares and Isabella and Harry King 250. Douglas and the Kings agreed to vote their shares as a unit and not to sell without first making an offer to the other party.

In January 1951 Douglas was named chairman of the board of directors of SAB. The Kings also served on the board. Douglas bought a 167-acre tract of land on East Fort Lowell Road in Tucson so he could be close to the bank. His son James also worked at the bank, becoming assistant to the president in 1953.

During his first year as chairman of the board Douglas's commitment to Helen d'Autremont was put to the test. Frank Brophy offered to sell Douglas his controlling interest in the Bank of Douglas for the purposes of merger, which would have made SAB the second largest bank in the state. Douglas declined Brophy's offer on the grounds that it would have violated, at least morally, his obligation. Later, Douglas conceded that he had made a mistake with that decision.

Then, in the summer of 1954 the First National Bank of Arizona, a subsidiary of Transamerica Corporation, announced plans to open a branch in Tucson. Douglas unsuccessfully sought ways to improve his bank's financial position in order to compete. The following summer Transamerica offered to exchange SAB stock for its own shares at a 1-to-14.6 ratio. The transaction required the consent of 80 percent of SAB stockholders.

Eager to maintain the bank's independence and local flavor, Douglas initially resisted the proposal. He called a meeting of the stockholders in August to discuss the offer and the alternative of remaining independent. Douglas pointed out the financial advantages and the trend in banking toward mergers and consolidations. "There are," he observed, "on the other side of the coin, weighty sentimental, emotional and philosophical considera-

tions." Those "considerations," he emphasized, "move me very deeply and weigh with me heavily." He made it clear that he was "perfectly willing to go any way the stockholders want to go," to accept or repudiate the proposal. Still, he could not "recommend that you decline this offer on financial and economic grounds." The bank would retain its name and its officers and employees. Moreover, the majority of its directors would be local.

When the meeting concluded, every member present, including Charles d'Autremont, a large stockholder, voted to accept the offer. Unfortunately, Helen d'Autremont, who did not attend the meeting, voiced her disapproval and accused Douglas of going back on his word. The charges deeply hurt Douglas, who cherished his reputation for integrity. At any rate, by late November 1954 the deal was completed and SAB, with assets of $81 million, became a subsidiary of the Transamerica bank chain. As a consequence, Douglas emerged as the largest shareholder in Transamerica and won a seat on its board of directors.

After the consolidation, Southern Arizona Bank thrived. Under Douglas's direction the bank embarked upon an aggressive expansion program. In 1958 it constructed a new bank building in the Spanish renaissance style on Stone Avenue. As Tucson's leading banker, Douglas played a prominent role in boosting tourism and attracting new industries to southern Arizona. In 1958 he announced a three-year $90,000 program, financed mainly by the bank, to lure electronics and other light industries to Tucson. That booster program successfully helped promote Tucson's impressive growth. Douglas also opened three branch offices in Phoenix and another in Nogales. He introduced a new $1 million computer center to process more than 40,000 checking accounts. Under Douglas's guidance, bank deposits climbed from $47 million in 1949 to more than $150 million in 1965.

Douglas headed the SAB board of directors until 1965, when he retired to become honorary chairman. In that capacity he told a friend, he would "continue to do approximately the same things I have always done, except to preside at board meetings." Three years later, Douglas's son James Stuart became president of the bank. In 1975, a year after Douglas's death, the Western Bancorporation, successor to Transamerica, merged the First National Bank and the Southern Arizona

Bank. James Stuart Douglas stepped down as president but continued to serve on the board of directors. Eventually, Western Bancorporation and its subsidiaries, including the Southern Arizona Bank, joined the First Interstate Bank System.

During his later years, Douglas served on the boards of numerous civic, business, and charitable organizations, including the General Motors Corporation, the American Philosophical Foundation, and the Sloan and Rockefeller Foundations. The recipient of 20 honorary degrees, he promoted the study of meteorology and weather modification at the University of Arizona. He donated his voluminous papers to the University and established a museum at SAB to honor his family's contributions to the state's history. The museum holds books, guns, Indian artifacts, mining paraphernalia, and a priceless collection of western art that includes the works of N. C. Wyeth, Frederic Remington, and Charles Russell.

Lewis Douglas, like his father before him, was a prominent Arizona banker. As SAB chairman he helped his bank and his community expand and prosper. Plagued by ill health during his later years, Douglas underwent surgery for an abdominal obstruction in January 1974. After the surgery he failed rapidly and died at his Tucson home, Pantano Farm, on March 7, 1974. His remains were scattered over the hills of Jerome, the mining town where he brought his bride some 50 years before.

Publications:

The Liberal Tradition: A Free People and a Free Economy (New York: Van Nostrand, 1935);

There Is One Way Out (Boston: Atlantic Monthly, 1935);

The Obligations of Leadership: Address of the Hon. Lewis W. Douglas . . . before the Chamber of Commerce of the United States, May 2, 1940 (Washington, D.C.: U.S. Government Printing Office, 1940);

"Dr. James Douglas: An Appreciation," in *The Golden Spike: A Centennial Remembrance* (New York: American Geographical Society, 1969), pp. 49-53.

References:

Frank Brophy, "The Reluctant Banker: From the Reminiscences of Frank Cullen Brophy," *Journal of Arizona History*, 15 (Summer 1974): 159-184;

Robert Paul Browder and Thomas G. Smith, *Independent: A Biography of Lewis W. Douglas* (New York: Knopf, 1986);

Bernice Cosulich, "Mr. Douglas of Arizona: Friend of Cowboys and Kings," *Arizona Highways,* 29 (September 1953): 2-11;

John G. Forrest, "Personality: Novice Banker Spurs Expansion," *New York Times*, March 2, 1963, pp. 9, 12;

William H. Jervey, Jr., "When the Banks Closed: Arizona's Bank Holiday of 1933," *Arizona and the West*, 10 (Summer 1968): 127-152;

Larry Schweikart, *A History of Banking in Arizona* (Tucson: University of Arizona Press, 1982);

Thomas G. Smith, "Lewis Douglas, Arizona Politics, and the Colorado River Controversy," *Arizona and the West,* 22 (Summer 1980): 125-162.

Archives:

The papers of Lewis Williams Douglas, including an unpublished biography by Douglas Martin, "The Douglas Family of Arizona," are located in the Special Collections Division of the University of Arizona Library, Tucson.

George S. Eccles

(April 9, 1900 - January 20, 1982)

by Leonard J. Arrington

Utah State University

CAREER: Assistant cashier (1922-1923), vice-president, Ogden First National Bank (1925-1934); director and secretary-treasurer (1928-1931), treasurer and vice-president (1931-1945), president and general manager (1945-1975), chairman and chief executive officer, First Security Corporation (1975-1982); president (1934-1970), chairman, First Security Bank of Utah, N.A. (1970-1982); director and chairman of the executive committee, First Security Bank of Idaho, N.A. (1945-1975).

George Stoddard Eccles, internationally known financier and chairman and chief executive officer of First Security Corporation, the leading bankholding company in the intermountain West, from 1975 to 1982, was born on April 9, 1900, in Baker City, Oregon, the third son and the sixth of nine children born to David and Ellen Stoddard Eccles. David Eccles, son of a nearly blind, poverty-stricken Scottish woodturner, migrated with his parents from Scotland to Ogden, Utah, in 1863; Ellen, the daughter of Scottish migrants who went to Utah in 1850 and 1863, grew up in Wellsville, Utah. David Eccles spent his teenage years working in sawmills and lumberyards, gradually earned enough to buy "an outfit," and eventually formed the Oregon Lumber Company. By reinvesting profits he came to own several lumber companies, banks, railroads, beet sugar refineries, canning factories, and construction companies. He is generally regarded as Utah's first millionaire.

George Eccles grew up in Logan, Utah, where he went to grade and middle school. He worked each summer on his father's Utah-Idaho Central Railroad and in his father's lumber mill in Oregon. He attended Utah State Agricultural College (later Utah State University), served briefly as a lieutenant in the U.S. Army in 1918, and then attended the University of California at Berkeley. In 1920 he enrolled in the School of Business at Columbia University,

George S. Eccles

where he studied under H. Parker Willis, a noted authority on banking. A member of the university's tennis team, Eccles served as president of the local chapter of Alpha Kappa Psi, a national business honorary fraternity. He graduated from Columbia in 1922. After a brief internship with the Irving Trust Company in New York City, he went to Ogden, Utah, to begin his banking career as assistant cashier with the Ogden First National Bank, an institution his father had assisted in founding.

At Columbia Eccles had met Dolores (Lolie) Doré, the daughter of a car wheel manufacturer in Houston, Texas. They were married in 1925 and remained lifelong companions. Lolie was George's ever-cheerful associate in skiing, swimming, golf, tennis, hunting, traveling, and philanthropy, as well as an enthusiastic hostess. The couple had no children.

After the death of David Eccles in 1912, leadership of many of his enterprises passed to twenty-two-year-old Marriner S. Eccles, George's oldest brother. When George returned from Columbia he persuaded Marriner to strengthen their father's banking enterprises by acquiring several small country banks. Among other things, George undertook to determine how many banks they needed to justify hiring a professional staff. In 1925, in cooperation with the Browning family in Ogden, the Ecclese's organized the Eccles-Browning Affiliated Banks, and within three years the group owned banks in Ogden, Logan, Hyrum, Brigham City, and Richmond, in Utah; Idaho Falls, Preston, Montpelier, Blackfoot, Pocatello, Boise, Nampa, Jerome, Shoshone, Gooding, and Ashton, in Idaho; and Rock Springs, in Wyoming.

With those assets, valued at $28 million, Marriner and George Eccles, Marriner Browning, and Idaho banker E. G. Bennett, on June 15, 1928, organized the First Security Corporation to manage the assets of the 17 Eccles-Browning affiliated banks and one savings and loan company. First Security quite possibly constituted the first multibank holding company in the United States. Member banks included the oldest bank in Idaho, the Anderson Brothers Bank, founded in Idaho Falls in 1865. In 1931 George Eccles became vice-president of the corporation, in charge of most of the banks in Utah. After Utah adopted a law permitting branch banking in 1933, First Security placed its banks in Utah, except those in Salt Lake City and Tooele, under the management of the First Security Bank of Utah, National Association, for which George Eccles served as president from 1934 to 1970. He retained his position with the parent company, First Security Corporation.

A personal triumph accompanied George Eccles's rise to business prominence. From the time he studied at Columbia he had experienced a steady deterioration in his hearing due to a hereditary disease known as otosclerosis. Reconstructive ear surgery had not yet developed at the time, so he learned lipreading and much of the time wore the type of bulky hearing aid typical of those years. Not until 1947, through a successful "window operation" perfected by Dr. Julius Lempert and performed by his student Dr. Howard P. House, did Eccles achieve restoration of his hearing in one ear.

Eventually doctors fully restored his hearing. In 1962 Eccles received the Personal Achievement and Distinguished Public Service awards of the Deafness Research Foundation. In 1977, before a star-studded audience, he received the Distinguished Service Award of the Ear Research Institute in Los Angeles.

Under the energetic leadership of Marriner and George Eccles and E. G. Bennett, First Security Corporation acquired other banks to add to its original 17. By the end of 1929 the corporation listed assets in excess of $50 million. Twenty-five member-banks served two communities in Wyoming, eight in Utah, and fourteen in Idaho. Small farming communities in the tri-state area could not have enjoyed such full service and excellent security without such a banking system. As a holding company, First Security concentrated banking resources, increased professionalism in management, permitted safer and less-costly operations, provided greater variety in customer service, made possible local financing of businesses that became units of national chains, and provided an alternative to rural bank mergers.

The events of 1929 to 1933 dramatically emphasized the advantages of the system. Although the effects of the stock market crash of 1929 and the ensuing depression came to Utah and Idaho more slowly than to the industrial Northeast and Midwest, increasing unemployment, plant closings, and bank failures in those regions portended calamity in the intermountain West as well. Marriner and George Eccles held a strategy meeting of First Security managers and officers in Salt Lake City in February 1930. The firm obtained a blanket surety bond to protect its banks against embezzlement and burglary. When the first panicky bank runs hit Utah in 1931, the leaders of First Security had made preparations to deal with them. Thanks to centralized management economies and credit controls, the firm did not lose a single bank during the Depression and in fact acquired several smaller banks that sought haven in the more solidly based First Security system.

In 1934 President Franklin Roosevelt called Marriner Eccles to Washington, D.C., to serve as assistant secretary of the Treasury and made E. G. Bennett head of the Federal Deposit Insurance Corporation. George Eccles stayed in Ogden to "mind the store." Although George remained predominantly a banker, by the time his brother entered government service he had already extended his interests, serving as president of the Ogden Chamber of Commerce and the Ogden Livestock Show. In addition, he served as a director of the Anderson Lumber Company, the Western Gateway Storage Company, the Utah Construction Company, the Mountain States Implement Company, the Ogden Union Railway & Depot Company, the Lion Coal Corporation, the Oregon Short Line Railroad Company, the Los Angeles & Salt Lake Railroad Company, and the Eccles Hotel Company. He also represented his region on the National Industrial Conference Board. During the 1920s and early 1930s Eccles accepted many invitations to speak to civic groups in cities where First Security banks had located, and he actively served in the Utah Bankers Association and the American Bankers Association.

George Eccles also enjoyed competition. When he assumed the presidency of the First Security Bank of Utah in 1934, Marriner Eccles acknowledged his brother's exceptional managerial ability. "Things go well when George is on the job," he declared.

With the approach of World War II in 1939 First Security assisted with the expansion of defense production in the intermountain West by making loans to defense contractors, opening new bank branches near defense plants and installations, and helping to absorb the tremendous issues of government bonds and securities. President Roosevelt made Eccles a member of the National Defense Loans Committee.

On the local level Eccles proved instrumental in the establishment of Hill Air Force Base, Ogden General Depot, Clearfield Naval Supply Depot, and the Internal Revenue Service Center for Western America in northern Utah. He also aided in the expansion of Ogden's canning and packing industry, the McKay-Dee Hospital, and Weber State College. He vigorously promoted small business in the intermountain area. "Banks like ours," he once said, "must make legitimate credit available to small business. It is easy for banks to sit back and invest in government bonds. They will make money, but that will bring about a concentration of wealth that will cause the props to fall from our economic structures."

In 1945, at the end of World War II, when the First Security board discovered that Marriner Eccles would not return to Utah but would remain with the Board of Governors of the Federal Reserve System (a position he had held since April 1935),

George Eccles was elected president and general manager of First Security Corporation. He held that position until 1975, when he became chairman and chief executive officer of the firm. During Eccles's years as president and board chairman of First Security Corporation the firm's assets grew from less than $300 million to $4.2 billion. By 1982 the corporation operated more than 150 banking offices in Utah, Idaho, and Wyoming and three mortgage companies serving 11 western states.

Corporations for which Eccles served as director during the 1960s and 1970s included Utah International, Husky Oil Ltd. of Canada, Amalgamated Sugar, Union Pacific Railroad Company, Texasgulf, Farmer's Insurance Group, American National Insurance Company of Texas, American Bankers Life Assurance, and Aubrey G. Lanston & Company, of which he was one of the founders and chairman of the executive committee.

During the early postwar years Eccles served as chairman of the Utah Committee on International Economic Policy, a group affiliated with the Carnegie Endowment for International Peace. He worked tirelessly on behalf of the $3.5 billion British loan to help pay for purchases made in the United States during the war, and in 1949-1950 served as a consultant to the Economic Cooperation Administration (Marshall Plan). In the latter connection, as financial observer and adviser, he made inspection trips to more than 20 nations receiving Marshall Plan aid. Interspersed between those visits he conducted "a one-man Chautauqua circuit," speaking to groups of bankers and businessmen around the nation on the benefits of the Marshall Plan. Eccles also represented American bankers at monetary conferences and World Bank meetings in many parts of the world, and in 1964 was general chairman of the International Monetary Conference in Vienna. He also served as a member of the National Advisory Committee on Banking Policies and Practices for the comptroller of the currency and for several years served on the Government Borrowing Committee of the American Bankers Association. He also assisted in organizing and then presided over the Reserve City Bankers Association and the Association of Registered Bank Holding Companies.

Eccles had a long involvement in community activities, serving as general chairman of the University of Utah Medical Center expansion fund drive, director and treasurer of the Salt Lake City Chamber of Commerce, and treasurer of the University of Utah. For more than 30 years he held a seat on the board of the Utah Symphony, a directorship of Ballet West, and the honorary consulship of Finland for Utah, Idaho, and Wyoming.

As president of First Security Corporation, Eccles sponsored programs to promote the cause of economic literacy by encouraging communication between businessmen and the public. First Security Foundation, of which Eccles was president and trustee, granted hundreds of thousands of dollars in scholarships and library grants to 22 intermountain West schools. Eccles also established the Presidential Endowed Chair at the University of Utah and the George S. Eccles Distinguished Lecture Series at Utah State University. He sat on the board of trustees of the Foundation for Education in Economics.

Eccles held honorary degrees from the University of Utah, Utah State University, Brigham Young University, Weber State College, and Westminster College. He received awards from professional, philanthropic, and governmental organizations, including a Distinguished Service Award from the Utah State Medical Association and the Brotherhood Award of the National Conference of Christians and Jews. The business building at Utah State University bears his name.

Despite his involvement in national and international monetary conferences and civic and educational affairs, Eccles remained a senior executive of First Security and its predecessors for 60 years, coping with the problems of recession and depression, war and peace, and inflation and "stagflation" while developing new ways of banking and improving upon old ones. Under his leadership First Security helped start or expand thousands of businesses, created a wide variety of jobs, brought in crops through loans to farmers, and built more than 100,000 homes. Even when he had passed the age when most people step down from responsibility, Eccles continued to do his homework. He ran the First Security system right up to the end. Eccles died in Salt Lake City on January 20, 1982.

Publications:

Europe Today and the ECA (Chicago: Committee for Economic Development, 1950);

"Credit and Monetary Policy," *Analysts' Journal* (New York Society of Security Analysts) (May 1953): 3-6;

"Registered Bank Holding Companies," in *The One-Bank Holding Company*, edited by Herbert V. Prochnow (Chicago: Rand McNally, 1969), pp. 82-103;

First Security Corporation: the First Fifty Years, 1928-1978 (New York: Newcomen Society, 1978);

The Politics of Banking, edited by Sidney Hyman (Salt Lake City: University of Utah Graduate School of Business, 1982).

References:

Herbert Bratter, "Banking's Spotlight on George Stoddard Eccles," *Banking*, 60 (July 1967): 62-63;

"The Eccles Brothers: A Team That's Moving Fast," *Business Week*, no. 1301 (August 7, 1954): 40-41, 44-47;

Sidney Hyman, *Challenge and Response: The First Security Corporation, First Fifty Years, 1928-1978* (Salt Lake City: University of Utah Graduate School of Business, 1978);

Hyman, *Marriner S. Eccles* (Stanford: Stanford University Graduate School of Business, 1976).

Archives:

First Security Corporation maintains a library at its headquarters in Salt Lake City that contains an extensive clipping file, a file of typescripts of several hundred addresses by George S. Eccles, and a complete set of company magazines, circulars, and annual reports recording the activities and decisions of Eccles and his associates.

Marriner S. Eccles

(September 9, 1890 - December 18, 1977)

by Leonard J. Arrington

Utah State University

CAREER: Director and vice-president, Thatcher Brothers Banking Company (1912-1928); president, Eccles Investment Company (1916-1970); president, Ogden First National Bank (1920-1926); director and/or president of Sego Milk Products Company, Stoddard Lumber, Eccles Hotel Company, Anderson Lumber, Mountain States Implement, Utah Home Fire Insurance, and other companies (1919-1930); partner, Eccles-Browning Affiliated Banks (1925-1928); president (1928-1934), chairman (1951-1975), honorary chairman, First Security Corporation (1975-1977); president (1933-1934), chairman, First Security Bank of Utah, N.A. (1955-1977); president (1920-1940), chairman (1940-1971), honorary chairman, Utah Construction Company [later Utah International, Inc.] (1971-1976); treasurer and vice-president (1921-1940), chairman (1941-1976), honorary chairman, Amalgamated Sugar Company (1976-1977); chairman, Utah Emergency Relief Council (1932-1933); assistant to the secretary of the treasury (1934-1935); governor, Federal Reserve Board (1935-1936); chairman (1936-1948); vice-chairman, Board of Governors of the Federal Reserve System (1948-1951).

Marriner Stoddard Eccles, leading banker and businessman in Utah from 1912 to 1934, principal architect of federal fiscal and monetary policies from 1934 to 1951, outspoken opponent of the Vietnam War in the 1960s, and critic of other national policies in the 1960s and 1970s, was born on September 9, 1890, in Logan, Utah. He was the oldest of nine children born to Mormon converts David and Ellen Stoddard Eccles. David Eccles migrated to Utah with his parents in 1863, when he was fourteen. Industrious and enterprising, he gained a vision of industrial possibilities in Oregon when his

Marriner S. Eccles (courtesy of the Marriner S. Eccles Foundation)

family went there in 1867; he worked in lumber mills and on railroad construction.

After the family's return to Utah in 1869, David Eccles, then twenty, struck out alone to make his way in the lumber business. He first took a job as a logger, then as a partner in a sawmill operation, then as a supplier of lumber in Ogden. As his ventures expanded, he contracted to supply lumber for the Denver & Rio Grande Western, Utah & Northern, and Oregon Short Line railroads. With the assistance of the John Stoddard family and Charles W. Nibley, also Scottish-Mormon convert-immigrants, Eccles founded the Oregon Lumber Company and established prosperous lumber mills at several locations in Oregon. He invested his earnings primarily in Utah, where he founded lumber mills, beet sugar factories, railroad lines, farm machinery shops, flour mills, condensed milk plants, canneries, banks, and the Utah Construction Company. Having started out in the poorest of immigrant families, he had become Utah's first millionaire.

As a youth, Marriner Eccles worked on his father's railroads and in lumber mills and banks. He attended elementary schools in Logan, Utah; went to Logan's Brigham Young College, which doubled as a high school and junior college; then served as a proselyting missionary for the Mormon Church in Scotland for two years. There he met May Campbell "Maysie" Young, who soon migrated with her parents to Utah. Marriner and Maysie were married in the Salt Lake Mormon Temple in 1913; they had four children: Marriner Campbell, John David, Eleanor May, and Maysie Ellen.

In December 1912 David Eccles died. His first wife, Bertha Marie Jensen Eccles, lived in Ogden with their 12 children; his second (plural) wife, Ellen Stoddard Eccles, lived in Logan with their nine children. Eccles died intestate, and after a suit the law recognized a third wife and one son. Under Utah law Eccles's children inherited equally, but only the first wife could inherit. Thus, the court awarded the Ogden family five-sevenths of his estate and the Logan family two-sevenths.

As the oldest child in the Logan family, Marriner Eccles assumed control of several of his father's business enterprises, including the Hyrum State Bank and the Thatcher Brothers Banking Company of his native Logan. A careful analyst and a tough business negotiator, his early responsibilities, crucial to the well-being of his mother and young brothers and sisters (seven of the nine Logan children were minors at the time of their father's death) proved good training for his later national and international roles.

In order to handle the variety of interests in his father's estate, in 1916 Eccles formed the Eccles Investment Company, a family holding company. His businesses thrived, while those of his Ogden half-brothers and -sisters did not fare so well. In 1919 Eccles, representing his mother and his brothers and sisters in the Logan family, assumed control of several of his father's most promising companies—Ogden First National Bank, Ogden Savings Bank, Utah Construction Company, Amalgamated Sugar

Company, Stoddard Lumber, Anderson Lumber, Mountain States Implement, Eccles Hotel Company, and Sego Milk Products Company. Under his sound management, coupled with the general growth in the intermountain economy during World War I, those companies flourished.

Eccles's interest in banking increased, and in 1925 he joined with the Browning family of Ogden to form the Eccles-Browning Affiliated Banks. With the help of his younger brother George, who had recently graduated from the Columbia University School of Business, Eccles acquired several country banks in the region. Marriner and George wanted banks enough to make up an economic unit and to justify employing a professional staff. Within three years they had acquired control of banks in 17 locations in Utah, Idaho, and Wyoming. On June 15, 1928, Marriner and George Eccles, Marriner Browning, and E. G. Bennett of Idaho organized the First Security Corporation as a holding company to manage the 17 banks and a savings and loan institution. First Security is touted as the first multibank holding company in the United States. As president Marriner Eccles assumed the role of the leading banker in the intermountain West. Often called upon to speak to bankers' associations, civic clubs, and university classes, Eccles's diverse business interests kept him on "the circuit."

The onset of the Great Depression following the stock market crash of October 1929 presented seemingly insoluble problems for Eccles's banks and other businesses. Standing to lose much of what he had worked for, he came to realize that the values on which he had been reared—hard work and thrift—provided no answer to the debacle. He read, talked with informed people, attended conferences where national leaders discussed the calamity, and met often with his managers.

In addition to trying to understand the cause of the nation's financial collapse, Eccles faced the immediate problem of keeping his own businesses afloat. Even if Eccles's banks remained sound, a sudden run on a weak bank in the same or a neighboring community posed a danger through association. First Security obtained a blanket surety bond to protect its banks. Eccles also developed a method of dealing with the psychology of a bank run. Jonathan Hughes writes that the story of how managers coped with the first run on a First Security bank, which occurred in the late summer of 1931 and is recounted in Eccles's 1951 memoir *Beckoning Fron-*

Eccles (left), as chairman of the Federal Reserve Board of Governors, with Franklin D. Roosevelt and James Roosevelt at the 1937 dedication of the Federal Reserve Building (Special Collections, Marriott Library, University of Utah)

tiers, is often read to beginning economics students and excerpted in texts on money and banking. On the first day of the run cashiers slowly paid depositors with small bills while talking about the weather. They clandestinely checked the signatures on the withdrawal slips and extended bank hours. The next day the bank opened early, paid quickly in large bills, and let no lines form for any reason. Armored carriers accompanied by police cars brought more money to the bank, reassuring depositors. Despite several close calls, every First Security bank managed to stay open during the Depression. In fact, First Security Corporation expanded by absorbing banks that could not have survived on their own. Among those merged into the system in 1932 was Deseret National Bank, the oldest national bank in Utah, founded by Brigham Young in 1871.

In protecting itself from collapse First Security had to adopt a rough and distasteful credit and col-

lection policy. Not everyone remembered the corporation as generous and forgiving during the Depression.

Eccles wondered whether his efforts to maintain liquidity helped the economy. By forcing the liquidation of loans and securities to meet the demands of depositors, was First Security not helping to drive prices down, making the deflation worse? By seeking individual salvation, did the bank contribute to collective ruin? Would it not be more rational for the central monetary authorities to stimulate an increase in the supply of money and credit? Each banker, pursuing his own best interests, only made things worse for his depositors and borrowers.

Eccles knew with certainty that the Depression was not, as many bankers and politicians asserted, simply a failure of confidence. "If it were simply a condition of psychology which existed

Cartoon by C. K. Berryman lampooning New Deal finance under Eccles's orchestration (Washington Star, December 4, 1938)

only in the minds of people and due only to a state of nerves," he told a Salt Lake bank management conference in 1931, "or if all that was needed was the optimism which has been pumped into the air in vast quantities by political and business leaders for more than a year, then our problem would be much simpler." The bankers and politicians needed to realize that there was something wrong with the basic structure of the economy; people could not buy as much as industry could produce. The popular sin-and-repent theory of depression, which held that people had spent extravagantly and had to pay the consequences, Eccles thought ridiculous. Depressions came not through the scientific operation of God-given economic laws, but through faulty social institutions and economic policies. Capital accumulation, Eccles believed, had gotten out of balance with consumption. No amount of hard work and thrift could protect an individual from the general failure of the system. Hard work meant more production, but frugality resulted in less consumption, so then-current remedies actually contributed to the production-consumption disparity. Only the govern-

ment, with its power to control money and credit, could generate the purchasing power necessary to put idle laborers and machines to work. Such a course promised to stimulate private enterprise and preserve capitalism. Those who failed to advocate that the government use the resources at its disposal to increase employment and production on the grounds that it would result in an unbalanced budget resembled "the stewards on the doomed Titanic who locked all the staterooms so nothing could be stolen as the ship sank."

Barely a high school graduate, Eccles had never heard of John Maynard Keynes, but his advocacy of a compensatory fiscal and monetary policy as early as 1931 remarkably resembled the Keynesian position advanced several years later.

In addition to the benefits of his own probing intelligence and his varied financial and business experience, Eccles had the advantage of his family's Mormon pioneer heritage. As Dean May has demonstrated, Eccles grew up in a society in which the centralized planning authority of the Mormon Church attenuated the ruggedness of individualism. Since the days of Brigham Young, Mormons had recognized the responsibility of that central authority to plan and direct the economy of the region and to provide the needy with jobs and the basic necessities of life. Frontier Mormonism emphasized group welfare, collectivization of investment, and extensive group efforts (through central church authorities) to overcome famines, sieges, and depressions. Eccles merely applied to the federal government a familiar principle of church interventionism. As a banker, he also saw some wisdom in the prescriptions of popular economists William Trufant Foster and Waddill Catchings in their book *The Road to Plenty* (1928).

Eccles had joined an organization of Ogden businessmen called the "Freidenkers" (German for free-thinkers). Another member of this group, Robert H. Hinckley, later served in the Franklin Roosevelt administration. Hinckley, a regent of the University of Utah, often attended a monthly Forum series sponsored by the university and invited Eccles to attend a lecture by Paul H. Douglas, a University of Chicago economist and later U.S. Senator from Illinois. In his talk Douglas expressed ideas similar to those of Eccles. Hinckley also was a nephew of Senator William H. King, a Utah Democrat who served on the Senate Finance Committee chaired by Senator Pat Harrison. The committee had to determine the causes of the Depression and suggest legislative remedies. Hinckley recommended to Senator King that he invite Eccles to testify before the committee. Eccles would do so in February 1933.

In the meantime Hinckley invited Eccles to a businessman's luncheon in the Hotel Utah at which economist and author Stuart Chase was scheduled to speak. A snowstorm delayed Chase's arrival. After going through the motions of introducing the absent Chase, Hinckley announced that a friend of his in the audience (Eccles) had some strong views about the economy, and he asked Eccles to take over until Chase arrived. Eccles expressed to the crowd his usual reservations about the balanced budget philosophy and laissez-faire government. After Chase arrived, he had time for a few words, and then while he ate his lunch Eccles explained at length what he would do to achieve recovery. Chase suggested that Eccles go to New York to see Rexford Tugwell, soon to be one of the early New Deal "braintrusters," after testifying before the Finance Committee in Washington.

Chairman Eccles in his Federal Reserve office (courtesy of the Marriner S. Eccles Foundation)

Eccles's February testimony before Harrison's Washington "Depression Clinic" advocated a gift of $500 million to the states to take care of the destitute and unemployed, a $2.5 million loan to the states for self-liquidating public-works programs, a domestic allotment plan to regulate agricultural output and raise farm prices, a program to refinance farm mortgages, federal child-labor and minimum-wage laws, unemployment insurance, old-age pensions, federal insurance of bank deposits, revisions in the Federal Reserve System to give the Fed greater control over the banking system, and the creation of a national economic planning agency. Contradicting the testimony of nearly all the others who appeared before the committee—including Bernard Baruch (longtime adviser to presidents), Myron S. Taylor (president of U.S. Steel), and General W. W. Atterbury (president of the Pennsylvania Railroad)—Eccles also called for deliberate deficit financing. The *New York Times* described Eccles's hard-hitting testimony as "inflamed" and "bombastic." But Archibald MacLeish, writing for *Fortune* in 1935, declared that Eccles's program so closely resembled that adopted by Franklin Roosevelt's New Deal that the Utahan was not only a Mormon but also a prophet.

Thanks to the recommendations of Chase, Tugwell, and George Dern, ex-Governor of Utah and secretary of war in the Roosevelt administration, and others, Henry Morgenthau, Jr., asked Eccles to join the administration as assistant secretary of the treasury. Eccles assumed his Washington duties in February 1934. He had already helped formulate the Emergency Banking Act of 1933 and aided in the establishment of the Federal Deposit Insurance Corporation (FDIC), created in June 1933 to guarantee individual bank deposits up to $5,000 against bank failures. Eccles's Idaho partner, E. G. Bennett, became the Republican member of the first three-member board of directors of the FDIC.

In one of his first activities as assistant to the treasury secretary, one in which he took immense pride, Eccles helped draft the Federal Housing Act, passed in June 1934, which established the Federal Housing Administration to insure housing loans made by private financial organizations. The agency later received the authority to extend loans to local governments for public housing.

In November 1934 Eccles's influence in government increased when Roosevelt nominated him to the governorship of the Federal Reserve System; the Senate approved the appointment in April 1935.

As governor of the Federal Reserve Board, Eccles sponsored the Banking Act of 1935, which, although it did not meet all of his specifications, restructured the Federal Reserve System, gave a new Board of Governors discretionary controls over bank reserves and margin requirements for loans against securities, and moved the renamed Federal Open Market Committee from New York to Washington. The act removed the secretary of the Treasury and the comptroller of the currency from the government of the Fed, consolidating the nation's monetary power. Roosevelt appointed Eccles as chairman of the Board of Governors, and he served in that position for 15 years. He was also a member of the Board of Economic Stabilization from 1936 to 1948.

In the spring of 1935 the stock market started a year-long climb, a phenomenon that ought to have delighted the American people, for it demonstrated investors' confidence in the nation's future and reflected income increases generated by various anti-Depression programs. But some, remembering

1929, remained fearful of inflation. Many called for an end to government borrowing and spending programs, but Eccles saw no reason to retrench. "Inflation," he told the American Bankers Association, "implies a state where an excess of dollars competes for a limited amount of goods and services on the existing market." High unemployment still existed; a large percent of the nation's industrial capacity still lay idle or underutilized. Eccles argued that the federal government must not cut its spending programs until private industry took over the employment load. Any reduction in consumer buying power threatened to retard, if not reverse, the progress of recovery. The government had to maintain and increase the flow of money as the economy expanded. Eccles pointed out that the federal debt had risen only $7 billion from 1933 to 1936, equal to about 8 percent of national income in fiscal 1928-1929, and the carrying charges on the debt comprised less than 1 percent of the national income. During the same period national income increased from $40 billion to $60 billion, industrial output climbed 65 percent, bank deposits rose $10 billion, and tax collections rose by $2 billion per year from 1932.

But Secretary Morgenthau, whose view seemed the prevailing one, still argued for a balanced budget, and most businessmen, bankers, and "sound money" advocates shared that attitude. Undeterred, Eccles tried to convert the president, preached the doctrine of compensatory spending to business groups, appeared on national radio talk shows, and gave interviews to journalists. In a 1936 cover story, *Time*, echoing the sentiments of many, reported, "A good many people believe that Marriner S. Eccles is the only thing standing between the United States and disaster." Others, however, while acknowledging his business and financial acumen, found his ideas heretical. "Eccles is like a poker player. He plays tight and talks loose."

In 1936 the Treasury Department, with Roosevelt's approval, advanced the idea of an undistributed profits tax as one means by which it could pump idle funds back into the nation's economy. Such a tax would cut the amount the government had to finance by selling bonds, thus increasing the debt and bringing in added tax revenue from another source. Eccles favored the proposal as a means of checking the growth of huge aggregations of idle capital. Eccles's studies showed that during

Eccles with New York senator Robert F. Wagner, 1944 (courtesy of the Marriner S. Eccles Foundation)

the years since 1929, many large corporations reduced their debt and increased their liquidity even though they had suffered operating losses. Cash holding of corporations comprised a larger percent of the total supply of deposit currency in 1936 than in 1929, and a substantial part of the new money created through government financing went into the hands of those corporations, but they did not distribute it. By draining off great portions of the government's newly created money, they had not pumped it back into the expenditure stream in the form of dividends or higher wages or lower prices. In short, the undistributed profits tax would increase investment and consumption expenditures and also improve the effectiveness of the Federal Reserve System in monitoring capital markets.

Those factors argued for the tax. But Congress refashioned and gutted it, and the tax ended up, in Eccles's view, as a prohibitive punishment for small corporations, permitting wealthy stockholders to continue to evade their fair share of taxation. It favored the growth of uneconomic bigness, and would be ineffective in forcing more purchasing power into circulation. Nevertheless, on bal-

ance, Eccles thought the arrangement was better than nothing, and worth retaining. But Congress allowed the 1936 tax to expire at the end of 1939.

The supreme moment for Eccles in Washington came during the recession crisis of 1937-1938, when he persuaded the fiscally conservative Roosevelt to stand foursquare behind an antirecessionary policy of deficit spending.

Unquestionably, as Dean L. May points out, the recession represented a major economic downturn. During the six months from August 1937 to January 1938 economic indicators registered as sharp a drop in industrial production as had occurred in the 13 months following the stock market crash of 1929. Stock prices declined dramatically, with a sharp break in April 1937 and sharp waves of selling in mid October, and by early November "the Roosevelt Depression" had arrived. Industrial production, stock-price averages, employment, payrolls, and income payments turned sharply down and showed no signs of leveling out. From April 1937 to April 1938 stock prices fell 58 percent, employment 28 percent, and payrolls and industrial production 43 percent. Just when it seemed that five years of costly effort might witness a return to 1929 prosperity, the structure collapsed.

Even New Dealers had doubts about the effectiveness of their programs. Were they headed the wrong way after all, as their vocal opponents gleefully charged? A particular poignancy marked the decline. The totalitarian states of Europe and Asia posed a serious challenge to American democratic values. Continuing economic stagnation would discredit free enterprise capitalism, America's liberal democracy, and Roosevelt's leadership. When the recession struck, the Spanish Civil War was seemingly ushering in a division of Europe into warring fascist, communist, and democratic nations. The democracies seemed hardly a match for the regimented efficiency of Germany and Italy. America felt the burden of proving that a liberal democracy, a "free society," had the capacity to solve the economic crisis and provide social justice for its citizens.

A furious debate ensued over administration policy. The president's closest adviser on economic policy had been his former Hyde Park neighbor, Treasury Secretary Henry Morgenthau, Jr. He and Roosevelt had a standing appointment for lunch each Monday. Indeed, Morgenthau told his staff in October 1937 that the president consulted him "on everything"–"almost constantly." When the sharp recession began to take its toll in the spring of 1937, Morgenthau contended that the administration must pull back, abandon some of its reform programs, and cut expenditures to the bone. Abundant support for that point of view existed among businessmen and politicians who thought government should cut taxes and retrench.

Eccles was furious. Why cut expenditures, he asked, when the spending stream had already started to dry up? He thought it preposterous. Eccles wanted the spending flow of consumers, businesses, and the government accelerated; a reduction in government spending was precisely the wrong action to take.

While Eccles had difficulty obtaining the president's ear, he gave forceful and persuasive speeches and commanded the support of a small but significant group of persons outside and inside the administration. In particular, he had the friendship and support of Harry Hopkins. Moreover, with his macroeconomic approach Eccles had a plan to end the recession–compensatory fiscal and monetary policies. Although he wanted to listen to Morgenthau,

Roosevelt, always the activist, wanted to *do* something, and he had lost confidence in leading bankers and corporate spokesmen.

Eccles won the war of wills, and Roosevelt embarked on a deliberate policy of increased public spending in April 1938. A slow recovery followed, and the New Deal spending program evolved into far more than a form of temporary pump-priming and act of political expediency; it officially recognized the use of macroeconomic insights to increase national income. Although historians have tended to credit the transformation in policy to the influence of John Maynard Keynes and his American followers, a careful study of the period shows that the key influence came from a Mormon banker from Utah who had independently arrived at the basic concepts described so elegantly by Keynes in his *General Theory of Employment, Interest, and Money* (1936). Concepts such as the multiplier, the propensity to consume, liquidity preference, and equilibrium at less than full employment, while not named and precisely formulated by Eccles, emerged in his thinking in 1932, 1933, and 1934 and formed the basis for his recommendations. With full confidence that it had adopted a rational policy, the administration in 1938 expanded its programs of public construction, social welfare, cultural development, and military preparedness.

Paradoxically, as Eccles pointed out in *Beckoning Frontiers*, the first promise of success in the recovery effort brought new demands to curtail the spending program. In December 1938, in an address broadcast nationally, Senator Harry F. Byrd of Virginia demanded an end to "nine years of fiscal insanity." In the speech Byrd paid his respects to Eccles's frequently expressed economic philosophy by declaring that it indicated "to what depths of false reasoning we have sunk in the crackpot legislative ideas of those holding important public positions." Encouraged by some editorial writers and some highly placed figures, Eccles quickly responded to Byrd's "misstatements of economic truths and distortions." Eccles checked with Roosevelt and then drafted a long letter to Byrd containing a "correct statement" of his point of view and philosophy. He explained the economics of spending, the national debt, private debt, taxation, and the general program of work relief and public works, contending that federal deficits should continue until the budget could be balanced out of a national income of about $80 billion, a figure supposedly representing full employment and satisfactory investment in industry. Byrd replied to the widely published letter with quotations from *Poor Richard's Almanac* and *Bartlett's Quotations*, Will Rogers's aphorisms, condensed versions of the lives of Thomas Jefferson and Andrew Jackson, and the history of the Federalist party.

Sensing the opportunity for a national debate, the National Broadcasting System invited Senator Byrd and Eccles to a radio debate in January 1939. Eccles challenged the budget-balancers to go ahead and cut work-relief projects, CCC camps, road construction and other public-works projects, veterans' benefits, farm benefits, and national defense, and then, as prices decline, unemployment mounts, and investment plummets, try to justify those policies to the electorate. The reaction from Eccles's opponent was "a long sputter."

The perceived positive response of the economy to the spending program did much to elevate deficit spending from a worrisome necessity to a central point of economic doctrine for New Dealers. By the time the recession ended, Eccles had supplanted Morgenthau as the president's most important adviser on economic policy.

It is important to note that Eccles's proposals relied solely on taxing and spending, long-accepted and legitimate powers of the federal government. Eccles had little sympathy for the structural reforms dear to the hearts of some New Dealers. He opposed the Tennessee Valley Authority, which he thought repelled private capital; he disliked the Agricultural Adjustment Administration, the National Recovery Administration, and industrial planning in general. An appropriate monetary and fiscal policy, he believed, would raise the level of demand and make it unnecessary for the government to regulate the market in other ways.

By the spring of 1939 the nation, growing stronger economically every month, turned its attention more systematically to the problems in Europe. America began to rearm, and the Federal Reserve and the Treasury Department united their policies to strengthen the war effort.

During World War II Eccles served on the National Advisory Council on International Monetary and Financial Problems. He was a delegate to the 1944 Bretton Woods Conference that laid out the agreements creating the World Bank and the International Monetary Fund, and he was the leading spokesman in obtaining approval for the $3.5 billion British loan of 1946. He also strongly advocated the Marshall Plan of 1948-1949, in which his brother George played an active role. At the end of the war Marriner also served on the Advisory Board of the Export-Import Bank.

Meanwhile, during the years Eccles and his family lived in Washington, Eccles's brother George and other associates looked after his businesses in Utah, although Marriner Eccles continually gave them counsel.

Eccles had hoped the Banking Act of 1935 would unify the nation's banking system. That did not happen. He accepted reappointment to the Board of Governors in 1944 on the basis of Roosevelt's implied endorsement of the Eccles Unification Plan. But unification did not occur until the mid 1970s, when Fed chairman Arthur F. Burns accomplished most of the objectives Eccles had attempted to achieve four decades earlier.

The other issue that concerned Eccles as World War II came to a close involved the confrontation with the Treasury Department's Morgenthau, Fred Vinson, and John W. Snyder over the best way to resolve inflationary pressures resulting from the war. Eccles believed that the Treasury's insistence on selling bonds to refinance the war debt had stoked the engine of inflation. True, bonds sold to individuals took away purchasing power, but banks buying bonds could use them to generate additional credit—precisely the wrong action in a time of scarcity, "full" employment, and price inflation. Eccles pointed out that a truly compensatory fiscal policy required higher taxes and tighter credit.

Eccles's skirmish with the Treasury probably played a part in President Harry S. Truman's decision not to reappoint him as chairman of the Board of Governors in 1948. Contemporary speculation held that Bank of America president A. P. Giannini, a heavy Democratic campaign contributor, had asked the victorious Truman to "get rid of Eccles." At any rate, Truman must have been surprised when Eccles, who still had more time on his 14-year appointment to the Board of Governors, swallowed his pride and, at the insistence of his many supporters, remained on the board as assistant chairman. He actually spoke out more openly about his disagreements with the administration, something he probably had yearned to do. Through his influence, the Fed exerted enough pressure on the Treasury to reach an accord in 1951 whereby it finally freed itself of Treasury domination.

During the years his professional career flourished, Eccles's relationship with his family deteriorated. His wife did not enjoy Washington and his family was not a high priority. He and Maysie were divorced in 1950, after 37 years of marriage.

In 1951, as his Washington career wound down, Eccles began writing his memoir, assisted by Sidney Hyman, a regular contributor to the *New York Times*, *Washington Post*, *Harper's*, and *Saturday Review* and a former staff member in the offices of Senators Paul Douglas and William Fulbright. The finished book, *Beckoning Frontiers*, was published in 1951, the same year Eccles resigned from the Board of Governors. He remarried that year as well, to Sara (Sallie) Maddison Glassie, a socially prominent Washington, D.C., divorcée.

After Eccles's return to Utah, he entered into a brief and unsuccessful campaign in the fall of 1952 to wrest the Republican senatorial nomination from Arthur Watkins. He then resumed active participation in his family's businesses, a corporate empire that had grown considerably larger from the time he left for Washington in 1934. The holdings for which he served as chairman of the board included First Security Corporation, Amalgamated Sugar Company, and Utah Construction Company (then based in San Francisco).

Although his Depression monetary policies had caused some to regard him as an unorthodox financier, Eccles unquestionably held orthodox business views. First Security Corporation, the largest intermountain banking organization, had resources of more than $400 million and 54 offices in Idaho, Utah, and Wyoming in 1954. Amalgamated Sugar Company had become a $25 million beet sugar manufacturer with factories and distribution plants in Oregon, Washington, Utah, and Idaho. Utah Construction Company, which had been one of the six companies that built the Hoover Dam, was one of the nation's largest and was topped in the intermountain area only by Morrison-Knudsen Company of Boise. Utah Construction operated from Alaska and Kansas to Indonesia and Peru. Certain that the nation was proceeding along an inflationary path, Eccles moved the company into the purchasing and working of physical assets—minerals—and with that new emphasis renamed it Utah Construction and Mining. Other family companies of which he was chairman, president, or director, and which continued to prosper, included Anderson Lumber Company, with mills and 20 retail lumber

Eccles in front of the Federal Reserve Building on the day of his retirement in 1951 (courtesy of the Marriner S. Eccles Foundation)

yards in Utah and Idaho, one of the area's largest; Eccles Hot ' Company, which owned Ogden's and Logan's largest hotels and many other hotels, apartments, stores, and office buildings in Utah and Idaho; and Mountain States Implement Company, one of the biggest farm implement distributors in Utah and Idaho.

Because of those interests Eccles divided his time between Salt Lake City, where he and Sallie Eccles kept an apartment in the Hotel Utah, and San Francisco, where they lived in a French provincial home in Pacific Heights. Since Eccles's role was primarily that of policymaker, planner, financial expert, and decisionmaker, he left the details of administration to his brother George and other business associates. Eccles pursued golf, his favorite pastime, and he belonged to several country clubs in Washington and Palm Springs. He also served as a member of the Federal Commission on Money and Credit from 1958 to 1961.

In the 1960s Eccles became more active in speaking and writing about three issues of critical concern to him. For the first, world overpopulation, he recommended a worldwide birth-control program and served as an honorary director of Planned Parenthood and World Population. The second was U.S. involvement in the war in Vietnam, which he had opposed with vigor since 1965. His persuasive talk to the San Francisco Commonwealth Club in 1967, "Vietnam: Its Effect on the Nation," was distributed to 20,000 commercial banks and was reprinted in *Vital Speeches*. Third, he advocated U.S. recognition of the People's Republic of China. He delivered his last public speech, mostly devoted to those three issues, before the World Trade Club in San Francisco in 1972, at which time they presented him with their International Achievement Award and applauded him enthusiastically.

Eccles's honest, straightforward, outspoken character is perhaps best encapsulated in his taking President Lyndon Johnson to task for the Vietnam War. By June 1965, 23,000 U.S. troops served in South Vietnam, fully committed to combat roles, and waves of U.S. Army reinforcements were landing in the country on a regular basis. Student protests, public unease, and calls for a cease-fire and the opening of negotiations swept the United States. In July, Joseph Fowler, secretary of the Treasury, at Johnson's behest, invited Eccles and 70 other members of an "independent committee" of businessmen that had backed the 1964 Johnson-Humphrey ticket to a dinner at the White House. After cocktails, the businessmen were ushered into the East Room where they were seated in three rows facing President Johnson. The full cabinet, White House staff members, the chief of staff of the Armed Services, and the chairman of the Board of Governors were among those present. Eccles soon realized that the "social event" was not merely an effort on the part of the president to express appreciation to his supporters but was intended to convert the 1964 "independent committee" to Johnson's escalation of American involvement in the Vietnam Conflict.

The president welcomed the guests, outlined American policy in Vietnam, introduced Secretary of State Dean Rusk, who spoke on the importance of the policy to world peace, and the secretary of defense, Robert McNamara, who declared that U.S. military strategy had worked so well that American military forces could be withdrawn within a year.

After the presentations the guests were shown to their tables. Place cards stood next to the name of each guest, some marked "writer" and some "speaker." The speakers had three minutes each to

express their views; the writers wrote what they would have said if they had had an opportunity to speak. Eccles, directed to table eight, saw that he had a card marked "speaker." He began to sweat. One after another of the seven speakers who preceded him arose to praise Johnson in extravagant terms and to endorse his course of action in Vietnam. When it came his turn to speak, Eccles asked the president if he really wanted him to say what he thought. The president nodded.

"Well, I regret that I cannot follow or subscribe in any sense to what the seven preceding speakers have said concerning Vietnam, or what I heard a while ago from members of the Cabinet. I believe the administration's policy toward Vietnam to be based on fatal errors, and that our national interest would best be served if the administration disentangled itself from a course of action that is bound to be ruinous."

At that point Eccles recalled that he had in his coat pocket a resolution he had prepared deploring the escalation of hostilities and calling for an immediate cease-fire and the beginning of negotiations. Eccles took out the documents and said: "My own position of opposition to your administration's Vietnam policy—as well as what I think should be done to reverse it—is laid out in something which I brought with me from Utah. Let me read from the texts."

As Eccles's biographer, Sidney Hyman, reported, "There was a stunned silence while Marriner was speaking and reading, and an uneasy silence when he was through. . . . Marriner had dueled with other presidents and their chief advisers over other major public policies, and had lived to see *his* judgment, and not *theirs*, confirmed by the march of events. . . . That was the last White House function Marriner was ever invited to attend."

In the 1970s Eccles wound down his business commitments. Utah Construction (which had become Utah Construction and Mining) became Utah International, Inc., in 1971. That year Eccles stepped down from his active board chairmanship and took the position of honorary chairman of the board. In 1975 Eccles also stepped aside to allow his brother George to become chairman of the board of First Security Corporation. The Eccles Investment Company was disbanded in 1970, and its assets, except the stock in Utah Construction, were sold and the proceeds used to buy stock in Utah International. In 1976 Utah International merged with

General Electric Corporation in the largest corporate merger in U.S. history to that time.

In addition to the attention he devoted to his public concerns and business interests, Eccles served on the Board of the American Assembly sponsored annually by Columbia University from 1959 to 1977. He founded the Marriner S. Eccles Library of Political Economy at the University of Utah, established the Marriner S. Eccles Graduate Fellowship in Political Economy, and created the Marriner S. Eccles Foundation, which has funded various charitable, scientific, and educational organizations for the benefit of the citizens of the state. Eccles also established the Marriner S. Eccles Professorship of Public and Private Management of the Stanford University School of Business in 1973. Eccles was awarded an honorary doctor of laws degree from the University of Utah in 1943 and an honorary doctor of laws from Utah State University in 1963.

Eccles died in Salt Lake City on December 18, 1977, at the age of eighty-seven. In 1982 the Federal Reserve Building in Washington, D.C., was named in his honor. Along with A.P. Giannini, Eccles stands as one of the two most important American bankers of the twentieth century.

Publications:
Economic Balance and a Balanced Budget: Public Papers of Marriner S. Eccles, edited by Rudolph L. Weissman (New York: Harper, 1940);
Beckoning Frontiers: Public and Personal Recollections, edited by Sidney Hyman (New York: Knopf, 1951).

References:
Leonard J. Arrington, *David Eccles: Pioneer Western Industrialist* (Logan: Utah State University Press, 1975);

"Banks and Brakes," *Time*, 27 (February 10, 1936): 59-64;
John Morton Blum, *From the Morgenthau Diaries: Years of Crisis, 1928-1938* (Boston: Houghton Mifflin, 1959);
"The Eccles Brothers: A Team That's Moving Fast," *Business Week*, no. 1301 (August 7, 1954): 40-41, 44-47;
Arch O. Egbert, "Marriner S. Eccles and the Banking Act of 1935," dissertation, Brigham Young University, 1967;
Jonathan Hughes, "Marriner Eccles: Logician in Wonderland," in *The Vital Few: The Entrepreneur and American Economic Progress*, expanded edition (New York: Oxford University Press, 1986), pp. 504-557;
Sidney Hyman, *Challenge and Response: The First Security Corporation, First Fifty Years, 1928-1978* (Salt Lake City: University of Utah Graduate School of Business, 1978);
Hyman, *Marriner S. Eccles: Private Entrepreneur and Public Servant* (Stanford: Stanford University Graduate School of Business, 1976);
Dean L. May, *From New Deal to New Economics: The American Liberal Response to the Recession of 1937* (New York: Garland, 1981);
May, "Sources of Marriner S. Eccles's Economic Thought," *Journal of Mormon History*, 3 (1976): 85-99;
Herbert Stein, *The Fiscal Revolution in America* (Chicago: University of Chicago Press, 1969).

Archives:
The Marriner S. Eccles Papers are in the Eccles Room at the Marriott Library, University of Utah, Salt Lake City. They include correspondence, speeches, clippings, transcripts of congressional hearings, publications, annual reports of the companies with which Eccles was associated, and dozens of scrapbooks.

John Evans, Sr.

(September 24, 1884 - April 23, 1970)

by James Smallwood

University of Texas at Tyler

CAREER: Engineer, Denver Tramway Company (1907-1916); director (1911-1970), president, International Trust Company of Denver [merged with First National Bank of Denver in 1958] (1916-1932); director (1916-1970), president, First National Bank of Denver (1928-1959); director (1935-1970), chairman, Denver & Rio Grande Western Railroad (1947-1970).

John Evans, Sr., was born on September 24, 1884, into the elite class of the society of Denver, Colorado. A member of an illustrious pioneer family, he was the grandson of Colorado's second territorial governor, also named John Evans; his father, William Gray Evans, was a successful financier and a major stockholder of several corporations, including the Denver Tramway Company, a company that later employed Evans, Sr. During his youth in Denver, Evans attended Miss Street's School, a private academy, and later the Denver University Preparatory School. In 1903 he entered the Massachusetts Institute of Technology (MIT). After graduating from MIT with a degree in engineering in 1907, he returned to his hometown and took a job as an engineer with the Denver Tramway Company.

The competent young Evans quickly impressed Denver's businessmen and bankers. Moreover, his physical stature was such that he attracted attention wherever he went: he was six feet four inches tall, had blond hair and blue eyes, and was sapling lean but also strong.

After watching Evans develop for four years, Gerald Hughes, an attorney and a member of the board of directors of the International Trust Company of Denver, invited the young man to join the company board. Evans accepted, continuing a relationship with Hughes that his father had developed years before. The "team" of Gerald Hughes and John Evans continued to work together until Hughes's death in 1956.

John Evans, Sr. (Eugene Adams, Lyle W. Dorsett, and Robert Pulcipher, The Pioneer Western Bank —The First of Denver: 1860-1980 *[1984])*

Five years after Evans had accepted Hughes's first offer, the older man made another. In 1916 Mahlon D. Thatcher, Sr., president of International Trust, died, and Hughes offered the presidency of the company to Evans. At first the younger man protested, arguing that he lacked the qualifications of a banker. Hughes then asked an associate, Absalom V. Hunter, to convince the hesitant Evans. To Hunter, Evans continued his protest, remarking, "But, Sir, I know nothing about banking." Hunter calmly responded, "Just remember that every cent [in International] belongs to someone else, and your obligation is to render an accounting and make a reasonable profit on it." Evans accepted the position.

The new president of International Trust established three rules he always followed in the years ahead. He decided that to ensure safe and stable operations, the institution should always operate in the black. He also decided to dedicate a portion of the house's money to building up the community the bank served, which would in turn increase business. Most important, he mandated that the trust company maintain funds enough to pay off its depositors at all times.

Evans's conservatism paid "dividends" for mentor Hughes in the early and mid 1920s. Due to an agricultural recession, four overextended banks in Colorado failed in 1920. The next year 11 more folded. In 1922 and 1923 a total of 26 more collapsed. Denver banks possessed no immunity in the crisis; between 1923 and 1927 ten financial houses in the city closed their doors. International Trust remained sound, however, as Hughes and his protégé remained set on a conservative course. The two men closely monitored their farm loans, refusing to involve themselves in what one historian of Colorado called the "frenzied expansion" of the postwar agricultural sector. Nor did they commit too strongly to the "installment buying craze" of the 1920s. Although by 1928 millions of automobiles operated on America's roads, Evans and Hughes had made only $375,000 in car loans.

As events demonstrated, Hughes made a good choice in appointing Evans, so good, in fact, that the older man developed more plans with Evans in mind. In December 1916, due to influence exerted by Hughes, Evans became a member of the board of the First National Bank of Denver. A dozen years later, when Evans was only forty-four years old, he became president of First National. For four years he functioned as the head of both International Trust and First National, but in 1932 he left the presidency of International Trust to devote more time to banking. He remained on the board of International Trust along with Hughes, and continued to control the trust company until it merged with First National in 1958.

As president of First National, Evans continued to cultivate relationships with the corporate clients Hughes had recruited, including the Adolph Coors Company, the Western Sugar Company, and the Denver Tramway Company. He also located other corporate customers, such as the Mountain States Telephone Company, the Gates Rubber Company, and the Montgomery Ward department store

chain. As the years passed, Evans's increasing contacts with area businesses made him more and more valuable to First National.

Although in the 1920s Evans sometimes attracted criticism for his conservatism, that course proved wise when the Great Depression began in 1929. Between that year and 1935, 78 of Colorado's banks collapsed. More than 400 banks operated in the state in 1920; by 1941 only 150 remained. But First National and International Trust still thrived. For one thing, the institutions led by Hughes and Evans maintained low loan-to-deposit ratios, 22 percent and 26 percent respectively. At that time the national average hovered at almost 50 percent. Furthermore, while many financial leaders opposed New Deal interference in the banking field, Evans welcomed significant federal reforms such as the Glass-Steagall Act of 1933, which created the Federal Deposit Insurance Corporation.

Throughout the Depression the careful Evans closely watched his loan policies, but he did not "freeze." He continued to support financially stable farmers and ranchers and aided industrialists who had favorable financial histories. For example, in late 1935 the Denver & Rio Grande Western Railroad declared bankruptcy. Two trustees for the railroad contacted Evans, who gave the organization strong financial backing, the kind of commitment that allowed the trustees to continue a climb and eventually stabilize the company in 1947. Beginning in 1935, Evans also served as a director of the Denver & Rio Grande, becoming its chairman of the board in 1947, a post he held until 1970.

In the 1930s First National Bank also became active in the petroleum industry and in aviation. It acquired such customers as the Continental Oil Company, Union Oil Company, Chevron Oil Company, Colorado Interstate Gas Company, and Moffat Coal Company. In the expanding field of aviation, Evans furnished Robert F. Six, founder of Varney Air Transport, with the money to buy a single aircraft. Six used the loan to build what would later become Continental Airlines. Evans eventually collected other customers in the aviation industry, including Delta, Trans World, United, Western, and Republic.

Even in the depths of the Depression First National continued to invest in Denver and the western region. Evans purchased bonds that allowed Denver's public school system to expand and modernize. He purchased municipal bonds to help mod-

Cartoon illustrating Evans's dominance over the Colorado economy (Eugene Adams, Lyle W. Dorsett, and Robert Pulcipher, The Pioneer Western Bank—The First of Denver: 1860-1980 *[1984])*

ernize area communities such as Gunnison and Glenwood Springs. He also purchased bonds to construct improved roads in states such as Montana and Idaho. For Albuquerque, New Mexico, he purchased bonds that benefited several of that city's utilities.

With the onset of World War II, Denver and the rest of the United States snapped out of the Great Depression. In Colorado salary and wage statistics reflected the new boom. In the Depression year of 1935 total wages and salaries paid in the state amounted to $447 million. That low figure jumped to approximately $1.4 billion by 1940. The numbers continued to escalate during the war years.

First National benefited from the wartime prosperity. Agriculture boomed; Colorado farmers and ranchers expanded (and made money) as never be-

fore. Coal and oil production increased, and Colorado continued to industrialize. First National supported the expansion; both loans and deposits increased. As of 1939 First National claimed assets of $67.7 million and deposits of $62.4 million. By 1945 assets soared to $186.55 million and deposits to $180 million, increases of almost 300 percent.

During the war Evans proved, as always, to be community-minded. He headed the Colorado Victory Fund Committee, which sold war bonds and coordinated civilian contributions to the war effort.

In the prosperous postwar years Evans continued to oversee First National's growth and the progress of his community. The bank helped alleviate a postwar housing shortage by putting millions of dollars into real estate, much of the amount going for government-sponsored GI home loans. Yet Evans kept the loan-to-deposit ratio at approximately 25 percent, still well below the national average. He did experience one great blow, when on August 27, 1956, his mentor and friend, Hughes, died. Hughes had helped Evans build solvent yet expansive institutions based on sound financial policies; thus, Evans went on along, following the same policies. Nevertheless, the aging Evans decided to retire from First National's presidency in October 1959; he remained honorary chairman of the board until his death. In his retirement Evans continued to spend part of every day doing business. He also devoted more time to civic affairs. Late in life he served as a trustee of the Denver Museum of Natural History, as a director of the Colorado Historical Society, and as a director of the Air Force Academy Foundation. In 1966 *Fortune* magazine named him one of 19 American "grand old men of business."

Evans died on April 23, 1970, at the age of eighty-five. He was survived by his son, John, Jr.; by two daughters, Alice Evans Moore and Ann Evans Freyer; by 12 grandchildren; and by 11 great-grandchildren.

Like his mentor, Hughes, Evans left a legacy to the banking industry and to the residents of the Colorado region. He left behind a solvent, stable, and expanding bank that proved a financial boon.

Statistics told of his success: in 1928 International Trust and First National controlled $34 million in combined assets. When Evans retired in 1959, First National alone claimed $314 million.

References:

Eugene Adams, Lyle W. Dorsett, and Robert Pulcipher, *The Pioneer Western Bank—The First of Denver: 1860-1980* (Denver: First Interstate Bank of Denver, N.A., 1984);

Kenneth H. Hunter and William G. Philip, *The Adequacy of Banking Facilities in Colorado* (Boulder: Colorado Bankers Association, 1938);

Fred R. Niehaus, *Development of Banking in Colorado* (Denver: Mountain States, 1942);

Niehaus, *Seventy Years of Progress: History of Banking in Colorado, 1876-1946* (Washington, D.C.: Federal Deposit Insurance Corporation, 1948).

Archives:

Much of the business and personal papers of John Evans, Sr., are located in the First National Bank Historical Collection, housed in the library of the First Interstate Bank of Denver. The Colorado Historical Society also houses a collection of Evans's papers. Some primary material relating to Evans's business career can also be found in Record Group 101, Comptroller of the Currency Files, National Archives, Washington, D.C.

Federal Home Loan Bank System

by Marc A. Weiss

Columbia University

Starting in the middle of the nineteenth century, bankers created savings and loan associations (S&Ls) for the purpose of pooling small savings deposits in order to extend loans to enable people of modest means to build or purchase homes. Also known as building and loan institutions, cooperative banks, homestead associations, and thrift institutions, by 1930 S&Ls had become the largest institutional home mortgage lenders in the United States. They had grown enormously during the 1920s, riding a boom in the housing industry and in the economy in general. When the Depression hit, many borrowers found themselves unable to repay their mortgages, and most depositors wanted to withdraw their savings. A great many S&Ls got

caught in a terrible squeeze, lacking sufficient cash reserves, credit with commercial banks, and liquid assets. Thousands of S&Ls went insolvent in the early 1930s. The Federal Home Loan Bank System was created in 1932 to provide a liquidity reserve system and regulatory mechanism for those S&Ls that got into financial trouble as a result of this dual pressure.

Modeled on the Federal Reserve Act of 1913, the Federal Home Loan Bank Act of 1932 created 12 regional Home Loan Banks initially capitalized by the U.S. Treasury (independent of the Federal Reserve System). Congress established the banks to provide short-term credit to member institutions based on certain underwriting criteria and using

John H. Fahey, chairman of the Federal Home Loan Bank Board from 1933 to 1947 (courtesy of ACME)

their existing mortgages as collateral. S&Ls, mutual savings banks, and insurance companies qualified for membership, but the system excluded commercial banks. The act also established a five-member Federal Home Loan Bank Board with supervisory and regulatory powers.

After the passage of the initial act, Congress added two key pieces of legislation to the home lending system. The Home Owners' Loan Act of 1933 created a federal chartering system for S&Ls that was designed to enhance the credibility of the industry. The act also established the Home Owners' Loan Corporation, a temporary agency run by the Federal Home Loan Bank Board that refinanced $3 billion worth of home mortgages before it stopped making new loans in 1936. One of the provisions of the National Housing Act of 1934 established the Federal Savings and Loan Insurance Corporation (FSLIC) to insure S&L deposits along the lines of the Federal Deposit Insurance Corporation (FDIC) established the previous year for commercial banks.

President Franklin Roosevelt appointed John H. Fahey to chair the Federal Home Loan Bank Board in November 1933, and he ran the system until 1947. Home ownership grew slowly before World War II, but after the war the baby boom, suburbanization, and Sunbelt migration created an explosion in housing construction and a corresponding S&L boom. But inflation and competition from commercial banks and other financial services firms created a substantial drop in S&L deposits by 1966. That year the federal government initiated the first in a series of reforms of the S&L industry that culminated in the virtual deregulation of S&Ls by 1982. After more than fifty years of limiting the industry to housing loans, S&Ls had won permission to engage in a wide variety of lending and investment practices, from financing speculative real estate deals to purchasing "junk" bonds.

While many well-managed S&Ls continued to specialize in home mortgage lending during the 1980s, others suffered from bad management, corruption, and regional economic downturns. Worse, the S&Ls remained outside the regulatory and examination framework of the Federal Reserve Board or the Federal Deposit Insurance Corporation, and the Federal Home Loan Bank Board lacked the authority or the wherewithal to take up the slack. By the end of the 1980s, S&Ls had collapsed by the thousands.

In August 1989, Congress passed the Financial Institutions Reform, Recovery, and Enforcement Act, which created the Resolution Trust Corporation, run by the FDIC, to take over failing S&Ls, manage and liquidate their assets, and pay off their insured depositors. The FSLIC became part of the FDIC and an Office of Thrift Supervision replaced the Federal Home Loan Bank Board as the main arbiter of the crisis. As American taxpayers prepared to spend billions of dollars to bail out the S&Ls, long-term forecasts suggested a far more modest future role for S&Ls in home mortgaging than in their heyday from the 1940s to the 1960s.

References:

James Ring Adams, *The Big Fix: Inside the S&L Scandal* (New York: Wiley, 1990);

Frederick E. Balderston, *Thrifts in Crisis: Structural Transformation of the Savings and Loan Industry* (Cambridge, Mass.: Ballinger, 1985);

Paul Zane Pilzer and Robert Deitz, *Other People's Money: The Inside Story of the S&L Scandal* (New York: Simon & Schuster, 1989);

Stephen Pizzo, Mary Fricker, and Paul Muolo, *Inside Job: The Looting of America's Savings and Loans* (New York: McGraw-Hill, 1989);

Franklin J. Sherman, *Modern Story of Mutual Savings Banks* (New York: Little & Ives, 1934);

Alan Teck, *Mutual Savings Banks and Savings and Loan Associations* (New York: Columbia University Press, 1968).

First Interstate Bancorporation

by Lynne Pierson Doti

Chapman College

First Interstate Bancorporation is a bank holding company that as of 1989 owned 21 banks in 11 western states and had issued franchises to another dozen banks. The activities of the franchises allowed First Interstate to operate in all the major cities and many of the smaller communities in the West, even in cases where laws prohibited banks from operating across state lines.

The historical origins of First Interstate Bancorporation gave rise to the company's unique position in the economy of the western United States. During the 1930s and 1940s A. P. Giannini purchased about 200 small banks and combined them into 46 banking companies, with the intention of merging them with his voracious giant, California-based Bank of America. Giannini parked the 46 banks in a diversified holding company, Transamerica Corporation, awaiting the time when bank regulators would permit the larger merger. In Transamerica the 46 banks coexisted with Bank of America and many other companies, including insurance companies, tuna packers, tobacco concerns, and an airline. In 1948 the Federal Reserve Board charged Transamerica with monopolizing western banking.

The court battle lasted five years, and Transamerica emerged victorious. But the victory was hollow, because in an effort to divert the regulators Transamerica divested itself of Bank of America years before. Although the corporation hoped to include the other 46 banks in the sale, the courts blocked that action.

Once the courts settled the suit, Transamerica rebuilt its banking empire. Between 1953 and 1956 the corporation grew to include 226 bank branches in 11 western states. Again the government halted its growth. The federal Bank Holding Company Act of 1956 made bank holding companies subject to the same restrictions on crossing state lines that individual banks endured. The same law forbade hold-

Edward M. Carson, chairman and chief executive officer of First Interstate Bancorporation after the June 1990 retirement of Joseph J. Pinola (courtesy of First Interstate Bancorporation)

ing companies that controlled more than one bank from operating any other kind of business. Unlike the act's prohibition of interstate banking through holding companies, that provision was made retroactive. Transamerica chose to maintain maximum flexibility by selling its remaining banks. To hold the banks it formed a new company, Firstamerica Corporation, under Delaware law and distributed its stock to Transamerica shareholders in 1958.

While arrangements for the stock transfer progressed, Firstamerica executives arranged a merger with the Los Angeles-based California Bank, headed by Frank King. That merger brought experienced top management to the new system. Composed of 322 offices, the new Firstamerica stood ready to become the fourth-largest bank holding company in the country. Unfortunately, as arrangements for the merger neared completion, the U.S. Department of Justice objected. The new combination would give the Bank of America strong competition in some areas of the West, but the Justice Department expressed concern about the situation in small communities where Firstamerica would control all the banks. Firstamerica went ahead and purchased stock in California Bank and made Frank King president of the holding company. He negotiated a settlement with the Justice Department that carved off $500 million in Firstamerica assets to create a new retail bank called First Western. Firstamerica sold that bank to Greatamerica Corporation, and it was resold several more times, finally losing its name when Lloyds Bank of California purchased it. The California assets remaining under the control of Firstamerica after the King settlement (California Bank and some of the California offices of First Western) were renamed United California Bank (UCB), and Firstamerica, the holding company controlling UCB and the banks outside California, was renamed Western Bancorporation (WBC).

After its complicated birth in 1961, Western Bancorporation grew even more rapidly than the burgeoning western economy as a whole. New industries such as aerospace, entertainment, electronics, and air conditioning created an exciting atmosphere for regional growth. UCB moved heavily into retail banking, searching for prospective branches in every part of California and even in foreign countries.

The most innovative move, however, came in 1980, under the chairmanship of Joseph Pinola. The new chairman, like other American financial officials, believed that the increasing tendency of inflation-strapped depositors to convert their time and demand deposits to high-yield money market accounts gave the federal government reason to repeal the law prohibiting interstate bank mergers. Pinola decided to exploit Western Bancorporation's unique position as the country's most expansive bank holding company by positioning its banks, then numbering 21 with combined assets of $48 billion, for the anticipated deregulation. He brought all WBC banks together under a common name, First Interstate Bank. The branching law had not yet changed, but the name sounded prophetic. The holding company, renamed First Interstate Bancorporation (FIB), also standardized bank logos, automatic teller machines, and certain policies so that a uniform system existed in the 11 WBC states.

Once FIB completed conversion of its banks to the First Interstate system, it launched an even more innovative plan. It franchised the First Interstate package. Participating banks not owned by FIB paid a fee plus royalties to use the First Interstate Bank logo, its automatic teller system, and a pool of loan funds. The participating banks gained exclusive rights to operate in certain territories, and FIB gained the right to make a first offer if any of the banks were sold. Franchising quickly filled holes in the western banking market in places such as Hawaii and Alaska, where no FIB bank had operated before, and the company also extended eastward.

By the end of the 1980s, as Pinola planned his retirement, observers still described FIB with the word "potential." Profits never quite matched the glitzy FIB image as "the McDonald's of banking," but the franchised network remained largely intact, waiting on the federal action that would permit it to become truly the first interstate bank in the United States.

References:

Robert Bryan, "First Interstate: California's Restless Giant," *Bankers Monthly*, 103 (October 1986): 23-26;

Daniel C. Kibble, *Their Bank-Our Bank; The Quality Bank: A History of First Interstate Bank of California* (Costa Mesa, Cal.: First Interstate Bank of California Professional Publications, 1981);

"Western Bancorp: A Waking Giant Merges Its Far-Flung Fiefdoms," *Business Week*, no. 2575 (February 23, 1981): 134-137.

Fractional Reserve Banking (*see* **Deposits, Reserves, and Fractional Reserve Banking**)

Franchising (*see* **Branch Banking, Interstate banking, and Franchising**)

Milton Friedman

(July 31, 1912 -   )

by Michael D. Bordo

Rutgers University

CAREER: Researcher, National Resources Committee (1936); member, National Bureau of Economic Research (1937-1977); economist, U.S. Department of the Treasury (1941-1943); researcher, Statistical Research Group, U.S. Office of Scientific Research and Development (1943-1945); professor, University of Chicago (1946-1977); senior research fellow, Hoover Institution, Stanford University (1977-   ).

Economic thinkers, politicians, and the general public alike regard Milton Friedman as the most influential economist of the second half of the twentieth century. His achievements have had a profound impact on economic science, and his advocacy of classical liberal views has influenced public opinion on the social role of Western governments. Friedman's ideas presaged and may even have influenced the rise of free-market economies in Asia and the decline of state socialism in Eastern Europe.

Friedman was born on July 31, 1912, in Brooklyn, New York, the youngest of four children of a Jewish emigrant family from Carpathia-Rumania, then a part of the Austro-Hungarian Empire. The family moved to Rahway, New Jersey, when Friedman was one year old. He attended public schools there, excelling especially in mathematics, and graduated from Rutgers College in 1932 after studying economics and statistics. At Rutgers, Friedman received encouragement in his economic studies from Arthur F. Burns, later chairman of the Federal Reserve Board, and Homer Jones, later research director of the Federal Reserve Bank of St. Louis. After graduation Friedman won a fellowship to study economics at the University of Chicago, where he received an M.A. in 1933. There Frank Knight, Henry Simons, and Jacob Viner trained him in the Chicago tradition of classical economics. As a research assistant to Henry Schultz, Friedman learned to appreciate the importance of testing the-

Milton Friedman

ory through rigorous statistical procedure. At Chicago he also met Rose Director, an excellent economist in her own right, whom he married in 1938. The couple has two children. Over the years the Friedmans have collaborated in the publication of several books on political economy, including *Capitalism and Freedom* (1962), *Free to Choose* (1980), and *Tyranny of the Status Quo* (1984).

In 1934 Friedman spent a year at the Columbia University graduate school, where he studied under the mathematical economist and statistician

Harold Hotelling and the institutional and empirical economists Wesley Clair Mitchell and John Bates Clark. His work in 1936 with the National Resources Committee in Washington, D.C., served as a building block for his path-breaking study, *A Theory of the Consumption Function* (1957). In 1937 Friedman began a four-decade association with the National Bureau of Economic Research (NBER), collaborating with Simon Kuznets on a study of professional incomes. He then began work with Anna J. Schwartz of the bureau, studying the role of money in business cycles. He took his Ph.D. in 1946.

Friedman spent World War II engaged in research. At the Department of the Treasury from 1941 to 1943 he participated in the wartime reform of the personal income tax system as well as in a variety of other immediate action issues. As a member of the Columbia University Statistical Research Group, a subsidiary of the Office of Scientific Research and Development, he applied statistical methods to military problems in collaboration with W. Allen Wallis, Abraham Wald, Jacob Wolfowitz, and Hotelling.

After the war, following a teaching stint at the University of Minnesota, Friedman was appointed an associate professor at the University of Chicago, filling Jacob Viner's position. In 1962 he was made the university's Paul Snowden Russell Distinguished Service Professor of Economics. He remained at Chicago until 1977 except for occasional visits to universities and government agencies in the United States and abroad. He spent the year 1950 in Paris as a consultant with the Marshall Plan and taught at Cambridge University in 1953-1954. He served as president of the American Economic Association in 1967 and nine years later received the Nobel Prize in economics. After leaving Chicago, Friedman has served as a senior research fellow at the Hoover Institution at Stanford University.

Parallel to his distinguished career as a professional economist, Friedman has engaged in extensive extracurricular activity as an advocate of the free market and the classical liberal order. With Fredrick Von Hayek he founded the Mount Pellerin Society in 1947. He served as a special adviser to three presidential candidates: Barry Goldwater in 1964, Richard M. Nixon in 1968, and Ronald Reagan in 1980. He has also served on several public-service commissions, including the Presidential Commission on an All-Volunteer Armed Force in 1969-1970. From 1967 to 1984 he wrote an influen-

tial column for *Newsweek* magazine. In 1980, Friedman's television series *Free to Choose* was shown on the Public Broadcasting System and around the world. The book with the same title remained on the *New York Times* best-seller list for many months and finished as the best-selling nonfiction publication for that year.

In the early years of his career Friedman, alone and with others, introduced the use of rank-order statistics to avoid making the assumption of normality in the analysis of variance. He also pioneered a novel method for separating the utility function to measure price elasticities from budget studies, and a method of "sequential sampling." In addition, his work with Kuznets and his *Theory of the Consumption Function* introduced the distinction between the permanent and the transitory in the analysis of data on expenditures by different income groups.

Friedman wrote "Methodology of Positive Economics," an essay in his 1953 volume, *Essays in Positive Economics*, both as a prescription for the practice of economic science and as a critique of the formalism of mathematical economic theory. In the essay he made a distinction between positive economics—the practice of economic analysis to solve a problem—and normative economics—the way to solve the problem. Positive economics was concerned with the question of "what is" and normative economics with the question of "what ought to be." Friedman himself has practiced both positive and normative economics. As a positivist he has developed theoretical and empirical tools to analyze real-world problems. As a normative he has prescribed solutions to the problems.

A Theory of the Consumption Function provides the best example of the methodology of positive economics in action. In that book Friedman resolved a major anomaly in the Keynesian idea of the consumption function—the inconsistency between time series and cross section (budget study) data sets. Unlike the Keynesian theory, which posited consumption as a function of current income, Friedman followed Irving Fisher and treated consumption as a function of the present value of long-run income expectations, or permanent income. Rigorous tests with both time series and cross section data gave strong confirmation of the prediction of the theory. The cross section anomaly of a lower marginal propensity to consume at lower rather than higher levels of income occurred because consumption and income as measured in the data combined permanent and transitory components. On a time series basis the permanent average (and marginal) propensity to consume were constant.

Friedman's best-known work in monetary economics, his attack on the Keynesian orthodoxy that dominated immediate postwar economics, helped generate a renewal of interest in monetary theory and policy in the 1950s. Friedman challenged the Keynesian idea of the impotence of monetary policy (based on the belief that money velocity was unstable and characterized by a high interest elasticity), the belief that a free-market economy could not maintain full employment without government intervention, and the Keynesian case for an active countercyclical fiscal policy. The modern quantity theory of money, which Friedman redefined as a theory of the demand for money as a stable function of permanent income and the opportunity cost of holding money (represented by the rate of interest and expected inflation), provided the theoretical background for the attack. Evidence produced by Friedman, his students, and others confirmed the stability of money demand under various historical and institutional circumstances. Based on the interaction of the stable demand for money with an independently determined money supply, the modern quantity theory of money proposes that changes in the rate of money growth produce a corresponding but lagged change in the rate of growth of nominal income. In the short run, changes in money growth lead to changes in real output. In the long run, changes in prices fully reflect changes in the money supply.

Friedman holds that monetary disturbances affect nominal expenditures through the community's adjustment of its actual to desired holdings of real cash balances. The adjustment affects a wide range of assets and a wide array of explicit and implicit interest rates connecting assets to permanent income streams, but it ultimately impinges on total spending. The breakdown and timing of changes in nominal spending into changes in real output and the price level depend on factors such as the speed of adjustment of price and wage expectations and the presence of price and wage rigidities.

The National Bureau of Economic Research provided massive support for Friedman's approach. Friedman's collaboration with Schwartz resulted in three volumes, *A Monetary History of the United States, 1867-1960* (1963), *Monetary Statistics of*

the United States (1970), and *Monetary Trends in the United States and the United Kingdom, 1867-1975* (1982), and several articles, including "Money and Business Cycles" (1963). The *Monetary History* provides long-run historical evidence for the modern quantity theory of money; "Money and Business Cycles" provides short-term cyclical evidence; and *Monetary Trends* provides long-run econometric evidence.

The *Monetary History* studies the economic influence of money quantity in the U.S. economy over a nearly 100-year span marked by drastic changes in monetary arrangements and the structure of the economy. Friedman and Schwartz found principally that changes in the behavior of money were closely associated with the rate of change of nominal income, real income, and the price level. Secularly, a close relationship existed between the growth of money and nominal income, independent of the growth of real income. Cyclically, a close relationship existed between the rate of change in the money supply and of subsequent changes in nominal income. The authors also found that the money-income relationship was invariant to changes in monetary arrangements and the banking structure, that in major business-cycle downturns changes in the quantity of money were independent in origin from changes in economic activity, and that although an influence from income to money existed in mild business cycles, the main influence ran from money to income.

Of special importance in the book is the evidence on monetary disturbances: the authors showed that sharp reductions in the money supply precipitated sharp declines in economic activity while monetary growth in excess of real output invariably produced episodes of sustained inflation. According to the historical record, inappropriate actions by monetary authorities could be blamed for both types of disturbance. Thus, the Great Depression resulted from an unprecedented reduction in the quantity of money that the Federal Reserve could have prevented, and wartime issues of fiat currency produced corresponding postwar episodes of inflation.

The evidence in "Money and Business Cycles" complemented the evidence in the *Monetary History*. The article showed that specific cycles in money growth preceded reference cycle turning points, that the degree of severity of business cycles closely correlated with the amplitude of cycles of

Friedman after his 1977 move to the Hoover Institution (courtesy of the University of Chicago)

money growth, and that evidence contradicted the view that cycles in money growth were merely a lagged response to changes in the business cycle. The article concluded that "appreciable changes in the rate of growth of the stock of money are a necessary and sufficient condition for appreciable changes in the rate of growth of nominal income."

Using reference cycle phase-averaged data to remove the influence of the business cycle, *Monetary Trends* examined the relationship between the money stock, nominal income, the price level, and real income in the United States and the United Kingdom. In that work, Friedman and Schwartz identified a stable long-run money demand, or velocity function, for both countries. A common set of determinants affected each country's money demand function. The authors also found that movements in money paralleled movements in nominal income. Given the stability of money demand and the variability in the conditions of the money supply, that par-

allelism primarily reflected an influence running from money to income. Finally, Friedman and Schwartz found evidence to support the idea of the "neutrality" of the money supply. Except in the interwar period, a sustained one-percentage-point change in the money supply led to a sustained one-percentage-point change in the price level in both countries.

Related to the evidence on the long-run neutrality of money presented in *Monetary Trends*, Friedman's 1967 American Economic Association presidential address presented a "natural rate" hypothesis that challenged evidence given in several influential studies published in the 1950s and 1960s arguing for the existence of a stable tradeoff (negative association) between inflation and unemployment. In the address Friedman argued that the tradeoff evidence reflected a statistical illusion produced by lags in the adjustment of expected to actual inflation. Faced with inflation, workers may temporarily be fooled into believing that real wages have declined and hence into supplying more labor. Once they realize that prices have risen, they will reduce their labor accordingly. In the long run, Friedman declared, the unemployment rate would converge to its natural level (determined by the law of supply and demand for labor, a function of demographic and institutional factors) uninfluenced by monetary and price changes.

Friedman's writings on economic policy changed both the ways economists approach problems of policy and the actual policies governments have implemented. His views are grounded in the belief that the minimum amount of government intervention (mainly to protect property rights) produces the maximum amount of prosperity. Within that context he recognizes the necessity for the government to control the money supply to achieve stable prices but feels that implementing a fiscal policy above and beyond the monetary role is unnecessary and potentially counterproductive.

Friedman has long championed the case against discretionary monetary and fiscal policy made by Henry Simons and Lloyd Mints, two of his predecessors at the University of Chicago. For discretionary action to have its desired effect, the argument goes, the responsive shocks exerted by the government would have to be of equal but opposite magnitude to the shocks produced by random economic movements. Producing that kind of precision is so difficult as to be impossible. Furthermore, the influence of discretionary action would have to be precisely timed to offset the inevitable lags that occur between the implementation of any government policy and its effect. Since the movement of the economy is impossible to predict precisely, government can never completely account for future developments as it formulates its solutions. The best government can do, therefore, is follow simple, predetermined rules of action.

Based on evidence he and colleagues have gathered linking economic instability to erratic Federal Reserve policy, Friedman has vociferously criticized the Fed in that regard. The *Monetary History* documents three episodes in which Fed policy actions led to economic contraction. A delayed and overly contradictory rise in the discount rate produced the contraction of 1920-1921, and a rise in reserve requirements for Fed members implemented to sop up idle reserves (which were in fact held for precautionary purposes) created the contraction of 1937-1938. A preventable decline in the money supply produced the great contraction of 1929-1933.

Over the years Friedman has devised several rules for policy formulation, which have reflected his developing views on money and the economy. The first rule (1948) would maintain full employment by offsetting negative (positive) departures by money-financed budget deficit (surpluses). The second (1960) would have monetary authorities preserve price stability by expanding the money supply at a steady and known rate sufficient to finance the growth of real output while allowing for a trend in velocity. A 1982 revision to that rule would have monetary authorities freeze the monetary base. To promote an efficient set of monetary arrangements (the optimum quantity of money), the rule would set the rate of deflation equal to the rate of interest or, alternatively, would pay interest on currency and reserves and allow competing banks to pay interest on all deposits. Friedman has also made a strong case for flexible exchange rates to govern the economic relationship between nation-states (1953) and against a return to the gold standard (1962).

In his 30 years at the University of Chicago, Friedman was a powerful and convincing teacher. His lectures, characterized by both simplicity and elegance, were thought-provoking and often amusing. Over most of the period he taught courses in price theory and monetary theory, which developed and applied basic Marshallian tools of supply and demand, and strongly influenced the intellectual development of several generations of economists. By applying price theory and the methodology of positive economics to novel fields of interest, Friedman's teachings spawned new insights into the traditional fields of labor economics, industrial organization, and public finance as well as the creation (with Theodore Schultz) of the new field of human capital. Friedman's influence (with George Stigler) on Gary Becker, one of his outstanding students, in turn has generated a vast outpouring of research on the economics of subjects long deemed to be beyond the province of the discipline, such as the economics of crime, medicine, education, and the family.

Friedman has been a strong practitioner of normative economics. For close to three decades he has acted as the leading American advocate of the classical liberal order—free markets and free speech. His 1962 work *Capitalism and Freedom* made a strong case for limited government intervention in the economy. In the book Friedman documented that the cost of government intervention in various sectors of the economy vastly outweighed its benefits. In addition to the traditional economic arguments against tariffs, subsidies, licensing arrangements, rent control, and the like, Friedman also made telling arguments against government involvement in social policy. Instead, to address social ills he has proposed schemes based on free-market solutions: tuition vouchers to improve education, a negative income tax to help lower-income families. Friedman has also remained highly critical of command economies for not allowing the price mechanism to allocate scarce resources.

Friedman has popularized his free market proposals through public lectures, television and radio appearances, magazine interviews, and books. Various governments and agencies in the United States and abroad have adopted some of his proposals. Dramatic examples include the volunteer American army, tuition vouchers, the placing of ceilings on bank deposits, and the privatization of state industry.

True to his classical liberal roots, Friedman has leveled strong criticism not just against government intervention in private markets but also against private monopolies and restrictive business practices. Because he believes the sole responsibility of a business is to its shareholders, he has argued that it is harmful for society to urge corporations to act socially responsible.

Friedman has had an enormous impact on technical economics and on the way economists and the public view government's role in society. His contributions to economic science lie in the areas of methodology, applied theory, macro/money, and policy. In each of those areas the questions asked and the approaches used to provide answers have been fundamentally changed by Friedman's insights. His contribution to the understanding of the role of money in the economy has been largely responsible for the abandonment of the Keynesian approach to macroeconomic policy. His passionate advocacy of the benefits of the free market has led to considerable controversy, but he is, arguably, the intellectual father of the Reagan and Thatcher "revolutions" of the 1980s and a prominent source of insight as Eastern Europe abandons social planning.

Selected Publications:

Income from Independent Professional Practice, by Friedman and Simon Kuznets (New York: National Bureau of Economic Research, 1945);

Essays in Positive Economics (Chicago: University of Chicago Press, 1953);

Studies in the Quantity Theory of Money, edited by Friedman (Chicago: University of Chicago Press, 1956);

A Theory of the Consumption Function (Princeton: Princeton University Press, 1957);

A Program for Monetary Stability (New York: Fordham University Press, 1960);

Capitalism and Freedom, by Friedman and Rose D. Friedman (Chicago: University of Chicago Press, 1962);

A Monetary History of the United States, 1867-1960, by Friedman and Anna J. Schwartz (Princeton: Princeton University Press, 1963);

"Money and Business Cycles," by Friedman and Schwartz, *Review of Economics and Statistics*, 45 (February 1963): 32-64;

Dollars and Deficits: Inflation, Monetary Policy, and the Balance of Payments (Englewood Cliffs, N.J.: Prentice-Hall, 1968);

The Optimum Quantity of Money and Other Essays (Chicago: Aldine, 1969);

Monetary Statistics of the United States, by Friedman and Schwartz (New York: Columbia University Press, 1970);

A Theoretical Framework for Monetary Analysis (New York: National Bureau of Economic Research, 1971);

Price Theory (Chicago: Aldine, 1976);

Free to Choose, by Friedman and Friedman (New York: Harcourt Brace Jovanovich, 1980);

Monetary Trends in the United States and the United Kingdom: Their Relation to Income, Prices, and Interest Rates, 1867-1975, by Friedman and Schwartz (Chicago: University of Chicago Press, 1982);

Tyranny of the Status Quo, by Friedman and Friedman (San Diego, New York & London: Harcourt Brace Jovanovich, 1984).

References:

Eamonn Butler, *Milton Friedman: A Guide to His Economic Thought* (New York: Universe, 1985);

William Frazer, *Power and Ideas: Milton Friedman and the Big U-Turn*, 2 volumes (Gainesville, Fla.: Gulf-Atlantic, 1988);

Abraham Hirsch, *Milton Friedman: Economics in Theory and Practice* (Ann Arbor: University of Michigan Press, 1990);

Kurt R. Lenke, *The Essence of Friedman* (Stanford, Cal.: Hoover Institution, 1987);

Thomas J. Sargent, *Some of Milton Friedman's Scientific Contributions to Macroeconomics* (Stanford, Cal.: Hoover Institution, 1987).

Futures (*see* **Securities and Futures Markets**)

Garn-St Germain Act (*see* **Depository Institutions, Deregulation, and Monetary Control Act of 1980**)

A. P. Giannini

(May 6, 1870 - June 3, 1949)

by Michael F. Konig

Westfield State College

CAREER: Produce worker (1885-1902); estate administrator (1902-1912); director, Columbus Savings and Loan Society (1902-1904); president (1904-1936), chairman, Bank of America [Bank of Italy to 1928] (1904-1945).

Amadeo Peter Giannini, arguably the most important American banker since J. P. Morgan, was born in San Jose, California, on May 6, 1870, in a 20-room hotel operated by his father, Luigi Giannini. His mother, Virginia, was not quite sixteen at the time of his birth. The family moved from the hotel to a 40-acre ranch outside San Jose, where a workman killed Giannini's father in a dispute over a dollar. Shortly after that, Giannini's mother married a ranch produce hauler named Lorenzo Scatena.

In 1882 Scatena moved the family to the Italian colony of North Beach in San Francisco. There Giannini attended Washington Grammar School, where he compiled a respectable if not overly impressive record. He spent a good deal of his youth working in his stepfather's wholesale produce business, L. Scatena & Company. By the age of fifteen he could hold his own during the postmidnight waterfront trading sessions. He purchased produce for his stepfather from fruit and vegetable sellers who arrived by riverboat from Sacramento and the San Joaquin Valley. It was a rough and tumble business, and Giannini's size at that young age—six feet tall and 170 pounds—served him in good stead. By the age of seventeen he made buying trips for the firm that reached into the Santa Clara, the Napa, and

A. P. Giannini

the Sacramento valleys. He worked hard, and the fact that business for L. Scatena & Company became exceedingly prosperous reflected the effort.

Giannini married Clorinda Cuneo in 1893. The death of his father-in-law, Joseph Cuneo, in 1902 played a major role in shaping the future of the young man. Upon his death Cuneo left a rather large estate. He also left a widow and 11 children, but, surprisingly, no will. The Cuneo family kept the estate intact and appointed Giannini to manage it for ten years. As a means of recompense for his services, Giannini received 25 percent of whatever increase he effected in the capital value of the estate. Ultimately his fee for his ten-year stewardship totaled nearly $37,000. The payment was justified, as Giannini looked after more than 100 real estate parcels under the arrangement. He also administered shares in a small North Beach savings bank, the Columbus Savings and Loan Society. Cuneo had been on the board of that institution. Thus Giannini received his first experience in the world of banking.

At the time of Giannini's 1902 ascension to the Columbus board, founder John F. Fugazi controlled the bank. The institution performed a valuable service to the North Beach community, where the Italian immigrant residents still distrusted paper money and hid their coins in their homes. The bank provided an alternative where the "hard" money remained safe and earned interest. It also provided much-needed credit for local home builders and merchants.

The Columbus Savings and Loan Society had its competitors, and Fugazi's policy of preferring large loans to small credit packages ignored many potential customers within the North Beach community. Giannini, then thirty-two, criticized the policy, much to the irritation of his colleagues. Specifically, Giannini complained that the bank "warehoused" too much of its funds and failed to earn adequate profits on real estate loans. Giannini understood the real estate business, as he also held a position with Madison and Burke, one of San Francisco's larger realty firms. He recognized that the rapid population growth of the North Beach area would continue and that relatively poor newcomers comprised the majority of the upsurge. Those newcomers resembled Giannini when he first arrived in the area, and he foresaw them as community leaders in future years, leaders running profitable businesses that badly needed initial financing. Giannini urged his institution to venture forth, make contact with the newcomers, and solicit their business. He believed that the profit potential could be extremely lucrative even though few within the banking community made those kinds of loans. According to Marquis James and Bessie R. James, the young banker "had touched a weak spot not only in the management of the Columbus Savings and Loan So-

ciety but in the financial machinery of San Francisco as well."

Through much of the twentieth century San Francisco has been the financial center of the West Coast, providing funds for the development of the region from Los Angeles to Seattle. San Francisco had also provided much of the funding in California's profitable agricultural industry as well. But during Giannini's early years, many San Franciscans, especially recently arrived foreigners, found it difficult to borrow $100 from a local bank. Many of the North Beach Italian residents had been driven into the jaws of loan sharks. Giannini recognized the need and the profit opportunities that would become available if the Columbus Savings and Loan Society catered to those residents.

Giannini also advocated that Columbus Savings and Loan look beyond North Beach and its resident Italians for patrons and work to appeal to individuals from varied ethnic backgrounds. Giannini's stepfather-in-law, who also served on the bank's board, supported those positions, but Fugazi and his two sons, also directors, did not. Giannini appealed to the bank's adviser, the conservative Isaias W. Hellman of the powerful Farmers and Merchants National Bank, who saw no merit in the young man's program. Realizing that his position had become untenable, Giannini resigned from the board, determined to start his own financial institution.

In order to raise capital for the new undertaking, Giannini solicited financial support from local men of means within the North Beach Italian community. The original articles of incorporation stipulated a capital investment of $300,000, and the bank accepted both savings and commercial accounts, which the bank's 11 directors divided into shares of $100 each. The directors purchased much of this stock, although, according to Giannini's orders, no one director held more than 100 shares.

The initial location of the new Bank of Italy gave rise to an interesting story. The Columbus Savings and Loan Society was located in the Drexler Building on Washington Street in the North Beach financial district. A saloon stood between the bank and a travel agency. Giannini learned that the saloonkeeper wanted to retire, and he purchased the saloonkeeper's lease. Next, Giannini leased from the Drexler estate the entire Drexler Building. Columbus Savings and Loan found itself a tenant of its former director, who had established his own rival bank. Unsatisfied with that situation, the Columbus Savings and Loan officers moved their institution across the street. Even at that early date in his career, Giannini demonstrated the skills with which he later confounded his competitors.

The Bank of Italy commenced operations on October 17, 1904, with Giannini as its president. By December of that year the bank's deposits totaled more than $109,000. What made that modest growth remarkable was the fact that many of the Bank of Italy's patrons had never before done business in a bank. The institution also initiated liberal lending policies. In fact, by the end of 1904 loans and overdrafts amounted to considerably more than deposits, a rather risky situation requiring that the bank keenly scrutinize the recipients of its loans. Giannini directed primarily toward profitable real estate ventures in and out of the North Beach community. The amounts of those loans generally remained small, roughly between $25 and $375.

Such policies contributed to the rapid rise of the Bank of Italy's fortunes. By the end of 1905 its assets totaled slightly more than $1 million. Small deposit accounts, which Giannini and other members of the Bank of Italy's directorship board openly solicited, comprised the vast bulk of that asset total. The directors made their solicitations by traveling throughout North Beach and explaining the functions of their bank in the simplest terms and, most important, in Italian.

A natural disaster temporarily halted the development of the bank. By the evening of April 21, 1906, most of the city of San Francisco lay in ruins from a devastating earthquake and fire. The fire destroyed the Bank of Italy, but Giannini had managed to remove the institution's money beforehand. Nearly all the bank's depositors had lost their homes and their places of business.

Giannini viewed the calamity as an opportunity for the Bank of Italy even though he had only $80,000 in available cash to cover more than $840,000 in deposits. He opened a temporary headquarters at the home of his brother, Attilio H. Giannini, in the Washington Street wharf district. Most of the city's larger banks could not resume operations as quickly because their vaults remained too hot. The governor declared a bank holiday that lasted for more than a month. The financial community's Clearing House Association helped facilitate the gradual reopening of San Francisco's larger banks.

While the Clearing House Association did not include the Bank of Italy within its membership, Giannini still attended that organization's meetings. He also determined that he could assist his stricken community better by attending to the interests of depositors who came to the Washington Street wharf area seeking relief. Giannini conducted much of his business right on the wharf, with his facilities consisting of a plank counter and a bag of money. The Bank of Italy could resume its operations more quickly than the city's larger banks because it depended less on extensive records. Those documents for almost all the San Francisco banking institutions had gone up in flames or lay buried under rubble, but Giannini knew many of his small depositors and their accounts personally. He also exuded a spirit of confidence when other financiers reflected only doom and despair. He exuberantly foresaw a new San Francisco bustling with people who rolled up their sleeves to work to rebuild their lives. He spread his $80,000 of remaining assets among small personal and business borrowers and helped launch a rebuilding effort in North Beach. San Francisco's Italian-language newspaper, *L'Italian*, acknowledged Giannini's "energy and initiative" during the period.

Before the earthquake and fire, the Bank of Italy had seen substantial growth. The disaster only made business increase. During 1906 the institution doubled its business. Assets totaled nearly $1.9 million, and deposits exceeded $1.35 million. The most noteworthy aspect of this activity involved the addition of new investors. Savings accounts also increased. The San Francisco earthquake and fire effected one final event with respect to the Bank of Italy. The response Giannini received from the residents of North Beach in return for his efforts at community rebuilding convinced him to make banking his lifelong career.

In early 1907 the board of the Bank of Italy granted Giannini a leave of absence so that he might enjoy the first vacation of his life. When Giannini departed the bank, San Francisco and the nation as a whole were experiencing almost unprecedented prosperity. But cracks had already appeared on the facade. International banking firms, overcommitted to large-scale speculative programs, had dangerously reduced their cash reserves. At the same time the United States had one of the most inadequate banking systems of any major commercial nation. The nation's monetary system was equally confused: everything from gold and silver to nickel and copper, as well as notes issued by the federal government and various national banks, circulated at the same time. The National Banking Act of 1863 established only a rudimentary support system. While it established a network of national and state banks, the outmoded legislation did nothing to provide for currency elasticity, and unwisely decentralized deposit reserves. Finally in March 1907 the Bank of England, the world's most influential monetary institution, attempted to reduce worldwide speculative trends by raising its own interest and discount rates. That action effected a catastrophic break on the New York Stock Exchange.

By the late spring of 1907 Giannini had reached the East Coast and realized that the problems incurred by the New York Stock Exchange could affect the nation's banking industry tremendously. He cut short his vacation, returned to San Francisco, and prepared the Bank of Italy for what he believed would be a general business and banking panic.

Those preparations involved the entailment of loans, an increase in the bank's gold reserves, and a vigorous campaign to build up deposits. Giannini's efforts proved necessary. During the summer and early fall of 1907 credit tightened abroad and in the United States. Heavy industrial failures and additional stock market breaks followed. Many trust companies, which had entered the field of general banking and kept no substantial reserves, closed their doors as the stampede of the Panic of 1907 worsened. Only the financial sagacity of J. P. Morgan prevented further collapse.

The measures taken by Giannini enabled the Bank of Italy to weather this financial downturn. He stacked the gold reserves he had accumulated inside the bank's cages for anxious depositors to see. In addition he directed that the bank pay out that gold on demand, and at no time did he place limits on withdrawals. In fact, the Bank of Italy turned over some of its gold to the much larger and more prominent Crocker National Bank. That institution had been caught short of reserves during the panic and had even paid $50,000 in premiums to banks in Chicago and New York to obtain gold and to stem runs on its reserves. The Crocker National Bank repaid Giannini's favor. At the start of the panic the Bank of Italy held certificates of deposit from Crocker National Bank, which served essentially as a drawable account totaling nearly

$150,000. After the Bank of Italy exhausted that sum, Crocker honored Bank of Italy overdrafts totaling $154,000. Thus the Bank of Italy, through its mutually beneficial relationship with Crocker, could meet all withdrawal demands and remain solvent. The ability of the institution to perform that function during the difficult weeks and months of 1907 greatly enhanced its reputation within the San Francisco financial community.

By the latter half of 1908 much of the distress incurred by the panic had subsided. The experience had taught the San Francisco and the national banking industry some valuable lessons. Various associations of state and national bankers met in conferences that fall. At one of those meetings Giannini heard Lyman J. Gage, a former U.S. secretary of the Treasury, and Woodrow Wilson, then president of Princeton University, extol the virtues of branch banking. Wilson argued that branch banking would open wider channels of credit to local merchants and farmers and would bolster the image of banking among the general public. With regard to the limits of local banking practices, Wilson stated, "What have you done to your banking system? The local bank is built up by local resources. Only the local resources for the most part can be called upon for local advantages. . . . You have set this country a task of developing in the most difficult and most improbable way."

Few bankers agreed with Wilson's message. Surprisingly, Wilson's farsightedness in the world of finance outstripped that of many of the nation's dominant banking figures. Still, some important large bankers, including James B. Forgan of Chicago's First National Bank, favored the branch concept. Most small bankers, however, viewed the arrangement as a threat to their independence and their profits.

Giannini regarded Wilson's branch concept positively. He understood the intricacies of the Canadian branch banking system and believed that it could be adapted, at least in the state of California. In 1909 California enacted a new banking law that authorized the state superintendent of banks to approve branches when in his opinion they satisfied "the public convenience and advantage." The statute gave Giannini the impetus to start a vast banking empire.

Giannini established the first branch of the Bank of Italy by acquiring the troubled Commercial and Savings Bank of San Jose. One of the oldest fi-

Giannini and his wife, Clorinda Cuneo Giannini, whom he married in 1893

nancial institutions in California, the Commercial and Savings Bank had nearly defaulted during the 1880s and barely managed to survive through 1909. The new California banking law proved the death knell for the institution, as the state banking superintendent Alden Anderson ordered it to dispose of its landholding subsidiary, the Commercial Land Company. The bank had created the company as a device to remove the many land foreclosures it had carried for too long on its books. The directors of the Commercial and Savings Bank needed to convert those landholdings into liquid assets.

Superintendent Anderson consented to the acquisition of the Commercial and Savings Bank by the Bank of Italy, but the new California banking law prohibited the purchase of one bank's stock by a second bank. Giannini solved that legal obstacle by insisting that Commercial and Savings convert its stocks to assets. The law permitted the purchase of assets and allowed for the rapid consolidation of the two banks. Giannini utilized the formula on several occasions in later years.

Giannini chose the Bank of Italy's expansion strategy well. San Jose served as an agricultural

county seat, and prior to World War I agriculture produced the majority of California's wealth. Giannini also realized that his branch banks must do more for California ranchers and farmers than the existing unit banks in the state. He accomplished that by retaining local advisory boards and local employees in the branches. Those branches in the state's agricultural regions retained their local character and thus their appeal to their traditional patrons, yet they still benefited from the strength of the Bank of Italy.

During the next few years the Bank of Italy continued its expansionist policies within an urban as well as an agricultural setting. In 1910 it purchased two San Francisco banks and a suburban San Mateo bank. Citizens National Bank constituted the first San Francisco institution. Similar to the Commercial and Savings Bank, Citizens National had experienced a series of financial difficulties. The second San Francisco purchase involved the Mechanics Savings Bank, an institution that had been established around the same time as the Bank of Italy and had been fairly prosperous. Several of San Francisco's leading financial figures served on the board of the Mechanics Savings Bank, and its deposits amounted to just less than $600,000. But the institution had constructed an expensive new headquarters that it could not afford.

By the end of 1910 the Bank of Italy possessed resources of more than $6.5 million. Its branch acquisitions and operations had allowed the institution to double nearly in size in the span of roughly one year. It accrued one-half of those assets from purchase of the two San Francisco branches. Profitable real estate loans comprised the bulk of the remainder of the assets.

The growth and profitability of the Bank of Italy was quite remarkable. But Giannini realized that he would have to establish a presence in southern California if he was to demonstrate the merits of branch banking statewide. He therefore looked to Los Angeles. The City of Angels offered tremendous prospects. Between 1900 and 1910 its population doubled to 319,000. Much of that growth occurred through the city's annexation of surrounding suburban communities. The wealth accrued from California's agricultural, mining, and industrial sectors also found its way to the booming Southern California metropolis. As a result, many of San Francisco's leading financial men hesitated to extend monetary support to the city, which had rapidly emerged as a powerful rival. That hesitant policy did little to slow the development of Los Angeles. Much of the capital for the city's expansion came from the Midwest in the form of tourist and winter resident spending and from investments provided by permanent residents who migrated to the area to enjoy the amenities of sunshine and a relaxed outdoor lifestyle. Giannini felt loyalty to San Francisco, but also to California. The only issue that remained was how he planned to penetrate the Los Angeles financial community.

Again Giannini focused his acquisition attempts on smaller institutions that had experienced difficulty. The Park Bank of Los Angeles, with assets totaling just less than $2 million, constituted the first target. Giannini quickly effected the purchase of Park Bank and sought further Los Angeles acquisitions. Not all of his efforts met with success, but by 1913 he had acquired the Bank of Italy's third Los Angeles branch, the City and County Bank. Similar to the precedent he had established in San Jose with the Commercial and Savings Bank, Giannini established a strong advisory board of Southern California bankers to assist in the administration of the Bank of Italy's Los Angeles branch operations.

Yet all did not proceed smoothly. Domestic immigration, largely from the Midwest, made up a large part of the population growth of Los Angeles. The newcomers descended from largely native-born American stock and brought with them significant prejudice. For example, a Los Angeles newspaper "heralded" the new presence of the Bank of Italy in a curt and almost hostile statement: "Park Bank Taken Over by Italians."

Giannini correctly surmised that branch banking operations fit in with exigencies of urban life. Los Angeles and San Francisco, like many large cities, had developed major traffic problems. Customers of downtown unit banks had to make arduous journeys through congested central city streets to handle their financial affairs. Branch banks eliminated those inconveniences. At the same time many unit banks in smaller communities could not completely care for all of their clients because of legal limitations that permitted only a certain percentage of a bank's capital and deposits to be loaned to any one borrower. The larger businesses in smaller communities needed to utilize the services of two banks, one at home and one located in a larger financial center. The considerable financial resources of the Bank of Italy, made available to those businesses through its expanding branch system, provided a more convenient and sensible alternative.

Giannini also used the power of advertising to facilitate his financial "invasion" of Los Angeles. After the earthquake and fire of 1906, the Bank of Italy purchased space in both Italian- and English-language San Francisco newspapers. Realizing that residents of Los Angeles responded to bravado and aggressive marketing tactics, Giannini purchased substantial newspaper space in their newspapers as well. On certain occasions he took out half-page advertisements that proclaimed the Bank of Italy's attractive loan policies to Los Angeles residents. Giannini took personal charge of the small-loan campaign. He traveled throughout the Los Angeles area appraising the properties of loan applicants. That proved a slow process. While the net deposits of Los Angeles branches grew, the small size of the increases discouraged several Bank of Italy directors in San Francisco and physically exhausted Giannini. In January 1914 he threatened to retire from the bank. While several of the directors felt that the Los Angeles ventures had not been overwhelmingly successful, they could not envision the Bank of Italy continuing without its dynamic president. The board persuaded Giannini to resume his duties after a lengthy West Indian vacation.

After returning from his leave, Giannini found that the bank's Los Angeles affairs still required a great deal of his time and energy. The economic picture in Los Angeles and the rest of the state in 1915 was not particularly strong. The slump forced Giannini to reduce the Bank of Italy's branches to two. But no sooner had the consolidation taken place than the San Mateo branch encountered difficulties in the form of inherited, doubtful loans. Events shaped Giannini's management style. He almost ceased to direct the Bank of Italy's operations from its San Francisco center. Instead he became a type of traveling troubleshooter as he journeyed from branch to branch in order to keep each profitable.

The coming of World War I in Europe bolstered the prospects for an economic upsurge in Los Angeles and throughout all of California. International expositions in both San Francisco and San Diego in 1915 reflected the growing vitality. Giannini took advantage of the improved climate to extend the Bank of Italy's branch activities and increase its total assets. Between 1915 and 1917 assets grew from $22 million to more than $77 million.

In February 1916 the Bank of Italy made the Santa Clara Valley Bank a new branch. The bank's purchase of the First National Bank and the Commercial Savings Bank, the Bank of Gilroy, the Bank of Hollister, and the Savings and Loan Bank of Senito County further augmented the Bank of Italy's branch facilities in the Santa Clara Valley region. By 1917 the bank had established branches in Modesto, Madera, Santa Rosa, Napa, Livermore, and Redwood City and had purchased the International Savings and Exchange Bank of Los Angeles, the San Joaquin Valley National Bank, and the San Joaquin Valley Savings Bank.

Most of the acquisitions reflected Giannini's realization that rural California provided a profitable environment for branch banking. Farms in California required a sizable monetary investment, but because of the diversity of the state's agricultural base they could be extremely profitable. Items such as dates, avocados, cactus pears, citrus fruits, cotton, grapes, grain, and dairy goods could also be produced throughout most of the state if an adequate water supply was secured, and specialized machinery relevant to highly perishable crops provided.

Such infrastructure needs required that California farmers become sizable debtors. The dearth of banks in California's agricultural areas had created a fierce competition among farmers for money. The competition drove up the price of borrowing. The region's lending agencies, which included banks as well as insurance companies, private individuals, and even meat and fruit packers, creameries, and wineries, offered credit to California farmers at sometimes ruinous rates of interest.

The financial prospects for an increased agricultural banking program in the form of branch facilities presented Giannini with profit opportunities he could not ignore. His energetic and accessible personality impressed potential customers. Giannini spent considerable time with grain and dairy farmers and grape growers to learn their businesses and tailor his financial offerings accordingly.

Giannini's personal dedication could not offset certain state regulations that tended to hinder his branch expansion plans. One of those regulations specified that no bank could carry real estate on its books for longer than five years. The regulation made it difficult for any bank to exploit the real estate market to its full potential. Giannini sought to circumvent the regulation by forming an entity known as the Stockholders' Auxiliary Corporation. The stockholders of the Bank of Italy owned the corporation, which could act in a variety of ways denied the parent bank. For example, it could hold developable property for an unlimited time, and its officers became adept at making landholdings more profitable. More important, the Stockholders' Auxiliary Corporation could buy, hold, and sell banks. It functioned to keep the bank, in Giannini's words, "cleaner." If a particular asset of the bank became less viable, the bank transferred it to the corporation, which could revitalize the impaired holding. The bank's stockholders at least had an opportunity to benefit from the original investment. Giannini's branch expansion and acquisition efforts as well as the new development opportunities afforded by the Stockholders' Auxiliary Corporation resulted in a substantial increase in the Bank of Italy's assets, which by 1918 totaled more than $83 million.

At the same time Giannini involved himself with financial matters related to U.S. participation in World War I. The Bank of Italy floated a significant amount in Liberty Loan bonds, and Giannini toured with popular entertainment figures such as

The Bank of Italy after the 1906 San Francisco earthquake

Charles Chaplin, Mary Pickford, and Douglas Fairbanks to promote the sale of the securities.

During the war years Giannini also traveled to New York City, where he purchased the East River National Bank. James A. Stillman, president of National City Bank, initiated the episode by appealing to Giannini to examine East River National closely. The institution had been founded in 1852 and by 1919 had $3.5 million in deposits and a capital of $250,000. The Italian Chamber of Commerce in New York also supported the purchase, as its members desired to secure the type of personalized banking service that Giannini had brought San Francisco's Italian immigrants. Giannini stipulated that he required $1.5 million in local funds to assist in the purchase of the East River National Bank and that no one could own more than 100 shares of the bank's stock. He maintained that the diverse pattern of stock ownership would help attract customers since the stockholders would encourage their friends to do business with the bank. The Italian Chamber of Commerce worked successfully to solicit the funds Giannini required.

Giannini's involvement with the East River National Bank is especially important from an historical perspective. In 1919 federal law prohibited interstate branch banking, so Giannini devised the Bancitaly Corporation as a holding company through which he could secure the East River National Bank and other banking institutions outside the state of California. The organization of the Bancitaly Corporation foreshadowed that of the Transamerica Corporation, one of Giannini's most powerful and prosperous endeavors. In 1919 Giannini also extended his financial affairs abroad with the acquisition of the important Italian branch banking system, the Banca dell' Italia Meridionale. After gaining control he changed the name of the institution to Banca d'America e d'Italia. Finally, in 1919, a thoroughly eventful year for Giannini, the Bank of Italy became the first state bank in California to join the Federal Reserve System.

Those events, in addition to the growth of the Bank of Italy through the continued establishment of new branches, brought Giannini into conflict with Charles F. Stern, the new superintendent of banks in California. A petition by San Luis Obispo residents seeking a Bank of Italy branch escalated the confrontation. The unfavorable attitude of Stern toward further expansion by the Bank of Italy reflected the concerns of much of the California banking community. According to Stern, the Bank of Italy had grown so large and powerful that if it faltered it could be catastrophic for the state's economy. He refused to consider the San Luis Obispo petition and even made public his assertions that the Bank of Italy had grown too quickly and might be unsound.

The statement made by Stern had the effect of producing a run at the Bank of Italy's Santa Rosa branch. To forestall the run, Giannini rushed $3 million in coin and currency to Santa Rosa with orders to keep the bank open and to allow depositors to make their withdrawals. That decisive action dispelled rumors that the Bank of Italy was under financial stress, rumors that had possibly emanated from the state banking superintendent's office.

While Giannini's actions in the Santa Rosa affair impressed Stern, the superintendent still denied the permit to establish a new branch in Fresno. But larger occurrences provided Giannini with new possibilities for branch acquisition and expansion, again especially in California's agricultural regions. The deflation of the agricultural boom following World War I resulted in the failure, or near failure, of banking institutions in the Sacramento and San Joaquin Valleys. Those failures allowed the Bank of Italy to come into possession of two of the best-known banks in the areas, the National Bank of Visalia and the Visalia Savings Bank and Trust Company. While Superintendent Stern opposed, at least in principle, the acquisition of the institutions, the actions by the Bank of Italy circumvented a great deal of economic stress. In his final days before his resignation as state bank superintendent, Stern agreed to support further branch expansion on the part of the Bank of Italy.

Prior to the Visalia takeover Giannini had sought permits from the superintendent's office to acquire branches in Fresno, Centerville, Hayward, King City, Los Banos, Paso Robles, and Sunnyvale. Stern had denied the permits. But because of the Bank of Italy's stabilizing role in the state's agricultural economy, Stern decided to grant the permits. The situation involved some complications. Because of the longstanding policy against branch expansion, Stern would have preferred that his successor, Jonathan S. Dodge, a former banker and Los Ange-

les attorney, actually carry out the licensing of the new branches. But that scenario would have given the California banking community the impression that Giannini controlled the new superintendent. Stern decided to grant the branch permits to resolve the antagonism between himself and Giannini and steer the way clear for Dodge.

Giannini faced difficulties from other quarters. Superintendent Dodge granted several licenses for Bank of Italy branch acquisitions in Bakersfield, Oakland, Chico, Shafter, Hanford, and San Diego. While conducting his first examination of the Bank of Italy's affairs, Dodge determined that Giannini had failed to move quickly enough to fully assimilate the new branches into the larger institution. Dodge criticized the Bank of Italy for "unsafe banking practices including sloppy record keeping and a lack of inspection of the new branches on the part of the head office." Dodge particularly condemned the Bank of Italy's management practices, stating that Giannini controlled the operation of the bank and its branches too closely. Tasks such as branch inspection, which could have best been handled by a subordinate, occurred only infrequently. Dodge assumed such a strong position against the Bank of Italy that he disallowed further attempts at branch expansion until Giannini "more strictly regulated" his institution.

Dodge made the situation worse for the Bank of Italy by reporting the findings of his examination to John Perrin, chairman of the Federal Reserve Bank of San Francisco. Perrin in turn forwarded the report to the Federal Reserve Board, which at that time was considering branch banking issues. The conflict between Giannini, the state superintendent of banking, and the Federal Reserve Bank of San Francisco helped shape a national branch banking controversy.

Giannini complicated matters when, in the face of the Federal Reserve's apparent opposition to branch expansion, he attempted to open a new bank in San Francisco. He wanted the Stockholders' Auxiliary Corporation to control the new institution and applied for a national charter. He mistakenly permitted local newspapers to announce the opening of the new institution–Liberty National Bank–and to make public his choice of officers. Federal Reserve Bank president Perrin took exception to Giannini's precipitous actions and refused to forward the charter application to the Federal Reserve Board. He also stipulated that the

Stockholders' Auxiliary Corporation function only within jurisdictional guidelines set forth by the Federal Reserve Board. W. P. G. Harding, governor of the Federal Reserve Board, supported Perrin and went further by demanding from Giannini "definite advice" as to "the maximum number of branches it was contemplated that the Bank of Italy shall have." Giving such "advice" would require Giannini to impose a limitation on expansion. Clearly, Giannini's association with the Federal Reserve System had become a bag of mixed blessings.

Giannini reacted to the threat by retaining the services of William G. McAdoo, secretary of the Treasury during the presidential administration of Woodrow Wilson, as the Bank of Italy's counsel. McAdoo's meetings with Federal Reserve Board officials went far in resolving the conflict. McAdoo allayed the fears of Federal Reserve officials that the Bank of Italy did not possess sufficient capital for new expansion efforts and also helped construct a 1922 agreement whereby the Bank of Italy would not acquire an interest in another bank or make an arrangement to acquire such an interest without first obtaining permission from the Federal Reserve Board. Giannini solidified the agreement by traveling to Europe for a year, thereby demonstrating that the Bank of Italy could remain strong without its founder.

While the agreement between the Bank of Italy and the Federal Reserve Board put a temporary hold on Giannini's expansionist efforts, it also resulted in a Federal Reserve investigation of the nature of branch banking in California. A series of conferences held in 1922 made public the findings of the investigation and demonstrated the soundness of branch banking enterprises and their relevance to the business of the state. The investigation convinced the Federal Reserve Board to assume a stronger position in favor of California branch banking. The performance of the state's banks in the ensuing decade justified the board's position. From 1921 to 1931, 19 percent of American banks failed, but only 4 percent of California banks went under, even though farm overexpansion during the war years and a postwar drop in world demand for farm products depressed the state's agricultural industry and therefore threatened many banks. But branch operations such as the Bank of Italy's could save crippled institutions before they collapsed.

During the 1920s Giannini also inaugurated policies that benefited farmers who had fallen upon difficult circumstances. One such policy allowed a delinquent borrower to match his labor against the capital of the bank and thereby escape foreclosure. Even if the bank found it necessary to foreclose, it sometimes kept the owners on as tenants with the right to buy back the property later.

Problems for the state's agricultural community did not necessarily translate into difficulties in other areas of the economy. In many respects California enjoyed a tremendous period of prosperity during the 1920s. That economic strength derived from an upsurge of population, real estate speculation, and, in some cases, the entertainment industry. Filmmakers located their operations in Hollywood because consistently good weather presented favorable conditions for year-round shooting. The movie industry employed thousands and served as an important economic generator, especially in the Los Angeles area.

Giannini possessed a special interest in motion pictures. As early as 1909 he had toyed with investments in the San Francisco nickelodeon industry. By 1920 the Bank of Italy led all other financial institutions in investment in the state's filmmaking industry. The bank financed the films of such notable Hollywood personages as Douglas Fairbanks, Charles Chaplin, and Harold Lloyd. Giannini also involved film producers in his movie investment policy by appointing such luminaries as Joseph M. Schenck, Cecil B. de Mille, Conrad Nagel, and Sol Lesser to the board of the Bank of Italy's Culver City branch.

The close tie between the Bank of Italy and the entertainment industry involved the financing not only of Hollywood films but also New York plays, and the relationship continued for many years. By 1952 the bank had invested $50 million in the film industry, supporting a list of clients that included the highly successful Walt Disney.

The high-profile status Giannini cultivated through his association with the filmmaking industry reflected the magnitude of the Bank of Italy's expansion during the 1920s. But during the decade Giannini also faced significant competition in the field of California branch banking. The state banking department and the Federal Reserve Board still constituted some of the principal obstacles to the expansion of the Bank of Italy's operations. Giannini often maintained that those agencies denied the Bank of Italy's branch permit applications at the behest of his competition, but he could not prove it.

He finally decided to address the problem through a massive program of consolidation. In January 1926 he formally presented the application for such a consolidation and stunned the California financial community. The proposal involved 155 branches with deposits totaling nearly $500 million.

By February 1927, Giannini had successfully implemented the statewide consolidation effort. The resulting conglomeration was called the Bank of Italy Trust and Savings Association. A national bank system, the institution fell under the control of federal regulations. But Giannini perceived that as only a partial victory. He was still determined to achieve interstate branch banking, which would require the reconfiguration of the national banking system into something akin to the arrangement that existed during the presidency of Andrew Jackson after he had vetoed the bill to recharter the Second Bank of the United States. Giannini decided to become first in the field, as he had been with branch banking in California, but he wanted no monopoly. He envisioned regional or even transcontinental institutions handling most of the nation's banking functions.

Giannini proceeded with nationwide branch banking efforts despite the existence of federal regulatory obstacles, most conspicuously the McFadden Act. That law, which became operative in February 1927, had substantially aided the Bank of Italy as it had all nationally chartered banks. It allowed national banks to make real estate loans for five years instead of one and also permitted them to include safe-deposit and savings departments within their operations. Giannini's attempt to establish a nationwide branch banking institution would require those sections to be amended and state branching laws overridden. Giannini did not wait for federal lawmakers to make the changes. He assumed that they would recognize the benefits of his California-wide branch system and establish a regulatory policy favorable to a nationwide version. But amendment to the act did not occur. Along with other important factors, such as the Great Depression and new leadership at the Federal Reserve Board, Giannini's assumptions doomed the effort.

While Giannini's attempt to establish an interstate bank system proved unsuccessful, and almost disastrous for him personally, it constituted an important chapter in American banking history. In order to increase the strength of Bancitaly, the agency Giannini wanted to use to establish the inter-

Mario Giannini, A. P. Giannini's son and colleague in the financial industry

state system, he sent representatives throughout the country to sell stock in the corporation. At the same time, through the Bancitaly Corporation, Giannini purchased banks and bank shares. He targeted entrenched institutions for that purpose, since they would add to the prestige of Bancitaly. A New York bank, Bank of America (unrelated to Giannini's later California institution) constituted one such institution acquired by Bancitaly. While not particularly large nor strong, Bank of America was one of the city's oldest and most respected banks, largely because of its association with J. P. Morgan & Company.

In February 1928 Giannini paid $17 million for a controlling interest in the Bank of America of New York. Then he applied for a national charter, which constituted a key step toward his goal of building a nationwide bank. But because it distrusted holding companies, the Federal Reserve demanded that Bancitaly sell its Bank of America stock to the public. Only by ensuring that Giannini would not engage in the trust business would the Federal Reserve agree to grant the charter. Although disappointed, Giannini agreed with the stipulations. He sold shares of the Bank of America to his friends within the San Francisco banking community but also began to formulate a plan to develop a new holding company, the famous Transamerica Corporation.

Another factor complicated the expansion efforts, the rapid increase of stock values in 1928. In the short term this soaring rise of stock prices dramatically increased the profits of Bancitaly and the Bank of Italy in California. Giannini cautioned his stockholders about the rise and attempted to discourage them from purchasing stocks on margin. He saw problems on the horizon and desperately wanted to expand his operations, especially those of Bancitaly, but a serious decline in the company's stock prices could damage his and his institutions' prestige.

Fatigued by his recent work schedule, Giannini decided to vacation in Europe. He even believed that his personal absence might help quiet the tumultuous stock market. But his trip could not have been more ill-timed. Stock prices continued to soar.

The stockholders of those institutions retained their confidence in Giannini's leadership. That support enabled Giannini to continue with his expansion endeavors. New York still remained the primary target of those endeavors, but the working relationship he had established with J. P. Morgan & Company for the purpose of purchasing the Bank of America of New York had yielded no further acquisitions. At the same time, the comptroller of the currency required that Bancitaly never own more than a one-fourth interest in any California bank. Giannini hoped to include the Bank of Italy under the Bancitaly umbrella, but the comptroller's stipulation obviously made that impossible. Thus, Giannini's expansion and consolidation efforts required another corporation, Transamerica.

In 1928 Giannini chartered Transamerica in Delaware with an authorized capital of $250 million. After the absorption of Bancitaly and the Bank of Italy and its affiliates, Transamerica controlled corporations with assets of $1.29 billion with $816 million to be added later. Of that later total, $400 million came from the Bank of America, formed in December 1928 from the amalgamation of the United Security branch system and the

recently purchased Isaias Hellman's bank, Farmers and Merchants National of Los Angeles. The remainder of the additional total ($416 million) represented the resources of the Bank of America in New York. Giannini served as president, son Mario Giannini as executive vice-president.

As a westerner, Giannini sometimes received curt treatment from established eastern financiers. Such had been the case during his association with J. P. Morgan & Company. Therefore, for Transamerica Corporation to succeed, Giannini needed a well-respected eastern moneyman to break ground for him along Wall Street. Giannini found such an associate in the person of Elisa Walker, a well-known and astute financier and also president of the powerful New York investment house of Blair & Company. Transamerica absorbed Blair & Company and with it the services of Walker.

Thus Giannini prepared Transamerica for what he believed would be great undertakings. He formed subsidiaries to help facilitate the operations and announced a 150 percent stock dividend distribution. But, suddenly, knowledgeable insiders began selling Giannini stock in large quantities. Prices fell precipitously, and those who purchased their shares on margin quickly faced ruin. Giannini and his son Mario fruitlessly attempted to shore up the stock values with a $60,000 infusion of capital. In the end, Bank of Italy stock declined 36 percent in value, and Bancitaly stock fell nearly 50 percent.

Giannini proceeded with his reorganization efforts undismayed. He removed himself from Transamerica, and Walker became chairman of the executive board. Mario Giannini became president. Other important Transamerica executives came with Walker from Blair & Company. Giannini viewed those men as energetic and sympathetic to his cause of interstate branch banking. They included Jean Monnet, a French industrial and financial expert, as vice-president.

Actually, the stock market debacle had only a negligible effect on Transamerica. By year's end its principal holdings, the two California branch banking systems and the New York bank, reported fairly strong earnings. The Bank of Italy had taken the first $4 million block of a bond issue to complete the San Francisco Hetch-Hetchy water system, and later Giannini arranged for his banks and others to move the balance of that issue, which amounted to $37 million. In March 1930, Transamerica bought Occidental Life Insurance Company of Los Angeles, valued at $150 million, and proceeded to expand that company's operations. In April of that same year, Transamerica acquired a million shares, and controlling interest, of General Foods Corporation.

While Transamerica operations demonstrated growth during the early years of the Great Depression, other financial institutions across the country did not fare so well. Transamerica felt the first impact of the long decline in wages and prices and spiraling effects of growing unemployment when it initiated an effort to increase the body of its stockholders from 175,000 to 300,000. Falling far short in its attempt to attract new investors who would purchase 25 shares or less, Transamerica increased its stockholders total to only 217,000.

That disappointment reflected the worsening of economic conditions. Obviously Walker had started his regime as head of Transamerica at an especially difficult time. In June 1930 the corporation's stock began to decline. By August it had fallen from 45 to 20. Furthermore, Walker cut more than half the quarterly dividends. On the basis of the net asset value of its stocks reaching $14.50, Transamerica's net worth by the end of 1930 had fallen to $335 million.

Those conditions caused strains between Walker and the Gianninis. In particular, Mario objected to what he perceived as Walker's panicked reduction of the dividend. Ultimately Mario lost complete confidence in Walker and resigned as president. Giannini then implemented several alterations in the operational structure of Transamerica. The decision to merge the Bank of Italy and the Bank of America of California under the title of the Bank of America National Trust and Savings Association constituted the most important of those. The resources of that institution totaled more than $1 billion.

Yet the difficulties involving Transamerica persisted with the worsening national economy. Earnings declined precipitously, and Walker initiated proceedings to liquidate Transamerica and abandon entirely the transcontinental banking project so painstakingly constructed by Giannini. Walker's severe measures also required the separation of various banks from their principal affiliates, and some even folded. Walker particularly targeted the Bank of America in New York as a likely institution for the block.

In reality, creditors pressed Walker on every side. Transamerica owed $51.8 million, and the comptroller of the currency demanded $15 million

to cover bank loans that the national examiners had marked off as losses. In addition, the comptroller indicated that Transamerica might have to produce another $20 million to cover loans granted by the Bank of America National Trust and Savings Association, which examiners had labeled "slow" or "doubtful." Walker naturally responded to those circumstances by calling for contraction and liquidation, but the Gianninis perceived his actions as "unconditional surrender" and an entirely too-ready willingness to dismember their financial empire.

Giannini, recuperating in Badgastein, Germany, from the severe and potentially crippling disease of polyneuritis, received word of Walker's plans. He cabled his outrage at such designs to Mario, referring to Walker's intentions as a "plot" and a "conspiracy" to harm the stockholders unduly. Giannini also perceived the incident as a deliberate attempt by Wall Street financiers, who had become uncomfortable with his financial strength, to destroy him.

At the same time, a group of stockholders representing about two million shares organized into the Associated Transamerica Stockholders and petitioned Giannini to head a movement to take the corporation away from Walker and assume control once again. In order for that to occur, however, Giannini needed to win the majority of support from the owners of Transamerica's 24.8 million shares.

Walker struck back by threatening to dismiss any Bank of America employee who participated in the activities of the Associated Transamerica Stockholders. At the same time, Walker attempted to eliminate the only possible means remaining through which Giannini could reestablish control of Transamerica without a direct appeal to the corporate stockholders. That involved the election of a new proxy committee that, for the first time, did not include Giannini or any of his supporters and that controlled the majority of Transamerica's nearly 15 million voting shares.

The reversal meant that Giannini could only continue his fight to regain control of Transamerica as an ordinary stockholder. The Gianninis countered by transforming the proxy fight into a type of public crusade whereby they traveled throughout California and beyond, soliciting monetary and moral support. In that respect, Giannini had returned to the original tactics that had so successfully built the Bank of Italy. In the public's eye, visiting branch banks and renewing contacts with old friends placed Giannini comfortably in his element. Because he was a rather poor public speaker, Giannini designated A. J. Scampini, a young lawyer in the bank's trust department and a fine orator, to deliver attacks against Walker and his supporters at gatherings of California Bank stockholders. Scampini's speeches often played upon recurring western fears of the moneyed elite of the East Coast and as such almost evidenced a rather populist flavor:

> Do two or three Wall Street bankers imagine we are a bunch of fools—20,000 California investors who will sit still in the face of a financial element carrying the economic and political control of California to two or three persons in New York? Do you think they can get away with Russian methods in giving orders to their employees that if they do not dissuade stockholders from joining our organization, they will be fired?

Those types of attacks translated into a continual growth of proxy support for Giannini. Walker countered by retaining a staff of publicity agents and proxy solicitors from the East. That infuriated Giannini, who saw the action as an attempt to fight Transamerica stockholders with their own money.

While not admitting defeat, Walker finally sent word to Giannini that he would accept a compromise. At the same time, the Federal Reserve Bank of San Francisco, which had become increasingly disturbed over the condition of the Bank of America, pressured both Walker and Giannini to reach a settlement. Giannini resisted a compromise settlement by unequivocally stating, "Throw the rascals out!," and rather unfairly blaming the considerable decrease in the bank's deposits on Walker. Giannini ultimately won a convincing victory at a proxy vote convention in Delaware and reassumed control of Transamerica in February 1932.

The events at Transamerica reflected both the difficulties of the nation's economic situation and the nature of Walker's management. *American Banker* described Walker's proclivity toward liquidation as a policy "born in fear." Yet Giannini's return did not signal the end of his banking empire's difficulties. John Calkins, the governor of the Federal Reserve Bank of San Francisco, perceived Transamerica as on the verge of bankruptcy and pressed Giannini as to how he would pay back loans outstanding from the government.

A. P. Giannini in 1927 (courtesy of Bank-America Archives)

In spite of the terrible condition of the economy in 1932, Transamerica emanated signs of resurgence. Turning his attention to the Bank of America National Trust and Savings Association, Giannini cut the salaries of almost all employees but refused to fire anyone. Through a dramatic program of expense reduction and confidence rebuilding, Giannini reversed the steady drain on the bank's deposits.

The confidence-building campaign involved a huge advertisement program. Through the use of newspaper advertisements, billboards, direct mail, and radio, Giannini stressed the theme that fear produced depressions. His methods caught the attention of Wall Street, as the Pacific Coast edition of the *Wall Street Journal* stated, "Giannini Scores Over Deflation." In fact, by mid June 1932 Transamerica's California banks added more than $50 million in deposits while other institutions in the state experienced continual erosion of their reserves. Giannini quickly put the infusion of funds to work in a variety of projects, including the financing of highway construction in Southern California and the purchase of the first bonds issued to support the construction of the Golden Gate Bridge.

The worsening financial situation of the state and nation could not be ignored, however. President Herbert Hoover created the Reconstruction Finance Corporation (RFC) to support the ailing financial and business community. Partisan national politics limited the effectiveness of the agency, which involved the federal government in private financial matters to a greater extent than at any previous time in the history of the nation. The short-term low-interest loans provided by the RFC to various banks were intended to bolster their liquid reserves and therefore lessen the impact of customer runs on their deposits. Certain Democratic political leaders, most notably John Nance Garner of Texas, made public the lists of institutions receiving the RFC loans, and thereby helped to destroy public confidence in the stability of the nation's financial sector. Problems within the structure of the RFC also presented difficulties. Most notably, the RFC demanded the highest quality collateral available from recipient banks, thereby significantly diminishing their investment capabilities. Bank runs proceeded at unprecedented levels, to the point that when Franklin Delano Roosevelt assumed the presidency he declared a national banking holiday to protect the few institutions that still remained operative.

California, similar to the rest of the nation, continued to experience tremendous economic difficulties. Still, Giannini attempted to remain optimistic, even though the Bank of America suspended operations because of the banking holiday. A staunch Roosevelt supporter, Giannini even attended the incoming president's inaugural. Returning to San Francisco, he confidently awaited authorization from the secretary of the Treasury to resume operations. The authorization did not come, which essentially meant that the Bank of America could not reopen with the rest of the nation's banks. Federal Reserve Board governor Calkins's highly critical report of the financial condition of the Bank of America resulted in the Treasury Department's decision. Giannini argued against the decision by informing Treasury Secretary William Woodin that Calkins based his report on outdated financial information that did not fully account for more recent increases in the bank's deposit levels. But Woodin would not relent, describing the bank as "hopelessly insolvent." Bank of America faced probable dissolution through reorganization if Giannini could not alter the Woodin assessment. At the same time Woodin

asked Calkins whether the Federal Reserve Board governor would assume responsibility if the requirement that the Bank of America remain closed turned out to be a mistake. Calkins balked at this stipulation. Therefore, Woodin reversed his decision and decided to allow the Bank of America to reopen. That episode constituted the last time during Giannini's lifetime that the Bank of America faced possible dissolution.

Throughout the remainder of 1932 and into 1933 the deposits and earnings of the Bank of America rose. During that period Giannini completely eliminated the bank's indebtedness and declared the first stockholder dividends since 1931. Transamerica also resumed dividend payments.

Yet during those years a disturbing situation developed with California Lands, Incorporated, the Bank of America affiliate that administered foreclosed farms. Established in 1929, the institution purchased, at cost, foreclosed farms from the Bank of America and later from the Central Bank of Oakland, the First National Bank of Reno, the Occidental Life Insurance Company, and the California Joint Stock Land Bank. About one-fifth of the foreclosures grew out of loans originally made by the Bank of America, while the balance derived from purchased banks and from the above-named institutions. By the mid 1930s, California Lands had come into the possession of 2,642 ranches that made up more than 531,000 acres. Many viewed the foreclosures as a reflection of a land-hungry and unsympathetic Bank of America. John Steinbeck's *The Grapes of Wrath* and Casey McWilliams's *Factories in the Fields* portrayed the bank and Giannini in that light.

Such a perspective may have been overly simplistic. California Lands ultimately functioned to transform the foreclosed properties into productive farms that would operate under individual ownership. That proved a difficult task, and for long periods during the Depression, California Lands had to run the farms—either by direct operation or by lease to individuals. While the situation made California Lands and the Bank of America appear as ruthless landholders who had created a tenant-farming situation, in truth just the opposite occurred.

The rehabilitation of the foreclosed properties involved considerable expense, often incurred by California Lands. The farming operations of the company lost more than $500,000 each year from 1930 through 1932. But by 1937 the corner had been turned, and California Lands realized an operating profit of more than $640,000. Factors that led to the positive reversal included better prices and improved marketing conditions, more leased farms and fewer farms operated directly by the company, and a revision of tax assessments.

Giannini also had to identify and remove those responsible for sending up the profits of California Lands too quickly. He made his position in regard to the matter clear by stating that California Lands would not remain in the farming business "except for the purpose of developing and caring for properties awaiting sale." He also disapproved of "first class" properties that generated substantial income being withheld from sale.

The lease arrangement implemented by California Lands did not resemble the southern sharecropping or crop lien systems, though many critics made that assertion. The most conspicuous difference involved Giannini's investment in farm equipment and livestock. More than half of the farmers who rented acreage through California Lands also owned other property. Thus, the turnover rate for renters remained at a fairly low level.

Giannini and California Lands actually pioneered a new method of agricultural leasing. Previously, renting had been done on cash terms or on a crop-percentage basis. During the Depression many farmers could not meet their rental payments. In order to alleviate the situation, Giannini developed a sliding rental scale for many crops and a system whereby California Lands charged only minimum rentals when return on farm products was low and higher rentals when better market conditions existed. Thus farmers could continue during difficult years, and during more favorable economic conditions the system guaranteed the landlord a larger income. Those practices assisted California Lands in accomplishing its ultimate purpose—the renovation of farms and ranches and their profitable sale on the open real estate market.

By 1936 the Bank of America had restored its power and prestige to pre-Walker regime levels. It achieved its resurgence by continuing to serve small businessmen and customers. The bank also prospered because of its innovative lending policies pertaining to automobiles, appliances, and its support of government programs, which loaned funds to veterans, farmers, and home buyers.

Following that formula, Giannini and his successors retained at least the aspiration of continuing

to develop a nationwide branch banking empire. But in reality expansion occurred at a slow pace. Other than the stock ownership in the National City Bank, which Walker purchased when he sold Bank of America of New York, Transamerica held only minor assets beyond the western United States. Within California, the Bank of America became supreme in several markets, most notably city and county bonds, which it continued to underwrite during the Depression. The bank also controlled 85 percent of all California automobile loans.

Those occurrences still spawned federal regulatory action. During the mid 1930s Congress passed legislation that limited banks to commercial banking activity at the exclusion of insurance and investment banking. Congress also placed bank holding companies such as Transamerica under the control of the Federal Reserve. The federal government continued to assume an anti-interstate banking position in such pieces of legislation as the 1937 McAdoo bill after Giannini had passed from the center of the nation's financial scene. Much of the legislation stemmed from continuing fears and suspicions regarding the size and power of the Giannini financial empire.

In 1936 Giannini retired as president of the Bank of America and was succeeded by his son, Mario. The elder Giannini retained the chairmanship of the board and continually made himself available for advice and counsel. That guidance remained an important factor in the formulation of bank policy. In fact, Giannini developed the concept of the Bank of America's famous "Timeplan" lending programs after he stepped down as president. Under the provisions of Timeplan, individuals borrowed at a low rate of interest with no collateral. Timeplan loans were also especially flexible and thus applicable to a variety of financial needs and situations.

Giannini's close relationship with the bank after his retirement seemed to imply that he still managed the institution, but that was not the case. Mario ran the Bank of America and brought to it a somewhat different style of management. At age forty-one when he assumed the presidency, Mario had worked for the bank since he was a schoolboy on summer vacations. Most likely no one knew as much as Mario of the details of the bank's operations. One reason A. P. Giannini had succeeded had been his ability to groom self-reliant subordinates who could handle detailed responsibility, so he could devote more of his energies to formulating grand designs and fostering positive public relations. Thus Giannini, especially during the latter years of his career, came to rely more and more on Mario's detail-oriented administrative support.

A hemophiliac, Mario had spent much of his early years as an invalid. Gary Hector, who has written an excellent study on the Bank of America, maintains that Mario adhered to and even in some cases developed standard bank procedure. His father, on the other hand, often ignored rules and "developed grand schemes." Mario focused more on detail and tried not to project a public persona. Both Gianninis demonstrated the rather distasteful trait of suspecting plots against their institution and their individual authority. Employees suspected that Mario placed "spies" among their number to ferret out possible disloyalty.

Mario's illness often forced him to work at home. This home was situated atop Nob Hill, and to it he summoned the bank's senior executives to various meetings. According to Hector, "He exerted control by scrutinizing expenses, salaries, corporate policies. He grilled executives, asking tough questions and digging for details. He kept track of all promotions, from the most junior to the most senior employee." All of that seemed to liken Mario to a king addressing his court. And because he regularly browbeat subordinates, Mario simply did not elicit the type of warm personal support enjoyed by his father.

Despite the limitations of his personality, Mario Giannini pioneered new trends in banking that helped to raise the Bank of America from fourth place among the country's banks to first. Under Mario's direction the Bank of America met its greatest challenges in the late 1930s and 1940s, that of attracting more depositors and finding additional borrowers. The bank retained its policy of making loans available to small borrowers, either individuals or businesses. The Bank of America became the principal backer of small industrial concerns that became so prominent on the California manufacturing landscape as the Depression receded and World War II began. The bank also sought individual borrowers that banks had previously considered poor risks because the lending amount appeared so trivial.

Under Mario's direction, the Bank of America also took quick advantage of the Federal Housing Act of 1934. That act fit perfectly with the bank's small lending policies. The federal government guaranteed the loans, and Title I of the act enabled a successful applicant to borrow up to $2,500 to enlarge or modernize a home. Title II offered loans up to $16,000 to build new homes or to refinance existing mortgages.

Bank of America led all banks in the country in making available loans under Title I and Title II. In later years the federal government broadened Title I to include the modernization of commercial properties such as hotels and apartment houses. In 1952, the year of Mario Giannini's death, Bank of America wrote its millionth Title I loan. Title II provided much of the basis for the huge, post-World War II home building surge in California. The Bank of America became the greatest single lending force in that surge.

Under Mario's direction the Bank of America also significantly expanded its international business. It opened branches in Manila, Bangkok, Guam, Tokyo, and Shanghai. The expansion reflected the emergence of California's commercial and financial influence in the developing international economy of the Pacific Rim.

In 1945 the Bank of America became the largest commercial bank in the world. It possessed more than $5 billion in assets and in the more than 40 years of its existence had been a major factor in transforming a previously rural and thinly populated California into an economic power of international proportions. The institution had provided a wide range of banking services to literally millions of Californians and had exerted a significant influence within the national banking and financial community.

In the same year that the Bank of America became the nation's largest commercial bank, A. P. Giannini retired as its chairman of the board. Seventy-five years of age, he still possessed almost a youthful energy. He traveled to Italy to inspect the Banca d'America e d'Italia as the Bancitaly was then called, and even assisted Mario in the Bank of America's expansion efforts in the Far East.

When the Federal Reserve Board made a formal complaint against Transamerica for unauthorized expansion, Giannini fought back hard. The conflict came to a head with official hearings scheduled in 1949. Shortly after those hearings began, A. P. Giannini died, on June 3, 1949. Claire Giannini Hoffman, A. P. Giannini's daughter, remained as the only immediate family member within the bank's management. She assumed A. P.'s position as director at the age of forty-five and remained on the board until 1985. At that date, she resigned in outrage at what she perceived as the inability of the management of the Bank of America to address several financial reversals, and especially expressed her anger over plans to sell the Bank of America's headquarters building in San Francisco.

Biographers have described A. P. Giannini as "sharp" and "aggressive," as an innovative banker not tied to tradition and conservative financial practices. Those attributes often created a ruthlessness and arrogance in his nature. Yet, it must be stressed, Giannini not only built his financial empire out of motives for self-aggrandizement but also out of a genuine desire to bring the valuable services of commercial banking to as many people as possible. Perhaps that remains his greatest legacy.

References:

Gary Hector, *Breaking the Bank: The Decline of BankAmerica* (Boston: Little, Brown, 1988);

Marquis James and Bessie R. James, *Biography of a Bank: The Story of Bank of America N.T. & S.A.* (New York: Harper, 1954);

Paul Rink, *Building the Bank of America: A. P. Giannini* (Chicago: Encyclopaedia Britannica Press, 1963).

Seymour Parker Gilbert, Jr.

(October 13, 1892 - February 23, 1938)

by William C. McNeil

Barnard College, Columbia University

CAREER: Attorney, Cravath and Henderson, New York (1915-1918); War Loans Staff (1918), assistant secretary in charge of financial affairs (1918-1921), undersecretary, U.S. Department of the Treasury (1921-1923); attorney, Cravath, Henderson and de Gersdorff, New York (1923-1925); agent general for reparations (1925-1930); partner, J. P. Morgan & Company (1931-1938).

For a brief time in the late 1920s Europe appeared to have found the political and economic stability that would allow a real recovery from the devastation and dislocation of World War I. The years of financial stability from 1925 to 1929 were based on the Dawes Plan, with its compromises on German reparation payments and its promise of American loans to finance European recovery. The financial experts who wrote the Dawes Plan created the powerful position of agent general for reparations and assigned him the responsibility for ensuring the success of the plan. In 1925, Seymour Parker Gilbert, Jr., a young American banking expert, was named to fill the post. Only thirty-two years old when he assumed that responsibility, Gilbert soon became one of the most powerful voices in international economic affairs. From 1927 to 1929 he played a central role in shaping American

Seymour Parker Gilbert, Jr. (courtesy of Harris & Ewing)

foreign monetary policy and was the decisive agent in arranging for a new conference to settle German reparation debts. The resultant Young Plan represented the last cooperative attempt to solve the international debt crisis left over from the war.

Seymour Parker Gilbert, Jr., was born in Bloomfield, New Jersey, on October 13, 1892. His father, active in state Republican politics, had served as a New Jersey assemblyman. The family was of moderate means, and Gilbert attended the local public schools and Rutgers University. He graduated at the head of his class at Rutgers in 1912 and then went on to law school at Harvard, graduating cum laude in 1915.

While at Harvard, Gilbert established himself, as the *New York Times* would later write, "as one of the truly brilliant young men of his time." After graduation he began his law career in the New York firm of Cravath and Henderson, where his extraordinarily long work hours and keen mind attracted unusual attention.

In 1918 one of the firm's senior partners, Russell Leffingwell, then a senior Treasury Department official, asked Gilbert to work on the Treasury War Loans Staff. In that post, helping arrange the government's wartime finances, Gilbert won a reputation as a man willing to work around the clock. He quickly became one of the most influential financial experts in the Wilson administration.

When Carter Glass took over as U.S. secretary of the Treasury in 1918, he asked Gilbert to take on the post of assistant secretary in charge of financial affairs. In that position Gilbert took charge of dealing with short-term government securities as they came due. The position was one of the most delicate in the government, since the vast expansion of government debt during the war threatened the nation's monetary stability. Gilbert's task involved paying off some of the debts and converting the rest into longer term, more stable bonds.

Gilbert won such acclaim for his work that when the Republican administration of Warren G. Harding came to office, the new secretary of the Treasury, Andrew Mellon, asked Gilbert to stay on. When Gilbert expressed a desire to return to his more lucrative Wall Street law practice, Mellon created the new position of undersecretary of the Treasury especially for him and doubled his former salary of $5,000.

With that inducement Gilbert stayed on with the Treasury until November 1923. In those years he became one of Mellon's most valuable and trusted confidants. When he finally resigned to go back into law, he was regarded, according to the *New York Times*, as the "most extraordinary man of his years in the field of public finance since Alexander Hamilton." He had supervised a major transformation in the American public debt. Under his care the government had reduced its total debt from $25 billion to $18 billion, and it had consolidated the remaining debt into long-term bonds.

While the accomplishment was indeed great, the management of the American war economy involved serious social costs. As a technical expert, Gilbert had helped the government shape policies that stimulated an inflationary boom in 1919. Then, under the Republican administration, he had managed the introduction of a sharp fiscal contraction that helped push the American economy into a short but severe depression in 1920-1921. Neither American nor foreign policymakers nor Gilbert himself seem to have understood the social costs of the unemployment caused by the contractionary fiscal policies of those years. But the short duration of the crisis and the move to steady growth after 1921 allowed Gilbert and the administration to look upon their management of monetary policies with considerable satisfaction.

Gilbert left the government in November 1923 to go back to his old New York firm, then known as Cravath, Henderson and de Gersdorff. But his reputation as a financial expert able to work intimately in both a Democratic and Republican administration soon pulled him back into an important role in international finance.

Just as Gilbert returned to private legal practice the long-simmering conflict over German reparation payments reached its climax. Since the end of the war in 1918 Germany had been locked in a bitter struggle with the Allied governments to determine who would bear the economic costs of the war. German determination to pay nothing for the damage its armies inflicted on occupied territories was matched by French determination to use economic pressure to reduce German power. In early 1923 French troops occupied Germany's Ruhr River basin in an attempt to force Germany to meet its obligations under the Versailles Treaty.

Rather than submit to French pressure, Germany closed its mines, factories, and railroads in a massive demonstration of passive resistance. The costs of the occupation and the resistance soon proved intolerable. By September 1923 hyperinflation and civil war threatened to tear Germany apart. On September 27, 1923, the new German chancellor, Gustav Stresemann, reluctantly gave up and accepted German responsibility to pay reparations. At the same time France, which appeared to have won the argument, approached its own economic limits and no longer had the will to carry the struggle to a successful conclusion.

The parallel exhaustion of both France and Germany following the Ruhr occupation set the stage for the most active participation in European affairs on the part of the United States during the interwar period. Appealing to President Calvin Coolidge, Stresemann urged the United States to send a representative to a new reparations conference along lines that had been set out nearly a year earlier by Secretary of State Charles Evans Hughes. American leaders in the State Department, Commerce Department, and banking circles, as well as the new president, hoped that the United States would be able to exert its influence to stabilize European economies and, through economic stabilization, promote social order. Yet they were reluctant to allow the government to assume responsibility for European affairs or for international financial stabilization. Instead government officials insisted that private American economic experts could advise Europeans, but they could not act as agents of the U.S. government.

With the provision that American delegates to the new reparations conference would serve only as private experts, the governments made arrangements, and the conference met from January to April 1924. Two Americans took the lead in the negotiations. Charles Dawes served as chairman of the most important committee, which investigated how much Germany could pay in reparations. Dawes proved instrumental in bringing the negotiations to a successful conclusion. The committee and the ensuing plan that emerged from it were named after Dawes, and as a mark of his success the Republican party named Dawes its vice-presidential candidate on the 1924 ticket.

The other American, Owen Young, head of General Electric Company, was even more instrumental in the Dawes Plan's evolution. Young, a financier of exceptional skill, had won support from all Europeans for his impartiality and knowledge. Most acknowledged him as the man who worked out the vital compromises and the man most committed to making the plan work.

Under the terms of the Dawes Plan, Germany was to begin reparation payments at a very low level in 1924. To help Germany stabilize its currency and cover some early reparation costs, it also was to receive a very large international loan. Over a four-year period the plan called for reparation payments to rise to an annual sum of 2.5 billion Reichsmarks (RM) in 1928. They would be maintained at that level for an indeterminate time.

Even as the participants accepted the plan, officials in the British Treasury, German government, and American banking circles expressed doubt that Germany could actually pay. In recognition of that fear, and believing that no one could foresee how much Germany would actually be able to bear, the experts tried to create a system flexible enough to respond to any eventuality. If Germany proved extremely prosperous, an escalator clause would increase the payments above the annual 2.5 billion RM limit. In the event that any complications arose in the system, the position of agent general for reparations was created to oversee the plan's operations. The reparations agent had the task of ensuring that Germany paid the maximum amount possible without threatening the stability of German currency. As the balance wheel between the allied governments and Germany, the agent general would act as the mediator of European affairs under the Dawes Plan.

The experts understood that in order to pay reparations without creating a new inflation, Germany had to create a budget surplus large enough to cover the costs of reparations. In fact, Germany's primary responsibility under the Dawes Plan was to raise its taxes high enough to provide that surplus. It would use the surplus to deposit Reichsmarks with the reparations agent, who would then transfer the funds in gold or dollars to the allied governments.

The power and delicate position of the reparations agent meant that it was vital to find the right man for the job. To guarantee that Germany loyally did its part to transfer all the payments possible to the Allies, the reparations agent would have to review Germany's taxing and spending policies. Yet he had no real authority over German policy and could use only his moral influence to shape decisions. The experts recognized that only a very powerful and influential man could step into the situation and make the plan work.

To find a leader with the authority to bring the plan to life, Bank of England governor Montague Norman turned to the most powerful banker in America to name a candidate. J. P. Morgan, Jr., had financed the Allied cause during the war, had worked to stabilize the international monetary system after the war, and now was called upon to support this last attempt to bring the financial catastrophes of the war to a satisfactory resolution. Morgan himself and the other principal partners in the firm, Russell Leffingwell, Dwight Morrow, and Thomas Lamont, had serious reservations about the plan. Despite those doubts, Morrow, regarded as the most brilliant of the partners, and who later served as American ambassador to Mexico and U.S. senator from New Jersey, agreed to take the position of agent general.

Morrow's nomination foundered on erroneous reports that the German government would not accept a Morgan partner as overseer of their economy and the more realistic fear of the Coolidge administration that naming an eastern banker promised to alienate midwestern German-American voters. With Morrow out of the running, the administration and the Morgan partners could not agree on a candidate. Herbert Hoover, then secretary of Commerce, was mentioned, but he refused to be considered. Owen Young was considered, but Morgan blamed him, again erroneously, for undermining Morrow's candidacy, and the Morgan partners felt Young might not be vigorous enough in protecting the international loan that was to be floated under the plan.

In the end the parties reached a compromise. Young would serve for three months, and then Gilbert, known only for his financial expertise, would take over for the longer term. They asked Gilbert, then only thirty-two years old, to take on a position that would play a crucial role in determining Europe's international financial future.

When Gilbert took the job as reparations agent, he had just returned to New York to make the money he hoped would guarantee his financial future. His salary was going to be far less than he would have received as a lawyer, and he did not have the personal resources to supplement his income. To meet that concern, arrangements made (probably by the Morgan partners) increased his salary from the originally estimated $7,000 per year to $50,000—a far from inconsiderable sum in 1925. After Gilbert accepted the position he traveled to Lexington, Kentucky, married Louise Ross Todd, and then, three days later, sailed for Europe and his new job in Berlin with his wife.

Brilliant, determined, and strong-willed, Gilbert aggressively pursued his duties during his five years as agent general. But German officials, especially those in the Finance Ministry, found it difficult to work with him. Finance Minister Heinrich Koehler, who engaged in bitter disagreements with Gilbert, described him: "Reserved and taciturn, the tall lanky man with the impenetrable features appeared considerably older than he really was and . . . made an eery impression." "Here," in Germany, Koehler went on, "he did nothing but work without interruption. No theater, no concert, no other cultural events intruded into his life. . . . The 'Plan' must function. To this everything else was subordinated."

Since Gilbert apparently did not learn German in his five years in Berlin, he conducted all business between himself and German officials in English or through translators. That left Gilbert isolated in German society and created awkward confrontations when English and German transcripts of conferences did not match. Conducting business in English was also not always easy. Another German finance minister, one who did not have a personal ax to grind, found Gilbert only a little more agreeable than Koehler had. Describing his first meetings with Gilbert, Paul Moldenhauer wrote, "These, like subsequent [meetings] were never pleasant. Parker Gilbert had a peculiar way of speaking. He spoke with a mixture of awkwardness and arrogance, mumbling the words so that one could hardly understand his English." British officials tended to share that view. British Ambassador Sir Ronald Lindsay believed that Gilbert found verbal exchanges difficult and often adopted "a self-protective attitude of abstract detachment. . . . He is really a bad man at verbal discussion and I should think he would be at his worst at a conference." Sir Frederick Leith Ross, the guiding light in the British Treasury, expanded on Gilbert's liabilities with the observation that "Gilbert is one of Mellon's pupils and has the same defects as his master. His mind is impervious to considerations of political and national sentiment."

Despite those complaints, German officials knew that Gilbert offered their best hope for proving to the world that reparations would have to be reduced. During the Dawes Plan years, Gilbert assumed tremendous responsibility, and he demonstrated that, despite his youth, he could use his banker's view of the world to shape the framework of the continuing reparations debate.

Until the summer of 1927 reparation payments remained small, and American bankers made such large loans to Germany that the Dawes Plan worked on a modestly low key. In that atmosphere German authorities paid only scant attention to Gilbert. The state secretary in the Foreign Ministry met with him for the first time in early 1926, after Gilbert had been on the job more than a year, and talked with him only once again late in the year. Government files indicate that few people had an interest in Gilbert's views at that time. By mid 1927 that was no longer true, and the files fairly bulged as Gilbert came to symbolize the twin constraints on German policy imposed by American capital and the reparation debts.

As Gilbert established his credentials and reputation as arbiter of the Dawes Plan, his influence increased. Already, in February of 1927, German ambassador to the United States Ago von Maltzan reported from Washington that on American policy toward reparations, Gilbert's influence was "decisive." Later in the year the German embassy in Washington amplified that impression. It reported that most Americans understood that at some future date Germany would face a crisis because it would not have enough foreign currency to pay both reparations and the loans Americans continued to make to Germany. But the embassy declared, "At the present time neither those involved in German business, nor public opinion are racking their brain. They soothe themselves [in the knowledge] that a confidant of the administration and big finance keeps guard in Berlin as Agent General."

If the Germans respected Gilbert because of his influence on American policy, French observers admired him for broader reasons. Bank of France governor Emile Moreau wrote in his diary that "M. Gilbert is always very conscientious and very firm in regard to the Germans. In him, we have not only a friend but even more, an excellent agent general of reparations." Gilbert became so friendly with French premier Raymond Poincaré that Germans regarded them as collaborators, and French Foreign Ministry reparations expert Jacques Seydoux told Germany's ambassador to France that "he held Par-

ker Gilbert in extraordinarily high esteem and could call him his friend."

As Gilbert's ties to French policymakers grew, his relations with British officials, particularly in the Treasury, deteriorated. The Treasury viewed Gilbert's determination to make the Dawes Plan work as an impossible task. When he insisted, as he always did, on proceeding about his business without consulting the Reparations Commission, the British resented the very independence that the French applauded. The British expected that the Dawes Plan would fail and that until then the Transfer Committee and Gilbert should keep the issue quiet. A senior official in the Treasury, Otto Niemeyer, expressed the British view when he observed that "the Transfer Committee is a useful bogey so long as the bogey is kept in a background of helpful obscurity: but if it faces midday sun everyone will see that it is only a turnip draped in a sheet." The American turnip refused to accept the passive role assigned him by the British Treasury, and the British eventually granted him their grudging respect.

By mid 1927 Gilbert's ties to American financial leaders and his influence as reparations agent made him arguably the most powerful individual in international financial affairs. Yet he exercised that power in near total isolation from other policymakers and the public. Rarely has a man had so much power about whom so little is known. British ambassador to Germany, Sir Ronald Lindsay, captured the uncertainty that surrounded Gilbert's personality and goals. "As for Gilbert," he wrote: "I am on good terms with him, but God forbid that I should pretend to be able to influence him. I never knew a man who could take his resolutions in such solitude. He is surrounded at his office with Commissioners, but not one of them ever knows what he is planning or thinking. I believe he sinks his character of American—and I say this though I know he is in close touch with Mellon, Ben Strong, and other great ones in New York. He regards himself, I believe, as an international person, charged with the duty of administering THE PLAN, and honestly determined to give it a fair chance."

As an American, and indeed as an American who hoped to become a Morgan partner, Gilbert surely worked to protect American interests, yet he was determined that his duty as reparations agent would not be compromised by his upbringing or his aspirations. As Lindsay noted, Gilbert tried to

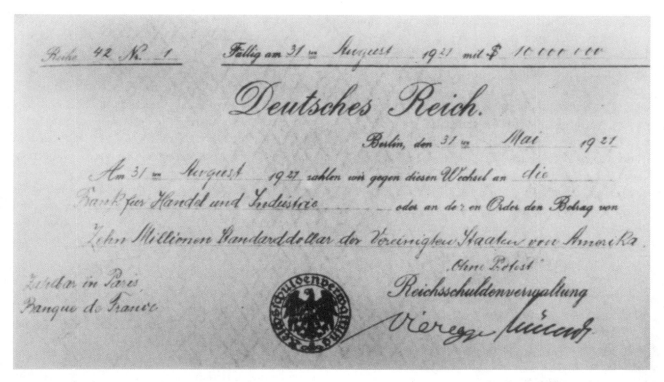

German check paying war reparations due in August 1921. Germany made no further reparations payments until the Dawes Plan went into effect in late 1924.

submerge his American character and deal with reparations as a protector of international stability.

German officials assumed that Gilbert's ties to New York financial circles meant that he would protect American investments in Germany. They misunderstood the situation on two scores. First, Gilbert, as the innovator in reparations policy, pulled other Americans along behind him. Second, Gilbert's ties in New York were to J. P. Morgan and partners, and those men, like Gilbert, had no sympathy for the "second-rank" banks that sold German loans. In reality, American capitalists did not have any agreed-upon policy or interest. Gilbert, like the Morgan partners, firmly believed in conservative, orthodox fiscal policies, and he had no sympathy for governments that tried to finance uncontrolled deficit spending through uncontrolled international borrowing. That issue thrust Gilbert into the limelight in 1927.

In the autumn of 1927 Gilbert's determination to make the Dawes Plan work led him into an open and public conflict with the German Finance Ministry. German social instability and the weakness of German political parties had led the government to permit growing fiscal deficits at the local, state, and federal levels. Gilbert argued that the deficit spending violated the rules of the Dawes Plan. His inability to get the German government to reverse its policies made him so angry that he refused even to speak with some of the bureaucrats in the German Treasury.

Gilbert's irritation with German fiscal policy grew so strong that he openly expressed his regret that the reparations agent had not received the power to control German spending. His only tool was the threat that he would allow all reparation transfers to continue regardless of the consequences. Gilbert anticipated that the threat "would be sufficient to bring them to their senses."

By mid 1927 Gilbert had gone far toward establishing himself as an independent, highly critical observer of German financial policy. His semiannual reparations reports in November 1926 and June 1927 demonstrated his increasingly active intervention in German affairs. His interest and concern focused on two closely related areas. First and always foremost, Gilbert held the firm conviction, expressed by the Dawes Plan itself, that unless the German budget remained balanced, inflation and an inability to pay reparations would inevitably result. The increasing debt of the Reich and its manipulations to hide the debt by expanding the capital budget while leaving the operating budget in balance caused him particular distress. As he wrote in June 1927, "the problem of checking the rising tide of government expenditures has, in fact, become acute."

The Reich's inability to reach a satisfactory financial arrangement with the states and cities constituted Gilbert's second major concern. Rejecting a trend accepted in almost all modern states, Gilbert argued that "it is, on the whole, a sound principle of taxation that taxes should be levied by the same Governmental authority that makes the expenditures." Since the Reich collected taxes and the local governments spent them, the German system "tends to relieve the states and communes from the pressure for economy in expenditure that would certainly exist if theirs was the responsibility to levy taxes necessary to meet their own expenditures."

The continued and mounting spending by German governments, at the federal, state, and municipal levels, led to an open break with the reparations agent, and ultimately to a revision of the Dawes Plan. The Reich's decision to increase pay for government employees brought the issue to a head. In spite of Germany's economic recovery, the real salaries of German government employees remained 25 percent lower than before the war. Although most observers recognized their plight, when Finance Minister Koehler proposed a 25 percent pay increase to bring salaries up to former levels, everyone recognized that the increase would put a heavy strain on the government's budget. Even more serious, with most state and city wages pegged to federal wage levels, an increase in federal employee wages would have to be matched by increased pay for local officials and by increased war pensions and family allowances. Since states and cities employed six times more workers than the Reich, Koehler's proposal promised not only to disrupt Reich finances but municipal and state finances as well.

Gilbert, as one might well expect, found the huge increase in government spending totally unacceptable. Already concerned about excessive municipal spending, he regarded the civil service pay raise as irresponsible and virtually an attack on the Dawes Plan. Within the German government, only Reichsbank president Hjalmar Schacht agreed with Gilbert's conviction that the government needed to reduce spending.

In the late summer and early autumn of 1927, Gilbert and Hjalmar Schacht formed an alliance to pressure the German government to reduce Germany's foreign borrowing and the size of its deficits. After a conversation with Gilbert, a German Finance Ministry official understood that Gilbert's effort to prevent further foreign borrowing was an attempt "to force in this indirect way, a reduction in our entire budget and financial behavior." Gilbert explained to Benjamin Strong that "the very great overexpansion of German Government spending is tending to restrict the possibilities of transfer, by over-stimulating internal consumption and encouraging increased imports of commodities for purposes of internal consumption."

Gilbert correctly understood that the deficits had stimulated the economy and induced greater German imports of foreign goods. He correctly argued that less spending would automatically improve the balance of payments. In the finest tradition of economists of the day, he ignored the reverse side of the coin, which German politicians saw all too clearly. If the government cut spending and increased taxes, it created greater unemployment and risked an economic crisis.

Gilbert remained unconvinced that the foreign loans helped Germany transfer reparation payments. He explained to Strong that "the advantages of foreign loans from the point of view of transfer are . . . greatly exaggerated. It is true that the loans do provide foreign exchange in the first instance, but . . . for the most part, the proceeds of foreign loans to Germany go to finance German imports." The problem, from his point of view, was that the foreign loans counteracted the conservative fiscal policies that allowed Germany to pay reparations. The foreign loans, instead of allowing Germany to pay reparations, as Schacht and others, including Benjamin Strong, believed, had the effect, in Gilbert's more theoretical view, of undermining the policies that would allow Germany to pay.

Gilbert knew that if he could stop German governments from borrowing on the American market, they would have to balance their budgets. By raising taxes and cutting spending, German income would fall, and that in turn would lead to a drop in imports and an improvement in Germany's balance of trade. Thus, while Schacht wanted to stop loans in order to prove that Germany could not pay reparations, Gilbert believed that by stopping the loans German income and imports would fall, and Germany would be able to pay. The two men allied themselves in pursuing the same policy with the ironic difference that they expected precisely opposite results.

Gilbert's determination to reduce American loans to Germany indicates that if he was a tool of American finance capitalists, he was a very odd tool indeed. He demanded firmly that Americans make fewer loans to Germany out of a desire to avoid losing American money, but, even more important, out of his determination to see the Dawes Plan work. Gilbert let his antagonism toward American bankers show when he told Britain's ambassador to Berlin, Sir Ronald Lindsay, that he used the reparations issue as a way to reduce American loans to Germany "because if he did not, he would 'merely' clear the decks for those issuing houses in America" that required restraint. In order to make the Dawes Plan work, Gilbert expressed his willingness to use every means at his disposal to slow or even stop the flow of American money to Germany.

In the late summer of 1927 Gilbert initiated his attack on German deficit spending. To prevent the flotation of a Prussian state loan on the American market, he wrote a protest to the German Finance Minister and wired the Federal Reserve Bank in New York urging the Americans to help impose financial discipline. When the American State Department proved reluctant to get involved in effective loan regulation, Gilbert moved to take matters into his own hands.

On October 20, 1927, Gilbert delivered a memorandum on German financial policy to Reich finance minister Heinrich Koehler. Although he intended it to remain secret, a *New York Times* reporter found out that a memorandum had been sent and guessed that it contained criticism of the finance minister's policies. Koehler attempted to prevent publication of the memorandum by telling his fellow Cabinet ministers that Gilbert opposed its publication and that releasing it to the press violated his confidence. That assertion appears to have been a total fabrication on Koehler's part, since two days later Gilbert wrote him a letter, with a copy going to the Reich chancellor, stating that "I have no objection to the publication of the full text of the Memorandum," and adding that he had already verbally informed Koehler to that end. Several days later when the full text of the memorandum appeared, it revealed even sharper criticisms of Reich policy than press reports had guessed.

Gilbert charged the German government with "developing and executing constantly enlarging programs of expenditure and of borrowing, with but little regard to the financial consequences of their actions." As he had in the past, Gilbert warned that "if present tendencies are allowed to continue unchecked, the consequence is almost certain to be serious economic reaction and depression." Growing Reich deficits and the Reich's agreement to increase state revenues without reaching a long-term settlement on state budgets comprised his principal concern. In spite of higher payments to the cities and states, and in spite of the Reich's coverage of more unemployment relief, the cities and states borrowed more than ever. "The question underlying state and communal borrowing," Gilbert wrote, "is not whether individual loans should be placed in the domestic market or in the foreign market, or at short or long term, but whether they should be placed at all."

He then went on to criticize the civil service pay raise, initially proposed as a reasonable 10 percent in July, which had suddenly ballooned up to the dangerously expensive 18 to 25 percent increase that finally passed. That, plus plans to compensate owners of private property damaged during the war and plans for school reforms, could lead Germany into a fiscal catastrophe. Gilbert warned that "the Reich, by failing to exercise proper restraint in its expenditures, is endangering the stability of its budget, the establishment and maintenance of which is the cornerstone of the expert's plan." Gilbert, like most conservative, orthodox economists, expressed further concern that the growing public outlay deprived agriculture and industry of the investment capital essential for a healthy economy. Finally, he mentioned the failure of the Reichsbank to control all public funds, which made an effective credit policy impossible. Summing up his impressions, Gilbert wrote, "These tendencies, if allowed to continue unchecked, are almost certain, on the one hand, to lead to severe economic reaction and depression, and are likely, on the other, to encourage the impression that Germany is not acting with due regard to her reparations obligations."

As one might well expect, publication of that critique had widespread repercussions. American investors grew anxious about buying German bonds. Prices for many German bonds fell several points in the next weeks, and issuing of new bonds ended. The memorandum created new divisions within the

German government and generated a great deal of bitterness toward Koehler. The Foreign Ministry in particular found Koehler's handling of Gilbert embarrassing. In early October, Stresemann had approached Gilbert to try to patch up relations and get a feel for what he really wanted. Gilbert complained that he did not understand Koehler and Koehler did not understand him. He agreed with Stresemann's suggestion that the country had done much better with Peter Reinhold as finance minister. Gilbert suggested that the government really needed a state secretary in the Finance Ministry to handle reparations problems and give the ministry some sense of direction. Closer and more open communications between Gilbert and the German government were also essential. Stresemann did not fail to quote Gilbert, who added that "it would be extraordinarily pleasing to me, if I had the opportunity to speak with you more often about these things," and concluded that if Stresemann were Finance Minister they could no doubt soon reach an understanding.

When it became apparent that Gilbert had written the memorandum because Koehler had ignored verbal warnings, Gilbert's irritation increased. Gilbert told State Secretary von Schubert that he had many conversations with Koehler, "perhaps too many," and had suggested that the differences might be clarified if he presented his views in writing—to which Koehler had agreed. Karl Ritter, head of the German Foreign Ministry's reparations division, told a British official that things had gone smoothly until that "old muddle-headed fool" Koehler asked for Gilbert's complaints in writing. He added that "even cumulative stupidity could be productive of real good. The 'Dummheit' of Dr. Koehler had produced the Gilbert memorandum, for which Ritter was truly thankful, since some objective outside judgment was necessary to bring the Reich Finance Ministry to a proper sense of its duties." Lindsay, too, found Koehler hard to understand. He wrote, "I have much sympathy with [Gilbert's] difficulties. Before Dr. Koehler's unfailing aimiability [*sic*], his ceaseless volubility, and his complete disregard of all suggestion, combined with the utter disorganization of the Ministry, Mr. Gilbert has been absolutely baffled." He added as a final coup, "Dr. Koehler's personality and incompetence is [*sic*] an important and unpleasant feature of the situation." Pierre Jay wrote Benjamin Strong that "one of the jokes going around German bank-

ing circles is that it would be a good thing for Germany if Gilbert were Finance Minister and Koehler were Agent General."

In July 1927, German industrialists found Gilbert's interference in German domestic affairs and his insistence that Germany could pay reparations so offensive to German national pride that they joined together to create an "anti-reparations agent" who would mount a propaganda campaign to isolate Gilbert. However, in November they fell all over themselves supporting his attack on public spending. Gilbert reported that shortly after he presented his memorandum he had received a visit from a "very important German industrialist, a man of almost violent Nationalistic policies, whom he had never made the acquaintance of. This gentleman had called uninvited to say that it was high time the German Government was called to order in Finance, and to express the hope that his, Mr. Gilbert's, memorandum was couched in the strongest possible language, as nothing else could have any effect." Gilbert added that eight or ten of the most powerful industrialists in Germany had hired Hans Luther to head a private lobby to force a reduction in government spending.

The leadership of the Reich Association of Industrialists concluded that "the discussion and conclusion of the Reparations Agent coincide with the fruitless demands made not only by industry but by all circles of the economy for the past two years." And they speculated that unless the government brought spending to heel, foreign faith in German credit could erode entirely. The industrialists even went so far as to accept the fulfillment policy toward reparations that had come to dominate government thinking. They agreed with Gilbert's accusation that Germany had failed to practice fiscal responsibility, which "must, unfortunately, be seen as a sign that all future prospects for a revision of the Dawes Plan, at least insofar as raising the funds internally is concerned, has been very seriously endangered if not completely ruined." The government had to cut spending, as only that would "let foreigners and especially the creditor states see that we are serious about our obligations and that we will strive to fulfill them." Germans, of course, expected that even their good faith effort at fulfillment would lead to failure, but German industry agreed to throw its support behind Gilbert in order to further its attack on government spending. Gilbert indeed was delighted by his new support and felt confident in reporting that he was "sure that the Germans didn't mind his 'kicking them in the pants pretty hard and strong': indeed, they appeared to like it."

As a result of the furor created by Gilbert's memorandum, Stresemann started to sit in on meetings between Gilbert and the finance minister. That seemed particularly necessary, since Gilbert told several people that he could no longer talk to the representatives of the Finance Ministry, and that he especially did not want to see Geheimrat Karlowa again. The government took Gilbert's complaint to heart, and within months Karlowa either quit or was removed from his post as one of the Finance Ministry's most powerful bureaucrats, transferred to the Foreign Service, and sent to Mombasa, East Africa, as consul.

Although German officials decided to cooperate with Gilbert, they took some pleasure in learning that the British Treasury had sharply criticized him. By late 1927 Gilbert and the most powerful official in the Treasury, Frederick Leith-Ross, verged on an open feud. Leith-Ross resented Gilbert's autonomy and thought that only the cancellation of reparations and war debts could restore international monetary stability. He, along with German officials, also believed that domestic economic needs might well differ from the policies that Gilbert demanded to make the Dawes Plan work. As one German official wrote, "It is not always the case that a sound financial and economic policy from our point of view is identical with one which makes transfers easier."

The crisis induced by Gilbert's memorandum forced Germans to think about the ties between their own national goals and the American loans. Some officials clung to the belief that American bankers would protect their loans by forcing a lower reparations settlement. Hans Luther, past chancellor, future Reichsbank president, and in 1928 employed as a propagandist for German industry, shared that opinion. But a far more perceptive (although perhaps less well-understood) counterview circulated in industrial circles: the United States had loaned to many nations, with Germany taking about one-quarter of America's foreign loans, so the Americans had interests in many markets, and J. P. Morgan had no interest in protecting Germany. Thus, as one observer put it, Luther's faith in American help was more an "illusion" than a reality.

Gilbert and his wife, Louise Ross Gilbert, on their way to Washington, D.C., in late 1928, during Gilbert's effort to prepare for a renegotiation of German war reparations in 1929 (courtesy of Underwood & Underwood)

How successful were Gilbert's pressures in forcing the German government to balance its budget? Despite the apparent desire of most German officials to meet his demands, it never occurred. Referring to Gilbert's June 1928 report, which contained no further criticism of municipal borrowing in spite of its continued volume, Ritter commented, "this sympathetic attitude deserves special interest when we realize that . . . when one critically considers the results, the actual development of the issues raised in the memorandum and the last report have not been entirely in line with the wishes expressed in the memorandum." Especially noteworthy was the fact that public loans had become even a greater share of total borrowing than they had been before the memorandum. Ritter summed up Gilbert's dilemma with the observation, "Just as in the conversations on Reich finances, the Agent General had to bow to the force of reality. . . . The law of supply and demand has once again soon prevailed."

After the long and bitter exchanges between the reparations agent and the German government, the moderate tone adopted in the agent general's report of December 1927 surprised officials. Even more surprising, Gilbert suggested that the time for consideration of a final reparations settlement had come, and he emphasized that in the settlement the transfer protection given to Germany under the Dawes Plan had to end.

In a memorandum presented to the Reparations Commission, Gilbert spelled out clearly and precisely why he had concluded that revision was necessary. He wrote that one of the foundations of the Dawes Plan was the concept "that Germany herself should exercise prudence in the management of her affairs and not dissipate her resources and her credit through overspending and over-borrowing by the public authorities." In his memorandum to the Finance Minister in October and in his December report he had "made it clear that the transfer protection which is given to Germany by the Plan involves reciprocal obligations on the part of the German Government, and . . . presupposes that Germany on her part will do everything within her power to facilitate transfers on reparation account." Gilbert argued that the Dawes Plan itself bore partial responsibility for the problems he had with the German government. "The very existence of transfer protection, for example, tends to save the German public authorities from some of the consequences of their own actions." He all but charged that the growing Reich budget was permitted because German officials hoped that when a transfer crisis came, the transfer clause would be used to end reparations payments.

Somewhat more sympathetically, Gilbert noted that uncertainty over the final reparations debt made it difficult to carry through such essential reforms as the final financial settlement with the states and cities. Until the Reich knew the limits of its reparations debt, it could not agree to fixed payments to the local governments. Summing up his concern, Gilbert wrote, "In other words, there will surely come a time, and in the not too distant future, when the system of protection established by the Plan will be less productive of reparations for the creditor Powers themselves than a system which gives Germany a definite task to perform on her own responsibility, without foreign supervision and without transfer protection." Gilbert considered the last point so important that he said it twice. The entire thrust of his argument contended that transfer protection had to end, and that would force Germany to accept the "responsible" policy he so unsuccessfully had promoted during the past year.

The motive force, then, behind Gilbert's call for a new reparations settlement came from his experience with German finance and his inability to induce a more conservative policy. In the summer and autumn of 1927, as a transfer crisis seemed to be brewing, Benjamin Strong urged him to seize the initiative in heading off a crisis. Less hopeful than Gilbert that Germany could pay large reparations, Strong conceded Gilbert's point that conservative fiscal policies could greatly strengthen German transfer capacity. While hoping that Gilbert's quick action might prevent a transfer crisis, Strong expressed his pessimism about the possibility. "I am not," he wrote Pierre Jay, "looking forward with any comfort or satisfaction to the possibilities of any sort of crisis, but this transfer problem is of a sort which usually cannot be solved without the influence or impact of some sort of a crisis. . . . I see no possibility of anticipatory action," he went on, "except through the intervention of Gilbert."

While in the United States in December and January, Gilbert talked with American officials. A consensus emerged that they desired some sort of settlement, and that the American capital market had grown strong enough to absorb the bonds that would constitute a crucial part of any settlement. Gilbert had consistently believed that, in revising the Dawes Plan, "the fundamental thing from every standpoint is that there should be a final settlement." Germany, he insisted, had the most to gain by a final settlement because it would remove the uncertainties plaguing Reich financial policy. But, he warned, "Germany must be prepared to pay, and to pay high, for the sake of getting a settlement." He added, "I think it is clear also that in order to get a settlement, Germany must depend largely on the use of her credit. It is vitally important, therefore, to keep Germany's credit at the highest possible level and to deal with the whole situation while her credit is unimpaired." Gilbert used the promise of large volumes of negotiable German bonds to win French support for a Dawes Plan revision. The security and immediate availability of the funds made the option very attractive to French officials who, as always, found themselves in financial trouble in late 1927.

Germans who hoped that Germany had indebted itself so heavily to the United States that Americans would demand lower reparations and war debts settlements to protect their private loans soon saw their dreams sour. Secretary of the Treasury Andrew Mellon publicly and firmly refused to consider any connection between reparations and Allied debts.

Germans found it nearly impossible to believe that the American government would continue to insist that no direct link between reparations and war debts existed, but Mellon's position remained firm. He based his view, like Gilbert's, on the belief that, given the correct fiscal and monetary policies, Germany could raise and transfer very large sums. In Gilbert's view, the British "had always underestimated German capacity to pay." And in the final settlement he had in mind, Germany's obligations would nearly total those under the Dawes Plan. The next year demonstrated that Gilbert and the American government would hold to their longstanding reparations and war debt policy, and that Germany badly misplaced its hope that the large volume of American loans would win American support for a vastly reduced settlement.

In order to eliminate the politically and economically destabilizing influence of reparations and war debts, the Americans discussed and may have tried to formulate a comprehensive and final settlement. As generally interpreted, that plan called for a revision of the Dawes Plan to reduce reparations and to end foreign intervention in German affairs. Yet, no one ever fully spelled out the American, or "Gilbert," plan, and if indeed such a thing existed, events soon superseded it. Gilbert made one thing clear: he primarily wanted to force Germany to balance its budget and help transfer reparations. But far wider schemes may also have been involved. Gilbert had long insisted that Germany must save its railway and industrial bonds created by the Dawes Plan for use in the "final" settlement. Germany might sell those bonds—worth nearly RM 16 billion ($3.8 billion)—on the American market and turn the proceeds over to the Allies as reparations. The Allies in turn could approach the American Treasury with cash in hand and offer to repay their war debts early in return for a "substantial discount."

British officials were quite rightly very skeptical of the whole scheme. They believed that Gilbert had proposed the deal because it was the only way to get around American insistence that the Allies make war debt repayments for 62 years. If that were true, the scheme in effect may have been intended as a way to permit the United States to agree to a substantial reduction in Allied war debts by allowing a heavy discount in return for a large cash payment. In any event, the British thought that the huge sums involved could never be sold, and any attempt to do so would create a "world shortage of credit." When Gilbert insisted that the Allies should first reduce reparations and then see if the United States would not reduce war debts, the British responded that they would never allow the United States to say to them, "Open your mouth and shut your eyes and see what I will give to you."

Gilbert flatly denied the existence of any "Gilbert Plan" for revision and quite obviously was not wedded to the scheme. By mid 1928 American interest rates rose, and any hope of selling large volumes of foreign bonds on the American market faded.

Throughout the second half of 1928 Gilbert traveled to the capitals of Europe to line up support for a new and final reparations conference. He found little support in Britain, where the Treasury made no secret of its belief that Europe could not long pay either reparations or war debts. But German leaders, cowed by Gilbert's influence over the American capital market, allowed themselves to be pulled into negotiations despite their repeated and emphatic protestations that they could not pay large scale reparations.

Gilbert's only strong support came from the French government of Raymond Poincaré. The two men shared the belief that the German government had to be forced to accept responsibility for its fiscal policies. If it raised taxes and reduced spending, it could afford to pay more in reparations than either the Germans or the British wanted to admit.

In meetings with Britain's chancellor of the exchequer, Winston Churchill, and with Poincaré, Gilbert established the minimum sum that the Allies would accept from Germany. It had to cover all Allied payments to the United States for war debts, plus something beyond that to cover French and Belgian reconstruction costs. That amounted to about RM 2 billion per year—a payment far beyond what Germans contended they could pay.

Despite German reservations, they found themselves unable to stop the new conference from meeting. They had to hope that their negotiators could win a lower settlement.

When the Young Plan negotiations got under way in Paris in February 1929, both Gilbert and the Germans found their hopes quickly disappointed. The Germans insisted that they could not pay the RM 2 billion that the Allies expected, and

Gilbert charged that the Germans had reneged on their earlier agreement. Although it is true that Gilbert had informed German leaders of what he expected them to pay, it is also true that in the obscure and often circular discussions that led up to the Young Plan, German leaders had persistently declared their inability to pay the sums suggested by Gilbert.

In the end, Gilbert played only a minor role in the actual Young Plan negotiations. Instead Owen Young carried the burden and won some concessions from the American government that made a last minute settlement possible. The German government grudgingly accepted an agreement that nearly matched the one worked out by Gilbert prior to the official meetings. Fear that collapse of the conference would destroy the German currency played the decisive role in that decision.

With the introduction of the Young Plan, Gilbert had successfully brought an end to his job as reparations agent. The position was no longer needed, since Germany now was given full responsibility for raising the foreign currency needed to pay reparations. Gilbert left his post in Berlin in May 1930. In January 1931 he joined J. P. Morgan & Company as a partner and expert on European affairs.

In the years after his tour as reparations agent, Gilbert played almost no public role. In the middle of the 1930s he took only two positions that brought him into the public eye.

In December 1935 Gilbert issued a warning about the dangers of large foreign currency deposits made in American banks. He argued that the Federal Reserve System should not increase reserve requirements in an attempt to immobilize the foreign deposits. He feared that if reserve requirements were raised and then the foreign holders of the funds took them out of the United States, the American banking system could face a crisis, as it would not have enough gold to cover reserve requirements. That theme clearly resonated with his experiences in Germany in the 1920s.

In November 1937 Gilbert made his last public appearance. Speaking at the Academy of Political Science meetings in New York, Gilbert attacked American tax and fiscal policies. He received loud applause when he declared that the United States probably had "the worst tax system of any civilized country." But he saved his strongest words to attack New Deal fiscal policies. He declared that federal spending at $7 billion per year was "far too heavy a burden for the people to bear." He warned that this burden was "gradually lowering the general standard of living," and that, unless checked, federal expenditures would become a threat "to the country's substance." Again Gilbert returned to the themes that had most occupied him during his years in Berlin. The call for fiscal responsibility and the fear of international monetary deficits that rested at the center of his reports as Agent General for Reparations remained with Gilbert to the end of his life.

After several months of illness Gilbert died on February 23, 1938, of cardio-nephritis, a disease of the heart and circulatory system. He was forty-five years old.

Publication:

Report of the Agent-General for Reparations Payments, May 30, 1925-May 21, 1930, 10 volumes (London & Berlin, 1925-1930).

References:

Kenneth Paul Jones, "Discord and Collaboration: Choosing an Agent General for Reparations," *Diplomatic History* (Spring 1977);

Melvyn Leffler, *The Elusive Quest: America's Pursuit of European Stability and French Security* (Chapel Hill: University of North Carolina Press, 1979);

William C. McNeil, *American Money and the Weimar Republic: Economics and Politics on the Eve of the Great Depression* (New York: Columbia University Press, 1986).

Archives:

Seymour Parker Gilbert, Jr., left no personal papers. The best sources available include the Thomas Lamont Papers in the Baker Library, Cambridge, Massachusetts, and the Benjamin Strong Papers at the Federal Reserve Bank of New York.

Carter Glass

(January 4, 1858 - May 28, 1946)

by **Eugene N. White**

Rutgers University

CAREER: Reporter (1876-1880), editor (1880-1899), owner and publisher, *Lynchburg News* (1888-1946); delegate, state of Virginia, Democratic National Convention (1892, 1896); state senator, Virginia (1899-1902); delegate, Virginia Constitutional Convention (1901); U.S. representative, Virginia (1902-1918); U.S. secretary of the Treasury (1918-1920); U.S. senator, Virginia (1920-1946).

Carter Glass was born on January 4, 1858, in Lynchburg, Virginia, into a family that settled in the Old Dominion in the seventeenth century. Politics and the press flowed in his blood. His father, Robert Henry Glass, an ardent supporter of the Virginia Democratic party and owner of the *Lynchburg Republican*, served as a major in the Confederate Army. In the hard times of postbellum Virginia, Carter Glass left school at the age of thirteen to learn the newspaper business with his father. He started in the printing shop and, except for a brief stint as a railway clerk, worked his way up in the profession.

In 1876 Glass took a job as a reporter for another Lynchburg paper, the *News*, and in 1880 he became its editor. He began his political career at about the same time as his newspaper career, serving as a clerk of the Lynchburg City Council, winning distinction for his handling of the negotiations for a railroad right-of-way through the city. In 1886 he married Aurelia Caldwell. Two years later Albert Waddill, publisher of the *Lynchburg News*, retired and sold the paper to his young editor. In announcing the sale, Waddill declared that he was "gratified that the ownership of the paper has fallen to one who, while as yet a very young man, has achieved an enviable fame for character, capacity, and indomitable energy." The *News* prospered under its new ownership, and Glass repaid in two

Carter Glass

years the $13,000 loan from relatives that he used to buy the paper.

In 1891 another rival Lynchburg paper, the *Virginian*, came on the market. The second oldest paper in the state, the *Virginian* had previously merged with Glass's father's *Lynchburg Republican*. Glass purchased the *Virginian* and merged it with his newspaper. That move left the town with two newspapers, the *Advance*, edited by Glass's father, and the *Lynchburg News*, owned and edited by Carter Glass himself. Later Carter Glass acquired the *Advance* as well. The father and son pilloried the Republican party and supported a conservative "redemption" in Virginia under the Democrats. The young publisher was elected as a Virginia delegate to the Democratic National Convention of 1892. Glass's election as a convention delegate signaled his arrival as a political force in Lynchburg. Two years later friends asked him to run for mayor of the city. In a letter to one of those friends declining the nomination, Glass expressed characteristic self-effacement. "After the fullest deliberation," he wrote, "I have cheerfully concluded that I was not cut out for a politician in any particular."

Attending the 1896 convention, again as a delegate, Glass found himself swept along with the rest of the assembly by presidential nominee William Jennings Bryan's "Cross of Gold" speech. During the campaign Glass avidly supported Bryan in a losing effort. Glass was himself elected to the Virginia senate as a Democrat in 1899.

In the legislature Glass acted as a mainstream state Democrat with populist leanings. He successfully fought against attempts by the Virginia Telephone Company to obtain a charter with special privileges. He also served as a member of the Board of Visitors to the University of Virginia and unsuccessfully attempted to reorganize the institution.

In 1901 Glass served as a delegate to Virginia's constitutional convention, its objective being to replace the state's Reconstruction constitution. Glass worked on the critical issue of suffrage. Under his leadership the convention disenfranchised people who could not prove they could read and required payment of a poll tax six months prior to every election, barring most former slaves and many poor whites from voting. The convention did not submit the new constitution to the electorate because it would have asked many voters to disenfranchise themselves. Instead it proclaimed the agreement by fiat.

In 1902 Glass won election to the U.S. House of Representatives. There he developed friendships with many key figures in the Democratic party, including Woodrow Wilson, governor of New Jersey, and key House and Senate leaders, including minority leader John Sharpe Williams. Owing to those close ties, Glass secured the unusual favor of a place on the important Banking and Currency Committee in 1904. When Williams had asked him if he would welcome an appointment, Glass replied, "I don't know anything about it [banking], but I guess I can learn."

The years following the Panic of 1907 proved a crucial time to hold a place on the Banking and Currency Committee. While the American banking system experienced persistent financial crises in the nineteenth century, attempts to reform the regulations governing banking and to establish a central bank had received relatively little consideration. The panic gave a new impetus to reform. As a temporary measure Congress passed the Aldrich-Vreeland Act in 1908, which created voluntary "currency associations" empowered to issue emergency notes. Those associations were patterned on existing clearinghouse associations and their emergency currency on the issues of clearinghouse loan certificates that had traditionally provided liquidity in times of crisis. Congress established a National Monetary Commission to study the problems of the banking system. Senator Nelson Aldrich, coauthor of the 1908 act bearing his name and longtime Republican party leader, took the chairmanship of the commission.

After studying the issue and surveying the opinions of bankers, Aldrich and his advisers drew up a bill that proposed the creation of a National Reserve Association. The association, composed of 15 regional reserve banks, was to be operated by member banks that subscribed to their stock. That structure and the placement of the head office in Washington, D.C., aimed at satisfying country bankers' demands that the New York banks not dominate the organization. The regional reserve banks would have counted endorsed notes and bills issued by member banks. The rediscount facility was aimed at providing banks with additional liquidity in times of crisis or, in contemporary terms, giving the currency more elasticity. National banks would have been compelled to join, but membership was voluntary for state banks. The Aldrich Commission carefully prepared the ground for the passage of the bill sponsoring the National Reserve Association and founded a National Citizens' League to propagandize on its behalf.

Like many Democrats, Glass had opposed the Aldrich-Vreeland Act as a Republican bill designed, he thought, to benefit big bankers. He also denounced the reports of the National Monetary Commission and blasted what had become known as the "Aldrich Plan" to set up a central bank. As the minority party, the Democrats might have found themselves confined to denouncing the Aldrich bill, but just as it was reported to Congress, the Demo-

Secretary of the Treasury Glass displaying the first Victory Bond. Like the wartime Liberty Bond issues, the Victory Bond program of 1919-1920 met with great success (courtesy of Underwood & Underwood).

crats gained control of the House of Representatives in the elections of 1910. With control of the two houses split, the bill stalled.

The presidential victory of Woodrow Wilson and the capture of the Senate by the Democrats in the elections of 1912 gave Glass's party control of bank reform legislation. Moreover, the chairmanship of the Banking and Currency Committee passed to Glass. Before the elections, the Democrats began an investigation of the big banks' control of the money markets. To handle that project and banking reform, two Banking and Currency subcommittees were formed in the Democratically controlled House. The first, chaired by Representative Arsène P. Pujo of Louisiana, investigated the "Money Trust," the alleged monopoly of the New York banks. The second, chaired by Glass, worked to formulate another reform bill.

Although he had sat on the Banking and Currency Committee since 1904, Glass did not possess as intimate a knowledge of banking as Aldrich. To remedy that deficiency he hired H. Parker Willis, professor of economics at Washington and Lee University. As most committee members were also

relatively unfamiliar with the details of the business of banking, Willis exercised considerable influence in the writing of the Democrats' bill. Significantly, he had actively worked in the National Citizens' League propaganda campaign and had generally favored the Aldrich Plan. Although the Democrats denounced the plan in debate, their substitute, the result of the efforts of the Glass committee and a new Senate Banking and Currency Committee chaired by Robert L. Owen of Oklahoma, closely resembled its predecessor.

Both the Aldrich Plan and the Glass-Owen version featured a decentralized system of banker controlled reserve banks that were to carry out clearing and discounting operations coordinated by a central board. The Republicans' bill left the governance of the central board to the bankers, while the Democrats could not stomach that idea. In the place of a banker controlled central board President Wilson recommended a Federal Reserve Board made up entirely of presidential appointees. Owen and the Senate Banking and Currency Committee approved the bill as reported from the House with only a few changes, notably a decrease in the num-

The Federal Reserve Board, December 1919. Glass, secretary of the Treasury, is seated fifth from the left (courtesy of Underwood & Underwood).

ber of Reserve Banks from 15 to 12. After conferencing, both houses passed the Federal Reserve Act on December 23, 1913, and President Wilson signed it into law on the same day.

Glass's views on banking and finance had been strongly colored by adviser Willis's adherence to a prominent banking theory of the day, the "real bills" doctrine. Proponents of the real bills doctrine maintained that banks should discount only short-term commercial bills used to finance goods in the process of production or exchange. If the banks limited themselves to making those kinds of loans, they could meet the legitimate needs of business for credit without inflating the currency. Although regarded as a panacea by modern analysts, contemporaries viewed the real bills doctrine as the solution to problems of American banking. As one of its strongest academic supporters, Willis claimed that the Federal Reserve Act put the doctrine into effect, although other academics and members of Congress did not fully share that view. More important, few members of the Federal Reserve Board of Governors adhered to the doctrine as strongly as Willis and Glass, setting the stage for future con-

flict. The outbreak of World War I delayed confrontation over the issue of Reserve Bank discounting practices. Meeting the government's war finance needs required the full attention of the Board of Governors.

As a chief architect of Democratic banking reform, Glass enjoyed great favor in the Wilson White House. When Secretary of the Treasury William G. McAdoo resigned in December of 1918, Wilson appointed Glass in his place. Almost immediately a crisis confronted the new secretary, as resistance to government borrowing mounted once the war ended. Glass fought a bitter battle over the issue of a "Victory Loan" for 1919-1920. In spite of the experts' pessimism, the loan was oversubscribed. One of Glass's great frustrations was that as interest in the Victory Loan waned, the stock market started to boom. The advance of the market could have been slowed by raising the discount rate, but that would have forced the government to borrow at higher rates itself.

Glass also faced the seemingly intractable problem of reorganizing postwar international finance. The French and the other Allies attempted to discuss the issue of allied government loans during the Paris Peace Conference. Glass resisted their efforts and any attempt to write off the loans or to link economic and political issues in the debate.

Glass served only briefly as secretary of the Treasury. The death of Senator Thomas S. Martin of Virginia in late 1919 left a vacancy that the governor wished to fill with a popular figure. Glass was probably happy to leave the troubled Treasury, and resigned from the cabinet February 2, 1920, to receive the appointment. He became a fixture in the Senate, winning election in 1924 and reelection in 1930, 1936, and 1942. Initially, as a former cabinet member, he did not entirely escape the problems of the Wilson administration. He found himself defending its policies, arguing soon after he assumed office, for example, on the losing side of the League of Nations debate.

Glass considered the establishment of the Federal Reserve System the finest achievement of his political career. He opposed tampering with his creation and often fought on the defensive, responding to criticism from inside and outside of Congress. In the Senate, when the post–World War I recession and deflation hit, Glass defended the operation of the Federal Reserve System against critics who wanted to see a quick expansion of credit. Sniping by populist opponents of the banking establishment continued through the 1920s. Glass's most extensive reply to critics of the Federal Reserve came in response to the publication of a history of the Federal Reserve Act written by Charles Seymour, a professor at Yale. Seymour gave President Wilson's friend and adviser Colonel E. M. House a key role in the legislative process that created the system. To give the public his perspective on the origins of the Federal Reserve, Glass published *An Adventure in Constructive Finance* in 1927. The book chronicled the events leading up to the passage of the act and lavished praise on Wilson while playing down House's role.

Although Glass staunchly defended the Federal Reserve, the growing speculative activity that he perceived in the stock market alarmed him. In letters to the *New York Times* and the *Journal of Commerce* in 1928 and early 1929 Glass warned the public of the dangers of speculation. He pointed to the rapid rise of brokers' loans as proof that the Federal Reserve System had failed to prevent excess and implored the Board of Governors to take action. He grew increasingly concerned and lashed out at "stock gambling," contrasting it to "productive" activities such as farming.

The Federal Reserve was not unmoved by events. The rapidly rising stock market worried the Federal Reserve Bank of New York, which applied to the Reserve Board to increase its discount rate. The board declined that request nine times until August 1929, leaving the Federal Reserve Banks with only moral suasion to deter member banks from making speculative loans. In spite of most critics' complaints about the Federal Reserve's laxity, it had maintained a tight policy since early 1928. By the time it raised the discount rate in August, the economy had already slumped into a recession. The stock market collapsed in October, but not in direct response to tight money. The market had boomed even when the rate of interest on brokers' loans soared in 1929. The crash constituted a reaction to the dramatic decline in the economy that was itself partly propelled into recession by the rise in the discount rate.

The October crash of the stock market appeared to fulfill Glass's predictions. In 1930 he began an investigation of activities of commercial banks that might have contributed to the boom and crash. He focused on securities affiliates, the organizing means by which banks had successfully penetrated the investment banking business in the late 1920s. The rapid growth of those affiliates and their ability to reach out to new customers made them likely offenders.

Although Glass began his investigation in 1930 the Republicans still controlled the Senate. They did not obstruct Glass in his investigation, but he knew that he could not propose any major reforms. Hearings of the Senate Banking Committee were held in the winter of 1931 before a subcommittee chaired by Glass, and a year later before the full committee. To assist him with the preparation of legislation to correct the defects in the Federal Reserve System, Glass again turned to H. Parker Willis.

Glass and Willis viewed the Federal Reserve System as a failure because it allowed commercial banks to venture into the business of investment banking, thereby violating the real bills doctrine. To rectify the situation they composed a bill to divorce the two activities over a five-year period. Although many of the carefully selected witnesses they called advocated a complete separation of commercial and investment banking, few congressmen and bankers shared that view. Most congressmen would have been reasonably satisfied merely by subjecting the se-

Glass with Federal Reserve Board chairman Marriner S. Eccles and Alabama representative Henry B. Steagall admiring Glass's commemorative plaque in the Federal Reserve Building, 1937 (courtesy of the Marriner S. Eccles Foundation)

curities affiliates to federal regulation and examination.

Glass, however, was determined to obtain a complete separation. At his insistence the Democratic platform for the 1932 election campaign called for the severance of securities companies from their parent commercial banks. On the campaign trail for the Democratic presidential nominee, Franklin D. Roosevelt, he blasted the Herbert Hoover administration for its failure to prevent the "lawless affiliates" of the big banks from unloading billions of dollars of worthless securities on the public. The Democratic victory in 1932 gave the persuasive and obstinate Glass an agreeable president and the Senate majority he needed to obtain the separation in the face of heavy banker opposition.

The final collapse of the banking system in March 1933 and the Roosevelt "bank holiday" brought further discredit on the banks and gave Glass and his supporters an easy victory. The bill that engineered the separation, the Banking Act of 1933, commonly referred to as the Glass-Steagall

Act, also provided for the establishment of the Federal Deposit Insurance Corporation (FDIC). Glass was no friend of deposit insurance, and he recognized many of its inherent problems. Nevertheless, he accepted the FDIC in order to secure quick passage of those provisions of the bill that he earnestly desired. The passage of the Glass-Steagall Act represented a major achievement. The senator won regard as one of the most influential Democrats in the area of economic policy.

Before assuming office Roosevelt had offered Glass his old post, secretary of the Treasury, but Glass declined the appointment. The senior senator from Virginia had been enthusiastic about the party's platform demand for a balanced budget and a reduction in government spending, but he disagreed with the President about the dangers of inflation and resented the fact that he would not have received a free choice of Treasury subordinates.

Although virtually all of Virginia's leading Democrats looked favorably upon the New Deal legislation passed during Roosevelt's "hundred day

Glass, senator from Virginia, with House Speaker John Nance Garner at a Washington, D.C., baseball game

honeymoon," Glass soon stood apart. He warned that Roosevelt was driving the country to destruction and that Congress had granted the president more power than Mussolini and Stalin put together. Glass antagonized the Roosevelt administration, but he never got out of touch with his constituency. Along with fellow Virginia senator Harry F. Byrd and key state politicians he tenaciously resisted demands that Virginia make state appropriations to match federal funds designated for poverty relief. Virginia's monthly relief payments remained among the lowest in the nation during the Depression. The primary recipients of Federal Emergency Relief Administration aid, poor rural whites and urban blacks, were the groups that had been largely disenfranchised by the Virginia constitution of 1901.

Glass and his junior colleague Byrd soon stood out among Senate Democrats in their opposition to the New Deal. They led the fight against the $4 billion appropriation funding the Works Progress Administration in 1935. Glass condemned the bill, which gave the President enormous discretionary power over how to spend the appropriation, then the largest peacetime appropriation in Ameri-

can history. The Virginians' opposition probably cost the state dearly.

Although Glass did not attack the president personally, he kept up his attacks on the New Deal and continually voted against the administration's proposals. Glass topped all Democratic senators in that regard, casting a "no" vote 81 percent of the time. He denounced Roosevelt's proposal to devalue the dollar and was the only Democrat to vote against the devaluation bill. He also voted against the regulation of utility holding companies, "soak-the-rich" taxes, and most spending measures and became a favorite of conservatives. Typical of his uncompromising opposition, he wrote to Representative James Beck concerning the pending National Industrial Recovery bill, "The so-called Recovery Act is not only unconstitutional, but it has been administered with a degree of brutality that has created a reign of terror and put industry, and individual business, in involuntary servitude." To liberal journalist Walter Lippmann he wrote that the National Recovery Administration created by the act was an attempt "to transplant Hitlerism to every corner of this nation." In mild rebuke, Roosevelt described the caustic Virginia senator as an "unreconstructed rebel."

Even though Glass scourged the New Dealers, he was not averse to ensuring that Virginia obtained her share of appropriations. Relations with the administration grew particularly bitter when Secretary of the Interior Harold Ickes attempted to withhold Public Works Administration (PWA) funds from Virginia because of Glass's attacks in Congress. Ickes described Glass as "typical of the political hypocrites that bite the hand that feeds them. . . . No Senator comes oftener and with more insistence for PWA grants than does . . . Senator Glass."

Roosevelt's enormous victory in Virginia in the presidential election of 1936, in which he garnered more than 70 percent of the vote, represented a threat to Glass. Roosevelt shifted his support to committed New Dealers in Virginia and might have challenged the senator, except for the recovery of the economy. With conditions improving, Glass's attacks against the programs of the administration seemed less dangerous. Pleas for states' rights and Jeffersonian opposition to big government offered by the aging politician retained their appeal with the electorate, however. Although in failing health, Glass easily won reelection for the last time in 1942, at the age of eighty-four. He continued to serve in the Senate until his death on May 28, 1946.

In many respects Glass typified the Democratic politicians of the South in the first half of the twentieth century. He presided over a powerful political machine created, in part, by the disenfranchisement of poor blacks and whites. He attempted to preserve the status quo and resisted political and social change.

In economic matters Glass fought, at least rhetorically, the growth of federal bureaucracy and big spending under the New Deal. Ironically, the two pieces of legislation he considered his finest achievements, the Federal Reserve Act and the Glass-Steagall Act, represented major interventions by the federal government in financial matters. He saw such intervention necessary in that single area, because the system needed legislation to enforce the operation of the real bills doctrine. Glass's legacy was, however, costly. The weak and decentralized character of the Federal Reserve System contributed to the collapse of the economy in the 1930s, and the Glass-Steagall Act tended to reduce efficiency and competition in the banking industry.

Publication:

An Adventure in Constructive Finance (New York: Doubleday, Page, 1927).

References:

Ronald L. Heinemann, *Depression and New Deal in Virginia the Enduring Dominion* (Charlottesville: University Press of Virginia, 1983);

James E. Palmer, Jr., *Carter Class, Unreconstructed Rebel* (Roanoke, Va.: Institute of American Biography, 1938);

Rixey Smith and Norman Beasley, *Carter Glass: A Biography* (New York: Longmans, Green, 1939);

Robert Craig West, *Banking Reform and the Federal Reserve, 1863-1923* (Ithaca, N.Y.: Cornell University Press, 1977);

Eugene N. White, *The Regulation and Reform of the American Banking System, 1900-1929* (Princeton: Princeton University Press, 1983).

Glass-Steagall Act

by Eugene N. White

Rutgers University

One feature of the American financial system after the New Deal that distinguished it from the systems of European nations was the separation of commercial and investment banking. This division was created by the Banking Act of 1933, generally known as the Glass-Steagall Act after its sponsors, Senator Carter Glass of Virginia and Representative Henry B. Steagall of Alabama. The act forbade member banks of the Federal Reserve System from affiliating with any firm engaged in the issue, flotation, underwriting, public sale, or distribution at wholesale or retail through syndicate participation of securities. It also restricted the underwriting activities of commercial banks, prohibited partners or officials of securities firms from serving as directors or officers of member banks of the Federal Reserve System, augmented the supervisory power of the Federal Reserve, and established the Federal Deposit Insurance Corporation. Congress passed the law in June 1933, during the flurry of activity following Roosevelt's assumption of the presidency, in reaction to the widespread belief in Congress that the connection of securities affiliates and commercial banks had contributed to the Depression and threatened the control of the Federal Reserve over the nation's credit.

The passage of the Glass-Steagall Act represented a response not only to the Depression but also to the rapid penetration of the securities business by commercial banks. In the Banking Act of 1864, Congress had originally intended to restrict commercial banks to a narrow range of investments—short-term paper financing only goods in the process of production or exchange. But it wrote a loophole clause into the law, permitting banks to perform "incidental" activities to further their business. Courts interpreted the clause to mean that banks could take up any activity not specifically prohibited in the law. As markets for financial services grew more competitive in the post-Civil War period

of industrialization and urbanization, commercial banks found themselves pressured by new rivals—trust companies, savings banks, and investment banks take up new activities. While the Federal Reserve Act prohibited commercial banks from providing many types of financial intermediation directly, the banks discovered that they could establish affiliates to provide the additional services. Banks created their first affiliates to compete with trust companies, which were able to offer both trust services and commercial banking services.

The First National Bank of New York created the first investment banking, or security, affiliate in 1908. National City Bank followed in 1911. Before the creation of the securities affiliates banks already offered brokerage and investment services to their customers for bonds. The affiliates offered a key additional advantage in that they could also underwrite and distribute stocks, which federal law barred the commercial banks from handling.

The demand for investment banking services increased rapidly during World War I. Many banks got their first taste of the business when the federal government pressed them to sell "Liberty" bonds. After gaining the wartime experience, in the 1920s commercial banks quickly shifted to other types of securities. Two factors played important roles in the creation of this new business: first, foreign securities markets boomed after the war, as Americans assumed the role of creditor nation, lending funds to reconstruct Europe and the world, and, second, modern corporations more often met their financing needs through the issue of stocks and bonds rather than commercial loans. To follow their customers, banks were forced to provide them with investment banking services.

The commercial banks had other reasons for favorably viewing an increased connection between commercial and investment banking. Commercial banks traditionally enjoyed a larger clientele than

President Franklin D. Roosevelt signing the Glass-Steagall Act, June 16, 1933. Cosponsors Senator Carter Glass of Virginia and Representative Henry B. Steagall of Alabama stand third from the left and sixth from the left (courtesy of Keystone).

the investment houses, and they used that greater customer base to expand the securities market into the middle class. The research staffs employed to analyze securities enabled the banks to improve their portfolio selection. The growth of a bank's securities business also diversified its operations, helping to minimize fluctuations in its earnings. By the end of the 1920s those advantages and the growth of the securities markets gave commercial banks a major influence in the investment business. Banks and their affiliates, for example, gained approximately 50 percent of bond originations and participations.

The October 1929 stock market crash and the subsequent collapse of the securities market led investors to the conclusion that the banks were responsible. Yet during the decade of expansion few had publicly criticized the growing interconnection, and Congress had ignored separation proposals. Still, after the onset of the Depression critics uncovered a case for reform, pointing to the possible conflict of interest arising from a bank serving customers both as depositors and investors and claiming that the securities affiliates threatened the soundness of the banking system as a whole.

In retrospect, however, little economic rationale seems to have existed for divorcing the commercial from investment banking. The affiliates appear not to have contributed to the Depression banking crisis. The liquidity and solvency of banks were not affected by their affiliates. Most significant, the failure rate for banks with affiliates was much lower than the failure rate for banks without affiliates. Banks with affiliates were generally much larger than average, which gave them protection through diversification of their activities. Abuses in sales and manipulation of securities occurred, but non-bank-affiliated firms committed offenses as often as did affiliated firms. The New Deal legislation regulating the sale and distribution of securities, the Securities Act of 1933 and the Securities Exchange Act of 1934 generally solved those problems. The laws applied to the securities affiliates without separating them from their parent organizations.

A key participant in the design of the Federal Reserve System, Glass had specific views concerning how the country's banking system should operate. When the issue of the relationship of commercial and investment banking first arose in Congress in 1930, Glass found little support for his view that they should be separated. The Federal Reserve Board, the Treasury Department, the White House, and the banks opposed him as well. As chairman of the Senate Banking and Currency Committee, he put the bankers on trial. His chief counsel, Ferdinand Pecora, blamed them for fostering speculation. Glass concluded the hearings, arguing: "The more intensive participation by commercial banks in the capital market exaggerates financial and business fluctuations and undermines the stability of the economic organization of the country."

While the Glass-Steagall Act forced a dissolution of the securities affiliates and a split in the banking industry, commercial banks retained some investment banking functions. The act implicitly established a cost-benefit test, allowing banks to participate in certain parts of the securities business. That arose from the fact that commercial banks were permitted to underwrite debt instruments of the federal government and general obligation municipal bonds, considered lower-risk paper than corporate securities. The act also allowed affiliates of commercial banks to engage in some investment banking activities provided they were not principally engaged in those activities. In 1947 the Supreme Court in *Board of Governors of the Federal Reserve System* v. *Agnew* further defined the extent to which commercial bank affiliates could engage in investment banking, by setting upper limits on the percentage of income, number of transactions, and the market value of dealings in corporate securities.

Given those loopholes in the Glass-Steagall Act, banks and securities firms have continually tested its limits. In the 1960s commercial banks began to offer common trust funds for agency accounts, automatic investment services, dividend reinvestment plans, individual portfolio management services, and advice to investment companies. Litigation has arisen challenging those newer commercial bank functions, including the 1971 Supreme Court case *Investment Company Institute* v. *Camp*, in which the court decided that commercial bank operation of a commingled investment fund for large investors violated the act.

The growth of multinational banking led to a partial circumvention of the act in the 1970s and 1980s. Many large American banks employ overseas affiliates that engage in underwriting and Eurosecurities market. Foreign bank affiliates in the United States manage to offer both commercial and investment services through subsidiaries. The securities firms have begun to mimic the commercial firms, by offering a variety of accounts that resemble checking accounts. They have also formed alliances with foreign banks and set up their own commercial affiliates.

Recognizing the increasing difficulty of controlling the gradual reintegration of commercial and investment banking, Congress has considered scrapping the Glass-Steagall Act, but so far attempts have met with little success. The investment banks firmly oppose a change, preferring to do business without full competition from the commercials, which came close to domination in the industry before the Depression. The act continues to impose substantial costs on the banking industry by preventing the combination within individual firms of strongly complimentary activities. Lack of full competition in the investment industry, moreover, has probably raised the cost of capital to issuers, and commercial bank customers must go elsewhere to secure some investment services.

References:

Vincent P. Carosso, *Investment Banking in America* (Cambridge, Mass.: Harvard University Press, 1970);

Franklin R. Edwards, "Banks and Securities Activities: Legal and Economic Perspectives," in Lawrence G. Goldberg and J. White, eds., *The Deregulation of the Banking and Securities Industries* (Lexington, Mass.: Heath, 1979), pp. 273-304;

Thomas F. Huertas, "The Economic Brief Against Glass-Steagall," *Journal of Bank Research*, 15 (1984): 148-159;

W. Nelson Peach, *The Securities Affiliates of National Banks* (Baltimore: Johns Hopkins University Press, 1941);

Edward J. Perkins, "The Divorce of Commercial and Investment Banking: A History," *Banking Law Journal*, 88 (1971): 483-529;

Eugene N. White, "Before the Glass-Steagall Act: An Analysis of the Investment Banking Activities of National Banks," *Explorations in Economic History* (January 1986): 33-55.

Joshua Green

(October 16, 1869 - January 25, 1975)

by Barry Provorse

Documentary Book Publishers

CAREER: Railroad surveyor's assistant (1888-?); partner, LaConner Trading and Transportation Company (?-1903); president, Puget Sound Navigation Company (1903-1923); director, National Bank of Commerce (1906-?); chairman, Peoples National Bank of Washington [Peoples Savings Bank to 1927, Peoples Bank and Trust Company to 1937] (1925-1962); chairman, Peoples Corporation (1929-1962).

The first member of the Green family to get involved in banking was Maryland druggist John Green, who began accepting deposits from his customers in the early 1800s. Two of his three sons, Joshua and Thomas, settled in Jackson, Mississippi, in the late 1840s and founded the J. and T. Green Bank there. The third brother, George, moved to Texas and also entered the banking business. Joshua Green's son, William Henry Harrison Green, was born an aristocrat, served in the Confederate army, and returned from the Civil War to find the J. and T. Green Bank looted. His talents as a banker were wasted in a region ravaged by war and bereft of cash and commerce.

William Henry Harrison Green married Bentonia Harrison and, on October 16, 1869, the couple had a son they named Joshua after William's father. For the next 20 years the family struggled to make a living in the depressed southern economy. In 1888 William Green moved his family to what he hoped would be greener pastures in Seattle, Washington. There he worked as a salesman.

In Seattle, Joshua found work as a railroad surveyor's assistant, but he made more pocket money on the side as a "banker" without portfolio, discounting and cashing pay vouchers for cash-hungry construction workers who could not or would not wait for payday. Soon he and two partners borrowed enough money to purchase a steamboat, the *Fanny Lake*. Later, with more borrowed money,

Joshua Green (courtesy of PeoplesBank Archives)

Green and his partners formed the LaConner Trading and Transportation Company, which they merged with other interests to form the Puget Sound Navigation Company in 1903. The new company became the largest inland steamship company on Puget Sound, and Green, who owned 40 percent of the stock, assumed its presidency. He ran the company for 20 years in near autonomy, but in 1923 one of his partners' sons, Alexander Peabody, took an interest in the management of the company, and

Green sold out. He took a few years off to figure out what he wanted to do with his money.

In 1925, somewhere among 18 holes of golf, attorney E. S. McCord offered Green a majority interest in a small Seattle bank, Peoples Savings Bank. McCord represented the Edward C. Neufelder estate, which had owned 88 percent of the institution. After a brief negotiating period, Green wrote out a check for $308,000 and the same day wrote to his banker at Chase in New York, M. G. B. Whelpley: "I found it necessary today to close the purchase of the Peoples Savings Bank. . . . I paid $350 a share and bought 880 shares of their stock. They have 1,000 altogether." Green also advised Whelpley, "I am afraid the check will arrive in New York before your note for $350,000 reaches me and I can sign it and return it to you, so I wish you would protect the check."

His father had always counseled Joshua Green to steer clear of banking, but on several occasions the younger Green had successfully invested in several start-up banks around Puget Sound. He used that method to tie Puget Sound Navigation Company to the communities it served; in addition, the investments often proved profitable.

In 1923 Green tried to acquire a small Seattle bank, Bank for Savings, from its mostly French absentee stockholders. Although unsuccessful in his bid for a controlling interest in that bank, he later sold what he had to the bank's management at a substantial profit. Green also invested in Washington National Bank, which later merged with another institution and became the National Bank of Commerce of Seattle (NB of C). He had served as a director of that bank from 1906.

With Peoples Savings Bank, Green felt that he could not lose. Though it was too small to compete against other commercial banks, it was situated on prime real estate, and the value of the land and the bank building exceeded $650,000. Green also knew through his friendship with NB of C president Manson Backus that Seattle's larger banks were following the national trend toward consolidation and wanted to acquire his bank if given the opportunity.

Green was not much of a banker, but then Peoples was not much of a bank either. Though the bank's assets were small, its pedigree was solid. It had been founded in 1889 by several of Seattle's most noted pioneers, including famed bankers Bailey Gatzert, Arthur Denny, and Jacob Furth. It had

seen remarkable periods of growth, but the most remarkable thing about it was the fact that it had survived the panics of 1893 and 1907 and the recent World War I recession.

Green made his intentions clear when he wrote to his banker, Whelpley: "I mean to retain the present staff, which is an excellent one and add to it one or two young Seattle men with push and energy to make a lively little bank out of it." By the end of the year Green had hired Albert Brygger, a tough former professional boxer, as Peoples' president. Brygger was an experienced banker who had served as a vice-president of NB of C when he and Green first became acquainted.

Green and Brygger thought Peoples was too small to service even the corner grocer. After 37 years in business, its assets totaled only $5.2 million, and its capital stock had not increased since its founding. Green's goals for his first year with Peoples were to increase its pitifully small capital base of $100,000 and increase its deposits by $1 million. Brygger's task was to manage the bank, assess its growth needs, and recharter it into a commercial bank.

The Green-Brygger tandem proved a good marriage of talent and personality. The flamboyant Green knew little of banking regulations, but he did know how to raise capital and how to sell. Brygger knew how to run a bank.

To solicit business, Green wrote to virtually all of his friends and business associates. To the head of the Standard Oil Corporation he explained, "Through the Peoples Savings Bank my close friends in Seattle have . . . purchased about 25,000 shares of your company's stock." Then Green asked for and got Standard Oil's Seattle banking business. Green also opened accounts for the Northern Pacific Railway and the Chicago, Milwaukee, St. Paul & Pacific Railroad as well as many other businesses.

Green used Peoples Bank stock to lure local accounts. To Whelpley he wrote: "I mean from time to time to place it [Peoples Bank stock] among influential friends that will give the bank business." He also recognized Peoples' need for a stronger board, and by the end of 1926 its directors included Nathan Eckstein, Edward Garrett, Fred Struve, and Bennett McCord, whom he chose for "their financial position in the community and because they all live well-balanced wholesome lives, have fine wives and families, and are held in the highest respect in the community."

By the end of 1927 the bank had its new board, new customers, new capital, and also a new state charter. It had been reorganized as a state commercial bank: Peoples Bank and Trust Company. In a letter to steamship magnate Stanley Dollar, Green summed up his quick success: "When I bought it a year ago, it had five million dollars in deposits and capital of one hundred thousand dollars. I have increased the capital to one-half million, and deposits today are over eight million. It is earning between thirty and forty percent on the capital and doing it very conservatively."

While Peoples restructured, Andrew Price and the Price holding company, Marine Bancorporation, acquired NB of C in 1928. Using the holding company to circumvent the state's prohibition of branch banking, Price had acquired control of banks with combined assets in excess of $50 million. Then came the $80 million consolidation of three major Seattle commercial banks to form Seattle-First National Bank. Green valued control over size, and he refused to trade stock for size. Subsequently Peoples experienced less vigorous growth. But in 1929 Green formed Peoples Corporation, a holding company that owned all of the stock in Peoples Bank and Trust Company, and with handpicked partners he formed Peoples First Avenue Bank and Peoples Security Company.

Peoples Corporation experienced considerable shrinkage during the nation's slide into depression. Its book value fell to $15 a share, but the company survived. The national banking holiday in 1933 forced Green to commit nearly all of his assets to secure Peoples Bank, and following the holiday the bank reopened with a clean bill of health from the federal bank examiner's office.

Even in the face of a failed Peoples Security Company and an extended absence of dividends,

Green still loved the exhilaration of the banking business, and when the opportunity arose for Peoples to take over a small, failed West Seattle bank, Green accepted the challenge. Washington State bank regulations changed in 1933 to allow branch banking, and Peoples' West Seattle location became the first branch of Peoples Bank and Trust Company and the first branch bank in the state of Washington.

In 1937, basking in a slow but steady recovery with operating profits in excess of $200,000, Peoples converted to a national charter and changed its name to Peoples National Bank of Washington. Its branch network development continued in western Washington, and by the end of 1939 the bank's capital had increased by $1.5 million, and its deposits exceeded $30 million.

Rampant growth followed the outbreak of World War II in 1941, and by 1945 the bank's war-swollen deposits surpassed $160 million, and its list of depositors had tripled to 95,000. But Green had lost some of his fire, and the bank's president, Albert Brygger, resigned for reasons of health and moved south to Arizona. Philip G. Strack was elected president and served out the decade in that capacity. By the end of the 1940s Peoples National Bank capital had grown to exceed $6 million.

Green married Laura Moore Turner on April 24, 1901. The couple had three children. Green continued as chairman of Peoples National Bank until his retirement, at the age of ninety-three, in 1962. He served as honorary chairman of the bank until his death on January 25, 1975, at the age of one hundred five.

Reference:

Barry Provorse, *The PeoplesBank Story* (Bellevue, Wash.: Documentary Book Publishers, 1987).

Joshua Green, Jr.

(December 9, 1908 - October 18, 1985)

by Barry Provorse

Documentary Book Publishers

CAREER: Messenger, assistant cashier, vice-president, executive vice-president (1929-1949), president (1949-1962), chairman, Peoples National Bank of Washington [Peoples Bank and Trust Company to 1937] (1962-1979).

During his steamboating days Joshua Green invested in the future in more ways than through the acquisition of stocks and bonds. On December 9, 1908, a son and namesake was born to the steamboat man and his wife, Laura Moore Turner Green. Joshua Green, Jr., was not raised to become a banker: as a steamboat man's son with no interest in his father's enterprises. He attended prep school in Lawrenceville, Kansas, when his father purchased Peoples Savings Bank in 1925; following his graduation he attended Harvard University and planned his own career in the East, far away from the family's interests.

Rightfully worried about orderly transition in the event of the elder Green's death, Peoples president Albert Brygger argued against the patriarch's view that "a family shouldn't put all its eggs in one basket." Brygger pointed out that if Green died, Green, Jr., would have to face the problem of controlling the bank. Brygger pointed out, "We'd have a helluva time with a greenhorn in that situation." The president offered to train Green, Jr., and guaranteed to "make a first-class banker out of him."

By June 1929 Green, Jr., had already accepted a job in Boston with the engineering and construction firm of Stone and Webster when he received a telephone call from Brygger. "Mr. Brygger, whom I had never met, called me and asked me to come out and join the bank. His interest was flattering and his argument compelling, so I came out from the East and got a lucrative job with the bank, starting at $60 a month as a messenger."

At first Green, Jr., felt indifferent to banking, and the constant prodding he received from his father made the task of learning more difficult. Though impatient with his son, Green told the bank's attorney, Phillip MacBride, "It's most important that he [Green, Jr.] learn to love the Bank like you and I do, and the only way to love a bank or a child or anything else is to have it make you work hard, give you a little trouble, and occupy a lot of your time."

The economy, more than the bank, tempered Green, Jr.'s, career. He recalled, "I started banking when the nation's economy was at its peak and I watched it drop to a point where everything was almost worthless, and I think that the most valuable part of my education came in 1929. We had a large and very active investment company and we were doing a very large volume of business before everything went sour. It was a real learning experience to see how fast good things could go bad."

Brygger served as young Green's mentor, and in December 1931 he became his father-in-law when Green married Elaine Brygger. In June 1936 the Green line was lengthened by the birth of Joshua Green III. Green, Jr., spent most of his time managing the family's holding company, the Joshua Green Corporation, until December 1941, when he joined the U.S. Navy and served until the end of World War II.

Upon his return to Seattle following his military service, Green, Jr., found a different and much larger Peoples National Bank. Brygger had taken up other interests and moved to Arizona, and Phillip Strack had replaced him as the company's president. The bank's deposits had grown from the 1939 total of $30 million to almost $160 million. It served 95,000 customers where in 1939 it had just more than 30,000 accounts. The bank's book value had almost doubled in five years.

Joshua Green, Jr. (courtesy of PeoplesBank Archives)

A different Green returned to the bank: self-confident, quiet, with a cautious sense of purpose. He slowly took charge, and on October 11, 1949, he became president of Peoples National Bank of Washington. Strack moved to a new position: chairman of the executive committee.

By 1950 Peoples had 11 offices. Green, Jr., and Strack preferred to build new branches from the ground up. Neither had a taste for bidding wars. Most banks were being purchased at the time at book value plus a percentage of the bank's deposits, which was paid as a premium. Since the war's end, a rival Seattle bank, National Bank of Commerce, had purchased ten banks, and another rival, Seattle-First National, had acquired nine banks and also established seven new branches.

Like his father, Green, Jr., was an avid bird hunter with a preference for eastern Washington duck and pheasant. In his quest for game he estab-lished many relationships east of the Cascade Mountains. In 1953 Peoples acquired Grant County Bank and Othello State Bank. During the remainder of the 1950s Green, Jr., expanded the bank's interests in eastern and western Washington, and by the end of the decade Peoples had 11 branches in Seattle, eight branches in outlying western Washington, and five offices in the eastern part of the state. Total assets exceeded $221 million.

In 1962 Green, Jr., replaced his ninety-three-year-old father as chairman of Peoples National Bank. He served in that capacity until 1979, when he was made honorary chairman. He died on October 18, 1985.

Reference:

Barry Provorse, *The PeoplesBank Story* (Bellevue, Wash.: Documentary Book Publishers, 1987).

Joshua Green III

(June 30, 1936 -)

by Barry Provorse

Documentary Book Publishers

CAREER: Auditor and other positions (1960-1972), president (1972-1979), chairman, Peoples National Bank of Washington (1979-1987); vice-chairman and chief executive officer, U.S. Bancorporation (1987-).

On June 30, 1936, banker Joshua Green, Jr., and Elaine Green had a son, Joshua "Jay" Green III, in Seattle, Washington. Both Green's grandfather, the first generation of the Green family of bankers in Washington State, and his father gave him an appreciation of the out-of-doors as a youth. Green attended the Lakeside School in Seattle before leaving for Harvard University to pursue interests in geology and invertebrate paleontology. He graduated from Harvard with a degree in English.

After graduation from Harvard, Green accepted a management training position with the Citicorp financial services organization in New York, where he gained not only a knowledge of banking operations but also, as part of a group of aggressively trained entry-level managers, exposure to Citicorp's strong work ethic. Green learned that he liked banking and that he could compete in the banking industry, but he did not like living in New York. In 1960 he returned to Seattle and a position as auditor for his grandfather and father's Peoples National Bank of Washington. During the 1960s he served in several other positions with the bank, moving up in the corporate hierarchy. In 1969 he assumed a director's position at Peoples.

Some time after Green assumed the director's position, longtime Peoples' director L. K. Lyle observed that the third in the Green line "learned how to use the bank's board from his father and grandfather. Peoples was the only bank in town where the head completely controlled the bank. Therefore, they really didn't have to listen very hard to their board. They really never had to take the board's recommendations, yet they seemed to bend over back-

Joshua Green III (Courtesy of PeoplesBank Archives)

ward to see that they did listen. The board of Peoples throughout the years had more influence, independent of the management of the bank, than others, and the Greens wanted the benefit of their board's opinion and they did more than other banks in keeping us informed on areas they felt needed discussion."

Following 12 years of preparation and the unexpected death of bank president Harold Rogers, Joshua Green III assumed the Peoples' presidency in 1972. He chose to become a strong leader. He took special interest in the expansion of the bank's electronic and computer systems, believing that greater investment in technology meant increased competitiveness. In 1975 he approved the addition of the

BankAmericard (later VISA) credit card system to the bank's services offerings, arguing successfully against an old guard on the Board of Directors (led by his father) that opposed credit card issues. That same year Green's grandfather, still a significant presence at the bank at one hundred five years of age, died. Green's father retired from active participation in the daily affairs of the bank in 1979. Peoples had tallied an impressive array of accomplishments by that time. Deposits had increased from $160 million in 1949 to nearly $1.5 billion. The number of Peoples' branches had expanded from 11 in 1949 to more than 80. Capitalization had increased from almost $15 million to more than $93 million.

In his first years as Peoples president Green also oversaw an increase in Peoples' commercial loan business. By 1980 commercial loans made up $245 million of the bank's total loan portfolio of $837 million. The bank's share of the area's commercial loan business increased still further in 1983, following the near failure of the Seattle-First National Bank due to an overconcentration in energy loans during a period of consolidation in that industry. By 1985 Peoples' commercial loan growth rate stood at 40 percent per year.

Increased competition in the retail side of the business resulted from growth in money market accounts after 1978 and from an increase in the number of nonbank financial services firms. With margins shrinking, banks, including Peoples, began looking for new markets and services. In 1980 the bank formed a holding company, Peoples Bancorporation, to aid interstate expansion. A brokerage company followed in 1983. The bank also implemented an increased fee structure.

On July 1, 1987, the state legislature amended Washington State's banking laws to permit out-of-state financial institutions to acquire Washington banks. Peoples had clear options. It could either continue to grow within its marketplace and possibly acquire new markets, or it could sell. As early as 1982 the bank had explored merger opportunities. Following the sale that year of Old National Bancorporation, with which Peoples had discussed a merger, to U.S. Bancorporation of Portland, Oregon, Green commented, "There were not many banks of any size that were available for purchase after we lost out on the Old National Bank deal. We really thought we could operate quite profitably and compete at the size we were, and that over time we could acquire small independent banks and grow somewhat, but we wouldn't be able to make a quantum leap in size."

Peoples turned from potential buyer to seller, especially after loan shrinkage in 1986 silenced merger talk. The next year, after a return to profitability, Peoples accepted an offer by U.S. Bancorporation of 2.6 shares of its stock for each share of Peoples stock. Peoples contributed $2.2 billion in assets to the new $14 billion corporation. The Green family became the largest single stockholder. As part of the deal, U.S. Bancorporation merged Peoples and the Old National Bank to form U.S. National Bank. Green became vice-chairman and chief executive officer of the holding company. That firm entered the 1990s on a sound footing to compete in an increasingly competitive financial services environment.

Reference:

Barry Provorse, *The PeoplesBank Story* (Bellevue, Washington: Documentary Book Publishers, 1987).

Alan Greenspan

(March 6, 1926 -   )

by Douglas K. Pearce

North Carolina State University

CAREER: Research associate, National Industrial Conference Board (1948-1953); economic consultant (1953), president and chairman, Townsend-Greenspan & Company (1954-1974, 1977-1987); chairman, Council of Economic Advisers (1974-1977); member, President's Economic Advisory Board (1981); partner and chairman of the investment policy committee, Greenspan O'Neil Associates (1984-1987); chairman, Board of Governors of the Federal Reserve System (1987-).

Alan Greenspan is one of the most influential business economists of the post-World War II period. In addition to being a consultant to some of America's largest businesses, he has served as chairman of the Council of Economic Advisers under President Gerald R. Ford and is currently chairman of the Board of Governors of the Federal Reserve System.

Greenspan was born on March 6, 1926, in New York City, the only child of Herbert and Rose Greenspan. His father, a stockbroker, was a staunch New Deal supporter: he published a book in 1935 entitled *Recovery Ahead!* that predicted the policies of President Franklin D. Roosevelt would end the Depression. Greenspan's parents divorced in 1931, and mother and son moved into the home of her parents in the Washington Heights section of Manhattan. His mother's father was a Russian immigrant and a cantor, and Greenspan was raised in an atmosphere dominated by religion and music.

Greenspan went to George Washington High School, where he was an average student except in mathematics and music. Those two interests continued throughout his life. In Greenspan's own words: "I get the same kind of joy from solving a hard mathematical problem as I do from hearing a Haydn quartet." He first pursued music, and after graduating from high school in 1943 he enrolled at the Juilliard School to study clarinet. Then he joined a

Alan Greenspan

swing band and toured the country, but he soon tired of the musician's life. While on tour he began to read about economics and decided to pursue that interest.

Returning to New York, Greenspan entered New York University in 1945 and graduated summa cum laude in economics in 1948. He continued his studies there part-time, earning an M.A. in economics in 1950. His thesis investigated the relationship between income and consumption during the Depression. Greenspan continued his graduate work at Columbia University under Arthur F. Burns but left without earning his Ph.D.

Greenspan took his first job with the National Industrial Conference Board in 1948, estimating the demands for metals by the aircraft industry. He enjoyed plowing through the statistics and coming up with forecasts. Frank Ikard of the American Petroleum Institute, recalling Greenspan's early work, described him as the "kind of person who knew how many thousand flat-headed bolts were used in a 1964 Chevrolet and what it would do to the national economy if you took out three of them." Greenspan himself stated that "my key skill is knowing how to take fragmented numbers and develop from them a general picture of what's going on."

In 1953 Greenspan married Joan Mitchell, an artist, but the marriage was annulled after one year. Greenspan apparently has always put his job ahead of his personal life. His former wife has commented that "He's devoted to his work and he loves it—it's an all-consuming interest."

Also in 1953 Greenspan and William Townsend, a Wall Street bond trader, formed the economics consulting firm of Townsend-Greenspan & Company. The firm specialized in providing companies with forecasts specific to their industries. When Townsend died in 1958, Greenspan became the firm's president and principal owner. Townsend-Greenspan continued to prosper, and by 1974 Greenspan reportedly averaged more than $300,000 per year in income from the firm.

In 1952 Greenspan met the novelist and philosopher Ayn Rand. He was profoundly influenced by her "Objectivist" philosophy, in which the pursuit of the narrow self-interest of the individual is viewed as leading to the greatest social good. Objectivism has been closely linked to the laissez-faire capitalist outlook of eighteenth-century economist Adam Smith. Greenspan has said of Rand's influence, "What she did was to make me see that capitalism is not only efficient and practical, but also moral."

Rand's impact on Greenspan's views is evident in the three essays he contributed to Rand's *Capitalism: The Unknown Ideal*, published in 1966. In "Antitrust," a paper originally given at a meeting of the National Association of Business Economists in September 1961, Greenspan argues that the monopoly power that enables companies to charge higher prices than would prevail in a competitive industry can only arise from government action. He asserts that "the ultimate regulator of competition in a free economy is the capital market. So long as capital is free to flow, it will tend to seek those areas which offer the maximum rate of return." Greenspan's faith in the benign effects of unregulated competition is further reflected in his essay "The Assault on Integrity," in which he argues that consumer-protection laws are unnecessary because it is in firms' own self-interest to establish a reputation for quality. He views government regulation as stifling to innovation: "The guiding purpose of the government regulator is to prevent rather than to create something." Greenspan's belief that unregulated industry best satisfies social needs is consistently apparent throughout his career.

Given Greenspan's later appointment as chairman of the Federal Reserve System, his early views on the appropriate monetary system for the United States contained in his third essay in the Rand volume are of particular interest. In the essay "Gold and Economic Freedom" Greenspan asserts that the lack of a gold standard allows governments to run budget deficits that in turn cause central banks to accommodate the deficits through money creation. Because central banks cannot be relied upon to discipline fiscal policy, he recommends returning to a system of unregulated or "free" banking along with a strict gold standard, a combination that is "the protector of an economy's stability and balanced growth."

Greenspan's conservative views led him to the Republican party. After serving as an adviser to Richard M. Nixon during the 1968 presidential campaign, Greenspan turned down offers of official positions in the Nixon administration. He did, however, serve on three presidential committees. In March 1969 Greenspan was appointed to the President's Commission on an All-Volunteer Armed Force. Not surprisingly, he strongly supported the commission's basic recommendation, issued in February 1970, that the United States move toward a volunteer military with only a standby draft. In October 1969 he was appointed to the President's Task Force on Economic Growth. That 13-member bipartisan committee made recommendations for improving efficiency and protecting the environment in a report published in May 1970. Along with two other committee members Greenspan dissented from the general tone of the report, arguing that the committee had placed too little emphasis on promoting economic growth through private investment.

Greenspan's third committee appointment was to the President's Commission on Financial Structure and Regulation, popularly known as the Hunt Commission after its chairman, manufacturing executive Reed Oliver Hunt. The commission's final report dealt mainly with the need to deregulate the financial industry. In particular the commission recommended eliminating interest rate ceilings on savings and time deposits (the Federal Reserve System's Regulation Q), broadening the asset choices of depository institutions, and allowing nonbank depository institutions to offer demand deposits but forcing all institutions that issued demand deposits to join the Federal Reserve. Although Congress enacted none of the recommendations, the Hunt Commission proposals laid the groundwork for the passage of the Depository Institutions Deregulation and Monetary Control Act of 1980.

True to his free-market beliefs, Greenspan strongly opposed the Nixon administration's wage-price controls program begun in August 1971 and its loan guarantee for Lockheed Aircraft. Despite his opposition, in the summer of 1974 Greenspan was asked by his friend and former professor Arthur F. Burns, then chairman of the Federal Reserve System, and William E. Simon, secretary of the Treasury, to take the job of chairman of President Nixon's Council of Economic Advisers. Greenspan agreed, but before his Senate confirmation Nixon resigned. President Ford continued to support the appointment, however. The most visible opposition came from Senator William Proxmire, who sent letters to each member of the Senate Banking Committee questioning Greenspan's suitability. Proxmire's concerns focused on Greenspan's negative view of antitrust laws, consumer protection laws, and government regulation of business and finance in general. In addition, Proxmire stated that Greenspan "has the almost incredible posture for an economic realist in these days–of opposing the progressive income tax."

Despite Proxmire's efforts, the Senate confirmed Greenspan without a roll call, and on September 4, 1974, he took the oath of office. When asked why he decided to enter public service and take a pay cut of 85 percent, Greenspan replied, "What is at stake is so large that if anyone has the possibility of making a contribution, he should. It's one of the rare instances when the issue of patriotism comes up." Greenspan left his consulting firm

in the hands of employees, with his share of the profits going to employees and charities.

Greenspan took the job as the president's chief economic adviser at a time when the economy was arguably in the worst shape since the Depression. While 1971 and 1972 had been years of above-average real growth and relatively low inflation, the Nixon wage-price controls coupled with an expansionary monetary and fiscal policy built up inflationary pressures. In 1973, also a year of above-average growth in real output, the rate of consumer price inflation more than doubled from the previous year. The Arab oil embargo, beginning in the last quarter of 1973, further aggravated the situation by simultaneously raising the inflation rate and lowering domestic aggregate demand. The unemployment rate stood at 5 percent at the beginning of 1974 but rose continuously throughout the year, reaching 7.2 percent by December 1974–the highest level since the recession of 1958. As a result real output growth fell by 1.4 percent for the year. The severity of the recession was exacerbated by the highest annual inflation rate in the post-World War II era–11 percent.

According to traditional "Phillips curve" prescriptions, the twin problems of rapid inflation and high unemployment meant that the administration had to choose between stimulating the economy–with the risk of worsening the inflation–and slowing the economy–with the risk of aggravating the recession. The administration chose initially to fight inflation, with Greenspan arguing that "if we allow inflation to run wild and get away from us we run the more serious risk of even higher unemployment down the road." Accordingly, he supported Ford's fall 1974 proposal to increase taxes. The administration's emphasis on fighting inflation was likely due in part to a failure of economists to forecast the severity of the downturn. Greenspan later recalled, "In my last forecast as a private consultant, in the summer of 1974, I predicted 1975 would be a year of very shallow recession. When I arrived in Washington, I eventually presided over something that could more readily be described as the roof caving in." Critics accused the administration of insensitivity to the problems of the unemployed, and Greenspan did not help when he told a group of labor leaders that those who were hardest hit, in terms of percentage declines in income, were Wall Street stockbrokers. Nat Goldfinger of the AFL-CIO described Greenspan as one who "believes that everything

Greenspan (left) and Martin Anderson advising candidate Ronald Reagan during the presidential campaign of 1980 (UPI)

that has happened in the United States since about 1870 has been a mistake. And there aren't any people in his equation—just abstract numbers."

The rapid rise in unemployment in the latter half of 1974 convinced Greenspan that the government should redirect policy toward stimulating the economy, a view reflected in the opening statement of the 1975 *Economic Report of the President*: "The economy is in a severe recession." The policies recommended in the report remained consistent with Greenspan's conservative approach. To stimulate the economy the report recommended tax cuts totaling $23 billion for households and businesses. To ameliorate severe energy shortages Greenspan proposed the deregulation of oil and natural gas prices to spur the private sector to develop new sources of supply. Not surprisingly, given Greenspan's views on the pernicious effects of government regulation, the report devoted one chapter to the desirability of deregulation, especially in the transportation and financial services industries. Many of the recommendations for deregulating the financial sector looked similar to those proposed by the Hunt Commission.

Congress passed the proposed tax cuts in 1975 but successfully opposed decontrol of energy prices. Greenspan strongly urged Ford to allow the

price controls to lapse and veto any further restraints. At the end of 1975, however, Ford bowed to Congress and extended the controls. Although inflation moderated in 1975 and fell below that forecasted in the 1975 *Economic Report*, unemployment remained higher than anticipated at 8.5 percent. As a result, the Council of Economic Advisers recommended further fiscal stimulus in the form of more tax cuts. Fearing that another round of tax cutting would lead to larger budget deficits, higher interest rates, and a crowding out of private investment, the administration proposed tax cuts matched by spending cuts. Congress passed most of the tax cuts but not the cuts in spending.

The council's economic predictions for 1976, given in the 1976 *Economic Report of the President*, turned out to be quite accurate. Real output grew at a rapid 6.2 percent annual rate, right in the middle of the council's forecast range of 6 to 6.5 percent, and the unemployment rate for the year averaged 7.7 percent, slightly higher than predicted. The pattern of the unemployment rate posed the greatest problem for the administration: unemployment bottomed out in May at 7.3 percent and then rose during the presidential election campaign. Many observers thought that that sign of a deteriorating economy significantly damaged Ford's election chances.

The 1977 *Economic Report*, written after the Democratic presidential victory, gives a good summary of Greenspan's conservative economic views. The *Report* argued in favor of an expansionary fiscal policy implemented through tax cuts rather than spending increases, which would allow the government sector of the economy to shrink in importance over time. It stressed the need for reducing government regulation and, moreover, for reducing uncertainties about future government regulation. Regarding monetary policy, the *Report* was more monetarist than Keynesian in tone, recommending relatively low rates of growth in the money supply and the abandonment of interest rate targeting. It expressed pessimism about the likelihood of reducing unemployment through such government policies as public employment or tax incentives.

With the change to a Democratic administration, Greenspan returned to his consulting firm in January 1977. He also rejoined *Time* magazine's Board of Economists–he had initially served from 1971 to 1974–giving him the opportunity to comment from time to time on the general state of the economy. His government service made him a popular candidate for corporate directorships, and he joined the boards of the Aluminum Company of America (in 1978), Automatic Data Processing Corporation (1980), Capital Cities / American Broadcasting Corporation (1984), General Foods Corporation (1977), J. P. Morgan & Company (1977), Morgan Guaranty Trust Company (1977), Mobil Corporation (1977), and the Pittston Company (1985). Greenspan also joined the boards of the Rand Corporation and the Institute for International Economics and returned to the Board of the Hoover Institution and the Brookings Panel on Economic Activity. In addition to those activities, he finally completed a Ph.D. from New York University in 1977.

When the Republicans regained the White House in 1981, Greenspan agreed to become a member of President Ronald Reagan's Economic Advisory Board. Shortly after the new administration took office, concern grew over the solvency of the Social Security System. Increases in benefits, the generous indexation of benefits to inflation, and slower than expected wage growth had led to continuous increases in the payroll tax. Projections indicated that unacceptably large increases in the payroll tax

would be necessary in the future to protect the integrity of the system. President Reagan asked Greenspan to chair a national commission to recommend reform.

Few issues were as politically sensitive as changes in Social Security, and skepticism concerning the effectiveness of the bipartisan commission abounded. Greenspan was widely credited with forging a consensus for action. The commission urged Congress to retain the basic structure of the system rather than convert to voluntary participation or tie benefits strictly to need. It also recommended extending coverage to Federal employees, reducing indexation to inflation, taxing half of the benefits of higher-income recipients, relating benefit amounts more closely to contributions, and increasing the payroll tax. A minority of the commission, including Greenspan, also pushed for a gradual increase in the retirement age. Congress adopted most of the recommendations, and as of 1989 experts generally considered the Social Security System secure.

Although Greenspan's consulting firm continued to prosper, its entry into the portfolio management field proved disappointing. In 1984 Greenspan and two partners formed Greenspan O'Neil Associates to manage pension funds. The firm failed to generate much business, however, and disbanded in early 1987. According to the April 20, 1987 issue of *Forbes* magazine, the firm "turned in one of the least impressive records of all pension fund advisers."

Greenspan had long been considered a good candidate for the chairmanship of the Federal Reserve System. In 1983, when then-chairman Paul A. Volcker was up for reappointment, Greenspan was rumored to be a likely replacement. But Volcker's reputation as an inflation fighter and a supporter of a strong dollar, combined with the prevailing concern about a falling dollar, virtually forced President Reagan to reappoint Volcker, despite Reagan's reluctance to retain a Democratic appointee. In June 1987, near the end of his second four-year term as Fed chairman, Volcker informed Reagan that he did not wish to serve a third term. Apparently, little debate ensued over who should replace Volcker, and the White House announced the Greenspan nomination simultaneously with Volcker's resignation. Although financial markets initially reacted negatively to the announcement, they quickly rebounded as economists and policymakers praised Greenspan.

Greenspan well knew the difficulty of replacing Volcker, who had been called the second most powerful man in the United States. He admitted that "trying to fill Paul Volcker's shoes is going to be an extraordinary challenge." He tried to reassure the financial markets that he would also be a staunch inflation fighter: "It will be up to those of us who follow him [Volcker] to be certain that those very hard-won gains are not lost."

The confirmation hearings went relatively smoothly. Greenspan's previous adversary, Senator Proxmire, then chairman of the Senate Banking Committee, even admitted that he regretted opposing Greenspan's earlier nomination as chairman of the Council of Economic Advisers. Greenspan emphasized he would uphold the tradition of a politically independent central bank: "My advice may turn out to be wrong, my actions may turn out to be wrong, but it certainly would not be on the basis of politics rather than economics." Greenspan's testimony in the hearings indicated he would push for broader powers for banks, particularly in the area of investment banking. He also stressed the need to cut the government deficit in order to raise the level of private investment. With respect to monetary policy, he shied away from his earlier belief that the gold standard should be reestablished. He voiced somewhat monetarist views, stating "that money does matter, that at least a significant aspect of Federal Reserve [money supply] targeting has to be the monetary aggregates or something related to them." In answering a question on exchange rate policy, Greenspan stated that intervention in the markets is "a useful adjunct to other policies" but that it "cannot and should not be relied upon to have large or lasting impacts on exchange rates."

The Senate committees considering Greenspan's nomination recommended his confirmation unanimously, and the Senate voted 91 to 2 for confirmation. Greenspan disbanded his consulting firm and on August 11, 1987, took the oath as the 13th chairman of the Board of Governors of the Federal Reserve System.

The Fed chairmanship put Greenspan at the head of an organization with a budget of more than $1.3 billion and employing more than 24,000 people. The system is composed of 12 regional banks, most with branches, and the Board of Governors in Washington, D.C. The regional banks, the op-erational arms of the system, supervise the nation's commercial banks, supply its currency, and make loans to depository institutions at the discount rate. The seven-member Board of Governors dominates monetary policy-making—the regional bank presidents have little power in this area—and oversees the operations of the regional banks. Governors are appointed to nonrenewable 14-year staggered terms. The chairman serves a four-year term but can remain on the board if his chairmanship is not renewed. The length and staggered nature of the terms supposedly provide political independence and a degree of continuity to the board. At the time Greenspan became chairman, however, all of the governors had been appointed by President Reagan, making them relatively inexperienced. Governors increasingly have resigned early, perhaps due to relatively low compensation.

One of the board's main duties is to consider the regional banks' requests to change the discount rate (the rate at which the Fed lends to commercial banks needing liquidity). The board denied two requests to raise the rate shortly after Greenspan became chairman in August, but on September 4 the board approved an increase, the first since April 1984. The increase reflected the board's growing concern over inflation, but some analysts have also suggested that Greenspan used the increase to signal his forceful intentions. David Jones, chief economist at the firm of Aubrey G. Lanston, contended that "Greenspan wanted to make it clear that he wasn't a wimp and that he would have a strong backbone in fighting inflation."

On October 19, 1987, the New York Stock Exchange suffered its worst day in history. The Dow Jones Industrial average plummeted 508 points, a 22 percent decline that exceeded even that of "Black Tuesday" in October 1929. Greenspan acted quickly to allay fears that the collapse of stock prices would cause a liquidity crisis. Before the markets opened on October 20, he issued a statement affirming the Fed's "readiness to serve as a source of liquidity to support the economic and financial system." James E. Annable, chief economist at the First National Bank of Chicago, told the *Wall Street Journal* the next day that Greenspan's statement "was the most calming thing that was said yesterday." The Fed supplied the bank reserves needed to avert a liquidity crisis by buying large amounts of government securities on the open market. The resulting fall in short-term interest rates cushioned

Greenspan (second from left) with President Reagan and administration officials, 1988 (courtesy of Peter Souza, the White House)

the economy from the aftershock of the crash so effectively that by the end of 1987 stock prices returned to where they had been at the year's start. Lyle Gramley, past Fed governor and chief economist for the Mortgage Bankers Association, argued Greenspan's actions "successfully walled off the stock market's crash and prevented a flood of financial problems from cascading through the economy."

In the aftermath of the crash, pressure mounted for tighter regulation of the financial markets. Greenspan generally opposed the pressure, especially the suggestion that the Fed become the prime regulator for the broader financial markets. In testimony before the Senate Banking Committee in May 1988, he argued against raising the margin requirements on stock-related loans and against restrictions on the kinds of financial instruments traded: "What many critics of equity derivatives fail to recognize is that the markets for these instruments have become so large not because of slick sales campaigns but because they are providing economic value to their users."

Several themes have marked Greenspan's tenure as Fed chairman. First, he has consistently stressed the need to keep inflation under control, stating that "if there is even the slightest whiff that inflation is drifting up, then some action is in order." Accordingly, money growth has been slow since his appointment. From mid 1987 through the first quarter of 1989, M1, the narrow definition of money that includes only currency and checkable deposits, grew at a mere 3.2 percent per year, while M2, a broader measure that adds savings and time deposits plus money market mutual funds, grew at a 4.5 percent rate. The corresponding figures for the seven quarters prior to Greenspan's appointment were 13.8 percent for M1 and 7.6 percent for M2. The Fed increased the discount rate in August 1988 and again in February 1989, in both cases due to concern about inflation. Greenspan's long-term goal is to achieve "price levels sufficiently stable so that expectations of change do not become major factors in key economic decisions."

A second theme is the need to reduce federal budget deficits. Before the Senate Committee on the Budget in March 1988 Greenspan asserted that it was "crucial that further actions in support of a long-term policy of reducing budget deficits and the associated claims on the nation's supply of saving be implemented." Doubting that domestic saving rates would rise, Greenspan contended that if the nation achieved adequate rates of private net investment, government had to reduce its demands on saving. He rejected deficit reduction through general tax increases in favor of reduction through spending cuts, although he favored raising the tax on gasoline.

A third theme is the need to deregulate banking. Despite the stock market crash, Greenspan supported the repeal of the 1933 Glass-Steagall Act, which split commercial banking from investment banking. He favored allowing bank holding companies to own subsidiaries that underwrite and deal in securities, arguing it would lead to a more competitive investment industry and lower consumer costs. He also maintained that technological advances have made deregulation a necessity. Greenspan's views are well summarized by the following statement made to a House subcommittee on financial regulation: "Attempts to hold the present structure in place will be defeated through the inevitable loopholes that innovation forced by competitive necessity will develop, although there will be heavy costs in terms of competitive fairness and respect for law that are so critical to a safe and sound financial system."

Greenspan enjoyed his Fed chairmanship. He was much less aloof from the Fed staff than his predecessor, Volcker. Andrea Mitchell, NBC News correspondent and close friend, said that "He's like a kid in a toy store; he loves all the numbers and the marvelous staff." Although usually described as shy and modest, he was well known on the New York social circuit. His main recreational activities included golf, tennis, and music. He has received honorary doctorates from Pace University (1981), Hofstra University (1984), and Colgate University (1987). He was awarded, jointly with Arthur F. Burns and William Simon, the Thomas Jefferson Award for the Greatest Public Service Performed by an Elected or Appointed Official by the American Institute for Public Service in 1976. He was also a fellow and past president (1970) of the National Association of Business Economists.

Critics viewed Alan Greenspan's first two years as Fed chairman a success. Inflation had been held in check while the unemployment rate fell. He acted decisively to avert a liquidity crisis after the stock market crash of October 1987. His policies remained consistent with his conservative economic philosophy: keep inflation low, reduce government's share in the economy, and rely on competitive forces to regulate the system.

Publications:
"Antitrust," "Gold and Economic Freedom," and "The Assault on Integrity," in *Capitalism: The Unknown Ideal*, by Ayn Rand (New York: New American Library, 1966).

References:
Lyle Gramley, "Happy Anniversary, Alan Greenspan," *Mortgage Banking* (July 1988): 38-42;

Joseph Kraft, "Right, for Ford," *New York Times Magazine*, April 25, 1976, pp. 96, 108-110;

Dyan Machan, "One plus one plus one equals zero," *Forbes* (April 20, 1987): 58-60;

Nathaniel C. Nash, "A Laissez-Faire Pragmatist," *New York Times*, June 3, 1987, D1;

Nominations of Phillip A. Loomis, Jr. and Alan Greenspan, Hearing before the Committee on Banking, Housing, and Urban Affairs, U.S. Senate, 93rd Congress (Washington, D. C.: U.S. Government Printing Office, 1974);

Nomination of Alan Greenspan, Hearing before the Committee on Banking, Housing, and Urban Affairs, U.S. Senate, 100th Congress (Washington, D. C.: U.S. Government Printing Office, 1987);

Richard L. Strout, "Chairman Greenspan," *New Republic* (September 14, 1974): 13-14;

"Supercapitalist at the CEA," *Time* (August 5, 1974): 61;

"Testing Time for Greenspan," *U.S. News and World Report* (September 21, 1987): 49;

Louis Uchitelle, "Alan Greenspan, Caution at the Fed," *New York Times Magazine*, January 15, 1989, pp. 18-21, 37, 41-42, 63.

George L. Harrison

(January 26, 1887 - March 5, 1958)

by Diane B. Kunz

Yale University

CAREER: Assistant general counsel (1914-1917), general counsel, Federal Reserve Board (1919-1920); deputy governor (1920-1928), governor (1928-1936), president, Federal Reserve Bank of New York (1936-1941); president (1941-1948), chairman, New York Life Insurance Company (1948-1958).

George Leslie Harrison played a pivotal role in the formation of the American central banking system. Born on January 26, 1887, in San Francisco, he attended Yale College, graduating in 1910. After completing his three years at Harvard Law School he became the law clerk for Supreme Court Justice Oliver Wendell Holmes. Thereafter he lived in Washington and remained in government service, joining the Federal Reserve Board as assistant general counsel in 1914. Since the board had just come into existence, Harrison had the opportunity to help create the framework within which he would work for the next two decades. During World War I Harrison took a leave of absence to serve in France with the American Red Cross. In 1919 he returned to the Federal Reserve Board, which promoted him to the position of general counsel.

In 1920 Harrison moved to New York to serve as deputy governor of the Federal Reserve Bank of New York. He had reached the seat of real power. The war had seriously disrupted the international economy, mangling European trade relations and transforming the United States from a debtor nation to the world's largest creditor. Because the American government had ostensibly opted out of international financial affairs, a vacuum developed that the New York Reserve Bank filled under the leadership of its first governor, Benjamin Strong. In the international sphere, the New York Reserve Bank, not the Federal Reserve Board in Washing-

George L. Harrison

ton, acted as the nation's central bank. Strong, who enjoyed longstanding friendly relations with the influential House of Morgan, worked in partnership with Montagu Norman, governor of the Bank of England, to restabilize European currencies and return to an international gold standard as modified by the 1922 Genoa Conference. With Harrison at his side, Strong presided over efforts to aid Britain, France, Belgium, and other nations. Furthermore, he gave the imprimatur of the Federal Reserve Bank of New York to the Dawes Plan, which restructured German reparations in 1924.

Upon Strong's death in 1928 Harrison was appointed his successor. Many had doubts whether the younger man had the ability to fill the position. But Morgan partner Russell Leffingwell wrote: "George Harrison has been under the disadvantage of being young and new and he has inherited all the antagonisms that poor Ben left behind him. But I have confidence in the soundness of his view and his ability to work out the situation ultimately." Had Harrison's problems been confined solely to the national sphere, Leffingwell's sanguine view might have proven accurate; instead Harrison presided over the worldwide catastrophe known as the Great Depression.

The new governor's first test of strength, however, came in 1929, during the last days of the legendary bull market. From February through August of that year Harrison engaged in a major struggle with the Federal Reserve Board over the question of the discount rate. At that time all 12 federal reserve banks set their own rate subject to the board's approval. In order to curb Wall Street speculation Harrison pushed for a higher rate. For six months the board denied his request. By the time the board permitted the New York Reserve Bank to raise its discount rate to 6 percent, it had little effect on the market.

The rapid deepening of the Depression forced Harrison to fight constant financial fires. The threatened unraveling of the Dawes reparations settlement led to the 1930 Young Plan, in which the New York Reserve Bank again took an interest. Among other things the agreement called for the creation of the Bank for International Settlements (BIS), an institution designed to improve the workings of the international financial system. While President Herbert Hoover forbade official American participation, Harrison kept in close touch with the BIS, headed at the time by Gates McGarrah, a former director of the New York Reserve Bank. As the banking system of Central Europe started to collapse during 1931, Harrison joined with other central bankers in various attempts to prop up the system. The Federal Reserve Bank of New York organized support loans for the Bank of Austria, the Reichsbank, and the Bank of England, but to little avail. By autumn the financial networks of Germany, Austria, and Hungary had been derailed, Britain had abandoned the gold standard, and the United States faced a run on its own gold reserves.

Harrison handled those problems as best he could while coping with the increasing paralysis of the domestic banking system, which during 1932 became the most difficult problem facing the country. Conditions deteriorated further during the interregnum prior to the inauguration of Franklin D. Roosevelt as president: Britain, France, and four other countries defaulted on their war debts, and one state after another declared bank holidays.

The Roosevelt "Hundred Days" brought hope and a new regime on both the domestic and international fronts. Believing that the United States always came out the loser in international conferences, Roosevelt sent his famous bombshell message barring American participation in joint monetary stabilization actions to the London World Economic Conference in July 1933. That act signaled the American government's three-year withdrawal from international financial cooperation. It also marked the fall of Harrison from his peak of influence. Instead of cooperating with Wall Street, the New Dealers were determined to drive the moneychangers from the temple. Partly they aimed to move the locus of American financial power from New York to Washington. They accomplished that by amending the Federal Reserve Act in 1935. Combined with isolationism in fact as well as word, the Democrat regime increasingly cut off Harrison's influence. He remained as president of the Federal Reserve Bank of New York (as the position was known after 1936) until 1941, when he assumed the presidency of the New York Life Insurance Company. During World War II Harrison earned the Medal of Merit for serving as chairman of the government's Interim Committee for Development and Use of the Atomic Bomb. In 1948 he became chairman of the board of New York Life.

A gentle, affable man, Harrison walked with a limp as a result of a childhood accident. In 1940 he married Gertrude Gordon Grayson, widow of his close friend, Admiral Cary T. Grayson, who had served as Woodrow Wilson's personal physician. In 1951-1952 Harrison served on a Yale University Alumni Committee, investigating the influence of communism on campus. During the 1950s he participated actively on the Board of Trustees of Columbia University, where his voluminous and exceedingly useful papers are housed. Harrison died on March 5, 1958.

References:

Lester V. Chandler, *Benjamin Strong, Central Banker* (Washington, D.C.: Brookings, 1958);

Stephen V. O. Clarke, *Central Bank Cooperation, 1924-31* (New York: Federal Reserve Bank of New York, 1967);

Diane B. Kunz, *The Battle for Britain's Gold Standard in 1931* (London: Croom Helm, 1987).

Archives:

The papers of George L. Harrison are housed at Butler Library, Columbia University.

Home Equity Loans (*see* **Mortgage Lending, Mortgage Pools, Home Equity Loans, and REITs**)

Gerald Hughes

(July 8, 1875 - August 27, 1956)

by James Smallwood

University of Texas at Tyler

CAREER: Attorney and partner, Hughes law firm (1897-1911); state senator, Colorado, (1901-1905); attorney and partner, Hughes and Dorsey law firm (1911-1956); director (1907-1924), chairman, First National Bank of Denver (1924-1956); director, International Trust Company of Denver (1911-1956).

Born on July 8, 1875, in Richmond, Missouri, about 20 miles northeast of Kansas City, Gerald Hughes was the son of Charles J. Hughes, Jr., and Lucy S. (Menefee) Hughes. The elder Hughes moved his family to Denver when Gerald was four years old. Beginning in 1881 Gerald Hughes attended Denver's public schools and then transferred to an exclusive college preparatory school, Holbrook Academy, in New York. In 1893 he enrolled at Yale, where he received his A.B. degree in 1897; then he returned to Colorado to attend the University of Denver's law school. After earning his law degree in 1899 he entered his father's long-established firm in Denver.

The younger Hughes later called himself a "darling of the gods," his open admission that he was no self-made man. He humbly recognized that his father's success had laid the foundation for his own,

but the young Hughes was determined to build upon that foundation.

The association of the Hughes law firm with the First National Bank of Denver began in 1894 when bank president David H. Moffat retained Charles Hughes as legal counsel. The firm became increasingly more involved in the affairs of the bank as the years passed, and Charles Hughes also became more prominent in Colorado politics and society. After refusing many times to run for political office early in his career, he relented in 1908 and won a seat in the U.S. Senate, but he died in 1911, in the third year of his term.

By the time his father died Gerald Hughes had come into his own as Colorado attorney and financier. He had become a partner in the Hughes firm in 1897 and had assumed management responsibilities after his father's election to the Senate. He served two terms in the Colorado state legislature, from 1901 to 1905. His transition to dominant partner had in effect already taken place by the time of his father's death. At that point the firm's major clients included not only the First National Bank of Denver but also Great Western Sugar Company, Adolph Coors Company, Denver Tramway Company, and the International Trust Company of Denver.

In 1907 Hughes joined the board of First National. Bank president Moffatt and the board were sinking large amounts of the bank's funds into investments, most prominently the Denver, Northwestern & Pacific Railway (called the "Moffatt Road"), that were turning out to be financially unsound. In 1911, after Moffatt's death, to keep the bank solvent Hughes arranged for the Moffatt estate to exchange cash for the bank's railway stock. Then he brought in Colorado financier Absalom V. Hunter to serve as the bank's president and soon after as a director of International Trust. By 1913 Hughes, Hunter, and associates had acquired a controlling interest of International's outstanding stock; First National and International thereafter operated in tandem, though a formal merger did not take place until 1958, two years after Hughes's death.

Hughes had taken on a new law partner after his father's death and thus created more time to devote to managing First National and International Trust. As a financier his style was conservative. He was once overheard to remark that "if the loan-to-deposit ratio of The First ever exceeds 32 percent, I will liquidate the bank." He and Hunter also recruited a quick-minded young man who shared their views, John Evans, Sr., an engineer for the Denver Tramway Company, who took a trustee's position at International Trust in 1911 and the trust's presidency five years later. Also in 1916 Evans joined the board of First National, and he assumed the bank's presidency in 1928. For four more years Evans held the presidency of International Trust, but in 1932 he vacated that position to devote more time to First National.

The conservatism of Hughes, Hunter, and Evans sometimes came under criticism in the recession of 1920-1921 and into the 1920s. In an era of ever-increasing installment buying, Hughes seldom approved consumer loans for automobiles with the result that First National stayed solvent when four Colorado banks closed in 1920, when eleven more collapsed in 1921, when nine more went under in 1922, and when yet another seventeen collapsed in 1923. The trio carefully monitored farm loans, and when Colorado's agricultural sector went into a recession in the mid-1920s, First National and International remained stable.

First National not only weathered the economic flux of the early 1920s and the agricultural depression of the mid 1920s but also survived the Depression of the 1930s. In 1920 there were 404 banks in Colorado and only 150 by 1941. During the entire depressed decade, Hughes, Evans, and Hunter remained cautious. The bank's loan-to-deposit ratio, for example, ranged from 22 to 25 percent, a "blessing" in the hard times of the Depression era.

Hughes's conservatism did not stop him from heartily endorsing several economic reforms of President Franklin D. Roosevelt's New Deal. He strongly endorsed the Glass-Steagall Act, the legislation that created the Federal Deposit Insurance Corporation (FDIC) in 1933. Although many bankers opposed the new FDIC because it involved federal regulation of private enterprise, Hughes believed that the FDIC would restore the public's confidence in the banking system (which it did).

Though careful in the 1930s, Hughes did not allow First National to atrophy. The bank invested in the petroleum industry, destined to become a "giant" of modern business. The bank served Continental Oil Company, Chevron Oil Company, Colorado Interstate Gas Company, and other oil and gas producers. Similarly, despite the Depression, First National became involved with the burgeoning aviation industry. In the late 1930s Robert F. Six, a pilot and an engineer, had assumed management of Varney Air Transport of Colorado, and Six went to Hughes and Evans to ask for a series of loans, first to buy a single aircraft, later to buy more. The bank found enough money for Six, and he developed the company that became Continental Airlines. Other aviation-related customers of First National included Delta, Trans World, United, Western, and Republic.

During the World War II years First National experienced rapid growth as Colorado's economy boomed along with the national economy. Total salaries and wages paid in the state of Colorado in 1935 were $447 million. That figure had jumped to about $1.4 billion by 1940. The numbers continued to soar though the war years. As of 1939 First National had assets of $67.7 million and deposits of $62.4 million. By 1945 assets had soared to $186.55 million and deposits had climbed to $180 million, increases of almost 300 percent.

In the postwar era, expansion continued as a population explosion occurred in the Denver area. Through the mid 1950s that expansion continued, and Hughes and Evans guided First National into the modern era in the banking industry. Gerald Hughes was still actively leading his bank as its long-time board chairman when he died on August 27, 1956.

Hughes left behind a solvent, expanding bank, a bank that was a financial boon to Colorado's thriving economy. Moreover, he had passed on his knowledge of the banking business to his colleague Evans. Those two men together trained a younger generation of banking executives who would make subsequent positive contributions to the economy of Colorado and the west.

References:

Eugene Adams, Lyle W. Dorsett, and Robert S. Pulcipher, *The Pioneer Western Bank—The First of Denver: 1860-1980* (Denver: First Interstate Bank of Denver, N.A., 1984);

Kenneth H. Hunter and William G. Philip, *The Adequacy of Banking Facilities in Colorado* (Boulder: Colorado Bankers Association, 1938);

Fred R. Niehaus, *Development of Banking in Colorado* (Denver: The Mountain States Publishing Company, 1942);

Niehaus, *Seventy Years of Progress: History of Banking in Colorado, 1876-1946* (Washington, D.C.: FDIC, 1948).

Archives:

The First National Bank Historical Collection housed in library of The First National Bank of Denver contains a voluminous collection of Gerald Hughes's business and personal papers. Another collection of Hughes's papers is found at the State Historical Society of Colorado, Denver. Other primary material relating to Hughes's career may be found in Record Group 101, Comptroller of the Currency Files, National Archives, Washington, D.C.

Individual Retirement Accounts (*see* **Money Instruments**)

Interest, Inflation, and Deflation

Interest represents the lender's profit for making a loan. It is usually made up of two components, the cost of the loan money to the lender and a return based on risk and time. Modern banks often charge compound interest, in which the interest itself generates interest over and above the principal.

The interest rate on a loan generally reflects expectations about the rate of inflation, which constitutes a risk to the lender. If the lender expects inflation to be 3 percent a year, he must include an additional 3 percent when calculating the interest on the loan. Inflation in its simplest form is a greater proportional increase in the amount of dollars (money) than goods and services in the economy. Cost per good increases because money is worth less. Deflation, on the other hand, involves a slower rise in the volume of money than goods and services. Goods are cheaper. Because of the profit component, even under deflationary conditions lenders would charge interest, but it would represent a much lower component of the cost of loan funds.

Modern debate over inflation in the American banking system (no prolonged deflation has occurred since the 1800s) centers on the budget deficit of the federal government, which since the 1960s has become a seemingly permanent feature of the economy. Economists differ on the relationship between inflation and interest rates. When John Maynard Keynes wrote his influential *General Theory of Employment, Interest and Money* (1936) he expected the beneficial effects of deficit spending to offset concerns over inflation. For some time, Keynes's American supporters argued that the federal government could ensure full employment through deficit spending. But the closer the economy got to eliminating all unemployment, the higher the rate of deficit spending and the higher the rate of inflation. Economist A. W. H. Phillips described the relationship, which, represented graphically, is known as the "Phillips Curve." Phillips held that high unemployment and high rates of inflation could not coexist. The "stagflation" of the 1970s, in which the American economy witnessed high unemployment and high inflation, disproved Phillips's contention.

Economists led by Milton Friedman—the monetarists—increasingly saw deficit spending as dangerous. They argued that monetary authorities should increase the rate of money growth in increments related to price levels. If price levels started to rise, authorities needed to restrain money growth.

The federal deficit worked its way into the American banking system when the Federal Reserve Banks purchased government securities on the open market, thus putting cash reserves into the Reserve Banks, which then loaned to member banks. More

reserves meant more loans. To restrain monetary growth, the Fed sold securities, essentially "calling in reserves," reducing the amount available for commercial banks to lend. One group of economists, called the "Rational Expectations School," maintained that businesses and consumers did not even need to experience the actual effects of inflation before they responded. Instead, as soon as they saw the government run a deficit, they immediately adjusted their price levels for the inflation they knew would appear at some point anyway.

Whereas under the gold standard the banks' gold reserves served as the basis for loans, in the modern system only the banks' cash reserves limit their lending: while the gold standard required that an increase in gold back increased lending, modern banks need only accomplish an increase in reserves to increase lending. However, the public, through price levels and interest rates, still provides the ultimate information about the value of money loaned, regardless of the volume.

—Editor

International Bank for Reconstruction and Development (*see* Bretton Woods Conference, the International Monetary Fund, and the World Bank)

International Banking Act of 1978

Concerned about growing foreign investment in the United States, in 1978 Congress passed the International Banking Act, which provided federal supervision of foreign banks operating in the United States and required a foreign bank to obtain deposit insurance for its branches (if those branches accepted deposits of less than $100,000) unless the branches

did not engage in domestic retail banking. The act gave the Federal Deposit Insurance Corporation (FDIC) primary supervisory responsibility for FDIC-insured state-chartered branches of foreign banks.

—Editor

International Monetary Fund (*see* Bretton Woods Conference, the International Monetary Fund, and the World Bank)

Interstate Banking (*see* **Branch Banking, Interstate Banking, and Franchising**)

Investment Banks (*see* **Commercial Banks and Investment Banks**)

W. W. "Hootie" Johnson

(February 16, 1931 -   )

by Olin S. Pugh

University of South Carolina

CAREER: Assistant cashier and other positions (1953-1965), president and chief executive officer, Bankers Trust of South Carolina [State Bank and Trust Company, Greenwood, South Carolina, to 1969] (1965-1986); chairman of the executive committee, North Carolina National Bank Corporation (1986-   ); chairman, North Carolina National Bank South Carolina Corporation (1986-   ).

William Woodward "Hootie" Johnson joined his father's small Greenwood, South Carolina, bank, the State Bank and Trust Company, in 1953 and by 1960 had emerged as a prime mover in expanding the bank into a metropolitan setting. In 1969 Johnson and the board of directors changed the bank's name to Bankers Trust of South Carolina and pursued the objective of placing the company at the forefront of statewide financial services organizations. Through mergers and acquisitions engineered by Johnson, the bank acquired a major market position. With the advent of a regional banking compact in 1986, Bankers Trust became part of the North Carolina National Bank (NCNB) Corporation. Johnson continues to play a significant role as chairman of the executive committee of NCNB and as chairman of the board of directors of the South Carolina division of that bank's operations.

Johnson was born on February 16, 1931, in Augusta, Georgia, the son of Dewey H. and Mabel Johnson. The family moved to Greenwood, South Carolina, in 1943, when Johnson's father became head of that city's State Bank and Trust Company. Johnson starred on the football field at the Univer-

W. W. "Hootie" Johnson (courtesy of NCNB South Carolina Corporation)

sity of South Carolina, where he attended from 1949 to 1953. In 1951, two years before his graduation from the university, he married Pierrine Baker of Greenwood. The couple has four daughters.

Upon graduation, Johnson took a position as assistant cashier at State Bank and Trust. He rose in the company hierarchy until in 1965 he became one of the youngest presidents and chief executive officers of a South Carolina bank. By that time he had decided to take advantage of the economic growth in South Carolina by instituting an accelerated policy of mergers and acquisitions, expanding the bank statewide. Johnson realized that he had to build from the bank's individual consumer base and that he had to exercise caution in developing corporate accounts. That "household" legacy made it possible for the bank to develop extensive consumer services and an image as a responsive servant of the interests of South Carolinians. In recognition of the bank's status as a leader in the South Carolina financial services industry, the bank's name changed to Bankers Trust of South Carolina in 1969.

Johnson recruited bright young people to staff his aggressive and growing bank. The staff contributed extensively to the program of innovation in service and delivery systems. Bankers Trust became known for the sophistication of its operations. While Johnson did not attempt to know all of the details of day-to-day business, he did know how to obtain and motivate good managers.

Johnson has recognized that for generations South Carolina has been a capital-poor state. One of his motivations for building a major banking institution in South Carolina was to facilitate the accumulation of capital funds. He carried that idea into the 1986 merger with NCNB Corporation. Johnson became chairman of the executive committee of the expanded organization and chairman of the board of directors of the South Carolina portion of its banking operations. The merger greatly enlarged the resources available in South Carolina to the state's venture capitalists.

As of 1989 Johnson served on the boards of several other corporations, including NCNB Texas National, Duke Power Company, and the Liberty Corporation. He served in the South Carolina general assembly from 1957 to 1958, as chairman of the South Carolina Ports Authority from 1968 to 1981, and as chairman of the South Carolina Research Authority from 1981. He has also served as chairman of the committee charged in 1981 with developing a plan to desegregate the colleges and universities of South Carolina, as a member of the board of the South Carolina Foundation of Independent Trustees, as a trustee of Benedict College of Columbia, South Carolina, as a member of the board of the University of South Carolina Business Partnership Foundation, and on the University of South Carolina Educational Foundation.

Reference:

John G. Sproat and Larry Schweikart, *Making Change: South Carolina Banking in the Twentieth Century* (Columbia: South Carolina Bankers Association, 1990).

Jesse H. Jones

(April 5, 1874 - June 1, 1956)

by Walter L. Buenger

Texas A&M University

CAREER: Branch manager (1894-1898), general manager, M. T. Jones Lumber Company (1898-1905); chairman, South Texas Lumber Company (1902-1956); chairman, Jesse H. Jones Lumber Company (1905-1956); director, Union National Bank [Union Bank & Trust Company to 1910] (1905-1917); president, Texas Trust Company (1909-1911); chairman, Bankers Mortgage Company (1911-1956); chairman, Houston Harbor Board (1913-1917); president (1922-1929), chairman, National Bank of Commerce (1929-1956); publisher, *Houston Chronicle* (1926-1956); director (1932-1933), chairman, Reconstruction Finance Corporation (1933-1939); federal loan administrator (1939-1945); U.S. secretary of commerce (1940-1945).

Asked to sum up the life of his old antagonist at the time of his death, Henry A. Wallace declared that Jesse H. Jones "wielded greater power for a longer period than any human being in the history of the United States." That power came from Jones's position as the lender of last resort for the troubled businesses of the New Deal and the overstressed businesses of World War II. As head of the Reconstruction Finance Corporation (RFC) and as federal loan administrator, Jones presided over the key distributors of credit in the 1930s and 1940s. In the age of blossoming state capitalism, he was perhaps the country's greatest banker.

Jesse Holman Jones was born in Robertson County, Tennessee, on April 5, 1874. His father, William Hasque Jones, was a prosperous farmer and tobacco dealer. His mother, Anne Holman Jones, died when Jesse was six, and most of his early care came from Nancy Jones Hurt, his father's widowed sister. Jones's father and his deceased uncle Hurt had both served in the Confederate army, but another uncle, Martin Tilford Jones, had moved to Illinois before the war and served in the Union army.

Jesse H. Jones

Next to his father and aunt Nancy Hurt, M. T. Jones influenced Jesse's early life more than anyone.

M. T. Jones had moved from Illinois to Texas in 1875 and engaged in various business activities. Among them were lumber and banking, the two earliest career areas for his nephew. M. T. Jones headquartered his operations in Houston, but by 1883 he needed someone to help manage his concerns in the Dallas area, the other center of urban growth in the state. William Hasque sold his Tennessee farm, moved the family to Dallas, and assumed a managerial role in his brother's lumber business. Although young Jesse Jones wandered back and forth between Texas and Tennessee for the next few years, when William Hasque died in 1894 Jesse returned to Texas and took a job as branch manager with his uncle's lumber company.

M. T. Jones, a pioneer Texas lumberman, was one of the first to employ extensive vertical integration in the lumber business. He purchased or leased acreage, built mills, processed the timber into finished products, and sold those products at his own yards. Lumberyards commonly supplied lumber and hardware on credit and built homes and businesses. They also acted as the mortgage banker of homeowners and businessmen, and used those mortgages as collateral for loans at local banks. While Jones had no formal education beyond the high school level, running a lumberyard taught him a variety of useful business skills and helped him develop important personal relationships in lumber, construction, and banking. By the close of 1894 Jones managed the Dallas yard, the largest of M. T. Jones's outlets in the state.

In later years Jones and his apologists liked to depict him as a rags-to-riches type who made it to the top entirely on his own hard work. Nothing could be further from the truth. Jones's father was not a dirt farmer. At the end of his life he owned 600 acres of tobacco land worked by sharecroppers, bought and sold the tobacco raised by his neighbors, and evidently made a substantial profit in his dealings with his brother M. T. Jesse Jones inherited from his father not only modest wealth but also the attitudes, manners, and personal connections essential to his later acquisition of truly great wealth. Chief among those personal connections was Uncle M. T. When M. T. died in 1898, Jones found himself named as an executor of the estate and the general manager of the company. He quickly moved to Houston, a city that by the 1920s would be synonymous with his name. Few twenty-four-year-olds in 1898 had control of an estate in excess of $1 million.

Through his father and uncle as well as his work as a branch manager in Dallas and general manager and executor in Houston, Jones formed close ties to two of the most significant banks and bankers in turn-of-the-century Texas: Royal A. Ferris, president of one of the forerunners of First National Bank of Dallas, and T. W. House, Jr., president of T. W. House and Company, the largest bank in Houston and one of the largest private banks in the state. House was also one of the execu-

tors of M. T. Jones's will. From 1902 to 1907, when Jones went into business on his own, he borrowed most of the money for the expansion of his enterprises from Ferris and House.

Jones entered business on his own as a typical lumber dealer, but he soon specialized in building. That in turn led to banking, for as Jones's projects grew they exceeded the credit limits of a lumber company. Instead he sought to develop local credit by helping found Union Bank & Trust, the first state bank organized under the new Texas banking laws of 1905, and by organizing two trust companies. He also proved remarkably adept at securing credit outside of the state. For example, he made it a habit to borrow twice what he needed and keep the balance in a non-interest-bearing account at the bank that lent him the money. Since he also took out substantial life insurance, had good family connections, and exhibited a growing record of successes, banks were increasingly willing to extend their credit. Anticipating the Panic of 1907, Jones took advantage of his good standing and extended the terms of his loans. Once the crash came, a crash that took down his lead bank, T. W. House and Company, Jones called on the New York banks to which his notes with T. W. House passed and assured them of his creditworthiness. Most already had heard of his value as a customer, and some even lent him additional funds with which he bought up real estate bargains in depressed Houston.

Jones emerged from the Panic of 1907 a wealthy and respected businessman. He increasingly turned to public service and politics to bolster his own wealth and to increase his standing in the community. His activities were not entirely self-serving, and some truth resided in his argument that he built his city first, and riches and prestige followed in the wake.

Jones first took an interest in politics in about 1905, and, not surprisingly, the creation of a state banking system attracted much of his attention. Texas had never utilized a state banking system but had instead relied upon private banks and national banks to supply its credit needs. Jones and others argued that private banks were too erratic and insecure and that national banks were too restricted by federal lending regulations and required overly high start-up costs. A well-designed state system would make more credit available in capital-starved Texas and would make banking services available to the av-

Jones with President Woodrow Wilson

erage citizen. Jones had no aversion to government taking the lead in business. Indeed, he believed it often advisable. He also had a strong streak of anticolonialism. One of the prime reasons he desired a state banking system was to free Texas from dependency upon outside sources of credit. For that reason and to ensure the strength and stability of the system, Jones also supported the two other major state business reforms of 1900-1910: the Robertson Insurance Act, which forced increased investment in Texas by non-Texas insurance companies selling policies in the state, and the Deposit Guaranty Law, which insured deposits in state banks against the failure of the bank. Later in life Jones described himself as a "liberal." Judged alongside others of his economic class, perhaps he was. He naturally emerged an early and influential supporter of Woodrow Wilson's 1912 presidential campaign. Wilson's southern roots and anti-big-business rhetoric appealed to Jones's anticolonialism, and his philosophy of governmental activism matched Jones's Texas experience. Wilson represented to Jones the example of all that was good in politics and the anchor that held him in the Democratic party until late in life.

One of the things Jones admired about Wilson—his example of public service—led Jones to perform what he considered acts of public service even before 1912. Most of those acts of public service involved improving Houston's link to the sea or stabilizing the city's banking structure. In 1907 he acquired the stock of the struggling Planter & Mechanics Bank and merged it with Union Bank. He claimed at the time that he acted to prevent the failure of a Houston bank, which he believed would damage the image of Houston as a city on the make. In 1910 Jones repeated his actions by acquiring the near-defunct Merchants National and merging it with Union to form Union National, then the largest bank in Houston. Those mergers left Jones the bank's largest stockholder. In both cases he preserved the stability of Houston's banking system and the image of the city. In the long run he also made a substantial profit on his stock.

Much the same pattern characterized Jones's work on behalf of the Houston ship channel and the port of Houston. After his move to Houston in 1898 he supported construction of the ship channel and helped raise local funds needed for the enterprise. In 1913 he chaired the city harbor board and

Jones (seated, right) with the board of the Reconstruction Finance Corporation, 1933

again spearheaded fund-raising for construction of port facilities. The channel and port opening in 1914 sparked an extended economic boom in Houston, which drove the value of Jones's real estate higher and higher.

Jones's connection with Union Bank and the ship channel also illustrates other facets of his character: an almost obsessive need for total control of any enterprise with which he was connected and a compulsive desire to maximize profit. In 1917 Jones severed his ties with both the harbor board and Union. The city government accepted a gift of land that carried with it an obligation to build a wharf downstream from the foot of Main Street, the traditional terminus of navigation. Jones resigned because he favored a wharf on Main Street even though engineers told the city it involved too high a cost to bring deep water to that point. Jones also sold his stock in Union to W. T. Carter, the other major owner of the bank, when Carter accused him of billing the bank for the electricity used in a Jones-owned adjacent building. Later, Jones, using the *Houston Chronicle* (of which he acquired a half interest in 1908 and complete owner-

ship in 1926) as a mouthpiece, opposed bond issues to build downstream wharfs, and he took great delight in building up his almost wholly owned National Bank of Commerce to a size greater than Union's. As Henry Wallace learned, Jones could exhibit vindictiveness, pettiness, and an unforgiving nature.

The year 1917 marked a turning point in Jones's life, for not only did he sever ties to Union and the harbor board, he went to Washington to help in the war effort. From that time until his death he participated intimately in national politics. He advanced in politics much as he had in business: through kinship and friendship ties. E. M. House, the brother of Jones's old banker, first brought him to the attention of President Woodrow Wilson. Jones's friendship with Stockton Axson, the president's brother-in-law and a professor at Rice Institute in Houston, strengthened the link to Wilson. Jones did not marry Mary Gibbs Jones until 1920, and the two never had children, but members of his extended family always played a role in his life. For example, his ties to the Texas congressional delegation and the Democratic party were enhanced by his own brother-in-law, Representative Daniel E. Garrett of Houston. When Jones became director-general of Military Relief for the Red Cross he rapidly added to his kinship and friendship ties. Using methods reminiscent of those he used to build up Houston, he gave service to his party and gained benefit for himself and his city. In 1924 he worked as the chief fund-raiser for the Democratic party's presidential campaign. In 1928 he convinced the party to hold its convention in Houston. As a reward for Jones's activities, in 1932 Democratic leaders in Congress, including two close friends of Jones, Speaker John Nance Garner and Senator Carter Glass, helped secure his appointment by President Herbert Hoover to the bipartisan Reconstruction Finance Corporation. In 1933 newly elected President Franklin D. Roosevelt appointed Jones chair of the RFC. Jones had first met Roosevelt during his World War I service and had grown closer to him during the 1924 campaign.

While Jones might have had reasonably close ties to Roosevelt in 1933, his relationship with Woodrow Wilson proved far different. Jones worshiped Woodrow Wilson, and if this highly pragmatic and in many ways traditional member of the southern urban elite had an ideology it was Wilsonian. Jones along with a handful of others supported Wilson financially after he left office. After Wilson's death Jones made a point of taking his widow to prominent political gatherings. Edith Bolling Wilson, for example, attended the 1928 Democratic convention in Houston and several other conventions thereafter as Jones's guest, as if, through her, Jones wanted to keep the memory of her husband shining brightly. Wilson served as a strong and enduring link between Jones and the Democratic party. Prominent Democrats who shared some of Jones's affection for Wilson, such as Garner and Glass, were Jones's closest friends in Washington. Perhaps of most importance to understanding his actions in the 1930s, while Jones evolved in his thinking about the role of government in the economy, his ideology always retained a strong dose of Wilsonianism. While accepting the need for an active government in the economy, Jones advocated decentralized growth and local control. The Federal Reserve Board served as his model for government action. In theory at least, it preserved some level of regional autonomy. An appointed board insulated the group from partisan politics. Cooperation, not coercion, marked the agencies' dealings with the regulated industry.

The doctrine of voluntarism preached by Herbert Hoover also influenced Jones to some degree. The concept that government and industry could through close communication and goodwill cooperate for the public good appealed to him. He considered his service to the government as voluntary, and he never accepted payment for his work in the Red Cross or in the Hoover and Roosevelt administrations. Wilsonianism inclined him, however, to a more active government than envisioned by Hoover. Besides, his experiences in Houston on the eve of the Depression demonstrated the limits of voluntarism.

In 1931 two large Houston banks stood on the verge of failure. As at the time of the Panic of 1907 Jones was determined to prevent bankruptcy. He called a meeting of the prominent business leaders of Houston in his office near the top of the building that housed his National Bank of Commerce. The first evening's session proved fruitless, but Jones would not give up. A second session yielded a plan that brought new ownership to one bank and the merger of the other bank with National Bank of Commerce. The city's banks, utility companies, and Anderson, Clayton (the world's largest cotton company) all contributed to a fund to take out suspect loans. Humble Oil bought some of the assets of one of the banks, giving it a cash infusion. Besides the cotton company and Humble, the third major corporate entity doing business in Houston was the Southern Pacific Railroad. Jones tried repeatedly to get that company, which from 1886 on had close ties to the city and its banks and law firms, to contribute to the bailout fund. Management of the company refused. Voluntarism would not work in an economy in which the major participants were often large corporations whose interests were scattered across the country. Voluntarism also failed when it lacked a forceful personality such as Jones to lead the way. Thus Jones arrived in Washington, D.C., in 1932 well aware of the limits of Hoover's philosophy of voluntarism and ready to pursue a more active course by the government in dealing with the Depression.

The RFC of which Jones was at first simply a director came about because Hoover's orchestrated attempt at voluntarism through the National Credit Corporation failed. It became increasingly obvious that the government, not business, had to take the

Jones taking the oath as secretary of commerce from Supreme Court justice Stanley Reed as President Franklin D. Roosevelt looks on (courtesy of Harris & Ewing)

lead in supplying credit and energy to the floundering economy. The RFC faced two immediate problems: the collapse of the banking and railroad industries. It steadily increased its powers and soon lent billions to both industries. When Jones headed the RFC, most thought of him and the agency as one and the same. No loan was made without his approval. No policy existed that he disliked. Indeed, he dealt with Congress so adeptly that he drafted legislation expanding or changing the role of the RFC as he saw fit.

In the early days of the New Deal Jones believed the RFC should concern itself primarily with infusing more capital into the system, having government share some of the risk traditionally born by depositors, and preserving as many banks as possible. Along with others in Congress and the executive branch, Jones played a major role in developing deposit insurance and certifying banks as eligible for that insurance. Purchase of preferred stock in banks by the RFC was more clearly the responsibility of Jones. He had to convince suspicious bankers, particularly New York bankers, that the purchase of preferred stock would infuse needed capital and

prevent the failure of marginal banks. On several occasions Jones spoke before the American Bankers Association and lobbied with major bankers. Gradually he overcame their reluctance to have government play a more direct hand in their business. As more and more banks sold preferred stock to the RFC, their legal loan limit rose, and in theory at least they had the resources to make more loans. Over the course of several years the RFC invested more than $1.2 billion in some 6,000 banks. By the 1950s almost all that money had earned a profit, as banks paid dividends and repurchased the stock from the RFC. Thus, in the indirect way that Jones preferred, the government, acting through local bankers, increased the availability of credit across the country, and in the long run it avoided taking a loss.

Local bankers often expressed their reluctance to lend money in such key industries as railroads and agriculture. The RFC found itself filling the gap left by traditional bankers. Jones not only brokered loans as banks had once done but also lent to the various railroad companies. As a condition of those loans Jones sometimes required changes in management or the placement of an RFC director on the board of the company. As in the case of any other banker, he wanted to protect his investment and ensure the best use of public funds. Ironically, the so-called representative of business in the New Deal did as much as any other New Dealer to extend the control of government over business.

Jones also helped to develop new types of loans, including loans secured by equipment trust obligations and other new categories of collateral. The RFC lent money to railroads to buy equipment. The railroad issued equipment trust securities and turned them over to the RFC. The RFC then marketed the securities for a profit. In so doing Jones accomplished one of the objectives of the New Deal in helping to put railroad equipment builders back to work. He combined the traditional profit-making function of the banker with public service.

A similar child of the RFC, the Commodity Credit Corporation, for six years in the 1930s acted to stabilize the price of farm commodities and to restore credit to farmers. The corporation set a fixed price that it would lend farmers with commodities as collateral. For example, one of its first acts was to lend 10 cents a pound on cotton when cotton sold for 9. That had the effect of raising the price of cotton to 10 cents and established a ready source of credit for farmers, as it encouraged local bankers to lend to cotton farmers because the government had set a floor price.

Eventually almost all industries and many state and local governments borrowed from the RFC. An RFC Mortgage Company bought and sold mortgages just as Bankers Mortgage once had, and the government made loans for small business and loans for rural electrification to qualified cooperatives and other organizations. The RFC lent the Metropolitan Water District of southern California $208 million to build a 244-mile aqueduct from the Colorado River to Los Angeles. An Export-Import Bank was formed under supervision of the RFC and helped restore international trade. Until 1945, all remained under Jones's direction either as head of the RFC or as federal loan administrator.

Jones's position as federal loan administrator brought him supervision of new areas of lending. After 1939 not only did he have charge of the Export-Import Bank and the RFC, but also the Federal Housing Administration and the Home Owners Loan Corporation.

War, and appointment as secretary of commerce in 1940, brought Jones even more control over the nation's credit supply. By a special act of Congress Jones retained the position of federal loan administrator when he became secretary of commerce. Added to the bureaus and agencies he already headed, Jones took on the Disaster Loan Corporation, the Federal Savings and Loan Insurance Corporation, and the Electric Farm and Home Authority, to name only a few. Wartime brought the creation of the Rubber Reserve Company, the Metals Reserve Company, the Defense Supplies Corporation, and the Defense Plant Corporation. All lent money for the construction of plants or purchase of needed raw materials. In some cases they purchased materials directly.

From 1932 to 1945 Jones presided over a gigantic expansion of the role of government in the business of banking. He became not only the lender of last resort but the head of a vast array of government-backed entities that stabilized prices, infused credit, developed new lending techniques, and served the aims of government by trying to restore full employment and win the war. Jones did all of that while trying to preserve a role for local businessmen and limit centralized control of the economy. For more than a dozen years he remained the key figure in the development of American-style state capitalism, the merging of the roles of government and business.

Jones made an ungraceful and bitter exit from Washington. He had shared some of the reservations of his friend John Nance Garner about Roosevelt's third term, but wartime emergency kept him and the president working in harness. Jones, however, became increasingly estranged from Henry Wallace, who served as vice-president in Roosevelt's third term. When a party revolt kept Wallace off the ticket for Roosevelt's fourth term, Jones was asked to step aside so that Wallace could be secretary of commerce. Other appointments were offered Jones, but he resigned all of his government positions in 1945 and drifted back to his beloved Houston. There he built a few more buildings, ran his bank, and took an increased interest in the *Houston Chronicle*. In the mid 1950s his body gradually wore out, and on June 1, 1956, he died following an operation for a kidney blockage the previous April.

In many ways Jesse H. Jones was a transitional figure. He stood between the nineteenth-century community where friendship and kinship often explained economic and political success and the emerging world of national corporations closely linked to government. He stood between a banking industry jealous of its private rights and suspicious of government and the public's need to increase the role of government in business to end the Great Depression and win the war. By increasing the role of government and the acceptance of that role by bankers and businessmen, Jones became one of the chief architects of the modern age.

Publication:

Fifty Billion Dollars: My Thirteen Years with the RFC, 1932-1945, by Jones and Edward Angly (New York: Macmillan, 1951).

References:

Walter L. Buenger, "Between Community and Corpora-

tion: The Southern Roots of Jesse H. Jones and the Reconstruction Finance Corporation," *Journal of Southern History* (forthcoming, August 1990);

Buenger and Joseph A. Pratt, *But Also Good Business: Texas Commerce Banks and the Financing of Houston and Texas, 1886-1986* (College Station: Texas A&M Press, 1986);

James S. Olson, *Herbert Hoover and the Reconstruction Finance Corporation, 1931-1933* (Ames: Iowa State University Press, 1977);

Olson, *Saving Capitalism: The Reconstruction Finance Corporation and the New Deal, 1933-1940* (Princeton: Princeton University Press, 1988);

Bascom N. Timmons, *Jesse H. Jones: The Man and the Statesman* (New York: Holt, 1956).

Archives:

A collection of early and personal papers of Jesse H. Jones is in the Barker Texas History Center at the University of Texas, Austin. Material dealing mostly with his career in government service is at the Library of Congress.

John Maynard Keynes

(June 5, 1883 - April 21, 1946)

by Douglas Fisher

North Carolina State University

CAREER: Civil servant (1906-1909, 1915-1919); lecturer (1908-1915, 1919-1920); Fellow, King's College, Cambridge (1909-1946); chairman, National Mutual Life Assurance Company (1921-1938); bursar, King's College, Cambridge (1924-1946); director, Bank of England (1941-1946).

John Maynard Keynes, economist, statesman, and originator of the branch of modern macroeconomic theory and policy known as "Keynesian economics," was born on June 5, 1883, in Cambridge, England, and died at Tilton, Sussex, England, on Easter Sunday, April 21, 1946. Keynes was the eldest of the three children of John Neville and Florence Ada Brown Keynes of Cambridge. His father was an economist and university administrator at Cambridge University and the author of *The Scope and Method of Political Economy* (1891), an analysis of orthodox economic thought. His brother, Geoffrey, was also an economist, but was also known as a collector of rare books. Margaret, his sister, earned a C.B.E. for her work on retirement homes; she mar-

ried Professor A. V. Hill, winner of the 1922 Nobel Prize in Physiology.

The Cambridge society into which Keynes was born stood at the forefront of Western intellectual life. Most important for Keynes's intellectual development was the ferment in Cambridge surrounding Fabian Socialism, the Aesthetic Movement of the 1880s and 1890s, woman suffrage, and the decline of religious orthodoxy. Keynes's parents were, in fact, religious nonconformists (meaning they were not communicants of the Church of England), and Keynes ultimately adopted a life-style that encompassed the famous artistic and literary Bloomsbury Group as his closest and longest-standing friends. It is hard not to link the Cambridge freethinking tradition and the sometimes Bohemian and homosexual life-style of Keynes with the man who ultimately led the "Keynesian Revolution" against classical orthodoxy in economics.

Keynes, a precocious child, received his early education at home and, from 1891, at St. Faith's Preparatory School in Cambridge. Keynes's parents wanted their sometimes sickly son to obtain a schol-

John Maynard Keynes (courtesy of Milo Keynes)

arship to Eton and from there to obtain the Eton Scholarship to King's College, Cambridge. Keynes did not disappoint the family ambitions, attaining the Eton prize in 1897 and entering Cambridge in 1902 on the Eton Scholarship. Keynes showed a special facility at mathematics—especially algebra—and through much of his education studied mathematics formally. At Eton, aside from placing first in mathematics, he won an astonishing number of prizes in other areas, including classics and chemistry, showing the precision of mind, energy, and intellectual curiosity that characterized his life. He also displayed both charm and a manner of treating those he took to be his intellectual inferiors that became increasingly rude through the years.

At Eton, Keynes participated fully in all aspects of life at the school, including sports, at which he was never very good. But at Cambridge his wide range was especially notable. He ultimately held the positions of president of King's College and president of the Cambridge Union (the debating society) but he also gained induction into the Apostles, a group of intellectuals then headed

by the philosopher G. E. Moore that included the philosopher Bertrand Russell and the economist Ralph Hawtrey among its members; this "secret" society had once initiated Alfred, Lord Tennyson and later included the famous spies Guy Burgess and Anthony Blunt. Keynes, an outstanding debater and orator, spoke on a wide variety of topics covering historical, political, and social themes, and his skills apparently carried over to the economics conference table, where his best-known efforts included the Macmillan Committee's 1930-1931 post-mortem on the Great Crash of 1929 and the Bretton Woods Conference in 1944 (out of which grew the International Monetary Fund), both of which he dominated.

His biographers have made much of Keynes's social and literary pursuits while he attended Cambridge, and the most important of these seem to have revolved around the Apostles. Aside from Moore, the most important member of the Apostles from the point of view of Keynes in later life, was the critic Lytton Strachey. There he also came to know Leonard Woolf and the painter Duncan Grant, the latter with whom he fell in love. His circle of friends ultimately included the Cambridge daughters of Sir Leslie Stephen (the editor of the monumental *Dictionary of National Biography*), Virginia (later Virginia Woolf) and Vanessa (later Vanessa Bell). The Bells, along with their brother Clive, Roger Fry, E. M. Forster, and David Garnett, formed the core of the Bloomsbury Group that dominated the English literary scene from 1915 or so until the mid 1930s. This informal postaesthetic assemblage, founded partly on the philosophy of Moore, held freethinking principles (as documented in his monumental *Principia Ethica*, published in 1903) and had a studied disrespect of authority that predates much of the tone of late-twentieth-century artistic and literary style. That Keynes remained a full partner in the association for the rest of his life, while steadily improving his position as an eminent economist and statesman and financial wizard, ultimately becoming knighted in 1942 for his contributions to the British nation, continues to pose a major puzzle. The "Keynesian Revolution" constitutes, of course, the missing piece.

At Cambridge Keynes majored in mathematics, and he took the Mathematics Tripos in 1905. The results failed to meet Keynes's usual standards (he finished as 12th Wrangler in the First Class). He then turned his attention to the Civil Service Examination, in which he finished second, ultimately entering the Civil Service in the India Office in 1906. Keynes first formally studied economics in 1903 and at the time was especially taken with the work of William Stanley Jevons, one of the founders of the marginal utility approach to the determination of relative value. Jevons (who died in 1882) and Alfred Marshall of Cambridge adhered to a rigorous, partly mathematical approach to economics, and, through Marshall and Keynes's father, Keynes turned to economics. Curiously, the only period of time in which Keynes formally studied economics came during the short period between his disappointing performance on the Mathematics Tripos and his entry into the British Civil Service.

Keynes did not find the India Office much to his taste, and it took little effort on the part of Marshall and Keynes's father to entice him back to Cambridge in 1908 as a lecturer in economics, with his salary of £200 paid jointly by Professor A. C. Pigou (who at that time succeeded Marshall in the principal economics chair) and his father. He did not abandon Indian affairs (later serving on the Royal Commission on the Indian Currency and Finance), nor did he appreciably lessen his contacts with the British governmental bureaucracy, with whom he had already earned a reputation for clear thinking and an ability to manipulate statistics. The position he took while with the Indian Currency and Finance Commission was essentially that of a classical economist in linking the price level to the quantity of money (along the lines of the quantity theory of money) and in promoting the establishment of a central bank (modeled upon the Bank of England) for India. The final report rejected (although later adopted) the central bank and accepted the quantity theory. Ironically Keynes himself later made the rejection of the quantity theory of money the backbone of his economic theory.

At Cambridge, Keynes sought to support himself and in 1909 he applied for and won a fellowship at King's College, a position he held for life. At that time he undertook a thesis on probability theory (later published as *A Treatise on Probability* in 1921), and it is fair to summarize his economics at that time as very much mainstream neoclassical in content, much like that of Marshall and Pigou. If one is to locate the beginning of the Keynesian theory, it is not here. In 1911 Keynes took over as editor of the *Economic Journal*, the official organ of the Royal Economics Society that Alfred Marshall

had founded in 1890. He remained as editor or coeditor until 1945, a position that enabled him to see and comment on much of the latest and best work in the field. His authorized biographer, Roy F. Harrod, joined him as coeditor in 1937, after Keynes's first heart attack, and he had other coeditors over the years.

Keynes continued in his Cambridge lectureship until 1915, when he resigned to join the Treasury because of World War I. There he became intimately involved in the economic affairs of Great Britain, an involvement that continued for the rest of his life. Keynes's analytical skills and his knowledge of monetary economics (in which he had specialized while lecturing at Cambridge) brought him to the front line in the Treasury, and during the Paris Peace Conference in 1919 he represented the Treasury as its principal representative. The issue of the conference concerned how much and when the German government was to pay reparations to the victorious Allies, and the French and British delegations dominated the conference, themselves reflecting the strongly nationalistic view that Germany should pay heavily. Keynes and the British Treasury, and some of the American delegation, favored a more moderate scheme, based on the ability of the Germans to pay. That ability required the reconstruction of German industry and the possibility of earning enough foreign exchange from exports (or private capital imports) to protect the value of the German mark. But the revival of the German economy did not rank well on the postwar agenda of most European nations.

Keynes steadfastly advanced the Treasury position, but grew increasingly despondent as the conference moved toward punitive and, ultimately, uncollectible reparations. On June 28, 1919, the Treaty of Versailles was signed, but by then Keynes had resigned. Following a brief recuperation from an illness possibly brought on by the strains of the conference, Keynes published *The Economic Consequences of the Peace*, his scathing denunciation of the terms of the Treaty. Appearing in December 1919, it was an international best-seller—especially in the United States where its negative view of European politics coincided with a movement toward American isolation—and turned Keynes into an international celebrity. The theme of the book, that economic considerations should have dominated political, and its drastic predictions of what would happen should the treaty be enforced, found a responsive audience. Keynes worried that the terms of the Treaty would stunt the European economy that was itself necessary to stave off the dangers to society brought on by rapidly rising population. (He saw starvation and Bolshevism, not Fascism, as the principal evils.) Ironically, some have posited that Keynes's book, by effectively labeling the terms of the treaty impossible, later gave Hitler the excuse he needed to dismantle the economic terms of the treaty in the 1930s. In fairness, Hitler probably would have done that anyway, and most believe that the treaty, and not Keynes's book, contributed significantly to the German disaster. Keynes merely predicted the danger, not the direction from which it would come.

In 1919 Keynes returned to Cambridge as a lecturer—turning down prestigious chairs at the London School of Economics and Political Science and at Leeds University. But the income from other activities soon dwarfed his academic earnings (he still held the King's fellowship and in 1924 took up the position of bursar of King's College), and he formally abandoned the lectureship in 1920. His considerable investment skill, aided at times by his numerous contacts in the City, London's financial district, enabled him to manage both his and his friends' financial affairs and those of King's College. On the whole he successfully speculated in foreign exchange (although a disaster in 1920 almost ruined him), at that time usually taking a bullish position on the dollar and a bearish one on European currencies. He also held several directorships, the most important being with the National Mutual Life Assurance Company (for which he was chairman of the board from 1921 to 1938) and the Provincial Insurance Company (1923-1946). Keynes ultimately became quite wealthy and indulged his passion—first cultivated at Eton—for collecting rare books, especially of the Renaissance, Elizabethan, and Stuart periods. He also collected art and was a generous supporter of the arts, becoming first chairman of what ultimately became the independent Arts Council in Britain. At his death he owned works by Ingres, Degas, Seurat, Cezanne, Picasso, Matisse, Renoir, and many others.

When Keynes returned to London in 1919, the Bloomsbury Group was spreading its influence; by then the group had expanded to include other artists and even stage and dance personalities. Keynes entertained frequently at his London home, 46 Gordon Square, and made frequent visits to the ballet

and, most particularly, to Sergey Diaghilev's 1921 production of Tchaikovsky's *The Sleeping Princess* in which Lydia Lopokova occasionally danced the part of the Princess. Lopokova, already known in Bloomsbury, had recently separated from her husband and lived at the Waldorf Hotel, but Keynes persuaded her to move to 41 Gordon Square. They married in 1925.

During 1922, Keynes contributed to the *Manchester Guardian* Supplement, a monumental survey of the problems of the reconstruction of Europe. Keynes wrote major articles for this paper, including work on "purchasing power parity" and exchange rates that he later incorporated into his orthodox and important *Tract on Monetary Reform* (1923). He argued—in both venues—for a return to the Gold Standard, but in the form of the Gold Exchange Standard (in which central banks traded gold for currencies but private individuals did not). Those views were quite orthodox. Keynes saw the chief advantages of his plan as deriving from the benefits that would accrue to foreign trade and investment through a stable exchange rate. Keynes believed exchange rates and domestic price levels to be tied together—an idea known as purchasing power parity—but he also vehemently opposed using a deflation policy (defined as a fall in the price level induced by a contractionary monetary policy) as a tool for restoring exchange parity, partly because it would lead to depression and unemployment. That proved the first mention of one of the major themes of his monumental *General Theory of Employment, Interest and Money* (1936). The *General Theory*, of course, launched the Keynesian Revolution. The reason the issue came up is that classical economists, including Keynes's former mentor Pigou, tended to recommend deflation as a way to deal with exchange rate problems *and* to deal with general depression in the economy. Keynes criticized the former but not (yet) the latter in those important early works.

Keynes's politics bear mentioning at this point, since the Keynesian approach to economics is generally associated with the liberal position in the United States. Keynes was always a member of the Liberal party (at that time the party's platform came reasonably close to the current Libertarian position in the United States), but on many important issues his positions fell definitely to the left of the party. He especially had his doubts about the effectiveness of the traditional laissez-faire policy of the

Keynes (center) with Bertrand Russell and Lytton Strachey, circa 1915 (courtesy of Richard Keynes)

Liberals, both nationally and internationally.

The *Tract on Monetary Reform* is also the source of the famous Keynesian retort to the generic classical theorist that "in the long run we are all dead," an epigram used to dramatize the point that classical theories–such as the Quantity Theory of Money–presented long-run but not short-run solutions to economic problems. Keynes felt the classical model did not grapple with the problem of the business cycle–a short-run problem. Keynes, indeed, advocated considerably more governmental intervention, in the form of manipulating interest rates to control the price level, than was typical of Liberals. As a consequence, therefore, at the time the book met a hostile reception from both left and right.

In 1924, England suffered from one of its periodic bouts of unemployment, and the questions arose as to what the government could or should do. Keynes's proposal to remedy the situation–increase spending on public works–appeared in the Liberal party weekly, the *Nation* (which Keynes supported both financially and intellectually) in May 1924. But the argument connecting the proposed fiscal policy with the problem of unemployment

lacked a theoretical basis. The construction of that theoretical superstructure occupied Keynes for the next dozen years. Along the way, the two great books of the Keynesian canon, *A Treatise on Money* (1930) and *The General Theory of Employment, Interest and Money* (1936), appeared.

The two-volume *Treatise* took five years to write and appeared in December 1930. That comprehensive survey of both theory and policy represents a fair summary of much of Keynes's work as an economist for the preceding twenty years. Indeed, his particular professional expertise lay as an expert on money. The *Treatise* has suffered historically because it was sandwiched between the Great Crash of 1929, against which its policies seemed ineffective, and the stronger medicine of the *General Theory*. Even so, it not only contained many of the insights of the later work but also presented essential parts of the entire project that Keynes did not repeat in the *General Theory*. This was particularly true of many institutional issues (such as how the financial system works) and its detailed discussion of macroeconomic equilibrium systems. Nevertheless, the central proposition of the *Treatise*–the fact that spending and producing decisions might not coincide—is shared with the *General Theory*, although in the early work the full implications of such an imbalance are not fully worked out. In the *Treatise*, Keynes was at pains to demonstrate that if savings exceeded investment there would be a depression and there would be inflation if the converse held. This is, therefore, an important early statement of the demand-pull theory of inflation generally associated with the Keynesians.

To combat depressions, Keynes recommended policies to discourage saving, or encourage consumption, and to stimulate investment spending. He recommended the latter because of the view that—in more modern terminology—there was a failure of aggregate demand (in this case consumption demand plus investment demand). This point, incidentally, had appeared in the work of another Cambridge economist, Dennis H. Robertson (in *Banking Policy and the Price Level*, 1926), but Keynes certainly explained it in a way that made it accessible to a much wider audience than had ever grappled with Robertson's slim but quirky volume. Robertson, incidentally, had studied under Keynes at Cambridge before the war.

When it came to policy, however, the *Treatise* did not really enlarge the arsenal, and this, certainly, contributed to its cool reception both academically and practically. The standard view of monetary policy at the time favored the use of the lending rate of the central bank (known as Bank Rate in England) as the chief tool of policy and basically took as its objective the stabilization of the external value of the currency, usually in a Gold Standard context. Keynes, in the *Treatise*, discussed both open market operations, including the control of the money supply, and Bank Rate as policy tools, but he felt that the latter, because of its effect on investment spending, held the key to restoring balance between savings and investment. He reinforced that perception by his view that excesses of investment spending created business cycles. This emphasis on the destabilizing effects of investment is in keeping with informed opinion at the time and has remained a central part of orthodox Keynesian theory ever since, although in recent years other sorts of shocks, such as changes in basic commodity prices, have become more important in theory and in practice.

Little doubt exists that few envisioned the calamity that befell the Western world in the decade before World War II, with recorded unemployment reaching a quarter of the work force (in the United States) and equivalent slumps in production, consumption, and even prices, but Keynes, at least, had predicted some of the ingredients in his *Economic Consequences of the Peace* and *Tract on Monetary Reform*. During this period, he served on the Macmillan Committee (1930-1931) and on the Economic Advisory Council (in 1930), and the agenda, in both cases, saved Great Britain from economic disaster. Characteristically, he dominated these groups on the macroeconomic issues, and it is arguable that the Keynesian Revolution itself was forged on the conference table at this time, in that his basic ideas took shape under that stimulus. Keynes himself realized quite early that Bank Rate was inadequate to the task at hand and began to formulate his new theories.

In June 1931 a student and protégé of Keynes, Richard F. Kahn, published an article in the *Economic Journal* outlining the theory of the "investment multiplier." That simple and elegant theory, that a sudden change in investment would have a cumulative effect on the economy, dragging it upward or downward depending on the direction of the initial thrust, provided the missing link for Keynes's *General Theory*. One could explain business cycles, on the one hand, as the result of anything that shocked the economy and hence investment such as the stock market crash of 1929 clearly did. And one could recommend a policy, such as "public works" (a particularly aggressive fiscal policy) to countershock the system so that it could react (cumulatively) in the opposite direction to the original and undesired shock. Because the cumulative forces were so strong—the multiplier so large— bold measures would be needed.

The *General Theory* was four years in the making and, like the rest of Keynes's books, was essentially produced (and priced) by Keynes to reach as wide an audience as possible. The book did not spring out of thin air, of course, and there are extant several drafts and a voluminous correspondence with (mainly) the economists Ralph G. Hawtrey and Dennis H. Robertson. Richard F. Kahn also worked closely with Keynes, but the final product is, by all accounts, vintage Keynes, both in style and content. Evidence of this abounds and is colored by the famous rift between Keynes and his former student Robertson over both the substance and style of the *General Theory*. Two things proved troublesome, and have remained so to some

Keynes and his wife, Lydia Lopokova, in 1929 (courtesy of Milo Keynes)

extent, and these are the numerous sallies against other theories designed to accentuate the differences between the new theory and the old, and the rather casual scholarship of the book. Keynes proved, indeed, an indifferent reader of other people's work, partly out of conceit. At the same time, he was determined to present his case with as much forcefulness as would carry the day. In any case, Keynes's work had the effect he desired, and Robertson left Cambridge in 1939 for a chair at the London School of Economics and Political Science, somewhat justifiably miffed at the way in which his important contributions were lost in the rush toward Keynesianism.

The *General Theory*, unlike the *Treatise*, was the right book for the times, producing powerful and persuasive answers to difficult and important questions, and the Keynesian Revolution was not long delayed. With its undertone of mathematical reasoning, with its messianic overtones, and with its system for analyzing general depressions, it appealed to scholars on both sides of the Atlantic. At that point American economists adopted Keynes. In

the United States there was almost a complete annihilation of existing and competing macroeconomic theory, such as it was, in favor of what Seymour Harris of Harvard University called the "new economics." In the hands of talented and basically liberal economists such as John R. Hicks and Roy Harrod in England and Paul Samuelson, Alvin Hansen, Franco Modigliani, and James Tobin in the United States, the basic Keynesian model was constructed from the elements in Keynes and turned toward the policy problems that emerged from World War II. The resulting business-cycle theory, in the form of the "accelerator-multiplier" model and a static policy framework, found a home (mostly in textbooks) in the IS-LM model, which describes the modus operandi of both monetary and fiscal policy. The Employment Act of 1946 and its establishment of a Council of Economic Advisers to the president linked those academic exercises to the political process. By the mid 1960s, Keynesian economics were firmly entrenched and a succession of American presidents—Eisenhower, Kennedy, Johnson, Nixon, and Carter—pursued Keynesian-style policies that emphasized fiscal policy, but also made some use of monetary policy for fine-tuning the economy.

For a time, and this was through no fault of Keynes who always insisted that his two great works should be read together, Keynesians promoted fiscal policy and totally ignored monetary topics; partly as a result, the Monetarist counterrevolution took hold. That was engineered in the 1960s, largely by Milton Friedman of the University of Chicago, where it had brewed at least since the mid 1950s. Fiscal policy had proved unwieldy for fine-tuning, partly because of its political basis, and monetary policy turned out to be feasible in the same role. The still on-going debate has resulted in a plethora of Monetarist, Neo-Keynesian, Marxo-Keynesian, Neo-Monetarist, Supply-Sider and Rational Expectations positions, all carrying something from the *General Theory* into battle.

Following the publication of the *General Theory*, almost immediately Keynes suffered the first of a series of heart attacks. He redirected his activities in the last ten years of his life, but, remarkably, that right up until the end he remained a central figure in many important issues. He never again wrote anything of special importance, although a small book and his letters and an occasional article exist to tantalize scholars, but his work on committees and, most especially, before and during the Bretton Woods Conference that produced the International Monetary Fund showed that his powers were far from exhausted.

Putting aside his participation in the debate over exactly how to interpret the *General Theory*, Keynes's major concern in this period focused on the question of war finance, and a small book, *How to Pay for the War*, appeared in February 1940. He wanted to finance increased government expenditures without inflation, in the likelihood that voluntary savings would fail to fund the deficit. Governments usually raise taxes in such circumstances, but Keynes proposed, instead, to persuade workers to accept deferred wage increases. In fact, in the United Kingdom and the United States, the governments made orchestrated appeals to savers, enacted price controls, and undertook rationing, so they clearly did not apply Keynes's prescription. It did, however, provide a model for a discussion and, by linking inflation to the relation between aggregate demand and supply, provided an "inflation-environment" version of the *General Theory* that

effectively counteracts the argument that his masterpiece was just "depression economics."

During the war, Keynes assisted the Treasury once again, seeking to solve the problem of paying for the American supplies. Keynes's group, with Richard Stone and James Meade, the well-known and ultimately eminent economists, the principal collaborators, implemented modern national income accounting, already under way in the United States. Lend-lease offered the answer, although politicians more than economists laid out the solution. Also during the war Keynes participated in the formation of the Committee for the Encouragement of Music and the Arts. The resulting Arts Council of Great Britain, a publicly funded agency, fostered and supported professional artists. Keynes served as its first chairman, and the agency continues to this day, operating largely independently of the political milieu as, indeed, the founders originally intended.

In some ways, Keynes's finest hour on the international stage came at the Washington Conference in September 1943 and in the subsequent Bretton Woods Conference in New Hampshire in July 1944. The conferees sought to redesign the collapsed international-payments system so as to promote economic recovery after the war, in a climate of exchange-rate stability. That sent the world back to some sort of Gold Standard, of course, but by that time the Gold Exchange Standard, which Keynes had promoted for 20 years, finally had its chance. Keynes, as usual, was one step ahead, and won over the British delegation to his view that the conference should create a new means of international liquidity—dubbed "Bancor"—to bolster the traditional means of supporting currencies against undesired drains. Until then, countries defended their exchange rates with gold and "convertible currencies" (internationally accepted foreign currencies), but to that total Keynes proposed that the superinternational agency that was to be created should be empowered to issue its own liabilities (Bancor). The existence of an agency to manage the Gold Exchange Standard was readily accepted, but Bancor proved unacceptable, especially to the Americans, led by Harry Dexter White. Ironically, the Gold Exchange Standard did not survive for very long—although it certainly assisted in the postwar reconstruction effort—and in 1968, just before its demise, was patched up with a Bancor-like instrument known as the Special Drawing Right. All along, Keynes's insistence that the system needed a provision for greater flexibility to reserve creation if one wished to have a system of fixed exchange rates emerged as correct, and subsequent experience vindicated it. Whether the fixed exchange-rate system was a good idea is another matter, and the possible revival of a Gold Standard of some sort would be difficult to implement in the modern climate of relatively uncontrolled movement of goods and capital among the advanced nations. Keynes wanted a fixed-rate system, in any case.

In June 1942, Keynes was awarded a peerage, making him Baron Keynes of Tilton, the home he had made with Lydia since 1925. In March 1946, Lord Keynes traveled to Savannah, Georgia, participating in the sometimes acrid discussions over the proposed location of the International Monetary Fund. He opposed the final Washington, D. C., location, but his arguments failed to persuade. While returning to Washington on the train, he suffered the worst of his heart attacks. He recovered briefly, but finally succumbed on Easter Sunday, April 21, 1946, at his home at Tilton. A memorial service was held at Westminster Abbey. Both of Keynes's parents attended. Aside from substantial gifts of literary and artistic items to King's College and the *Nation*, he left behind the legacy of a brilliant man whose energy and insight fashioned a revolution in the way economists think about the economic problems of a nation. His system has been much modified as the theory has been upgraded, and empirical work has called into question many of his premises. But an identifiable Keynesian position on macroeconomic questions still remains, as do economists willing to call themselves Keynesians. In many respects, John Maynard Keynes was to the mid twentieth century what Karl Marx was to the nineteenth and Adam Smith was to the eighteenth. What the world has gained is a Keynesian Revolution that has pro-

vided governments with many of the tools they might use in the broad task of safeguarding the standards of living of their people. In 1929 the British and American governments found themselves unable to think of vigorous and effective remedies while scarcely 30 years later, when the revolution itself had subsided, the tool kit was well stacked with fiscal and monetary means.

Publications:

The Collected Writings of John Maynard Keynes, 30 volumes (Cambridge: Cambridge University Press, 1971-1989);

Polly Hill, and others, *Lydia & Maynard: Letters Between Lydia Lopokova & John Maynard Keynes* (New York: Macmillan, 1990).

References:

Peter Clarke, *The Keynesian Revolution in the Making, 1924-1936* (New York: Oxford University Press 1988);

Athol Fitzgibbons, *Keynes's Vision: A New Political Economy* (Oxford: Claredon, 1988);

Roy Forbes Harrod, *The Life of John Maynard Keynes* (London: Macmillan, 1951);

Elizabeth Johnson and Harry G. Johnson, *The Shadow of Keynes: Understanding Keynes, Cambridge, and Keynesian Economics* (Chicago: University of Chicago Press, 1978);

Richard F. Kahn, *The Making of Keynes's General Theory* (New York: Cambridge University Press, 1984);

Alan H. Meltzer, *Keynes's Monetary Theory: A Different Interpretation* (New York: Cambridge University Press, 1989);

Don Patinkin, *Keynes's Monetary Thought: A Study of Its Development* (Durham, N.C.: Duke University Press, 1976);

Robert Skidelsky, *John Maynard Keynes: Hopes Betrayed, 1883-1920* (London: Macmillan, 1983).

Archives:

John Maynard Keynes's personal papers are located in King's College Library, Cambridge. His economic papers are located in the Marshall Library, Cambridge.

Thomas W. Lamont

(September 30, 1870 - February 2, 1948)

by David M. Fitzsimons

University of Michigan

CAREER: Reporter, *New York Tribune* (1893-1894); secretary, Cushman Brothers (1894-1898); director, Lamont, Corliss & Company (1898-1925); secretary, treasurer (1903-1905), vice-president, Bankers Trust Company (1905-1909); vice-president, First National Bank (1909-1911); partner, J. P. Morgan & Company (1911-1948); owner, *New York Post* (1918-1922); chairman of executive committee (1940-1943), chairman of the board, J. P. Morgan & Company, Incorporated (1943-1948).

Thomas William Lamont was a noted banker, diplomat, and philanthropist. For two decades, until the death of J. P. Morgan, Jr., in 1943, Lamont was second only to Morgan himself in directing the fortunes of the international banking house of J. P. Morgan & Company. In 1937 the radical journalist Ferdinand Lumberg said with only some exaggeration that Lamont "exercised more power for 20 years in the western hemisphere, has put into effect more final decisions from which there has been no appeal, than any other person."

Born on September 30, 1870, in the small rural town of Claverack, New York (near Albany), Lamont was the youngest child of Caroline Deuel (Jayne) Lamont and the Reverend Thomas Lamont, a Methodist minister who served at a series of churches in the Hudson River Valley. The elder Lamont, of Scottish descent and a former teacher of Greek, raised his three children in strict accordance with the tenets of Methodism. He encouraged the children to read extensively, and his youngest child enjoyed recalling that he had read the Bible twice through by the time he was fourteen. With the aid of scholarships, Thomas Lamont graduated from Phillips Exeter Academy in 1888 and Harvard College in 1892.

Lamont liked to refer to himself as "an old newspaper man." At Harvard he contributed to

Thomas W. Lamont

The Crimson and two Boston newspapers, and after graduation he hired on as a reporter at the *New York Tribune.* In 1918 he purchased the *New York Post* from Oswald Garrison Villard. He sold it to a newspaper syndicate in 1924 but retained its literary supplement and operated it as the *Saturday Review of Literature* until 1938. Throughout his life Lamont indulged his journalistic and literary interests by acting as a financial angel for several daily newspapers and cultivating literary friends such as Robert Frost, Walter Lippmann, and H. G. Wells.

In 1894 Lamont left the *Tribune,* borrowed $5,000, and invested it in the troubled import-export firm Cushman Brothers, where he accepted the position of secretary. Through clever newspaper advertisements he saved the firm and reorganized it as Lamont, Corliss & Company in 1898.

His rescue of Cushman Brothers and successful reorganization of other firms brought him to the attention of Henry P. Davison, who made him secretary and treasurer of Bankers Trust Company in 1903. Two years later he was promoted to vice-president and in 1909 was appointed to a comparable position at First National Bank. In January 1911, at age forty-one, he became a partner at J. P. Morgan & Company.

Until his death in 1948, Lamont participated in the most important business decisions the House of Morgan made, and after the death of Harry Davison in 1922 he exercised day-to-day executive command until 1943. In addition, beginning with the famed Pujo hearings in 1912, Lamont planned and orchestrated the extensive public-relations efforts of the House of Morgan for more than a generation. As Wall Street put it at the time: "Mr. Morgan speaks to Mr. Lamont and Mr. Lamont speaks to the people."

When Lamont received an honorary LL.D. from Harvard in 1931, the commendation declared: "By nature a statesman, by occupation a financier; sagacious in council on the affairs that affect all nations." The declaration was appropriate, for Lamont was the quintessential and premier banker of the Diplomatic Age of American financial history. His interest in foreign affairs started at the beginning of World War I and accelerated toward the end of his career. In 1915 he helped secure a $500 million loan for Britain and France, and he served on the Liberty Loan committees that helped the Department of the Treasury sell bonds after America entered the war. In the autumn of 1917 he traveled to Europe with Wilson adviser Colonel Edwin House, and he represented the Treasury Department as a financial adviser in the American delegation at the Paris Peace Conference following the war.

In Paris, Lamont and Woodrow Wilson developed a mutual admiration for each other, and Lamont became a strong advocate of world peace organizations. He directed money into associations advocating American entry into the League of Nations and even went so far as to cast his lone Democratic presidential vote for James M. Cox because of Cox's support for the League in the 1920 election. He made sizable contributions to both the League of Nations Association and the Foreign Policy Association, and in 1940 he helped found the Committee to Defend America by Aiding the Allies.

Lamont was involved very much in the debt-settlement and reparations negotiations during the interwar years. Feeling that a strong Germany was central to European economic health, he advocated a reparations amount at the Paris conference of approximately $40 billion, modest compared to British and French demands. He participated in the drafting of the Dawes Plan in 1924 and the Young Plan in 1929, and in 1935 he negotiated a 70 percent repayment of the interest due on the German loans associated with those plans.

As the chairman of the International Committee of Bankers on Mexico, Lamont worked under close State Department supervision as its key man in the delicate Mexican debt negotiations that followed World War I. In the eyes of the Mexicans he exemplified American economic power: in 1921 a Mexican journalist noted that Lamont "is not the man behind the throne, he is the man on the throne. He is the most clever, the most listened to, the most powerful of the partners of Morgan." In spite of that power, Lamont returned only a fraction of the investments of the bondholders whom he represented, due to Mexican expropriation.

He was more successful in Japan, where he floated substantial loans, helped arrange a merger between Tokyo Electric Power and Tokyo Electric Light, and, in 1930, worked to restore Japan to the gold standard. In 1927 the emperor of Japan invested Lamont with the Order of the Rising Sun. Lamont had a special fondness for Japan and worked to support the liberal forces there against their militarist opponents.

He shared Japan's perception of the Chinese as cunning and deceitful. Immediately after the Mukden incident Lamont drafted a press release that was modified and released by Japan's Ministry of Finance to exonerate Japanese conduct in Manchuria. But in the wake of the bombing of Shanghai in 1932, and after several influential Japanese friends of the liberal persuasion were assassinated, Lamont reversed his support for the Japanese in 1934.

Lamont's relations with the Italian Peninsula resulted in early success and later embarrassment. A converted Presbyterian, Lamont was granted the Grand Cross of St. Gregory the Great by Pope Pius XI in honor of the investment advice he provided for the Vatican. Benito Mussolini was a close acquaintance of Lamont, and Lamont created a New York publicity office to enhance the dictator's overseas image. Lamont proved instrumental in securing huge loans for the government of Il Duce. In 1925 he coached Mussolini in the fine art of manipulating Anglo-American opinion, and in a 1926 speech before the Foreign Policy Association he strongly praised Mussolini's economic policies. Soon after, the U.S. government granted Italy a lenient settlement on its war debt. Lamont's announcement that the House of Morgan granted Italy a $100 million loan quickly followed.

As one of the few people who could count both Herbert Hoover and Franklin D. Roosevelt as friends, Lamont moved comfortably in both Republican and Democratic circles. His son Corliss, who was a chairman of the Friends of the Soviet Union and a socialist professor of philosophy at Columbia University, admired his father's internationalism and saw his own views as an extension of his parents' liberalism.

Lamont's ideology, a mixture of the classical liberalism common in the United States during his youth and the modern liberalism that it developed into during his lifetime, can be most clearly seen in his attitudes toward the Great Depression. On the one hand, as Wall Street's point man during the Great Crash, he advised President Hoover to pursue a hands-off policy toward the stock market and grant a temporary cessation on war debts and reparations in 1931. That same year he also helped enlist 110 banks to save the British gold standard, albeit without success. He advocated a repeal of capital-gains taxes and "excess profits" taxes, and he praised Britain for overcoming the Depression without resorting to the deficit spending advocated by John Maynard Keynes. On the other hand, Lamont supported Hoover's Reconstruction Finance Corporation, a boon to Morgan interests, and was less hostile to the New Deal than most bankers, approving of government relief for the poor and of inflationary measures such as the purchase and sale of government securities by the Federal Reserve Banks.

Before Pearl Harbor and the German declaration of war on the United States, Lamont opposed American entry into World War II but helped Roosevelt lobby for Lend-Lease aid to the Allies. He drew closer to Roosevelt during World War II because they both had the same enemy—the isolationists. In early 1942 Lamont and Roosevelt discussed for almost an hour the possibility of using American gold reserves to stabilize the world economy after the war. As historian Ron Chernow adroitly observed, "This was the relationship Lamont had craved—full of secrets, confidences and back scratching." Lamont was a charming and intelligent man who respected and was attracted to power; that is why he was successful as an international banker and a diplomat.

Lamont replaced J. P. Morgan, Jr., as chairman of the board of J. P. Morgan & Company, Incorporated, in 1943. Rather than signaling an increase in Lamont's power and authority at Morgan, the promotion merely reflected the enormous influence he had exercised within the firm for more than a generation.

That same year Lamont developed a heart ailment that forced him to reduce his time at the bank. During his declining years, he authored *My Boyhood in a Parsonage* (1946), which detailed his early life, and *Across World Frontiers* (1951), originally printed for private circulation but ultimately published, with favorable reviews, for a larger audience after his death.

With his wife of 53 years, Florence Haskell (Corliss) Lamont, at his bedside, Lamont died late in the evening of February 2, 1948, at his winter home in Boca Grande, Florida. Russell Leffingwell replaced him as chairman of J. P. Morgan, and his estate sold his nearly $6 million bloc of J. P. Morgan stock, the largest then in existence. His bequests to charitable and educational institutions totaled nearly $10 million, with the largest donations going to Harvard University ($5 million), Phillips Exeter Academy ($2 million), and the Metropolitan Museum of Art ($1 million).

Selected Publications:

Henry P. Davison: The Record of a Useful Life (New York & London: Harper, 1933);

My Boyhood in a Parsonage (New York & London: Harper, 1946);

Across World Frontiers (New York: Harcourt, Brace, 1951).

References:

John Brooks, *Once in Golconda: A True Drama of Wall Street, 1920-1938* (New York: Harper & Row, 1969);

Vincent P. Carosso, *Investment Banking in America: A History* (Cambridge, Mass.: Harvard University Press, 1970);

Ron Chernow, *The House of Morgan—An American Banking Dynasty and the Rise of Modern Finance* (New York: Atlantic Monthly Press, 1990);

Warren I. Cohen, *The Chinese Connection: Roger S. Greene, Thomas W. Lamont, George E. Sokolski and American-East Asian Relations* (New York: Columbia University Press, 1978).

Archives:

Thomas W. Lamont's papers are housed at Harvard University.

James M. Landis

(September 25, 1899 - July 30, 1964)

by John Majewski

University of California, Los Angeles

CAREER: Clerk for Supreme Court justice Louis Brandeis (1925); professor of law (1926-1933), dean, Harvard Law School (1937-1945); commissioner (1934), chairman, U.S. Securities and Exchange Commission (1935-1937); director, U.S. Office of Civilian Defense (1942-1943); U.S. economic minister, Middle East (1943-1945); chairman, U.S. Civil Aeronautics Board (1945-1947); private law practice (1948-1960, 1961-1964); special assistant to President John F. Kennedy (1961).

James M. Landis, a brilliant legal scholar, helped engineer the securities and banking legislation of the New Deal. Although his later career was beset by personal and emotional tragedies, he continued to exert a major influence in the regulatory world until his death in 1964.

The son of a Presbyterian missionary, Landis was born in Tokyo, Japan, on September 25, 1899. At age fourteen he moved to America to study at Mercersburg Academy in Pennsylvania. Thanks to the stern discipline of his father, he was far ahead of most of the other students. He was accepted to Princeton University at age sixteen and graduated at the head of his class. After the *Harvard Law Review* published one of his undergraduate papers Landis decided to accept a fellowship at Harvard Law School, where his intellectual brilliance and work ethic became almost legendary. Contemporaries regarded Landis as one of the most brilliant students of his day.

The most important influence on Landis's career at Harvard was Felix Frankfurter, a legal scholar who already had a reputation for spotting exceptional talent. After Landis graduated first in his law school class, Frankfurter invited him to spend an additional year at Harvard as a research assistant. He eagerly accepted the offer, and in 1925 he co-authored a series of articles with Frankfurter on the mechanics of the federal judiciary. The articles later appeared in the 1928 publication *The Business of the Supreme Court*. Frankfurter awarded Landis by arranging for him to clerk with Supreme Court justice Louis Brandeis. Brandeis, a leading progressive, strongly supported government regulation of big business, especially through strong antitrust legislation. Not surprisingly, Brandeis encouraged Landis to pursue his interests in regulatory law. In 1926, at the age of twenty-eight, Landis was appointed to Harvard's new professorship of legislation.

The early political attitudes of Landis helped make him the ideal New Deal regulator. His political ideology is best described as pragmatic progressivism. Since his days at Princeton he had deplored the materialism of American society (though his antimaterialistic attitudes did not inhibit him from starting a profitable business selling class notes and academic advice at Princeton). Working closely with Frankfurter and Brandeis put Landis in touch with many of the leading intellectuals of the Left and helped solidify his progressive instincts. Although he made his disdain for big business and commercial mentality evident, he had no wish to destroy capitalism. On the contrary, he wished to save capitalism by curbing what he saw as its excesses of greed and power. Such a pragmatic political philosophy drew attacks from both the Left and the Right. As the *New York Times* once noted, Landis "achieved the rare distinction of being regarded as a conservative by liberals and an extreme liberal by conservatives."

Landis's legal philosophy mirrored his political attitudes. While he worked at Harvard, legal scholarship shifted away from formalism to realism. Legal formalism taught that law established

James M. Landis (courtesy of the National Archives)

a series of precedents outside the influence of economics or society. But by the turn of the century scholars had begun to relate law to its social and economic contexts, arguing that it could be used as a vehicle for social reform. Always the moderate, Landis rejected the more extreme versions of legal realism but still accepted its basic framework. He conceived of law as an "umpire," a moderator between competing interest groups that naturally arose in a pluralistic society. As Landis's biographer Donald H. Ritchie argues, "Regulatory decisions, in his [Landis's] 'umpire theory,' were simply wise compromises between conflicting claims."

Landis put his expertise with legislation and regulation to practical use beginning in April 1933, when Frankfurter arranged for him to visit Washington to observe the genesis of the New Deal. Landis thought he would return to Harvard by the end of the weekend; he ended up staying in the capital for four years. Frankfurter, Roosevelt's recruiting agent for top academic talent, gathered Landis and two others of his top students (Thomas Corcoran and Benjamin Cohen) to write the Securities Act of 1933. Most New Dealers contended that wide-spread abuses in the securities industry had contributed to the speculative fever of the 1920s. The Securities Act sought to force stock issuers to provide potential buyers with accurate purchasing information. By forcing issuers to provide balance sheets, the government could stop fraudulent sales and slow risky speculation. Landis, Corcoran, and Cohen undertook the laborious task of writing the detailed registration procedures that the government required of all new stock issues. The three quickly became symbols of the New Deal brain trust, and the Washington press promptly labeled them the "Happy Hot Dogs."

Landis made three important contributions to the Securities Act. First, he made ignoring a Federal Trade Commission (FTC) subpoena a penal offense. Before the passage of the act, stock issuers often ignored the subpoenas of the regulatory agency, forcing it to go to court and prove the appropriateness of the action. In the long and costly legal procedure that followed, the resulting testimony was usually outdated. Under the Securities Act, a person who ignored an FTC subpoena could go to jail. Second, Landis inserted a cooling-off period in the legislation. That meant that the security issuer had to wait 20 days after stock had been registered with the FTC before putting it on the market. The cooling-off period gave regulators an opportunity to verify the registration information. If the FTC registered no complaints with the proposed sale, it could proceed without hindrance. Third, the provision also allowed the issuer to proceed with the sale even if the FTC had not rendered a judgment within the 20-day period, ensuring that delays in stock sales would result from legitimate causes, not administrative backlog. If regulators did find something wrong within the 20-day period, they could issue a "stop order," suspending the sale until the mistake was corrected. Since a stop order resulted in a loss of investor confidence, it provided security issuers with a big incentive to provide the FTC with accurate information.

Although Landis often bickered with Cohen and Corcoran, his work earned him considerable praise. President Franklin Roosevelt appointed Landis head of a new securities department of the FTC, where he supervised the monumental task of implementing the new regulations. More important, Landis began work on the Securities Act of 1934, which attempted to regulate the stock exchanges. The exchanges had often acted as private clubs, the rules set by a small group of influential traders. New Dealers argued that those traders could manipulate the rules to their own advantage, an unacceptable situation given the importance of the exchanges to the national economy. Another concern of the New Dealers, margin buying, allowed stock purchasers to make a small down payment on a purchase and make up the difference in loans. Margin buying, the New Dealers contended, provided the impetus behind the wild Wall Street speculation of the 1920s. Finally, Landis and his colleagues wanted to force all security-issuing corporations to provide complete annual reports for public access, since the 1933 act only covered new issues.

Opposition to the 1934 legislation proved difficult to surmount. Entrenched interests within the securities and banking industry—especially on the powerful New York Stock Exchange—resented the loss of power the bill would entail. Despite the opposition the New Dealers managed to implement a revolutionary regulatory program. The 1934 act prohibited trading practices that manipulated prices, extended the requirements of the 1933 act

to all corporations, provided for federal regulation of the securities exchanges, and gave the Federal Reserve Board power to set margin-trading requirements. The act also created a new regulatory agency—the Securities and Exchange Commission (SEC)—to enforce both the 1933 and 1934 laws.

Roosevelt appointed Landis one of the five commissioners of the SEC. Along with Joseph P. Kennedy—an influential Wall Street banker who was appointed Chairman—Landis sought to fashion a pragmatic strategy that would allow businessmen, accountants, and government officials to work together to regulate the securities business. Businessmen, worried about the antibusiness rhetoric of the New Deal, issued new stock only hesitantly after the formation of the SEC. The assurances of Kennedy combined with the practical administrative procedures of Landis, however, revived business confidence, and by the spring of 1935 a flood of new stock issues appeared. Although many of the most liberal New Dealers (including Landis's former mentor, Frankfurter) resented Landis's accommodative policies, in September 1935 Landis—then thirty-six years old—became chairman of the SEC. He continued his work of setting tough federal regulations while remaining attentive to the concerns of business.

As chairman of the SEC Landis tried to persuade rather than force businessmen to accept the new regulations. In speeches before stock exchanges he stressed the need for self-regulation. In an October 1935 speech to the New York Stock Exchange Institute, he declared that "it has always been my thesis that self-government is the most desirable form of government, and whether it be self-government by the exchange or self-government by any other institution, the thesis still holds." As Thomas McCraw has observed, such emphasis on self-government "served to make the specter of government regulation far less threatening." Although the powerful New York Stock Exchange still opposed federal regulations on disclosure, Landis's cooperative approach produced the desired result. When former New York Stock Exchange president Richard Whitney was convicted of embezzlement in 1938, the last of the old guard fell. Government regulation could proceed with cooperation, not opposition, from businessmen.

In 1937 Landis left the SEC to take the position of dean of Harvard Law School. Despite the prestigious appointment, he found academic life

Chairman Landis (center) with the Securities and Exchange Commission, 1936 (courtesy of the Securities and Exchange Commission)

dull and uneventful after the heady days of leading New Deal regulatory efforts. During World War II he managed the Office of Civilian Defense, and in 1945 he was appointed chairman to the Civil Aeronautics Board (CAB). His tenure at CAB was rocky: he found little support for his efforts to formulate a coherent set of regulatory objectives, and established carriers strongly opposed his goal to open the industry to more competition. The CAB experience exposed an important weakness in Landis's umpire theory of regulation: established interests usually had more influence on the umpire than would-be competitors. Landis's policies generated so much pressure from large airlines that President Harry Truman refused to renominate him for the post in 1947. After his tenure on the CAB, Landis started a private law practice and became a leading adviser of his SEC friend Joseph Kennedy. In 1959 Landis worked full-time for John F. Kennedy's presidential campaign and became a special assistant to the president in charge of federal regulatory efforts after Kennedy took office. His 1960 *Report on Regulatory Agencies to the President Elect* proposed wide-scale regulatory reform that Landis would spearhead himself. But a divorce suit suggesting marital impropriety soon forced him to resign.

Landis was plagued by personal problems throughout his life. His devotion to work led to the breakup of his marriage to Stella Landis, by whom

he had two daughters, Ann and Ellen. During his tenure as civilian defense administrator, Landis fell in love with his secretary, Dorothy Brown. The resulting divorce and marriage scandalized Harvard, where Landis still held his post as dean of the law school. His failure at CAB added to his personal woes, leaving him without the prestige that accompanied important government postings. He also often neglected his own finances, and between 1955 and 1960 he failed to file income tax returns. He fell into a deep depression when the personal financial scandal finally broke. Psychiatric examination revealed that he suffered from an acute lack of self-esteem. He tried to compensate for that lack through academic and professional achievement. But he never quite succeeded. Depressed and alcoholic, he died from a heart attack on July 30, 1964.

Landis's career as regulator left an ambiguous legacy. Although the New Deal regulations he helped devise and implement were revolutionary, critics of all ideological stripes have criticized them. Those on the Left have argued that the SEC mainly served the interests of business; those on the Right contend that the SEC represents counterproductive economic interference. By the 1950s Landis himself had become remarkably more market-oriented. The CAB ordeal demonstrated that special interests could use regulation to thwart legitimate competition. His experience in private practice, where he frequently defended business clients before government commissions, gave him even greater insight into the anticompetitiveness of government regulations. In a 1962 speech, for example, Landis declared that regulators should "allow the forces of competition to provide a free market, and to permit the entry into that market of new creative forces, as well as to keep the market reasonably clean so that seller and purchaser will deal fairly with each other at arm's length." Although the final verdict on his New Deal regulatory efforts may be negative, none can deny that Landis played a major role in shaping modern financial institutions.

Selected Publications:
"Constitutional Limitations on the Congressional Power

of Investigation," *Harvard Law Review*, 25 (December 1926);

The Business of the Supreme Court, by Landis and Felix Frankfurter (New York: 1928);

Report on Regulatory Agencies to the President Elect, 86th Congress, second session (Washington, D.C.: U.S. Government Printing Office, 1960).

References:
Thomas K. McCraw, *Prophets of Regulation* (Cambridge, Mass.: Harvard University Press, 1984);

Donald H. Ritchie, *James M. Landis: Dean of the Regulators* (Cambridge, Mass.: Harvard University Press, 1980).

Hugh C. Lane

(March 5, 1914 -   )

by Olin S. Pugh

University of South Carolina

CAREER: Assistant cashier, Exchange National Bank, Albany, Georgia (1936-1937); assistant to the president (1937-1940), first vice-president (1940-1944), president (1944-1962), chairman (1962-1974), chairman of the executive committee, Citizens & Southern National Bank of South Carolina (1974-   ).

Hugh C. Lane was known as an aggressive and innovative lender during a period when change and aggressiveness in lending were not commonplace in South Carolina banking. He led his bank, Citizens & Southern (C&S) Bank of South Carolina, to a strong statewide position from its base in Charleston. He has also served in major capacities in public service and civic organizations and has become a leader in his state.

A third-generation banker, Lane was born on March 5, 1914, in Savannah, Georgia, the son of Mills B. Lane, founder of the Citizens & Southern Bank of Georgia and the Citizens & Southern Bank of South Carolina. He graduated from the University of South Carolina in 1935 and married Beverly Glover of Charleston in 1946. The couple had four children.

Lane started his banking career in 1936 with the Exchange National Bank of Albany, Georgia. A year later he moved to Charleston to become assistant to the president at C&S. In 1944 he took the president's office at the bank.

When Lane became head of C&S he objected to many of the practices of the Charleston Clearinghouse. Customer charges and practices by banks were expected to be uniform, and banks were not expected to open for business before mid morning. Within his first year as president, he resigned from membership in the clearinghouse in order to compete more aggressively and to express his belief in an open financial services market.

Lane recruited Willis Cantey to C&S in 1958 to diversify and expand the bank's top management. When Cantey became C&S president in 1960, Lane became chairman, a position he held until 1974.

Lane did not believe that check clearings and routine customer services cost as much as the industry commonly charged. He prepared C&S for the advent of computers, ordering one of the first International Business Machines computers to be developed for use in banking. In the process he reduced customer charges and lowered the minimum

Hugh C. Lane (courtesy of the South Carolina Bankers Association)

balance for free checking to $100. Such actions jolted the banking industry. But the public loved the change, and the bank grew rapidly during a period when other South Carolina banks struggled to adopt the use of computers.

Lane bristled at the attitudes of the officials of bank regulatory agencies, who tended to put bankers on the defensive and made them act on the basis of fear. He believed that if bankers tried to do the right thing they would succeed regardless of general economic conditions.

Lane's greatest pride as a banker was his creativity as a business lender. He could accurately appraise entrepreneurs and identify opportunities. As a result he had a great impact on the South Carolina business community. He developed an almost in-

nate ability to finance successful ventures and had the courage to back his convictions. He never believed that the decision-making process in banking could be computerized.

The C&S leader ran his bank with a disciplined approach. Some would say he was an autocrat. He held strong beliefs and seemed to enjoy defending them against contrary views. Certain changes in the industry did not meet with his approval. He disapproved of credit cards and did not want to compete aggressively for time deposits. He did, however, establish a bank holding company, a special housing corporation, and a mortgage financing corporation.

Housing always held a special interest for Lane. By the late 1960s he endeavored to compel federal authorities to establish a system of home financing through tax-exempt security issues with lowered mortgage rates for eligible borrowers. While he did not meet with success in that venture at the national level, he did succeed in convincing the government of the state of South Carolina to establish a housing authority on such a basis. He served as chairman of that organization from 1971 to 1981, during which more than $250 million in bonds were issued for lower-income home purchasers.

During and after his full-time banking career, Lane served as president of the South Carolina Bankers Association, on the boards of several historic foundations, as a member of the state insurance commission, and as an official for the Radio Free Europe organization. In 1985 he was inducted into the South Carolina Business Hall of Fame. In 1982 a special chair in economic theory was established in his honor at the University of South Carolina.

Lane's contributions to the banking industry in South Carolina depended upon his ability to make wise financing decisions and his belief in providing quality customer service. His legacy as an astute banker and state leader will carry the industry into the twenty-first century.

Reference:

John G. Sproat and Larry Schweikart, *Making Change: South Carolina Banking in the Twentieth Century* (Columbia: South Carolina Bankers Association, 1990).

Russell Cornell Leffingwell

(September 10, 1878 - October 2, 1960)

by W. Elliot Brownlee

University of California, Santa Barbara

CAREER: Partner, Guthrie, Cravath & Henderson law firm (1907-1917); assistant secretary of the Treasury (1917-1920); partner, Cravath, Henderson, Leffingwell & de Gersdorff law firm (1920-1923); partner (1923-1960), director (1940-1960), vice-chairman, executive committee (1940-1943), chairman, executive committee (1943-1948), chairman of the board (1948-1950), vice-chairman of the board, J. P. Morgan & Company (1950-1955).

Russell Cornell Leffingwell, an influential corporate lawyer, banker, and assistant secretary of the Treasury during World War I, was born on September 10, 1878, in New York City, the only son among the three children of Charles Russell Leffingwell and Mary Elizabeth Cornell Leffingwell. His father's family had an eight-generation history in Connecticut and New York, and his mother's family owned the Cornell iron business (J. B. and J. M. Cornell Company), in which his father worked as an executive. Leffingwell grew up in affluence and received an excellent education at the Yonkers (N.Y.) Military Academy, the Halsey School, and Yale University, where he graduated with a B.A. in 1899. He obtained his LL.B. in 1902 from Columbia Law School, where he edited the first edition of the *Columbia Law Review* and became its second editor in chief.

Leffingwell joined the well-connected New York law firm of Cravath & Henderson (then Guthrie, Cravath & Henderson) immediately after graduation. He married Lucy Hewitt in 1906 and in January 1907 became Cravath's youngest partner. Leffingwell specialized in corporate finance during a hectic period of intense corporate reorganization. His clients included New York City's major investment bankers, J. P. Morgan & Company among them, and he became a specialist in railroad and international bonds. He formed a particularly strong relationship with the investment banking house of

Russell Cornell Leffingwell (courtesy of Harris & Ewing)

Kuhn, Loeb & Company, handling, along with Paul Cravath, most of Kuhn, Loeb's bond issues. For example, he represented Kuhn, Loeb and the Morton Trust Company between 1906 and 1908 on a $20 million bond issue of the Dominican Republic. Most significantly, in 1911 and 1912 Leffingwell represented Kuhn, Loeb in the negotiations over the proposed six-nation $300 million loan to the new Chinese republic by an American syndicate. Kuhn, Loeb played the leading role in scuttling American participation after the Chinese government refused to accept the bankers' conditions. In his work for the Cravath firm Leffingwell became noted for his extensive research, his meticulous attention to clarity of expression, and his interest in the financial viability of the transactions he handled.

Leffingwell grew bored with the practice of corporate law and at Paul Cravath's urging took a six-month holiday at Lake George in the winter of 1914-1915 to contemplate a career in teaching and writing. He remained at the firm, however, until World War I spun his career in a new direction, widening his intellectual horizons and the scope of his life.

A vigorous Anglophile and defender of America's international rights, Leffingwell eagerly volunteered for the Plattsburgh Reserve Officers Training Camp in the summer of 1916 and hoped America would enter the war in Europe. In May 1917, as he prepared to take up his commission, he received a request from the secretary of the Treasury, William G. McAdoo, to join the Treasury as special counsel for Liberty Loan matters. McAdoo was in the process of assembling a staff appropriate for wartime mobilization and had recognized his need for a legal expert in designing bond issues. McAdoo discussed his need with the Treasury committee supervising the Liberty Loan, and Paul Warburg, member of the Federal Reserve Board and former partner in Kuhn, Loeb & Company, nominated Leffingwell on the basis of his work for the firm, which had strong ties with the Wilson administration and McAdoo. As it turned out, McAdoo had been a neighbor of the Leffingwell family in Yonkers and had known Leffingwell since his boyhood. (Leffingwell apparently never represented McAdoo, but the Cravath firm did handle the refinancing of McAdoo's Hudson & Manhattan Railroad in 1912 and 1913.) McAdoo was certain that Leffingwell followed the family's Republican tradition, but McAdoo set aside narrow partisanship and appointed him.

At the Treasury, Leffingwell played a central role in organizing the first Liberty Loan. While McAdoo focused on setting the outlines of loan policy and on personally leading the sales campaign through an extensive speaking schedule, and while Leffingwell's immediate superior at the Treasury, Oscar T. Crosby, concentrated on the financial relationship with the allied powers, Leffingwell assumed responsibility for the operational details of the Liberty Loan. He worked closely with the governors of the Federal Reserve Banks and developed the techniques of bond marketing and financing that prevailed throughout the war.

Following the success of the first Liberty Loan, McAdoo reorganized the Treasury. He sent Crosby to Europe as the special commissioner to the Inter-Ally Council and, in October, rewarded Leffingwell for his extraordinary service by naming him as Crosby's replacement as assistant secretary. Leffingwell's administrative zone was the most powerful in the Treasury: "fiscal matters," including the Treasury's borrowing and debt management policies. In the course of the two subsequent Liberty Loans, Leffingwell became increasingly expert in all aspects of public borrowing and debt management. In managing the Treasury's borrowing activity, he served, in effect, as director of the Federal Reserve System, which functioned during the war as an arm of the Treasury. Leffingwell led the effort of the 12 Federal Reserve Banks to coordinate the Liberty Loans in their districts. Working together, Leffingwell, the Treasury, and the Federal Reserve Banks devised innovative techniques for federally sponsored installment credit. Moreover, Leffingwell proved particularly innovative in creating techniques of short-term borrowing, developing the instruments known as Treasury certificates.

In the process of working with the Federal Reserve System and the major banks, Leffingwell acted as the focal point of communication between the banking community at large and the Treasury. Thus, when McAdoo overruled the Advisory Board's recommendation that corporations under financial stress be allowed to defer their payments of taxes due in 1918, Leffingwell defended that policy to the bankers. And, when McAdoo had difficulty convincing investment bankers that they should support the creation of the War Finance Corporation, Leffingwell took up the task of persuading Thomas W. Lamont that it was in his self-interest to do so. The "mere existence of the Corporation," Leffingwell explained to Lamont in February 1918, "with power to give relief in case of necessity will have the effect of restoring confidence to such an extent as to make financing through the ordinary channels of the banks and banking houses possible, which is not now possible."

In April 1918, because McAdoo's responsibilities had increased, he created an additional assistant secretary of the Treasury with responsibilities for the Liberty Loan and foreign lending and made Leffingwell de facto undersecretary of the Treasury.

Leffingwell, of all of McAdoo's assistants, had the breadth of vision and comprehensive knowledge required to supervise all aspects of Treasury operations. He supervised all the other assistant secretaries, oversaw all Treasury affairs, including personnel matters, and assumed complete control of the department during McAdoo's frequent absences on Liberty Loan promotions, tours of railroad facilities, vacations, and sick leave.

In his new position, Leffingwell, as supervisor of the Bureau of Internal Revenue, also played a major role in shaping revenue legislation, an activity that grew increasingly important for the Treasury during the war. McAdoo gave Leffingwell substantial room to maneuver within the Treasury despite the fact that Leffingwell's views on central issues, such as the taxation of corporations, differed sharply from McAdoo's. For example, in discussing the controversial excess-profits tax within the Treasury, McAdoo allowed Leffingwell to develop and defend his own position—one of opposition to excess-profits taxation and, instead, support for "war-profits" taxation. Leffingwell's view was quite simple: "the trouble" with the excess-profits tax was that it "carried to an extreme [Claude] Kitchin's [the chairman of the House Ways and Means Committee] desire to throw the burden on the profiteers and the rich."

Simultaneously, in his new position Leffingwell expanded the Treasury's program of systematic investigation, which included estimating future revenues and reviewing tax options. Most notably, his hostility to excess-profits taxation led him in 1918 to conduct an extensive investigation of that practice. The results of the study tended to supplement his arguments that the tax was either ineffective or impeded industrial expansion. He suggested, for example, that some corporations had increased their capital issues to reduce their rates of return and slip into lower tax brackets under the excess-profits tax, and that the highest rates of return on capital, and thus the highest tax rates, often rested on the smallest corporations.

Armed with those findings Leffingwell fought a bureaucratic battle within the Treasury against the Treasury's principal tax adviser, Yale economist Thomas S. Adams. On the most significant tax issue during the war Leffingwell lost the contest for the support of Secretary McAdoo. Adams convinced McAdoo to adopt a "dual-basis" tax under which corporations would pay the higher of an in-

creased excess-profits tax or the British-style war-profits taxation. Despite his opposition to such a tax, Leffingwell remained the good soldier. In August 1918, while McAdoo was out of town on a Liberty Loan speaking tour, Leffingwell carefully explained the principles of war-profits and excess-profits taxation to President Woodrow Wilson and Joseph Tumulty. Setting aside his personal preferences, he arranged for Wilson to intervene in the congressional debate over the Revenue Act of 1918 on behalf of the dual-basis tax. That laid the basis for the enactment of Adams's formula early in 1919.

When McAdoo left the Treasury at the end of 1918, Leffingwell emerged as the dominant figure there. His expertise, energy, and loyalty to his superiors greased the transition for the new secretary, Carter Glass, who had one eye fixed on the Senate. And Leffingwell was an even more appropriate second-in-command for Glass, who was more conservative than McAdoo and believed that the Wilson administration should counter growing Republican support by moving the Treasury away from McAdoo's anticorporate, statist policies. Glass wanted to establish what Leffingwell later called a "non-partisan" Treasury; he and Leffingwell hoped to lift department policy above politics—by which they meant political controversy and, in particular, the hostility of business. More important, they sought a Treasury that promoted investment but avoided intervention in corporate decision making. In the process of working toward that goal Leffingwell and Glass formed a close friendship.

Establishing the "non-partisan" Treasury required, in particular, substantial tax reform. Leffingwell hoped to substitute a noncontroversial income tax system for the tariff system, which he described as having been "the football of politics for several generations." The new income tax system would protect corporations as the major engines of economic progress, but it would also mediate class conflict. Leffingwell proposed retaining income taxation as the federal government's primary revenue instrument, but he wished to repeal the excess-profits tax and make the individual income tax more uniform and efficient. During his postwar service, however, Leffingwell succeeded only in undermining the excess-profits tax—by blocking the creation of the administrative structure that would have been necessary to make the tax permanent. Thus, under Glass, Leffingwell's approach won out over that of Adams; in 1919 Adams announced that he had developed serious reservations about excess-profits taxation as a permanent part of the nation's revenue system.

Leffingwell's continued effort to repeal excess-profits taxation made up part of his effort to concentrate the energies of the Treasury on restoring business confidence and, more generally, easing the reconversion of the economy to peacetime. With regard to fiscal policy his approach revealed the kind of awareness of the potential impact of taxing and spending on the business cycle that would figure centrally in Keynesian countercyclical policy. Preoccupied with the mounting problem of inflation, he urged immediate curtailment of military spending (which increased even in 1919), disarmament, and defeat of spending for veterans' bonuses. He also stressed the importance of maintaining high taxes (with the exception of the excess-profits tax).

In the area of monetary policy Leffingwell was the first Treasury official faced with the necessity of using the instruments of the Federal Reserve System to cope with severe peacetime inflation. He was convinced that, for the sake of international economic recovery from war, a substantial deflation had to take place in both the United States and Britain. Both he and Benjamin Strong, chairman of the Federal Reserve Bank of New York, agreed on that point, and both worked together to achieve it by moderating postwar inflation and engineering a gradual deflation, but they disagreed as to how to accomplish that end. Leffingwell had left the Treasury by the time the bubble burst in 1920, which was followed by a sharp depression that continued into 1921. Strong believed, as have most economists since, that the Federal Reserve, under Leffingwell's de facto leadership, acted too slowly to restrict the growth of the money supply and then jammed on the brakes too hard. Leffingwell discussed that episode, and monetary policy in general, with Benjamin Strong until the latter's death in 1928, and Leffingwell, throughout his career, agonized over his decisions in the 1919-1920 period of reconversion.

Leffingwell's approach to economic stability was global in scope. Most important, he devoted great attention to the promotion of European economic recovery as something that served the best interests of the United States. He thought European prosperity crucial to American prosperity and to the prevention of revolution and war. Enlightened self-interest, he maintained, argued that the United States should reconstruct the gold standard system, ease the terms under which Europeans repaid their loans, reduce tariff barriers, and join the League of Nations. He supported a close Anglo-American partnership as an instrument to promote his plan. He advanced the program in his supervision of the work of Treasury representatives Norman Davis and Thomas Lamont in Europe, in his relations with Congress, and in his public forums. He was, of course, ahead of his time; the kind of program he advocated did not win acceptance until the United States had gone through a major, worldwide depression and fought another world war.

Leffingwell nearly became the final secretary of the Treasury in the Wilson administration after Carter Glass resigned in November 1919. Both Glass and Benjamin Strong supported him, but his candidacy hit a major snag when ex-secretary McAdoo, then a potential presidential candidate, objected to Leffingwell as too close to Wall Street and as a former registered Republican, although Leffingwell claimed that he had shifted his loyalties to Woodrow Wilson and the Democratic party. McAdoo strongly preferred two other candidates (Daniel Roper, the commissioner of revenue, and John Skelton Williams, the comptroller of the currency), primarily on the grounds that the party needed to have the Treasury under control of a Democrat during an election year. President Wilson rejected McAdoo's choices, apparently because he wanted to avoid a secretary associated with the South, but he passed over Leffingwell in favor of David Houston, his secretary of agriculture.

Leffingwell apparently never learned about McAdoo's objections or received an explanation of Wilson's decision. But he never complained, and he served David Houston loyally until May 1920, when Leffingwell resigned. Secretary Houston and Leffingwell never became close friends, but Houston was as cognizant of Leffingwell's abilities as Glass had been. In fact, Houston, with little experience in financial matters, never sent a major memorandum or letter that Leffingwell had not drafted. During that transition period, Leffingwell and Houston continued the policies that Leffingwell had developed under Carter Glass.

Leffingwell's influence over Treasury matters remained powerful even after he had left the Treasury. His policies had acquired institutional momentum and, after he left, Secretary Houston turned immediately for support to S. Parker Gilbert, who

Assistant Secretary of the Treasury Leffingwell (second from left in the front line) in a gathering of Liberty Loan administrators listening to an address by Treasury Secretary Carter Glass

had succeeded Leffingwell as first assistant secretary. Leffingwell had drafted Gilbert from Cravath & Henderson in 1918 to serve as counsel to the War Loan staff, and Gilbert had become Leffingwell's understudy in the Treasury. In the Republican administration that followed, secretary of the Treasury Andrew Mellon persuaded Gilbert to continue, offering him the newly created official post of undersecretary. Gilbert served until 1923, continuing his strong relationship with Leffingwell. In both Houston's and Mellon's Treasury, Gilbert continually asked for Leffingwell's advice on the full range of Treasury matters, and Leffingwell provided him with the long, thoughtful letters for which he became famous.

Leffingwell had favored Benjamin Strong over Mellon for secretary of the Treasury in 1921 but, through Gilbert as an intermediary, the approach that Leffingwell had outlined for restructuring the wartime revenue system won Mellon's approval. On the one hand, Andrew Mellon expanded the attack on the most redistributional parts of the wartime tax system. Most importantly, the Revenue Act of 1921 abolished the excess-profits tax. On the other hand, Mellon protected income taxation

against the threat of a national sales tax, which most Republican congressmen preferred. Using Leffingwell's arguments, Secretary Mellon persuaded corporations and the wealthiest individuals to accept, instead, *some* progressive income taxation as a way of proving their civic responsibility and defusing more radical attacks on capital. In effect, Leffingwell was the architect of the transition from McAdoo's democratic statism to a policy of "corporate liberalism."

Leffingwell, however, disapproved of some Mellon policies. He felt, for example, that Mellon had not done enough to establish the uniformity of the income tax and had gone much too far in advocating major income tax loopholes, such as the preferential taxation of capital gains. In contrast, Leffingwell supported a constitutional amendment allowing federal taxation of the interest earned on state and municipal bonds. Moreover, the defeat of American membership in the League of Nations at the hands of Republicans (described by Leffingwell as making "the peace of the world the plaything of politics"), the high-tariff policy of the Republican administrations during the 1920s, the restriction of immigration, and Republican pressure on the Allies for debt repayment convinced Leffingwell that he should continue his wartime Democratic affiliation. Working with Carter Glass, he wrote much of the Democratic national platform in 1920 and supported all the Democratic presidential candidates during the 1920s.

After resigning his Treasury post, Leffingwell rejoined the Cravath firm. There the firm assigned him to breaking up the coal property holdings of the Reading Company following a U.S. Supreme Court order. More important, he continued his interest in international lending. In 1921 he represented J. P. Morgan & Company in negotiations for an Austrian loan, and Kuhn, Loeb & Company for a $30 million loan to Argentina's state railroad. He tackled his legal work with enthusiasm, often working into the late evening. However, his restlessness appeared not only in the irregular hours he kept but also in his extensive correspondence over public issues and his writing on economic issues, particularly his stewardship of the Treasury and the international debt situation. In that correspondence and in his writing for publication, Leffingwell launched a lifelong effort to communicate his views to leading politicians, experts in foreign relations, economists, financial analysts, and the informed public. Though not a prolific writer, his thoughtful essays won a wide following among those policy makers, and his correspondence helped him cultivate a great array of influential friends.

Surprising no one at the Cravath firm, Leffingwell, on July 1, 1923, left to become a partner in J. P. Morgan & Company. There he quickly developed a reputation as one of the three most powerful Morgan partners, along with J. P. Morgan, Jr., and Thomas Lamont. He assumed major responsibilities in the financing of foreign governments and specialized in the financial analysis of their offerings. Leffingwell was proud of his work. In 1932 he told Carter Glass that not one of his foreign government loans had defaulted, despite the collapse of world capital markets that began in 1931. In 1949 he pointed out to John J. McCloy that the discrimination and restraint Morgan & Company had employed in its lending to foreign governments had resulted in a better record than the other investment houses—a record of success in retiring almost 80 percent of all such loans, including those made to Germany and Japan.

In Leffingwell's mind, his work at Morgan & Company was all of a piece with his earlier service at the Treasury. He was involved, or so he was convinced, in an effort to replace the international economic system shattered by World War I with a new order, which would provide for the free movement of goods, capital, and people under a reconstructed gold standard administered by the United States and Britain. At Morgan & Company, he helped to rebuild capital markets and promoted the economic recovery of Britain and Western Europe, and he understood that the financial system created by Republican administrations of the 1920s depended to an unhealthy degree on heavy flows of American capital to Western Europe. That system carried political as well as economic risks. In 1925, he wrote to his partner Thomas Lamont criticizing high tariffs and immigration restriction; he complained that the "United States having obtained possession of about the most desirable territory is now trying to build a ring fence around it to keep out goods and human beings." The United States "is, therefore, in my view, doing the best she can to bring on another war."

The onset of the Great Depression in 1929 and its worsening in 1931 confirmed Leffingwell's belief in the importance of countercyclical monetary policy and in a foreign policy that sustained economic expansion. He criticized the Federal Reserve Board's contraction of the money supply in 1931 and the Revenue Act of 1932, both of which figured centrally in the disastrous deflation and depression between 1931 and 1933. Those policy errors confirmed Leffingwell's identification with the Democratic party during the agony of the Depression crisis. He complained in 1932 that Republican policies had in six months swept away "the work of eight years of my life . . . trying to rebuild the world which the war destroyed, to rehabilitate the currencies of Europe."

Leffingwell alone among the Morgan partners supported the presidential candidacy of Franklin D. Roosevelt in 1932, and he decided to accept appointment as undersecretary should Roosevelt appoint Carter Glass secretary of the Treasury. Leffingwell advised Roosevelt regarding monetary policy and enthusiastically supported Roosevelt's decision to suspend gold payments and devalue the dollar as a means of reflating the economy. "Cheap money," Leffingwell told the Academy of Political Science, "opens the door to recovery." As the New Deal progressed, he worried about New Deal reforms that shook business confidence or increased public employment, but he supported the bank holiday, encouraged the Reciprocal Trade Agreements Act, supported a vigorous Reconstruction Finance Corporation, contributed to money and banking reforms, and supported the Wagner Act. Also, he consulted extensively with secretary of the Treasury Henry Morgenthau, Jr., over fiscal and monetary policy, and in 1936 he alone among the leading bankers warned against just the kind of monetary contraction that led to the sharp recession of 1937-1938. In 1936 he was one of the few New York bankers to support Roosevelt's reelection. That year, Leffingwell told Lamont that while "Roosevelt's sayings and doings have distressed me beyond measure time and again," Roosevelt "did follow the principal major monetary policy which I believed in." Moreover, Leffingwell added, "He did save capitalism." However, Roosevelt's assault on the Supreme Court and the New Deal's sponsorship of the undistributed profits tax led Leffingwell to oppose Roosevelt's election to a third term in 1940.

The crises of the Great Depression and World War II only increased the value of Leffingwell to the House of Morgan. Because of his experiences in international economic life and national policy, his intellectual flexibility, and his ability to think strategically, Leffingwell acquired significantly greater responsibilities at the firm. In 1935, the company had divested itself of its investment banking business, with several of the partners withdrawing to form the investment banking house of Morgan, Stanley & Company. Leffingwell, however, remained a partner of the original firm, which continued to conduct the general banking and trust business. When the firm was incorporated in 1940, Leffingwell became one of its directors and vice-chairman of the executive committee. In 1943 he stepped up to chair the executive committee.

As the movement toward World War II gathered force, Leffingwell's interest in foreign policy intensified, as did his preoccupation with the tragic defeat of Wilsonian internationalism after World War I. He opposed the neutrality program of the 1930s, writing to Lamont that "the present policy of assuming that we must do nothing to avoid a conflagration and nothing to put out a conflagration if it occurs, and that by some magic we can keep ourselves from being burnt in it, is not only degrading and pusillanimous but perilous to the last degree." He urged assistance to Britain and may well have been the first to suggest the lend-lease program. Thus, World War II confirmed Leffingwell's reputa-

tion as a foresighted leader in fostering a stable international order. Walter Lippmann, who carried on an extensive correspondence with him, expressed a high regard for his views on the tariff, international debts, and foreign policy. Describing him as "enlightened," Lippmann declared in 1942 that "Your views are not, and never have been, typical of the great mass of American businessmen, and those who think as you do have never been able to lead them during these twenty years."

During and after World War II, Leffingwell, from his senior position in the nation's financial community, worked to promote fiscal and monetary policies that not only helped win the war but also restored economic stability. He supported the adoption of "mass-based" income taxation during the war but advocated, as well, a greater diversification of the tax system. He criticized the Treasury for fostering excessive monetary expansion during the war but after the war urged against deflationary measures, clearly remembering the disaster of 1920-1921. "I dread deflation even more than inflation," he wrote in *Fortune* in 1948. He remained an advocate of an active use of monetary policy, but only if monetary authorities exercised great care. They should "sail the narrow channel between Scylla and Charybdis, between inflation and deflation, between cheap money and dear money; but not with the tiller tied like a toy yacht on the pond in Central Park."

Leffingwell's economic thinking was often eclectic and unconventional, but events seemed to confirm the importance he attached to monetary variables and monetary policy. He kept up with professional economists, whom he respected. He was an early reader of John Maynard Keynes, and in 1944 he described him as "one of the greatest men of our day." However, Leffingwell maintained a lifelong commitment to the gold standard even though he willingly endorsed tactical departures from it if circumstances warranted, as he believed they did in 1932 and 1933. He disagreed with Keynes's criticism of Britain's return to the gold standard in 1926 and concluded that Keynes made assertions primarily for effect. In 1931 Leffingwell told Lamont that Keynes "is just a bright boy shocking his admiring elders by questioning the existence of God, and the Ten Commandments!" And, while the events of 1929-1933 led Keynes to postulate a "liquidity trap" rendering monetary policy ineffective, Leffingwell maintained and elaborated his belief in

Leffingwell at about the time of his 1955 retirement from J. P. Morgan & Company

the efficacy of monetary policy. Leffingwell, however, cautioned against using it rashly. He favored, instead, fine-tuning monetary policy. Thus, after World War II he argued that "Between the wars our money was managed too much, and too roughly." He declared that "our country cannot endure another inflation like that of 1919 or 1929, nor another deflation like that of 1921 or 1932 or 1937."

As early as 1940 Leffingwell planned for the postwar international economy, and after the war he was a vigorous supporter of the Marshall Plan (including extending to the Soviet Union an invitation to participate), the Bretton Woods agreements, and the United Nations—all of which he regarded as necessary for domestic prosperity, international economic order, world peace, and the fruition of Wilsonian internationalism. Reflecting the same interests, Leffingwell was a founder of the Council on Foreign Relations after World War I and served as chairman of the board of that organization (1946-1953), and of the Carnegie Corporation, where he served as a trustee beginning in 1923. He was, in addition, a member of the Alumni Council of the Yale Institute of International Studies.

In 1948, after the death of Thomas W. Lamont, Leffingwell became chairman of the board of Morgan & Company. He served for two years and then, at age seventy-two, he stepped down to vice-chairman, with George Whitney succeeding him. During this period of reduced activity he retained his intense interest in promoting effective countercyclical economic policy. In 1951 he urged president Harry S Truman to restrain the Treasury in promoting an inflationary monetary policy. Three years later he advised president Dwight D. Eisenhower to ignore the federal deficit and cut taxes to stimulate recovery from recession. "Heretofore," Leffingwell wrote, whether under "Wilson or Harding or Hoover or Roosevelt, our government's remedial action has been too little or too late."

In 1955 Leffingwell retired but remained a director of the House of Morgan until his death from cancer on October 2, 1960. He was survived by his widow and their only child, Lucy (Mrs. Edward Pulling).

During his long and accomplished career Leffingwell had his greatest influence on American economic life during World War I, when he played an instrumental role in the development of modern central banking, public finance, and monetary policy. Drawing on his wartime experience he became a vigorous internationalist and a farsighted analyst of monetary policy. As a powerful Morgan partner he played a key role in the flow of American private capital to Western Europe during the 1920s and in the restoration of economic order in the trans-Atlantic trading community after World War II. Through his thoughtful and original articles, essays, and correspondence he established a reputation as an enlightened conservative and, as such, influenced the formation of national economic policy, particularly as it affected international relations, from World War I through the early 1950s.

Publications:

"The Soldier and His Bonus," *Saturday Evening Post*, 192 (May 15, 1920): 6-7, 58, 61-62;

"Treasury Methods of Financing the War in Reference to Inflation," *Proceedings of the Academy of Political Science*, 9 (June 1920): 16-41;

"Some Problems of Future Government Finance," *Coupon* (March 1921);

"The Discount Policy of the Federal Reserve Banks," *American Economic Review*, 11 (March 1921): 30-36;

"Federal Tax Revision," *Baltimore Evening Sun*, April 22, 1921;

"Retrenchment in National Expenditure," *Proceedings of the Academy of Political Science*, 9 (July 1921): 486-502;

"An Analysis of the International War Debt Situation," *Annals of the American Academy*, 102 (July 1922): 108-115;

"America's Interest in Europe," *Foreign Policy Association Pamphlet No. 14* (July 1922);

"The War Debts," *Yale Review*, 12 (October 1922): 22-40;

"Reserve Banks and the Future," *Saturday Review of Literature* (September 27, 1930): 153-154;

"Causes of Depression," *Proceedings of the Academy of Political Science*, 14 (June 1931): 69-77;

"The Post-War Years," in *Hearings before the Committee on Banking and Currency*, U.S. Senate, 72nd Congress, first session, *Stock Exchange Practices*, part 2, exhibit 53 (Washington, D.C.: U. S. Government Printing Office, 1933);

"The Gold Problem and Currency Revaluation," *Proceedings of the Academy of Political Science*, 16 (April 1934): 69-82;

"Statement before Senate Committee on Agriculture, February 1, 1935," in *Causes of the Loss of Export Trade and the Means of Recovery, Hearings before the Committee on Agriculture and Forestry*, U.S. Senate, 74th Congress, first session (Washington, D.C.: U. S. Government Printing Office, 1935);

"Economic Recovery and Monetary Stabilization," *Proceedings of the Academy of Political Science*, 17 (May 1936): 105-114;

"Notes for T.N.E.C.," *Wall Street Journal*, January 19, 1940, pp. 1, 11;

"Managing Our Economy," *Yale Review*, 34 (June 1945): 603-617;

"Make-work and Full Employment," *New York Times*, July 22, 1945;

"Our Monetary Problems," *Commercial & Financial Chronicle*, May 2, 1946, pp. 2349, 2397-2398;

"Trade and Taxes After the War," *Commercial & Financial Chronicle*, February 13, 1947, pp. 861, 902-903;

"How to Control Inflation," *Fortune* (October 1948);

"Treasury Methods in Two Wars," *Proceedings of the Academy of Political Science* (1948);

"Devaluation and European Recovery," *Foreign Affairs*, 28 (January 1950): 203-214;

"Our Fiscal and Banking Policy," *Barron's* (November 13, 1950).

References:

Vincent Carosso, *Investment Banking in America* (Cambridge, Mass.: Harvard University Press, 1970);

Ron Chernow, *The House of Morgan* (New York: Atlantic Monthly, 1990);

Charles Gilbert, *American Financing of World War I* (Westport, Conn.: Greenwood, 1970);

Hearings before Special Committee Investigating the Munitions Industry, U.S. Senate, 74th Congress, 2nd session, part 32 (Washington, D.C.: U. S. Government Printing Office, 1936);

Stephen A. Schuker, *The End of French Predominance in Europe* (Chapel Hill: University of North Carolina Press, 1976);

Lloyd Milton Short, *The Development of National Administrative Organization in the United States* (Baltimore: Johns Hopkins University Press, 1923);

Robert T. Swaine, *The Cravath Firm and its Predecessors, 1819-1948* (New York: Privately published, 1948);

Carroll H. Wooddy, *The Growth of the Federal Government, 1915-1932* (New York: McGraw-Hill, 1934).

Archives:

The most important collections of Russell Leffingwell's papers are in Yale University Library and the Library of Congress, which holds his Department of Treasury letter books. His business papers after 1923 are at J. P. Morgan and Company. There is additional material regarding his Treasury service and episodes thereafter in the Carter Glass Papers, University of Virginia Library, and the William G. McAdoo Papers, Library of Congress. Other collections with Leffingwell correspondence include the Norman Davis Papers, Library of Congress; Thomas W. Lamont Papers, Baker Library, Harvard University; the Dwight W. Morrow Papers, Amherst College Library; and the Franklin D. Roosevelt Papers, Roosevelt Library.

Charles A. Lindbergh, Sr.

(January 20, 1859 - May 24, 1924)

by Tiarr Martin

University of Dayton

CAREER: Lawyer, Minnesota (1883-1907); director, First National Bank of Little Falls, German-American National Bank, Transcript Publishing Company, and other businesses in Little Falls, Minnesota (1889-1924); U.S. representative, Minnesota (1907-1917).

Charles Augustus Lindbergh, Sr., businessman, attorney, politician, author, social scientist, and father of the famous American aviator Charles A. Lindbergh, Jr., became an outspoken critic of the "money trust" and the Federal Reserve system after the passage of the Federal Reserve Act in 1913. A member of the House Banking and Currency Committee when the legislation was drafted, Lindbergh characterized the act as "the greatest of all public gifts" given to the industry that least needed or deserved special privileges. He predicted that booms and panics would become more frequent and increase in magnitude, just the opposite of what the act's supporters claimed would happen. Lindbergh did not live to see the startling fulfillment of his prophecy: the Roaring Twenties and the Great Depression.

Born on January 20, 1859, in Stockholm, Sweden, Lindbergh immigrated later that same year with his parents, August and Louise (Carline) Lindbergh, and settled on a farm near Melrose, Stearns County, Minnesota. In the mid nineteenth century most Swedes immigrated to the United States for economic reasons, but the Lindberghs left Sweden to escape political controversy.

August Lindbergh, known as Ola Mansson in Sweden before changing his name just prior to leaving, was a leading member of the Riksdag (the Swedish parliament) and a director of the Bank of Sweden in Malmo. His liberal political views, which included advocacy of increased rights for women, full citizenship for Jews, reduced trade restrictions, and the abolition of the whipping post as

Charles A. Lindbergh, Sr. (courtesy of Anne Morrow Lindbergh)

a form of punishment, made him many enemies, who eventually trumped up a financial scandal to disgrace him. Against that backdrop, he left his native country and came to America with a new name, a new wife, and a new son, Charles, named in honor of Crown Prince Charles, a personal friend of August's who later became King Charles XV.

The Lindbergh homestead, located along a road traveled by practically all newly arriving immigrants to northern Minnesota, became a popular stopping place for many of them, especially those from Scandinavia. The resulting favorable name recognition certainly accounted in part for the political success of Charles A. Lindbergh, Sr., several decades later.

While working at a sawmill in 1861, August Lindbergh suffered an accident in which he lost his left arm. As soon as he was old enough, Charles shouldered many of the responsibilities once assumed by his father, including hunting, fishing, and defending against Indian attacks. His resulting expert marksmanship enabled him to sell enough game to pay for a significant portion of his later school expenses.

Lindbergh's early education consisted of home instruction and attendance at a grammar school located in a granary donated by his father. Eventually the community built a permanent school and hired a teacher named Jennie Stabler, who boarded with various families, including the Lindberghs. During that time Lindbergh attended school only sporadically, partly due to his family responsibilities and partly due to his fiercely independent personality. From 1879 to 1881 he attended Grove Lake Academy, a nearby prep school specializing in individualized instruction and 12-hour school days. It proved a more than adequate preparation for law school. In 1881 he entered the University of Michigan law school and graduated on March 28, 1883, with a Bachelor of Laws degree.

On June 22, 1883, Lindbergh was admitted to the Minnesota bar and for the next year worked in the law office of Judge Searle in St. Cloud before moving to Little Falls to start his own practice. He quickly established a reputation for honesty and integrity, refusing to take any case where he thought the potential client in the wrong. According to biographers Lynn and Dora Haines, Lindbergh turned down more cases than he accepted during the fledgling years of the practice. He eventually specialized in real estate law, and his clients came to include many of the town's leading businesses, including the Weyerhauser Company, which operated several large mills in the area.

In April 1887 Lindbergh married Mary La Fond, youngest daughter of Moses and Harriet La Fond. The couple would have three children: Lillian, born in 1888; Edith, born in 1891 and died ten months later; and Eva, born in 1892.

Lindbergh's brother, Frank, came to Little Falls in 1889 and joined Lindbergh's law practice, and that same year Lindbergh's parents also moved to the town. The Lindbergh name attained local

prominence. Also in 1889, Lindbergh became one of the original directors and shareholders of the First National Bank of Little Falls, owning ten shares valued at $1,000 each in a bank capitalized at $50,000. Lindbergh later joined the board of directors of the other bank in town, the German-American National Bank.

Lindbergh won election as Morrison County attorney in 1890 but served only one two-year term, deciding not to seek reelection because the job took him away from his very successful law practice. He also had a running feud with the county commissioners over the $900-a-year salary he considered inadequate.

During the 1890s Lindbergh's extensive landholdings and reputable business practices attracted the attention of Howard P. Bell, a wealthy East Coast capitalist. The two men established a business and personal relationship that later proved somewhat of a political liability for Lindbergh when he campaigned as a progressive Republican against eastern financial interests.

In the spring of 1899 Lindbergh's wife died following surgery for the removal of an abdominal tumor. Two years later Lindbergh began courting Evangeline Lodge Land, who had come from Michigan to teach in the local high school. Her father, Dr. Charles Henry Land, a dentist, invented the porcelain jacket crown. Lindbergh and Evangeline exchanged marriage vows on March 27, 1901, and their only child, future aviator and American hero Charles Augustus Lindbergh, Jr., was born the following year on February 4. Within five years Lindbergh and Evangeline separated, and Charles, Jr., lived with his mother most of the time. Lindbergh and Evangeline continued to care for each other, however, "attuned mentally, but not emotionally," according to daughter Eva.

On February 28, 1905, Lindbergh, Frank Lindbergh, Carl Bolander, Arthur Blanchard, and Charles Land incorporated the Industrial Adjustment Company. Interestingly, the company published a quarterly journal, entitled *The Law of Rights: Realized and Unrealized, Individual and Public*, for which Lindbergh served as editor. He used the journal as a vehicle to express his reformist views on politics and economics, including his concern that the family farmer, always unorganized, continuously faced a disadvantage when doing business with organized merchants, railroads, express companies, and the like. According to Lindbergh, because of their lack of vision and leadership the fault of the farmers' plight rested with the farmers themselves. But he sympathized with the farmers and hoped to help them gain a more prominent place in the economy.

As with most new small businesses, the Industrial Adjustment Company never really became viable, and the journal ceased to exist after publication of only three quarterly issues. One reason for the enterprise's failure involved Lindbergh's campaigns for Congress, which took almost all of his time. On June 20, 1906, he announced his candidacy for the Republican nomination in Minnesota's Sixth Congressional District. Although his views were heavily populist, Lindbergh saw the Republican party as the most effective vehicle for change. His opponent in the primary, popular two-term incumbent Clarence B. Buckman, accused Lindbergh and his law firm of profiting from the many farm foreclosures during the period from 1894 to 1896 and also characterized Lindbergh's association with the wealthy Howard Bell as inconsistent with Lindbergh's professed ideology. But Lindbergh prevailed in a divisive campaign by a vote of 9,962 to 8,709. The general election campaign against Democrat Merrill C. Tifft unified the Republican party behind Lindbergh and produced a victory of 16,752 to 13,115 on November 6, 1906.

Lindbergh's freshman year in Congress found him uncharacteristically but understandably voting "with the herd" on several votes, including one returning the powerful but controversial Joseph G. Cannon of Illinois as Speaker of the House. By his second year, however, Lindbergh established himself as an independent thinker and outspoken opponent of party politics and political patronage, which he regarded as a "curse which came with the job." Always a nondrinker and nonsmoker and somewhat of a loner, he chose not to involve himself in Washington social life, preferring instead to keep long office hours and to spend time with his young son, Charles, Jr., who frequently accompanied Lindbergh on the House floor.

On March 4, 1908, in his first speech to Congress, Lindbergh discussed why a government guarantee of bank deposits proposed to help prevent a repeat of the Panic of 1907 would at best only delay future downturns. He claimed a deposit guarantee could actually precipitate a panic if banks pursued more aggressive lending practices as a result. He argued further that if the government decided to provide deposit guarantees it should also exert a measure of regulatory control to protect itself.

Later that year Lindbergh spoke against the Aldrich-Vreeland emergency currency bill. He complained that American banks could secure with watered securities the $500 million in currency issues authorized by the bill. He also objected to the provision appointing a National Monetary Commission "chiefly made up of bankers, their agents and attorneys," who would likely propose legislation favorable to the banking industry. With those objections and with the added discouragement of having to deal with what he considered the ramrod tactics of the Republican leadership under Senator Nelson Aldrich of Rhode Island, he voted against the bill in vain, solidifying his belief in a "money trust" that unduly influenced legislation.

The elections of 1908 found Lindbergh with no opposition in the Republican primary and only token Democratic opposition in the general election. By that time he had identified with the progressive wing of his party, and when Congress reconvened, he participated in the unsuccessful insurgency against Speaker Cannon. Fellow insurgent Victor Murdock of Kansas described Lindbergh as "absolutely independent, one of those marvelous souls who lived out of his time and in the midst of an environment absolutely independent of him." His one-word description: "unowned."

When the House debated the controversial Payne-Aldrich tariff bill in 1909, Lindbergh came out in favor of protective but not prohibitive tariffs. The debate inspired him to compose a poem, which he included in a speech on the House floor: "Fence our European rivals out, / Keep the duty steep, / Save our honest workingman / From foreign labor cheap. / Build a tall old tariff wall, / Thus produce a dearth, / And make the honest workman pay / Twice what things are worth. / When his cheek is thin with want / And thinner is his calf, / Fill his place with an immigrant, / Who'll do his work for half."

In 1910 the Republican insurgents finally enacted long-awaited reforms of House rules and removed Cannon from the Rules Committee. In the 1910 elections Lindbergh claimed that his Republican primary opposition represented the "interests" in Washington, namely Cannon and Aldrich. But Lindbergh won the primary and general election easily and returned to the House, now controlled by the Democrats, for a third term.

Lindbergh on the campaign trail. He served in the U.S. House of Representatives from 1907 to 1917 (courtesy of the Minnesota Historical Society).

In 1911 the National Monetary Commission completed its work, 23 volumes of printed material that examined the banking and currency systems of Europe and Canada as well as the monetary history of the United States. According to a newspaper reporter, only Lindbergh, of all the men he knew, had read all 23 volumes.

A proposal that became known as the Aldrich Plan, after Senator Aldrich, who chaired the National Monetary Commission, grew out of the studies of the commission. The plan featured a National Reserve Association consisting of 15 branches spread throughout the country and a central board in Washington, capitalized at roughly $300 million and authorized to issue its own currency based upon gold as well as paper securities. It would carry member banks' reserves, determine discount rates, perform open-market operations, and handle the deposits of the U.S. government.

Lindbergh described the plan as "the greatest monstrosity ever placed before the American people." He objected to a majority of its provisions, including the stipulation relieving the association of the burden of having to pay interest on government deposits. Lindbergh declared, "If the people asked the government to furnish them with money without interest, it would be charged by Aldrich . . . that they were socialists." He also claimed that under the plan, control of American finance would go to Wall Street at the expense of the rural West. His biggest objection, however, was that the government was relinquishing its constitutional mandate to issue and control the nation's money supply to a centralized private monopoly.

Lindbergh vowed to do everything in his power to derail the Aldrich Plan. He presented an alternative reform plan in which administrative power rested solely with the Department of the Treasury and submitted a resolution calling for a congressional investigation of the "money trust." He established the National Bureau of Money Reform Literature to counter what he considered the propaganda of the National Citizens League (Lindbergh claimed the league was an agent of Wall Street) and wrote his first book, *Banking and Currency and the Money Trust* (1913), as an exposé of the "real" nature of the developments in Washington. Congress adjourned in 1912, before Lindbergh's book saw publication, and the House never seriously considered his alternative reform package. The National Bureau of Money Reform Literature never found a level of viability. But Lindbergh's money trust investigation resolution, although blocked by the Rules Committee (controlled by Democrats), led to an increased interest in Congress on the subject. Shortly thereafter two similar resolutions were introduced by two Democratic members, Robert L. Henry of Texas and Arsène Pujo of Louisiana.

The Pujo resolution, passed overwhelmingly by the House, empowered a House Banking and Currency subcommittee to investigate the money trust rather than an independent committee, which Lindbergh had favored. But he accomplished his goal. Public and congressional attention turned to the money trust investigation, which proved fatal for the Aldrich Bill.

According to Lindbergh the Pujo Committee pursued its investigation only halfheartedly. Nevertheless, the committee confirmed much of what Lindbergh had been saying, concluding that "if, by a money trust, is meant an established and well-defined identity and community of interest between a few leaders of finance, created and held together through stock holdings, interlocking directorates, and other forms of domination over banks, trust companies, railroads, public-service and industrial corporations, and which has resulted in a vast and growing concentration of control of money and credit in the hands of a comparatively few men ... your committee, as before stated, has no hesitation in asserting as the result of its investigation up to this time that the condition thus described exists in this country today."

In the 1912 presidential election Lindbergh refused to support his own party's sitting president, William Howard Taft, preferring Theodore Roosevelt, who almost wrested the Republican nomination from Taft. Roosevelt went on to run in the general election as head of the Progressive "Bull Moose" party with continued support from Lindbergh. Lindbergh chose to run for reelection as a progressive Republican and won easily, returning to a more heavily Democratic Congress and gaining a seat on the House Banking and Currency Committee.

The Banking and Currency Committee busied itself with drafting an alternative currency reform bill, which became the Federal Reserve Act, to replace the dead Aldrich bill. According to Lindbergh the Democrats on the committee routinely held secret meetings with administration officials and members of the banking establishment at the exclusion of the Republicans on the committee. Lindbergh denounced the secret meetings as a contravention of the Constitution and a violation of House rules. He called for a special committee to investigate, but the resolution failed on a point of order. He served notice, however, that he and his fellow Republicans expected to participate in the drafting of the bill, although the committee ended up accepting only one of the many amendments offered by Lindbergh.

The final version of the Federal Reserve bill was approved on September 4, 1913, and was reported to the House on September 9. On that same day six members of the committee, including Lindbergh, submitted and signed a minority report. Five of the members objected because they claimed the bill gave too much power and control to the federal government, while the sixth dissenter, Lindbergh, objected because the government retained too little control. He claimed that the bill "proposes to incorporate, canonize, and sanctify a private monopoly of the money and credit of the nation. . . . It violates every principle of popular, democratic, representative Government and every declaration of the Democratic Party and platform pledge from Thomas Jefferson down to the beginning of this Congress."

Lindbergh did acknowledge that a few key amendments could make the Federal Reserve bill "less severe on the people" than the existing system. Even though the House never made his proposed changes, Lindbergh surprisingly voted for passage on September 18. The Senate version, drawn up under the direction of Robert Owen of Oklahoma, passed on December 19, 1913. It contained more than 40 important differences from the House version, to be ironed out in conference committee. Opponents of the bill believed that it would take several weeks to negotiate and that the traditional courtesy of not bringing important legislation to a vote during the week prior to Christmas would apply to the Federal Reserve bill as well. However, the House-Senate conference committee somehow managed to iron out all 40 differences in a single day, Sunday, December 21, and the bill was quickly brought to a vote in the House on December 22, with many members already gone for the holidays. It passed 282 to 60, and later the same day the Senate voted 43 to 23 in favor. President Wilson, like many others surprised at the speed with which the bill was finalized, then refused to sign it because of his objection to the provisions for the selection of Class B directors. But after receiving assurances from future War Industries Board chairman Bernard Baruch that administrative processes could rectify this minor matter, Wilson signed on December 23.

Lindbergh did not vote for the Federal Reserve Act the second time around. He blasted it for creating "the most gigantic trust on earth." He chided Congress for creating the Sherman Antitrust Act to break up other trusts while they continued to pander to the "father of all trusts." He also warned that under the new act the "intermingling of finances" between the United States and Europe could unnecessarily draw the United States into a European conflict.

After war broke out in Europe the following year, Lindbergh advocated a policy of strict neutrality. In 1914, after reelection to a fifth term, he began to edit a new journal entitled *Real Needs: A Magazine of Co-ordination*, in which he charged that the "Wall Street end of the Federal Reserve System" indirectly used Treasury and depositors' funds to aid the Allies and encouraged, via the "subsidized press," American entry into the war.

In order to seek a wider audience for his antiwar views, Lindbergh decided to run for governor of Minnesota, officially announcing his candidacy on October 2, 1915. He withdrew his candidacy when the sitting Democratic governor, Winfield Hammond, died suddenly in December and the Republican lieutenant governor, J. A. A. Burnquist, took over. Lindbergh then filed for the Republican nomination for the U.S. Senate. Three other contenders also vied for the Republican nomination in 1916: incumbent senator Moses Clapp, a progressive like Lindbergh; former governor A. O. Eberhart; and Frank B. Kellogg, a nationally known trustbuster during the Roosevelt administration. Despite heavy campaigning with fourteen-year-old Charles, Jr., acting as his chauffeur, Lindbergh suffered his first political defeat, finishing last with 14 percent of the vote. Kellogg won the primary and went on to win the general election.

During the waning months of Lindbergh's final congressional term he introduced a resolution to investigate the Catholic church because of charges made by the Free Press Defense League and others that the church conspired to "bring the United States of America under the complete domination of the Pope of Rome and the Catholic hierarchy." That politically naive move did incalculable damage to his political career and haunted him the rest of his life.

In a parting shot at the new Federal Reserve Board, Lindbergh introduced during the lame duck session of 1917 articles of impeachment against five members of the board: W. P. G. Harding, governor; Paul M. Warburg, vice-governor; Frederick A.

Delano, Adolph C. Miller, and Charles S. Hamlin. The matter was referred to the Judiciary Committee and subsequently shelved.

Three days before leaving the House to return to Minnesota, Lindbergh, responding to all the war hysteria, prophesied: "The man who reasons and exercises good sense today may be hung in effigy tomorrow by the jingoes."

The brutal fulfillment of Lindbergh's prophecy occurred little more than a year later, when he campaigned for the Republican nomination for governor with the endorsement of the Non-Partisan League. While not technically a political party itself, the Non-Partisan League's tremendous growth and popularity in Minnesota threatened both the Democratic and the Republican parties' ability to run their political machines, because league-endorsed candidates could and did run in each party's primaries. Considered to be the most acrimonious election campaign in Minnesota's history, the 1918 Republican primary pitted Lindbergh against J. A. A. Burnquist, the same man Lindbergh, as a political courtesy, opted not to oppose two years previously. The Minnesota Republican party organization painted Lindbergh as disloyal, anti-Catholic, anti-God, and pro-Bolshevik, citing passages in his recently published book, *Why Is Your Country At War and What Happens to You After the War* (1917), as proof of his disloyalty. But Lindbergh's consistent position in his book and in his speeches revealed that, while he most definitely had opposed entry into the war, he nevertheless supported the president once the nation entered the war and insisted that we "fight this through to victory with the least possible delay." He vigorously denied that it was disloyal to advocate neutrality before an official declaration of war.

During the campaign Lindbergh drew huge crowds, some as large as 15,000, consisting mainly of farmers and agricultural workers. Toward the end of the campaign, he found meeting halls for which he had prepaid the rent locked by local officials with no satisfactory explanation. Lindbergh eventually resorted to speaking in barns and other farm buildings on private property. When throngs of people continued to flock to hear him, county officials in 19 of Minnesota's 86 counties outlawed public appearances by Lindbergh or anyone connected with the Non-Partisan League.

Gunfire was commonplace on the campaign trail, and protesters frequently pelted Lindbergh with rotten eggs and stones or ran him out of town. He often encountered his likeness dangling in effigy from telephone poles and lampposts. On June 8, 1918, while addressing a crowd on a farm in Martin County, he was arrested and charged with unlawful assembly and conspiracy to violate the law against interfering with enlistments. He was released the same day on a $1,000 bond. Even the federal government contributed to the melee when agents entered the premises of National Capital Press and seized and destroyed the original plates of Lindbergh's two books. When Lindbergh biographer Bruce Larson attempted in 1966 to persuade the FBI to confirm the event, director J. Edgar Hoover claimed that as far as the FBI was concerned it had never happened.

In the end Lindbergh's opponents convinced enough people of his alleged disloyalty. On June 17, 1918, in a record turnout with many Democrats voting in the Republican primary, Burnquist defeated Lindbergh by almost 50,000 votes. The 349,951 votes cast almost doubled the vote in the 1916 Republican primary. Serious questions arose regarding procedures employed by county election officials in the vote count, but no recount ever took place. Officials quietly dropped the conspiracy and unlawful assembly charges against Lindbergh in Martin County after his defeat.

Two months later, in a curious, almost bizarre, turn of events, President Wilson, apparently convinced of his loyalty and his ability to work with Bernard Baruch, appointed Lindbergh to a position on the War Industries Board (WIB). Lindbergh readily accepted the position and indicated his willingness to "serve anywhere for the general (war) cause." However, both Lindbergh and the Wilson administration underestimated the political fallout from the appointment. A firestorm of protest emanated from Minnesota, forcing Wilson to ask for Lindbergh's resignation. Without malice Lindbergh tendered his resignation on September 10, 1918, and reemphasized his willingness to serve should another opportunity arise.

Physically and emotionally exhausted from the primary campaign and the WIB affair, Lindbergh retired to a lakefront cottage with a friend to recuperate. After that, instead of reestablishing his law practice, he opted to edit and publish a new monthly farm journal, entitled *Lindbergh's National Farmer*. The first issue appeared in March 1919. Pressruns averaged between 1,500 and 5,000 copies but never approached the 25,000 that Lindbergh had anticipated. Consequently, the journal ceased publication in March 1920.

The approaching elections brought strong pressure on Lindbergh to make another run for governor, especially since incumbent governor Burnquist did not seek reelection. Lindbergh declined, citing the memory of the previous campaign. He decided to run for his old House seat if he could get enough signatures to run as an independent. By September he obtained the necessary signatures, but the campaign was severely underfinanced and disorganized, which resulted in Lindbergh losing his first Sixth District and third consecutive election, this time by a margin of 2 to 1.

After the election Lindbergh participated in the chartering of a new bank, the People's National Bank, in Shakopee, Minnesota, and bought a significant portion of the original stock in the bank. He also had invested heavily in land in the Miami, Florida, area, accurately predicting the development boom and personally favoring the mild climate.

During the 1920-1921 school year, Charles, Jr., studied mechanical engineering at the University of Wisconsin, but in the summer of 1922 he quit and moved to Lincoln, Nebraska, where he enrolled in flying school at the Nebraska Aircraft Corporation. Lindbergh did not approve of the change, fearing for his son's safety. But he may have been partly responsible for Charles, Jr.'s, decision, because the elder Lindbergh ceased funding the younger Lindbergh's education in 1922.

The election year of 1922 again found Lindbergh involved in politics, this time serving in party offices rather than as a candidate. He served as treasurer and state campaign manager of the newly organized Farmer-Labor party of Minnesota. Although it is difficult to assess accurately his contribution, the fledgling third party encountered enormous success in the fall elections. The party's candidate for the Senate, Henrik Shipstead, trounced both the Republican incumbent, Frank Kellogg, and Democratic contender, Anna Olesen. The new party almost captured the governorship and won an incredible 70 seats in the state legislature.

In addition to his political activities in 1922, Lindbergh finished the manuscript for his third book, *The Economic Pinch*, published by Dorrance of Philadelphia in April 1923. Familiar Lindbergh themes ring throughout the book, including the assertion that both major parties had been captured by

Lindbergh with his son and namesake, the future aviation pioneer (courtesy of Anne Morrow Lindbergh)

someone sabotaged the plane's rudder, causing a minor accident on a takeoff. Lindbergh lost the primary election to Magnus Johnson, who went on to defeat both the Democratic and Republican nominees in the general election, making both of Minnesota's senators Farmer-Laborites.

Lindbergh spent the next year shoring up his finances. The Panic of 1920-1921 hurt him badly, as land values plummeted, especially in Florida. The heavy use of his own money to finance his publishing ventures and political campaigns also took its toll. But when the 1924 campaign season arrived he could not resist and filed for the Farmer-Labor nomination for governor.

Before any campaigning occurred, Lindbergh became seriously ill and was taken to the Mayo Clinic, where doctors found an inoperable brain tumor. He was eventually transported back to St. Vincent's hospital in Crookston, Minnesota, where he died on May 24, 1924. At his request, Lindbergh's remains were cremated and later distributed by his son, Charles A. Lindbergh, Jr., from his airplane over the original Lindbergh homestead near Melrose, Minnesota.

After his father's death, Lindbergh, Jr., went on to become an American hero as a result of his pioneering, nonstop flight from New York to Paris in 1927, for which he received the Congressional Medal of Honor. His definitive account of the venture, *The Spirit of St. Louis* (1953), gained him the 1954 Pulitzer Prize in American biography. The infamous kidnapping and murder of his firstborn infant child prompted Lindbergh to move to Europe in 1935, where he made airpower surveys of several European countries and the Soviet Union. After war broke out, he became a leading isolationist prior to U.S. involvement in the conflict. Mirroring his father, he supported the war effort after the American entry, serving as a civilian consultant for several aircraft companies and the Air Force. His fervent desire for historical accuracy led him to keep diaries of his activities and observations during the war. Those controversial accounts detailing what Lindbergh described as "disgusting conduct" on the part of American troops toward German civilians after the Allied victory were published in 1970, four years prior to his death.

In his *Autobiography of Values* (1976), Lindbergh espouses many of the political and economic views of his father, including his opposition to the collusion between government and monopoly capi-

special interests who in turn controlled legislation to their advantage. He accused the Federal Reserve System of deliberately allowing the Panic of 1920-1921 and predicted that it would "ease up" and create a period of prosperity in order to "prepare the people for a worse fleecing" down the road. He called upon the "three useful groups in society"—small businessmen, farmers, and labor—to inform themselves politically and participate more in government. If they did not, the significant unequal distribution of wealth in the country would only worsen as politicians continued succumbing to capitalists' lobbying efforts for more governmental favors.

Within a month after the publication of the book, Minnesota's senior senator, Knute Nelson, died, and the state held special elections, including primaries. Lindbergh filed for the nomination in the Farmer-Labor party primary. He and Charles, Jr., barnstormed from town to town in the younger Lindbergh's government surplus Curtis "Jenny" biplane. The airplane campaigning ended prematurely after talism, which he felt threatened the American form of government and way of life. Both Lindberghs, "Lucky Lindy" and "C.A.," will be remembered for their honesty, integrity, and outspoken support of Jeffersonian principles.

Publications:

Banking and Currency and the Money Trust (Washington, D. C.: National Capital Press, 1913);

Why Is Your Country At War and What Happens to You After the War, and Related Subjects (Washington, D. C.: National Capital Press, 1917); republished as *Your Country At War and What Happens to You After the War* (Philadelphia: Dorrance, 1934);

The Economic Pinch (Philadelphia: Dorrance, 1923).

References:

Lynn Haines and Dora B. Haines, *The Lindberghs* (New York: Vanguard, 1931);

Bruce L. Larson, *Lindbergh of Minnesota: A Political Biography* (New York: Harcourt Brace Jovanovich, 1973);

Charles A. Lindbergh, Jr., *Autobiography of Values* (New York: Harcourt Brace Jovanovich, 1976).

Archives:

The papers of Charles A. Lindbergh, Sr., are at the Minnesota Historical Society in St. Paul.

James G. Lindley

(June 13, 1931 -   )

by Olin S. Pugh

University of South Carolina

CAREER: Various positions, Manufacturers Hanover Trust Company of New York (1957-1975); president, Bank of North Carolina, Raleigh (1975-1979); chairman and chief executive officer, South Carolina National Corporation (1979-   ).

James G. Lindley developed rapidly Manufacturers Hanover Trust Company of New York and served in several capacities in regional as well as general banking areas. His relatively brief career with the Bank of North Carolina proved highly successful in stabilizing and strengthening a bank that faced financial difficulties. As chairman and chief executive officer of the South Carolina National Bank he has overseen a period of growth and development while maintaining the bank's independent status. South Carolina National remains one of the largest independent banks in the southeastern United States, a region in which many interstate mergers have taken place in recent years.

Lindley was born on June 13, 1931, in Greensboro, North Carolina. He graduated from the University of North Carolina in 1953 and from New York University with an M.B.A. in 1960. He married Jane Kennedy of Asheville, North Carolina, and the couple had three children. Lindley served in the U.S. Navy from 1953 to 1957 and in the naval re-

serves from that date until he retired as a captain in 1977.

Lindley's years with Manufacturers Hanover gave him broad experience in many facets of banking. After serving in the national division of the organization until 1971, he joined the metropolitan division and became officer in charge of the New York office until 1973. He entered the regional banking field in that year, as senior vice-president of the Delaware through Florida region of the bank, specializing in corporate lending. His broad experience made him an attractive candidate for the presidency of the Bank of North Carolina in 1975. That bank suffered from serious credit problems and from inadequate cost controls in a period of rapid expansion. Lindley's staff changed the direction of the bank and returned it to a level of good earnings and equity.

When Lindley accepted the positions of chairman and chief executive officer of the South Carolina National Bank in 1979, he faced the challenge of guiding a profitable and well-run independent bank through the intricacies of deregulation and a period of instability in the economy and the money markets. In 1980 more than half of South Carolina National's deposits consisted of demand deposits; by 1988 only about 20 percent were demand deposits. In the face of dramatic interstate mergers and ac-

James G. Lindley (courtesy of South Carolina National Bank)

quisitions throughout the Southeast, Lindley's South Carolina National remained as of 1989 the largest independent bank in the region. Lindley has maintained that an independent can serve local customers more effectively than an interstate and that banking services and products can be designed for local needs.

As of 1989 Lindley did not hold that banks should specialize in originating credits that they might later sell to other investor groups. He believed in the wisdom of providing "base banking" services on a full-service basis. Maintaining a feeling of personalized customer service has become a tremendous challenge to modern bankers. Lindley had aspirations of continuing the personal approach even though South Carolina claimed assets of nearly $5 billion in 1989. He has expressed reluctance to diversify but might modify that position as

long as diversification does not harm the emphasis on base banking.

Lindley has maintained a flexible management style, communicating directly with all levels of service but keeping out of the details. By establishing and keeping a strong capital position for South Carolina National he has sought to be ready to enter diverse financial service fields. Throughout his career Lindley has contended that the effective manager must be able to deal with many inconsequential things without getting frustrated, so that he may make a few wise high-level decisions.

Reference:

John G. Sproat and Larry Schweikart, *Making Change: South Carolina Banking in the Twentieth Century* (Columbia: South Carolina Bankers Association, 1990).

Marine Midland Banks

by Barry Koling

Marine Midland Banks

Marine Midland Banks has engaged in banking and financial services for six decades through a network of branches in New York State and nationally through offices in some two dozen states. Founded in Buffalo, New York, in 1929 as the Marine Midland Corporation, it was the nation's first multibank holding company. That structure enabled it to expand throughout New York State during an era when state law prohibited bank branching.

Marine's roots date back to the 1850s when a group of Buffalo businessmen won a charter to establish a bank on the shores of Lake Erie—at that time a focal point for shipping and barge traffic along the Erie Canal. Focusing at first on trade finance, the new Marine Bank grew quickly, expanding its product line to serve the needs of shipping company employees and other individuals.

The success of that diversification led to more growth, and Marine acquired several banks, first in Buffalo itself and later farther inland. Eventually Marine acquired some 80 banks in all—most of them well away from the waterfront where Marine had its start. To reflect the company's new geographic diversity, its principals changed its name to Marine Midland Bank.

Early in 1929, George Rand, Jr., the son of one of Marine Midland's founders and an architect of its expansion strategy, assumed leadership of Marine and listed its stock on the New York Stock Exchange as a prelude to national expansion. But by late in the year, as the market began to signal its impending collapse, Rand and Marine's senior managers decided to curtail national expansion until the economic picture became clearer. Still, the new Marine Midland Corporation started life with a capital base of nearly $60 million and a network of 17 affiliated banks in New York State, the result of merging some of its smaller subsidiaries in overlapping markets.

Geoffrey A. Thompson, president and chief executive officer of Marine Midland Banks from 1988 (courtesy of Marine Midland Banks, Inc.)

Marine's capital base enabled the company to weather the economic storm of the 1930s. In fact, its stability and multibank structure made Marine a case study for regulators during the Depression, when some 9,000 banks closed their doors for good.

As the Depression waned and war loomed, Marine began to experiment with new types of financial services, including personal loans and automobile financing. Innovation led to additional growth as Marine continued to expand through acquisition. It added some 56 banks to its affiliate list between the late 1930s and early 1950s, in many cases combining the smaller institutions. By 1955, Marine's assets reached $2 billion, and the company's structure was streamlined to form ten large regional banks.

In the early 1960s, while Marine's domestic expansion continued, the company made its first step overseas. The Marine Midland International Corporation was launched in 1963 under the Edge Act, which permits banks to finance overseas investment and trade from U.S. bases while enjoying tax benefits comparable to those offered in offshore locations. In 1964 Marine opened its first overseas branch in London, and, with the purchase of the Grace National Bank of New York City in 1965, Marine inherited a significant book business and office network in Central and South America.

On the home front, meanwhile, Marine continued to cultivate new lines of business and new markets in New York State. In 1961 Marine became one of the first banking companies to step into the computer age with the purchase of a single General Electric computer. In 1962 its fledgling credit card business broke into the black, and by 1965 was the largest in the country.

Marine's assets in the 1970s approached $8 billion, and the company increased its lending to small and medium size businesses in New York State. Overseas, business continued to grow, fueled in large part by a merchant banking unit in London operated by Marine's New York City affiliate. The picture began to change, however, when rising oil prices coupled with a severe recession at home led to increasing loan losses. Marine's earnings, which had climbed for 24 consecutive years, dropped sharply in 1974 and remained depressed for the next two years.

Taking advantage of New York State's deci-sion to rescind its century-old restriction on branch banking, Marine in 1976 merged its ten affiliate institutions into a single bank in what was then the largest bank merger to date. The consolidated bank, with assets of $10.6 billion, had 316 offices in New York State. The merger represented the first step in an effort to reorganize and restore profitability. Faced with a choice between shrinking the bank or raising new capital, Edward W. Duffy, the Marine chairman who engineered the statewide merger, began to explore the possibility of a merger with the Hongkong and Shanghai Banking Corporation, whose chairman, Michael G. R. Sandberg, was looking for a way to diversify and expand in North America.

Those talks proved fruitful. After overcoming or circumventing procedural and regulatory obstacles, Hongkong Bank acquired 51 percent of Marine Midland in 1980, injecting some $236 million in new capital into the company. With that capital infusion, Marine built on its traditional strengths and expanded in selected markets nationally. In 1987, Hongkong Bank acquired the remaining 49 percent of Marine Midland, making the bank one of the largest foreign-owned financial institutions in the United States.

As a full member of the Hongkong Bank group, Marine in 1989 was among the nation's largest banking concerns, serving consumers and commercial customers through its New York State bank and a commercial banking subsidiary in Delaware. Some of its early expansion efforts foreshadowed its modern strengths. As of 1989, Marine was the country's largest bank financier of automobiles, the fifth largest credit card issuer, and one of the top three lenders to small businesses. Its roots remained solidly planted in New York State, where it operated 324 branches in more than 200 communities from Buffalo to Long Island.

William McChesney Martin

(December 17, 1906 -   )

by Walter L. Buenger

Texas A&M University

CAREER: Examiner, St. Louis Federal Reserve Bank (1928-1929); investment banker (1929-1931), partner, A. G. Edwards (1931-1938); governor (1935-1938), president, New York Stock Exchange (1938-1941); U.S. Army (1941-1945); chairman and president, Import-Export Bank (1945-1949); U.S. assistant secretary of the Treasury (1949-1951); chairman, Board of Governors, Federal Reserve System (1951-1970).

William McChesney Martin was born on December 17, 1906, in St. Louis, Missouri, the son of attorney, banker, and financier William McChesney and Rebecca Woods Martin. He had the benefit of an elite education and easy access in the financial communities of St. Louis and New York and rose quickly to become president of the New York Stock Exchange and chairman the Federal Reserve Board. As head of the Fed he espoused sound money and anti-inflationary policies. But ideology did not prevent him from becoming the consummate bureaucrat who protected the power and independence of his agency by repeatedly compromising with Congress and the executive branch while achieving the mission of the agency as he conceived it. He often summarized that mission by saying the Fed should "lean against the wind" to even out business cycles. By that he meant the Fed should tighten interest rates during times of inflation and loosen them during times of depression.

Martin's father helped draft the Federal Reserve Act of 1913 and later became president of the St. Louis branch of the Federal Reserve Bank. A serious student of banking and monetary policy, he also authored a book and several pamphlets on the subject. Evidently he encouraged the same interest in his son, who took an undergraduate degree from Yale University and almost completed a Ph.D. from Columbia University.

William McChesney Martin

The father also secured the son his first job, in the bank examiner's office of the St. Louis Federal Reserve Bank in 1928. From there Martin moved to the St. Louis investment firm of A. G. Edwards the following year, becoming a partner in 1931. He took a position on the Board of Governors of the New York Stock Exchange in 1935 and in 1938 became the first—and youngest ever—president of that organization.

After a distinguished career in the military during World War II, in which he helped coordinate the American Lend-Lease program to the Soviet Union, and four years as chairman and president of the U.S. Import-Export Bank, Martin became assistant secretary to the Treasury for international finance in 1949. He soon found himself drawn into a controversy between the Treasury Department

Federal Reserve Board chairman Martin with President Lyndon B. Johnson (AP/Wide World Photos)

and the Federal Reserve over the independence of the Fed. During World War II the Fed had firmly supported the price of government securities. By 1950 members of the Fed wanted to reassert its independence from the executive branch and counteract inflation. Martin entered the fray as a mediator and soon worked out a compromise that gave more to the Fed than it did to the Treasury.

In 1951 President Harry S Truman appointed Martin to fill the unexpired term of Federal Reserve chairman Thomas McCabe. Despite some criticism, the Senate confirmed the appointment. During his first years in office Martin worked diligently for sound money and an independent Federal Reserve. His policy of tightening credit by raising the rediscount rate in times of inflation fit in well with the anti-inflation policy of President Dwight D. Eisenhower. Relatively stable economic conditions allowed him to avoid sharply raising the rediscount rate until after he received an appointment to a full 14-year term as chairman of the Board of Governors in 1956.

By 1960 Martin had pushed the rediscount rate from 1.5 percent, where it had stood through much of the early 1950s, to 3 percent. In doing so

he came under attack by prominent Democrats including Wright Patman, chairman of the House Banking and Currency Committee. In the 1960 presidential campaign he also became a frequent target for candidate John F. Kennedy. When Kennedy won the election, Martin proved flexible enough to ease access to credit in accord with the attempts of first Kennedy and then President Lyndon B. Johnson to stimulate the economy.

In the mid 1960s, however, Martin found himself increasingly at odds with the Johnson administration's attempts to finance both the Vietnam War and the war on poverty. In December 1965 the Fed, led by Martin, raised the discount rate from 4 to 4.5 percent. President Johnson and Representative Patman questioned the wisdom of Martin's anti-inflationary efforts. Indeed, Patman predicted a sharp decline in home building and in the savings and loan industry. When that came to pass, he stepped up his efforts to force Martin to resign. Martin countered by calling for a tax increase to fight inflation and refused to resign. Over the protest of Patman and other Democrats, Johnson reappointed Martin to another term as chairman of the Federal Reserve in 1967 and agreed to a tax increase.

In his last years as Fed chairman, Martin cooperated with Johnson and his successor Richard M. Nixon in attempts to combat rising inflation. In the spring of 1969 he presided over a hike in the discount rate to 6 percent, at that time a record high. He also increased the reserve requirements of member banks by .5 percent and by the end of 1969 had extended those reserve requirements to commercial paper issued by bank affiliates.

After leaving office in early 1970 Martin served on a committee to reorganize the New York Stock Exchange and on the boards of several corporations. He continued to comment on U.S. economic policy throughout the 1970s. Martin is probably best remembered for his tight money policies, but he also reestablished the independence of the Federal Reserve, which during the Great Depression and World War II had become virtually another part of the executive branch. He also proved politically astute enough to cooperate with both Democratic and Republican presidents in his almost 20 years as Fed chairman. For those latter accomplishments he is best remembered within the Federal Reserve itself.

References:

William Greider, *Secrets of the Temple: How the Federal Reserve Runs the Country* (New York: Simon & Schuster, 1987);

Elgin Groseclose, *America's Money Machine: The Story of the Federal Reserve* (Wesport, Conn.: Arlington House, 1980);

William S. Melton, *Inside the Fed: Making Monetary Policy* (Homewood, Ill.: Dow Jones-Irwin, 1985).

William Gibbs McAdoo

(October 31, 1863 - February 1, 1941)

by W. Elliot Brownlee

University of California, Santa Barbara

CAREER: Lawyer, Chattanooga, Tennessee (1885-1892), New York City (1892-1913, 1920-1922), Los Angeles, California (1922-1933); president, New York & New Jersey Railroad Company (1902-1906); president, Hudson & Manhattan Railroad Company (1906-1913); U.S. secretary of the Treasury (1913-1918); U.S. senator, California (1933-1939); chairman, American President Lines (1939-1941).

William Gibbs McAdoo, secretary of the Treasury during World War I and most of the presidency of Woodrow Wilson, was born on October 31, 1863, in Marietta, Georgia. He was the second of three sons and fourth of seven children of William Gibbs McAdoo and his second wife, Mary Faith Floyd. His mother came from an old slaveholding family and authored romantic fiction. His father, from an east Tennessee family, had practiced law in Knoxville and dabbled in Whig politics before moving to Georgia to be closer to his wife's family home during the Civil War. Losing the slaves his wife inherited, he maintained a modest legal practice in Milledgeville, Georgia, until 1877, when he accepted a position teaching English and history at the University of Tennessee. That meant that young McAdoo, who had already received an excellent education from his parents, received the financial support to attend the university.

McAdoo left the university after three years (1879-1882) in order to accelerate his legal studies. In 1885, after working as a law clerk and studying law at night with a local judge in Chattanooga, he won admission to the bar and married Sarah H. Fleming. He established a law practice in Chattanooga, prospered from investments in a local real estate boom, and began his lifelong fascination with developing transportation systems. He purchased and then electrified Knoxville's streetcar line. Overextended, however, the line went into receivership, and McAdoo moved to New York City in 1892 to increase his income, pay off his debts, and practice closer to the nation's financial center.

In New York McAdoo survived the depression of the 1890s by practicing law, selling railroad securities, studying railroad economics, and restlessly dreaming about grand development projects. Finally, in 1901, on a ferry ride to New Jersey, he hit upon the idea of a railroad tunnel under the Hudson River. With advice from his friend John Dos

William Gibbs McAdoo

Passos, he decided to revive a failed project that had left an abandoned stretch of tunnel, rusted machinery, and disappointed stockholders. McAdoo formed the New York & New Jersey Railroad Company in 1902, and, winning crucial financing from Walter G. Oakman of the Guaranty Trust Company and Pliny Fisk of Harvey Fisk & Sons, bought the old project and completed the tunnel. In 1904 McAdoo's company completed two midtown tunnels. Meanwhile, in 1903 McAdoo had formed a new corporation, the Hudson & Manhattan Railroad Company, to build two downtown tunnels that would connect with the Pennsylvania Railroad. In 1906 McAdoo consolidated the tunnel companies into the Hudson & Manhattan company, and in 1908 train service commenced through the midtown tunnels, with President Theodore Roosevelt switching on the power. In 1910 McAdoo completed his system, which included 19 miles of subways and office buildings that occupied two city blocks, all of which was valued at $72 million.

McAdoo ran his railroad by what were then called "progressive" practices. He paid union wages and adopted an eight-hour day, introduced equal pay for women, experimented with separate cars for women passengers, invited complaints from riders, introduced improved cars—all steel with automatic doors—and he forthrightly publicized accidents. He publicized his management style with the motto "The Public Be Pleased." In 1911, however, his plans to expand his railroad network failed in competition with railroad interests with better access to city government and to capital markets. In his battles, especially with the Interborough "traction trust" controlled by J. P. Morgan & Company and with Thomas Fortune Ryan's Metropolitan Street Railway Company, McAdoo developed a strong antipathy to the financial power of the largest New York investment bankers.

McAdoo's public relations efforts, his contests with the Morgan interests, and the widespread urban dissatisfaction with corporate insensitivity to the public interest made him a highly popular figure in New York. His popularity, his business defeat in 1911, and the inspiration of Theodore Roosevelt's style of leadership fed McAdoo's political ambitions. A lifelong Democrat, he attached himself to the fortunes of fellow-Southerner Woodrow Wilson, first supporting Wilson's successful race for governor of New Jersey in 1910 and then in 1911 winning support for Wilson's presidential campaign among both progressive Southerners and New York investment bankers, including Jacob Schiff, the senior partner of Kuhn, Loeb & Company. In 1912 McAdoo assumed the management of Wilson's successful presidential campaign.

President-elect Wilson, looking for a secretary of the Treasury who understood the nation's capital markets but was independent of the largest—and usually Republican—financiers, asked McAdoo to serve. McAdoo accepted and resigned as president of his railroad. His resignation came none too soon because the competitive problems of the Hudson & Manhattan Railroad, combined with McAdoo's extravagant management, put the line close to bankruptcy and required major refinancing by Kuhn, Loeb & Company in 1913.

As secretary of the Treasury, McAdoo played a role in the enactment of the important financial legislation of Wilson's first term. His contributions were not decisive, but during the debate over the Federal Reserve Act in 1913 McAdoo's proposal to make the central bank a formal part of the Treasury dramatized the issues of public control and centralization and helped offset pressure from the banking community to establish the bank as a purely private enterprise. During the debate over the Underwood Tariff he helped highlight, as well, the commitment of the Wilson administration to progressive income taxation, which the tariff act implemented following the ratification of the Sixteenth Amendment. The income tax, although modest by modern standards, still represented a dramatic new course. Like most champions of the tax, McAdoo favored keeping the rates low until the government settled on appropriate definitions of income and proved its ability to administer the tax effectively.

World War I gave full play to McAdoo's ambitions, energy, organizational skills, salesmanship, and imagination. By the wartime years he had already emerged as the most powerful member of Wilson's cabinet. McAdoo's first wife died in 1912, and in 1914 he married Wilson's daughter, Eleanor, possibly cementing his influence with the president, although some evidence suggests that the president discounted McAdoo's family status. More important were McAdoo's abilities and the fact that Wilson offered all of his cabinet officers "discretionary space" for entrepreneurship. By 1914 McAdoo had succeeded in establishing independence even from Colonel Edward M. House, Wilson's closest adviser. As the president's attention turned more toward foreign policy after 1914, McAdoo expanded his power even further.

During the war McAdoo presided over and guided the dramatic transformation of American public finance. The federal government raised $13.5 billion in wartime tax revenues and in the process ended its reliance on import duties and began its use of heavy progressive taxation of incomes and profits. Of the remaining $38 billion required for the war effort, the government borrowed slightly less than two-thirds (about $24.5 billion) from the American people. In so doing, the Treasury revolutionized the techniques of debt finance, and the Federal Reserve System assumed its modern role in American financial life.

As early as 1915 McAdoo and Wilson knew that an American war effort would require revenues of unprecedented magnitude. Because the disruption of international trade had ruined the tariff as a source of new tax revenues, the alternatives were national sales taxation or income taxation. In the single most important decision in the financial history of the war and perhaps of the century, McAdoo chose to cooperate with a powerful group of insurgent Democrats who opposed preparedness but whose concepts of social justice led them to champion redistributive taxation. Those insurgents, led by Representative Claude Kitchin of North Carolina, who chaired the House Ways and Means Committee and served as majority leader of the House, carried remnants of republican, antimonopolist, and populist traditions. Focusing on taxation issues, they attacked concentration of wealth and special privilege.

McAdoo made a partisan decision to work with the insurgents. He knew he could have engineered passage of a much less progressive tax system—one relying more heavily on consumption taxes and mass-based income taxes—in cooperation with Republicans and a minority of conservative Democrats. But he also knew that if he did so he would have betrayed the heritage and program of his political party—a party with strong traditions of representing the disadvantaged, of opposition to the taxation of consumption, and of support for public policies designed to widen access to economic opportunity. Without a highly progressive tax program he would have bitterly divided the party, spoiled opportunities for attracting Republican progressives to the party, and destroyed Wilson's strong partnership with congressional Democrats—a partnership required by Wilson for his parliamentary-style government.

But McAdoo's decision involved more than partisanship. He regarded tax policy as an important means to achieve social justice through a restructuring of the economy according to the ideals of nineteenth-century liberalism. His program, with its promise to tax monopoly power, constituted an important dimension of Wilson's "New Freedom" approach to the "emancipation of business." McAdoo and Wilson, along with Louis Brandeis and Colonel House, held the view that taxation should discipline the large corporations to promote a more competitive economic order. McAdoo presumed that the largest corporations exercised inordinate control over wealth and that a "money trust" dominated the allocation of capital. He based his belief in the strength of monopoly power partly on the investigations of the Pujo Committee, the special committee that investigated the "money trust" in 1913 and established the committee's counsel, Samuel Untermyer, as an influential adviser to McAdoo. Also influential was Louis Brandeis's exposé, *Other People's Money*, published in 1913 and 1914, which McAdoo had assisted by providing Brandeis

Secretary of the Treasury McAdoo (seated, center) with the rest of the Federal Reserve Board as constituted from 1914 to 1918 (courtesy of Clinedinst Studio)

with Treasury Department information on corporations.

The Democrats enacted their plan for financing the war and adopting "soak-the-rich" taxation through the Revenue Acts of 1916 and 1917. Those acts transformed the experimental income tax into the foremost instrument of federal taxation; introduced federal estate taxation; imposed the first significant taxation of corporate profits and personal incomes, but rejected a mass-based income tax—one falling most heavily on wages and salaries; and established the concept of taxing corporate "excess profits" on a permanent basis. In contrast with Britain, which taxed only "war profits"—the excess of wartime over peacetime profits, the United States imposed a graduated tax on all business profits earned above a "normal" rate of return. By 1918 corporations paid more than $2.5 billion annually in excess-profits taxes—more than half of all federal taxes, which in turn amounted to more than one-third of all federal wartime revenues, a share that ranked the highest among the belligerent nations.

The Treasury's decision to place excess-profits taxation at the center of wartime finance shocked business leaders, including some of the nation's foremost investment bankers, corporations, and the Wilson administration's own business supporters. Cleveland H. Dodge (Wilson's Princeton classmate and largest campaign contributor) and Jacob Schiff, the senior partner in the investment banking house of Kuhn, Loeb & Company, lobbied McAdoo directly. Schiff told McAdoo that heavy reliance on income taxation for financing the war would "curb the push and ambition which is at the bottom of all material progress and development." Schiff singled out the excess-profits tax as "a measure which is economically unsound and which will strike at the very foundation of . . . prosperity." The businessmen preferred greater reliance on consumption taxes and on income taxes that reached middle-class families, arguing that such taxes would discourage consumption and encourage investment.

McAdoo remained confident that he could impose the radical tax program without damaging the nation's basic economic infrastructure because of the second major aspect of his wartime financial policy: minimizing borrowing. Such a policy would, he hoped, restrain inflation. McAdoo managed to fund the initial program of preparedness with no borrowing at all through the Revenue Act of 1916. By March 1917 McAdoo and House agreed that "a large part of the war's cost should be met by taxation." In April 1917, after America's entry into the war, they decided to limit wartime borrowing to no more than one-half of expenditures. In June 1917, after the success of the first Liberty Loan and a substantial increase in their estimates of the costs of war, they loosened their restraint on borrowing, raising their planned borrowings to two-thirds of expenditures. But even that higher level of borrowing left a degree of reliance on taxation that represented a notable departure from historic practice and exceeded the level of any of the other World War I belligerents.

In adopting his limited borrowing policy McAdoo had turned his back on the advice of the business community, which had traditionally assumed major responsibility for managing the public debt. J. P. Morgan, Jr., had recommended that only 25 percent of expenditures be financed through taxation, and the Federal Advisory Council of the Federal Reserve Board recommended an even lower share, 20 percent. Among the business supporters of the Wilson administration, only Benjamin Strong, governor of the Federal Reserve Bank of New York, favored heavy reliance on taxation.

The third element in the McAdoo program of war finance involved floating long-term loans at interest rates consistently and substantially below those available on relatively risk-free investments. The decision to borrow at submarket rates ran contrary to the best information available to the Treasury and was very much McAdoo's personal decision. Virtually all commercial and investment bankers pressed for materially higher rates. Investment bankers did not believe the public would buy the subpar issues in great quantities, and commercial bankers disliked the downward pressure on interest rates. Even Benjamin Strong, who favored a long-term strategy of offering submarket rates, urged the Treasury to set a premium for the first Liberty Loan in order to guarantee its initial success.

McAdoo favored low rates because, for one thing, he wanted to limit the future, and especially the postwar, burden of interest payments on the federal government. Confronting an ambitious, capital-intensive military effort of unpredictable duration and potentially great pressures on existing capital resources, McAdoo knew that the long-run interest charges to the federal government could be crippling in the postwar world, particularly in the face of postwar deflation. A closely related objective was to keep the federal government from becoming dependent on wealthy creditors. He feared that if the Treasury did not reduce dependency on the wealthiest borrowers, a small class of wealthy capitalists would gain control of the state, just as had happened, McAdoo believed, after the Civil War. In October 1917 he declared that "in a democracy, no one class should be permitted to save or to own the nation."

McAdoo's approach to war finance contained a fourth component—a "statist" or administrative, rather than market, approach to converting capital to the conduct of the war. Rather than relying on higher interest rates to allocate capital, McAdoo sought to borrow capital at low rates and then develop new government machinery to guarantee American business adequate access to the resources for maintaining health and productivity in the postwar period. In implementing this fourth policy, McAdoo led a Treasury effort to gain control of the nation's capital markets. He pressed Wilson, other members of the cabinet, and Congress to increase the federal government's control over prices and the allocation of capital and to coordinate and centralize all wartime economic powers in the Treasury. In August 1917 Colonel House commented on McAdoo's program: "When you sum up, it means he would be in complete control of the Government," and, "taking his demands as a whole, it would leave him as arbiter not only of the United States but of the European nations as well."

McAdoo pushed for his statist initiatives late in 1917, when the difficulties that the railroads and other utilities were having in financing wartime expansion began to concern him. He knew that the railroads could not, because of a critical Interstate Commerce Commission decision in December, raise their rates; that the Revenue Act of 1917, through a provision that established high rates of taxation on holding companies, further compounded their problems; and that those problems of finance threatened the stability of bond and stock markets and the ability of the government to raise taxes. McAdoo received the details from a wide assortment of investment bankers, including J. P. Morgan, Jr.,

Thomas W. Lamont, and S. R. Bertron. Most of them urged McAdoo and the president to declare, as Bertron put it, "that no further war taxation need be enacted in the near future," but McAdoo rejected the advice. Working closely with the members of the Federal Reserve Board, particularly Benjamin Strong and Paul Warburg, he devised proposals to block any private expenditures of capital that did not advance the war effort and to give priority to the capital needs of railroads and the Treasury. In November 1917 McAdoo proposed that Congress empower him to appoint a commission to review "all applications for new capital expenditures" and to impose a 10 percent tax on those expenditures if they were not appropriate for the war effort. That proposal led to the formation of the Federal Reserve Board's Capital Issues Committee, which McAdoo chaired. One month later, in December 1917, he proposed, with the support of the Federal Reserve Board, the creation of a War Emergency Finance Corporation funded with $500 million. That led to the creation of the War Finance Corporation, which he also chaired. McAdoo attached great importance to both organizations, seeing them as instruments for rationing scarce capital resources, providing public capital for critical private needs unserved by the marketplace, and enhancing confidence in the banking system.

In addition, McAdoo used the issues of war finance to advance his campaign to take over the railroads. On December 10, 1917, he wrote to the president, "The railroad situation is inextricably bound up with the vital and major problem of Government finance," adding that "we shall have to handle these two problems with very great care and skill" and that "future financial operations of the Government will be seriously affected by your action, and whoever you may choose to direct this operation should work in the most harmonious relationship with the Treasury Department." Four days later he wrote again, this time confidentially, warning Wilson of the demoralization of New York security markets and urging him to "take action in the railroad matter at the very earliest possible moment" because if "a panic would set in, grave injury would result and the financial operations of the Government would be seriously imperiled." Within a few days Wilson had decided to name McAdoo the director general of the railroads.

McAdoo's desires to keep interest rates down, reduce government dependence on the wealthy, and

increase the capital available for problem industries led to the fifth element of the Treasury's financial program: maximizing the sale of bonds to middle-class Americans. Congress left the marketing procedures for these loans almost entirely to Treasury discretion. Free to act, McAdoo attempted to persuade middle-class Americans to change their economic behavior: to reduce consumption, increase savings, buy bonds and thus become creditors of the state. After the conclusion of the war, he hoped, revenues raised from taxing corporations and the wealthiest Americans would repay the bondholders.

Selling the subpar, high-priced bonds—the Liberty Loans—directly to middle-class Americans on a multibillion-dollar scale required campaigns of unprecedented scope. McAdoo personally led the campaigns with extensive speaking tours across the country. But, most important to the success of the four Liberty Loans was the fact that McAdoo and the Treasury expanded the federal government's, and the nation's, knowledge of the social basis of capital markets. Largely through trial and error, they formulated a vast array of state-controlled national marketing techniques, including the sophisticated analysis of national income and savings and the identification of groups of middle-class Americans who could save at higher rates and invest in federal bonds.

The Treasury succeeded in placing the Liberty Loans deep in the middle class. In the third Liberty Loan campaign (conducted in April 1918), for example, more than 18 million people, accounting for nearly 18 percent of the American population and probably representing at least one-half of all American families, subscribed. Consequently, the borrowing stimulated considerable savings, just as McAdoo had hoped. Personal savings, the crucial component for McAdoo's borrowing strategy, nearly doubled between 1916 and 1917, increasing from $5.56 billion to $10.07 billion; savings increased further in 1918, to $12.69 billion. Most or perhaps nearly all of the increase was a consequence of the investments in U.S. government securities. And, largely because of those investments, personal savings as a share of gross national product increased by about 50 percent between 1916 and 1918.

To reach success the complex and ambitious program of taxing and borrowing required a vast expansion of the administrative capacity of the

Treasury. Following McAdoo's recommendations, Congress increased the number of assistant Treasury secretaries from three to five and created a sixth position of comparable status, the special commissioner to the Inter-Ally Council, who supervised the complex economic relations between the United States and the Allies. McAdoo assembled a management group in the Treasury appropriate to meet the severe demands of the wartime financial crises. His lieutenants included Russell C. Leffingwell, assistant secretary of the Treasury for "fiscal matters" (including the Treasury's borrowing and debt management policies), Daniel C. Roper, the commissioner of internal revenue, whose empire grew from 4,000 to 15,800 employees during the war, and Thomas S. Adams, the Treasury's principal tax adviser. Lacking a formal civil service presence adequate for his ambitions for the department, McAdoo had fashioned within the Treasury what political scientist Hugh Heclo has called an "informal political technocracy." It was an early example of what would become a typical expression of America's unique form of a "higher civil service." In the Treasury this group of talented, entrepreneurial advisers developed a significant degree of autonomy and served as the Wilson administration's primary instrument for learning about financial policy and its social implications, shaping the definition of financial issues and administration programs, and mobilizing support for those programs. The group provided the necessary means for McAdoo to form and dominate networks linking together competing centers of power within the state and linking the state with civil society.

The Federal Reserve System served as a major tool for success in fulfilling the Treasury's new responsibilities. In fact, during the war it functioned as an arm of the Treasury, working in close harmony with Leffingwell's borrowing and debt management operations. Treasury control over the Federal Reserve developed in part because McAdoo had succeeded earlier in cutting off an attempt to establish a council of bankers that would advise the Treasury. McAdoo then dominated the Federal Reserve System's policies by cultivating a solid relationship with Benjamin Strong, the powerful chairman of the New York Federal Reserve Bank, and by maintaining control over three of the Wilson appointees to the Federal Reserve Board, Boston lawyer Charles Hamlin, Birmingham banker Warren P. G. Harding, and McAdoo's close friend John Skelton

McAdoo giving a speech in support of the U.S. Liberty Bond drive (courtesy of Underwood & Underwood)

Williams (who served ex officio as comptroller of the currency).

To support the administration's program of mass-marketing bonds, the 12 Federal Reserve banks coordinated the Liberty Loans in their districts, and the Federal Reserve Board and the Treasury devised innovative techniques for buying the bonds with federally sponsored installment credit. Milton Friedman and Anna Schwartz have described the Federal Reserve during the war as becoming "to all intents and purposes the bond-selling window of the Treasury." In addition, McAdoo used the Federal Reserve System as a source of national information gathering. The Federal Reserve Board and John Skelton Williams kept McAdoo supplied with detailed reports on corporate bank balances, particularly those of the munitions, steel, iron, and coal companies, for the purposes of monitoring the taxpaying capacity and capital needs of corporations. The centralized collection of business information on a national scale enhanced the ability of McAdoo's Treasury to respond to and to shape economic change.

The new combination of redistributional and significant "state-building" components in the Treasury's financial program constituted a strategic threat to the nation's corporate infrastructure. Most severely threatened were the large corporate hierarchies who believed their financial autonomy to be in jeopardy. In fact, no other single issue aroused corporate hostility to the Wilson administration so much as the financing of the war. In 1918 the corporations found an opening to attack McAdoo.

That year, McAdoo decided that the war effort, which the Wilson administration believed might continue for two more years, would require greatly increased revenues. After a thorough investigation of the options, McAdoo proposed *doubling* federal taxes in fiscal 1919 by, among other means, requiring corporations to pay 80 percent of the higher of their "excess profits" or "war profits." The new tax, McAdoo declared, would place a relatively heavier burden on the largest corporations. In May, after complaining to the president about the monopoly power of J. P. Morgan & Company and "the financial bosses of Wall Street," McAdoo told him, "A proper war-profits tax will have a salutary effect upon these gentlemen."

McAdoo hoped to focus attention during the 1918 campaign on war "profiteering" through the tax issue. As he put forward his tax program, he worked with Senator William E. Borah, who launched an attack on "war profiteers," attempting to hold up to public scorn those corporations that had exploited the war and had not paid their fair share of taxes. The Treasury agreed to produce a list of all corporations that had earned more than 15 percent on their capital stock in fiscal 1917. In July, Thomas S. Adams and his staff had produced an extensive compilation of critical data on more than 30,000 corporations. McAdoo wrote to his friend Representative John Nance Garner that "indefensible profits are being earned in various lines of industry," and in August McAdoo placed on the record more of the Treasury's analysis—estimates by Adams that the 80 percent tax on war profits would bear more heavily on a great many of the largest corporations, including all the steel companies (producing $100 million more in revenues from U.S. Steel alone) and the Standard Oil group ($60 million more).

McAdoo had to make the case for dramatic tax increases during an election year, 1918. Corporate efforts to shift the blame for inflation and economic distress to the wartime financial program delayed consideration of the tax bill until after the November elections and the armistice, helped Republicans gain control of Congress, and set the stage for the 1920 elections. (In February 1919, however, Congress passed the Revenue Act of 1918, which established the main element of the Adams-McAdoo compromise—the hybrid "excess-profits" and "war-profits" tax.) McAdoo attributed the Democratic loss of Congress in 1918 to the "unpopularity of the proposed legislation with its proposal to increase taxes generally and to bear heavily on large corporate and individual incomes." Acutely aware of historical contingency, McAdoo later wrote that "if the Armistice had occurred a month earlier," in October, then "the Democrats would have won the election and . . . the history of the next two years would have been vastly different."

Acknowledging the seriousness of the 1918 electoral defeat, having been spared a fiscal emergency by the armistice, and perhaps trying to build conservative support for a Democratic coalition that he might lead in 1920, McAdoo quickly moved away from supporting even "war-profits" taxation. Immediately after the armistice, McAdoo called for the elimination of all excess-profits and war-profits taxation (after the collection of those taxes on incomes earned in calendar 1918 or on contracts entered into during the war). In November 1918, assessing the new conditions, McAdoo warned of the possibility of a postwar depression and urged Congress "to look ahead to the future of American business and industry." Taxation, he told Congress, "should be devised as to encourage and stimulate rather than to burden and repress them."

McAdoo left the Treasury for the practice of law in New York immediately after the armistice. He did so in part because he recognized that the elections of 1918 had destroyed the congressional base that was necessary for effective Wilsonian party government. But he left as well in order to recoup his finances, which expensive tastes and a large family had drained; to recover his health, which his strenuous Liberty Loan campaigns had taxed; and to position himself as a candidate for the presidency in 1920.

McAdoo ran an ineffective campaign for the nomination in 1920. He was reluctant to challenge or embarrass President Wilson, who as late as convention time still considered running for a third term. Shifting his hopes to 1924, McAdoo moved his law practice to Los Angeles in 1922 so that he might more effectively lead the western-southern wing of the Democratic party.

McAdoo's California clients included movie stars, real estate developers, A. P. Giannini of the Bank of Italy, and, unfortunately for his presidential ambitions, Edward L. Doheny—the man who had bribed Secretary of the Interior Albert B. Fall to obtain an oil lease at Elk Hills. When Doheny testified in 1924 that McAdoo had represented him before government agencies, many progressives felt betrayed. Nonetheless, McAdoo defended himself well against the charges, and, with the support of Bernard Baruch, his 1924 campaign was well funded. He won a majority of the convention delegates, defeating Governor Alfred E. Smith of New York, the candidate of the eastern wing of the party. But the progressive defections denied McAdoo the two-thirds majority he needed under party rules. After 103 ballots the nomination went to John W. Davis.

McAdoo's involvement in California's Democratic party continued. In 1932 he led the state's delegation to the national convention and played a crucial role in the presidential nomination of Franklin D. Roosevelt. McAdoo received control of the New Deal's California patronage and won election in 1932, at age sixty-nine, to the U.S. Senate, where he served one term as a loyal New Dealer. Still interested in transportation, he ended his public career as chairman of the board of the government-owned American President Lines, serving until his death from a heart attack on February 1, 1941. Surviving him were five of the six children from his first marriage; the two children from his sec-

ond marriage; Eleanor Wilson, who divorced McAdoo in 1934; and his third wife, Doris I. Cross.

McAdoo's most significant legacy was the permanent transformation of the Department of the Treasury during World War I. As he managed wartime financial mobilization, he pioneered in federal income taxation, made a success of the first mass-marketing of federal securities, poured content into the Federal Reserve Act, and organized in a permanent fashion the modern Treasury.

Publication:
The Crowded Years (Boston: Houghton Mifflin, 1931).

References:
John J. Broesamle, *William Gibbs McAdoo, A Passion for Change, 1863-1917* (Port Washington, N.Y.: Kennikat, 1973);

W. Elliot Brownlee, "Wilson and Financing the Modern State: The Revenue Act of 1916," *Proceedings of the American Philosophical Society*, 129 (1985): 173-210;

Charles Gilbert, *American Financing of World War I* (Westport, Conn.: Greenwood, 1970);

Seward W. Livermore, *Politics Is Adjourned: Woodrow Wilson and the War Congress, 1916-1918* (Middletown, Conn.: Wesleyan University Press, 1966);

Daniel C. Roper, *Fifty Years of Public Life* (Durham, N.C.: Duke University Press, 1941);

Dale Norman Shook, *William G. McAdoo and the Development of National Economic Policy, 1913-1918* (New York: Garland, 1987);

Lloyd Milton Short, *The Development of National Administrative Organization in the United States* (Baltimore: Johns Hopkins University Press, 1923);

Carroll H. Wooddy, *The Growth of the Federal Government, 1915-1932* (New York: McGraw-Hill, 1934).

Archives:
The public and personal papers of William G. McAdoo are in the manuscript collections of the Library of Congress.

Louis Thomas McFadden

(July 25, 1876 - October 1, 1936)

by Tiarr Martin

University of Dayton

CAREER: Assistant cashier (1898-1899), cashier (1898-1916), president, First National Bank, Canton, Pennsylvania (1916-1926); U.S. representative, Pennsylvania (1915-1935).

Louis Thomas McFadden, orphaned farm boy turned bank president turned powerful and controversial Republican chairman of the House Committee on Banking and Currency, authored the McFadden Banking Act of 1927, the most important revision of national banking laws since the passage of the Federal Reserve Act in 1913. After the act's passage until his death in 1936, McFadden bitterly opposed actions of the Federal Reserve Board and the 12 Federal Reserve Banks. McFadden asserted that Fed policymakers routinely accommodated the wants and needs of international financiers and foreign central banks at the expense of domestic economic priorities.

Born on July 25, 1876, near Granville Center, Troy Township, Bradford County, Pennsylvania, McFadden was the only child of Theodore L. and Julia (Babb) McFadden. Theodore McFadden, a wounded Union Civil War veteran of Irish and Dutch descent, settled in Granville Center in 1872 to engage in farming and the poultry business. Louis McFadden, orphaned at an early age, was raised by Dr. T. A. Gamble of East Troy, Pennsylvania, and earned his keep by farming.

McFadden graduated from the Bradford County school system and Warner's Commercial College in Elmira, New York. At age sixteen he took a job at the First National Bank of Canton, Pennsylvania, as a floor sweeper and night watchman. In 1898 the bank promoted him to assistant cashier, and on January 10, 1899, the bank's stockholders elected him head cashier. He was the youngest bank cashier in the state of Pennsylvania in 1899.

Louis Thomas McFadden (photograph by Bachrach; World's Work, *August 1921)*

McFadden married Helen Westgate, daughter of Orrin Ballard Westgate of Canton, in October 1898. They had three children: Theodore Westgate, Leslie Benjamin, and Barbara.

In 1906 McFadden became treasurer of the Pennsylvania Bankers Association, a position he held for one year. In 1913 he was elected vice-president of that body and in 1914 was elected president, again serving for one year. In the mid 1920s McFadden served as chairman of the association's Robert Morris Memorial Commission, which completed the erection of a monument to Robert Morris in Philadelphia in 1927. Several years earlier, in 1910, he had presented a resolution calling for the erection of a monument to Morris, financier of the American Revolution and founder of the Bank of North America–the first bank in the state of Pennsylvania.

By 1900 McFadden had become active in politics and was named to the Pennsylvania Republican party's Vigilance Committee. He won election to Congress in 1914 on his first attempt, representing the 15th district of Pennsylvania. He immediately gained a seat on the House Banking and Currency Committee and became chairman of that body in 1920. In 1916 the stockholders of the First National Bank of Canton elected McFadden bank president, a position he held until 1926, when he resigned to devote more time to his political activities.

The McFadden Act, which became law on February 25, 1927, removed many of the handicaps under which national banks had competed with state banks in the area of branch banking. Many states allowed branch banking by state banks, but the law theretofore had prohibited national banks from branching. As a result many banks had renounced their national charters in favor of state charters in states that allowed branch banking, threatening the power, if not the existence, of the Federal Reserve System. The purpose of the McFadden Act, therefore, was not to encourage branch banking but rather to equalize the powers and privileges of national banks and state banks. The act also liberalized capital requirements, permitted par values of less than $100 per share, granted national banks the right to deal directly in investment securities, and relaxed some of the restrictions on national banks in the area of real estate loans.

During the late 1920s McFadden grew increasingly suspicious of the activities of the Federal Reserve Board. Specifically he accused the Federal Reserve of bowing to pressure from international bankers and European central banks to pursue a domestic easy-money policy that facilitated a gold flow out of the United States and into Europe. McFadden claimed that international bankers wanted to return to Europe the gold it had lost to the United States during World War I and put Europe back on the gold standard. McFadden also blamed the easy-money policy for the stock market run-up and crash of 1929. In December 1931 McFadden introduced a resolution calling for an audit of the Federal Reserve Board and the Reserve Banks. The resolution failed, and the Federal Reserve System continues to operate as of 1990 without ever having received a comprehensive audit from a governmental agency.

On December 13, 1932, McFadden introduced a resolution calling for the impeachment of President Herbert Hoover for his moratorium on German war debts owed the United States. McFadden claimed the moratorium violated a law passed by the 72nd Congress prohibiting cancellation in whole or in part of war debts owed by foreign nations. The House tabled the resolution by a vote of 361 to 8, with 60 members abstaining.

On May 23, 1933, McFadden introduced a lengthy resolution calling for the impeachment of members and former members of the Federal Reserve Board and others for their part in causing and exacerbating the Depression. He accused them, among many other things, of having "treasonably conspired and acted against the peace and security of the United States, and with having treasonably conspired to destroy constitutional government." The House referred the resolution to the Judiciary Committee, which never reported it to the floor.

Charges of anti-Semitism were leveled against McFadden after his assertion on the House floor that "international money Jews" lay behind President Franklin Roosevelt's national bank holidays, his repudiation of the gold standard, and the confiscation of gold from private citizens by Roosevelt's "Jewish-controlled administration." As a result, both the Democratic and Republican parties, which had endorsed him for reelection in 1932, repudiated him in the 1934 election. McFadden consequently lost the election, despite having won with increasing majorities in his previous reelection bids.

In 1936 McFadden failed in an attempt to win the Republican nomination for his former House seat. He died later that year, on October 1, of coronary thrombosis while on a visit to New York City. He is buried in the East Canton Cemetery in Canton.

Despite his meteoric rise from humble beginnings and his many accomplishments in both the public and private sectors, no comprehensive biography of McFadden exists. Despite his position as House Banking and Currency Committee chairman during one of the most economically volatile periods in American history, McFadden's insightful, though controversial, analysis of Federal Reserve policies and actions remains largely ignored by historians and economists.

Publication:
Collected Speeches of Congressman Louis T. McFadden
(Hawthorn, Cal.: Omni, 1971).

Reference:
Pat Barber, *First National Bank of Canton—A 100 Year
Start on Tomorrow, 1881-1981* (Troy, Penn.: Troy
Gazette-Register, 1981).

McFadden Act of 1927

On February 25, 1927, President Herbert Hoover
signed into law a bill drafted under the direction of
the comptroller of the currency and introduced by
the chairman of the House Banking and Currency
Committee, Louis T. McFadden. Created specifically to respond to the numbers of national banks
that had abandoned their charters and converted to
less restrictive state charters, the McFadden Act expanded the branching powers of national banks by
allowing them to do so when state laws allowed it.
In other words, the act allowed national banks to
conform to state laws if those laws were more generous than federal law.

Any state bank that joined the national system
could retain all its branches in existence when the
act went into effect. The act prohibited a bank
from opening branches outside the city in which it
maintained its home office and also prohibited state
banks that joined the system from keeping out-of-
town branches they acquired after the signing of
the bill. National banks still found themselves somewhat disadvantaged compared to state banks that
could branch outside their home-office cities, but
the act represented a major step toward redressing
a serious inequity.

Other specifics of the McFadden Act prohibited national-bank branches in towns of less than
25,000 in population; restricted towns of 25,000 to
50,000 to only one branch; and limited towns of
50,000 to 100,000 to two branches. The comptroller of the currency reserved the right to determine
the number of branches in cities of more than
100,000 in population.

The McFadden Act became necessary only because of a precedent set by the second comptroller
of the currency, Freeman Clarke, who served in
that office from 1865 to 1866. Clarke interpreted
Section 8 of the National Banking Act of 1863 in
such a way as to prohibit branching by national
banks. The section stated that banks receiving a na-

tional charter had to conduct business at an office located in the place given on the certificate of organization. Clarke decided that a bank could *only* do
business in that location, and subsequent comptrollers accepted the interpretation.

Some historians maintain that the McFadden
Act developed out of a compromise to admit A. P.
Giannini's Bank of Italy and its 300 branches to
the national system. Admission of the Bank of Italy,
a California-based bank, not only promised to
bring in all those branches but would also send a
message that the government stood ready to compromise on the issue of national bank branching.
Giannini, sources suggest, saw the McFadden Act
only as the first step in uniting his *interstate* network under a single corporate entity. The second
step, interstate banking, never occurred in his lifetime. But the McFadden Act, as Eugene White has
pointed out, "helped to end the erosion of the national system and put national banks and state members on an equal footing." Not only did the Bank
of Italy come in with its branches in 1930, but
shortly thereafter the Los Angeles First Security National Bank and Trust joined the system and
brought in its 100 branches.

Gradually authorities reinterpreted branching
restrictions by recalling the McFadden principle of
the supremacy of liberal state law: if states could permit branching, then they could also permit interstate banking. In 1980, South Dakota allowed
Citibank of New York to open a "home" office in
the state, and Citibank moved its credit card operations there. Starting in the 1980s, states engaged in
reciprocal agreements to admit each others' banks.
The first such agreement, the New England Compact, involved several northeastern states. In 1984,
Georgia, Florida, and the Carolinas worked out an
agreement to allow their banks to cross each others' state lines freely. States in the Far West have
also concluded such an agreement. The most impor-

tant interstate arrangement, however, came when New York and California agreed to banking reciprocity beginning in 1991. All that remained was for the several states not involved in interstate agreements to conclude them on their own. With the major states already involved, those left out stand to incur economic damage if they remain outside the emerging interstate system.

References:
Benjamin J. Klebaner, *American Commercial Banking: A History* (Boston: Twayne, 1990);
Eugene White, *The Regulation and Reform of the American Banking System, 1900-1929* (Princeton: Princeton University Press, 1983).

                                                         —*Editor*

Robert S. McNamara

(June 9, 1916 -   )

by Larry Schweikart

University of Dayton

CAREER: Accountant, Price Waterhouse (1939-1940); instructor and assistant professor of accounting, Harvard University Graduate School of Business Administration (1940-1943); consultant, U.S. Department of War (1942-1943); consultant, U.S. Army Air Corps (1942-1943); U.S. Army Air Force (1943-1946); management consultant (1946-1949), comptroller (1949-1953), assistant general manager, Ford Automobile Division (1953-1955), general manager and vice-president, Ford Automobile Division (1955-1957); vice-president and group executive, car and truck division (1957-1960), president, Ford Motor Company (1960-1961); U.S. secretary of defense (1961-1968); president, World Bank (1968-1981); director, BankAmerica Corporation (1981-1987).

Best known for his role as U.S. secretary of defense during the Vietnam War, Robert Strange McNamara had a powerful impact on American and international finance in his position as president of the World Bank. He also experienced a lengthy and influential career in auto manufacturing, and after his years as president of the World Bank he participated in crucial decisions at BankAmerica as a director.

Born on June 9, 1916, in San Francisco to Robert James and Claranel (Strange) McNamara, McNamara grew up in Piedmont, California, where he attended public schools. His father, the son of Irish immigrants, worked in Buckingham & Hecht, a wholesale shoe firm, as an executive. Robert James McNamara was a lapsed Catholic, while Claranel

Robert Strange McNamara

was a Protestant; Robert S. split the difference somewhat by becoming an Episcopalian. Not only did religion separate his parents, they also had a 20-year age difference. Although Robert J. made enough that the family could live where it chose, they eventually settled in Oakland. Robert S. grew up on the border of an extremely affluent section called Piedmont, which provided him a better-than-average education. An excellent student who made "B"s only in French and physical education, he participated in many school organizations, including student government, and was president of Rigma, a secret group pledged to service (called by a faculty member "more of a nuisance than anything else"). During his high school years, he apparently exhibited little of the drive that later characterized his career.

After high school McNamara attended the University of California at Berkeley, where he majored in economics and served on the Men's Judicial Committee. On the committee he developed a reputation as having "too much faith in his fellow man." He also belonged to all the honor societies. At college McNamara also cultivated a liberalism that he offset with stubbornness. While those traits kept him unattached emotionally, they endowed him with an intellectual desire for social involvement without the ability truly to immerse himself in the problems of others. At Cal, McNamara picked up his hobby of mountain climbing during a brief fling at prospecting.

McNamara graduated Phi Beta Kappa from Cal in 1937. Later that year he attended Harvard Business School, where he steeped himself in the techniques of cost control. He became enamored with planning and management and did so well that classmates often found themselves letting McNamara handle the projects. During McNamara's Harvard years, his father died. McNamara went on to obtain his M.B.A. in 1939 and then took a job with the accounting firm of Price Waterhouse in San Francisco, where he met his future wife, Margaret Craig. They married on August 13, 1940, and later had three children, Margaret, Kathleen, and Robert. Margaret McNamara went on to found the education program "Reading is FUNdamental." In 1940 McNamara left Price Waterhouse to take a position as an instructor in accounting at Harvard, where he remained until 1943.

While teaching at Harvard, McNamara volunteered to teach Army Air Corps officers systematic management principles through a program at Harvard. He also served as a consultant for the U.S. Department of War, working on statistical control systems for the U.S. Army Air Force under a program created by a young officer, Charles B. Thornton. (The Navy had rejected McNamara when he tried to enlist because of poor eyesight.) He took a leave

from Harvard and went to England in 1942 for the Air Corps to establish statistical control systems, and in 1943 he received a commission as a captain in the Air Force, and he was later promoted to lieutenant colonel. His work took him to India, China, and the Pacific and earned him the Legion of Merit. McNamara's job, according to his biographer Henry Trewhitt, "was to make things work the way they were supposed to work." Despite his success in the military, McNamara intended to return to teaching after the war.

McNamara's experience in managing control systems and his military contacts stood him in good stead for the remainder of his career. Along with Thornton, he formed a group that studied the prospect of moving the American B-17 bomber force from Germany to Asia. The group concluded that the United States could achieve more cost efficiency by keeping the B-17s in Europe and building B-29s for the Far East. Thornton and McNamara soon were called the "Whiz Kids," a name that stuck with McNamara for the rest of his life. On the basis of their statistical studies, the Pentagon made several important decisions, and those events convinced McNamara of the power of statistics. When the war ended, Thorton convinced McNamara, whose wife had contracted polio, that private industry would pay better than academia. As a result, McNamara and Thornton planned to start a management consulting team focusing on market research for Allegheny Corporation, but before they started that project McNamara caught the corporate eye of Ford Motor Company, which employed him and his team to perform financial analyses for the company. The Ford group marked the birth of a new style of manager—one who had little production experience and whose knowledge was completely abstract. They knew about systems, not about products. The group viewed work "as a statement of class," as David Halberstam put it.

Ford had fallen on hard times despite the wartime contracts. When McNamara arrived the company was losing $9 million a month. Henry Ford II sought out consultants such as Thornton and McNamara. He hired those two and eight others in February 1946. Until 1949, McNamara managed Ford's Planning Office and Financial Analysis Office, after which time Ford named McNamara as its comptroller. As comptroller he developed a reputation for his thorough command of the company's books. He also, in the words of Trewhitt, "made the right moves in the automobile jungle when they counted most." Although he helped drive a remarkable comeback for the automotive giant, McNamara soon alienated many in the manufacturing side of the company because of his sterile, accountantlike approach to automaking. He and his minion pried into the activities of everyone at Ford, and asked so many questions that people started referring to them as the "Quiz Kids." Viewed as humorless and passionless, he soon inspired distrust among the production people, who feared his facility with the ledgers. One executive remarked of McNamara, "He's mature to the point that he eliminates his own feelings, and thereby eliminates the feelings of others."

The auto companies had just entered a new era in which the "bean counters" reigned supreme, and McNamara marched up the corporate ladder at Ford without missing a beat: assistant general manager, Ford Automobile Division (1953-1955); general manager and vice-president, Ford Automobile Division (1955-1957); vice-president and group executive, car and truck division (1957-1960); president (1960-1961). Part of his success hinged on his work habits—he spent from 7:30 A.M. to 6:30 P.M. each day at the office—and part came from pure luck. The Edsel disaster narrowly missed him, even though the company's misjudgment of the market for such a car resulted from its reliance on the types of statistical inputs McNamara championed, while he received much of the credit for the Falcon's success.

With each step up by McNamara, Ford's production men groaned. McNamara could "prove" that new investments, in such equipment as painting facilities large enough and hot enough to accommodate the new, larger-model cars, were not cost effective. He argued against expansion when Lewis Crusoe, Ford's general manager, fought desperately to modernize the plants. McNamara did not so much oppose the expansion as much as he wanted to study it further. But Henry Ford II, torn between his appreciation for McNamara's caution and the need to improve the facilities, finally decided in favor of new investment for expansion. He reportedly said, "Bob, the problem with you is you always want to study things. You never want to do anything." Still, McNamara won a small victory in that Ford only recommended $500 million for the modernization, or about half what the plants needed. When McNamara took over Crusoe's job in 1955, he ordered a study that at his insistence

"concluded" that delaying the expansion had produced profits for the company. That study only proved McNamara's conclusion under a very narrow set of circumstances, but McNamara needed the vindication.

Nothing captured the "McNamara v. Manufacturing" struggle as did the "battle of the paint ovens," or so termed by Halberstam. The old ovens proved far too small for contemporary autos and had created a bottleneck in the entire assembly process. Rather than build modernized paint ovens, McNamara sought to have the cars built in two parts, then painted, then welded together, a process guaranteed to weaken the chassis and subject it to incredible stress. McNamara never got cars built in parts, but he succeeded in purging most of the strong voices on the manufacturing side of Ford.

Other problems pitted McNamara against the "real car men," as they called themselves. He had a difficult time with the final stages of the Ford Falcon, because mileage varied from test to test. McNamara could not understand that wind, test conditions, and drivers all caused variations in mileage; he wanted the same mileage on each test. His aloofness and fascination with numbers and precision led one longtime marketing Ford man to comment to him, "It's too bad, isn't it, Bob, that the place has to be run with people—they have so many flaws." Yet he often biased his arguments through his statistics while professing objectivity. His favorite rejoinder—"that's irrelevant!"—abruptly terminated discussions at meetings. He also sought to inject a note of social responsibility into the design and manufacturing process, favoring padded dashboards and deep-dish steering wheels as safety features. The idea backfired: When Ford made safety a focal point of its advertising, people associated the company's cars with accidents.

Before McNamara could do much in his capacity as president at Ford, John F. Kennedy named him his secretary of defense. Kennedy had only been president a few weeks, and McNamara jumped at the opportunity. He disposed of his interests in Ford and assumed his cabinet position. He had been a registered Republican but supported liberal Democrats regularly and had voted for Kennedy in the election. He also made his liberal positions clear when he joined local movements in Ann Arbor to end discriminatory housing practices. Beneficiaries of his contributions included both the National Association for the Advancement of Colored People and the American Civil Liberties Union.

Called by Robert F. Kennedy "the most dangerous man in the Cabinet because he is so persuasive and articulate," as secretary of defense McNamara undertook some radical reorganizations of the nation's defense and procurement policies. One of his programs, the famous PPBS, or planning programming budgeting system, established five-year defense budget plans and brought together all the activities that supposedly were related. That system sought to keep the nation's overall military needs from falling prey to individual service pressures. He also introduced widespread reorganization of the Department of Defense (DOD) based on his management principles. First, he attempted to integrate all procurement under the PPBS, wherein he emphasized the areas of programming and cost-analysis. Programming sought to bridge the gap between military needs and civilian budgets. In fact, program reviews came to dominate the process, even dictating budget decisions. McNamara also brought all DOD activities under a new approach to American defense policy wherein he viewed the nation's defense posture as a whole. Rather than allow the Air Force, for example, to establish its procurement goals and operational roles in isolation, McNamara insisted that the Air Force's requests for new aircraft enhance and compliment the missions of the Navy, and so on. That approach, in turn, led to a review of the entire American strategic approach, which had been known as "Massive Retaliation."

Under McNamara's guidance, the United States formulated a new strategic defense policy that sought to maintain enough of a retaliatory force to sustain a Soviet nuclear attack and still destroy enough Soviet targets to deter them from launching such an attack in the first place. That strategy, known as "Mutually Assured Destruction," or MAD, remained the cornerstone of American defense policy until the Reagan administration. But McNamara gently shifted to a variation of MAD that envisioned circumstances in which a less than all-out nuclear exchange might take place. Rather than destroy population centers, the new strategy planned to retaliate based on necessity. No massive retaliation need occur in certain scenarios: the new objective was to destroy the enemy's military forces, not civilian population. (Whereas the strategy of attacking populations had the name "countervalue" strategy, the plan to attack mostly

weapons or military centers had the name "counterforce.") Counterforce gave the United States the ability to retaliate in increments, avoiding, at least in theory, an escalation to the point of an all-out nuclear exchange. As McNamara successfully pushed the new doctrine through the administration, he saw that it had beneficial effects for the Pentagon budget he managed, for no longer did the nation need to build greater numbers of nuclear weapons simply to "stay ahead." Fortunately, the new strategy also fit into McNamara's view of Soviet capabilities. He did not think that the Soviets, "in our lifetime," he said in 1963, "will reach parity with us." In that prediction, as in others, McNamara erred. Most observers put the two countries' nuclear forces at parity around the end of the decade, and the Soviet heavy missile forces soon surpassed those of the United States in number and in destructive capability.

The MAD policy dictated a subtle change in force structure, with McNamara pressing for expansion of the sea-based nuclear force and a shift away from manned bombers. No new strategic bombers went into production during his tenure, and indeed he essentially killed the B-70. And although he supported the antiballistic missile proposal (ABM) as a bargaining chip for arms negotiations, he personally thought it destabilizing and unworkable. Eventually, McNamara supported a modest ABM system as a political compromise providing a limited defense against nuclear attacks from nations such as China.

McNamara's strategy depended to a great extent on his faith in the sensibility of Soviet leaders. But they behaved differently than he expected, creating a massive, first-strike intercontinental ballistic missile force (ICBM) by the end of the decade and embarking on the largest peacetime shipbuilding effort in history. One scholar, comparing the rates of the Soviet buildup in the 1960s with that of Nazi Germany from 1933 to 1939, concluded that the Soviets had far surpassed what Hitler had achieved. For counterforce to work the Soviets had to respond properly: if the Soviets had enough missiles to strike first against military targets in a surprise attack and still have enough left over to threaten population centers should the United States retaliate, counterforce would be of little use.

To implement his new strategic theory, McNamara thoroughly reorganized the DOD, seeking to bring, as he called it, "a rational foundation as opposed to an emotional foundation" to decisions about the size and type of forces fielded by the United States. He ordered the consolidation of the position of assistant secretary of defense for properties and installations with that of the assistant secretary for supply and logistics into the office of assistant secretary for installations and logistics. At McNamara's order, the government created the Defense Supply Agency to manage and procure common supply items instead of having those operations performed by the Armed Forces Supply Support Center and the Consolidated Surplus Sales Office. He also established new agencies or offices, including the Office of Education and Manpower Resources and the private Logistics Management Institute, a research organization to improve procurement practices. Other reorganizations involved assigning to the assistant secretary of defense for manpower the duties of the assistant secretary of defense, health and medical. Foreign language training and intelligence gathering activities for all services were consolidated into the Defense Language Institute and the Defense Intelligence Agency, respectively. The latter agency also established a Defense Intelligence School to train officers for intelligence work. McNamara increased and expanded the activities of the Defense Communications Agency, which oversaw the massive interconnecting of all lines of communication within the armed forces. He combined the Tactical Air Command (TAC) with the Strategic Army Corps forces, calling the unit United States Strike Command (STRICOM).

The constant threat of nuclear attack led McNamara and President Kennedy to revitalize the civil defense program by putting it under the control of the DOD. McNamara appointed an assistant secretary for civil defense and undertook a massive assessment of the nation's fallout shelters, directing almost $700 million toward new civil defense activities. Under his supervision the nation designated 58,000 buildings as public shelters, and the DOD undertook an extensive program of shelter construction. Those civil defense activities, by the way, hardly adhered to the counterforce theory of limited nuclear exchange centered on military targets. Finally, McNamara oversaw completion of several radar and ballistic missile warning networks designed to alert the United States of a nuclear attack and to maintain presidential command and control in the event a war occurred.

Among McNamara's more serious flops, the TFX aircraft represented an ill-considered attempt to introduce commonality to weapons purchased by more than one service branch. Originally conceived as a fighter aircraft at a time when both the Air Force and the Navy needed a replacement fighter airplane, McNamara saw an opportunity to force both services to use the same basic airframe and engines. However, the Navy had vastly different demands for its carrier-based airplanes than did the Air Force for its land-based aircraft. Innovations such as variable geometry wings, introduced to address some of the Navy's objections, only added weight, thus eroding the aircraft's desirability to the Air Force. Ultimately the Navy refused to purchase any of the bloated planes, which had grown too large to be effective as fighters. Designated the FB-111s, the aircraft ultimately proved effective as fighter bombers based in Europe (and were effectively used in the raids on Libya in 1986), but they never served as the replacement fighter plane the Air Force and Navy needed.

McNamara also presided over the Skybolt missile disaster, though the missile itself had originated before he took office. Conceived as a long-range air-to-ground missile, Skybolt offered some of the advantages of modern cruise missiles, but, of course, used a rocket instead of an air-breathing engine and flew much faster and at higher altitudes. Because it could attack enemy targets after launch from a bomber stationed well outside enemy territory, Skybolt attracted the attention of the Royal Air Force (RAF). In Skybolt, the RAF saw the perfect weapon to justify continuation of its Vulcan bomber force, and with the United States picking up the development costs Skybolt offered a much cheaper alternative to a British-built missile. Unfortunately for its proponents, Skybolt did not work. McNamara desperately wanted to cancel the project even before mounting failure rates came to his attention. Britain thought that American attempts to cancel the missile amounted to reneging on its promise to support a British nuclear deterrent. Complained one British politician, "It's the greatest double cross since the Last Supper." In negotiations with the British, McNamara's style only made matters worse. George Ball, U.S. undersecretary of state, later charged that McNamara had partially bungled the affair because he lacked sensitivity to political issues. Subsequent dealings with McNamara by the

European allies on other issues repeatedly reminded them of Skybolt.

Other efforts at DOD won both praise and criticism. McNamara tended to take his "Whiz Kid" approach to the Pentagon, where the military viewed him as an intruding egghead at times. By insisting that the Pentagon "buy American" when the cost differential did not exceed 50 percent, he appeased union groups but condemned the DOD to substantially larger outlays. He tried to increase American military might, but not without direction. For example, although he supported expanding the Navy by two aircraft carriers and a support carrier, he favored the lower performing (but cheaper) oil-burning carriers instead of the more expensive (but better performing) nuclear carriers. With McNamara's support, the Navy placed orders for additional Polaris submarines, which McNamara liked, increased active-duty military forces by more than 325,000, and increased the number of tactical aircraft wings.

The Vietnam War, of course, drove many of McNamara's initiatives, although certainly not all of them. He favored expanding the war and supported Kennedy's escalation of the conflict. Under Kennedy's administration, the number of Americans in South Vietnam increased from 900 to 16,000. On his first trip to Saigon in 1962, McNamara personally observed the situation and upon his return pronounced "every quantitative measurement we have shows we are winning this war." While he also recognized that a war in Vietnam meant a "long, hard struggle extending over a period of years," McNamara thought that only a lack of correct information stood between the existing situation and victory for the United Sates and the South Vietnamese. He relied on "indices" of areas under government control or statistics showing "defection rates" as signs of progress in the war. A friend admonished that McNamara "was trying to quantify the unquantifiable." McNamara, instead, saw the war as an equation. Once the United States "learned how to analyze this thing," he responded, "we'll solve it."

Sent again in September 1963 to observe the situation in Vietnam firsthand, McNamara observed a rising tide of opposition against Vietnamese premier Ngo Dien Diem. The Kennedy administration vascillated between trying to pressure Diem to become more democratic, withholding American support altogether, or simply taking over. Kennedy

tended to rely on McNamara's advice more than others. But when Washington staff had to formulate the critical response to a cable by the new ambassador, Henry Cabot Lodge, who, having just arrived, was greeted by a surprise suppression by the Diem government of Vietnam's Buddhists, McNamara was out of town. So was Kennedy. Roger Hilsman drew up the response, suggesting that the United States would support a coup. McNamara recognized that as a death warrant for Diem and his brother, Ngo Dien Nhu. Kennedy, after studying the response, did not understand its implication, or so McNamara thought. At any rate, the administration quickly made public its endorsement of "personnel changes" in South Vietnam, which gave the conspirators, who awaited only a sign of U.S. approval, the green light. A coup by Vietnamese generals overthrew and assassinated Diem. Evidence now suggests they acted on assurances and with money given by the CIA with Kennedy's approval.

After Kennedy's assassination, McNamara continued to advise the new president, Lyndon B. Johnson, and threw himself into his job with renewed vigor. During the Johnson years McNamara appraised the Vietnam situation pessimistically, predicting the immediate collapse of South Vietnam without a greatly increased U.S. military involvement. For that reason, Senator Wayne Morse referred to Vietnam as "McNamara's War." Throughout the early years of the war, McNamara remained convinced that the United States opposed only the ill-supplied and poorly armed Viet Cong insurgents when evidence showed that North Vietnam's regular troops had already invaded the South in large numbers. Nevertheless, until 1964, McNamara insisted that the United States was only conducting a pacification effort in a few isolated areas, even as North Vietnamese general Vo Bam said he had been designated to lead "an invasion" of the South.

After the Gulf of Tonkin incident, however, McNamara told General William Westmoreland that the DOD would give him whatever he wanted. Just how many troops McNamara promised remains a matter of dispute. Westmoreland claimed he asked for up to 1 million men, although the United States had only 429,000 troops in South Vietnam by 1966. Even then McNamara let word circulate that he doubted the United States could win the war, and he privately put a ceiling on U.S. involvement at 543,000. Although he increasingly came to rely on statistical measures, especially the "body count" of Viet Cong and the North Vietnamese, to chart the progress of the war, he took unfair criticism for that practice, which was standard procedure. Quickly the troops in the field got the message, and body counts inflated wildly. Ultimately, estimates suggested that the number of enemy killed and dragged away or never counted actually exceeded the inflated counts: later evidence put North Vietnamese and Viet Cong casualties at one million. Nevertheless, one famous story, no doubt at least partially true, told of the DOD "brass" gathered around a computer in 1968, feeding in information on the relative troop strength, armaments, supplies, and so on about the United States and North Vietnam. "When will we win the war?" the warlords asked the computer. "You won in 1964," came the reply. McNamara's approach often featured proposals that seemed ill-grounded in reality, such as setting up an electronic "fence" across the South Vietnamese border with North Vietnam in order to prevent infiltration, or, at least, to identify spots where units had crossed. The new "high-tech" weapons procured by McNamara's DOD often proved inadequate for jungle operations. Jamming problems afflicted the M-16 rifle, and aircraft lacked cannon for close-in strafing and dogfighting.

McNamara's statistics also revealed that the North only had to deliver 60 tons of supplies a day to the South—just 20 truckloads—to sustain the war. Closing off the Ho Chi Minh Trail looked simple on paper: just cut it at one spot and keep the separation in place. In fact, the trail covered 3,500 miles of gullies, mountains, and jungles and consisted of not one trail but dozens. To accomplish the separation the Johnson administration intended to establish the "McNamara Line," an electronic fence projected to cost billions of dollars, comprised of traditional mines and barbed wire supplemented with electronic acoustic and seismic sensors. By 1968, 20,000 sensors covered the North-South border, including "people sniffers"—odor detectors—and other detectors disguised as trees and foliage. North Vietnamese troops expressed their contempt for the devices by urinating on them, which often set them off. Ultimately, the McNamara Line did reduce the amount of material shipped down the trail by two-thirds, but not below the 60 ton per day minimum needed to sustain the war. Many military figures, including Westmoreland, thought that had the war con-

tinued, the Line would have eventually delivered on its promise.

As the war dragged on, however, McNamara grew more pessimistic about the effectiveness of such policies as bombing North Vietnam. He established rigid guidelines for the bombing, trying to keep the attacks away from population centers. In doing so he firmly maintained that the United States should not provoke the Soviets or the Chinese. Privately he wanted to conduct a humane war. Well before he left office, whether he actually believed the bombing had become too brutal, as he later said, or whether, as was more likely, that the numbers simply did not show enough return on the investment, he had started to criticize the bombing policy internally. He had joined with Paul Nitze to try to draft a formula for deescalating the war (the San Antonio formula), and, according to Nitze, press reporting of the war convinced McNamara to resign. When McNamara had learned that errant artillery fire had destroyed villages, he reversed his fundamental position on the war. In 1966 he had written a memo to Johnson arguing "there may be a limit beyond which many Americans . . . will not permit the United States to go. The picture of the world's greatest super-power killing . . . one thousand non-combatants a week, while trying to pound a tiny backward nation into submission on an issue whose merits are hotly disputed, is not a pretty one." Nitze and others recalled McNamara's "agonizing over the difficulty of trying to wage war 'more intelligently and less brutally,' " and Lyndon Johnson's biographer described McNamara as "wracked by doubts," even to the point that "he was becoming emotionally disturbed." Johnson, who as early as 1966 had concluded that the United States could not win the war, liked to tell magnanimously that he allowed McNamara to head the World Bank "as a way of preserving his sanity." In reality, once the war ceased to be a sterile exercise in numbers and became a gory and human conflict, McNamara lost his most important talent as defense secretary—his objectivity. The war so disturbed him that even as late as 1981 he kept totally silent on the subject.

The presidency of the World Bank had come open, and in October 1967 Johnson, who increasingly viewed McNamara as soft on Vietnam, asked him if he had an interest in the position. By November 1967, McNamara had decided to resign, but Johnson wanted him to slip out quietly. They agreed that McNamara's departure should not be viewed as a defection, so McNamara planned to stay until the end of February 1968, when he took over as president of the World Bank. Unfortunately, that lame duck period coincided with the massive Tet offensive, which demanded consistency and determination from the secretary of defense. But the transition occurred essentially in the middle of Tet. Lyndon Johnson announced the appointment of Clark Clifford as McNamara's replacement on the eve of Tet. By the time Clifford actually took over, Tet had ended. In the meantime, McNamara passed on several policy decisions, such as giving Westmoreland additional troops, that would have involved fundamental changes in draft practices.

At the World Bank, McNamara found an entirely different challenge: bringing capital to bear on the needs of developing nations without allowing the institution to become simply a charity. In his 13-year term with the bank, McNamara presided over a major transformation of that institution into the world's largest and most important source of international development assistance. From 1968, when he replaced George Woods, to 1981, when former BankAmerica chairman of the board A. W. "Tom" Clausen replaced him, the World Bank had increased its lending by $11 billion a year. McNamara's final year involved overseeing lending totaling more than $100 billion on 1,600 projects. His role in the bank manifested his sense of liberalism. As he proclaimed in his first speech as World Bank president, "Aid does work, it is not money wasted, it is sound investment."

Concentrating his efforts on development of the non-oil-producing countries, McNamara expressed concern that their growth rates had fallen below the expected and predicted rates of around 5 percent, with many African and Latin American countries growing at a rate of only 3.5 percent, and other African states barely exceeding 1 percent. McNamara commissioned a survey team, led by Lester Pearson, former prime minister of Canada, to conduct a study of past aid programs to determine how the bank could use its resources more effectively. McNamara also established a "development plan" for each developing nation, under which the bank determined where it could best play a role and which states would actually repay their loans. Pearson's study, delivered in October 1969, was described by one historian as "guilt ridden": it surveyed the entire aid program since 1950 and "blamed its failures on the people who had supplied the money." Almost expectedly, the Pearson study showed that the World Bank could increase its lending without much added risk.

Thus McNamara anticipated having the bank lend, from 1968 to 1973, at twice the levels it had loaned during the previous five years. He also redirected lending away from the Asian subcontinent, where remarkable growth had appeared, toward Latin America and especially Africa, "where the greatest expansion of our activities should take place." But along with cash, McNamara planned to right "one upside-down aspect of our operations" by increasing technical and educational assistance to African borrowers. He also sought to emphasize education by investing in textbooks, audiovisual materials, and, most important, television. The bank also increased its efforts in agricultural lending for irrigation projects, pesticides and fertilizers, and agricultural research and extension services.

From the outset the McNamara World Bank saw population growth as a danger. Like the former chairman of the Federal Reserve Board, Marriner S. Eccles, who spoke against population growth frequently during the period, McNamara completely accepted all of the projections that showed the underdeveloped nations were facing a "population bomb" that could derail development. Most projections that McNamara and others relied on used the famous catch-all, "At current rates of growth. . . ." Ironically, at the very time McNamara took over at the bank, evidence had started to accumulate showing that developing nations themselves slowed their own growth automatically and naturally when their per capita income reached approximately $450. Consequently, at a time when statistics showed that increasing income led to decreased population growth, McNamara had put the bank on a course to lower population growth as a way to increase incomes. He argued that even if population rates fell by one-half, they would still exceed the rates in most developed countries (which, he failed to note, had almost fallen to zero in most industrialized European states, with white reproduction rates—even in the Soviet Union—dropping below replacement levels). More than any other single problem, McNamara repeatedly put population growth at the top of the World Bank's list, calling it "the most delicate and difficult issue of our era."

McNamara assumed an inverse relationship between population growth and wealth and proceeded to view that relationship as the main cause of the "chasm" between the rich and poor nations. According to McNamara, "the misery of the underdeveloped world is today a dynamic misery, continuously broadened and deepened by a population growth that is totally unprecedented in history." Or, as he said, "To put it simply: the greatest single obstacle to the economic and social advancement of the majority of the peoples in the underdeveloped world is rampant population growth."

To a man as obsessed with statistics as McNamara, the numbers could lead him to no other conclusion: his speeches frequently repeated the well-known formulae of how long it took the world's population to double and to double again. He rejected "the myth that 'more people means more wealth' " as "shallow" and "misleading" and ignored data that showed poverty-ridden states such as Chad, Libya, Tunisia, and most French-speaking African states all had small populations and low density, while populous Hong Kong, Taiwan, Malaysia, Singapore, South Korea, and above all Japan had surged into phenomenal growth trajectories. Indeed, by the 1980s, per capita incomes and standard-of-living indices of some of those nations equalled those of most Western European countries and the United States. Japan, for example, while pushing the United States in per capita income, had the highest density per cultivated arable land and permanent crop land in the world, *ten times* the ratio for Africa. And Taiwan, another rapidly growing state, had a population density almost double that of the Chinese mainland. Yet McNamara seemed hypnotized by Malthusian trend analysis that viewed population growth as "runaway" or "exploding." Typical of McNamara's fascination both with numbers and the population problem, his 1973 book, *One Hundred Countries, Two Billion People: the Dimensions of Development*, again focused on the geometric aspects of population growth statistics.

Beyond population, McNamara directed the World Bank to improve the creditworthiness of its borrowers and to make strides in debt management. Yet he also agreed that the bank needed to make more "hard loans," where the borrowing nation might not repay as easily or quickly as hoped. The Pearson study convinced him that the need for hard loans would increase by at least 100 percent.

To expand lending by 100 percent the bank needed to improve its liquidity. The bank had run into trouble borrowing in world markets, and by mid 1969 its liquidity had fallen by $400 million. McNamara therefore proposed not only that the International Bank of Reconstruction and Development (IBRD) arm of the World Bank increase its annual lending from $800 million to roughly double that amount, but that the bank add $500 million to its cash reserves, a feat he planned to accomplish by increasing the bank's own borrowing in the capital markets to $600 million. He had reason for optimism, as $600 million represented less than 1 percent of the long-term funds in the capital markets of the industrialized countries.

McNamara noted in 1969 that despite the backing of World Bank bonds by the "strongest industrial nations on earth," management had always proceeded as if no such protection existed. The bank acted in such a way that it would never have to use its security, which in 1969 came to $20.7 billion. Indeed, the bank maintained good profits, averaging $145 million in the five years before McNamara assumed the presidency and increasing to $170 million in fiscal year 1969, despite "concessionary" interest rates (6.5 percent for a 24-month loan). The cost to the bank for funds came to a relatively low 3.1 percent, allowing the bank to cover its administrative and managerial costs. McNamara maintained that the excellent performance was due to the good managerial staff at the bank.

In 1970, McNamara embarked on a campaign to persuade the major industrialized powers to increase their support to the developing areas. Among the nations that pledged greater support, the Federal Republic of Germany, Britain, Norway, New Zealand, and Japan all worked with the bank to meet goals established by the Pearson commission.

Based on a 1960 United Nations General Assembly resolution to increase aid from the developed countries, the World Bank expected to meet the target of approximately 1 percent of the combined national incomes of the economically developed countries. In the five years prior to the endorsement of that resolution by the Development Assistance Committee in 1964, the developed countries indeed met that goal. But they failed to attain the goal in any year since the endorsement until 1970, when McNamara expressed his concern. Nevertheless, the bank's call for a stronger effort received a surprisingly positive response from the industrialized countries. As a result of those governments' decisions to increase their official levels of aid, they agreed to support a third replenishment of the International Development Association for 1972, 1973, and 1974 at a rate of $800 million a year, which represented a 100 percent increase over the previous period.

McNamara joined the Third World nations in blaming the United States and Western Europe for world poverty. Although he muted his criticisms of American efforts at first (compared to later gatherings that denounced U.S. policies, such as the 1974 World Population Conference), McNamara gradually increased his criticism of the United States, pointing out that it did not lead the nations of the world in contributions as a percent of gross national product (GNP). He accepted the conundrum, then propagated on a regular basis at the United Nations "that the West was somehow to blame for world poverty," a notion that itself had originated among Western intellectuals such as McNamara.

At the beginning of the Marshall Plan, he observed, American economic aid came to 2.79 percent of GNP and 11.5 percent of the federal budget. But by 1970, American aid had dropped to .3 percent of GNP and scarcely 1 percent of the budget. As of 1970 the U.S. ranked 11th out of 16 members of the UN's Development Assistance Committee. However, much of the U.S. budget went to the Vietnam War, the loss of which only promised to add at least one nation—and possibly many others—to the ranks of underdeveloped countries. (Indeed, in retrospect, Communist domination of South Vietnam and Cambodia left both those nations, plus the North, permanently poor, and thus only added to the problems of the World Bank.) Worse, in his 1970 speech to the World Bank Board of Governors, McNamara, who had already proven himself vulnerable to accepting false maxims, repeated the charge that Americans "form[ed] 6% of the world's population but consume[d] almost 40% of the world's resources." He certainly knew better, and as a former president of Ford knew that Americans discovered or created far more resources than they used, that American farmers fed the entire nation and had enough left over to feed dozens of others, and that American-owned or -affiliated companies either invented or developed most of the technologies that gave any value to those resources, as in the case of Ford's automobiles. Indeed, the postwar pe-

riod as a whole witnessed the most massive transfer of wealth from rich nations to poor nations in the history of the world. As British historian Paul Johnson noted, that transfer "amounted to the largest voluntary transfer of resources in history." If McNamara was right, the knowledge was virtually useless.

To the Board of Governors in late 1970 McNamara proclaimed a "crisis." He admitted that even when the growth rates of the developing countries reached 5 percent, the problems of poverty and illiteracy still existed in many countries. For once, however, McNamara's faith in statistical analysis developed a crack: he noted "we lack the necessary understanding and expertise [in critical fields]." Calling for increased research, McNamara wanted to know, in the case of unemployment, for example, "its causes, its impact and the range of policies and options which are open to governments, international agencies and the private sector" to deal with it. Nevertheless, it was an important admission for a man who at Ford always knew the answers.

In 1972 McNamara introduced a new slant to the World Bank's lending. Acknowledging that even if the industrial countries met the Second Development Decade's 6 percent growth target, it would not in itself "guarantee a significant advance in the quality of life for the majority of the two billion people who live in our developing member countries." The problem, as McNamara saw it, lay in the fact that the poorer members of those societies never seemed touched by the aid. Special pockets of impoverishment existed, which were "readily identifiable geographically," making it possible to design special programs just to reach them. But the lowest 40 percent of the population of all developing countries were untouched by most aid, and McNamara thought that traditional assistance, public services, and market forces could not reach them. In ten countries with per capita incomes of $145 annually, the lowest 40 percent received only $50 a year, while in a second group of nations that had per capita incomes of $275 annually, the poorest 40 percent only received $80. McNamara rejected the view that entrepreneurial activities, necessary for growth, automatically produced such disparities, and he ignored evidence showing that rapid entrepreneurial growth always produced wealth disparities.

To attack the problem, McNamara first identified the need for the political resolve to make the effort. Typically, he then recommended "a clearer perception of the problem," meaning more data.

McNamara during his 1981-1987 tenure as a director of BankAmerica (photograph by William Smith; courtesy of Stanford University Visual Art Services)

He therefore proposed that the developing countries address the task of gathering income data. In other words, he wanted the poorest countries in the world to spend what precious resources they had on gathering data. Scarcely in a position to refuse, however, those countries set a target date of 1975 when they agreed to start collecting the information McNamara wanted. More important, the bank identified and started to pursue policies specifically directed at alleviating poverty among the poorest of the poor in the developing nations themselves. That included forcing the developing countries—by using the leverage of loans—to "establish specific targets" to bring the growth rates of the poorest 40 percent of the population at least up to the national average within 5 years. Furthermore, the bank wanted to see progress at "significantly faster than the national average" over a 10-year period.

The bank also intended to attack unemployment through a variety of make-work programs: construction of irrigation and drainage facilities, road construction, housing construction, reforestation, and so on. Perhaps the most controversial aspects of the bank's plan involved its demand for "institutional reforms to redistribute economic power" through a variety of "land reform" (collectivization), "corporate reform" (confiscation), and credit

and banking (usually, some sort of controlled inflation) reforms. McNamara intended to pressure the developing states into changing their tax laws and banking regulations. He also sought to change the patterns of public expenditures in those countries, which he alleged "end by benefiting the already privileged far more than the mass of the disadvantaged." Again, the solution required the developing countries to conduct studies and gather data "on the effects of their current patterns of disbursement: where do funds really go, and who benefits the most?" (Ironically, if indeed the elites so controlled the government and positions of power, as McNamara thought, they easily could have fudged the statistics to fit whatever criteria the bank established.) Finally, the new program aimed at eliminating what McNamara saw as "distortions in the prices of land, labor and capital," wherein capital for the wealthy was underpriced and wherein the wealthy had liberal access to scarce resources.

In light of the political-economic philosophy then in vogue–a Keynesian liberalism spiced with a Galbraithian contempt for entrepreneurship and wealth–those policies looked both just and sensible. Yet decades later, especially after the Iron Curtain collapsed and only Cuba, China, and Vietnam remained "true believers" in the promise of a socialized economy, McNamara seemed to be directing the developing countries in exactly the opposite way they needed to go. The examples of Hong Kong, Singapore, the Philippines, Taiwan, and many other once poor nations that blossomed under capitalism stood as a stark reminder of the difference that policies could make.

At the end of the five years McNamara had increasingly come to view the lack of growth in the underdeveloped countries as a failure on the part of the affluent countries to give enough. The World Bank, on the other hand, had met the goals it established in 1968. It indeed had doubled its financial commitments to the IBRD (up from $5.8 billion in the 1964-1968 period to $13.4 billion from 1969 to 1973). Projects in East Africa had increased from 78 to 104; in West Africa from 35 to 102; and in Europe, the Middle East, and North Africa from 113 to 168. As McNamara explained to the Board of Governors, which convened in Nairobi, Kenya, in late 1973, the bank sought more than quantity. According to McNamara's goal of increasing lending to the poorest 40 percent, the bank nearly tripled lending to those nations that had per capita incomes of $120 or less, initiating 217 separate projects. The five-year plan also succeeded in shifting the emphasis to lending in the agricultural and educational sectors. Finally, the bank established a Population Projects Department, which concentrated on seven countries, especially India and Indonesia. Other departments were added inside the bank, including Tourism Projects, Urban Projects, Industrial Projects, an Office of Environmental Affairs, an Operations Evaluation Unit, and, predictably, a new program of comprehensive economic reporting.

For the bank's second five-year plan McNamara had even more ambitious goals. He hoped, for example, to attack three interrelated difficulties that plagued the developing countries: an insufficiency of foreign exchange earnings from trade, an increasingly severe burden of external debt, and an inadequate flow of Official Development Assistance. Regarding the trade problem, most of the developing countries could not expand their exports rapidly enough to pay for their essential imports. Because those imports themselves often served to form the basis for greater export capability and higher foreign exchange earnings, McNamara saw the trade imbalances as "self perpetuating." The second problem, publicly guaranteed debt, by 1973 had reached $80 billion, with an annual debt service of $7 billion. Finally, McNamara identified as "acutely inadequate" the flow of Official Development Assistance. Against the goal of .7 percent of the developed countries' GNP by 1975, actual assistance came to roughly .35. McNamara contended that reaching the target did not require any great sacrifice but "only a tiny fraction of the *incremental* income—income over and above that which [the developed countries] already enjoy." Anticipated annual GNP of the affluent nations was expected to grow by $1.5 trillion from 1970 to 1980, an "increase in output virtually beyond one's capacity to comprehend."

Accelerating his verbal flagellation of the developed nations, McNamara noted a difference existed between "relative poverty and absolute poverty," the latter consisting of "disease, illiteracy, malnutrition, and squalor as to deny its victims basic necessities." The bank's program during the second of McNamara's five-year terms focused on expanding IBRD and IDA lending at a cumulative annual rate (in real terms) of 8 percent. Its $22 billion in new commitments would constitute a 40 percent increase in real terms over the 1969-1973 period. Under the new targeted approach to lending, the bank set a goal of increasing production on small farms in such a way that by 1985 their output would achieve a 5 percent annual growth rate. That growth rate depended on the acceleration of land reform, better access to credit, assured availability of water, expanded extension facilities, greater access to public services, and "new forms of rural institutions and organizations that will give as much attention to promoting the inherent potential and productivity of the poor as is generally given to protecting the power of the privileged." To that end the bank expected to lend $4.4 billion in agriculture, an increase of $1.3 billion over the previous five years and an increase of almost $3.1 billion over the period from 1964 to 1968.

In a single two-week period the bank approved $10.7 million in credit for agricultural development in the Sudan to provide a higher standard of nutrition for some 50,000 farm families through expanded food crops and to assist an additional 13,000 farm families through new cash crops. In that same two-week period the bank also approved an $8 million credit for rural development in Upper Volta to benefit 360,000 individuals; a $21.5 million credit for a livestock development program in Kenya, which would affect the incomes of 140,000 rural inhabitants; an $8 million credit for integrated rural development in Mali touching some 100,000 families; and a $30 million credit for dairy development in India directly benefiting 450,000 farm families.

McNamara also correctly assessed blame for the problems of the developing countries to the price increases by members of the Organization of Petroleum Exporting Countries (OPEC), many of whom had the highest per capita incomes in the world. He noted that the price rise generated "a global imbalance of payments on an unprecedented scale." Yet, unlike his sharp attacks on the Western nations, McNamara refrained from criticizing the OPEC countries directly. Whereas British historian Paul Johnson termed the OPEC policies "a catastrophe" for the Third World, McNamara ignored the vast shifts of wealth—perhaps $70 billion from 1974 to 1975—from the underdeveloped and industrialized countries to the Arab oil states. In his speeches he certainly never proposed any action specifically to disgorge the excess profits in the form of mandatory aid from OPEC. Indeed, the aloofness with which McNamara treated the price increases that generated a fall in income, which spelled malnutrition and epidemics in the underdeveloped world, was striking. Where Johnson contended that "the number of Africans and Asians who died in consequence . . . must be calculated in tens of millions," McNamara produced no calculations to the contrary. He only observed that the "countries least able to finance this cost increase have . . . had to curtail their development programs." Rather, McNamara saw the primary effect of the price increases in their impact on the Western world. He argued that the balance of payments deficits between the developing nations and the OPEC countries "would be so large as to exert a cumulative strain on the economies of the developed nations . . . making it more difficult for the developing countries to expand export earnings and to finance their balance of payments deficits." Not only did the price-income disparity have those harmful effects, it also helped generate an overall price inflation on commodities that eroded the terms of trade and the export volumes of the developing nations.

As a solution to the problems created by the OPEC price increases, McNamara wanted to force the industrialized nations away from imported oil to domestic sources. But he also (again) fell into the trap of noting that the "one billion people in countries with per capita incomes below $200 consume only about 1% as much energy per capita as the citizens of the United States," implying that an inverse relationship existed between energy use in the United States and in developing countries. He did admit that a shift to alternative energy sources in developing countries was a long-term, and in some cases, very uncertain, prospect.

The OPEC experience again underlined some of the basic pessimism in McNamara's worldview. He saw the price increases as slowing growth rates in the developed countries, which, in turn, meant that they would slow their giving. Or, without greater Western giving, the underdeveloped countries had no hope. However, that approach completely ignored entrepreneurial spirits at work in the developing countries. It also sadly misjudged the responses in the West. Growth rates slowed for a while, but that only reminded Americans and Western Europeans of the delicate relationships, not between energy and production, but between government regulations and energy. European nations embarked on an expanded program of nuclear energy

production, while Americans examined tax incentives to drill and pump oil and gas. More important, however, was the way Britain and the United States responded to their stagflation by revising their tax codes and the degree of government involvement in the market. In each country, by the early 1980s, those responses had led to renewed growth, a revitalized market, and, in America's case, some 14 million new jobs. Thus, in many ways, McNamara had a paternalistic, condescending view of the Third World. The underdeveloped nations could only expect minimal growth if left to the devices of their own entrepreneurs: real advances could only be made with the help of the industrialized countries, and therefore nothing could interfere with their pipeline of largesse.

The oil episode revealed other key aspects of McNamara's worldview. "What," he asked, "really constitutes wealth? And what more fundamental measures of wealth are there than the levels of nutrition, literacy, and health?" McNamara assumed that the "OPEC countries have gained huge amounts [of wealth]," ignoring the fact that they only had that wealth by virtue of the fact that they owned, by reason of geography, a natural substance that had no value until an American discovered a refining process, and until British, Dutch, and Americans developed engineering techniques to pump it out of the ground. McNamara frequently confused the physical manifestations of wealth with wealth itself. He compared caloric intakes and per capita incomes of developed nations with the underdeveloped nations, asking, "Are there any more basic terms in which to compare the wealth [of those two groups of nations]?" Yet the per capita income of Kuwait, at the time one of the highest in the world, rested entirely on the value of oil, subject to wild and surprising fluctuations, while the wealth created by the Vietnamese boat people did not rely on their caloric intake but on their ideas, spirit, and cultural heritage.

Inflation's effects on the industrialized nations concerned McNamara, in that he feared they would cut aid as a first, not last, resort. He argued that "aid is not a luxury" and that regardless of the problems caused by inflation, the developed nations had to continue their aid uninterrupted. Indeed, by 1976, he claimed for the World Bank partial credit for changing attitudes toward aid. He contended that the bank's policies had contributed to important changes in growth strategies at the national and international levels. Nations started to reexamine their strategies to focus more on the massive problems of the absolute poor, while on the international level growth strategies concentrated on the disparities between developed and developing nations. Despite that new attitude, McNamara glumly reported to the Board of Governors in late 1976 that "the weight of the evidence is that [the poorer nations] are continuing to worsen rather than improve."

Scarcely a year later, McNamara announced that "the immediate economic outlook, although still clouded, has measurably improved." Performance figures showed growth in the developing countries averaged 4.7 percent. McNamara offered no explanation to the Board of Governors, and indeed it flew in the face of most of the bank's pessimistic predictions. He still found reason for gloom. The protracted North-South dialogue in Paris and several other meetings by the international community failed to resolve fundamental differences. He commented, "neither the North nor the South are really satisfied with the outcome." McNamara recommended "a wholly independent, high level, but deliberately unofficial commission of experienced political leaders—drawn from developed and developing countries alike—that could assess and recommend feasible alternatives to the current North-South deadlock." Of course, the fundamental problem was that the very division of nations into "North-South" was completely arbitrary and did violence to simple geography as well as the facts of basic economics. Nations in the "South" included 11 countries north of the equator, including Saudi Arabia, which at the time had the world's highest per capita income. Countries in the "North" included Japan, the United States, Canada, the European Economic Community powers and Australia, the only continent entirely south of the equator (included presumably because "it was predominantly white and capitalist," quipped historian Johnson). Not surprisingly, that highly politicized conference omitted the Soviet Union altogether, even though that nation had a per capita income well above most nations in the South, was primarily white, and was located entirely in the North.

Nevertheless, former West German chancellor Willy Brandt answered McNamara's call for a commission by recruiting a group of members. Brandt's report, called *North-South: a Programme for Survival*, appeared in 1980. It echoed the Pearson report, blaming the West, or by then, the North, for the problems of the developing countries. The Brandt report called for a blatant transfer of wealth from North to South through an international taxation system generally resembling welfare.

McNamara's 1977 report did note with satisfaction that the recent record of development lacked historical precedent. More than 2 billion people had experienced a faster rate of growth than developing peoples at any previous time. Life expectancy had soared, and societies had eradicated major diseases. The developing world had absorbed 900 million people and still improved—if only marginally—its standard of living. McNamara also expressed optimism about the ability of developing countries to increase the productivity of their small farms, citing evidence from Taiwan, Korea, and Malaysia without noting that generally those nations had capitalist economies. Moreover, the bank had met its five-year goals announced at Nairobi: increasing agricultural lending by 40 percent and having 70 percent of all the bank's agricultural loans contain specific components for small landholders. A new emphasis on job creation in the developing countries also characterized the bank's 1977 and 1978 agendas. But most of what McNamara saw in 1977 and 1978 looked bleak. Further improvement, he argued, depended on the developed nations lowering their trade barriers, which could shift $24 billion a year to the poorer countries. The developing countries, however, also needed to modify their policies, which could lead to increased manufacturing exports of $60 billion over the decade 1975-1985. Therefore, in 1977 McNamara outlined a plan whereby the developed countries could reduce their tariffs. He also issued his perennial call for a new study, "a comprehensive analysis of economic and social progress," completed in 1978 and published as the *World Development Report*. The initial aspects of that analysis showed that even if growth rates improved slightly in underdeveloped countries, 600 million people would remain in poverty by the end of the century.

As for the World Bank's own strategy at the end of the 1970s, it moved toward a sixth replenishment of the IDA's resources and a capital increase in the IBRD. Without an increase the bank would have had to cut its lending. McNamara reported a "consensus" among the nations that had met in London and Paris in the previous years that favored such an increase.

McNamara viewed the talk of protectionism, which grew more heated in the late 1970s, as especially dangerous to the developing nations. In 1979 he took his campaign to roll back tariff barriers to the fifth United Nations Conference on Trade and Development, arguing that tariffs threatened to undermine the progress made over the past quarter century. He specifically recommended reviewing existing trade agreements for their impact on the developing areas. Of course, dismantling existing barriers continued to top the trade reform list of priorities for McNamara.

McNamara's appeals for tariff reform and aid usually relied on moral suasion, but he also appealed to the developed nations on the basis of good economics. He noted in his address at the University of Chicago, accepting the Albert Pick, Jr., Award, for example, that the value of American manufactured exports and the importance of imported raw materials made assistance to the developing nations "the economically advantageous thing to do."

By the time McNamara appeared before the Board of Governors of the World Bank in 1979 to outline the targets for the Third Development Decade, he had again swung back to pessimism. The major goals of the bank had not been achieved, he announced. Certainly the developing countries, with the exception of a short burst, had not come close to the 6 percent per capita growth the bank had envisioned. And the growth that had occurred reflected the distortions of the rich oil-producing nations. Thus, for the Third Development Decade, he saw "little point in establishing overall targets which the poorest countries . . . have no hope of achieving." Undaunted, the bank prepared exactly those kinds of projections, showing that the developing nations could attain a 5.6 percent annual growth. Softening the ground for the Brandt report he knew was coming, McNamara warned "the measures of the past are simply not going to be adequate in the decades that lie immediately ahead."

As the text for his 1979 speech went to press, the U.S. House of Representatives, dismayed at the atrocities that the North Vietnamese had perpetrated in the South after their victory a few years earlier, attached an amendment to the legislation appropriating funds for the replenishment of the IDA that precluded the use of funds for certain purposes (such as loans to nations that routinely violated human rights). The war that McNamara had presided over for almost eight years had ended with 1 million South Vietnamese civilians dead after the surrender, yet McNamara expressed his moral outrage only at the amendment that would have banned aid to the North.

In his final year as president of the World Bank, McNamara dealt with a revived oil price rise and a trade decline among the developed countries. He urged developing nations to produce more of their own energy and to substitute whenever possible. He expressed his concern that increased energy costs and inflation would drive developing countries to slash what small antipoverty programs they had.

Perhaps McNamara's greatest contribution to the World Bank involved the transformation he oversaw in the use of the equity base of the bank to mobilize larger amounts of borrowed funds. By fiscal year 1980 those borrowings totaled $30 billion while loans reached $27 billion. At the same time the bank's paid-in capital and reserves rose to $7 billion. When McNamara stepped down, he expressed his gratitude for the opportunity to serve. In his eyes, the bank had grown into "one of the world's most constructive instruments of human aspiration and progress."

McNamara's resignation was planned before he suffered the death of his wife in 1981. Despite that personal tragedy, he entered into new activities. His years at the bank only increased his marketability in the corporate world. He became a star on any corporation board that was fortunate enough to get him, and he took his duties seriously. He remained in banking and finance through his directorship in BankAmerica.

At BankAmerica, the nation's largest bank by the 1970s, McNamara served as a voice of caution and conservatism. Joining the 15-member board of directors in 1981, McNamara started to criticize the policies of Sam Armacost, BankAmerica's chairman. McNamara argued that Armacost had not put aside enough loans-loss reserves and that Armacost needed help running the bank. Armacost, who had enjoyed a meteoric rise, found the bank slipping into deep trouble even as he took over. But he had more than contributed to the decline, and McNamara proved a continual critic in board meetings. Especially after the failure of Continental Illinois in 1984, when the U.S. comptroller of the currency started to audit the big banks almost continually, BankAmerica's board grew increasingly critical of Armacost's policies. Several major problems had developed. It had made far too many bad loans, and even before Armacost took over, had started to suffer from an obsolete computer system, unfocused investments, the interest rate mismatch, and its negligence in installing automatic teller machines when most other banks had in the 1970s. McNamara often spoke in a lone dissenting voice against Armacost's policies. Because of his experience at the World Bank, McNamara well understood the interest rate mismatch and the problems inherent in BankAmerica's bad loans. He unsuccessfully attempted to eliminate the quarterly dividend to stockholders in August 1985, recognizing the grave cash drain the bank faced.

McNamara's continuing battle with Armacost put him in the position of leading the opposition. As a financial analyst, he could match Armacost's understanding of the numbers. To Armacost, "McNamara joined the Comptroller on [the] blacklist," according to Gary Hector's study of BankAmerica. In the case of the dividend, Armacost wanted to use the proceeds of the sale of its San Francisco headquarters building to provide the cash. That plan brought a quick reprimand from the comptroller and the Federal Reserve, which issued a joint policy statement known on Wall Street as the "BankAmerica decision," wherein the two agencies made known their displeasure at using the proceeds of the sale of assets to pay a dividend.

Behind the scenes McNamara worked to oust Armacost or at least dilute his power. He had considerable experience with corporate takeovers, as he had held a place on the board of Trans World Airlines during the takeover battle with Carl Icahn. When it came to BankAmerica, McNamara worked with Sanford Weill, a takeover specialist, to install Weill as chief operating officer in return for Weill's commitment to bring in $1 billion in additional cash. McNamara saw to it that Weill's proposal got to the board. Armacost and his allies managed to dismiss Weill's bid almost out of hand and also to sidestep a second buyout by First Interstate Bank.

McNamara pushed even harder for changes in 1986. Some speculated that he threatened to resign in a burst of bad publicity unless BankAmerica gave the board more autonomy and independence. Instead, Charles Schwab, whose profitable investment firm had been merged into the bank earlier, resigned. Still, by the end of the year McNamara and events themselves had convinced many of the other directors that Armacost had to go. Unfortunately,

they had no one to put in his place. Desperate, Armacost solicited plans for saving the bank, including one from Drexel's Michael Milken. But it was too late: McNamara and his allies had seized control of the board. In October 1986 the board voted to bring back Armacost's predecessor, Tom Clausen, who had replaced McNamara at the World Bank, and to fire Armacost. Despite the critics' constant attacks, Clausen sparked a revival at BankAmerica. By the late 1980s, *USA Today* characterized the bank as a reawakened giant. Its assets had fallen from $120 billion in 1984 to just more than $93 billion in 1987, while its problem loans went from $5 billion to just more than $4 billion in 1989. After losing $1.5 billion from 1985 to 1987, the bank reported earnings of $547 million in 1988 and $208 million in the first quarter of 1989 alone. By 1990, McNamara's positions on Armacost and Clausen appeared vindicated.

While still a director of BankAmerica, McNamara reentered the political arena as a coauthor, along with three other noted former foreign policy public servants, McGeorge Bundy, Gerard Smith, and George Kennan, to challenge the concept presented by President Ronald Reagan for a Strategic Defense Initiative (SDI). The authors portrayed SDI as a threat to world peace and as "a case of good intentions that will have bad results because they do not respect reality." They argued that SDI's objectives could not be achieved technically, and to hope for a shield from nuclear weapons was "a false hope." Arguing that even a few nuclear weapons penetrating such a shield would result in disaster, the authors dismissed SDI's promise of protecting populations. They similarly dismissed any chance that it might protect *some* weapons or populations and thus enhance arms control. In fact, they contended, SDI threatened greater destabilization because the Soviets would see it as an attempt to secure a first-strike capability. They urged the president to "seek arms control instead."

McNamara resigned from the board of BankAmerica in May 1987 (when he reached the mandatory retirement age of seventy-two), and he proceeded to devote his time to serving on the boards of several nonprofit or philanthropic groups. He also continued to serve on a variety of other corporate boards, most notably Corning. McNamara also served as a director of Strategic Planning Associates, the *Washington Post*, and several private institutions, such as the California Institute of Technology, the Overseas Development Council, and the Urban Institute. He authored *Blundering into Disaster: Surviving the First Century of the Nuclear Age* (1986). His awards and recognitions included the Medal of Freedom, the Legion of Merit, the Albert Einstein Peace Prize, and the Christian A. Herter Memorial Award. He also won the Olive Branch Award for the outstanding book on the subject of world peace in 1987. With the possible exception of the Founding Fathers, particularly Alexander Hamilton, few Americans had influenced American business, finance, politics, and national security as much as McNamara. To many an enigma, McNamara marched to a different drummer, and for years the United States–and the world–listened to his beat.

Selected Publications:

The Essence of Security: Reflections in Office (New York: Praeger, 1968);

One Hundred Countries, Two Billion People (New York: Praeger, 1973);

The McNamara Years at the World Bank: Major Policy Addresses of Robert S. McNamara (Baltimore: Johns Hopkins University Press, 1981);

The Future Role of the World Bank (Washington, D.C.: Brookings Institution, 1982);

"Time Bomb or Myth: The Population Problem," *Foreign Affairs* (Summer 1984);

"The President's Choice: Star Wars or Arms Control," *Foreign Affairs* (Winter 1984-1985);

Blundering Into Disaster: Surviving the First Century of the Nuclear Age (New York: Pantheon, 1986).

References:

Robert Coulam, *Illusions of Choice: The F-111 and the Problem of Weapons Acquisition Reform* (Princeton: Princeton University Press, 1977);

Gary Hector, *Breaking the Bank: The Decline of BankAmerica* (Boston: Little, Brown, 1988);

Paul Johnson, *Modern Times: The World from the Twenties to the Eighties* (New York: Harper, 1980);

William W. Kaufman, *The McNamara Strategy* (New York: Harper & Row, 1964);

James M. Roherty, *Decisions of Robert F. McNamara: A Study of the Role of the Secretary of Defense* (Coral Gables, Fla.: University of Miami Press, 1970);

Henry Trewhitt, *McNamara* (New York: Harper & Row, 1971).

Archives:

The papers of Robert S. McNamara relating to his position as secretary of defense are at the Library of Congress. Those pertaining to his tenure at Ford Motor Company are at the Ford Motor Company Industrial Archives in Redford, Michigan. McNamara's World Bank papers are at the bank's Washington, D.C., archives. His Bank of America papers are at Bank of America's archives in San Francisco.

Andrew Mellon

(March 24, 1855 - August 26, 1937)

by David T. Beito

University of Nevada, Las Vegas

CAREER: President, T. Mellon & Sons (1882-1902); president, Mellon National Bank (1902-1921); president, Gulf Oil Corporation (1907-1909); founder, Mellon Institute of Industrial Research of the University of Pittsburgh [later merged into Carnegie-Mellon University] (1913); U.S. secretary of the Treasury (1921-1932); U.S. ambassador to Great Britain (1932-1933); founder, National Gallery of Art (1937); director, officer, stockholder, more than 60 companies including the Aluminum Company of America [previously Pittsburgh Reduction Company], Union Trust Company [previously Fidelity Title & Trust Company], Gulf Oil Corporation [previously J. M. Guffey Petroleum Company and Gulf Refining Company], Standard Steel Car Company, McClintic-Marshall Construction Company, Carborundum Company, and Koppers Company.

Andrew William Mellon was notable in his time not only for the sheer size of his fortune but for the wide range of his business investments. Oil, banking, steel, and aluminum were among the sectors of the economy in which Mellon's involvement left a revolutionary and enduring legacy. After the close of his business career, he served as secretary of the Treasury for 12 of the most controversial years of that department's history.

Mellon was born in Pittsburgh, Pennsylvania, on March 24, 1855, to Thomas and Sarah Jane (Negley) Mellon. His father, an attorney, headed the prestigious Pittsburgh banking house of T. Mellon & Sons. Judge Thomas Mellon's political and social philosophy left a deep impression on his son. The judge was strongly influenced by nineteenth-century classical liberalism. He had such strong antistatist beliefs that while serving as a member of the Pittsburgh city council, he voted against accepting Andrew Carnegie's donation of a public library on the grounds that the taxpayers would have to maintain the institution in future years. The judge's privately printed autobiography has been characterized as "outstanding literature" by historian David E. Koskoff. In it, he expressed admiration for the laissez-faire political philosophy of Herbert Spencer.

As one commentator put it, Andrew Mellon studied entrepreneurship by way of the "Thomas Mellon school of finance." Judge Mellon not only put his son to work on the family farm baling hay and selling it to passersby but also set him up in business with a small newsstand. According to one account, "the Judge talked to his son not as to a little boy but as to one with a mature intellect and thereby challenged the youngster to think as a man." At thirteen, Andrew commenced studies at the University of Pennsylvania. He dropped out four years later, only three months before graduation, to run one of his father's business operations, a lumber and building company.

In 1874 he went to work at T. Mellon & Sons. He had won enough respect from his father to warrant a substantial salary and the authority to approve loans. Eight years later his father entrusted him with ownership and the presidency of T. Mellon & Sons and, in 1890, handed over the remaining family enterprises. In the late 1880s Andrew Mellon entered into a full partnership with his brother Richard, who also worked at the bank. The relationship was so close that each developed a habit of prefacing business decisions with the statement "My brother and I." As Koskoff noted, when "either one decided to buy a stock, he frequently ordered a like amount from his brother's money in the other's name. They approached the world as one." Their formal business partnership lasted until 1921, when Andrew Mellon became secretary of the Treasury.

Historian Allan Nevins wrote one of the best physical descriptions of Andrew Mellon: "A man of

Andrew Mellon (courtesy of the National Gallery of Art)

moderate height, slender build, long narrow head, chilly gray blue eyes, and tightly closed lips masked by a mustache, he possessed a quiet elegance of presence but lacked magnetism. He was reticent, soft-voiced, diffident in manner, and extremely reluctant to speak in public, a slight stammer indicating nervousness."

Mellon followed in the footsteps of his father in methods of conducting business. He financially underwrote a wide array of promising entrepreneurs but rarely involved himself in management. He had a talent for delegating authority to able men who would take the credit, and the blame, for the success and failure of particular investments. Only on rare occasions did either of the Mellon brothers directly interfere in the management of the enterprises they backed. As Albert Atwood, an editorial writer for the *Saturday Evening Post*, put it, Andrew Mellon was "never a plunger; he was a supporter."

The Pittsburgh Reduction Company, which eventually became the Aluminum Company of America (Alcoa), comprised one of the most substantial of the early investments by the Mellon brothers.

Charles Martin Hall, a young inventor, had formed the company to exploit his new process for refining aluminum. Hall shared management of the company with Arthur Vining Davis, a recent graduate of Amherst College. In 1889 Davis went to Mellon's office to ask for a $4,000 loan to expand operations. After inspecting the factory site, Mellon decided that the company needed much more money to succeed and advanced a longer line of credit. Mellon put his faith in the company's prospects to the test by making extensive stock purchases from the outset. He also provided Hall and Davis with four acres of land on the Allegheny River for use as a factory site. By the 1920s the Mellon brothers owned more than a third of Alcoa's preferred stock and a like amount of its common stock.

The Mellons avoided direct involvement in the management and put their full trust in Davis to run the company, although Richard Mellon acted as nominal president of Alcoa for several years and Andrew Mellon served as treasurer for a brief period in 1892. Vertical integration characterized Alcoa as well as other businesses controlled by the Mellons; Alcoa owned and controlled most of its transportation facilities, power generation operations, mineral sources, rolling mills, and sales outlets. The new metal was put to uses ranging from surgical instruments to cooking utensils.

Although its patents expired in 1909, Alcoa held an effective monopoly on aluminum production and sales in the United States until the 1940s. It retained that preeminent market position because of low prices, aggressive marketing, and efficient production techniques. A variety of factors kept prices low, including foreign competition, the easy substitution of other metals, and the ever-present possibility that new companies would enter the aluminum business.

While in his twenties Mellon began a long friendship with Henry Clay Frick. The two had met during the 1870s when Frick had established himself in the coke metal business largely through loans from T. Mellon & Sons. Soon Frick not only became a millionaire but a partner with steel producer Andrew Carnegie.

Mellon's most profitable business collaboration with Frick was the Union Trust Company, organized in 1894. Together Mellon and Frick owned 80 percent of the company's original stock. Union Trust had begun as the Fidelity Title and Trust Com-

pany, an appendage of T. Mellon & Sons, for the purpose of tapping the lucrative market in trust estates. It quickly surpassed T. Mellon & Sons in size and became a leading force in American banking. By 1903 Union Trust's capital surplus, $16 million, exceeded that of the Bank of England. Mellon and Frick selected Henry Clay McEldowney, a cashier at Pittsburgh National Bank, as president of Union Trust. McEldowney proved a wise choice, and he served in the office for the next 34 years.

Union Trust's rise coincided with the metamorphosis of the traditional base of the family's business operations. In 1902 T. Mellon & Sons became a subsidiary of Union Trust under a new name, the Mellon National Bank. The new bank rapidly expanded, acquiring the Pittsburgh National Bank of Commerce in 1903 and the Federal National Bank ten years later. Although Frick purchased large blocks of stock, Andrew Mellon remained the effective head of the transformed bank. Through the Mellon National Bank and the Union Trust Company, the Mellons continued their lucrative strategy of financing, and then purchasing stock in, up-and-coming companies.

By far their most profitable investment came in the oil industry. Throughout the last three decades of the nineteenth century, oil refining and the Standard Oil Company, owned by John D. Rockefeller, were virtually synonymous. The Standard Oil Company consistently controlled 80 to 90 percent of the country's refining capacity. Even so, it always had to guard against smaller competitors.

The flagship of the Mellon fortune, the Gulf Oil Corporation, started as one of those upstart competitors. It originated in 1893 when Captain Anthony Lucas, a mining engineer from Yugoslavia, organized a company to explore a promising oil field near Beaumont, Texas. After drilling 575 feet, Lucas ran out of money. Convinced that an oil strike was only a matter of time, he turned to J. M. Guffey and John Galey, two prominent Pittsburgh speculators, for financing. Guffey and Galey quickly negotiated a controlling interest for themselves. In exchange, Lucas settled for a one-eighth interest in the then reorganized J. M. Guffey Company. The partners soon encountered the same problem that had plagued Lucas: lack of money.

Unlike Lucas, Guffey and Galey had some valuable business contacts. Both the partners had dealt with T. Mellon & Sons. In 1900 Guffey traveled to Philadelphia to make an appeal to the Mellon broth-

Secretary of the Treasury Mellon (left) with the rest of the Federal Reserve Board of 1921-1922

ers. After hearing him out, Andrew and Richard Mellon agreed to approve for him a credit line of $300,000. Guffey and Galey had to pay a stiff price for the help. William Larimer Mellon, a nephew of the brothers, speculated, "A.W. [Andrew] and Dick probably were to get back their money and a profit by an agreement that gave them half of any oil until the loan was paid."

In January 1901 years of effort paid off with a major oil strike at Lucas, No. 1, the main well of the company, near Beaumont. Three months later the Mellons helped to organize a company to exploit the discovery. The new J. M. Guffey Petroleum Company purchased the properties of the old J. M. Guffey Company. The Mellons purchased 50,000 shares and Guffey, with 70,000 shares, became the president. Andrew Carnegie and Charles M. Schwab provided additional capital with extensive stock purchases.

From the beginning the Mellons planned to build facilities to refine the oil in their fields. In November 1901 they set up Gulf Refining Company with essentially the same officers as the production company, including Guffey as president. They would have called it Texaco had not a competitor already used that name. Shortly after its formation, the Gulf Refining Company ran into dire straits.

The wells appeared to be running dry, and Guffey's lax management generated complaints. Initially the Mellons tried to contain their losses by cutting a deal with the Standard Oil Company, but Standard officials quickly rebuffed them. Rockefeller had tangled with Texas antitrust laws in the past and did not want a repeat performance.

Once the option of a buy-out by the Standard Oil Company had been closed, the Mellons embarked on an aggressive strategy of vertical integration. They saw to it that the allied Gulf and J. M. Guffey companies owned not only their fields but also their refining, distribution, and retailing facilities. Standard, by contrast, had specialized almost exclusively in refining. To keep a watchful eye on Guffey and spearhead the reorganization, the Mellon brothers appointed their nephew William Larimer Mellon as vice-president of Gulf. The younger Mellon, in turn, hired a host of talented subordinates and embarked on a determined search for new fields. By 1907 the reorganization started to pay off: The J. M. Guffey Petroleum Company could boast of extensive fields in Texas, Louisiana, and Oklahoma. The Gulf Refining Company had already laid the longest network of pipelines in the United States not controlled by the Standard Oil Company. The Mellons completed the reorganization in 1907 by removing Guffey as president. They also consolidated both companies into the new Gulf Oil Corporation. In a rare departure from form, Andrew stepped out of the background and agreed to assume the presidency. He resigned in 1909 but remained a principal stockholder and member of the board of directors.

By the second decade of the twentieth century, the Gulf Oil Corporation had become the most valuable of the Mellon family enterprises. In descending order, the next largest family holdings were the following: Alcoa, the Standard Steel Car Company, the McClintic-Marshall Construction Company, the Carborundum Company, and the Koppers Company.

The Standard Steel Car Company started in 1902 as a producer of railroad cars. The founders, K. T. Shoen and his nephew W. T., had once controlled the Pressed Steel Car Company, the dominant producer in the field. The Shoens hoped to reenter this profitable market through Standard Steel, but they needed capital. They convinced the Mellons to approve a $200,000 line of credit. As the company turned into a major force in the railroad car industry, Richard and Andrew Mellon gradually purchased more stock. They also took an active interest in management decisions; becoming disillusioned with the abilities of the Shoens, they bought them out through stock purchases. Eventually they owned more than 80 percent of the shares. Government contracts during World War I fueled dramatic expansion in the company's operations.

The story of the McClintic-Marshall Construction Company is a textbook example of the business strategy of the Mellons. Engineers Howard McClintic and Charles D. Marshall had founded the company in 1900 to produce steel for building construction, in particular frames for skyscrapers. They approached the Mellons for a loan to build a plant. The Mellons realized that the skyscraper construction boom had every prospect of continuing, and they decided to give the loan applicants a test. They asked both McClintic and Marshall for their opinions on what to do about a steel plant the family had recently acquired. After the Mellons received candid and informed advice about the plant's prospects, they called McClintic and Marshall in to discuss the loan application.

Andrew Mellon opened the meeting by announcing the loan the applicants had sought was too small. "This is often the case with borrowers," he said. He offered to lend them $50,000 on the condition that McClintic and Marshall would put up an additional $50,000. When the applicants pleaded that it would be impossible to raise $50,000, Mellon had a ready reply. He suggested that they mortgage their houses to raise the money and ask Marshall's father for a loan. These draconian conditions left McClintic and Marshall flabbergasted, but they reluctantly agreed. William Larimer Mellon described what happened next: "It was A.W. who then breathed a sigh of relief. He told them he appreciated and sympathized with their feelings, not only as to mortgaging their homes but as to approaching Marshall's father. 'Neither of these steps will be necessary,' said A.W. 'My brother and I will lend you the money. You should be able to repay us out of the profits of the business.' " Even so, the Mellons had driven a tough bargain. As a condition for the loan, they received a half interest in the company.

The McClintic-Marshall Construction Company produced steel frames for such structures as the Grand Central Terminal, the Golden Gate Bridge, the George Washington Bridge, the Radio City Building in New York City, and the Waldorf-Astoria Hotel. It lost $2 million on its most famous commission, the locks for the Panama Canal, but recouped the money quickly in public relations. Until it merged into Bethlehem Steel in 1931, the McClintic-Marshall Construction Company had only four stockholders: Andrew and Richard Mellon and McClintic and Marshall. The Mellons gave McClintic and Marshall free rein in the management of the company.

As they had done in the case of the Standard Steel Car Company, the Mellons became involved in the management of the Caborundum Company, which had been incorporated in 1891 by inventor Edward Acheson. Acheson found that he could produce a powerful abrasive by applying electricity to carbon and clay. He also discovered that the abrasive, which he called carborundum, was useful not only for diamond cutting but for a variety of other industrial purposes. In 1895 he visited Andrew Mellon to ask for a loan to finance plant expansion for his still-obscure concern. During their meeting Acheson pulled out a chunk of carborundum and proceeded to slash an incision in Mellon's glass paperweight. That impromptu demonstration was all Mellon needed. He jumped at the chance to ad-

Mellon (center) with President Calvin Coolidge and Secretary of Commerce Herbert Hoover, whom Mellon only reluctantly supported for president in 1928 (courtesy of Paul Mellon)

vance a series of "interest free" loans in exchange for stock bonuses. Through the exchange of loans for stock, the Mellons acquired an ever-larger stake in the company. Increasingly they found themselves frustrated with Acheson's lethargic and disorganized management style, and after gaining control of more than 50 percent of the stock, they forced him out.

Andrew Mellon topped off his business career by helping to organize the Koppers Company. Shortly before World War I, businessmen Harry W. Croft, Hamilton Stewart, and Henry Rust asked the Mellons for loans to put to practical use a new coal distillation process invented by Dr. Heinrich Koppers. The Koppers coal-to-coke process made it possible to salvage gas that had been wasted in the earlier process and use it for cooking, lighting, and other domestic purposes. The Mellons loaned money to get the new Koppers Company off the ground and purchased 37.5 percent of its stock. They saw to it that the Koppers Company was vertically integrated: Koppers not only constructed and sold coke ovens to other companies, but also

owned its coal fields and coal processing plants. It purchased several utilities to serve as a distribution network for Koppers gas.

Koppers did a booming business during World War I. Ironically the war also brought the business downfall of Heinrich Koppers. Shortly after the United States entered the war in 1917, major stockholders in the Koppers Company, including the Mellons, tipped off the U.S. Alien Property Custodian that Heinrich Koppers, a German citizen, owned a large share of the stock. Following the letter of the law, the custodian auctioned off Koppers stock. The only bidders for the stock (sold at bargain basement prices) were the Mellons and Harry W. Croft.

Outside of direct business investments, Andrew Mellon's most enduring legacy from this period was the Mellon Institute of Industrial Research. The inspiration for the institute came to Mellon in 1909 after he read *The Chemistry of Commerce* by Robert Kennedy Duncan, a professor of chemistry at the University of Kansas. Mellon agreed wholeheartedly with Duncan's contention that modern businessmen had failed to put scientific knowledge to profitable use. Duncan had set up a program at the University of Kansas in which businessmen could endow research fellowships to tackle scientific problems. All concerned had a financial incentive to participate in the fellowship program. The university benefited from the additional endowments, and the business donor, who would be first in line to apply research findings, had a new source for profit.

In 1913 Mellon officially launched the Mellon Institute of Industrial Research (named for Thomas Mellon, who had recently died) of the University of Pittsburgh. He had no trouble persuading Duncan to assume the presidency. Under Duncan's leadership the Mellon Institute became a large-scale version of the University of Kansas venture. For its part, the University of Pittsburgh provided laboratories and other facilities. In exchange, the institute recruited donors to underwrite the full cost of finding solutions to specific problems. Probably the most notable early project involved the research program on synthetic rubber. In many ways the Mellon Institute provided an early example of business and academic cooperation to promote research and development. During the 1960s it merged into Carnegie-Mellon University.

By 1913 Mellon's wealth probably equaled that of Henry Ford. The only person richer than those two was John D. Rockefeller. Unlike Ford and Rockefeller, however, Mellon had not based his wealth on any single enterprise.

Mellon's many years of involvement in politics began rather modestly. At first he depended heavily on Henry Clay Frick for advice on candidates and causes to support. In 1912 he contributed $2,500 to the campaign of Republican presidential candidate William Howard Taft. Four years later he donated $6,000 to help Charles Evans Hughes in his bid to become president. After World War I he made substantial contributions to the campaign against the League of Nations. The organizer of the anti-League drive was his longtime acquaintance Senator Philander Knox of Pennsylvania, who had also been Frick's attorney. Knox's brother was an officer at the Mellon National Bank.

Mellon's relationship with Knox proved crucial to his political career. The two had drawn closer in 1920, when Mellon supported Knox's unsuccessful run for the Republican presidential nomination. Knox returned the favor by touting him to President-Elect Warren G. Harding for secretary of the Treasury. Mellon quickly became the preferred choice of the conservative "old guard" of the Republican party. After a short delay, Harding offered him the position. On Knox's recommendation Mellon resigned as a member of all the boards of directors (more than 50 at that time) to which he belonged. He kept his stock, with the exception of Union Trust, which he sold to his brother Richard. He retired (except for some rare occasions) from active business involvement and transferred full control of the family's investments to Richard.

Mellon exhibited a "penchant for anonymity" as both a businessman and a cabinet official. Except for the bank, none of the family businesses carried the Mellon name. His first inclination was to stay in the shadows, "preferring privacy to glory." By most accounts only a handful of family members and friends knew him well. *Who's Who in America* failed to list him until the 1918-1919 volume, and his name did not appear in the *New York Times Index* until December 1920.

Mellon probably made fewer speeches than any other cabinet official during the 1920s. Those that he did deliver, according to Koskoff, were generally "inaudible more than a few feet from the podium, and he was so nervous about their delivery that he sometimes became discombobulated in the course of them." Mellon's retiring nature also left an impression on Herbert Hoover, who remembered him as "a shy and modest man." Hoover participated in three administrations alongside Mellon, first as secretary of Commerce and later as President. Mellon excelled at small and informal gatherings. At press conferences, according to one participant, he "indulged in that dry wit which often pricked the pretensions of the world, slyly, slowly, showing that he knew within him that all was vanity and vexation of the spirit." Journalists found him approachable for interviews and unafraid to go on the record with candid statements. The good relations he cultivated with the press paid off. During the 1920s he received extremely favorable newspaper coverage.

Once in Washington, Mellon continued his characteristic management style, including the habit of delegating authority to talented subordinates. He reorganized the department in the corporate mode, with the secretary comparable to a chairman of the board and the first undersecretary to a corporate president. He displayed his legendary knack for ap-

Mellon, a longtime director of the Aluminum Company of America, with his unique all-aluminum automobile, the "Mellonmobile" (courtesy of Underwood & Underwood)

pointing talented underlings. The undersecretaries who fulfilled this role during Mellon's tenure were S. Parker Gilbert (1921-1923), Garrard B. Winston (1923-1927), and Ogden L. Mills (1927-1932).

Mellon kept his attention focused on broad policy questions. According to Chester N. Morrill, who worked at the Department of the Treasury during the 1920s, Mellon "always seemed dispassionate and always relaxed, and whenever any question came up he seemed to be quite willing to listen, to defer to the judgment of other people, and then say what he thought, but not expecting necessarily that everybody would agree with him." Although a delegator, he was also a workaholic, frequently logging 12 to 15 hours a day in the office.

Mellon maintained a cordial though distant relationship with all the presidents under whom he served. He liked Harding personally and generally shared his ideology but regarded him as a poor manager. In his professional capacity, Mellon often visited the White House to brief the president on important policy matters. He usually brought a neatly typed summary of recommendations, rarely more than a page long. Invariably Harding took

the summary, promised to "look into this," and then stuffed it into a pile of papers on his desk. Mellon also complained that Harding forced patronage appointments on the Department of the Treasury and was inconsistent in going to bat for his secretary on policy matters. "I am sure," William Larimer Mellon opined, "that A.W. never would have hired Harding to run any company in which he was interested."

Mellon had a much greater regard for Coolidge, whom he admired as a model of efficiency. Coolidge always kept his desk clear of backlog and carefully read every document Mellon gave him. Because both men agreed almost completely on policy, the two had a close working relationship. William Allen White went to the extreme of claiming that "so completely did Andrew Mellon dominate the White House that it would be fair to call the administration the reign of Coolidge and Mellon." White's characterization was greatly overdrawn. Mellon may have been philosophically close to Harding and Coolidge, but they, not he, pulled the strings of policy. As historian Robert K. Murray has put it, Mellon was "their spokesman, not their persuader."

The tax reductions of the Coolidge and Harding administrations have played a central role in analyses of Mellon's reputation. Unfortunately, this emphasis has obscured reality. A closer look reveals that Republican tax policy during Mellon's service exemplified continuity far more than a sharp break from the past. When the Harding administration began, the postwar demobilization continued in full swing. It was the consensus of both Republicans and Democrats that a healthy peacetime economy depended on reducing taxes and spending from high wartime levels.

In great part the Harding-Coolidge tax reductions merely codified this bipartisan sentiment. Mellon's first annual report set the tone for federal tax policies during the rest of the decade. The report called for reduction in surtaxes and elimination of both the excess profits tax, which taxed corporate gains higher than 8 percent, and several wartime nuisance taxes. To make up the revenue loss, Mellon recommended a revamped corporate profits tax, an automobile tax, and a boost in the price of stamps.

In particular Mellon focused on the excess profits tax, which he assailed as a dead weight on the economy. In 1921 a sampling of marginal income tax rates showed the following: 71 percent for incomes of more than $400,000, 51 percent for incomes of more than $90,000 and, 21 percent for incomes of more than $30,000.

Mellon charged that those high rates had created a cottage industry among the wealthy to find tax shelters. He singled out for denunciation tax-exempt government securities, arguing that they had become the favorite method for the wealthy to escape high rates. The combination of high tax rates and tax shelters led Mellon to put priority on two goals: first, reduction of surtax rates, and second, elimination, through constitutional amendment, of tax exemption for government securities.

He blamed government tax policy for establishing a perverse incentive system that threatened to "destroy the spirit of business adventure." On the one hand, the government levied confiscatory surtax rates, thus discouraging entrepreneurship and business innovation; on the other, it encouraged "safe" and unproductive investments, such as tax-exempt government securities. "An economic system," Mellon asserted, "which permits wealth in

existence to escape its share of the expense of the government, and wealth in creation to be penalized until the creative spirit is destroyed, cannot be the right system for America."

According to Mellon, tax exemption for government securities gave states and municipalities an incentive to go into debt: "The tax-exempt privilege, with the facility that it gives to borrowing, leads in many cases to unnecessary and wasteful public expenditure, and this in turn is bringing about a menacing increase in the debts of States and cities." Tax-exempt government securities, in his view, had deteriorated into an unfair federal subsidy to spendthrift states and municipalities. He rejected claims that tax exemption stimulated needed government projects at the local level. If those activities were so useful, Mellon asked, why did the bonds to finance them need a special exemption?

Mellon's plan to tax government securities ran into strong opposition from Congress. Opponents, such as Texas Democrat John Nance Garner, claimed it violated states' rights. To defend his proposal against that accusation, Mellon made two points. First, passage of a constitutional amendment would remove any doubts of the plan's constitutionality (and thus speak to the states' rights issue). Second, the amendment did not discriminate against the states because it also subjected federal securities to taxation. The "proposed Constitutional amendment," Mellon wrote, "involves no question whatever of States' rights and makes no attack whatever on [their] credit and borrowing power."

Mellon never persuaded Congress to impose a tax on government securities. The 1921 Congress did, however, substantially reduce surtaxes. Taxpayers in the higher brackets benefited the most from the first year's reductions while those at the lower end of the scale received only marginal relief. Surtaxes fell from 71 to 58 percent for taxpayers with a $400,000 annual income, 51 to 50 percent for those earning $90,000, and 21 to 20 percent for taxpayers in the $30,000 bracket.

The tax cuts continued throughout the decade. In the early stages the reductions were concentrated among higher incomes, but they soon spread to the lower brackets. In 1929 surtax rates had fallen to 24 percent (down from 71 percent in 1921) for taxpayers earning $400,000; 23 percent for $90,000 incomes (down from 51 percent); and 12 percent (down from 21 percent) for incomes of $30,000.

Historians have frequently portrayed the Republican tax program as biased in favor of the rich. Several of Mellon's critics during the 1920s made similar charges. Senator Robert M. LaFollette of Wisconsin, for example, accused the secretary of favoring "a system that will let wealth escape." That traditional interpretation has been persuasively challenged by historian Lawrence Leo Murray III. According to Murray, Mellon wanted first and foremost to stimulate the economy, not, as some have charged, to line the pockets of the rich. To be sure, the wealthy received substantial rate reductions, but so did the taxpayers in the lowest brackets. In 1921 the marginal rate for taxpayers earning $2,000 had been 4 percent; by 1929 it was .5 percent. Moreover, in 1921 taxpayers earning in the $6,000 bracket paid 9 percent of their income in taxes; in 1929 that had been reduced to 2 percent.

Those who benefited least from the tax program (although, they, too, received major reductions) were taxpayers in the middle brackets. For those earning $30,000, tax rates declined from 21 to 12 percent, a substantial but relatively smaller decline than for taxpayers at the bottom and top of the income scales. "What appears to have happened," Murray concluded, "was the government lowered its costs somewhat and that reduction was passed on to those at the extreme ends of the taxable population, those under $5,000 and over $100,000."

Although marginal rates fell substantially, wealthier taxpayers as a group paid a *larger* burden in taxes *after* the institution of the Mellon program. In 1921 taxpayers earning more than $1 million paid 4.37 percent of all income taxes collected; by 1929 their share had increased dramatically to 19.07 percent. At the bottom end of the income scale, the precise opposite occurred. Taxpayers earning less than $5,000 had paid 12.9 percent of all income taxes collected in 1921. By 1929 that percentage had been reduced to .44 percent.

At the beginning of the 1920s, Mellon had predicted that lower rates would bring in more revenue. The results of his tax program appeared to confirm his case. Koskoff wrote, "The Treasury's receipts seemed to bear out the wisdom of the plan; the statistics did not lie." In proposing his program, Mellon had asserted that, from the standpoint of a government seeking revenue, high surtax rates had long before passed the point of diminishing returns. They had become a drag on the economy by draining capital away from productive enterprise. Thus, the higher the rate, the lower the return to the tax collector. During a wartime crisis, Mellon observed, taxpayers usually paid high rates without much complaint. When peace arrived, however, their eagerness to demonstrate patriotism by paying more taxes quickly turned into resentment and the scramble for tax shelters began. During the 1920s that meant primarily tax-exempt government securities.

Conversely, lower marginal rates would motivate those same taxpayers to invest in more productive (and taxable) sectors of the economy. To illustrate his contention that lower rates would generate more tax revenue, Mellon compared the marginal rate to the price of goods on the market: "If a price is fixed too high, sales drop off and with them profits; if a price is fixed too low, sales may increase, but again profits decline." For any businessman, the key to profit was to find a price somewhere between these two extremes, one high enough to earn profits but low enough to stimulate sufficient demand. "Does any one question," Mellon asked, "that Mr. Ford has made more money by reducing the price of his car and increasing his sales than he would have made by maintaining a high price and a greater profit per car, but selling less cars?"

For that reason Mellon suggested that Congress reduce the tax rate to a point that would both maximize revenue and stimulate economic growth. He estimated the ideal rate at 15 percent or slightly lower. He held that "a decrease of taxes causes an inspiration to trade and commerce which increases the prosperity of the country so that the revenues of the Government, even on a lower basis of tax, are increased." Not surprisingly, Mellon's tax policies have been cited with approval by modern-day defenders of supply-side economics. James Gwartney and Richard Stroup have concluded that "as a result of the strong response of high-income taxpayers, the tax cuts of the 1920s actually shifted the burden to the higher income brackets even though the rate reductions were greatest in this area."

The two most influential figures in shaping Mellon's tax philosophy were his father and Adam Smith. Mellon approvingly quoted Smith's statement from the *Wealth of Nations* that while the government "obliges the people to pay, it may thus diminish, or perhaps destroy, some of the funds, which might enable them more easily to do so." Mellon regarded it as ironic that those who favored higher progressive rates to force the wealthy "to pay more" actually achieved the opposite of their goal. "It is a strange theory of taxation," he writes, "which, in order to make the gesture of taxing the rich, retains rates that are producing less and less revenue each year and at the same time discouraging industry and threatening the country's future prosperity."

Mellon profoundly disagreed with advocates of the theory that income redistribution was a proper goal of taxation. "I have never viewed taxation," he explained, "as a means of rewarding one class of taxpayers or punishing another." In his view, schemes to redistribute income through taxation constituted nothing less than "class legislation" contrary to American "traditions of freedom, justice and equality of opportunity." Mellon opposed tax exemption for any group for the same reason he rejected taxation as a method for income redistribution. He believed that every citizen should pay taxes (even if only a few dollars) to claim a stake in government.

In analyzing Mellon's tax proposals, historians have underscored the role of critics such as Senator Robert M. LaFollette of Wisconsin. Unfortunately, this focus has encouraged a neglect of the remarkably strong bipartisan support for tax reduction during the 1920s. Indeed, repeal of the excess profits tax first had been proposed by Mellon's Democratic predecessors Carter Glass and David Houston. In words that Mellon would later echo, Glass charged that the excess profits tax "encourages wasteful expenditures, puts a premium on overcapitalization, and a penalty on brains, energy and enterprise, discourages new ventures, and confirms old ventures in their monopolies." Mellon often stressed the continuity of his program with Democratic antecedents and the fact that Houston and several other former members of the Wilson administration had endorsed his proposals. The major sticking point between the Republicans and Democrats was not the desirability of surtax reduction but the means of implementation. In general the Democrats put greater stress on cuts for taxpayers in the lower income brackets. Representative John Nance Garner, the Democratic majority leader, exemplified that approach when, in 1924, he countered Mellon's tax proposals with a plan for larger reductions for those earning less than $50,000. Like its Republican counterpart, however, the Garner Plan

included substantial rate reductions for all taxpayers.

At times the Democrats outdid Mellon in their enthusiasm for tax reduction. In 1926 the Democratic leadership in Congress even proposed much larger tax reductions than the Republicans were willing to accept—between $330 million and $500 million. Only the secretary's determined opposition derailed the Democratic tax reduction demands. When the Revenue Act of 1926 finally came up for a vote, the Democratic leadership, including Garner, threw their support behind Mellon. The Revenue Act not only reduced the maximum surtax to 25 percent but halved estate taxes.

The continuity between Mellon and his Democratic predecessors extended to personnel as well as policy. He retained several holdovers from the Wilson administration, often to the consternation of patronage-hungry Republicans. In one of his first acts after taking office, he reappointed S. Parker Gilbert as undersecretary of the Treasury. Because Mellon had respect for Gilbert's abilities and the two men saw eye-to-eye on policy, they worked well together.

The passage of the Revenue Act of 1926 coincided with the high point of Mellon's tenure. His program had inspired a popular campaign of support. A network of local tax clubs and the American Taxpayers League of Washington, D.C., banded together to pressure Congress to pass his tax proposals. The League later took part in the tax revolts of the early 1930s. The popular campaign supporting the Mellon plan deserves study as a possible model for these later tax resistance movements.

Second only to taxation Mellon emphasized reduction and eventual elimination of the national debt. This program proved to be one of the great success stories of his tenure. The national debt stood at $24 billion in 1921; by 1931 it had dropped to $16 billion, producing an annual compounded savings of $40 million in interest payments. Mellon projected elimination of the national debt by 1942 by a slow process of retirement. From the start he sought a balance between tax reductions and debt retirement. Particularly after the passage of the Revenue Act of 1926, he pressed a strategy of devoting one year's surplus to tax reduction and the next year's to debt retirement. He fervently disagreed with Democratic proposals to shift money intended for debt retirement into tax reduction. Mellon considered any policy that allowed accumulation of a national debt "a sign of debility [that] denoted an absence of the essential vigor and foresight which insures future success. It is the policy of the thriftless, the ne'er do-well." He cited Germany's massive "inflation and financial pyramiding" during the 1920s to illustrate the dangers of excessive government debt.

As secretary of the Treasury, Mellon was a significant player in the debt and reparations negotiations of the period. After 1922 he served as chairman of the World War Foreign Debt Commission, which had been formed to find a solution to the problem of repayment. In general he steered a middle course, rejecting outright cancellation of debt but opposing demands for full repayment. He favored a "capacity to pay" approach that took into account the economic conditions of each country. Former British prime minister David Lloyd George found Mellon to be "keen, experienced, hard and ruthless" in this work, describing the encounter between Mellon and Prime Minister Stanley Baldwin as analogous to that "between a weasel and its quarry." In the end, the commission nailed down agreements pledging repayment of the debt over five decades. The agreements also scaled down the interest on the loans, in effect canceling 50 percent of the debt owed by the Europeans.

Mellon's opposition to the bonus for World War I veterans proved the most controversial of his initiatives during the 1920s. Bonus legislation was tremendously popular, particularly with politicians eager for support from such organizations as the American Legion. Mellon attacked the bonus in unequivocal language, stating that it "accomplishes nothing less than a redistribution of the wealth of the country by governmental operation, and constitutes a bad precedent, which is likely to prove more and more expensive to the country with each surrender to organized pressure."

Harding gave Mellon full backing on this issue. Putting Republican election prospects at some risk, the president lobbied hard against bonus legislation, warning that it would endanger tax reduction and lead to deficit spending. When both houses of Congress passed a bonus in 1922, Harding responded with a veto. Although the Senate sustained the veto by a narrow margin, it provided only a temporary victory for Mellon and the administration. In 1924 both houses of Congress overrode another veto by President Coolidge, and the bonus became law.

Treasury Secretary Mellon commencing a trip to Europe (Wide World Photos)

Mellon gained a justified reputation as one of the cabinet's most reliable voices for economy in government. During the brief but severe depression of 1921 and 1922, he resisted Secretary of Commerce Hoover's plan to spend more money on public works. Later he lined up against a proposal backed by Hoover and Hubert Work, secretary of the interior, to get federal funding for a high dam at Boulder Canyon on the Colorado River. He also led the charge against the various McNary-Haugen bills that proposed creation of a federal agency to set a minimum price for sales of selected agricultural goods. The bills would have authorized the government to purchase and then resell in foreign markets any goods that could not be sold at the fixed price.

Mellon stressed two themes in his drive against the McNary-Haugen legislation: first, it would add to the burden of taxpayers; second, it would raise food prices for the consumer. He attributed the slump in the agricultural economy to farmers having purchased too much land at inflated prices; he warned that government subsidies only would exacerbate the inevitable deflation and declared that "we cannot oppose fundamental economic laws."

Critics quickly pointed out how that statement contradicted others Mellon had made to justify protective tariffs for industry. If price controls on agricultural goods violated "fundamental economic laws," they asked, could not the same be said for controls on industrial imports through the tariff? Senator William Borah of Idaho, a supporter of McNary-Haugen, adeptly exploited this argumentative weakness. He read Mellon's critique of McNary-Haugen on the Senate floor "substituting the words 'tariff bill' for 'Haugen Bill' with telling effect," according to one account. Mellon's response to these allegations of inconsistency was evasive. "Our tariff policy," he declared, "has been mainly responsible for the development of manufacturing in America. Our tariff policy has brought to American labor the highest real wages in history."

Probably Mellon's least favorite duty involved presiding over the enforcement of prohibition; the Volstead Act lodged the most authority for carrying out the eighteenth amendment in the Department of the Treasury. Throughout his tenure Mellon tried to have this jurisdiction shifted to the Department of Justice, and finally succeeded after nine years in office. Mellon's family background made him an unlikely champion of the drys. His father had condemned excess in drink but saw nothing wrong with alcoholic beverages per se. The judge fondly recalled in his autobiography walking to work at age ten sipping from a half-pint flask of whiskey that he carried in his pocket. His sons were also introduced to drink at an early age. Like his brothers, as a child Andrew Mellon sampled spruce beer brewed by the family's housekeeper. In later years he counted a whiskey distillery among his investments.

In office Mellon tried to make the best of an uncomfortable situation. In general he let the drys have a free hand. He tried to appoint leading prohibitionists for enforcement positions. At the same time, he betrayed his own lack of enthusiasm for the program by allowing and even promoting reductions in funds for enforcement activities. By most indications Mellon wanted to distance himself from a

crusade he viewed as fated to fail. Dry forces quickly blamed him for the demise of prohibition. In 1934 James Cannon, who had been dubbed the "Dry Messiah," charged that when "prohibition control was turned over to the Treasury Department under Andrew W. Mellon, it was doomed."

Historians continue to debate what role, if any, Mellon played in precipitating the Great Depression. Most attention has centered on his involvement with monetary policy as the ex officio chairman of the Federal Reserve Board. Economic historian Murray Rothbard, for example, has blamed the board's easy-credit policies, which Mellon supported, for starting a chain reaction that led to the Depression. On one count several of the critics are wrong. They have tended to exaggerate Mellon's centrality in the making of monetary policy. His participation in the board's day-to-day affairs was minimal, and he turned in a poor attendance record for meetings. That he viewed credit expansion positively, however, few can doubt. Less than three months after he took office, he lined up behind the board's decision to lower the discount rate from 7 to 5 percent. Throughout the rest of the decade, he pushed for still lower rates.

The evidence indicates that Mellon had at least two motivations for becoming such a staunch defender of credit expansion. Along with the rest of the board, he wanted to help Great Britain return to the gold standard. This proved problematic, however, because the British insisted on returning to gold at the prewar par. Because the prewar par was 10 to 20 percent higher than the current free-market rate, such a change would necessitate a painful commensurate decline in British prices. One way to bring about a price decline of that magnitude was for the Bank of England to contract credit. For various political and economic reasons, it refused to take that risk. As a result, the British experienced a worrisome drain of gold to the United States. The gold drain had two possible antidotes: either the British could contract their own central bank credit or the Federal Reserve Board could lower its discount rate, which would inflate the American money supply. The board, partly at Mellon's behest, decided to institute the second option. Through this policy, Robert K. Murray has charged, "the Federal Reserve was being prostituted for international reasons as the American discount rate was kept lower than that of the Bank of England to prevent a gold drain from Great Britain to the United States."

The second probable reason why Mellon supported easy money was less elaborate: he may have viewed credit expansion as a useful device to keep the American economy booming. Easy credit had other virtues. It boosted Republican election chances and helped quiet agricultural discontent. Whatever his motivations, Mellon helped to derail several attempts to reverse the board's policy of credit expansion. He characterized as alarmist Hoover's warning that "inflation of credit is not the answer to European difficulties." In 1928, however, he went along passively with the board's reversal of policy. A majority of members had expressed concern that the inflationary boom was getting out of control. In three separate actions during the first six months of 1928, the board raised the discount rate to 5 percent, the highest since 1921. It followed those increases with a boost to 6 percent in August 1929. Some scholars have explained the stock market Crash of 1929 as a result of the board's belated attempts in 1928 and 1929 to stem the inflation tide it had been responsible for causing.

After Calvin Coolidge dropped out of the 1928 presidential race, important Republicans such as Governor John Fisher of Pennsylvania touted Mellon as a candidate. Mellon's base of support broadened when William Randolph Hearst, through his newspapers, gave him a ringing endorsement. Mellon, noncommittal at first, soon dropped out. His motivations were unclear but, at age seventy-two, he probably saw himself as too old to make a presidential bid. Mellon tried hard to persuade Coolidge, his first choice for the nomination, to change his mind and enter the race. His second choice was Republican Party elder Charles Evans Hughes. Hughes, like Coolidge, ruled himself out. Much lower on Mellon's list of preferences was Hoover, the front-runner for the nomination. The two had clashed repeatedly over policy at cabinet meetings. Hoover, as the representative of the cabinet's "progressive" wing, did not share Mellon's small-government views. Mellon had once complained, "Hoover is an engineer; he wants to run a straight line, just one line, and then say to everyone, 'This is the only line there is, and you must keep up to it, or else keep out.' "

Only days before the convention, Mellon threw his support to Hoover. It had not been an easy decision. Almost until the last minute, he had tried to get Coolidge to enter the fray. When that failed, Mellon realized that every sign pointed to Hoover's easy nomination. Had he opposed the front-runner, Mellon would have risked his credibility as a party leader. The fact that Hoover had the backing of undersecretary Ogden Mills may have also figured in Mellon's calculations. During the general election campaign, he worked actively for Hoover, although not with great enthusiasm.

When Hoover won, most observers expected that Mellon would step down. He had served for eight years and was approaching his seventy-fourth birthday in 1929. Because he did not share much of Hoover's political outlook, it was questionable that he would ever again enjoy the prestige and power he had achieved under Harding and Coolidge. Moreover, even if he wanted to stay, it seemed doubtful that Hoover would let him. The major reason Mellon continued as secretary of the Treasury, despite those drawbacks, may have been the unappealing alternative of retirement. Though he had an extensive stock portfolio, the business world offered few attractions. The family investments remained under the capable stewardship of his brother, Richard, and his nephew, William. Mellon did not want to repeat the experience of his father, who had spent years of retirement in frustrated idleness.

Hoover had more straightforward reasons for retaining Mellon. The secretary had won the confidence of the business community and Hoover saw no point in undermining this goodwill. Moreover, Hoover could easily bypass Mellon, if necessary: since about 1927, at Mellon's initiative, the Treasury's power had gradually been ceded to Hoover's trusted ally, Undersecretary Mills.

By most accounts, Mellon did not anticipate the stock market Crash of October 1929. In fact, in a private letter of April 1929 to Charles Hamlin of the Federal Reserve Board, he had predicted the continued expansion of the stock market. He echoed those sentiments in comments to the press. When the crash came, he expressed little alarm. Hoover wrote in his memoirs that Mellon initially reacted to the plunge by exclaiming, "They deserved it." He described Mellon as "in every instinct a country banker. His idea and practice had been to build up men of character in his community and to participate in their prosperity. He had no use for certain varieties of New York banking, which he deemed were too often devoted to tearing men down and picking their bones."

Hoover's account remains one of the few sources about Mellon's philosophy on coping with the Depression. According to Hoover, Mellon spoke for the "leave it alone liquidationists" in the cabinet "who felt that government must keep its hands off and let the slump liquidate itself." Readjustment through deflation, the secretary asserted, was the price that had to be paid for the "inflation brainstorm" of the 1920s. "He held," Hoover wrote, "that even a panic was not altogether a bad thing. He said: 'It will purge the rottenness out of the system . . . Values will be adjusted, and enterprising people will pick up the wrecks from less competent people.' "

Hoover spurned Mellon's advice, agreeing with other members of the cabinet (including Undersecretary Mills) that "we should use the powers of government to cushion the situation." The interventionist policies of the Hoover administration represented a sharp departure from the past. Previous presidents, when confronted with economic slumps, generally had followed the prescription recommended by Mellon: spending retrenchment and credit contraction. Hoover, by contrast, put forward a vast array of interventionist initiatives. These included the Reconstruction Finance Corporation (to subsidize business and banking), the Home Loan Bank Board (to stimulate the housing industry), and federal loans to agriculture. To persuade employers to maintain high wage rates in the face of massive price deflation, he convened a series of White House conferences with top corporate leaders. Hoover and Mellon may have disagreed over policy, but they respected each other. "Secretary Mellon," Hoover wrote, "was not hard-hearted. In fact he was generous and sympathetic with all the suffering. He felt there would be less suffering if his course were pursued."

Andrew Mellon's advice (as related by Hoover) could almost have been culled from the writings of Thomas Mellon. One particularly striking parallel was a favorite expression of Andrew Mellon: "there is a mighty lot of real estate lying around the United States which does not know who owns it." The elder Mellon had employed similar words to describe the depression of the 1870s. In his autobiography he had recalled that property "of all kinds remained, but it was set afloat in search of its true owners. Nothing but a process of general liquidation could determine what any man owned or was worth. And when in this way the

real owners of property and wealth were ascertained, they were found to be only the few who had paid as they went, or confined their business or speculative operations to what was clearly within their power to hold." Andrew Mellon, an enthusiastic booster of credit inflation during the 1920s, had emerged as the administration's leading spokesman for deflation. Ironically, as Koskoff points out, had Thomas Mellon been alive, he might have blamed policies supported by his son for causing the Great Depression. According to the elder Mellon's beliefs, all depressions sprang "from the same cause—excessive extension of credit and consequent expansion of values . . . The vitals of trade were destroyed by the canker work of credit; bloated inflation spread and increased until the decayed carcass dropped dead."

In the abstract, Andrew Mellon urged fighting the depression through a short, deflationary process of readjustment. On specific policy recommendations he was vague. Along with Hoover, he initially supported further reductions in both income and corporate tax rates, which Congress enacted at the end of 1929. As the depression deepened he completely shifted gears. Shortly before leaving office he backed the Revenue Act of 1932, one of the largest tax increases in American history. In any case, Mellon's recommendations had become largely irrelevant to policy. As far as Hoover was concerned, Ogden Mills, not Andrew Mellon, now ran the Department of the Treasury. One of the few times that Hoover sought Mellon's advice was on the worsening debt and reparations crisis of 1931. The secretary proposed a moratorium allowing the European powers to suspend debt payments for two years on the condition that reparation payments from Germany also be suspended. Both the "Hoover moratorium" and the Young Plan of 1932 later incorporated many of Mellon's recommendations.

Ineffectiveness on policy matters comprised the least of Mellon's worries. From 1932 until his death he remained the focus of almost constant investigation and litigation. In January 1932 Texas Democratic Representative Wright Patman, then in his second term, called for Mellon's impeachment. Later in the month he followed up with hearings, in which he alleged a conflict of interest between Mellon's extensive business holdings and his duties at the Department of the Treasury. The Patman hearings failed to uncover persuasive evidence of any direct conflict of interest. The adverse publicity, however, dealt another major blow to the secretary's severely shaken reputation.

Less than a month after the hearings began, Hoover appointed the beleaguered Mellon as ambassador to Great Britain. He named Ogden Mills as the new secretary of the Treasury. Patman and other members of the investigatory committee in turn agreed to call off the hearings. It was not clear who first suggested Mellon as ambassador. In any event, the change pleased him. "This is not a marriage ceremony," he told reporters, "this is a divorce." According to William Larimer Mellon, Andrew Mellon had become "completely worn out by the pressure of his Treasury duties." Mellon started his new job on April 7, 1932. His work load as ambassador proved lighter than expected. In probably his most important undertaking in that role, he helped lay the groundwork for the World Economic Conference in London, which met in June 1933.

Just after Franklin D. Roosevelt's inauguration in March 1933, Mellon resigned from his position and returned to work at the Mellon National Bank. His retirement from political life got off to a stormy start. In May 1933 Attorney General Homer Cummings announced that Mellon was under investigation for evading taxes on fraudulent stock sales. Mellon characterized the investigation as an attempt by the Roosevelt administration "to regularize a campaign of terrorism with the tax law as weapon." To the charge of tax evasion he responded that he had, in fact, overpaid his taxes. After a grand jury refused to indict him, he demanded a $130,045 refund from the Board of Tax Appeals. Instead of granting the refund, the board countersued for $3 million. The investigation dragged on for three years and failed to reach a conclusion until December 1937, four months after Mellon's death, when the board ruled that he owed $600,000 in back taxes but cleared him of all charges of fraud.

Other events in Mellon's life added an ironic twist to his tax troubles. Even while he came under investigation for tax evasion, he was in the process of giving the government a large grant for the erection of what became the National Gallery of Art. Mellon outlined the details to Roosevelt during a Christmas visit in 1933. He offered to donate his personal art collection, valued between $19 million and $50 million, and pledged $5 million for an endowment and $10 million for a building to house the collection.

Roosevelt accepted the donation on behalf of the government and even invited Mellon to have tea at the White House. "While Roosevelt and Mellon sipped their tea," Koskoff notes ironically, "their respective attorneys were contriving to paint each other in the worst possible light in their Board of Tax Appeals briefs." His legal troubles only grew worse when, in early 1937, the government named him as a defendant in its antitrust suit against Alcoa.

Mellon died on August 26, 1937, at the age of eighty-two. His survivors included his former wife, Nora McMullen Mellon (they had divorced in 1911); his daughter, Ailsa Mellon Bruce; and his son, Paul Mellon. In the years before his death he had transferred the bulk of his $200 million fortune to his children and to various philanthropies.

Publication:

Taxation: The People's Business (New York: Macmillan, 1924).

References:

D. T. Armentano, *The Myths of Antitrust: Economic Theory and Legal Cases* (New Rochelle, N.Y.: Arlington House, 1972), pp. 108-119;

Charles C. Carr, *Alcoa: An American Enterprise* (New York: Rinehart, 1952);

Herbert Hoover, *The Memoirs of Herbert Hoover: The Cabinet and the Presidency, 1920-1933* (New York: Macmillan, 1952);

Hoover, *The Memoirs of Herbert Hoover: The Great Depression, 1929-1941* (London: Hollis & Carter, 1953);

David E. Koskoff, *The Mellons: The Chronicle of America's Richest Family* (New York: Crowell, 1978);

Dwight R. Lee, ed., *Taxation and the Deficit Economy: Fiscal Policy and Capital Formation in the United States* (San Francisco: Pacific Research Institute for Public Policy, 1986);

William Larimer Mellon and Boyden Sparkes, *Judge Mellon's Sons* (N.p.: Privately printed, 1948);

Lawrence Leo Murray III, "Andrew W. Mellon, Secretary of the Treasury, 1921-1932: A Study in Policy," dissertation, Michigan State University, 1970;

Robert K. Murray, *The Politics of Normalcy: Governmental Theory and Practice in the Harding-Coolidge Era* (New York: Norton, 1973);

Lee Nash, ed., *Understanding Herbert Hoover: Ten Perspectives* (Stanford: Hoover Institution Press, 1987);

Murray N. Rothbard, *America's Great Depression* (Kansas City: Sheed & Ward, 1972).

Charles E. Merrill

(October 19, 1885 - October 6, 1956)

by Edwin J. Perkins

University of Southern California

CAREER: Various positions, Patchogue Plymouth Mills (1907-1909); bond department manager, George Burr & Company (1909-1913); sales manager, Eastman, Dillon & Company (1913-1914); founder, Charles E. Merrill & Company (1914); partner, Merrill, Lynch & Company (1915-1940); directing partner, Merrill Lynch, Pierce, Fenner & Beane (1940-1956).

Charles Edward Merrill, a cofounder of Merrill Lynch & Company in 1915, was one of the most dynamic and innovative leaders in the twentieth-century financial services sector. During World War II his reinvigorated enterprise became the nation's foremost stock brokerage firm and one of the most active investment banking houses. The internal reforms that he publicly advocated and successfully implemented at Merrill Lynch & Company after 1940 had a major and continuing impact on the business practices and ethical procedures of every Wall Street firm. In the brokerage field, Merrill has no peer in American history.

Born on October 19, 1885, he was the eldest of three children, and the only son, of a physician and drugstore proprietor in Green Cove Springs, Florida. His father, Charles Morton Merrill, was a native of Ohio, and his mother, Octavia Wilson, was born in Mississippi in 1861, the first year of the Civil War. In his youth Charlie Merrill sold newspapers and earned pocket money doing odd jobs around town. In his early teens he attended a college-preparatory school affiliated with Stetson University in De Land, Florida.

For more advanced academic training, Merrill was sent north to the Worcester Academy in Massachusetts, with part of his tuition covered by an athletic scholarship. As an undergraduate at Amherst College in Massachusetts from 1904 to 1906, he sold clothing and waited on tables and participated in sports. After leaving Amherst without graduat-

Charles E. Merrill

ing, Merrill spent the summer months working on West Palm Beach's *Tropical Sun* as reporter, editor, and occasional typesetter. He later recalled the job as "the best training I ever had; I learned human nature." That fall he enrolled in law school at the University of Michigan, but legal training had little appeal, and he did not return for a second year. He spent the summer of 1907 playing baseball for a Class D minor league team in Mississippi.

After the baseball season ended, Merrill, then twenty-two, went to New York City. His first position was in the city office of Patchogue Plymouth Mills, a textile firm that operated its main factory in Patchogue, New York. He rose to the position of credit manager and assistant to the president. "My two years there," he later remarked, "turned out to be the equivalent of a university course in general, and credit, finance, cost accounting and administration, in particular." Soon after arriving in New York, Merrill met Edmund Lynch while both men were exercising regularly at the 23rd Street YMCA. A Johns Hopkins graduate, Lynch at the time sold soda fountain equipment. The two young men became fast friends and apparently roomed together for a short time.

In September 1909 Merrill got his first job with a Wall Street firm. George H. Burr & Company, a commercial paper house, performed financial services for Burr's textile firm, and its owner had become aware of Merrill's abilities. Burr wanted to expand into handling corporate bonds, and he hired Merrill to head the newly created bond department. Merrill in turn hired his friend Lynch to work in sales. Merrill's main plan for attracting new customers was to rely on direct mail solicitations, and he concentrated on the dissemination of accurate, informative circulars devoid as much as possible of misleading statements and overblown optimism. In the early twentieth century any newspaper advertising that appealed blatantly for new accounts was still considered taboo by the most prestigious and high-minded securities firms.

An emphasis on straightforward dealing appears to have been one of Merrill's hallmarks from the outset. In an article entitled "Mr. Average Investor," published in the November 1911 issue of *Leslie's Illustrated Weekly*, he stressed the importance of knowing a customer's financial requirements before suggesting an investment vehicle. He lamented the industry norm, which consisted of promoting any security in which a given brokerage house had a direct financial stake and the tendency to place too much emphasis on opportunities for short-term, speculative gains. Merrill also discussed the advantage of attracting a broad clientele: "Having thousands of customers scattered throughout the United States is infinitely preferable to being dependent upon the fluctuating buying power of a smaller and perhaps on the whole wealthier group of investors in any one section." In another article he wrote, "The customer may not always be right but he *has* rights."

For the next half century Merrill remained at the forefront of the movement to make honesty and integrity the bywords of the securities industry. In addition he led in the movement to enlarge the customer base of securities firms to include millions of middle-class investors. Over the long term, he believed, truthfulness and full disclosure would benefit all parties involved in the routine trading of stocks and bonds—not just the public who were the major buyers and sellers, but sales personnel hoping to retain accounts over the long run as well.

Merrill made Burr's bond department a quick success, and the firm soon ventured into underwriting equities. In 1912 Burr sponsored an offering of $2 million in preferred stock plus 10,000 shares of common stock for the Kresge chain stores. That transaction launched Merrill's long association with chain stores, then a fresh and innovative concept in retailing; it was an involvement that continued, almost uninterrupted, over the next 40 years.

Dissatisfied with his compensation at Burr & Company, Merrill became sales manager of Eastman, Dillon & Company in 1913 but resigned within a year to establish his own small securities firm, Charles E. Merrill & Company, in January 1914. He persuaded Lynch to join the business before the year ended, and twelve months later, in October 1915, the partnership was retitled Merrill, Lynch & Company. (The firm included a comma after Merrill's name until the punctuation mark was dropped coincidental with incorporation in 1938, a few months after Lynch's death on a vacation trip to Europe.) The pair made a perfect team. An associate later remarked, "Merrill could imagine the possibilities; Lynch imagined what might go wrong in a malevolent world."

The firm's initial underwritings in 1915 included the securities for two chain stores—McCrory Stores and Kresge, with the latter's account won away from Merrill's former employer. Indeed, the partners made the emerging chain store industry their specialty. The timing was opportune since the public had started to cultivate an appetite for stocks of enterprises beyond the traditionally narrow circle of railroads and heavy manufacturing. When the partnership originated, the fighting in Europe had already begun, and after the United States entered World War I in 1917, Merrill, now thirty-two, volunteered for service. He became a combat flight instructor for the air division of the army but never left the United States.

Following the end of the war in November 1918 the partnership had poised itself for the stock market boom of the 1920s. Millions of Americans had acquired the investing habit as a result of their regular purchase of U.S. war bonds, and they were now prepared to venture into corporate securities. The partners' strategy of catering to a broad spectrum of middle-class investors fit perfectly with new trends within the financial services sector. Merrill aimed to overturn two popular images about the character of employees in the typical Wall Street firm—that they were either elitist stuffed shirts or sleazy, get-rich-quick speculators.

As in the past, Merrill stressed a flow of accurate information, simple honesty, and reliable service for clients of moderate means. In 1919 he hired Annie Grimes, Wall Street's first bond saleswoman. While he never even considered the possibility of launching a movement to bring more women into the financial services sector, Merrill nonetheless demonstrated by this move his ability to discard outdated customs and old taboos. In 1924, for example, the firm deviated from standard business hours by opening its uptown New York office every weekday from 7 P.M. to 9 P.M. for the convenience of customers who could not drop by earlier in the day. The firm was involved in a very competitive market, and the partners sought new ways to serve clients and expand the volume of their brokerage business.

In its underwriting activities, Merrill Lynch continued to concentrate on the expanding chain store sector. About half of its underwritings in the postwar decade included retailers, including J. C. Penney, National Tea, and two former clients, Kresge and McCrory. The firm also made several venture capital acquisitions in the 1920s. One acquisition was Pathè Exchange, the U.S. subsidiary of the early French filmmaker Pathè Freres, in 1921. The American unit was famous for its "Perils of Pauline" serials and its regular newsreels. When the partners learned that future success in the motion picture industry required a huge investment in a nationwide chain of theaters, they sold out to Cecil B. deMille and Joseph Kennedy (father of President John F. Kennedy).

With the cash from the sale of the movie company, the partners acquired Safeway Stores, a southern California food chain, in 1926. For the next two decades Merrill remained an active participant in overseeing the development and expansion of Safeway. In 1929 he formed another food chain under the name MacMarr Stores, starting out with

nearly 40 retail outlets. From his association with Safeway and other chain stores, Merrill had an opportunity to become familiar with the business principles behind the mass marketing of goods at high volume and low margins; eventually he got into the perfect position to transfer those ideas to the securities field.

As the stock market rose to spectacular heights in the late 1920s, Merrill became increasingly alarmed. In a letter addressed to all the firm's customers on March 21, 1928, a date well over a year before the great crash, Merrill warned: "Now is the time to get out of debt. We do not urge that you sell securities indiscriminately, but we do advise in no uncertain terms that you take advantage of present high prices and put your own financial house in order." Early in 1929 he finally persuaded Lynch, who remained more upbeat about market trends, to reduce the firm's own exposure to the possibility of a sharp decline in equity prices.

When the crash came in October 1929, Merrill's reputation as a forecaster of market trends soared. Customers who had heeded his advice avoided the worst consequences of the debacle on Wall Street. Merrill's conservatism and prudence had paid off for his associates and customers with the good sense to listen to his warnings about stock market excesses. Unfortunately, the firm could not profit from its enhanced public reputation over most of the next decade because brokerage and investment banking were two fields that contracted sharply in the 1930s.

The outlook for Wall Street firms, given the reduced volume of trading, was so uncertain that the partners decided to transfer all their brokerage business to E. A. Pierce & Company, an established firm with branches connected by private telegraph wires throughout the United States, including the West Coast states. Jointly Merrill and Lynch invested about $5 million of their own capital in the merged firm, while Pierce and his partners put up another $10 million. The public announcement of February 3, 1930, explained that the remaining New York office of Merrill, Lynch & Company would concentrate on investment banking. Since few new issues of securities appeared in the 1930s, the partners focused much of their attention on previously acquired investment properties. For Merrill that meant concentrating on the operation of the food chains in which he had invested heavily in the 1920s. The Depression may have curbed the public's interest in securities, but people were almost certain to continue patronizing local grocery stores, and Merrill relished the challenge of delivering quality foods at fair prices. In 1931 he arranged the absorption of the MacMarr chain, with 1,300 stores, by Safeway Stores, which had twice that many outlets. The new Safeway, with almost 4,000 retail stores, became the nation's third largest chain, trailing only A&P and Kroger.

Merrill emerged as the enlarged Safeway's largest stockholder, and he appointed M. B. Skaggs to serve as chief executive officer. In 1932, upon Merrill's urging, Safeway introduced *Family Circle*, the first magazine to rely strictly on point-of-sale purchases in grocery stores, and it proved enormously successful. To keep posted on his investments in California, Merrill made frequent cross-country flights in propeller-driven airplanes during the 1930s.

The aggressiveness of national chain stores threatened the economic viability of thousands of small "mom-and-pop" grocery stores, which typically did a low-volume business and maintained high prices to generate profits. The owners of small independent stores frequently denounced the low-price chains as insensitive interlopers determined to run local operators out of business. In California the legislature passed a punitive tax aimed at the chains, which would have cost Safeway about 20 percent of its net income. Safeway management led the movement to put the issue on the ballot for voters to decide. The advertising campaign emphasized that the tax on chain stores indirectly taxed consumers. In a statewide referendum in 1936 the voters repealed the tax on chain stores. Most people decided that they wanted what the chains delivered on an everyday basis: a huge selection of quality foodstuffs at low prices. Merrill later quipped: "If ever I get to heaven, it will be because I helped lower the price of milk by a penny a quart in Los Angeles."

On a vacation trip in May 1938, Edmund Lynch, at age fifty-two, died unexpectedly in London. Upon hearing the news Merrill wrote a mutual friend: "Eddie's death has been a terrific blow to me. For 31 years Ed and I were the best of friends and for 29 of these years the closest of business associates." In the months that followed, Merrill made an assessment of the outlook for E. A. Pierce & Company. The securities industry still languished in the doldrums, and the prospects for the Pierce network of offices across the nation still did not seem very favorable. Operating losses systematically depleted the firm's capital. As a result Merrill transferred his monies and that of Lynch's heirs out of the partnership equity account and converted the balance outstanding into a strictly interest-bearing investment account in November 1938.

Despite the generally bleak outlook on Wall Street at the close of the 1930s, a series of meetings in the last few months of 1939 rekindled Merrill's interest in reentering the brokerage and investment banking fields. The pivotal person in arranging the negotiations was Win Smith, a former trusted employee of Merrill, Lynch & Company in the 1920s, who had remained with the Pierce firm throughout the hard times of the last decade. Smith convinced Merrill that, given the proper reorganization of the Pierce branch network, they could convert the firm's losses into profits within a fairly short period of time. Merrill finally agreed to a realignment of the existing partnership based on his assumption of managerial control. The company made its announcement public on March 29, 1940. As new partners came and went over the next decade and a half, the firm's name occasionally changed, but the title Merrill Lynch was always listed first.

While the negotiations leading to Merrill's return to management continued, the New York Stock Exchange commissioned the Elmo Roper organization to survey public opinion about the securities industry. Its revelations were startling. The public believed that most stockbrokers were deceitful and dishonest. The same report also showed that many people were woefully uninformed about how the financial markets functioned. Merrill took the results of the opinion poll very seriously. He planned to create a different kind of brokerage firm for the growing American middle class—one that would educate customers about both the mechanics and principles of investing. In a memo to their other 65 partners and office managers, Merrill and Pierce assessed the challenge: "We in the securities business have a job to do—a job of reestablishing faith in the security markets as a place for sound investment."

During the years of Merrill's absence from active involvement in the securities sector, the federal government had passed a series of laws designed to clean up some of the worst abuses of Wall Street operators. The government created the Securities and Exchange Commission to monitor the industry and guarantee compliance with the law. It required

Merrill Lynch "wire room," the firm's operations center, circa 1952 (courtesy of Merrill Lynch Archives)

firms with securities listed on the major exchanges to file prospectuses for their new offerings and to make regular and fairly uniform reports of their financial condition to stockholders and the general public. Persons convicted of securities fraud were subject to criminal prosecution, which meant not only fines but jail terms as well. Governmental reforms had done much to produce at least minimum standards for Wall Street firms. Merrill would have preferred to see the initiatives come from within the industry, but he completely agreed with the thrust of the reform movement.

In one of his first acts as senior partner, Merrill had a small pamphlet prepared for the guidance of employees, which outlined, in no uncertain terms, the basic policies of the firm. At the heart of the document appeared the commandment: "The interests of our customers MUST come first." In advertising brochures prepared for the public at large Merrill promised to devote substantial resources to investigating thoroughly the securities recommended by sales personnel, to ban trading by partners and employees on the basis of advance information, and to give customers, not insiders, prior-

ity in filling orders for securities underwritten by Merrill Lynch. By the end of 1940 the firm had 50,000 accounts, and about 12,000 of them had opened within the previous 12 months.

Over the next decade and a half Merrill Lynch introduced a host of innovative policies. Starting in 1940 the firm voluntarily published an annual report, the first ever by a private firm on Wall Street. The initial report featured little to crow about, however. Trading volume on the New York Stock Exchange had dropped 20 percent in 1940, and the firm, despite massive cost cutting, recorded losses totaling more than $300,000. It was an inauspicious beginning.

The next year trading on the Big Board fell off even more. One of the firms that developed serious financial problems in 1941 was Fenner & Beane, the nation's second largest brokerage firm with more than 50 offices in cities across the country. Within a few days the firms arranged a merger, and the newly organized Merrill Lynch, Pierce, Fenner & Beane claimed representation in 92 cities from coast to coast. The organizational network was in place, but the public still held back from broad participation in the stock market. Due in large part to underwriting commissions on new securities issues for retail food chains, the firm reported net profits of $459,000 in 1941. The tide had finally turned.

But the firm was not yet out of the woods. Trading on the Big Board hovered at only 126 million shares in 1942, the lowest level since World War I. (By the 1980s that many shares often changed hands in a single day.) American entry into World War II had revived the manufacturing sector of the economy, but the financial markets responded at a much slower pace. In 1943 volume picked up substantially, however, and the partnership reported profits of $1.1 million.

In April 1944 Merrill suffered the first of a series of heart attacks. He recovered, but for the next 12 years he did not involve himself in the day-to-day administration of the firm. Indeed, he only rarely visited the office; he communicated with his partners over the telephone and through a steady flow of memos. His new role, chiefly that of policy maker, focused strictly on strategy and long-term planning. In that capacity he met regularly with Win Smith, the partner who had lured him back to Wall Street in 1940. Smith implemented many of Merrill's most innovative ideas.

Among the first areas to draw the senior partner's attention in the mid 1940s was the overall status of the firm's sales force. The average age of its brokers exceeded fifty; because of the low trading volume over the last decade and a half, few young peeople had entered the brokerage field. Merrill decided to establish an in-house training program designed to attract top-flight recruits and then to train them according to the highest standards. He aimed at giving his firm's brokers more of the background and education associated with recognized professionals in related fields, particularly accounting and commercial banking. One of the individuals recruited for one of the earliest training classes, Donald Regan, became chief executive officer of Merrill Lynch in the 1970s and then President Ronald Reagan's secretary of the Treasury and later his chief of staff in the 1980s.

Merrill Lynch expected its representatives to behave as expert investment advisers, not rumormongers trying to churn accounts to yield the maximum commissions. They dispensed essentially conservative advice regarding the performance of stocks. The analysts in the research department recom-

mended mainly reliable blue-chip stocks; their reports on publicly traded companies were realistic assessments, with the possible negatives listed along with the optimistic factors. The company instructed its brokers to stress the long-run gains accruing from a program of steady investments in a mix of bonds and equities. It encouraged its customers to formulate a financial plan for their future retirement and to stick with it throughout the upswings and downslides in the market. Rather than promise the middle-class client the opportunity for quick profits, Merrill Lynch presented him with an investment strategy that could enhance wealth slowly but steadily over a lifetime. Merrill wanted to attract new accounts, and he hoped to retain their loyalty for decades. He proposed a whole new way of conducting routine business on Wall Street.

Merrill was serious about educating the general public regarding the intricacies of the securities markets. He directed the advertising department to print a large volume of unbiased informational material. A booklet entitled "How to Read a Financial Report" came out in 1946, and updated versions are still distributed today. An earlier publication for persons interested in the commodities markets had this catchy title: "Hedging: Insurance Policy or Lottery Ticket." In 1948 the firm ran a full-page advertisement in leading newspapers across the nation that featured 6,000 words of copy in very small print entitled "What Everybody Ought to Know... about the Stock and Bond Business." In textbook prose the advertising copy explained the fundamental operations of the securities markets. Readers were directed to write their local Merrill Lynch office for extra copies of the advertisement, and over the next decade more than three million requests for reprints were filled. The firm ended the Wall Street taboo on creative and boldly solicitous newspaper and magazine advertising.

Merrill wished to demystify Wall Street and to overturn the elitist atmosphere that prevailed at one end of the spectrum and the unsavoriness associated with its bottom side. In the past most brokerage houses had reserved their most reliable and valued information for their wealthiest and best customers. Merrill Lynch made virtually all of the information generated by its research specialists available to all its regular customers, and indeed to almost anyone who made a legitimate request. Secrecy and special privilege undermined the integrity of the marketplace, Merrill had concluded, and he set out to raise the ethical standards not only of his own firm but of the financial services sector as a whole.

In the late 1940s and early 1950s Merrill Lynch continued to expand its branch network. In 1949 the 100th office was opened–in Omaha, Nebraska. With trading volume on the exchanges reviving in the wake of the postwar economic prosperity, the firm had its most profitable year to date in 1950. Pretax income was $12.5 million and after payment of the partners' taxes, averaging nearly 70 percent, net income climbed to $3.5 million–double the previous high in 1948. During the 1940s the number of offices grew to 138, and the number of accounts jumped to 400,000–a fourfold increase since the early 1940s. The firm as rapidly realized Merrill's dream of bringing Wall Street to citizens living on more ordinary streets in towns and cities across the nation.

In 1954 the New York Stock Exchange introduced the Monthly Investment Plan (MIP) for persons with moderate incomes who wanted to invest small amounts in the stock market on a regular schedule. Merrill Lynch emerged as the largest institutional supporter of that marketing concept. It provided a mechanism for small investors to accumulate their own stocks, not shares in a mutual fund, for as little as $40 per month without having commission fees swallow up a huge proportion of their capital investment. Moreover, by "dollar averaging" the regular investor could take advantage of the declines in market prices to acquire stocks at bargain prices. Securities firms expected to profit little from handling thousands of odd-lot transactions; breaking even was the aim. The underlying strategy was to cultivate new customers whose incomes would increase over the years and whose investment portfolios would grow steadily. One day the small account would become middle sized and evolve into genuinely profitable business. In the first year after implementation, Merrill Lynch had just under one-half of all MIP accounts, and a few years later the firm maintained the vast majority of them. No other brokerage house duplicated Merrill Lynch's service to the small investor.

In addition to developing its brokerage business, the firm actively traded in other financial markets. Its broad retail network made Merrill Lynch a likely candidate for inclusion in many new-issue syndicates, and by the end of World War II the firm had become the nation's 15th largest underwriter.

In 1956 it was one of seven lead managers for the Ford Motor Company's stock offering of $660 million. After his return to active management, Merrill had opted for continuing the provision of services for commodities traders both at home and abroad. One of the straightforward booklets issued to the public in 1940 was devoted to defending the practice of hedging in commodities; it explained how the buying and selling of options contracts acted to stabilize those frequently volatile markets. A brochure published in 1956 was titled "Handbook for Commodity Speculators." Some partners wanted to shy away from commodities because of their speculative reputation, but Merrill decided that he wanted to develop a full line of financial services for a wide range of customers, including clients prepared to accept high levels of risk.

Even before his death at his home in Southampton on October 6, 1956, Merrill won effusive praise from individuals both within the firm and in the wider world. In a 1947 poll of 50 outstanding business leaders, he was the only one listed with a background in the securities industry. In 1954 his partner and long-term business associate Win Smith wrote down these memories for a future biographer: "On balance, after some 37 years of intimate relationship, I know that CEM is innately a kindly gentleman, a financial genius, a courageous, pugnacious man, an individual who just plain likes people and one who can be an easy touch to an old friend." In *Wall Street: Men and Money*, published in 1955, Martin Mayer wrote: "He is the first authentically great man produced by the financial market in 150 years. Merrill brought in the public, not as lambs to be fleeced but as partners in the benefits." In discussing the transformation of the securities markets, Mayer added: "The climate of the 1930s helped, the New Deal laws helped, and many individuals helped, but the prime mover was Charlie Merrill."

In his will Merrill authorized the creation of a trust fund to benefit colleges, churches, and hospitals. The income from his capital left in the firm went directly to the trust fund. Over the years major grants went to Amherst College, Stetson University, and Harvard Medical School. A substantial share of his wealth went to support predominantly black colleges and universities in the southern states. When the Charles E. Merrill Fund closed its books in 1981, it had distributed a total of more than $110 million.

Merrill (left) with Winthrop H. Smith, who helped Merrill reorganize the Merrill Lynch brokerage firm after Edmund Lynch's death in 1938 (courtesy of Merrill Lynch Archives)

Merrill made the securities markets a vehicle for the emergence of mass capitalism. The ownership of stocks and bonds remained no longer the preserve of wealthy persons and institutions, but offered an investment vehicle for middle-class families of modest means across the nation. Merrill downplayed the speculative aspects of the stock market and emphasized the soundness of investments in the equities of American business firms listed on the organized exchanges. Along the way he was instrumental in introducing a host of internal procedures and principles based on the highest ethical standards. He believed straightforwardness and honesty were in the best interest of the whole market mechanism and that those attributes benefited his partners and all their sales personnel over the long run.

Merrill saw no conflict between profit and high principle. He strove to develop the same professional standards for retail brokers as for wholesale investment bankers. The innovations he sponsored at Merrill Lynch eventually spread to virtually every other brokerage and investment banking firm in the United States.

Publication:

"Mr. Average Investor," *Leslie's Illustrated Weekly* (November 1911).

Reference:

Henry Hecht, ed., *A Legacy of Leadership: Merrill Lynch, 1885-1985* (New York: Merrill Lynch, 1985).

Michael R. Milken

(July 4, 1946 -)

by Larry Schweikart

University of Dayton

CAREER: Assistant to the president (1970), broker, bond department (1971-1973), head, bond department, Drexel Burnham Lambert (1974-1989); president, International Capital Access Group (1989-1990).

Called by some the most important and influential venture capitalist in the twentieth century and the J. P. Morgan of the 1980s, Michael Robert Milken virtually single-handedly developed and marketed a wide range of innovative securities that by 1989 had provided more than $120 billion in growth capital to companies in almost every industry in America. His accomplishments, tainted by a 1990 conviction on fraud charges followed by a fine and a short jail sentence, nevertheless reflected a new democratization of American capital markets. His impact on American finance cannot be overstated.

Born to Fern and Bernard Milken on the Fourth of July in 1946, Milken grew up near Encino, California, in a relatively affluent Jewish household. His father was an accountant, and Milken studied his father's work on tax returns from the age of ten. Personally driven, even as a teenager, Milken slept only a few hours a night (a trait he shared with financiers such as Andrew Mellon and Ivan Boesky). His kinetic energy showed itself even during his high school years at Birmingham High School in Van Nuys, where he graduated in 1964. In addition to his other activities he was a cheerleader.

Milken's unmatched energy came from natural sources, as he never consumed alcohol, cigarettes, coffee, or even carbonated beverages. According to one Drexel Burnham Lambert official who later knew him, "Mike has an energy level that makes a nuclear plant look pathetic." He continued his education at the University of California at Berkeley, where he graduated Phi Beta Kappa in

1968. Connie Bruck described Milken's years at Berkeley by noting, "While that campus was roiled with the protests of the militant left, Milken majored in business administration, managed a few portfolios for investors, and was active in a fraternity, Sigma Alpha Mu." He married his high school sweetheart, Lori Anne Hackel, and they had three children.

Accepted at the Wharton School, Milken determined to finish at the top of his class. He received his MBA degree, but even before he completed his degree in 1970 he received his first break, when Anthony Buford, Jr., of the firm then known as Drexel Harriman Ripley, offered him a summer job. The company's Philadelphia office struggled under the burden of back-office paperwork, and Milken received his first assignment to reorganize that aspect of the business. He failed miserably, not because he lacked talent, but because his high-powered intellect endowed him with a phenomenal ego and general abrasiveness. Drexel wisely recognized both his talents and his weaknesses and transferred him to the position of assistant to the president. In that capacity he worked for both Bertram Coleman and James Stratton.

Milken started to earn his keep with Drexel when he analyzed the company's securities delivery system. Previously the company had used a system whereby it shipped securities to cities, borrowing the price until final delivery. If delivery took five days, Drexel paid interest for five days. Milken convinced Drexel to make overnight deliveries, cutting the interest paid to one day and saving the company a half-million dollars a year.

Upon leaving Wharton, Milken took a full-time position at Drexel in the bond trading department. That tradition-steeped company, once associated with J. P. Morgan, had not grown as had many of its competitors. Milken changed that. He developed a fascination for lower grade bonds–bonds

Michael Milken, 1978 (Neal Boenzi/New York Times)

below the "investment grade" of AAA. Some 800 American companies could boast a bond rating of triple-B or better from Moody's or Standard and Poor's, the major rating services. Major companies such as IBM or General Motors usually rated anywhere from A to triple-A. But Penn Central also qualified for a triple-B or better rating until two weeks before it went bankrupt, and, as Robert Lifton pointed out, "For all practical purposes, Argentina and Mexico did too, before the Latin American debt bomb blew up." On the other hand, some 21,000 companies did not meet triple-B standards in 1989, despite the fact that they produced the greatest job growth, income growth, and overall expansion of any sector of the economy. Among some 1,000 clients at Drexel that did not qualify for investment grade debt at the time Milken picked them up, Cablevision, Caesar's World, Fruit of the Loom, Hasbro, Holiday Inns, Lorimar, Mattel, MGM/UA Entertainment, Orion Pictures, Newreeveco/Shick, Revlon Group, Safeway, Uniroyal, and Zale constitute just a small sample. Moreover, not one business largely owned by minorities or women qualified for the higher bond ratings. Most entrepre-

neurial companies could never hope to "make the grade" for bond offerings.

Enter Michael Milken. Impressed with a study that showed that the yield on a diversified low grade bond portfolio exceeded that on a higher grade portfolio, Milken decided to make the low grade bonds his specialty. His unmatched energy allowed him to research the companies that issued the bonds, and he brimmed with enthusiasm for the offbeat securities. But his snobbish colleagues considered the low grade bonds "crap" and treated Milken like "a leper." Part of the hostility arose because of anti-Semitism, and some Drexel traders saw Milken as a "peddler."

Undaunted, Milken turned regular profits with the otherwise unwanted paper. When he threatened to leave, Drexel Burnham Lambert opened up the purse strings and gave him a $2 million trading position. In that year, 1973, Milken made a $2 million profit for the firm, whereupon the company quickly increased his position. Milken retained 35 percent of his group's profits as a bonus, and he distributed it as he saw fit. Indeed, he created a virtually autonomous unit inside Drexel, replete with its own sales force, research staff, and traders, known as the high yield and convertible bond department. (Most bonds paid off at maturity. Convertibles could be converted into common stock or other securities.) Ultimately, Drexel simply called Milken's group "the Department." As Milken went, so went Drexel, and the company started an impressive resurgence.

Milken and his group approached the high yield bonds as though they were stocks and traded them accordingly. Those high yield (and high risk) bonds, sometimes amalgamated with a variety of notes or other debt investments, soon acquired the name "junk."

Milken's best customers included David Solomon, Carl Lindner, Saul Steinberg, Meshulam Riklis, and Lawrence Tisch. They formed the core of a group that routinely took large blocks of Milken's junk at one time or another. Large institutions such as Massachusetts Mutual and First Investors Fund for Income (FIFI) also placed much of their portfolios in Milken's control. While the bond funds under the control of Milken's portfolio managers turned in impressive performances, Milken played a different angle, buying undervalued bonds and anticipating their recovery. He and his favored clients purchased undervalued bonds across an entire spectrum of near-bankrupt securities, in addition to the bonds of Real Estate Investment Trusts (REITs). REITs operated much like mutual funds whose portfolios consisted of real estate or financial instruments associated with real estate. When the REITs started to falter in the early 1970s, they provided a natural opportunity for Milken, who correctly anticipated that some of them would return to their prerecession value. When the company ordered Milken to get Drexel out of REITs, he formed a syndicate to buy out the firm's position and made "a fortune."

Among Milken's clients, Saul Steinberg's Reliance Insurance Company made a move to take over the Walt Disney empire financed by Drexel's junk. Meshulam Riklis, one of Milken's best customers, who controlled a conglomerate with sales of $2 billion, later claimed to have invented junk bonds. Even if he was correct, Milken made them practical instruments for actual financing. At any rate, Riklis's companies often purchased the junk bonds offered by Steinberg's Reliance, and vice versa, with Milken orchestrating the activity between them. When they had troubles—as Riklis did in the mid

1970s—Milken bailed them out. As Riklis recalled of Milken, "He oversaw everything I did . . . He had to be constantly monitoring what we were doing." Riklis considered Milken "a creative genius."

Milken's impact on Wall Street greatly resembled that of Merrill Lynch's founder, Charles E. Merrill, in that he democratized a Wall Street that since Merrill's time had again become elitist. By opening financing to anyone willing to take risks, Milken destroyed the aura of the snobbish brokerage houses, which accounted for some of his unpopularity on "the street." His junk broke down the barriers erected by the Wall Street firms and offered important alternatives to the traditional means of financing corporate activities. Milken, as Bruck observed, offered "low-rated companies a new financial instrument that blended the best of equity and debt: long-term, dilutionless compensated for the riskiness of the issue, and they also held out the hope of having their ratings upgraded in the future."

Milken's financial democracy extended even further, however. He knew he had to expand his base to a more diversified group of customers. To reach the retail buyers, Milken and his right-hand man, Fred Joseph (known as the "Dr. Feelgood" of Drexel), invented a class of high yield bond funds that provided diversified portfolios accessible to customers who had smaller amounts of money to invest. Indeed, David Solomon's FIFI had operated much along those lines since Milken had started tutoring Solomon in the intricacies of junk. Financed by Drexel in 1976, FIFI emerged as the first of a half-dozen junk funds, repackaged for the public as "high yield" funds. Those funds paid an average 2.5 percent more than U.S. Treasury bonds.

With the new retail outlets, Drexel steadily and dramatically increased its junk offerings, and in 1978 alone the company issued $439.5 million, taking close to 70 percent of the market. Given his new base of power, Milken persuaded Drexel to allow him to relocate his entire high yield group to Century City, Los Angeles. Although both Milken and his wife were California natives, he really wished to move his group far away from the prying eyes of anxious, more traditional senior partners, such as I. W. "Tubby" Burnham II. The relocation, however, did not materialize easily: several members of the firm expressed concern about moving Drexel's chief money-maker 3,000 miles away. But the independent Milken—who made virtually all of Drexel's profits—insisted, and in 1978 for the first time a major New York firm lost its central operation to California. With Milken went nearly two dozen top traders, all destined to become millionaires under his guidance. On his trip to California—by car—Milken, who had sold short some securities before leaving, essentially betting that the price would fall before he had to produce the securities for delivery, learned that the price had started to rise. He frantically checked in from phone booths across the country and managed to unload the securities on some of his clients and avoid large losses.

The hajj to Century City coincided with two long-term trends in American business that coalesced in the early 1980s. First, a decade of efforts to deregulate everything from banking to airlines had entered its final stages. Second, American business and industrial productivity had dropped to post-war lows. Those two factors made for a "fourth great merger wave"—the most important since the 1890s—by easing regulations against takeovers at the very time many bloated companies had become appealing takeover or merger targets. Milken provided a means, through his junk bonds, for corporate raiders to raise the millions of dollars they needed to put their takeover plans into action. Certainly not all of Milken's deals panned out: American Communications Industries and Drexel issued $20 million worth of bonds for a company that had virtually no assets and became the "first company in junk-bond history to default without making even one interest payment," according to Bruck. Nevertheless, investors knew the risks. Milken packaged the bonds with warrants (bonds that the investor could convert into the company's stock at a given price), high interest, and large discounts. He mixed and matched the packages until the investors found the issue attractive. He also learned that young companies, especially, ran into difficulties on interest repayments rather than on operating expenses. If he could find ways to satisfy the debt holders with payments in common stock, he could relieve the debt burdens of struggling companies whose operations indeed showed profits.

One other factor played a key role in Milken's operations. Due to the immediate pressures on the companies, the debt for equity swaps had to occur quickly. But the processes of registering a security with the Securities and Exchange Commission could take months, in which time a struggling company could go belly up. Milken thus created the unregistered exchange offer, with the conditions for converting the bonds into stock incorporated into the original offering, but covered by the little-used Section 3(a)9 of the Securities Act of 1933. Under that provision, as Drexel banker James Schneider discovered, companies could offer new paper in exchange for the old without registering, provided the investment bankers did not accept a fee for promoting or soliciting the exchange. However, investment bankers could inform the company of the particular exchange that it would find most beneficial. Schneider explained the provision to Milken, who saw its potential. While other traditional banking houses shied away from offerings based on Section 3(a)9, Milken treated it as the Holy Grail.

From 1981 to 1986, Drexel completed 175 3(a)9 exchange offers for a total of more than $7 billion of junk bond debt. More astounding, Drexel's rate of default came to less than 2 percent, whereas other investment houses' default rates ran as high as 17 percent on their traditional exchanges. So while critics complained that the junk bonds had ushered in a new era of recklessness and high risk, in fact Drexel's junk proved less risky than the traditional investments offered by the more conservative Wall Street houses. Even with the default rates on junk bonds experienced by the other investment houses, the amount of junk bond offerings by Drexel expanded by three times from 1982 to 1983. In one ten-day period Drexel underwrote seven issues totaling $500 million, and in April 1983 Drexel raised $400 million for MGM/UA Communications followed by a $1 billion issue for MCI Communications. The MCI deal had started as a $500 million deal that Milken continued to sell. When he could not sell an entire issue, Drexel purchased the rest. In the case of MCI, Drexel took $250 million through its own high-yield mutual fund.

Not only did Milken take firms on the verge of fantastic growth, such as MCI, but he also took on industries no other investment firms would touch. In the late 1970s, for example, Drexel, at Milken's recommendation, financed a $160 million package to build a Golden Nugget casino in Atlantic City. Other investment houses refused to touch the gaming industry. Drexel and Milken prospered with it.

Along with the rapid expansion of the junk bond market, Drexel—and Milken's group—expanded. The firm grew from eleventh among corporate bond underwriters in 1978 to sixth; its profits increased from $6 million to $150 million over the same period. Milken and his brother Lowell, who followed Michael's investments and had joined Drexel in 1978, made personal fortunes. Milken moved the Drexel operations from Century City to Beverly Hills in 1983.

By the mid 1980s, Milken had spread his and Lowell's wealth through numerous partnerships—GLJ, WB Associates, WRC Associates, Lobon Associates, and Carlyle Associates—as well as half a dozen more elite partnerships for their families. Those who followed Milken made fortunes, but he demanded complete dedication to trading. Quite egalitarian in some respects—he never had his picture on a Drexel annual report—Milken had no office. He operated from a single desk in the middle of the trading room. Other traders were welcome to use his desk. The company's Christmas card put all the names together on the list, including those of the parking attendants. When asked how many subordinates he had, Milken replied, "We don't really have a pecking order." When someone tried to draw an organizational chart of Milken's operation, it crisscrossed wildly into a maze. Yet if Milken ran an egalitarian shop, he demanded an intense workload from his personnel. He personally arrived at the office between 4:30 and 5 A.M., and, as he recalled, "Sometimes around ten forty-five to eleven fifteen they put some food on my desk which I eat in anywhere from one to five minutes." He once agreed to meet with a friend, but the only time available was 5:30 A.M. on a Sunday. Milken then called the friend to remind him that on that particular Sunday the clocks would be moved for daylight savings time—they had to meet at 4:30!

Milken's junk bonds found their way into the troubled savings and loan (S&L) industry when Congress deregulated the S&Ls with the Garn-St Germain Act in 1982. Suddenly thrifts could make commercial loans and invest in corporate debt securities. The S&Ls offered Milken a new pool of almost $1 trillion to tap. Because the S&Ls slumped, due to the mismatch of paying more for their short-term deposits than they received for their long-term mortgage loans, they desperately searched for high-yield investments that would allow them to recoup their outflow of interest to depositors. Virtually all of the nation's 3,000 S&Ls faced the same mismatch problem. A typical union of an S&L and

Milken was Columbia Savings and Loan in Beverly Hills, one of the first of the many S&Ls to move into junk bonds. It started buying Milken's securities in 1982. Columbia soon soared from $373 million in assets in 1981 to $10 billion in 1986.

By far, however, the most important—and disastrous—of the S&L wheeler-dealers to connect with Milken came in the person of Charles Keating. A war hero, devout Catholic, and antipornography crusader, the Cincinnati-based developer had studied deal-making under Milken supporter Carl Lindner. Keating had received $119 million in Drexel-underwritten bonds for his American Continental Corporation, a real estate development company in Phoenix, Arizona. Using $51 million of that pool of cash Keating purchased Lincoln Savings and Loan of Irvine, California. He then used the S&L to invest in junk bonds, with the company growing from $800 million in assets in 1984 to $5.5 billion by 1989. However, Lincoln lost at least $300 million by taking, as one regulator put it, "the junkiest of the junk." Keating also funneled money to Mizel Development Corporation (MDC) in Denver, which itself issued about $700 million worth of junk bonds through Milken from 1983 to 1986. MDC also invested $43 million in Silverado Savings and Loan in Colorado. Meanwhile, Keating's network also extended to Dallas financier Gene Phillips and his Southmark Corporation, which owned the Houston-based San Jacinto Savings Association. Drexel raised $450 million for Southmark, which went to purchase still other junk bonds.

Ultimately, the government alleged that Keating was guilty of mismanagement and fraud. The Resolution Trust Corporation, Congress, the Internal Revenue Service, the FBI, the Securities and Exchange Commission (SEC), and agencies in California and Arizona all investigated the case. Federal courts in Phoenix, Los Angeles, and Washington also examined Keating's activities. At that time the public learned of Keating's connection with Milken. Yet Milken maintained that high-yield bonds were not responsible for the S&L debacle. The S&L industry "didn't lose money by investing in [high-yield bonds]. They lost it by blindly investing in commercial real estate."

Long before the S&L troubles, to celebrate and advertise the virtues of high-yield bonds, Milken in 1979 had sponsored a conference at the Beverly Hills Hilton. The attendees met in an intimate setting where they exchanged information on

Milken and his attorney, Edward Bennett Williams, at a 1988 congressional hearing investigating charges of securities violations at the brokerage firm of Drexel Burnham Lambert (AP/Wide World Photos)

various companies. That event soon expanded, to the point that companies seeking financing appeared with slick video presentations. And the event itself took on an almost mythical quality, with the conferees simply referring to it as the Predators' Ball. To that audience in 1985 Milken had pointed out that they controlled more than $3 trillion in buying power. Reports circulated that in order to attract clients to the early conferences, Milken's troops had arranged for plenty of call girls to entertain the arbitrageurs and attorneys. Even years later, after the Ball gained widespread respectability, the call girls stayed.

Milken, with associates such as Steinberg, Lindner, Riklis, and Victor Posner, under normal circumstances could lay claim on access to $100 billion at a time. His expanded horizons led him to look at mergers and acquisitions (M&A), with its phenomenal fees. M&A had emerged in its own right as a major profit center for all of the large investment houses. The tax structure had encouraged the assumption of debt instead of equity, and the 1974 stock market crash had also turned many expensive companies into attractive targets. Drexel had specialized in "mezzanine debt"—the unsecured debt below the senior secured debt in a deal but above the equity. Companies increasingly looked to the mezzanine debt for leveraged buyouts (LBOs). As Bruck explains, in an LBO "a small group of investors, usually including management, buys out the public shareholders by borrowing against the assets being purchased and then repays . . . with cash from the acquired company or, more often, by selling some of its assets." And since the LBO shifted control of a company, often into the hands of more entrepreneurial-minded owners, Milken saw it as a natural area to pursue. Drexel needed a Fortune 500 client with a billion-dollar bank line to wage a takeover that would establish the firm as a legitimate power in the M&A field. However, Milken, confident he could raise a billion-dollar line, allowed Drexel to claim it had such a fund, even though it did not exist. Thus Drexel created the "highly confident" letter, known to insiders as the Air Fund. By simply announcing that it had such a fund—or was "highly confident" it could raise such a sum—Drexel obtained commitment letters in which its buyers agreed to purchase a certain amount of junk bonds, which then fueled the takeover. Using that basic strategy, Milken financed T. Boone Pickens's hostile takeover of Gulf Oil by Mesa Petroleum, Steinburg's Reliance and its attempted takeover of Disney, Carl Icahn's bid for Phillips Petroleum, Triangle's takeover of National Can, and several others. And in July 1984, Milken underwrote an additional $100 million worth of junk bonds for Triangle without identifying any target!

In each acquisition, Drexel—and Milken—received fees that ten years earlier would have seemed pure fantasy. Not only did the company receive a percentage of the total issue, it also tagged the borrower with advisory fees (up to $500,000) and, upon consummation of the deal, Drexel got an additional 3 to 5 percent minus the up-front amount. In the Triangle-National Can deal Drexel pocketed $25 million plus warrants for 16 percent of Triangle's stock.

Of course, Milken and Drexel could command such exceptional fees because of their extraordinary services. In one 1985 deal Drexel raised $3 billion over a five-day period from 140 institutions, tying up six telecopier machines. Milken raised the $365 million for Triangle in less than 36 hours. No doubt such feats would have impressed even J. P. Morgan. To make such rapid sales Milken relied on his loyal group of "high rollers," including Riklis, Steinberg, and the rest. Even when they did not want to buy the bonds, and even when they did not know anything about the company, the loyalists always took a healthy slice of each Milken offering. They did so because Milken would consistently finance their own activities and also because as soon as possible Milken moved the securities into another tier of investors at a higher price. The first group received a premium for their loyalty.

If done carefully, the entire process was completely legal, and, as Bruck observed, "sublimely purposeful." Milken kept the high rollers' cash free. Meanwhile, second-tier risk-averse groups that did not want to have the public image of dealing in junk bonds could come in at a later date and play. In the case of the Triangle deal, four-fifths of the bonds changed hands before they were registered. Evidence suggests that Milken deliberately did not always take care to register the securities quickly. Technically no violation of the law existed if the first-tier buyers simply changed their minds and decided to sell the bonds after purchase. But they violated the law if they intended to resell the securities all along.

Milken also financed the activities of another well-known takeover artist, Carl Icahn, who made his own imprint on American business. An expert chess player who had attended medical school thanks to his uncle, Icahn got a job at the brokerage firm of Dreyfus and Company. He promptly invested his Army poker winnings and made $50,000 in the stock market, which he soon lost. Icahn took a job with another trading firm where he specialized in options known as puts and calls—rights to buy and sell stock at a given price in the future. After forming his own company Icahn marched through several profitable but unsuccessful merger attempts in which he developed a new tactic in the takeover game, called greenmail. Greenmail involved mounting a takeover attempt on a company to force the owners to buy out the predator at a price not offered to other stockholders (blackmail, using green money). Steinberg's Reliance had mustered an attempt to take over Disney that resulted in greenmail.

In the case of Drexel's financing of Icahn's attempted takeover of Phillips Oil, Milken could not circulate the "commitment letter" for fear of running up the price. Instead Drexel gave Icahn its own commitment letter, which meant that the firm guaranteed the capital. That technique, known as bridge financing, represented a new manifestation of old underwriting techniques. The Icahn bid for Phillips represented Drexel's first tender offer in which the company had not already arranged the financing. Because Drexel received a percentage of all the cash it raised, Milken tried to raise more than Icahn actually needed. He ultimately started to raise $1.5 billion when Phillips instituted a "poison pill" defense, developed by Martin Lipton, in which the company gives the stockholders such lavish rights that a would-be acquirer loses interest. In 1986 Drexel completed the financing for Icahn's takeover of Trans World Airlines (TWA), and to everyone's surprise Icahn actually stepped in and started to run the airline himself. One year later TWA hit an all-time high in industry profits, earning $240 million. Milken was vindicated. In just a few months TWA pursued another airline, Ozark, in its own takeover bid.

The Drexel-sponsored takeovers brought an ethos to American business that, while not new, certainly reached new heights. By taking over a company that raiders thought had not performed well, the raiders forced all businesses to monitor constantly their profits and stock positions. If the raiders succeeded in obtaining an undervalued company, they could sell off unprofitable parts to pay for the borrowed amount. That meant, however, that many American businesses, whether successful or unsuccessful in holding off the raiders, had to take on new, and, to some, shocking levels of debt. Debt-to-equity ratios reached 71.4 percent in 1985 compared to 35.3 percent in 1961 (but below the 91.1 percent in 1974). The junk bond explosion coincided with rising U.S. trade deficits and with record American domestic deficits (at least, in nominal terms: as a share of GNP the deficits hardly differed from those in the 1960s). Total debt in 1986 came to $7 trillion. Many observers assumed that the three debt measures were related somehow. In fact, most serious economic studies found no correlation between the three, and many studies showed no correlation between any two of the three measures. Milken's critics claimed his bond empire would collapse with a recession, but the long-predicted recession did not come.

Milken maintained that American companies had not taken on too much debt. He certainly did not slow his financing of new takeovers. In 1985 he backed Ronald Perelman's Pantry Pride takeover attempt on Revlon, a company five times the size of Pantry Pride. Drexel had supplied about 40 percent of the money needed for Perelman's other activities, which included the purchase of the film processing company Technicolor. Bruck labeled the Pantry Pride raid as the "crucial campaign" in the junk bond war, because the "most impassioned corporate defenders were united against Milken's onslaught; where they unloaded everything in the takeover defense arsenal; where they fought down to the wire." Ultimately they lost because the money supplied by Milken was as good to the stockholders as anyone else's. The episode also proved that Wall Street traditionalists had underestimated both Milken's daring and stockholders' common sense. Pantry Pride also constituted Milken's first large hostile takeover that had gone to completion (he had a small previous triumph in Coastal Corporation's takeover of American Natural Resources Company).

When one of Milken's deals ended, the established holders of any high-grade bonds the company had usually fell because the company had so much new debt. Milken, of course, prophesied as much, saying that while low-grade bonds could always go up, there was only one way for high-grade bonds to go: down. As for Drexel-held or Drexel-initiated bonds that went up, in 1985 $4.6 billion worth of junk bonds advanced into investment grade. By contrast, more than $9 billion worth of in-vestment grade bonds moved downward, classified as junk. By 1986 Drexel's position had increased to the point that one large investor, in an issue of *Barrons*, commented, "Drexel is like a god.... They are awesome."

Having capitalized some of the largest and most unexpected deals in modern American finance, Milken expanded to Japan, where he held a Predators' Ball in 1986. Breaking into the Japanese securities market was almost impossible for American companies, but Milken confidently marched in. The prospect of linking the huge Japanese capital pool with Milken's investments produced visions of $10 billion to $20 billion deals.

Meanwhile, in the United States other firms started to copy Drexel's tactics. Milken responded, "I welcome competition. Other people might see things we don't see." In fact, Milken had presided over still more new debt instruments, such as the zero-coupon bond. It sold at a discount from its face value and paid no interest until maturity, at which time it paid the total accrued interest. Yet as the competition expanded the amount of junk debt, with $50 billion issued from 1985 to 1986, some studies showed that the credit quality of new junk issues started to slide. One study, which showed steady increases for junk from 1978 to 1984, claimed the market deteriorated after that. Part of the deterioration came from the bankruptcy of LTV Corporation, but Lehman and not Drexel had underwritten that debt. Milken reportedly lost $11 million on the LTV bankruptcy.

However, other warning flags started to fly. Columbia Savings and Loan, one of Milken's junk movers, had come under increased scrutiny from regulators. Milken's other clients increasingly found themselves getting, they thought, "gouged" on Drexel's fees. Most important, since 1984 the SEC had concluded two separate investigations of Drexel. Those investigations had centered on the timing of trades involving Casesar's World and raised questions of insider trading. Regulators taking testimony from Milken thought he stonewalled them and conveniently forgot information. But even if he wanted to reproduce the details of a deal, it seemed impossible: he made or took between 50 to 100 phone calls a day.

Certainly Milken and Drexel operated on the border of legality quite often. They worked with such innovative instruments and in such uncharted waters that frequently no one—including Milken—

knew if what Milken did was legal or not. No precedents existed. Unless specifically told that a particular offering violated the law, Milken proceeded. Thus, considering his arrogant attitude and his reputation as a wheeler-dealer, that the regulators and the legal authorities would investigate Milken and Drexel was inevitable.

The New York-based U.S. attorney Rudolph Giuliani had viewed Drexel as a prime target to show that his office was as tough on white collar crime as on violent crime. Moreover, the authorities certainly had the help of the established Wall Street firms, which wished to direct attention to what they considered unfair practices by the upstart Drexel. Consequently, Giuliani mounted a concerted and rather transparent effort to prosecute Milken and Drexel by applying a law usually reserved for Mafia killers, the Racketeer Influenced and Corrupt Organizations (RICO) Act. That law allowed the government to seize an individual's assets before a trial actually started. The government also conducted a publicity campaign against Milken's income. But it still needed inside information to make any kind of a case, because many of Milken's deals could have the appearance of insider trading, and stock market regulations made it virtually impossible to prove violations without proving the intent to defraud, which required a witness. In May 1986, Dennis Levine, a Drexel Burnham Lambert banker, was arrested on insider trading charges. The government pressured Levine to turn state's evidence with the intent of using Levine to get Milken.

Several months later the government got another break when one of Milken's "regulars" at purchasing the junk bond issues, Ivan Boesky, settled with the government on insider trading charges, with much of the government's case coming from Levine. Boesky paid a then-record $100 million fine and served five years in jail, but he had received a deal based on his willingness to cooperate against Drexel and Milken. The government used Levine only to get to Boesky and used Boesky to get to Milken. In 1988 the SEC charged Drexel with many violations of securities acts. Drexel, in December of that year, agreed to plead guilty to six securities-fraud felonies and to pay a $650 million fine. But as part of the agreement Drexel had to fire Milken and withhold $200 million in pay and stock purchases from him.

In March 1989, after years of rumors, federal authorities finally charged Milken and his brother Lowell with 98 counts of securities and fraud violations, including mail fraud, wire fraud, and leading a conspiracy to defraud. Most insiders considered the prosecution of Lowell Milken as leverage to force Michael to plea-bargain rather than go to trial, where he might possibly win. Nevertheless, at first Milken and his brother pleaded not guilty, and in June, Milken resigned from Drexel to form his own company, International Capital Access Group (ICAG). Milken also received a temporary boost when the California attorney-general's office announced in August that it had terminated its investigation of Milken. He continued to fight back in the press, arguing through his attorney that the U.S. Attorney's Office had deliberately leaked damaging information to the press.

As the government prepared its case, Milken continued to build ICAG, which he designed to help find capital for minority groups and unions. In the first four months after he formed ICAG he purchased $2.5 million worth of barges to lease to Unimar International, Inc. a shipbuilder and tugboat company based in Seattle that was bought out by its unionized employees in 1987 with help from Drexel. Milken also met with the publisher of New York's black-owned newspaper to develop a bid on the *New York Daily News*. He started plans to lend to developing countries such as Mexico and participated in lending efforts in Australia and Israel along with more mundane reorganizations—car dealerships, entertainment groups, and more than 25 other businesses. Milken also talked to many former Drexel clients, although the ongoing investigation frightened off many potential investors. One former Drexel client said he could not be identified publicly with Milken, and, he added, some banks "have decided that Milken is not a credible person right now." But hundreds of other companies beat down the doors of ICAG, and many other important business figures publicly praised Milken. Steven J. Ross, cochairman of the merged Time-Warner Inc. called Milken "one of the most brilliant financial minds of our time."

Even under the cloud of prosecution, Milken remained indefatigable. He always claimed to have little interest in money: "We're focused on creating value. Wealth is a by-product." That said, Milken had earned $550 million in a single year, and had by some estimates amassed a fortune totaling nearly $2 billion. Yet he still lived in a relatively modest home in Encino and took his kids, along with an entire group of neighborhood children, to the local supermarket on Saturday mornings. Certainly by the late 1980s Milken was not driven by money but by the challenge of completing bigger and more complex deals.

Nevertheless, the future of ICAG depended to a great extent on the outcome of Milken's legal difficulties. For example, he lost many of his trading privileges when Drexel severed its relationship with him in 1988. Possibly as a result of that pressure, and also because of the charges brought against Lowell, Michael Milken reversed his not guilty plea in April 1990. He pleaded guilty to six felony fraud charges in return for the government's agreement to drop all charges against Lowell. His arrangement meant that he would ultimately spend as many as five years in jail and pay a fine of $600 million. However, all racketeering and insider trading charges were also dropped.

Observers argued that three factors changed Milken's plea. First, he did not want to see his brother facing a sentence, especially if the government only used Lowell as leverage against Michael. Second, he saw the guilty plea as a way of clearing the deck for his ICAG. Finally, he made the plea based on an understanding with prosecutors that he and his family could keep the bulk of their personal wealth. And, certainly, the image that had appeared in the media of Ivan Boesky, who while in jail had pumped iron and gotten extremely fit, encouraged Milken in the opinion that he could survive a minimum-security prison.

Hailed as a "massive victory" by the government, according to many editorialists the Milken conviction represented an abuse of RICO and marked a clear-cut attack on capital. Even before the announcement of the deal commentators around the country denounced the government's war on Milken and other capital entrepreneurs. "Without Mike," wrote Martin Sosnoff in the *New York Post*, "MCI would have been crushed by Ma Bell." Milken was "anti-white shoe America." The *Kansas City Star* likened Milken to the 500-pound gorilla that sat anywhere it wanted, except Milken chose "to sit in Beverly Hills and not Wall Street." The *Memphis Commercial Appeal* called him the "free market's modern hero" and the "ultimate outsider."

That, of course, was Milken's greatest crime: he successfully challenged the established Wall Street maxims and also found ways to negate the scle-

rotic political regulatory system. Capital usually manages to do that eventually, but Milken gave it a push. Milken's prosecution raised a larger issue, again taken up by the editorialists, of the usefulness of insider trading laws. Ultimately any transaction is based on knowledge, and some people always have better information than others. Walter Williams argued that such laws were completely lacking in common sense and could be applied to any transaction at random.

Drexel, finding itself "in the prosecutorial hothouse," also cut a deal. The $650 million fine it paid not only cut profits but personnel. In 1986 the company had 10,500 employees and earnings of $522 million. By 1989 employment had dropped by 50 percent, and net income in 1988 sagged to a loss of $167 million. Ironically, Drexel's demise had an immediate effect on the rest of Wall Street. On the day the newspapers announced Milken's deal, rumors surfaced that Drexel sought a merger partner, and the stock and bond markets tumbled. After a brief recovery, Drexel filed for chapter 11 bankruptcy protection in May 1990.

Meanwhile Milken's supporters continued to trumpet his virtues. Not only did Milken's wealth allow him to pay almost half a billion dollars in taxes during his career, but he actively worked for a variety of charities through his Foundation of the Milken Families, founded in 1982. That foundation funded some 500 programs in education, welfare, community services, and health care. The chief charitable beneficiaries included HELP, a Van Nuys organization that cared for children with physical and mental problems.

Milken's long-term effect on American finance ran far deeper than the charities to which he contributed or the taxes he paid or even the companies he financed. In Nevada one estimate credited high-yield bond issues with creating one out of every three jobs. In communications, food products, gaming, movies and entertainment, and supermarkets, Milken and Drexel provided the necessary cash for expansion. "One MCI alone," Milken argued, "was testimony to what you can do to bring capital to a company that needs it but doesn't have an investment-grade rating." He added, "When you see companies growing, you will see people's dreams come true." Because he thought "we needed to find a place for kids when parents worked," he channeled high-yield money into Kinder-Care, Inc. He claimed to have "the honor of raising 60 percent of the dollars in home financing in the United States." Even on the eve of his jail term, Milken continued to sing the praises of junk.

Comparing Milken to J. P. Morgan, one writer sarcastically pointed out that Morgan "never copped a plea." But Morgan was dragged before the Pujo Committee, and he did business at a time before sophisticated securities laws existed. No one can doubt Milken's guilt—he has admitted to violating the law in his guilty plea. Yet future historians will have to determine whether the plea came as a result of the government's threats against Lowell or its determination to destroy the Milken family fortunes. Doubts will also remain, as they do in any state's evidence case, about Levine's evidence against Milken. Finally, observers have raised a new series of criticisms against "insider trading" laws as they now stand.

However, even if one ended Milken's career before he started to trade on insider information (that is, in 1984, according to the accounts of Levine and other witnesses), Milken's impact on corporate finance still would have equaled that of Benjamin Strong or Morgan. He single-handedly democratized the capital markets. He either invented or pioneered high-yield bonds, the use of the 3(a)9 clause, and a variety of warrants, including zero-coupon bonds. Most important, Milken demythologized capital. "Capital is not a scarce resource," he repeatedly taught. He thus supported America's fourth merger wave and helped create the debt explosion of the 1980s. Insofar as the companies he underwrote were concerned, that debt explosion had many beneficial consequences. As of 1990 critics still maintained that the nation's debt hovered at dangerously high levels, but no solid evidence had yet shown that the debt had produced any harm. Instead, Milken, through his junk bond raiders, had made corporate America much more responsive to

stockholders and had virtually ended random expansion by companies. Where Morgan's deals had centralized the railroads and utilities, Milken's deals forced a massive decentralization. Given that many analysts, such as Tom Peters, argued that large corporations had become too unresponsive and slow to the marketplace, and only smaller, more entrepreneurial companies could survive the new global competition, Michael Milken was a man for his age, every bit as much as Morgan was for his.

References:

Connie Bruck, *The Predator's Ball* (New York: Penguin, 1988);

"Drexel: Prosecution and Fall," *Wall Street Journal*, February 15, 1990, p. A14;

George Gilder, "The Drexel Era," *Wall Street Journal*, February 16, 1990, p. A 12;

Jerry Heaster, "Those Who Savage Milken Are Missing the Point," *Kansas City Star*, April 30, 1989;

Robert K. Lifton, "Twilight Zone Economics," *New York Times*, June 29, 1989, p. A23;

"The Man with the High-Yield Vision," *Insight* (June 12, 1989): 8-15;

"Milken Lawyers Say U.S. Has Argued Case Through Press," *Los Angeles Times*, September 15, 1989, section 4, p. 4;

Joe Mysak, "Putting Junk to Rest," *American Spectator*, 23 (May 1990): 34-36;

"The New Milken," *Los Angeles Times*, October 15, 1989, pp. D6, D8;

"Original Thinkers," *Life*, 12 (Fall 1989): 167;

"RICO: Only Repeal Will Do," *Los Angeles Times*, October 25, 1989, p. B6;

"RICO Overkill," *Washington Post*, October 25, 1989, p. A26;

"RICOteering," *Washington Times*, October 17, 1989;

Llewellyn H. Rockwell, Jr., "The Free Market's Modern Hero," *Memphis Commercial Appeal*, April 18, 1989;

Martin Sosnoff, "Milken a Scapegoat," *New York Post*, September 25, 1989.

G. William Miller

(March 9, 1925 -   )

by Robert D. Auerbach

University of California, Riverside

CAREER: Attorney, Cravath, Swaine & Moore, New York City (1952-1956); assistant secretary (1956-1960), president (1960-1968), chief executive officer (1968-1974), chairman, Textron Incorporated (1974-1977); chairman, Board of Governors, Federal Reserve System (1978-1979); U.S. secretary of the Treasury (1979-1981).

G. William Miller applied his exceptional managerial and negotiation skills to turn a relatively small Rhode Island textile firm, Textron Incorporated, into a multibillion-dollar conglomerate in the 1970s. During the presidential administration of Jimmy Carter he served as chairman of the Federal Reserve Board of Governors and then as U.S. secretary of the Treasury. As Federal Reserve chairman Miller, more than his predecessor, Arthur F. Burns, or his successor, Paul Volcker, negotiated the compromises between the executive branch and U.S. Congress that led to the passage of the Depository Institutions Deregulation and Monetary Control Act of 1980, a law that dramatically altered the American banking system.

George William Miller was born in Sapulpa, Oklahoma, on March 9, 1925, the son of James Dick and Hazle Deane (Orrick) Miller. In 1926 the Millers moved to Borger, Texas, where James Miller opened a furniture store that failed during the Great Depression. The young Miller attended Borger public schools and then Amarillo College for two years beginning in 1941. He then enrolled in the U.S. Coast Guard Academy at New London, Connecticut, where he received a B.S. in marine engineering in 1945. From 1945 to 1949 he served as ensign and then lieutenant junior grade in the Coast Guard, working as a line officer in the Pacific theater. He retained a lifelong interest in the Coast Guard, serving as director, president, and chairman of the Coast Guard Academy Foundation beginning in 1969, 1973, and 1977 respectively. Miller met

G. William Miller (Banking: The Journal of the ABA, *January 1979)*

Ariadna Rogojarsky, a Russian émigrée, in Shanghai in the first year of his Coast Guard service, and the couple married on December 22, 1946.

In 1949 Miller left the Coast Guard to attend the School of Law at the University of California, Berkeley, where he received a J.D. degree in 1952. His distinguished law school record includes scholarships and the attainment of the position of editor in chief of the *California Law Review*. He gained admission to the California Bar in 1952 and the New York Bar the following year. Declining higher paying offers from West Coast firms, he joined the New York City firm of Cravath, Swaine & Moore at a $4,000 salary and worked there until 1956. His success in helping Textron win a proxy fight for control of American Woolen Company in 1955 impressed Royal Little, chairman and chief executive officer of Textron.

Little hired Miller that year as an assistant secretary assigned to the examination of acquisition prospects. When Little retired in 1960 his successor, Rupert C. Thompson, Jr., appointed Miller, then thirty-five, president of the company. Miller instituted managerial reforms and continued diversification efforts. Textron products came to include Talon zippers, Polaris snowmobiles, Speidel watchbands, Homelite chain saws, Gorham silverware, Shaeffer pens, and Bell UH-1 ("Huey") helicopters–used extensively in the Vietnam War.

Miller became chief executive officer at Textron in 1968 and chairman in 1974, then left in 1977 to become chairman of the Federal Reserve. Textron sales grew from $246 million in 1956 to $2.8 billion in Miller's final year.

Vice President Walter Mondale conducted the search for a new Federal Reserve chairman in secrecy to keep from embarrassing the controversial but respected sitting chairman, Arthur F. Burns, who was appointed by former president Richard M. Nixon. Miller's appointment to what many consider the most powerful economic policy position in the government came as a surprise, and many experts expressed uncertainty over the qualifications of the dapper, gray-haired Miller. A Senate investigation of charges that Textron made "concealed foreign payments" to officers of the Iranian army in order to sell them helicopters delayed his confirmation. The potential illegality involved the Securities and Exchange Commission requirement to report such questionable payments. Miller testified that he did not know that Iranian general Khatemi owned a sales agency that received $2.9 million in commission on the sale of 500 Bell helicopters to Iran in 1973, and the Senate issued the confirmation in early 1978. In 1980 the Justice Department convened a grand jury to investigate charges that some Textron employees obstructed the 1978 confirmation hearings. Though the Justice Department gave no indication that Miller was the ultimate subject of the 1980 inquiry, the episode generated a further adverse public reaction, this time during a presidential election year. Neither episode appeared to impede Miller's job performance, however.

Miller's credentials included a dependable affiliation with the Democratic party and obvious managerial skill. But he had limited experience in banking and monetary policy.

In his confirmation hearings Miller noted his limited banking experience. He had served as a director of a private bank (the Rhode Island Hospital Trust National Bank) and the Federal Reserve Bank of Boston, both for seven years. He had also served as a member of the Business Council, an advisory board composed of prominent executives sponsored by the Commerce Department, and as a director of the U.S.-USSR Trade and Economic Council and the Polish-U.S. Economic Council.

But he had been an enthusiastic Democrat for years. In 1968 Miller served as a Rhode Island delegate to the Democratic National Convention and in the same year as chairman of Businessmen for Humphrey-Muskie, a campaign fund committee. He had made frequent contributions to the 1968 campaigns of prominent Democrats in the House and Senate. He also served as a panel chairman of the White House Conference "To Fulfill These Rights" in 1966, on the President's Task Force on Hard Core Unemployment from 1967 to 1968, on the Advisory Board of the Coalition of Northeastern Governors in 1976 and 1977, and as chairman of the President's Committee on HIRE (veteran's employment) in 1977. He had actively promoted the revitalization of downtown Providence, Rhode Island, headquarters of Textron, and job opportunities for minorities. Those activities won him praise from members of Congress and labor leaders.

Miller gave the Carter administration the easy money policy it desired. After Carter's election the Federal Reserve under Chairman Burns had increased the rate of growth of the money supply from what it had been during the Ford administration. The change, however, proved insufficient to save the chairmanship for Burns. Miller continued the growth policy, which reached an annual rate of 8.5 percent by October 1978, a fast rate by peacetime standards. But in a speech on November 1, 1978, Carter abruptly changed his priority from economic stimulation to anti-inflation and asked for slower money growth, and Miller complied.

Although Miller had moved to the job of U.S. secretary of the Treasury before the Depository Institutions Deregulation and Monetary Control Act of 1980 was passed, he did more than his predecessor, Arthur Burns, or his successor, Paul Volcker, to nego-

Miller after his terms as chairman of the Federal Reserve Board from 1978 to 1979 and secretary of the Treasury from 1979 to 1981 (by permission of Jeff MacMillan; Forbes, November 3, 1986)

tiate with Congress and the banking industry the details of the most important banking bill since the 1930s. The act authorized the payment of interest on consumer checking accounts for the first time since the 1930s. It applied legally stipulated cash reserve requirements to all commercial banks, credit unions, and savings banks when only member banks of the Federal Reserve System had previously been required to carry such reserves. That part of the bill was an answer to the perceived threat that substantial numbers of member banks would quit the Federal Reserve System to eliminate the reserve requirement.

Miller excelled in the business of negotiation. He was persistent, constructive, and congenial. On technical points he frequently consulted his staff and congressional staff economists, though his lack of training in the technical area placed him at a disadvantage in staff debates and congressional oversight hearings, as the April 17, 1978, excerpt from the *Wall Street Journal* indicates: "The other day, during an appearance before the House Banking Com-

mittee, Ohio Republican Chalmers Wylie questioned him [Miller] about the growth rate of the money supply. The Chairman quickly turned to Stephen Axelrod, a senior Board economist for help—something Mr. [Arthur] Burns, an acknowledged expert, never had to do. 'There are,' says a Fed man, 'a lot of subtleties of the field he doesn't know anything about.' "

Only 16 months after Miller took the chairmanship at the Federal Reserve, President Carter nominated him for secretary of the Treasury to replace Michael Blumenthal, whom Carter fired, apparently because Blumenthal had grown too independent.

The result of the easy money policy of the Federal Reserve under Miller was a 13.3 percent rise in the consumer price index in 1979. The attempt after November 1978 by the Carter administration to stop the inflation and its accompanying high interest rates brought high unemployment and a recession in 1980, the presidential election year. After a decline in the money supply in the first half of

1979, the Federal Reserve, in an attempt to stabilize interest rates, instituted a faster growth rate again. That change made it appear to experts that the Federal Reserve had lost control of money growth. There was fear of a precipitous fall in the international value of the dollar if monetary growth remained rapid. Summarizing views on Miller's reign at the Federal Reserve, one reporter observed that he "has left his successor a monetary policy in disarray." On August 6, 1979, Miller was replaced by Paul Volcker, an individual knowledgeable in banking and monetary policy who had been president of the New York Federal Reserve Bank. Carter nominated Miller for secretary of the Treasury, and the former Fed chairman won confirmation.

Five months after becoming secretary of the Treasury, Miller faced the management of the Chrysler loan bailout. Congress passed a loan guarantee bill on December 20, 1979, authorizing up to $1.5 billion in loan guarantees to Chrysler in a total aid package of $3.5 billion. Miller, made chairman of the Chrysler Loan Guarantee Board, found himself immersed in arguments over extending additional guarantees. The board had to determine whether Chrysler could regain its financial health. Miller monitored Chrysler up to the time he left the Treasury, when the Reagan administration took office in the beginning of 1981.

Miller returned to the private sector after Reagan's election. He was elected a director of Federated Department Stores in 1981, a position he had held previously. In 1983 he announced that a new company under his control, Private Satellite Network, would begin offering satellite television broadcasting facilities and services to businesses and institutions.

References:

Robert D. Auerbach, *Money, Banking, and Financial Markets* (New York: Macmillan, 1989);

Lindley H. Clark, Jr., "Miller's 16 Months," *Wall Street Journal*, July 24, 1979, p. 20;

Hearing Before the Committee on Banking, Housing, and Urban Affairs, United States Senate, Ninety-Fifth Congress, Second Session, on the Nomination of G. William Miller to be Chairman of the Board of Governors of the Federal Reserve Board. January 24, 1978 (Washington, D.C.: U.S. Government Printing Office, 1978).

Charles E. Mitchell

(October 6, 1877 - December 14, 1955)

by Thomas F. Huertas

Citibank NA

CAREER: Various positions, Western Electric Company (1899-1905); assistant to the president, Trust Company of America (1905-1911); founder and president, Charles E. Mitchell & Company (1911-1916); president (1916-1929), chairman, National City Company (1929-1933); president (1921-1929), chairman, National City Bank (1929-1933); chairman, City Bank Farmers' Trust Company (1929-1933); director, Federal Reserve Bank of New York (1929-1931); founder and president, C. E. Mitchell, Incorporated (1933-1935); chairman, Blyth & Company (1935-1955).

Called by many the greatest bond salesman who ever lived, Charles E. Mitchell was also singled out during the Depression as the man "more responsible than all the others put together for the excesses that have resulted in this economic disaster."

Acclaimed in the 1920s, Mitchell was despised in the 1930s and prosecuted by the U.S. government into the 1950s.

Mitchell was born in Chelsea, Massachusetts, on October 6, 1877, to middle-class parents. After graduating from Amherst College in 1899, he went to work for the Western Electric Company in Chicago, rising to assistant manager by 1905. He then moved to New York and into the world of finance, becoming assistant to the president of the Trust Company of America shortly before it was rescued by J. P. Morgan and his associates during the Panic of 1907. In 1911 Mitchell established his own investment banking firm, Charles E. Mitchell & Company.

The success of his investment firm brought Mitchell to the attention of Frank A. Vanderlip, president of National City Bank. In 1916 Mitchell be-

Charles E. Mitchell

came president of its security affiliate, the National City Company, and in 1921 he became president of the bank as well. He continued in both posts until 1929, when he was named chairman of each organization, as well as chairman of a second bank affiliate, the City Bank Farmers' Trust Company. He remained chairman of the bank and its two affiliates until he was forced to resign on February 26, 1933, reportedly at the insistence of president-elect Franklin D. Roosevelt. Shortly thereafter he was indicted for income tax evasion. Disgraced, in debt, and on a federal court docket, Mitchell did not disappear from the banking arena. He fought his way back to the summit of the financial world, beginning with his successful defense against the tax evasion charge.

Mitchell's National City career gave him a prominent place in the annals of business and economic history. During his tenure at National City he transformed the company into a modern, diversified financial services corporation. In managerial terms his accomplishments rank alongside those of executives such as Alfred Sloan of General Motors, who created modern manufacturing enterprises oriented toward the mass market.

As Mitchell put it, National City became the "Bank for all." It provided institutions and individuals around the world with a full range of commercial, investment, and trust banking services. Mitchell's vital contribution was twofold: he added individuals to the customer base, and he separated management from ownership. He started from a strong base. When he joined the National City Company in 1916 he became a participant in the comprehensive strategy developed by Frank Vanderlip and James Stillman to expand the business of National City Bank through product, geographic, and customer diversification. National City's core business had been the provision of commercial banking services to large corporations. Starting in the 1890s, the bank expanded from that domestic wholesale base into investment banking. By 1912–the year of Arsène D. Pujo's House subcommittee probe into the "money trust"–National City Bank had emerged as one of the leading underwriters and distributors of securities in the United States. Geographic diversification became a possibility following the passage of the Federal Reserve Act in 1913, which permitted national banks to open branches abroad for the first time. National City Bank made extensive use of that new power. By the end of 1916 it operated 26 branches in 14 countries.

Mitchell's arrival at National City Company in 1916 also signaled the start of a third thrust: extending the customer base to the individual investor. Vanderlip had long felt that middle-class individuals wanted to get involved in the burgeoning securities market. To tap the potential market, in 1915 National City Company acquired N. W. Halsey and Company, a relatively small investment banking house oriented toward the retail distribution of securities. At the same time, National City Company took over from the bank's bond department its traditional, institutionally oriented investment banking activities. Together with the Halsey acquisition, that made National City Company potentially one of the most dynamic forces in investment banking.

To Mitchell fell the task of transforming potential into reality. Blessed with what Vanderlip later called "an astonishing capacity to create energy," he built a nationwide retail distribution system within three years. By 1919 National City Company had offices in 51 cities across the United States, starting from four in 1916. The new distribution channels the offices provided added to National City Company's ability to place securities, enhancing its role as a leading underwriter.

During the 1920s National City Company participated in or originated nearly one-fourth of all bonds issued in the United States, placing it in the front rank of all underwriters. It actively floated bonds for new entrants to the domestic capital markets, such as foreign firms and governments. By 1929 the company was reputed to be "the largest agency in the world for the distribution of securities."

As president of National City Bank beginning in 1921, Mitchell energetically implemented Vanderlip's comprehensive strategy. Foremost among Mitchell's accomplishments, the bank brought its services to the individual customer. Prior to 1921 National City had predominantly served for large corporations and wealthy individuals. Mitchell changed that. As fast as changes in the banking laws would permit, the bank built up a local branch network in New York City to serve small businesses and individuals. To attract individual customers it offered passbook savings accounts and, starting in 1928, unsecured personal loans. By 1929 National City had more than 230,000 individual accounts.

Alongside that dramatic expansion in individual banking, National City under Mitchell also expanded its core business of commercial banking for domestic corporations and deepened its penetration of existing overseas markets (after rectifying some severe problems in its Cuban branches). By the end of 1929 National City had developed into the biggest bank in the world. It was also one of the strongest. During its expansion in the 1920s National City Bank maintained a high degree of liquidity and a low degree of leverage. That conservative financial posture enabled it not only to survive the banking panics that characterized the Depression but also to help stabilize the banking structure through such steps as the acquisition of the troubled Bank of America (New York) in 1931. According to *Time*, National City's policy made its balance sheet "the envy of every bank in the United States." To Mitchell himself the bank's financial strength was his "deepest source of pride."

The third component of this "financial department store" was trust banking. National City had established a trust department in 1919, soon after legislation clarified its trust powers. During the

1920s the department grew rapidly as a result of extensive marketing to individuals and a merger with People's Trust Company, a local Brooklyn bank. In 1929 Mitchell pushed National City into the front rank of trust companies through a merger with Farmers' Loan and Trust Company, one of the oldest and largest trust companies in the United States. Thus, at the end of 1929 the National City organization enjoyed a leading position in commercial, investment, and trust banking. It was without question the world's leading financial intermediary.

Management comprised the secret of Mitchell's success. Indeed, the inability of Vanderlip and Stillman to reach agreement on the division of ownership and control led to Vanderlip's resignation in 1919 and opened the way for Mitchell. His solution to the problem of ownership and control, the management fund, divorced ownership from management but married reward to performance. The management fund amounted to a contract between owners and managers of the firm concerning the division of risk and reward. Each side guaranteed the other a minimum return in the form of dividends and salary. After those amounts had been paid, remaining profits went to the owners and executives in a four-to-one ratio. The fund assured executives the sort of compensation they could have earned had they been important shareholders in their own institutions or partners in an investment bank. It also stimulated executives to greater efforts and the bank to greater profits.

In that, the management fund certainly succeeded. Profits at the bank more than tripled from 1923, the year of the plan's inception, to 1929. Profits at National City Company grew at a similar rate. Mitchell and other executives benefited accordingly. In the peak years of 1928 and 1929 Mitchell earned in excess of $1 million annually.

The million-dollar income and the accomplishments that justified it made Mitchell a prominent public figure. To many he was a hero, a self-made man who embodied the values future president Herbert Hoover had expounded in his 1922 book *American Individualism*. The press lauded Mitchell, calling him a "dynamic," "potent," "brilliant," "straight from the shoulder executive," and reporters regularly solicited his views on everything from the state of the market to the state of the world. For the *Saturday Evening Post*, the magazine of America's rapidly expanding middle class, what

Mitchell had to say was of "peculiar value and significance."

Then came the Depression. The stock market collapsed, output plummeted, and unemployment soared. As firms failed so did their banks. Depositors of failed banks and investors in securities lost money—in many cases, their life savings. Panic spread, and as the Depression deepened, the public and Congress sought a quick and simple explanation for the calamity.

They found their scapegoats in the "banksters," Mitchell foremost among them. In the midst of the banking panic of 1933 the Senate Banking and Currency Committee conducted hearings regarding stock exchange practices. Theories in vogue at the time, but later discredited, made it appear that banks and bankers were responsible for the economic slide. According to the prevailing credit view of the business cycle, economic stability depended on banks financing only "real bills"—short-term, self-liquidating commercial loans. If banks adhered to that policy, the real bills doctrine held, they would remain liquid, and the total amount of credit would expand in line with the "needs of trade." Banks would not fail, and the economy would remain stable.

From that vantage point activities of the banks in the 1920s seemed to have contributed heavily to the economic catastrophe of 1930-1933. Banks had not restricted themselves to "real bills." Indeed, total commercial loans fell during the 1920s, both absolutely and relative to the banks' holdings of marketable securities and call loans collateralized by securities. To the adherents of the real bills doctrine, that constituted speculation pure and simple. According to the real bills theory, big banks were the worst offenders, because they underwrote and distributed securities directly and through affiliates. Thus, they not only engaged in speculation but also encouraged others to do likewise. To Ferdinand Pecora, the chief counsel of the Senate Banking Committee, the "natural consequence" of such activity was "the catastrophic collapse of the entire banking system of the country." Pecora did not consider it necessary, nor did he try, to prove the link between alleged speculative activity of leading bankers and the failure of the banks they managed or of the banks to which they had sold securities. He felt it necessary only to show that leading bankers had fostered speculation and had personally engaged in it.

Mitchell naturally became Pecora's star witness in Senate Banking Committee hearings, for he was "a rampant bull," the personification of the union between commercial and investment banking. Other possible candidates for star witness did not possess so many useful characteristics. Alfred H. Wiggin, the chairman of the nation's then-largest bank, Chase National, by 1933 served largely as a figurehead and was in any event close to retirement. A. P. Giannini, the head of Transamerica Corporation and a staunch Democrat, had gone into semiretirement well before the crash. J. P. Morgan, Jr., and his partners ran a private bank and did not deal with the public. Pecora later wrote that he picked Mitchell because "National City was one of the very largest banks in the world, and had but recently been surpassed in this country by the Chase National. The prestige and reputation of these institutions were enormous. They stood, in the mind of the financially unsophisticated public, for safety, strength, prudence, and high-mindedness, and they were supposed to be captained by men of unimpeachable integrity, possessing almost mythical business genius and foresight." If Mitchell were convicted, then all banks would stand guilty.

The committee levied three principal charges against Mitchell: that he was personally corrupt, that he (National City Company) sold "unsound" securities, and that he (National City Company) financed speculation by others. Pecora began his questioning by probing into Mitchell's personal finances. He quickly established that Mitchell had earned much more than $1 million in salary and management fund bonuses in 1929 but had not paid any income tax that year because of a capital loss incurred in the sale of National City stock to his wife. Senator Burton K. Wheeler had an extreme but not atypical reaction: "The best way to restore confidence is to take these crooked presidents out of banks and treat them the same way they treated Al Capone when Capone avoided payment of his tax."

The new Roosevelt administration promptly followed Wheeler's advice. It indicted Mitchell for tax evasion on March 24, 1933. The *New York Times* reported that administration advisers felt that "the prosecution of an outstanding violator of the banking law would be the most salutary action that could be taken at this time. The feeling is that if the people become convinced that the big violators are to be punished it would be helpful in restor-

Mitchell at about the time he assumed the presidency of New York's National City Bank in 1921 (photograph by Paul Thompson; World's Work, *July 1921)*

ing confidence shaken by the Senate committee revelations." Despite his full agenda in the New Deal's first hundred days, Roosevelt kept a close watch on Mitchell's indictment and arraignment. In a personal response to a letter from Fredrick A. Houseman, a private citizen, Roosevelt rejected out of hand the former's assertions that the Pecora investigation represented "more of a persecution than an investigation" and that Mitchell had acted in accordance with the income tax law.

Pecora's original reason for probing into Mitchell's finances was probably not to indict him, but to discredit him. Although the public might have difficulty in comprehending the details of bond deals and call loans described in Mitchell's later testimony, it had no trouble at all understanding his failure to pay any income tax. Once the favorite of the press, Mitchell became, beginning in February 1933, "unscrupulous," "shameless," "arrogant," "morally obtuse," and a "consciousless manipulator."

Did those charges contain any substance? In the trial, evidence established that Mitchell had acted on the advice of counsel, that sales of stock to family members were legal, and that many peo-

ple commonly employed such sales to avoid paying tax. Mitchell was therefore innocent, and a jury acquitted him of the criminal charge of tax evasion on June 22, 1933. Attorney General Homer Cummings, aghast at the verdict, declared, "Nevertheless I still believe in the jury system." But, as Robert Winsmore commented in the *Philadelphia Inquirer*, "To pay no more taxes than the letter of the law demands is not only a settled universal custom, but an attribute of human nature. If it is a knavery, then the United States is entirely a nation of knaves."

After Mitchell's acquittal, the Roosevelt administration turned the matter over to the Internal Revenue Service. The commissioner found Mitchell's 1929 tax return deficient and ruled that he was guilty of civil fraud. The Board of Tax Appeals sustained that decision, but the Circuit Court of Appeals modified it, ruling that Mitchell's 1929 return was deficient, but that he was not guilty of fraud. Mitchell appealed the former point to the Supreme Court, but it refused to hear the case in October 1937. Roosevelt then commended E. S. Greenbaum, the government attorney who had worked on the case for four years, for contributing to the public service by "challenging the practices to which Mitchell resorted." The government finally settled Mitchell's tax lien for an undisclosed sum on December 29, 1938.

Was Mitchell's acquittal on the original criminal charge of tax evasion simply the result of the brilliant defense conducted by his attorney, Max Steuer, one of the foremost criminal lawyers in the country? The record suggests that Mitchell had acquired the stock that he later sold to his wife for quite responsible business reasons. Mitchell testified that he had purchased the shares on October 29, 1929, at the height of the panic, in order to offset certain purchases by the National City Company, made without his knowledge, that he thought imprudent. In effect, Mitchell employed his personal fortune to rectify questionable actions by the corporation for which he held ultimate responsibility. It was testimony to his belief that the American system of corporate organization concentrated responsibility "in the hands of one accountable individual."

In September 1929 National City Bank and the Corn Exchange Bank had agreed, subject to approval by the shareholders of the two companies, to merge via an exchange of shares. Each Corn Exchange shareholder was to receive four National City shares for every five Corn Exchange shares he held. Under the McFadden Act of 1927, however, Corn Exchange shareholders who did not assent to the merger had to have the option of receiving cash for their shares. To provide for that eventuality, National City Company agreed to purchase National City Bank shares in the open market for use as treasury stock. Upon completion of the merger, the bank would resell that treasury stock in the open market and use the proceeds to pay cash to the nonassenting Corn Exchange shareholders.

At the time of the merger agreement there was no reason to believe that a significant number of Corn Exchange shareholders would demand cash for their shares. The shares of National City Bank sold in the open market at $492, well above the $450 price below which it would have been more profitable for Corn Exchange shareholders to demand cash for their stock.

Then came the crash. In late October 1929 the stock market collapsed, and on October 28, National City stock threatened to fall below the $450 level. In an attempt to maintain the stock, the National City Company, during trading hours on Octo-

ber 28, purchased 71,000 shares of National City Bank stock at a total cost of $32 million.

Mitchell first learned of the extent of those purchases at 5:30 P.M. that day, when he returned to the bank after a series of meetings at J. P. Morgan & Company and at the Federal Reserve Bank of New York regarding the stock market crash. Mitchell was surprised by what National City Company had done. Its purchases had gone far beyond the incidental magnitude originally envisioned by all parties to the merger agreement, and posed a threat to the entire National City organization. National City Company did not have the cash to pay for the stock and could not borrow from the bank for that purpose. Dumping the stock back on the market would have driven the stock down further, produced a significant loss for National City shareholders, and undermined the program of steadying the entire stock market that Mitchell and other financial leaders had agreed to implement earlier that day.

Mitchell therefore decided to reverse the actions taken by the National City Company to the extent that he could. On the morning of October 29, before the market opened, he pledged the bulk of his personal fortune, 30,000 shares of National City stock, as collateral for a line of credit of $12 million from J. P. Morgan & Company, an amount equal to approximately 10 percent of the stockholders equity of National City Company. Mitchell then instructed the Company to sell him personally as much stock as needed in order to maintain its financial integrity. The National City Company did that, and Mitchell wound up at the close of business on October 29 with an additional 28,300 shares of National City stock at a total cost of $10.6 million. Although that failed to save the merger with Corn Exchange, it did keep National City Company and National City Bank in sound condition.

Mitchell did stand to benefit personally from his purchase of National City shares from the National City Company, since that helped the firm in which he had invested the bulk of his personal fortune. The action clearly placed Mitchell at risk, however, for it involved an increase in his personal leverage and a commitment to pay Morgan regardless of what happened to National City stock. The obligation to Morgan in fact grew quite burdensome to Mitchell. When the price of the stock fell in 1930 and 1931, Mitchell put up additional collateral, including second mortgages on his personal residences. At the time of the trial in 1933, the loan from Morgan was undercollateralized by $2.5 million, so that Mitchell was practically insolvent. However, Mitchell neither defaulted nor declared bankruptcy, nor did Morgan foreclose; Mitchell ultimately repaid the loan in full with interest.

To characterize Mitchell as "morally obtuse" thus seems too harsh. He had a strong sense of personal responsibility, which led him to put his own fortune at risk in order to correct a mistake made by one of his subordinates. He certainly acted naively in selling the stock to his wife. He failed to consider the adverse effect such a sale, no matter how legal, would have on his and National City's public image when the public learned of it. But then neither he nor anyone foresaw the economic catastrophe that would unfold during the three years prior to his testimony at the Pecora hearings. What might have been prudent tax planning in 1929 the public perceived by 1933 as callous greed.

Revelations about Mitchell's personal finances led to charges that he (National City Company) had sold unsound securities to the unsuspecting public. Congress and the media looked in 1933 at the prices of the bonds the company had underwritten in the 1920s, saw that many of them traded at a small fraction of their original issue price, and concluded that those bonds had been worthless all along, but that the investment bankers had hidden that "fact" from the public. Much of the criticism focused on foreign bonds, and National City Company had probably sold more foreign bonds to the public during the 1920s than any other investment house. According to Congress, National City Company and the other investment houses knew, or should have known, at the time of the original underwriting that the bonds were unsound—that is, certain to default. As Senator Hiram W. Johnson put it, in selling the foreign securities the investment bankers had abused the public's "childlike confidence." Historians have also judged Mitchell guilty as charged. Samuel Eliot Morison and Henry Steele Commager, for example, lampoon Mitchell and assert that "great banking houses palmed off on gullible investors South American bonds that they knew to be almost worthless."

National City Company advertising lent a certain credence to those charges. During the 1920s it had portrayed itself not as a salesman of securities but as a financial adviser to prospective investors. It realized that individuals knew little about investing,

and through its advertising and brochures it attempted to teach the rudiments to "person(s) of limited resources, all of whose capital and income are necessary to insure life's future comforts." And, if a customer had questions about investing, National City Company encouraged him to "be as frank and open in discussing his investment problems as he is discussing legal problems with his lawyer or his health problems with a doctor."

Following the crash, National City Company was charged with malpractice. But the plummeting price of bonds did not prove that National City had acted with negligence in the 1920s any more than a lost case or uncured patient would prove a lawyer or a doctor guilty of malpractice. What the investment bank knew, or could have known, at the time that it gave the advice is the pertinent factor. When underwriting a bond, National City Company did give its "seal of approval," meaning that it recommended the issue for purchase by its customers, provided the purchase of the bond did not disturb the portfolio diversification that it urged all customers to maintain. Thus, by underwriting a bond issue, National City Company asserted that the bonds carried a fair price, that is, a price that reflected the risk of the bond at the time of the original offering. It did not claim that the original bond price represented a fair price for the bond throughout the life of the issue. Indeed, both Mitchell and National City Company warned investors that bonds carried risk and that every added measure of security in a bond "has its own special price tag attached." External conditions could change, which might affect the ability of the borrower to repay. If those changes improved the borrower's ability to repay, the price of the bond would rise; if the changes reduced the borrower's ability to repay, the price of the bond would decline, and possibly decline sharply.

The latter occurred during the Depression. The rapid decline in output and prices in the United States and other industrialized countries drastically reduced the ability of all borrowers, domestic and foreign, to repay the debts that they had contracted in the 1920s. Prices of domestic and foreign bonds fell sharply during the Depression, and many borrowers went into default, including domestic corporations and municipalities and foreign governments.

To have expected investment bankers, or anyone else for that matter, to have foreseen the severity and duration of the Depression, an economic catastrophe without parallel in American history, is unreasonable. Yet Congress expected investment bankers generally, and Mitchell in particular, to have done just that.

What Mitchell and National City Company actually did was underwrite securities of high quality. From 1921 to 1933 National City Company played a role in bringing to market more than 1,200 issues with a value of more than $13 billion. Most of those issues were bonds, almost all of which carried a rating by Moody's, so that investors had an independent assessment of the risk. More than 85 percent of the 1,189 bond issues underwritten by National City Company during the years 1921-1933 had a rating as investment grade securities (Baa or better) when the bank offered them to investors. Even after the passage of the Glass-Steagall Act, such investment-grade bonds were judged safe enough for banks to invest in them.

The third charge against Mitchell claimed that National City Bank had financed speculation by others. Congress and later historians pointed specifically to National City's extension of call loans in March 1929 in apparent defiance of the Federal Reserve Board. That allegedly sustained the stock market boom, enabling stock prices to rise to ever greater heights until October 1929, thus making the ensuing crash all the more severe. Mitchell's statements were indeed provocative. When stock market prices broke sharply on March 1929 and call money rates shot up to 20 percent, Mitchell saw a panic in the making. To stem it he offered to lend up to $25 million in the loan market, "whatever the attitude of the Federal Reserve Board," which had for more than a year tried to limit such allegedly speculative loans. Senator Carter Glass of Virginia, coauthor of the Federal Reserve Act, accused Mitchell of "slapping the Federal Reserve Board squarely in the face" and with treating its policies "with contempt and contumely." In 1979 John Kenneth Galbraith wrote, "The Federal Reserve Board remained silent. . . . It meant that it conceded Mitchell's mastery."

That statement reverses the actual situation. Although Mitchell's words were ill-advised, his actions were not. He made the commitment to lend in the call money market only after receiving approval from George L. Harrison, governor of the Federal Reserve Bank of New York, and the assurance of the Reserve Bank's support at the discount window. When interest rates began to climb rapidly, Harrison telephoned Mitchell, stating that "in circumstances . . . bordering on the 'panicky' the Federal Reserve does not want and can not be in the position of arbitrarily refusing loans on eligible paper to member banks." Harrison told Mitchell, "The call money market is now the problem of the New York money market"; that is, the member banks and the private bankers. Even the Federal Reserve Board agreed that Mitchell had done the right thing. One member of the board, Charles S. Hamlin, noted in his diary, "None of the B[oar]d criticized what Mitchell did—it was merely what he said."

Was Mitchell then completely devoid of responsibility for the Depression? No, for he had the responsibilities of a central banker as well as a commercial and investment banker. In the former capacity Mitchell participated in the formulation of monetary policy—the root cause of the Depression.

Mitchell became a central banker on January 1, 1929, when he started a three-year term as a Class A director of the Federal Reserve Bank of New York. The position gave Mitchell some influence over policy, for many still considered the Reserve banks as "bankers' banks" and saw them as independent of the Federal Reserve Board in Washington. Moreover, of the 12 regional Reserve banks, the one in New York had the most influence. Thus, Mitchell was a member of a key policy making unit from 1929 to 1931, from the onset to the midst of the Depression.

Like his fellow directors, Mitchell viewed the economy as inherently stable and the business cycle as a natural, self-equilibrating phenomenon. In a speech to the shareholders of National City Bank on January 13, 1931, he outlined the position in more detail: "It is a well known fact that the course of business is subject to alternating periods of activity and depression, more or less pronounced according to the circumstances of the time and the extent to which the movements are carried by the prevailing spirit of optimism or depression. The slowing down of the industrial organization is evidence in itself that something is out of order in it, and that adjustments are necessary."

To Mitchell, recovery would result from a restoration of balanced economic conditions. He looked to retrenchment by firms and governments to eliminate waste and to provide a solid base for balanced expansion. Thus, the economy would ultimately

*Mitchell (center) with his attorney, Max Steuer (left), and a smiling U.S. marshal during Mitchell's
1933 tax evasion trial*

heal itself, despite the initial decline implied by retrenchment. As he commented at the start of 1931, "During the second half of the year [1930] the curtailment of expenditures of all kinds, on the part of consumers, distributors and producers, was very pronounced. The first effect of these economies undoubtedly was to intensify the position, and if everybody accomplishes this, the ultimate effect must be to strengthen the general situation. This process is the reverse of that by which, through individual expenditures and debt making, the general situation became seriously involved. It has been a year of debt paying on a great scale, which necessarily means curtailment of purchases and a check upon enterprise, but it also means that when this policy has run its course new sustained buying power will appear in all markets. Gradually the new conditions will make themselves felt."

Mitchell and other directors felt the Federal Reserve needed to facilitate, and perhaps accelerate, the natural self-adjusting process of the economy. The question was how and when to act. The answer depended on central bankers' assessment of where the economy stood and where interest rates stood relative to the equilibrium path.

In 1929 Mitchell and other central bankers agreed about the problem facing the economy but disagreed about what policy to adopt. To all concerned the problem seemed to be "overheating," especially in the stock market. To avoid a bigger bust later called for curtailing the boom then, either by raising interest rates or rationing credit. The New York directors pushed for the former, arguing that an increase in the discount rate would moderate the boom before it got out of hand. The Federal Reserve Board in Washington pushed for the latter, arguing that denying discount privileges to member banks that extended call loans would limit speculation and spike the boom in the securities markets before it threatened "legitimate" businesses.

By 1930 and 1931, in contrast, policymakers did not even agree about the problem facing the economy. Some thought that the deepening economic slide was part of the natural self-adjustment process and saw no need for intervention. Others thought that the slide was abnormally steep and that the Federal Reserve should take steps to brake and then reverse it. Still others shifted back and forth, from one position to the other, depending on their view of where the economy and interest rates stood at the time. A majority of the directors of the Federal Reserve Bank of New York, including Mitchell, comprised the third group.

In October 1930, April 1931, and December 1931, for example, Mitchell opposed open market purchases of securities by the Federal Reserve since he felt that such intervention would not help, and might possibly harm, the economy. He reasoned from the low level of rates relative to their historical averages that rates had already fallen low enough to spark a recovery. The markets needed confidence, and further declines might actually undermine confidence by depressing the earnings of already weak banks.

In contrast, in September 1930, May 1931, and August 1931, Mitchell favored intervention by the Federal Reserve in order to stimulate the economy. Moreover, he advocated that Federal Reserve intervention should be strenuous if it was going to act at all. Anything less would not have the favorable impact on confidence that was needed to lift the economy out of depression. Mitchell and his fellow directors ultimately refrained from such a bold policy, however, for fear of exhausting the Federal Reserve's supply of "free gold," the amount of gold over the 40 percent minimum required by law as backing for Federal Reserve notes. As late as December 1931 Mitchell recommended that "the Federal Reserve system conserve its ammunition." His fellow directors concurred.

The result of such vacillation was inaction. In the face of one of the worst economic declines in the nation's history the Federal Reserve did nothing. It failed to act as a lender of last resort, and it failed to maintain the money supply. Although done with the best of intentions, it produced the worst of results—the Great Depression.

For 50 years common wisdom held that banks and bankers helped cause the Great Depression. Bankers allegedly speculated outrageously in the 1920s and lured the public into following their example. The Depression was perceived as the consequence, and the New Deal banking legislation,

especially the Glass-Steagall provisions separating commercial and investment banking, was held to be necessary as a safeguard against the repetition of economic catastrophe. That premise must be subject to doubt. In a reexamination of the activities of Mitchell, the most notorious "bankster," evidence in his favor requires reconsideration. Congress and the Roosevelt administration, in their zeal to find a scapegoat for the Depression, chose to ignore that evidence. After his battle against tax evasion charges Mitchell then opened his own investment firm, C. E. Mitchell, Incorporated. In 1935 he became chairman of Blyth & Company, a West Coast investment banking house, and proceeded to build that firm into one of the nation's leading underwriters. His success prompted new prosecution by the government. In November 1950 Mitchell became a central figure in the government's antitrust suit against 17 investment banking houses "and especially Blyth"–a case that Judge Harold Medina ultimately dismissed on May 19, 1953, as based on "ill-founded rumors, conjecture and age-old suspicion." Mitchell died on December 14, 1955, again a multimillionaire and once more a respected figure on Wall Street.

References:

Milton Friedman and Anna J. Schwartz, *A Monetary History of the United States, 1867-1960* (Princeton: Princeton University Press, 1963);

John Kenneth Galbraith, *The Great Crash*, 50th anniversary edition (Boston: Houghton Mifflin, 1979);

Robert A. Gordon, *Economic Instability and Growth: The American Record* (New York: Harper & Row, 1974);

Thomas F. Huertas and Harold van B. Cleveland, *Citibank, 1812-1970* (Cambridge, Mass.: Harvard University Press, 1985);

Herman E. Krooss, *Financial History of the United States*, second edition (New York: McGraw-Hill, 1963);

Ferdinand Pecora, *Wall Street Under Oath* (New York: Simon & Schuster, 1939);

George Soule, *Prosperity Decade* (New York: Holt, Rinehart, 1947);

"Troubles of Mitchell," *Time* (November 18, 1929);

Elmus R. Wicker, *Federal Reserve Monetary Policy, 1917-1933* (New York: Random House, 1966).

Money Instruments: CDs, IRAs, NOW Accounts, Money Market Mutual Funds, and Travelers Checks

The negotiable certificate of deposit, or CD, pioneered by Walter Wriston of Citibank in 1961, allowed customers who could deposit larger amounts of funds over a predetermined length of time to earn higher interest rates. At first Citibank made CDs available only to corporations, set a minimum amount of $100,000, and paid 1.25 to 1.75 above normal passbook interest rates. The CD differed from the time certificate that had existed prior to 1961 because it was negotiable on the market: it could be exchanged before the time limit arrived. Citibank achieved that by persuading a New York dealer in securities to start a secondary market for CDs, thus ensuring a place to buy and sell them. Soon the amount required to purchase a CD fell to $5,000, then $1,000, making CDs a viable investment instrument for people of average means.

Individual Retirement Accounts, or IRAs, appeared in 1982, when Congress, concerned about the effects of taxation on savings rates, allowed individuals to put aside a sum of money each year and to deduct that amount from their taxes. The saver had to keep the money in an interest-bearing account until the saver reached the age of fifty-five and a half, at which time he could start withdrawing the money with only minor tax penalties. If the saver waited until age sixty, he paid no penalty whatsoever and had the benefit of tax-free compound interest as well as the deductions he had taken over the course of his working years.

In 1972 Massachusetts savings banks began to offer new interest-bearing draft and checking accounts, called NOW (negotiable order of withdrawal) Accounts, to circumvent laws that prohibited paying interest on checking accounts. Technically, NOWs constituted savings accounts having withdrawal slips that received the name "near money" and were negotiable and similar to checks. A legal provision subjected NOWs to a 40-to-60-day advance notice before withdrawal, a policy virtually no one followed. After much lobbying by commercial banks, Congress conceded that the sophistication of financial instruments had exceeded the limits of the law and in 1981 legalized NOWs and three other financial instruments: Automatic Transfer Accounts, wherein a depositor could request an automatic transfer from a higher-paying deposit account to cover an overdraft on a lower-paying checking account; share accounts at credit unions; and electronic terminal banking at Savings and Loan institutions.

Money Market Mutual Funds satisfied a need of individuals who wanted to invest in short-term paper but could not or would not invest heavily in stocks. A Mutual Fund constituted an open-end investment trust: an investment company whose capital was not fixed but which issued shares and purchased old shares according to demand. One type of mutual fund, the Money Market Mutual Fund, provided the investor with shares of stock representing a broad portfolio of short-term paper.

Travelers checks, although not strictly a money instrument, served as money for millions of travelers by the late twentieth century. Originated in 1891 by the American Express Company, the checks were 100 percent insured by the issuer against loss or theft in return for a fee. Companies' businesses depended on the quick and easy replacement of the checks.

—Editor

John Pierpont Morgan, Jr.

(September 7, 1867 - March 13, 1943)

by Steven Wheeler

New York Stock Exchange Archives

CAREER: Partner, Drexel, Morgan & Company (1892-1895); partner (1895-1913), senior partner, J. P. Morgan & Company (1913-1940); partner, J. S. Morgan & Company (1898-1909); director, United States Steel Corporation (1909-1943); partner (1910-1913), senior partner, Morgan, Grenfell & Company (1913-1943); chairman, J. P. Morgan & Company, Inc. (1940-1943).

Investment banker and heir to the Morgan banking empire, J. P. Morgan, Jr., continued many of his father's methods and policies in banking and corporate finance. During World War I he distinguished himself and J. P. Morgan & Company as a leader in financing foreign governments. He earned enormous international prestige and personally came to symbolize American wealth, privilege, and financial power.

John Pierpont Morgan, Jr., was born in Irvington-on-Hudson, New York, on September 7, 1867, the only son among four children, to Frances Tracy Morgan and banker J. P. Morgan. From his childhood he was known as "Jack" to distinguish him from his father. He was raised in the Episcopal church and remained an active layman throughout his life. He was educated at St. Paul's School at Concord, New Hampshire, and received his bachelor's degree from Harvard College in 1889. His academic career was undistinguished. Following graduation, young Morgan spent several months touring Europe before settling into his career.

In 1890 Morgan started working at the banking firm of Jacob C. Rogers & Company of Boston. Rogers was a former partner and the Boston agent of Junius S. Morgan, head of J. S. Morgan & Company in London and Morgan's grandfather. Later that year Morgan married Jane Norton Grew, and the couple moved to New York. They subsequently had four children, two sons and two daughters.

John Pierpont Morgan, Jr.

In 1891 Morgan went to work in his father's private banking house, Drexel, Morgan & Company, and received a promotion to partner the following year. Three years later the firm's name was changed to J. P. Morgan & Company. There Morgan learned the rudiments of banking and securities underwriting. During his apprenticeship, the firm managed many notable railroad reorganizations following the Panic of 1893: the Erie Railroad in 1894, creation of the Southern Railway System—a consolidation of 30 companies—in 1894, and the Northern Pacific in 1896. In 1895 the elder Morgan shored up the U.S. Treasury's dwindling gold reserves with an infusion of $65 million in gold, much of it obtained abroad. Under the shadow of his strong father, J. P. Morgan, Jr., exerted little influence over the course of the firm's business during these years.

On January 1, 1898, at the age of thirty, Morgan was made a partner in the London affiliate, J. S. Morgan & Company. Two weeks later Morgan and his family left for England. Founded by his grandfather in 1864, J. S. Morgan & Company remained the most important American banking house operating in London. Morgan's main objectives while in London were to learn the British central banking system and to look about London for English partners in order to convert the firm into a British concern. He ultimately chose the partners–E. C. Grenfell, Vivian Smith, and others–who eventually constituted Morgan, Grenfell & Company.

Morgan eagerly looked forward to his new assignment, but most of his work at J. S. Morgan & Company was routine and dull compared to the New York firm's business at the time. Virtually exiled by his domineering father, Morgan accepted his role at J. S. Morgan & Company resignedly. He amused himself with an active social life among the English titled nobility and developed a love for Britain that stayed with him throughout his life.

Morgan's most important responsibility during his London years involved negotiations for a loan to the Russian government. In October 1905 he traveled to St. Petersburg to consult with the Russian finance minister when the elder Morgan abruptly called off the deal from New York. Although J. P. Morgan, Jr., finally persuaded his father to reconsider, convincing him to authorize a loan of 100 million French francs, Russia's political unrest halted negotiations for the loan.

In 1905 Morgan and his family returned to New York where he worked diligently alongside his father at J. P. Morgan & Company for the next seven years. During the Panic of 1907 the elder Morgan helped stem the tide of panic by organizing a pool to stabilize the banks and the stock market, bringing some degree of order to New York's financial community. The junior Morgan went to France to negotiate a loan of gold from the Banque de France in order to stabilize the American financial system. To make the loan the Banque demanded a guarantee from the U.S. government that it could not legally give. Over the next month negotiations stalled, and Morgan returned to New York.

Following his missions of 1905 and 1907 Morgan's responsibilities at J. P. Morgan & Company grew. He acted as liaison between the New York and the London houses. Both firms actively participated in financing Latin American governments, a highly competitive area of international banking at the time. In 1909 the stockholders elected Morgan a director of the United States Steel Corporation, the giant conglomerate organized by his father in 1901.

Morgan oversaw the conversion of J. S. Morgan & Company to Morgan, Grenfell & Company at the end of 1909. The old firm was completely liquidated and a new partnership established with capital supplied by J. P. Morgan & Company and Drexel & Company, the Philadelphia affiliate. In reorganizing the London bank, Morgan intended "to bring all the houses closer together with more mutual information as to the condition, plans, and investments of each."

The prestige garnered by the senior Morgan during the Panic of 1907 also brought glaring publicity that seriously damaged the firm's public esteem. Charging that a "money trust" composed of Wall Street financiers controlled the majority of the nation's corporate financial resources, a special House committee on banking and currency–known popularly as the "Pujo Committee"–began hearings late in 1912. The investigation exposed the intricate structure of the financial system and highlighted the Morgan bank's alleged control of corporate America through interlocking directorates. The elder Morgan himself appeared as the investigation's star witness, and he died a few weeks after giving his testimony.

With the death of J. P. Morgan, Morgan, Jr., then aged forty-five, assumed responsibility as senior partner of J. P. Morgan & Company. He promptly dropped the "Jr." from his name.

Morgan inherited an estate from his father worth $78 million, much smaller than anticipated, with most of its value represented by his vast art collection. Short of cash to pay inheritance taxes and run the banking business, Morgan sold many important pieces of art that had been promised to New York's Metropolitan Museum of Art, raising about $8 million. The sale brought on a storm of public criticism, but Morgan chose not to explain or defend his actions. He later donated the rest of the huge collection to the Metropolitan and other museums.

Morgan (right) with colleague Henry P. Davison in 1913 (courtesy of the Pierpont Morgan Library)

Morgan soon took J. P. Morgan & Company in a new direction. He believed amalgamation and concentration had gone far enough and decreed that the firm would adhere to regular banking and securities underwriting business, lending money on security and floating high quality bond issues. Early in 1914 Morgan and his partners resigned from the boards of nearly 30 corporations. Morgan publicly acknowledged that the action came in response to a change in public opinion. Other investment banks divested themselves of many corporate directorships as well.

When World War I broke out in 1914, the financial havoc in Europe presented to U.S. investment bankers new demands for their services and unusual opportunities for profit. Morgan took a leading role in financing the belligerent governments, supplying them with war materiel and reorganizing their economies at war's end. While his father had developed American railroads and industry by attracting foreign capital, Morgan transformed the United States into a creditor to Europe

and firmly established New York as the international capital of finance.

In the two days following the assassination of Archduke Franz Ferdinand, investors throughout Europe began liquidating their security holdings, much of it top-quality American stocks and bonds. Stock exchanges throughout the world closed down, leaving the New York Stock Exchange the only major market where worldwide panic could vent itself. Morgan called two conferences of bankers and stock exchange officials to assess the situation and decide whether the stock exchange should remain open. Faced with a deluge of sell orders from Europe and with the brokerage community's need of $30 million credit to continue operating, the group decided to close the exchange just minutes before its usual opening hour on July 31.

In 1915 Morgan agreed to act as agent for Great Britain in the purchase of war supplies in America. Later the company signed a similar agreement with France. J. P. Morgan & Company set up an Export Department under the direction of partner Edward R. Stettinius, Sr., that furnished an ever-increasing supply of food and munitions to the Allies and organized the production of war materiel in the United States. The Allies channeled orders for more than $3 billion worth of war supplies through the Morgan bank and bought much of it on an enormous credit advanced by the Morgan firm. Morgan's handling of Allied war purchases earned the firm $30 million in commissions. The encouragement of war production in the United States provided a great service after America entered the conflict in 1917.

A staunch Anglophile, Morgan strongly supported the Allied cause from the start of the conflict, often in the face of President Wilson's policy of neutrality. In 1915 a radical German sympathizer attempted to assassinate Morgan, shooting him twice. His wounds were not serious, however, and he recovered quickly.

After Wilson lifted restrictions on loans to belligerents in 1915, Morgan organized a syndicate that floated $500 million in 5 percent bonds guaranteed by Great Britain and France. The loan proved difficult to place, given the opposition of German, Irish and peace groups in the United States but Morgan—without charging the usual fee—organized a syndicate of 2,200 banks that underwrote the loan. That represented the largest foreign bond issue ever sold in America by the Morgan bank and Morgan's most notable achievement. The Morgan bank itself subscribed $30 million of the loan. Additional loans to the Allies quickly followed. The firm negotiated a total of $1.5 billion in loans for the Allies in the years before the United States entered the war.

When America joined the conflict in 1917, the government took over the purchase and supply of war materiel to the Allies. The firm actively promoted bond sales and subscribed $50 million in the first Liberty Loan campaign. At Morgan's invitation, the Coast Guard pressed his yacht *Corsair* into war service as a submarine chaser.

In the postwar years Morgan arranged nearly $2 billion in loans to Great Britain, France, Belgium, Italy, Austria, Switzerland, Japan, Argentina, Australia, Cuba, Canada, and Germany. The firm also floated $4 billion in domestic bonds during the postwar decade.

In 1922 Morgan served on a Committee of Bankers that met in Paris to reconcile the reparations provisions of the Versailles Treaty to economic realities. The committee considered the possibility of selling a German loan abroad to repay the reparations debt but concluded that Germany's credit needed to be strengthened and her debts scaled down in order for a loan to be successful. The committee's work was an important preliminary to the Dawes Plan that two years later set annual reparations payments and attempted to stabilize the German economy. An integral part of the plan involved a German loan that the Morgan bank successfully floated in nine financial markets.

In 1929 Morgan served as a delegate to the Committee of Experts, under the leadership of Owen D. Young, to advise the Reparations Commission on revision of the Dawes Plan. The committee produced the Young Plan, which reduced the level of Germany's reparations payments and established the Bank for International Settlements. J. P. Morgan & Company served as the bank's American correspondent and headed a syndicate that floated the American portion of the Young Plan loan, amounting to nearly $100 million.

When the stock market crashed in October 1929, Morgan was abroad, but members of the leading financial institutions in New York met in his office to confer on the crisis. They organized a pool of $240 million to stabilize key securities on the stock exchange, but stock prices and the American economy followed a steady, disastrous decline over the next years.

The stock market crash and subsequent depression shone a spotlight on investment bankers and on Morgan in particular. The Senate Banking and Currency Committee launched an investigation led by counsel Ferdinand Pecora to determine the causes of the 1929 crash and examine the operations of investment bankers. Morgan's appearance as a witness in the spring of 1933 aroused intense public interest. The private banker, Morgan testified, unregulated by any government authority, was instead governed by "a code of professional ethics and customs which could never be expressed in legislation, but has a force far greater than any law." The key to that code was credit: the private banker's "most valuable possession; it is the result of years of fair and honorable dealing and, while it may be quickly lost, once lost cannot be restored for a long time, if ever."

Morgan reluctantly disclosed the firm's partnership agreement to the committee, making clear his absolute power in the firm's dealings and policies. He could fire any partner, remained the sole and final arbiter of any dispute in the firm, and alone determined the firm's assets and the amount due any departing partner. Nonetheless, Morgan's activity in the firm had decreased over the years, its day-to-day operations increasingly in the hands of the partners.

The Pecora hearings revealed no breach in Morgan's fiduciary responsibilities. Instead, the firm had conservative management and dealt mostly in bonds, avoiding speculative ventures and showing considerable responsibility to its clients. But the investigation renewed charges of concentration of power in Wall Street's financial circles and focused on the close, continuing ties between a few New York investment bankers and the great railroad and industrial corporations of the nation. The committee's investigation revealed that Morgan partners held 167 directorships in 89 corporations representing combined assets of $20 billion.

The most startling revelation of the investigation involved Morgan's underwriting of three holding companies during 1929: United Corporation, Allegheny Corporation, and Standard Brands, Inc. All three had issued a large amount of common stock—a type of security the Morgan firm had never before offered. Concerned about the risk of selling the securities to the public, the firm instead offered them privately, and at cost, to a select list of customers composed of prominent bankers, brokers, and businessmen. The list also included many well-known politicians and public figures. The press seized the issue of the preferred customer lists, characterizing them as polite bribes that offered favored friends an opportunity to make a profit without much risk.

In another greatly publicized revelation, Morgan and his partners paid no income tax during the depression years of 1931 and 1932. The public was unmoved by the explanation that the partners had suffered a capital loss of $73 million between 1929 and 1932. The sensation caused by the Pecora hearings paved the way for sweeping government regulation of the banking and securities business.

The Banking Act of 1933 forced the separation of commercial and investment banking. Morgan decided the firm would continue to accept deposits and operate as a private commercial bank and the firm gave up its securities business. Several Morgan partners left the firm to set up Morgan, Stanley & Company in 1935 as an investment bank.

In 1936 Morgan again testified before a senate committee investigating the activities of private bankers. Senator Gerald P. Nye accused Wall Street bankers of driving the United States into World War I in order to protect their investments in the Western Allies. Morgan consistently denied that the supplies and credits furnished by his firm to Britain and France in any way influenced President Wilson's foreign policy. Ultimately, all Nye's charges were discredited and the investigation ended in a shambles.

In 1940, J. P. Morgan & Company became J. P. Morgan & Company, Inc., a corporation chartered under the laws of New York. The firm found incorporation necessary because of the difficulties of keeping the bank's capital intact as elderly partners died or withdrew. Morgan assumed the position of chairman of the board of the new corporation, with Thomas W. Lamont as vice-chairman and head of the Executive Committee, and other partners became directors of the corporation. In 1942 the stock in J. P. Morgan & Company, Inc., was offered to the public.

Although Morgan remained titular head of the Morgan bank, his active participation in the firm had diminished since the end of World War I. Morgan skillfully chose able partners, and they often sought him out for advice, but Lamont effectively ran the business, presiding at the partners' meetings and providing the firm's leadership.

In his leisure years Morgan amused himself with frequent cruises on his yacht *Corsair*, annual trips to his English country estate, grouse shooting in Scotland, and hunting in North Carolina, the Adirondacks, and Jekyll Island, Georgia. He also actively raced smaller sailing vessels, served as commodore of the New York Yacht Club, and frequently financed the America's Cup defender.

One of Morgan's passions was the private book collection, known as the Morgan Library, that he inherited from his father's estate. The library constituted a magnificent collection of medieval and Renaissance manuscripts, early printed books, fine bindings, literary manuscripts, autograph letters, modern printed books, and prints and drawings. Morgan frequently started his day with a visit to the library, housed in a building next door to his mansion on East 36th Street. In 1924 he gave the library to a board of trustees to administer as a public research facility.

On a fishing trip to Florida in the spring of 1943 Morgan suffered a heart attack, followed by a stroke a few days later. He died on March 13 at Boca Grande, Florida, at the age of seventy-five. Funeral services were held in New York at the family church, St. George's, Stuyvesant Square, and in London at St. Margaret's, Westminster. Morgan's ashes were deposited in the family vault in Hartford, Connecticut. His two sons, Junius Spencer Morgan, Jr., and Henry Sturgis Morgan, inherited the bulk of his estate.

In addition to heading the various Morgan banks in New York, Philadelphia, London, and Paris, Morgan also served as a director of the Aetna Insurance Company, International Mercantile Marine, Northern Pacific Railroad, Pullman Company, New York, New Haven Railroad, and First Surety Company of New York.

Under Morgan's quiet leadership the Morgan bank financed and armed the Allied powers during World War I and aided the postwar reconstruction of Europe, earning for the senior partner even greater international prestige than his father. He materially aided the transformation of the United States from a debtor to a creditor nation and firmly established New York City as the international capital of finance. At his death he left the Morgan banking empire on a weaker footing than the elder Morgan, in large part due to differing economic times and government attitudes toward business.

Reference:

John Douglas Forbes, *J. P. Morgan, Jr., 1867-1943* (Charlottesville: University of Virginia Press, 1981).

Archives:

A private collection of the papers of J. P. Morgan, Jr., is on deposit at the Pierpont Morgan Library, New York City.

Henry Morgenthau, Jr.

(May 11, 1891 - February 6, 1967)

by Larry G. Gerber

Auburn University

CAREER: Publisher, *American Agriculturist* (1922-1933); chairman, New York Agricultural Advisory Commission (1928-1930); New York conservation commissioner (1930-1932); chairman, U.S. Farm Credit Administration (1933); U.S. undersecretary of the Treasury (1933); U.S. secretary of the Treasury (1934-1945); chairman, United Jewish Appeal (1947-1950); chairman, board of governors, American Financial and Development Corporation for Israel (1951-1954).

Henry Morgenthau, Jr., was one of Franklin D. Roosevelt's closest advisers and served as secretary of the Treasury longer than any other person in American history except Albert Gallatin. He helped shape the government's monetary and tax policies during the Great Depression and World War II. He also played a key role in the establishment of the International Monetary Fund and World Bank and advocated a controversial proposal, the Morgenthau Plan, for deindustrializing postwar Germany.

Morgenthau, the son of Henry and Josephine Sykes Morgenthau, was born in New York City on May 11, 1891. His father was a wealthy real estate investor, philanthropist, and prominent member of New York's German-Jewish community. The elder Morgenthau became an important financial supporter of Woodrow Wilson's initial campaign for the presidency and served as American ambassador to Turkey from 1913 to 1916.

The younger Morgenthau attended public schools in New York before enrolling in Phillips Exeter Academy. He went on to study at the Sachs Collegiate Institute and Cornell University, but he left Cornell in 1911 without having completed his studies in architecture. After trying several odd jobs, Morgenthau had finally begun to find a source of personal satisfaction doing volunteer work at the Henry Street settlement house in New York when he contracted typhoid fever, and doctors advised him to go west to convalesce. While re-

Henry Morgenthau, Jr.

cuperating in Texas, he made a decision to pursue a career in farming.

Once back in New York, Morgenthau returned to Cornell to study agriculture. School, though, was never much to his liking, and within months he again left Cornell without earning a degree. In 1913 he purchased several hundred acres of farmland in Dutchess County, New York, and embarked on a career as a "gentleman farmer," taking particular pride in his apple orchards and dairy herd. Three years later Morgenthau married Elinor Fatman, a graduate of Vassar and a relation of the wealthy Lehman family of New York. The couple eventually had two sons, Henry and Robert, and a daughter, Joan.

Morgenthau unsuccessfully tried to enlist in the army after the outbreak of World War I but the army rejected him because of poor eyesight. Before the war ended he visited his father in Turkey and also traveled to England and France, playing a role in arranging for a shipment of American tractors to France to increase farm production there.

During the war years Morgenthau also first met and became close friends with Franklin D. Roo-

sevelt, a Dutchess County neighbor whose Hyde Park home was 20 miles from Morgenthau's farm. Morgenthau's career in public life would subsequently be shaped by his enduring friendship with Roosevelt. In 1920 he served as Dutchess County campaign manager for the Cox-Roosevelt presidential ticket and continued throughout the 1920s to involve himself in local civic affairs.

When Roosevelt ran for governor of New York in 1928, Morgenthau acted as his advance man. After becoming governor Roosevelt named Morgenthau chair of New York's Agricultural Advisory Commission. Morgenthau had already established a reputation as an advocate of farm interests, having become publisher in 1922 of the weekly *American Agriculturist*. He remained personally involved in the paper until he moved to Washington in 1933. While serving as chair of the Agricultural Advisory Commission, Morgenthau proved influential in supporting tax reductions and increased state services for New York farmers. Following Roosevelt's reelection as governor, Morgenthau obtained a new appointment as New York's Conservation Commissioner. In that position he helped develop a reforestation program that later served as a model for the New Deal's Civilian Conservation Corps.

Roosevelt's election as president in 1932 resulted in speculation that Morgenthau would become secretary of agriculture. The president-elect, however, first asked Morgenthau to head a proposed new federal agency to deal with the problems of the unemployed. Morgenthau declined the offer but agreed to come to Washington with Roosevelt to take charge of all government lending programs for farmers. At that time American agriculture faced perhaps the greatest crisis in its history, with slightly more than one-half of all farm debt then in default.

Morgenthau accepted an initial appointment as governor of the Federal Farm Board, an agency established during the Hoover administration to help stabilize farm prices through the purchase of surpluses. After supervising the dismantling of the unsuccessful Farm Board, Morgenthau headed the newly created Farm Credit Administration (FCA). He moved energetically to reorganize the government's farm lending programs and to have the Federal Land Banks reduce interest rates on existing farm mortgages. Within its first year and a half of existence the FCA helped to refinance one-fifth of the nation's total farm mortgage debt.

Even though Morgenthau played an important role in the New Deal's early farm program, he was not very sympathetic to the production restrictions and processing tax that constituted central parts of the program of the Agricultural Adjustment Administration (AAA), the New Deal's principal organization dealing with the farm problem. Instead, he favored devising measures to increase the demand for farm products. Morgenthau never openly opposed the AAA, but the only production restrictions he believed to be justifiable were those resulting from the reforestation of marginal lands.

Morgenthau did not restrict his role in the early months of the New Deal to farm policy. Roosevelt called upon him to help initiate the contacts with the Soviet Union that led to the reestablishment of diplomatic relations in 1933. While still serving as head of the FCA, Morgenthau also became directly involved in formulating and implementing one of the most controversial policies of the early New Deal, Roosevelt's gold purchase program.

With a downturn in prices in July 1933, a major debate took place within the Roosevelt administration over various aspects of monetary policy. Most officials in the Treasury Department, the Bureau of the Budget, and the Federal Reserve supported international cooperation among the monetary authorities of the principal capitalist nations as the best means of stabilizing prices. Roosevelt, however, had recently rejected that approach with his "bombshell" message to the London Economic Conference.

In his quest for an alternative policy designed to raise domestic prices, Roosevelt asked Morgenthau to arrange a meeting at the White House with George F. Warren, a Cornell University economist and former member of the New York Agricultural Advisory Commission. Warren contended that increasing the price of gold through a sustained program of government purchases would result in an increase in the overall price level. In effect, a gold purchase program would serve as an indirect means of devaluing the dollar. Morgenthau had long known Warren and also eagerly sought a way to increase farm prices. He became an influential supporter of Warren's unorthodox monetary theories. When Treasury and Justice Department lawyers argued that the president had no legal authority to initiate a program of gold purchases, Morgenthau enlisted the services of FCA counsel Herman Oliphant, who found a legal basis for such action in existing statutes.

Operating through the Reconstruction Finance Corporation (RFC), Roosevelt undertook the gold purchase program in late October. At the time the market price of gold was $29 an ounce. Although Warren's plan required that the government pay more than the market price for the gold it purchased, it also needed to prevent speculators from accurately predicting the specific price the government would pay at any particular time. Consequently, while the gold buying program functioned, Roosevelt conferred each morning with Morgenthau, Warren, and RFC head Jesse Jones to set, in a rather arbitrary fashion, the price of gold for that day. Roosevelt finally put an end to the experiment in January 1934, signing into law at that time the Gold Reserve Act, which officially set the value of gold at $35 an ounce (up from the previous official value of $20.67).

Most historians and economists agree that Warren's monetary and price theories had little validity and that the government's gold purchase program proved ineffective in raising the general price level. Morgenthau and Roosevelt's willingness to follow Warren's advice is often cited as evidence of both men's economic ignorance. Yet, even if Morgenthau and Roosevelt failed to perceive the theoretical weaknesses of Warren's scheme, their support for the gold buying program proved a politically useful means of deflecting pressure from Congress for more radical inflationary measures. Indirectly, at least, the program also contributed to the evolution of a more flexible monetary system that depended less on a rigid international gold standard, an objective that John Maynard Keynes advocated in the 1930s.

In addition, the entire episode marked a first step in a shift in power over the nation's money supply and exchange transactions from the banks of the Federal Reserve System, particularly the New York Reserve Bank, to the executive branch. Before the new official value of gold went into effect, the Gold Reserve Act allowed the Treasury to take control of all gold held by Federal Reserve banks by paying the old official price of $20.67 an ounce. Out of the windfall profits resulting from revaluation, the act authorized the Treasury to create a $2 billion Exchange Stabilization Fund that henceforth enabled the Treasury to exercise some of the powers of a central bank, including the ability to add to the nation's bank reserves by purchasing government securities and foreign exchange, as well as gold.

A few weeks after Morgenthau's involvement in the implementation of the gold purchase program began, Roosevelt decided to move his trusted friend from the FCA to the Treasury Department. Roosevelt's first Treasury secretary, William Woodin, had developed a serious illness soon after taking office, and the undersecretary, Dean Acheson, vehemently opposed Roosevelt's unorthodox monetary policies. In mid November Roosevelt replaced Acheson with Morgenthau, whom he also then designated as acting secretary. On January 1, 1934, Morgenthau was officially sworn in as secretary of the Treasury.

Morgenthau brought to his high office a strong personal loyalty to President Roosevelt, a deep-seated humanitarian commitment to relieving the suffering of the millions of Americans impoverished by the Great Depression, and a firm belief in the wisdom of a balanced federal budget. As an ardent New Dealer, he supported an increase in the power of government to regulate business and to provide the destitute with some degree of protection from want. However, he never accepted the ideas of the Keynesian revolution. Throughout the 1930s he continued to call for fiscal conservatism within the Roosevelt administration. While he thought that large-scale relief expenditures were necessary to get the country through the crisis of the Depression, he never wavered in his belief that the country needed the restoration of a balanced budget to reestablish the business confidence required for a solidly based recovery.

From the moment he took over the Treasury, Morgenthau hoped to find suitable means of raising additional revenues in order to hold down the federal deficit. Thus, while favoring the development of the New Deal's Social Security program, he insisted upon a self-financing system based on payroll taxes. Morgenthau believed that other forms of new taxation could be developed not only to raise needed revenues, but also to achieve a more equal distribution of wealth and to eliminate what he considered to be undue concentrations of economic power in the business world.

Morgenthau presented his first comprehensive tax reform package to Roosevelt in December 1934. The proposals, drafted largely by Herman Oliphant, whom Morgenthau had brought over to the Treasury from the FCA, called for a graduated inheritance tax, new gift taxes, a reduction in oil, gas, and mining depletion allowances, and two new taxes then being urged on Roosevelt by Felix Frankfurter, one on intercorporate dividends and the other on undistributed corporate profits.

The Treasury secretary played a leading role in pushing the Revenue Act of 1935 through Congress, even though in its final form the law differed considerably from Morgenthau's original proposals. The tax bill omitted both the inheritance and undistributed corporate profits taxes that Morgenthau had wanted but included increased estate taxes, a surtax on upper incomes, an intercorporate dividends tax, and a graduated corporate income tax. In spite of being watered down significantly from Morgenthau's initial program, the bill came to symbolize what the business community widely perceived as the emergence of a more hostile attitude on the part of Roosevelt and the New Deal toward both the wealthy and business in general.

The Supreme Court's decision striking down the AAA's processing tax and the congressional passage of the veterans' bonus bill over Roosevelt's veto in 1936 forced the Treasury once again to look for new sources of revenue. Morgenthau opposed the adoption of a new comprehensive processing tax as placing too heavy a burden on the average consumer. Instead, he supported Oliphant's proposal to revive the idea of a tax on undistributed corporate earnings as a means of simultaneously raising revenue, increasing disposable income, and discouraging the growth of monopoly power in the economy. After a very heated debate in Congress, the Revenue Act of 1936 established, in token form, a graduated tax on undistributed profits. So strong was the opposition of business even to that minimal tax, however, that only two years later, Congress, in effect, repealed it over Morgenthau's strenuous objections. Although in his first five years as Treasury secretary Morgenthau devoted a great deal of time and energy to tax reform, the New Deal had actually done little by 1939 to change the nation's basic tax structure.

Morgenthau achieved more success in helping bring about changes in the Federal Reserve System. A conservative with regard to fiscal policy, Morgenthau at the same time generally supported "easy money" and tended to harbor suspicions of bankers, especially Wall Street bankers. During his first year as Treasury secretary he felt that the Federal Reserve's Open Market Committee had not fully cooperated with his efforts to expand the money supply and keep interest rates low. He believed that the members of the Open Market Committee, who were then elected by the boards of directors of the regional Federal Reserve banks, were more concerned with their own portfolios than with the well-being of the country as a whole. Consequently, Morgenthau became an influential supporter of Marriner Eccles's proposals to modify the Federal Reserve System, proposals that led to the Banking Act of 1935.

Morgenthau had first invited Eccles, a Utah businessman and banker who also emphatically favored "easy money" as a way to revive the economy, to come to Washington in early 1934 to serve as an assistant secretary of the Treasury. In June of that same year Morgenthau proved instrumental in getting Eccles named to the Board of Governors of the Federal Reserve System. Although Morgenthau and Eccles came to disagree over details, they both wanted to see legislation adopted to change the composition of the Federal Reserve's Open Market Committee in order to give the government, or at least individuals appointed by the president, more power over the money supply. In the course of the debate over the reform of the Federal Reserve System, Morgenthau's suspicion of bankers led him to suggest that the government purchase stock in the Federal Reserve to insure public control over not only the Open Market Committee but also the system's regional banks. In the end Morgenthau willingly accepted the compromise terms of the Banking Act of 1935. The bill reorganized the Open Market Committee, dominated henceforth by the members of a reconstituted Federal Reserve Board, and gave to the new board increased powers over reserve requirements and the selection of officers of the regional banks of the system.

Morgenthau's concerns about bankers and monopoly power also caused him to express doubt about the benefits of branch banking and bank holding companies. In the late 1930s he found himself involved in a lengthy and well-publicized dispute with A. P. Giannini's Bank of America and its parent company, the Transamerica Corporation, over the nature of the bank's investments and the level of dividends paid by the bank to its holding company. After a prolonged investigation Bank of America agreed in 1940 to make some essentially minor concessions in response to Treasury concerns.

Although as Treasury secretary Morgenthau's primary responsibilities involved financial and monetary matters, he also became one of the Roosevelt administration's earliest and most forceful advocates of a firm policy to deter Japanese and German expansionism. As early as 1937 he began to consider the possibility of freezing Japanese assets in the United States as a form of retaliation for Japanese aggression in China. In the wake of the Munich conference of 1938 he urged on Roosevelt "the need for *positive action*" to "check the aggressors," including a program of military preparedness, a billion-dollar effort of preclusive buying of strategic raw materials needed by the Germans and the Japanese, and a loan to China. Before the end of 1939 he called for an embargo on the sale of all strategic materials to Japan and Germany.

When war broke out in Europe in 1939 Morgenthau played a crucial role in helping the British and French make purchases of war materiel in the United States. To facilitate their procurement of materiel he convinced the British and French to set up a joint purchasing mission that would operate through the New York Federal Reserve Bank rather than through private banks, as the Allies had done in World War I. Subsequently, Roosevelt gave the Treasury the assignment of drafting the legislation creating the Lend-Lease program. Morgenthau himself served as the principal contact with the British delegation headed by Keynes in the early negotiations over the terms of Lend-Lease aid.

A staunch supporter of aid to Britain in the period before Pearl Harbor, Morgenthau had already concluded by May 1941 that American entry into the war would be necessary to prevent a British defeat. He insisted, however, that the British would have to sell off a significant portion of their foreign assets to make at least partial payment for the goods they would receive from the United States. Throughout the war years he remained a hard bargainer on that issue.

The coming of war greatly altered the nature of the problems confronting the Treasury Department. As depression gave way to a war-generated boom, Morgenthau found himself confronted with the task of financing unprecedented levels of federal spending while trying to hold down the inflation historically associated with full-scale war mobilization.

During the course of the war the Treasury secretary consistently called for tax increases that went far beyond what either Congress or Roosevelt wanted to support. In 1939, he pushed for strict excess profits taxes. Although Congress incorporated such taxes into the Revenue Acts of 1940 and 1941, their rates fell far below that advocated by Morgenthau. He unsuccessfully proposed major increases in social security taxes, with the condition that Congress increase significantly the retirement benefits paid in later years. Morgenthau sought to avoid making the tax system more regressive and effectively opposed calls for a national sales tax; but he did come to support the two most dramatic and long-lasting wartime changes in the American tax system, the implementation of payroll withholding and the extension of the income tax to millions of Americans who had never before been subject to it. Whereas in 1939 only four million Americans had filed income tax returns, the new tax system established by the Revenue Act of 1942 resulted in nearly 50 million Americans paying income tax by war's end.

Even with the increase of federal tax revenues from approximately $5 billion dollars in 1939 to nearly $45 billion in 1945, Morgenthau had the responsibility of directing the biggest borrowing program in the nation's history. Between July 1940 and July 1945 the Treasury had to finance an added federal debt of $211 billion. Morgenthau resisted calls to implement a program of compulsory saving, fearing that such a program would make Congress even less willing to pass needed taxes. Instead, he developed a two-pronged approach to the problem of financing the war debt. First, he initiated a massive campaign to convince Americans to buy government bonds voluntarily, building on the practice he had introduced in 1935 of selling to individual purchasers small-denomination savings bonds that would come to maturity after ten years. Nonbank investors, both private individuals and corporations, ultimately purchased almost 60 percent of the new debt generated during the war.

Second, Morgenthau won a commitment from the Federal Reserve Board to purchase any government securities that the government could not sell at par on the open market. That allowed the Treasury throughout the war to market government securities bearing remarkably low rates of interest and thereby to keep down both inflationary pressures and the long-term costs of war financing. Although relations between the Treasury and the Federal Reserve had often been strained during the 1930s, after the outbreak of war the relationship

grew more harmonious, as the Federal Reserve surrendered some of its control over the determination of the size and composition of its banks' portfolios. The Federal Reserve Board's cooperation added a critical component to the Treasury's success in bringing about a reduction in the average rate of interest on all federal obligations to less than 2 percent at war's end.

Within days after United States entry into World War II, Morgenthau considered the possibilities that might arise in the postwar world for a reconstruction of the international monetary system. He had little expertise in the complicated realm of international finance, but he generally understood that competitive devaluations and unstable exchange rates acted as disruptive influences on the world economy and had retarded worldwide economic recovery during the 1930s. Before World War II ended Morgenthau played an important role in the establishment of two new international institutions, the International Monetary Fund (IMF) and the International Bank for Reconstruction and Development (World Bank).

The roots of the IMF can be traced back to the Tripartite Agreement of 1936. Morgenthau played an instrumental part in working out that accord with the British and French as a means of trying to avoid competitive devaluations. Although the three nations did not agree to fixed exchange rates, the governments involved committed themselves to utilize their own stabilization funds to help maintain orderly markets for the currencies of each signatory to the agreement. At the time the pact was signed, Morgenthau saw it as an important expression of unity among the major Western democracies in the face of the growing threat of totalitarianism.

When in December 1941 Morgenthau asked his assistant, Harry Dexter White, to initiate plans for the postwar restructuring of the international monetary system, he had in mind the creation of a much more broadly based inter-Allied stabilization fund than had been possible in 1936. He envisioned building a world order in which a smoothly operating multilateral system for settling accounts and maintaining stable exchange rates would allow for an expansion of trade that would contribute to both peace and prosperity. Morgenthau also intended to create an international monetary authority that would act as an instrument of "sovereign governments and not of private financial interests," so that "the usurious money lenders" would be

Secretary of the Treasury Morgenthau and President Franklin D. Roosevelt (courtesy of the Franklin D. Roosevelt Library)

driven "from the temple of international finance." In the process, he hoped to "move the financial center of the world from London and Wall Street to the United States Treasury."

Given his own lack of technical expertise, Morgenthau relied on White to draft the specific plan the Treasury first put forward in 1942. Over the next two years White also did most of the negotiating with the British to try to resolve differences between the U.S. Treasury plan and the plan developed by Keynes on behalf of the British government. Morgenthau did, however, head the American delegation and serve as presiding officer at the Allied nations conference at Bretton Woods, New Hampshire, in July 1944 that produced the final agreement for the establishment of the IMF and World Bank. He also then directed the carefully orchestrated campaign that resulted in congressional approval of the Bretton Woods agreements the following year.

The IMF represented a major new effort at international cooperation to stabilize (though not fix) exchange rates and to tide over member nations ex-

periencing temporary balance-of-payments problems. To accomplish those purposes member nations committed to the IMF a total of $8.8 billion in gold and currencies, with the United States supplying slightly over one-third of the total. The Bretton Woods agreements recognized the dollar as an international reserve currency convertible to gold at a value of $35 an ounce. At the same time the World Bank, with a proposed capitalization of $10 billion, was also established to make or guarantee loans for reconstruction and development.

Throughout the planning stages for the IMF and World Bank Morgenthau hoped that the Soviet Union would actively participate in the new financial system. The Soviets did send a delegation to the Bretton Woods Conference, and Morgenthau's willingness to accede to their demands for a larger than originally proposed IMF quota helped convince the Soviets to sign the Bretton Woods agreements of 1944. The subsequent development of Cold War tensions, however, as well as the Soviets' reservations about involvement in international institutions designed principally for market economies, kept the Soviet Union from ultimately participating in either the IMF or the World Bank when those institutions began operations after the war.

Morgenthau also played a central role in the policy deliberations relating to another key issue affecting the postwar world, the fate of Germany. After learning in August 1944 of State Department proposals for a generous postwar treatment of Germany, Morgenthau took it upon himself to develop an alternative plan based on the assumption that future world peace required making "Germany so impotent that she cannot forge the tools of war." By September 1 the Treasury had prepared the first draft of what would come to be known as the Morgenthau Plan. In its final form the plan called for transferring East Prussia to Poland and the Saar to France and then dividing the remaining German territory into three separate states. Germany's industrial base was to be dismantled, even to the point of flooding the coal mines of the Ruhr. The plan envisioned sizable reparations payments, but only in the form of the removal of capital equipment, forced labor, and the confiscation of Germany's foreign assets. Since Germany was to be deprived of its industrial capacity, reparations out of current production would be impossible. In addition, Morgenthau called for a thorough campaign of denazification.

As a Jew, Morgenthau may well have had a special antipathy toward the Germans, but he did not base his approach to the problem of what do with Germany primarily on a desire for revenge. He was convinced that only through a concerted program of deindustrialization could Germany's future potential for waging war be eliminated. Such a policy, he believed, would have the added benefit of helping the postwar recovery of the British economy, since it would do away with a principal source of competition for British industry. Morgenthau also thought that a hard peace would be welcomed by the Soviets and thus contribute to postwar cooperation between the two emerging superpowers. In fact, since his plan would have prevented reparations payments to the Soviets out of current German production, Morgenthau advocated a $10 billion American credit for the Soviets to aid them in reconstructing their devastated country.

Morgenthau, moreover, did not consider it a terrible punishment to force the Germans to return to an agricultural lifestyle. Because of his own Jeffersonian agrarian bias, he thought that living in a pastoral environment would actually help the Germans

reestablish a sense of moral values in the aftermath of the disaster of Nazism.

Although Morgenthau's proposals met with strong opposition from both the War and State Departments, Roosevelt had the Treasury secretary present his views at the Quebec Conference with British prime minister Winston Churchill in September 1944. At the conference Roosevelt and Churchill signed a document that reflected the influence of Morgenthau's ideas in its call to turn Germany into "a country primarily agricultural and pastoral in its character." Morgenthau, at the time, considered the Quebec conference "the high spot of my whole career in the government." Roosevelt, however, quickly retreated from the Morgenthau Plan when it became an issue in that fall's presidential election.

More important, the Morgenthau Plan continued to receive harsh criticism from officials in the War and State Departments who argued not only that German industry was necessary for the restoration of a vigorous European economy but also that a weakened Germany would inevitably result in a more important role for the Soviet Union in central Europe. Roosevelt, Churchill, and Stalin subsequently discussed many aspects of the Morgenthau Plan at the Yalta meeting the following February but made no firm commitment to that approach to dealing with postwar Germany. When Harry Truman became president, what little chance remained that the government might adopt the Morgenthau Plan disappeared. Truman rejected virtually all the assumptions underlying the plan and refused Morgenthau's request to participate in the Potsdam Conference at which Allied policy for the occupation of Germany was to be decided. Their dispute over the issue led directly to the Treasury secretary's forced resignation from office in July 1945.

Clearly the influence Morgenthau exerted on the course of events during the 1930s and 1940s had depended on his special relationship with Franklin Roosevelt. He had proved himself an effective and conscientious administrator, but his loyalty and willingness to serve Roosevelt's purposes appeared the most distinctive aspect of his public career.

Following his departure from government Morgenthau became involved in various philanthropies. Even though he had not been a Zionist before World War II, his largely unsuccessful attempts to help find a safe haven for Jewish refugees during the war transformed him into an active supporter of Jewish causes in the later stages of his life. He served as general chairman of the United Jewish Appeal from 1947 to 1950 and as chairman of the board of governors of the American Financial and Development Corporation for Israel, which handled a $500 million bond issue for the new nation. He also collaborated closely with Yale historian John Morton Blum, who utilized Morgenthau's extensive diaries and papers to write *From the Morgenthau Diaries*, a three-volume account of Morgenthau's public career.

Morgenthau's wife of more than 40 years, Elinor, died in 1949. Two years later he married Marcelle Puthon Hirsch. Morgenthau suffered two heart attacks in the early 1950s but in subsequent years spent a good deal of time traveling. After a long illness, Morgenthau died on February 6, 1967.

Publications:

"Bretton Woods and International Cooperation," *Foreign Affairs*, 23 (January 1945): 182-194;
Germany is Our Problem (New York: Harper, 1945);

"Our Policy Toward Germany," *New York Post*, November 24-29, 1947.

References:

John Morton Blum, *From the Morgenthau Diaries: Years of Crisis, 1928-1938* (Boston: Houghton Mifflin, 1959);
Blum, *From the Morgenthau Diaries: Years of Urgency, 1938-1941* (Boston: Houghton Mifflin, 1965);
Blum, *From the Morgenthau Diaries: Years of War, 1941-1945* (Boston: Houghton Mifflin, 1967);
Milton Friedman and Anna J. Schwartz, *A Monetary History of the United States, 1867-1960* (Princeton: Princeton University Press, 1963);
Sidney Hyman, *Marriner S. Eccles: Private Entrepreneur and Public Servant* (Stanford: Stanford University Graduate School of Business, 1976);
Warren F. Kimball, *Swords or Ploughshares? The Morgenthau Plan for Defeated Nazi Germany, 1943-1946* (Philadelphia: J. B. Lippincott, 1976);
David Rees, *Harry Dexter White: A Study in Paradox* (New York: Coward, McCann & Goghegan, 1973).

Archives:

The papers of Henry Morgenthau, Jr., are at the Roosevelt Library, Hyde Park, New York.

Morris Plan Banks

by Martha May

Bowdoin College

Morris Plan Banks provided an important source of consumer credit during the first half of the twentieth century, primarily to individual borrowers for small purchases.

Founded in 1910 by Arthur J. Morris, a Norfolk, Virginia, lawyer, the first Morris Plan bank emulated the cooperative industrial banks of Europe and extended loans to working people "of good character." The banks generated approximately $8 in profit for every $100 loaned. They also tapped a large pool of customers unable to secure loans from commercial banks and unwilling to use the other common source of small loan credit, the pawnshops. The average Morris Plan customer obtained a loan of $250 in 1936.

Persons who could provide two cosigners or collateral such as stocks and bonds or personal property qualified for Morris Plan loans. The plan operated through the use of investment installment certificates. The borrower signed a note for a one-year loan and paid the bank 6 percent interest on the amount, then used the remaining money to purchase an investment certificate at the bank, payable in monthly installments. Occasionally Morris Plan banks also utilized the deposit account device, to which the borrower made payments.

The use of investment installment certificates and deposit accounts allowed Morris Plan banks to circumvent state usury laws while making the rate of interest twice the nominal amount. After the 1940s, as states changed banking laws to accommodate personal laws, the Morris Plan banks no longer resorted to certificates.

Morris initially developed his idea with franchising in mind. He organized the Norfolk-based Fidelity Corporation in 1912 to expand the plan, and by 1914 the Industrial Finance Corporation formed in New York to do the same thing. Those corpora-

Arthur J. Morris, originator of the Morris Plan cooperative bank system in 1910

tions usually held 25 percent of a Morris bank's capital stock. In 1925 the Morris Plan Corporation of America was incorporated in Virginia; that organization changed its name to Finance General Corporation in 1956.

Morris Plan banks flourished or declined along with fluctuations in the consumer economy. By 1920, 103 Morris Plan banks were operating, mainly in the East with the majority in Massachusetts. The Great Depression limited the growth of the system, and by 1940 only 87 of the banks remained. Most of those had entered the commercial business through the sale of investment certificates and the provision of other general banking services.

The Morris Plan Corporation also experimented with other consumer services. In 1917 the corporation formed the Morris Plan Insurance Society in New York City. Between 1918 and 1924 it contracted with the Studebaker automobile corporation to finance consumer purchases of Studebaker products. It also created the Industrial Acceptance Corporation to discount retail trade acceptances.

The Morris Plan Corporation continued as a force in the consumer loan business until the 1960s, when rising interest rates rendered its special services obsolete.

References:

Ira B. Cross, *Financing an Empire: History of Banking in California* (Chicago: Clarke, 1927);

Peter Herzog, *The Morris Plan of Industrial Banking* (Chicago: Shaw, 1928);

Ray B. Westerfield, *Money, Credit, and Banking* (New York: Ronald, 1947).

Dwight W. Morrow

(January 11, 1873 - October 5, 1931)

by Diane B. Kunz

Yale University

CAREER: Attorney, Reed, Simpson, Thatcher & Barnum (1899-1913); partner, J. P. Morgan & Company (1914-1927); U.S. ambassador to Mexico (1927-1930); U.S. senator, New Jersey (1930-1931).

Dwight W. Morrow was one of the century's most capable investment bankers as well as a prominent diplomat and politician. In his role as a partner of J. P. Morgan & Company he participated in many of the important post-World War I reparations negotiations and currency stabilizations. As ambassador to Mexico he helped ease some of the difficulties between his host nation and its overbearing neighbor. Advocacy of a moratorium on German war reparations highlighted his brief U.S. Senate career.

Morrow was born on January 11, 1873, and grew up in a poor family in Allegheny, Pennsylvania. His father worked as a teacher of mathematics and an elementary school principal. With scanty funds Morrow aimed toward an appointment at West Point. His campaign met with success until the nomination was withdrawn when the school learned that his older brother was already a student there. Fortunately, Henry Gibbons, a family friend, had recently received an appointment as professor of Greek at Amherst College. He arranged for Morrow to receive an Amherst scholarship, and Morrow entered there in September 1891.

For Morrow the next four years comprised a pivotal experience that remained central to his existence. He later devoted as much as 20 percent of his correspondence each year to Amherst matters. Academically, the college far expanded his horizons. Although very intelligent and scholarly in inclination, Morrow had received a poor secondary school education. He developed a particular interest in history. That fascination stayed with him and played a part in his successful diplomatic career. He also bene-

Dwight W. Morrow (courtesy of Harris & Ewing)

fited from living in a college environment and seeing how someone from a comparatively disadvantaged background could obtain prominence and influence. Finally, while at Amherst, Morrow met Elizabeth Reeve "Betty" Cutter, the Smith College student he later married.

After graduation Morrow worked for one year at his brother-in-law's Pittsburgh law firm and then, in September 1896, entered Columbia Law School. At that time Columbia attracted many socially prominent and wealthy students who did not wish to leave New York. Franklin D. Roosevelt attended (without graduating) a decade later. Mor-

Morrow (right) in Panama in 1922, during his tenure as a partner in J. P. Morgan & Company, with his brother, Canal Zone governor Jay J. Morrow, and their mother, Clara Johnson Morrow

row met many students there whose acquaintance proved helpful in years to follow. After Morrow graduated, his Amherst professor arranged for him to become a law clerk at the Wall Street firm of Reed, Simpson, Thatcher & Barnum in October 1899. While at that time Wall Street associates received no salary, the firm made an exception in Morrow's case when he said that without a salary he could not afford to join them.

Morrow's outstanding ability and willingness to put in long hours rapidly made his reputation at the firm. He still found the time to become engaged to Elizabeth Cutter in June 1901. She was the second major influence in his life. Betty Cutter, raised in Cleveland, Ohio, came from a poor branch of a wealthy family. Capable, intelligent, and ambitious, she provided the worldly presence that helped drive the more aesthetic Morrow to the heights of financial success. After their marriage they moved to Englewood, New Jersey. Morrow commuted daily to his Wall Street office, becoming a partner of his firm in 1905 and an even more prominent corpo-

rate lawyer. Then he found interesting diversions such as work for Amherst and foreign travel and began to tire of practicing law. Fortuitously, in late 1913 the firm of J. P. Morgan & Company invited him to become a partner.

J. P. Morgan then had the reputation as the most powerful and notorious firm of private bankers in the United States. Under the leadership of J. Pierpont Morgan, the firm created the U.S. Steel Corporation, the nation's largest company, and controlled the majority of the country's railroads. Morgan's overweening financial role in American financial affairs had recently been exposed by the Pujo Senate committee, charged with investigating the "money trust." But quietly the House of Morgan reached out to talented men from nondescript backgrounds such as Morrow and Thomas Lamont. That willingness to expand the firm's horizons partly accounted for its continued success during World War I and in the postwar period.

Morrow joined Morgan & Company in July 1914, emerging overnight as a nationally known figure. He simultaneously became a partner in Morgan Grenfell, the firm's London office, Morgan Harjes & Cie, the Paris branch, and the Philadelphia firm of Drexel & Company, all of which followed firm practice. The outbreak of World War I presented the Morgan firm with an opportunity to underwrite a revolution in world finance. Prior to the war, British bankers ran the international financial system, which was based on the gold standard. Not just European or colonial markets depended on London; American financial markets and the commodities trade so hinged on British finance that when the war erupted the value of the pound on American exchanges virtually doubled and the U.S. markets faced paralysis. The cooperation of the Treasury Department and American bankers signaled a fundamental shift in prevailing financial winds, led, in part, by the Morgan bank. More important, when the British government decided that it needed an American purchasing agent to coordinate the giant volume of war orders placed in the United States, it selected the House of Morgan. As the war continued Morgan also arranged massive loans for the British and French governments; Morrow worked on those and also worked on the New Jersey War Savings Committee once the United States entered the conflict.

The United States emerged from "the war to end all wars" as the world's largest creditor; Brit-

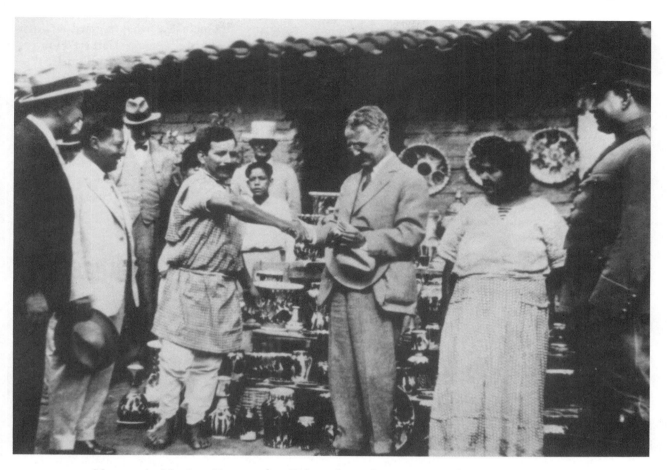

Morrow in Mexico. He served as U.S. ambassador to Mexico from 1927 to 1930.

ain owed $1.3 billion to American private creditors alone. That tremendous shift meant, among other things, an expansion of opportunity for American private bankers. The American political environment during the postwar decade produced an even larger bankers' role. The failure of the Senate to ratify the Versailles Treaty and the election of Warren G. Harding to the presidency signified that Washington would not take an official role in the economic recovery of Europe. Benjamin Strong, governor of the Federal Reserve Bank of New York, working in tandem with the House of Morgan, filled the vacuum.

Morrow was well equipped to aid in the task, having continued to pursue his love of history and his interest in world affairs. The interrelated questions of German reparations and Allied war debts to the United States dominated the financial affairs in the 1920s. The German decision to default on reparations led to the January 1923 occupation of the Ruhr region by French troops. German passive resistance as well as active financial sabotage brought hyperinflation and the virtual destruction of the German economy. Finally, in late 1924, an interna-

tional negotiating team obtained all parties' consent to the Dawes Plan, which revised reparations and called for the appointment of an agent-general for reparations. Morrow's name surfaced in discussions, and he accepted the position. But the erroneous announcement by the American ambassador to Germany, Alanson Houghton, that the German government would not accept any partner of Morgan's as agent-general, because of the firm's role as banker to the Allies during World War I, put an end to that notion. Reluctantly, Morrow withdrew his name from consideration and instead devoted a great deal of effort to currency restructuring for Belgium and France. World War I had devastated both countries' finances, both because of the enormous cost of the war and the immense destruction it caused. With the return of both currencies to the gold standard, the European financial environment once again appeared healthy.

By the middle of the 1920s Morrow again looked for new challenges. In 1925 President Calvin Coolidge, an old classmate from Amherst, appointed Morrow to an aviation commission charged with the purpose of reporting on the best means "of developing and applying aircraft in national defense." That commission, formed in response to the charges made by U.S. Army colonel Billy Mitchell that the nation lacked protection from the possibility of attack from the air, faced a dilemma. It had to avoid hysteria—a difficult task given the poor condition of the nation's antiaircraft defenses—yet it had to report the facts in a sober manner. Morrow, elected chairman, engineered a balanced report and in the process helped ameliorate the jealousy between the army, army air, and navy departments. Unfortunately Morrow and his colleagues, siding with the "battleship admirals," too hastily dismissed Mitchell's prescient comments on the importance of air power in the next war.

Morrow's success on the aviation commission partly contributed to his appointment in July 1927 as ambassador to Mexico. For all its attractions, the business world never fully satisfied Morrow. In 1921 he had considered accepting the position of president of Yale University, but former president William Howard Taft dissuaded him by maintaining that not being a Yale man constituted an insurmountable problem. Given the unhappy relations between Mexico and the United States since the Mexican Revolution of 1913, the Mexican post was bound to prove difficult. Many urged Morrow to turn down the offer; his wife, who thought only of the deprivations and not at all of the challenges, especially opposed taking the position.

But Morrow accepted the post, arriving in Mexico City in October 1927. The general unpopularity of the United States and Morrow's Morgan background ensured a cold welcome, but once again Morrow's ability and personality enabled him to move past initial feelings. The question of the status of oil concessions presented Ambassador Morrow with his most difficult problem. His overwhelming intelligence and careful negotiating produced a compromise settlement that pleased both the Mexican and American governments and the American oil companies. Morrow next mediated between the Catholic church and succeeded in increasing the church's social role under Mexican law. Finally, Morrow played a large part in the renegotiation and rescheduling of Mexico's massive external debts. In between those duties, he also had the pleasure of seeing his daughter Anne marry aviator Charles Lindbergh in May 1929.

Having accomplished what seemed impossible, Morrow accepted President Herbert Hoover's offer of an appointment to the American delegation for the London Naval Conference that opened in late January 1930. Working on the basis of the Washington Conference of 1922 and attempting to improve on the shambles of the 1927 Geneva Conference, Morrow, as chairman of the drafting committee, proved instrumental in drafting an agreement that settled the difficult cruiser question by allowing more cruisers for the United States and Britain which both preferred. Unfortunately neither France nor Italy signed the treaty, which went into effect on January 1, 1931, and Japan, increasingly resentful of its second-rate status, refused to participate.

In 1930 Morrow entered the U.S. Senate from New Jersey. Elected first as a replacement for ambassador Walter Edge, he won reelection in his own right that same year. His first session was marked by the increasing financial paralysis that gripped the United States and the world during 1930 and 1931. The failure of the Austrian Credit Anstalt and the resulting collapse of the Central European banking system allowed Morrow his opportunity to make an important if ultimately futile contribution to world affairs. Understanding better than most the depth of the crisis, he worked to persuade Hoover to accept the idea of a one-year moratorium on war debts and reparations. While the president ultimately acquiesced, he did not follow Morrow's advice to consult the French government before making a public announcement. The resulting objections from Paris led to a three-week delay that eroded the effectiveness of the initiative.

The resulting summer of financial chaos culminated in the British departure from the gold standard in September 1931. French premier Pierre Laval journeyed to the United States in order to attempt to recapture some control over reparations. On October 1-2, 1931, Morrow helped Secretary of State Henry Stimson prepare the American negotiating position. That contribution was his last public act; Morrow died on October 5, 1931.

References:

Hewitt Howland, *Dwight Whitney Morrow: A Sketch in Admiration* (London: Century, 1930);

Mary Margaret McBride, *The Story of Dwight W. Morrow* (New York: Farrar & Rinehart, 1930);

Richard Meltzer, "The Ambassador *Simpatico*: Dwight Morrow in Mexico 1927-1930," in *Ambassadors in Foreign Policy: The Influence of Individuals in United States-Latin American Policy*, edited by C.

Neale Ronning and Albert P. Vannucci (New York: Praeger, 1987);

Harold Nicolson, *Dwight Morrow* (New York: Harcourt, Brace, 1935).

Archives:

The papers of Dwight W. Morrow are located at Amherst College, Amherst, Massachusetts.

Mortgage Lending, Mortgage Pools, Home Equity Loans, and REITs

A mortgage constitutes a pledge of property against a debt. When a bank makes a loan to a farmer, it may choose to hold his land as security. The borrower acquires a deed (a title of ownership) once he satisfies the entire principal and interest on the debt.

In the case of the homeowner, the value of the payments made toward the principal constitutes equity (that is, the owner's stake or investment) in a house or farm. Banks often make loans against that equity, using the house or land as collateral in the form of a second mortgage. However, in the case of a default on the home equity loan, the second-mortgage holder, who could take legal action, would receive recompense only after the first holder's debt was satisfied. Thus, a default on the second could move the first mortgager to action. But normally borrowers use home equity loans to make major additions to their property—such as adding a swimming pool—to improve the value of the home.

Mortgage pools appeared when a single piece of property—an office building, for example—or several pieces of property—an office park—posed too great an expense for a single investor. A bank would offer the property or properties to a group of investors in a pooling arrangement, where each received (or lost) an appropriate share relative to his investment.

In the 1970s banks created Real Estate Investment Trusts, or REITs, which were trust companies that borrowed to purchase commercial real estate. The REIT provided a trust company umbrella for the investors but otherwise operated much like a mortgage pool. Chase, Citicorp, and Bankers Trust all loaned heavily to REITs when new downtown areas in the West and Southwest boomed. However, when the Arab oil embargo sent the economy into recession, real estate values plummeted, and investment in REITs nearly broke some banks. Bankers Trust, long considered a conservative bank, nearly failed due to its bad REIT loans.

—Editor

Mutual Funds (*see* Money Instruments)

National Banks and State Banks

The term "national bank" in American financial history referred to the type of charter under which a commercial bank originated. Until 1863, when Congress passed the National Banking Act, the only national banks to exist were the First and Second Banks of the United States (BUS). Those two institutions differed greatly from the national banks chartered after 1863. First, each BUS had some "central" bank powers, meaning that to a degree they could affect the money supply through loans and note issues based on their large gold and silver (specie) reserves. Second, each had a huge capital relative to other commercial banks of the day. Third, despite the fact that 80 percent of the stock remained in private hands, each was a public institution that had certain monopoly privileges in its charter. For example, the charters stated that the government would charter no other national banks as competitors during the length of either BUS charter. Perhaps their most important advantage over other commercial banks, and the most important difference separating them from the national banks created after 1863, was their ability to establish branches in any of the several states. Thus, the two banks of the United States could engage in interstate branching more than 100 years before the question of branching across state lines emerged as a controversial issue. States did not have the authority to regulate the BUS or its branches because the banks operated under federal law. Nor could they tax the BUS or its branches, as the Supreme Court ruled in the famous *McCulloch* v. *Maryland* case (1819).

The Second BUS failed to win recharter in 1832 when President Andrew Jackson vetoed the recharter bill and Congress could not override the veto. It limped along but no longer even had any effective banking power after 1833, when Jackson removed the government's deposits, taking much of the bank's deposit base. When its charter officially expired in 1836, the nation carried on without the services of a central bank until 1913, when Congress created the Federal Reserve System. From 1836 to 1913 the U.S. Treasury handled some of the tasks that the BUS had performed, including holding government specie deposits and making the government's international payments.

Under the National Banking Act the federal government granted charters to groups of five individuals or more, provided they met the relatively high capitalization requirements of $200,000 for banks in large cities or $50,000 for banks in cities with populations of 5,000 or less. The act also required that the bank hold U.S. government bonds as collateral. In return the bank used the term "national" in its title and on its notes. National banks also received the authority to issue national bank notes, which they obtained in exchange for ownership of U.S. Treasury securities. National bank notes soon circulated as the nation's only currency (with the exception of greenbacks, which existed for 20 years during and after the Civil War). National bank notes achieved their monopoly status because Congress had placed a 10 percent tax on all nonnational bank notes, effectively driving them out of existence.

Several differences existed between the earlier BUS variants and the post-1863 national banks. National banks were strictly commercial banks, and the only obligation they had to lend money to the government was an indirect one in that they held government bonds. The charters of national banks prohibited them from branching, although Congress later modified that restriction. However, they never received the privilege of interstate branching that the two banks of the United States enjoyed. Nor could national banks lend on real estate. Finally, their charters required a capitalization that many bankers considered excessively high, and states quickly discovered that they could undercut the national banks by lowering their state charter requirements.

States had chartered their own banks since the early days of the Republic, and usually the term "state bank" referred to a bank given a permit to operate by the state legislature. State charters set capitalization requirements, the length of the charter's life, and established conditions of operation. Almost all charters included a penalty, usually revoking the charter, if the bank "suspended" specie payments—that is, if the bank refused to convert the notes it issued into gold or silver coin on demand. Frequently during crises, however, when banks suspended, legislatures rattled their charter-revoking sabers a great deal but then passed laws exempting the banks from those provisions after the crisis passed. State banks, depending on their charters, could have branching privileges. After 1863, when the several states thought that the national banking system's high capitalization requirements were starving them of credit and money, many states lowered their state capitalization requirements. That liberalization process started a stampede toward state charters and away from national charters that continued into the twentieth century.

One special type of state bank lent confusion to the term: many states chartered a bank that they intended to serve as an agent of the state, and in some cases as a monopoly bank (the State Bank of Alabama, for example). While all other state-chartered banks were privately owned and operated for private profit, the legislators intended this variant of the state bank to operate for the benefit of the state. Tennessee, for example, required the profits of the Bank of Tennessee to pay for the state's educational system. Most state-controlled banks operated in competition with the numerous privately owned state-chartered banks, and despite the intentions of the legislatures, few state-controlled banks designed as monopoly banks ever really succeeded in achieving that status. When they did, they met with disaster. State monopoly banks in Arkansas, Alabama, and Missouri collapsed, usually because their lending practices were driven by political needs, not profit. A few state banks achieved some degree of success, especially the Bank of the State of Indiana, largely due to the efforts of its president, Hugh McCulloch.

The simultaneous presence of state banks and national banks led to the term "dual banking system." With the passage of the Federal Reserve Act in 1913, the government required all national banks to join the Federal Reserve System, thus placing a percentage of their deposits with the regional Reserve banks. The dual banking system continued and remains in place as of this writing, although it

has undergone considerable transformation since its origination.

In the late nineteenth century, continuing into the 1920s, the stricter provisions of national charters compared to state charters led to a migration of banks away from national charters. New banks being formed in the 1920s overwhelmingly had state charters: from 1921 to 1929 the states granted 79 percent of the charters issued to the 6,109 banks that were formed during that period. As early as 1919 the share of commercial bank assets held by national banks fell below 50 percent and sank to 44.4 percent in 1926.

The shift concerned national authorities all the more because it occurred in spite of the fact that from 1900 to 1920 more than 2,800 state and private banks had converted to national charters to escape the deposit guaranty laws many states had enacted. National bank numbers reached an all-time peak of 8,244 in 1922. To stem the tide of defections, Congress passed the McFadden Act in 1927. While it expanded the powers of national banks to open branches, invest in and underwrite securities, and make real estate loans, national charters still remained more restrictive than state charters, and national banks' share of commercial bank assets remained at just less than 44 percent. However, A. P. Giannini brought into the national system his Bank of America and its 300 branches, and other large California banks followed suit, thus bolstering the numbers of national banks during the period.

Fortunately for the Federal Reserve, a bank did not have to become a national bank to become a Federal Reserve member bank. By 1930 member banks held almost 70 percent of all bank deposits. The Glass-Steagall Act enabled state banks, and required national banks, to obtain federal deposit insurance, thus bringing them under the regulatory supervision of the Federal Deposit Insurance Corporation, as well as the comptroller of the currency (for national banks) or the appropriate state regulatory agency (for state banks). By 1988, as a result of deposit insurance, more than 98 percent of state banks came under FDIC jurisdiction. The federal government also received a greater degree of control in the Banking Act of 1935, which required the comptroller of the currency to consider several factors before granting a new charter or before the FDIC would insure a state nonmember bank, including its prospects for attracting a viable level of business.

High failure rates of state nonmember banks during the Great Depression fostered a resurgence in the number of national banks over state banks in the 1930s, but both national and state bank numbers declined sharply. After World War II, however, the number of state-chartered banks started to grow again, and by 1989 two-thirds of all banks held state charters. Moreover, recent trends showed at least half of all new bank charters were of the state variety. National banks did continue to hold the majority of deposits, and the state systems had seen important defections from their ranks from 1965 to 1990: Chase Manhattan (1965), Wachovia (1968), Wells Fargo (1968), and Marine Midland (1980). Nonmember banks have grown steadily since World War II, to 59 percent of all banks as of 1988. Member bank deposits fell from 86 percent in 1945 to 72 percent in 1979. The fall in deposits and the massive migration out of the Federal Reserve System in the 1970s was in part the inspiration for the Depository Institutions Deregulation and Monetary Control Act of 1980, which phased in uniform reserve requirements for all depository institutions, regardless of the agency that chartered them. Thus, in the words of Benjamin Klebaner, "One motive for conversions was eliminated." As of mid 1988, national banks comprised 4,459 of the nation's 13,274 banks. The dual banking system remains as of 1990, and it continues to serve as a useful check on regulatory excesses at either the state or federal level.

See also:

Banking Act of 1935, BankAmerica, Chase Manhattan Bank, Depository Institutions Deregulation and Monetary Control Act of 1980, A. P. Giannini, Glass-Steagall Act, McFadden Act of 1927, James J. Saxon.

—Editor

NCNB Corporation

by John Landry

Brown University

NCNB is a regional multibank holding company based in Charlotte, North Carolina. It evolved from the mergers of several North Carolina banks, the oldest of which was the Commercial National Bank, organized in 1874 in Charlotte. Primarily a retail bank, Commercial National flourished into the 1950s, when increased competition from other banks forced it to expand its resources. It went on to merge with its next-door neighbor, the wholesale-oriented American Trust Bank, founded in 1901.

The new American Commercial went on to absorb the First National Bank of Raleigh in 1959. The following year it gained a statewide banking network by merging with Security National Bank. Begun in Greensboro in 1933, Security had opened or acquired offices in six other towns in the state. The merged company took the name of the North Carolina National Bank (NCNB), with assets of $460 million.

The bank continued to expand, and in 1968 it formed the NCNB Corporation as a holding company. Its strategy of aggressive growth brought trouble in 1974. With archrival Wachovia Corporation holding the lion's share of the state's profitable consumer deposits, NCNB had to purchase money directly, then lend aggressively in order to meet the higher margins that money required. The bank prospered until the 1974-1975 recession made interest rates soar and left it with a portfolio of bad construction and consumer loans.

To clean up the balance sheet, NCNB followed a strategy of greater equity by swapping stock for debt, retaining earnings, and reinvesting dividends. By 1979 it was the largest bank in North Carolina but had little room to expand further. It and the second and third largest banks held almost three-fourths of all deposits in the state.

In 1981 NCNB tested an opportunity to cross state lines. Florida banking legislation prohibited the acquisition of Florida banks by out-of-state banks, but a grandfather clause gave NCNB, which had owned a trust company in that state since

1972, a base from which to acquire banks there. The Federal Reserve Board ruled in favor of NCNB and against objecting Florida bankers, and the company went on to buy First National Bank of Lake City. In the next three years it added Gulfstream Banks of Boca Raton, Exchange Bancorporation of Tampa, Downtown National of Miami, Ellis Banking Corporation of Bradenton, and the biggest, Pan American Banks of Miami. The purchases doubled NCNB's assets, from $7.7 billion to $15 billion, and by 1987 NCNB National Bank of Florida was the fourth largest bank in the state. The wealth of consumer deposits from the large population of retirees in the state gave the holding company funds for lending from Miami to Charlotte.

The advent in 1985 of reciprocal interstate banking in the Southeast allowed NCNB to expand into South Carolina (Bankers Trust Company of Columbia), Georgia (Southern National Bankshares, Incorporated, of Atlanta), and Virginia (Prince William Bank of Dumfries). The office in the thriving Atlanta market enabled NCNB to continue its position as a leading banker for middle-market companies.

In 1987 NCNB went out of its region by merging with Centrabank, a holding company in Baltimore. A year later it won a strong position in Texas, when the Federal Deposit Insurance Corporation selected it to manage, with an option to buy, the restructured subsidiary banks of the failing First Republic Bank Corporation, the largest bank in the state. By recognizing early the tax benefits of First Republic's losses for its healthy segments, NCNB managed to outbid Citicorp and other large banks. NCNB's 49 percent investment in First Republic placed it among the ten largest banking companies in the country, with nearly $60 billion in assets.

NCNB's brusque, aggressive style in acquiring out-of-state banks appeared to hurt the company in the late 1980s. The new subsidiary in Florida, with access to the holding company's funds, did well in commercial lending, but it lagged behind competitors in the retail side, a side of banking said to require more personal service and decentralized management. Three Georgia banks spurned NCNB and merged with Wachovia, including one for a significantly lower bid. Bankers' fear that NCNB would replace current managers with out-of-staters may have also played a part when the managers of C&S Corporation, another thriving regional banking company, successfully held off NCNB's offer of merger in 1989.

In 1984 NCNB combined its merchant banking and corporate finance areas with international banking activities in London to form NCNB Investment Banking Company. By 1987 it had a private placement department and was involved in leveraged leasing, venture capital, and capital markets, as well as merchant banking. This subsidiary was an unusual entry for a commercial bank, whose culture tends to differ greatly from that of investment banks. The subsidiary aimed to preserve a regional focus as a boutique operation directed more to problem solving for the middle market than to mass production of investment banking products.

As of 1989, NCNB Corporation held the following subsidiaries: NCNB National Bank of North Carolina; NCNB National Bank of Florida; NCNB National Bank of Atlanta, Georgia; NCNB Texas National Bank; NCNB Bank of Maryland; NCNB Financial Services Incorporated; Superior Life Insurance Company; NCNB Virginia; NCNB Leasing Corporation; NCNB Mortgage Corporation; and NCNB Securities Corporation.

References:

Alan Sloan, "Will NCNB Rise Again?" *Forbes*, 124 (October 15, 1979): 78-79;

Barry Stauro, "Breakthrough," *Forbes*, 132 (November 7, 1983): 144-146.

New York Stock Exchange

by Steven Wheeler

The New York Stock Exchange (NYSE) is the nation's premiere marketplace for corporate equity securities. By providing an efficient, central market for the stocks and bonds of a wide array of corporations it has fundamentally contributed to the growth and development of American industry.

As the twentieth century dawned the New York Stock Exchange was unquestionably the largest and most important market for stock and bond trading in the United States. More than 1,300 companies' securities had listings there. Nearly 105 million shares had changed hands in 1900. The new century introduced a host of new companies to an increasingly sophisticated investing public. Industrial corporations such as General Motors and U.S. Steel listed more than 3 billion shares of stock on the NYSE. Fueled by four years of prosperity, the accumulation of tremendous wealth, and consolidation in railroads and industry, the stock market rode high on a bull market like none before.

On April 26, 1901, the brokers moved to temporary trading quarters at the nearby Produce Exchange where, only days later, a new trading record was set at 3 million shares. The old NYSE building on Broad Street was demolished and a new Classical Revival edifice designed by George B. Post arose on its site. Its magnificent trading room, with a gilt ceiling and huge window walls four stories high, featured 16 trading posts. Five hundred telephones around the perimeter of the room provided a direct connection to members' offices. The new building's columned facade remains today a recognized symbol of Wall Street and finance.

The outbreak of World War I ushered in one of the greatest crisis periods for the NYSE and the nation. As international tensions mounted in July 1914, a "financial earthquake" rocked the world and stock exchanges throughout Europe and America closed their doors. On the morning of July 31, NYSE officials met to consider closing the market. After consulting with leading bankers and stock bro-

New York Stock Exchange (courtesy of the New York Stock Exchange Archives)

kers, just minutes before the opening hour, they decided to close the exchange until further notice. It remained closed for four and a half months.

After the United States entered the conflict in 1917, the NYSE threw its full support behind the war effort. The exchange helped finance the war by aggressively promoting, selling and buying war bonds. Four Liberty Loan drives and one Victory Loan raised more than $23 billion from 1917 to 1919. The NYSE sponsored huge rallies on the trading floor and outside on Broad Street, urging citizens to buy the Liberty bonds. It was the first time the exchange ever endorsed a particular security issue. The wide sale of Liberty bonds brought security ownership and a new familiarity with the stock

Brokers at the New York Stock Exchange, 1985

market to a broad class of Americans for the first time.

The 1920s brought a bull market that captured the public imagination and became central to American culture. Stock prices skyrocketed, and it seemed to some that a new day had dawned on the stock market—that fundamental economic changes had brought stock prices to a permanent new level. The Dow Jones Industrial Average marched to a high of 381 in September 1929. People invested in the stock market like never before, many hoping to get rich quick by "playing the market." A good number bought stock with a minimum of cash—as little as 10 percent margin. The end finally came when the market crashed on October 29, 1929. Stock prices plummeted, and more than 16 million shares traded hands, a record that was not broken for 39 years. Prices continued to decline over the next few years. The Dow Jones Industrial Average bottomed out at 41 in the summer of 1932—the darkest days of the Great Depression.

The 1929 stock market crash focused critical attention on the NYSE and the entire stock brokerage business. In 1932 the Senate Banking and Currency Committee began its much-publicized investigation of the causes of the crash. Led by counsel Ferdinand Pecora (dubbed "the hellhound of

Wall Street" for his relentless questioning of bankers and brokers), the hearings disclosed a number of alleged abuses in stock market practices and sparked a public clamor for reform.

As a direct outcome of the Pecora Hearings, Congress passed the Securities Exchange Act of 1934, which established the Securities and Exchange Commission (SEC). Creation of the SEC ushered in comprehensive federal regulation of the securities industry. The aims of the SEC were to ensure correct statements in the issuance and sales of securities, fair dealing in stock exchanges, and honesty and sound financing of public utilities. Overall, it intended to protect investment and strengthen public confidence in the nation's system of corporate finance. In one of the commission's first regulations, it registered the nation's stock exchanges and required a full disclosure of their rules and methods. The NYSE led the way by applying for registration as a national securities exchange on October 1, 1934. At the SEC's urging the NYSE underwent a considerable administrative reorganization in 1938. The Governing Committee was replaced by a Board of Governors, which, for the first time, included non-member public representatives.

During World War II activity at the NYSE dwindled as attention and resources were diverted to the war effort. As men reported for duty in the armed forces in unprecedented numbers, women worked as pages on the trading floor to fill the labor shortage. Again the stock market aided the Allies by selling war bonds.

In the decades following World War II the exchange embarked upon a comprehensive educational and advertising campaign to rebuild confidence in the stock market and to broaden share ownership. A share ownership census conducted in 1952 revealed that 6.5 percent of Americans owned securities. Advertising campaigns stressed the economic benefits of informed investments in common stocks and sought to increase the number of share owners with the slogan, "Own your share of American business." One crucial component of the campaign, the Monthly Investment Plan, offered the average worker the opportunity to buy common stocks with installment payments as low as $30 a month.

During the 1960s and 1970s rising share volume at the NYSE resulted in a devastating "paperwork crunch." Twelve-million-share days resulted in a ticker that ran hours late, requiring back-office personnel to work all night to keep up with the volume. The entire securities industry was swamped by the manual paperwork required to process stock transactions. The crisis prompted the brokerage community to begin automating its data-processing and communications systems. Computers and other new technological systems were introduced to speed and simplify operations on the trading floor and throughout the securities industry. The Designated Order Turnaround system (DOT), inaugurated in 1976, routed orders from member firms directly to the specialist at the trading post. The Intermarket Trading System (ITS), a key component of the National Market System, started in 1978. Through ITS, a computer network that links eight securities exchanges, a broker could buy or sell a stock at the market offering the best price. By 1980, the Exchange completely overhauled the trading floor facilities. New trading posts with an array of sophisticated computer support systems enabled the NYSE to handle trading of hundreds of millions of shares per day.

The bull market of the 1980s broke all price and volume records and raised the industry's standards of measurement to astounding new heights. The Dow Jones Average topped 2,700, daily volume reached more than 600 million shares, and a seat on the exchange fetched more than a million dollars. It brought drama in new proportions as well. The "market break" of October 19, 1987, when the Dow plunged more than 500 points, riveted the world's attention on the stock market and the NYSE. Critics cited program trading—computer-driven trading in many stocks simultaneously—as contributing to the stock market's new volatility.

The NYSE has responded to the new challenges in the market by upgrading its automated systems and expanding trading capacity, offering increased priority to individual investors and requiring stronger capital positions for specialists. Finally, coordinated regulation between equities and futures markets has set today's financial markets on a much firmer footing.

References:

Deborah S. Gardner, *Marketplace: A Brief History of the New York Stock Exchange* (New York: New York Stock Exchange, 1982);

Leonard Sloane, *The Anatomy of the Floor: The Trillion-dollar Market at the New York Stock Exchange* (New York: Doubleday, 1980);

Robert Sobel, *NYSE: A History of the New York Stock Exchange, 1935-1975* (New York: Weybright & Talley, 1975).

Norwest Corporation

by Rebecca Strand Johnson

Loyola University of Chicago

Norwest Corporation is one of the largest bank holding companies in the United States. It forms a confederation of banking institutions with interrelated goals and perspectives. Affiliated banks act independently within a well-defined framework of policies and performance goals.

The company, originally known as Northwestern Bancorporation, or "Banco," was consolidated on January 8, 1929, in response to the financial needs of the economically depressed Upper Midwest region of the United States. When the Depression threatened many of the small and financially insecure banking institutions in the Twin Cities, Minnesota, area, several bankers decided to organize a group to coordinate some of them through majority stock ownership by a central supervisory holding company. Governed by a local board of directors and financially supported by the Northwestern National Bank of Minneapolis, the strongest bank in the area, Northwestern Bancorporation acted as a protective organization for that group of small banks.

The strategy worked. In Banco's first year the company acquired 90 financial institutions, and by 1931, 37 more banks had moved under its umbrella. The company had far outstripped its initial regional boundaries, taking affiliates in Montana and Washington State. Moreover, it had also outreached its initial expansion goals by acquiring several investment companies along with the banks. The continu-

Lloyd P. Johnson, chairman and chief executive officer of Norwest Corporation from 1985 (courtesy of Norwest Corporation)

ing Depression of the 1930s forced Banco directors to prune those branches of growth somewhat and to reorganize the governing structure, with the goal of clarifying the organization's planning strategy. For example, membership on the board of directors, previously open to the presidents of all affiliated banks, was limited to 20 in 1933. Still, the central board continued to refrain from influencing the day-to-day operations of the individual banks.

Despite the continued attempts of the American Farmer-Labor Party to force Banco officials into legal difficulty, the company continued to receive the trust of the predominantly agricultural communities of the Upper Midwest throughout the

Depression period, during World War II, and into the postwar era. J. Cameron Thomson, who relieved Edward W. Decker as Banco president in 1933, brought a national and global perspective to the holding company through his previous work with the national Council for Economic Development (CED). Thomson strengthened farmers' understanding of financial issues and the midwestern economy by forming a regional group similar in purpose to the CED, eventually known as the Upper Midwest Council, which in essence served as an educational and promotional tool. He also increased the bank's responsiveness to changes in the character of the communities it served.

During the 1940s and 1950s the industrialization of Minnesota's iron range and the Dakotas' oil fields, with the increased mechanization of agriculture, and the development of a service-oriented urban economic segment in the midwestern region, provided more business for Banco's affiliates and expanded the company's mission. Throughout the 1950s and 1960s Thomson's successor as Banco president, Goodrich Lowry, pushed the holding company into new areas of growth, including international banking and trading on the New York Stock Exchange.

With the modern use of interrelated computer systems, Norwest Corporation has expanded into 47 states and provides consumer and mortgage banking and a variety of other financial services. Founded on the principle of the autonomy of the affiliate, the company has tried to achieve maximum efficiency in resource use without jeopardizing that autonomy. Its recent presidents, Henry T. Rutledge (1971-1977), Richard H. Vaughan (1977-1979), Chester C. Lind (1979-1982), John W. Morrison (1981-1985), and Lloyd P. Johnson (1985-), continue to follow that philosophy.

Reference:

Harold Chucker, *Banco at Fifty: A History of Northwest Bancorporation, 1929-1979* (Minneapolis: Northwest Bancorporation, 1979).

NOW Accounts (*see* **Money Instruments**)

Wright Patman

(August 6, 1893 - March 7, 1976)

by Gary M. Pecquet

Southwest Texas State University

CAREER: State legislator, Texas (1921-1923); U.S. district attorney, Bowie County, Texas (1924-1928); U.S. representative, Texas (1929-1976).

John William Wright Patman, populist Texas Democratic congressman, ardent easy money advocate, and opponent of the Federal Reserve System, was born on August 6, 1893, in the small community of Patman's Switch in Cass County, Texas. He was the only son of John Newton and Emma Spurlin Patman, both strict Baptists. His mother, the religious backbone of the family, brought the family to church every Sunday and regularly quizzed the children on the sermons. His father, a poor tenant farmer, adhered to the strict taboos of the church against liquor and tobacco. As a devout fundamentalist, John Newton Patman even refused to attend church when the congregation purchased a piano because he believed that the Bible did not permit music in a place of worship. These rural religious values helped shape Wright Patman's political thought.

Not wishing to remain a tenant farmer, young Patman pursued education, graduating first in his high school class. In his valedictory address he recommended that his classmates work for the "good of humanity" in order to secure a place in history. In 1916 Patman graduated from the law school at Cumberland University of Lebanon, Tennessee. He shortly passed the Texas bar examination, but his law practice proved unsuccessful. During World War I Patman volunteered for military duty, but he did not see active combat because of a minor heart deformity. On January 11, 1919, he was honorably discharged after advancing to the rank of first lieutenant.

Following military service, Patman married Merle Connor of Winnsboro, Texas, in 1919. The following year he won election to the Texas state leg-

Wright Patman

islature, where he served from 1921 to 1923. During his term he introduced measures to broaden the state property tax base and considered occupational taxes. He opposed the influences of the Ku Klux Klan, although later as a U.S. representative he consistently opposed civil rights legislation. As a religious fundamentalist, Patman spoke against the teaching of evolution in Texas schools, although he once voted against a bill outlawing the subject because it lacked an enforcement clause.

In February 1924 the local (Bowie County) district attorney resigned, and the Texas governor appointed Patman to fill the vacancy. From 1924 to 1928 Patman vigorously fulfilled those duties. He crusaded against the red light district in Texarkana and upheld Prohibition laws with the strictest possible interpretation. He enlisted the support of the

Texas Ministerial Alliance and the Lion's Club to clean up the city. Not only did he prosecute direct lawbreakers, he also held landlords legally responsible for the illegal activities of their tenants.

In 1928 Patman challenged Eugene Black, a 14-year incumbent, in a race for Congress. Patman accused his opponent of giving money away to foreign countries in the form of war loans while refusing to help Texas farmers and veterans. He specifically charged Black with being a friend of Wall Street, big business, and railroads. Patman claimed to be a strong supporter of Prohibition and a champion of the common man. Promising to urge new banking regulations, lower interest rates, stronger antitrust laws, immigration restrictions, and an end to foreign loans, Patman won the election and claimed the House seat in 1929, a seat he occupied for 47 consecutive years without a defeat or a runoff.

During the Hoover years of 1929 to 1933, the new congressman unsuccessfully supported federal assistance to agriculture and crop allotment schemes designed to reduce supply. He joined the Federal Trade Commission's investigations of antitrust violations. He introduced a bill to provide the immediate payment of veterans' benefits. In 1932 he filed impeachment proceedings against Andrew Mellon, U.S. secretary of the Treasury, charging numerous examples of conflict of interest.

Patman supported most of the New Deal programs of President Franklin D. Roosevelt. His chief personal crusade during the 1930s was against the "monopolistic tendencies" of chain stores, which eventually led to the enactment of the Robinson-Patman Act in 1936. Patman wrote the introduction and endorsed Charles Daughters's 1937 volume *Wells of Discontent*. That book presented the case for stronger antitrust laws designed to protect small independent stores from the rise of chains. Chain stores (such as Woolworth, Kresge, Penney, and Walgreen) led to absentee ownership, increased the concentration of business, and resulted in unfair quantity discounts. Daughters denounced the lobbyists and spokesmen who argued in behalf of the efficiency advantages of chain stores as proindustry propagandists. He also raised fears that business concentration could lead to revolution unless new restrictions could be established. The Robinson-Patman Act attempted to regulate the conditions under which large chain stores could obtain quantity discounts. The act, however, proved compli-

cated to interpret and enforce. Consequently, in 1938 Patman published a 401-page book entitled *Complete Guide to the Robinson-Patman Act* to help businessmen, accountants, and lawyers comply with the law.

The passage of the Robinson-Patman Act followed the collapse of the National Recovery Administration (NRA). The NRA, created in 1933 by the passage of the National Industrial Recovery Act, established industry codes on an industry-by-industry basis. The codes established minimum prices, restricted quantity, and imposed entry barriers on foreign goods. The Supreme Court ruled the NRA unconstitutional in 1935, and the law was soon replaced with Robinson-Patman, and amendment of the Clayton Antitrust Act of 1914. The Clayton Act established certain principles governing the general conduct of business. The Robinson-Patman Act regulated each sales transaction on a case-by-case basis. Businessmen were forbidden to do many things but required to do many others, and neither set of directives is clearly defined. The primary intent of Robinson-Patman was clearly to protect small independent middlemen, but a chief consequence of the act induced large chain stores to purchase directly from manufacturers, bypassing middlemen entirely.

During the 1950s and 1960s Patman chaired the House Select Committee on Small Business. He launched investigations and issued reports to the committee. One of those reports investigated the interlocking connections among the Federal Reserve member banks, or "chain banks," as he called them. That report, issued in January 1963, applied much of the same analysis used to criticize chain stores in the 1930s to the banking industry of the early 1960s. Patman favored independent banks over "chain banks" for two reasons: first, independent banks were small businesses in their own right, and, second, the lending policies of the independents were supposed to be based upon personal, firsthand knowledge of the borrower's credit worthiness rather than the published credit ratings used by larger lenders. He considered the lending policies of independent banks to be more favorable to small businesses. For those reasons, Patman opposed bank mergers and bank holding companies and supported more banking regulations. He sometimes claimed that he was not against banks per se, but rather that "banks should get back into the banking business." By that he meant that bankers should make more direct loans to businesses, especially small businesses, instead of purchasing government securities.

Congressman Patman will undoubtedly best be remembered as an unswerving critic of Federal Reserve tight money policies. An ardent champion of easy money in the same tradition as William Jennings Bryan and the other nineteenth-century populists who comprised the greenback and free silver advocates, Patman also opposed the Federal Reserve System as a source of monopoly privilege.

Patman published his early views on money and banking in the 1934 pamphlet *Bankerteering*. There he made several remarkable but unsubstantiated claims: "If the masses could only pierce the 'smoke screen of secrecy' and see what's going on behind closed doors in the financial world; could understand the plots and plans of these 'money changers' in their efforts to fleece and filch an innocent and unsuspecting public; things would be changed in the twinkling of an eye." He further contended: "With very few exceptions practically every large corporation in this country" is "under direct and absolute bank domination and control." (Small banks, however, he deemed blameless.) Patman then gave a lengthy quotation from the 1877 U.S. Monetary Commission Report, which blamed monetary contraction during the Roman Empire for causing the centuries-long impoverishment of the Dark Ages! He considered the quantity of money in circulation the primary cause rather than an effect of long-term progress: "Without money civilization could not have a beginning; with a diminishing supply it must languish and unless relieved finally perish."

During the depths of the Great Depression, with falling prices and receding economic fortunes, some of Patman's claims undoubtedly seemed to ring true for many people. He blamed the Federal Reserve System for the collapse of the monetary system and recommended that Congress resume its constitutional responsibility as overlord of the money supply. He called for the government to take over the Federal Reserve banks and coordinate them with the Reconstruction Finance Corporation.

Patman was assigned to the House Committee on Banking and Currency in 1937 and in 1963 became its chairman, filling the post until 1975. As chairman he published a 1964 report entitled *A Primer on Money*, which presented characteristic attacks upon the independence of the Federal Reserve System. Patman opposed the Fed, not because he objected to government intervention, but because he favored direct congressional control over the money supply. The *Primer* argued that the creation of the Fed constituted an abdication of Congress's constitutional mandate to "coin money and regulate the value thereof." Moreover, tolerating an independent Fed placed the country in the position of having two control centers independently attempting to guide the economy. The president and Congress enacted fiscal policy while the Fed determined monetary policy. "If they are not steering in the same direction, they can either neutralize each other or have the economy lurching in all directions," contended the report. Patman's major criticism of the Fed, however, was not that it was independent, but that it gave too much power to private interests. The Federal Open Market Committee (FOMC), responsible for monetary policy decisions, had 12 voting members, the seven members of the Federal Reserve Board of Governors appointed by the president and five representatives of the banking industry (such as presidents of the 12 Federal Reserve Banks). Moreover, since all 12 Fed Bank presidents typically attended FOMC meetings, the report contended that bankers exercised undue influence over monetary policy.

The *Primer* then proceeded to express the chairman's views on money and interest rates. It endorsed easy money, not only for periods of recession, but for normal periods as well. High interest rates choked off private investment and reduced the growth rate. Only when there was an excess demand for capital goods would an increase in interest rates ever be justified, claimed the report. Tight money (high interest rates) should never be used to fight inflation. The line of reasoning went as follows: (1) Interest rates are a cost of doing business. (2) High interest rates are passed on to consumers in the form of higher prices. (3) Tight money may worsen inflation. Patman summarized, "As a means of 'fighting inflation' tight money is like using a cannon to kill a fly. If it doesn't kill the insect, it will at least do a great deal of damage. The modern economy is just not an ideal patient for the tight money treatment for inflation." Consequently, he considered monetary restraint leading to high interest against the public interest in much the same way that a monopoly price enriches the monopolist at the public expense. He ridiculed arguments for monetary restraint as "inflation bunkum."

Armed with those theories, chairman Patman persistently pressed for easy money. While he sup-

Patman (right) conferring with House colleague Sol Bloom of New York in 1935 (courtesy of Harris & Ewing)

ported President Lyndon Johnson's Great Society programs (except the civil rights initiative) and backed the Vietnam War effort, Patman accused the president's aides of being soft on interest rates. When the Fed raised the discount rate to 4.5 percent in 1965, he began an investigation of the Fed as chairman of the Joint Economic Committee. He questioned Fed chairman William McChesney Martin and called for his resignation. In fact, following almost every subsequent uptick in interest rates, Patman publicly denounced Martin and the Fed, gaining newspaper headlines. In 1969, for example, Patman feared that increases in Federal Housing Administration and Veterans' Administration mortgages would plunge the United States into "the worst depression we ever had," and "whenever you exceed the usury laws you are robbing somebody."

Occasionally bankers arose to defend themselves. In a 1964 pamphlet the American Banker's Association (ABA) attempted to make a point-by-point refutation of a Patman speech called the "ABC's of Money." The ABA defended the Fed, arguing that the net effect of tight money would indeed restrain inflation, and criticized Patman for implying that the interest payments made on federal securities held by the Federal Reserve System were not repaid to the U.S. Treasury, as they indeed were. Patman, however, maintained the upper hand. As Banking and Currency chairman, he could and did launch investigations into various aspects of the banking industry that appeared dubious to outsiders. The bankers' lobby itself was investigated in 1969. Patman attacked one-bank holding companies and introduced regulations to tighten banking regulations. Fed chairman Martin agreed with Patman that bank conglomerates should be regulated.

Although the Patman-Martin confrontation over interest rates took center stage during the later 1960s, Patman also locked horns with the comptroller of the currency, James J. Saxon, who favored the liberalization of banking regulations. Specifically, Saxon proposed to permit branch banking in states, such as Texas, that required unit banking. Patman opposed "chain banking" and would allow none of the changes. To attack Saxon, in March 1965 Patman introduced legislation that would have abolished the office of comptroller of the currency and reorganized the Department of the Treasury.

The members of the House Banking and Currency Committee once revolted against their chairman during 1965. They held a committee meeting, without informing Patman, in order to approve a bill that would have relaxed regulations on banking mergers. Patman overruled their action on the ground that a quorum had not been present. Bitter feelings remained among the committee members.

Inevitably, both the easy money and fiscal policies of the 1960s led to inflationary pressures that could no longer be contained during the 1970s. The "Fisher Effect" (which defines inflation as a cost of interest charges) set in as a consequence of continuous monetary expansion. Fewer and fewer people paid attention to Patman's regular denunciations of higher interest rates. Moreover, congressional reforms weakened the House seniority system, and Patman was ousted as chairman of the House Banking and Currency Committee in January 1975. Before he could complete his term of office, he died of pneumonia on March 7, 1976. At that time Patman held many other influential committee positions, including chairman of the Subcommittee on Domestic Monetary Policy, chairman of the Joint Committee on Defense Production, vice-chairman of the Joint Economic Committee, and chairman of the Subcommittee on Economic Progress. He also held memberships on the House Committee on Priorities and Economy in Government, the Subcommittee on Energy, the Subcommittee on Financial Institutions Supervision, the Committee on Interior and Insular Affairs, the Subcommittee on Public Lands, the Public Policy Committee, and the Democratic Steering Committee. Patman was survived by Pauline Tucker Wright, his second wife, whom he married in 1968, and three children.

Publications:

Bankerteering, Bonuseering, and Melloneering (Paris, Tex.: Peerless, 1934);

Complete Guide to the Robinson-Patman Act (Englewood Cliffs, N.J.: Prentice-Hall, 1938);

Our American Government: The Answers to 1001 Questions on How It Works (Chicago: Ziff-Davis, 1948);

Chain Banking Stockholder and Loan Links of 200 Largest Member Banks (Washington, D.C.: U.S. Government Printing Office, 1963);

A Primer on Money, Subcommittee on Domestic Finance, Committee on Banking and Currency, House of Representatives, 88th Congress, second session (Washington, D.C.: U.S. Government Printing Office, 1964).

References:

American Bankers Association, "Comments on Mr. Patman's ABC's of Money" (New York: American Bankers Association, 1964);

Charles G. Daughters, *Wells of Discontent: A Study of the Economic, Social, and Political Aspects of the Chain Store* (New York & Chicago: Charles G. Daughters, 1937);

Nelson Lichtenstein, *Political Profiles: The Johnson Years* (New York: Facts on File, 1976);

Richard Posner, *The Robinson-Patman Act, Federal Regulation, and Price Differences* (Washington, D.C.: American Enterprise Institute, 1976);

Janet Louise Schmelzer, "The Early Life and Early Congressional Career of Wright Patman: 1894-1941," dissertation, Texas Christian University, 1978;

Eleanora V. Schoenbaum, *Political Profiles: The Nixon/Ford Years* (New York: Facts on File, 1979);

Burton A. Zora and George J. Feldman, *Business Under the New Price Laws: A Study of the Economic and Legal Problems Arising out of the Robinson-Patman Act and the Various Fair Trade and Unfair Trade Practice Laws* (Englewood Cliffs, N.J.: Prentice-Hall, 1937).

Archives:

The Eugene Barker Texas History Center at the University of Texas, at Austin contains a collection of newspaper clippings on Wright Patman's congressional career entitled "Biographical Scrapbooks."

Penn Square/Continental Illinois Bank Failures

by Larry Schweikart

University of Dayton

In the 1970s American energy prices rose to all-time highs. The embargo by the Organization of Petroleum Exporting Countries had helped drive up prices, but U.S. domestic drilling had also tailed off due to tax disincentives. As Congress changed the tax laws, drillers immediately started operations, while the demand for oil returned, starting a new oil boom. To finance the burst of new drilling, a small bank in Oklahoma City, Penn Square National Bank, triggered the largest bank bailout in American history.

Penn Square's vice-president in charge of energy lending, Bill Patterson, known for drinking champagne out of a cowboy boot in a local bar and wearing a Mickey Mouse hat to meetings, convinced the managers of several large banks in the money centers of the tremendous returns available in the Oklahoma oil fields. For several years Penn Square had funneled the deposits from those banks to local drillers. But as the oil ventures grew increasingly risky, Patterson started to repackage Penn Square's loans and sell them in total or in part to other out-of-state banks. Penn Square retained a service fee for those "participations," as the bankers called them. Using the participations, Penn Square grew from a $62 million institution in 1977 to a $250 million bank in 1982.

Penn Square used the proceeds from one participation to lend on another energy project, repackaging the participations in an almost endless chain. By 1982, the bank had set up more than $2 billion in oil and gas loans through its participations. Ultimately, not only did some of the loans themselves go bad, but oil prices flattened, then fell. As Federal Deposit Insurance Corporation (FDIC) director Irvine Sprague put it, "Drilling rigs used to secure loans had been worth millions. Now their worth added up to only dollars." The authorities moved in, closing Penn Square in mid 1982, and turned the bank over to the FDIC for liquidation in July of

Penn Square Bank depositors with accounts exceeding the Federal Deposit Insurance Corporation's $100,000 coverage limit in line at the bank after its June 1982 failure. The FDIC covered all uninsured Penn Square deposits (courtesy of the Oklahoma City Journal-Record).

that year. The FDIC covered both the insured and the uninsured deposits, making it the first bank in excess of $100 million to receive a bailout. As receiver, the FDIC estimated that uninsured depositors and other claimants would receive only 65 percent of their claims, compared with more than 90 percent in average closed-bank situations.

Penn Square's network of participations exposed many other banks, including some large institutions. Chase, a bank diversified enough to sustain such a shock, easily survived its participation but suffered some embarrassment. Northern Trust Company of Chicago had less invested in the loans than Chase or other large banks, and it too experienced little damage. Three other large banks did not fare so well. Michigan National almost fell to a takeover effort, and Seattle-First National had so many loans with Penn Square that regulators allowed an out-of-state bank holding company, BankAmerica Corporation, to take it over in 1983. The worst, however, was Continental Illinois, which by 1982 held $1.1 billion of Penn Square's oil and gas loans, 17 percent of Continental's energy loans.

Continental Illinois' failure proved especially shocking because as late as 1978 *Dun's Review*, a financial magazine, had named the bank one of the five best-managed in the nation. Even at the end of 1983 the bank showed a $25 million profit and declared a dividend for the fourth quarter. It had a reputation as one of the fastest growing banks in the nation, with loans totaling $34 billion in 1982.

Many of those loans came from Penn Square participations, but Continental Illinois survived the mid-1982 closing of that Oklahoma bank, even though the losses from the Penn Square oil and gas loans absorbed from Continental Illinois came to $800 million. It did not show any side effects until May 1984. Experts differ as to what caused the critical run—some blame a rumor that investment bankers had tried to drum up a takeover in Japan, while others point to the sale of Continental's credit card operation—but most agree that rumors of one sort or another sparked the initial runs on May 8 and 9. Within 10 days, outflows surpassed $6 billion. Even though 16 major banks supported a $4.5 billion 30-day credit line, the regulators knew that the bank needed much more.

More than 175 banks had at least half their capital in Continental Illinois' correspondent deposit accounts, and 66 had more than 100 percent. More than 2,100 small banks had $6 billion in deposits in the bank. Continental Illinois' collapse could thus have triggered a major nationwide run, so regulators acted quickly. The FDIC and the Federal Reserve agreed that the FDIC should make a subordinated loan of $2 billion to the bank, and another group of banks (including some in the former group that supported the credit line) later purchased $500 million of the note from the FDIC. However, the banks had not agreed to that proposal until the FDIC promised a 100 percent risk guarantee. The major participants agreed that Continental Illinois could not be saved without 100 per-

cent FDIC insurance and "unlimited liquidity support by the Federal Reserve," according to Sprague. Neither Continental Illinois nor the government could locate a suitable merger partner: the bank was just too big.

Ultimately, in a complex deal announced in 1984, the FDIC took over $4.5 billion in bad loans, for which it gave the bank $3.5 billion, meaning that Continental Illinois had to immediately write off $1 billion as a loss. Once that was written off, the FDIC injected $1 billion in new capital through a stock purchase in the holding company the government had set up. The bank then repaid the original $1.5 billion loan to the FDIC and the $500 million to the banks in stock, of which the FDIC had 80 percent of the total common stock. All outstanding common stock, which went into the holding company, had to remain there for five years. At the end of that time, if the holding company still had $800 million or more of the debt, the FDIC had the option to acquire all of the common stock at a nominal price, but if the loss had decreased below $800 million, the FDIC could only acquire a pro-rata share. Special stock prices gave inducements for shareholders to retain their shares or acquire still more stock and thus inject more capital into the bank. To oversee the reductions in bad loans, the FDIC named a new management team and left all operations to those managers, and it also agreed to take over all claims against the former management. Anything it recovered from those claims, it would apply to the current Continental Illinois Holding Company debt, although the FDIC expected to lose a total of $1.7 billion.

The Continental Illinois bailout represented the largest bank bailout on record up to that point. Continental Illinois gradually recovered and had its bond rating upgraded. According to Sprague the Penn Square failure disproved the myth that no bank in excess of $100 million would ever be paid off, because it would cause too much disruption in the system, while Continental Illinois showed that managers of large multinational banks were not necessarily any better managers than individuals who ran small banks. Those observations proved quite perceptive when taken in the context of the Savings and Loan debacle of the late 1980s.

References:

Gary Hector, *Breaking the Bank: the Decline of BankAmerica* (Boston: Little, Brown, 1988);

Benjamin J. Klebaner, *American Commercial Banking: A History* (Boston: Twayne, 1990);

Irvine H. Sprague, *Bailout: An Insider's Account of Bank Failures and Bank Rescues* (New York: Basic, 1986).

Joseph J. Pinola

(May 13, 1925 -   )

by Lynne Pierson Doti

Chapman College

CAREER: U.S. Navy (1942-1945, 1950-1952); Various positions (1953-1970), senior vice-president (1970-1974), executive vice-president, North American Division, Bank of America (1974-1976); president, United California Bank (1976-1978); president and chief executive officer, First Interstate Bancorporation [Western Bancorporation to 1981] (1978-1990).

Joseph J. Pinola

Joseph Pinola came to California without a vision of his future, but fate joined his career to the fortunes of two of the state's largest banks. At Bank of America he rose to executive vice-president, reporting to president A. W. "Tom" Clausen. When the troubled United California Bank needed new leadership, Pinola found the challenge intriguing, and he took the presidency there in 1976, becoming chairman of the board of the parent company Western Bancorporation, in 1978. Though Pinola instituted a bold and innovative management style, the bank still found high profits evasive, and as he retired in 1990, parts of the company were being sold.

Pinola was born in Pittston, Pennsylvania, on May 13, 1925, and raised in that mining area in a blue-collar environment. His high school years were marred by Pearl Harbor and the ensuing war, and like most of his class, he put his military career first. At age seventeen he passed through California on his way to the Pacific Theater. For more than three years beginning in 1942 he served in the navy, steering landing craft during the invasions of Okinawa and the Philippines.

After the war Pinola returned home to Pittston, married his high school sweetheart, Doris Jean Walker, and attended Wilkes College and Bucknell University, where in 1949 he received a B.A. in economics. A job in a department store supplemented his G.I. Bill funds while he went to

school; then world events again interrupted his career plans. He was called back to the navy reserves for the Korean War and was stationed in Long Beach, California. When he was discharged in December 1952, he and Doris already had two children and happily settled in Southern California. A help-wanted ad attracted Pinola to a trainee position at the Bank of America, at that time the nation's largest bank. As the bank continued its rapid growth, Pinola rose through the ranks of branch managers, then into corporate finance.

One of Pinola's early bosses, Tom Clausen, had a few years more age and experience and advanced a few steps ahead of Pinola in the corporate structure. Pinola never lagged very far, however, and in 1974 he attained the position of executive vice-president in charge of the bank's North American Division, as one of four regional vice-presidents reporting to Clausen, who had become president and chief executive officer of the bank's parent corporation in 1970. Each of the four vice-presidents had his territory. Pinola worked out of the Los Angeles regional headquarters; his responsibilities for corporate lending covered all of North America and Mexico.

Pinola had done well, but his chances for advancement at Bank of America seemed remote. When United California Bank (UCB) approached him with the offer of its presidency, he faced an obvious temptation. UCB comprised the largest bank in the portfolio of Western Bancorporation, a holding company with banks in 11 western states. Pinola reported agonizing over the move from Bank of America after 23 years there, but other reasons also caused him to hesitate. UCB had just recovered from an international scandal involving a Swiss subsidiary when the 1974-1975 economic downturn hit hard. Tight credit conditions stifled the national construction and real estate industries, where UCB had loaned heavily. Profits dropped from $35.2 million in 1974 to $27 million in 1975.

Knowing he faced a challenge, Pinola moved a few blocks to the newly built UCB corporate headquarters, the tallest building in the city. When he took over as UCB president, he first sought to control expenses and to make the bank more competitive in pricing loans and services. He quickly realized the bank had some valuable assets in its staff, its extensive branching system, and a healthy bank credit card division, and he moved to exploit those strengths. By trimming costs and writing off losses, the bank quickly showed improvement in profits.

That success brought Pinola to the attention of Ralph J. Voss, chairman of Western Bancorporation. Nearing retirement, Voss saw Pinola as a likely successor and named him to the holding company's board of directors on August 1, 1977. Simultaneously the company announced Pinola's appointment as president and chief executive officer of Western Bancorporation effective January 1, 1978.

While profits at Western Bancorporation soon underwent a healthy rise, the banking industry itself had drifted into some trouble. Inflation caused interest rates to soar. Since regulations prevented banks from passing those high rates along to their depositors, savvy customers replaced their savings, and sometimes even their checking accounts, with shares in high-yield money market mutual funds. This "disintermediation," as economists called the phenomenon, frightened the financial world, bringing pressure to deregulate. One massive step in that direction, the sudden congressional approval of the Depository Institutions Deregulation and Monetary Control Act of 1980, provided for the phaseout of interest-rate ceilings. Unfortunately, the phaseout provisions did not occur rapidly enough to slow the loss of funds from financial institutions, as interest rates rose even further in 1981. Again construction and real estate loans started to become burdens, and once-lucrative loans to Mexico and South American countries fell into default. In some parts of the country, oil producers also gave their bankers restless nights.

As banks and other financial institutions failed at an alarming rate, the regulators found antitrust and antibranching laws impeded their attempts to merge failing institutions with complementary healthy banks. After mergers of several institutions across state lines, many observers saw that confining a bank to just one state as mandated by the McFadden Act of 1927 no longer constituted a workable system. Interstate banking seemed inevitable.

Aware of the trend, Pinola decided to position Western Bancorporation for that eventuality. Because it owned 21 banks in 11 western states, the holding company already found itself uniquely well positioned in the event Congress legalized interstate mergers. Until then, however, the corporation had chosen to emphasize the local bases of those sometimes venerable institutions. Creating a common name for all of its banks constituted a first step toward eventual closer ties and helped WBC gain recognition in national and international loan markets. A committee settled on a suitable new name.

While the name "First Interstate Bank" seems in retrospect an obvious choice, the committee reviewed more than 45,000 possibilities. UCB and other banks quickly approved the new name while the corporation prepared to distribute 7,474 new signs and truckloads of forms, brochures, and stationery to 900 branch offices. On June 1, 1981, a year and a half after making the decision, the banks simultaneously made the switch. Although the public and many of the bank's customers often thought all of the banks had become one, in fact each bank still operated as an autonomous business, with its legal name including a tag to identify it. For example, the flagship bank became First Interstate Bank of California; the city or county name was added in cases where several of the company's banks resided in a single state. Federal law still required the separation of assets, so the combination gained none of the diversification benefits of branch banking, but all the banks shared in a massive advertising campaign that used $11 million the first year to forge a unified identity.

Another advantage of the more unified structure was the move to give each bank a market niche. First Interstate of California had handled initial contacts with foreign borrowers for several years; after the unification of the system individual banks accepted the task of representing the entire system to given industries.

While the renaming created the impression of a strong link between the banks, many regretted the loss of the old identities. For instance, the Walker Banks, with strong regional identification and a loyal customer base, suffered from the public's impression that the "big city" bankers had moved in, and Northwest Bancorporation of Minneapolis openly fought the new image. While dissension grew stronger, the holding company continued to handle advertising until 1989, when strategy changed, allowing individual banks to tailor their ads to local markets.

In spite of the opposition Pinola persisted. To ease further expansion he had the name "First Interstate" registered in all 50 states, then launched an unprecedented effort to expand by franchising the name, logo, and attendant systems to banks in states not represented in the holding company. That quickly earned the company the sobriquet "the McDonald's of banking."

Pinola positioned the company for deregulation in other ways as well. The data-processing facility reorganized along functional rather than geographical lines. First Interstate of Denver launched a pilot program for expansion into investment advising services for wealthy clients. Some California branches began selling casualty insurance through branches by cooperating with SAFECO Insurance Company.

While Pinola's vision became prophecy, it did not produce spectacular growth in earnings. Branch-

ing law was liberalized in the 1980s, but in unexpected ways. State-by-state reciprocal agreements allowed limited interstate branching, which forestalled a more comprehensive change in the federal law. The continuing problems of the financial industry slowed progress in legal changes needed to allow banks to move into new areas of business.

A most frightening problem arose at Bank of America. While First Interstate and other financial companies worked hard to cope with the changing environment, Bank of America had remained complacent in its bulk. A bureaucratic management system allowed some serious mistakes to go unchecked. Commercial loan officers charged only with unloading huge amounts of funds hopped planes to Mexico, Brazil, and Argentina, where interest rates and the need were high, even though the ability to pay became seriously impaired as interest rates increased. A new personal banking service ran rampant. Real estate lending continued its pace while foreclosures reached record levels. By mid 1985, many experts considered Bank of America so badly managed that it was an ideal acquisition target.

Corporate takeovers, often arranged against the wishes of the acquired company's management (called "hostile takeovers"), commonly occurred in the 1980s, but banks had remained immune. Several people recognized the potential in banking, however, including Robert Huret and Jim Hale of Montgomery Securities, who planned the acquisition of Bank of America. The merger partner, because of restrictions on bank ownership, had to be another banking firm. Huret and Hale quickly settled on First Interstate Bancorporation.

On July 12, 1985, Huret approached the management of First Interstate with the idea and soon afterward suggested it to Sam Armacost, Bank of America president. Armacost seemed interested and even willing to let Pinola run the combined company, although that interest probably stemmed from an even more immediate and personal threat to his future. Bank of America's board members had started to doubt his leadership ability. Discussions with the managers of both companies continued through the fall.

Armacost's problems worsened in 1986. Wealthy investor Sandy Weill thought he might like the challenge of turning around a troubled bank and offered his services as president to the Bank of America board. His offer included a commitment by the investment banking firm of Shearson Lehman to raise $1 billion for the bank. Armacost called his investment banker at Goldman Sachs and asked for that firm's help in analyzing the First Interstate offer. Goldman Sachs prepared an analysis, which, though it ignored the major problem of gaining regulators' permission, was only slightly optimistic about the results of a merger. Still, the Goldman staff had the impression Armacost wanted the deal. Armacost's main concern seemed to be how long Pinola would remain as president of the combined company before retiring, since Armacost built his succession into the merger plan. Armacost and Pinola arranged a meeting for Saturday, February 29, 1986.

Pinola flew to San Francisco. They planned to meet in the Goldman offices in the massive black tower Bank of America had sold to bolster its income statement. But at 11:00 A.M. someone called from Armacost's office to say he was too busy to come down. How Armacost could show so little respect is difficult to understand. Pinola was not only a former boss, a man with a long, distinguished banking career, but he came in the guise of white knight. Naturally, the meetings did not result in agreement. Pinola even volunteered to try again later in the day, but Armacost turned down the offer. Later in the week, after the Bank of America board meeting, Armacost called Pinola to arrange another meeting. That meeting never occurred, but Pinola stayed in persistent pursuit of the increasingly troubled giant. By the end of the year every business publication had explored the potential of the merger. The media cast Pinola as the "new Gianinni," a reference to the fact that A. P. Gianinni started both institutions as part of his plan to extend his banking empire throughout the world.

On Friday, October 3, 1986, a letter from Pinola arrived in Armacost's office with an offer to acquire BankAmerica. The offer included a promise to issue new securities to finance the acquisition at $18 per share, $8 above the market price. The value of those securities depended on the performance of Bank of America after the takeover. The BankAmerica board of directors met the following Monday. While they considered the offer, other matters seemed more urgent. By the end of that week, Tom Clausen had replaced Armacost as president of the company.

For several months, the two banks' investment bankers met and exchanged desultory proposals while the press carried on the battle between the banks. On the one hand, the media compared Pinola's visionary leadership with Clausen's bureaucratic style. On the other hand, some articles quoted Clausen as "unimpressed" with First Interstate's management, and First Interstate had the same problems as the bank it wanted to acquire: Latin American loans in default, agricultural land and development loans in foreclosure. By January 1987 the deal looked much less attractive to Pinola. If the merger went through, regulatory problems would force the sale of First Interstate Bank of Washington, and the newly merged bank would have to sell stock to increase capital. Its profits would go from lackluster to unacceptably low. BankAmerica sold its most marketable subsidiary, Charles Schwab & Company, at a bargain price, and profits continued to fall. On February 9 First Interstate withdrew its offer. The time had come for Pinola to focus on his internal corporate problems.

To fight falling earnings Pinola closed branches and cut staff. He sold many assets, although he followed through with an agreement to buy Allied Bancshares Incorporated, Texas's fifth-largest bank. Assets acquired in that agreement proved weaker than suspected, and the Texas economy deteriorated quickly. By the end of 1987, First Interstate wrote off $180 million in loans at Allied. Pinola sold more subsidiaries, including a commercial finance company and a government securities operation, and looked around for other nonessential assets to unload. Since the company's headquarters building was too small for the occupants and also out of date, he added it to the list. Then, one night in May 1988, the building burned. While the company's disaster recovery program won credit for minimizing problems (all major operations returned to business the next day), relocating the 1,700 employees and locating backups for the trading room, asset management department, and numerous lost personal computer programs presented a tremendous distraction. Publicity about Los Angeles's first major high-rise fire revealed the lack of a sprinkler system. Although a sprinkler system and other modernizations were completed along with the repairs, the event delayed the sale of the building until a replacement could be completed. The company proceeded with plans for the new building, which would raise the height of the Los Angeles skyline to 72 stories.

Other problems surfaced. In 1989 Allied Bancshares deteriorated further, racking up losses of almost $300 million and forcing the addition of another $400 million to reserves against loan losses. By 1990 stockholders openly rebelled. When Pinola went to see major stockholders to propose issuing new stock to bolster the company's equity, they attacked the proposal. The company was mentioned as a takeover target. On January 17, 1990, First Interstate Bancorporation announced Pinola would retire on his sixty-fifth birthday, to be replaced by Edward Carson, former Phoenix banker and president of First Interstate.

References:

Stephen Beitler, "Western Banks Unify in 'One Face' Plan," *Advertising Age*, 52, no. 23 (June 1, 1981): 36;

Robert Bryan, "First Interstate: California's Restless Giant," *Banker's Monthly*, 103 (October 1986): 23-26;

Teresa Carson, "First Interstate Puts All Its Eggs in Two Baskets," *Business Week*, no. 2881 (February 18, 1985): 72-73;

Carson, "Is Joe Pinola's Problem Bad Luck or Bad Management?," *Business Week*, no. 3073 (October 10, 1988): 39;

Theresa Conlon, "First Interstate, Los Angeles, CA: Outstanding Data Center," *Computer Decisions*, 17 (January 15, 1985): 81-86;

M. William Friis, "Call This Bank Fire Resistant," *ABA Banking Journal*, 80 (September 1988): 82-88;

Gary Hector, *Breaking the Bank: The Decline of BankAmerica* (Boston: Little, Brown, 1988);

"Interview with Joseph J. Pinola, Chairman and CEO, First Interstate Bank," *United States Banker*, 93 (February 1982): 36-38;

"ISM Interviews: Mark Barmann," *Journal of Information Systems Management*, 5 (Fall 1988): 84-88;

Daniel C. Kibbie, *Their Bank—Our Bank; The Quality Bank: A History of First Interstate Bank of California* (Costa Mesa, Cal.: First Interstate Bank of California Professional Publications, 1981);

Jeffrey R. Lauterbach, "Testing the Waters: With a Little Help from Its New York Subsidiary, First Interstate Bancorp Has Established a Foothold in the Financial Planning Market," *Financial Planning*, 14 (March 1985): 162-165;

"The New Giannini?," *United States Banker*, 97 (December 1986): 18-22;

Robert E. Norton, "The Man Who Would Be Boss At Bank America," *Fortune*, 115 (February 16, 1987): 88-94;

Jane Simon, "Franchised Banking Viewed Skeptically By Region's Bankers," *New England Business*, 8 (January 6, 1986): 33, 35;

"Western Bancorp: A Waking Giant Merges Its Far-Flung Fiefdoms," *Business Week*, no. 2676 (February 23, 1981): 134-137.

Charles Ponzi

(188? - January 15, 1949)

by Marcia Grodsky

University of Pittsburgh

Charles Ponzi, one of the most notorious swindlers of the twentieth century and the man responsible for such schemes as chain letters and pyramid sales being dubbed "Ponzi Schemes," was born Carlo Ponsi sometime in the 1880s in Parma, Italy. When he died in 1949 he was generally said to be seventy-one years old, although several sources state his age as sixty-six. He spent his younger years in constant trouble, living a life of petty crime. In 1903, after his family finally tired of his escapades, they purchased a one-way ticket on the S.S. *Vancouver* and sent him to Boston, and from there he took a train to Pittsburgh. A distant cousin

who had previously emigrated had reluctantly agreed to take Ponzi into his business, which involved shipping produce and other foodstuffs.

In a short time Ponzi tired of working for the cousin for such meager wages, so, having mastered the art of falsifying shipping orders, he left Pittsburgh to make his fortune in New York. The wealth about which he spent his waking hours fantasizing continued to elude him, as he spent the next several years in a variety of menial jobs in New York, New Jersey, and New England. At that point in his life Ponzi was convinced that games of chance were going to be his ticket to the life of

Charles Ponzi (courtesy of Underwood & Underwood)

riches to which he aspired, but a number of disheartening experiences finally convinced him that he did not have quick enough hands to make his fortune with a deck of cards. In despair he used the little money at his disposal to buy a ticket to Montreal, where he had heard of a compatriot who had achieved some success as a banker.

Louis Zarossi, who had started out in the cigar business, had founded the Banco Zarossi, funded largely by the savings of Italian immigrants. Zarossi found himself in over his head by the time he met Ponzi, having speculated heavily in real estate. Ponzi, after securing a teller's job in the bank, ingratiated himself with Zarossi and his daughter, Angelina, and soon saw a way to exploit the situation to his advantage.

Ponzi developed a scheme to enable him to take over the Banco Zarossi and enlisted the help of a friend, Angelo Salvati, to convince Zarossi to raise deposit interest rates (which at that time stood at about 2 percent) to 10 percent. Ponzi realized that many immigrant depositors wanted to send money home. Zarossi told them that he sent the money, but in actuality used it to make payments on his debts. In that manner he could stall while he

waited for a loan that Ponzi had assured him was on its way from mythical wealthy friends in Italy.

Ponzi, using the alias "Mr. Bianchi," and Salvati worked their way through Italian neighborhoods, gossiping and spreading word that the Banco Zarossi offered an unheard-of 10 percent return. For a time money poured into the bank.

When people grew suspicious, Ponzi convinced Zarossi to flee the country to avoid jail for embezzlement. However, just when the Banco Zarossi and the riches that Ponzi had dreamed of appeared to be in his grasp, Ponzi found himself double-crossed by his co-conspirator, Salvati. Salvati arranged for authorities to find out about a stolen check Ponzi had used to finance part of the venture, and the state sentenced Ponzi to three years in St. Vincent de Paul Penitentiary on charges of forgery.

Upon his release it took only a very short time for Ponzi to land again in prison. He spent two months in a Plattsburgh, New York, jail after being charged with smuggling illegal aliens into the United States. After pleading guilty he was sent to the Federal penitentiary in Atlanta, Georgia, where he befriended an investment banker named Charles Morse. Morse, who had been sentenced to 15 years in prison for misappropriation of funds (reputedly he had $7 or $8 million hidden away), served less than two years of his sentence before receiving a pardon from President William H. Taft. Ponzi compared his own situation with that of Morse and determined that in the future he would model himself after his friend and mentor and prove that he, too, could become a financial success.

After his release Ponzi spent the next several years drifting around the country, usually one step ahead of the law. His inability to hit upon the perfect money-making scheme frustrated him, and he blamed his failures on the small minds of other people, who failed to recognize his genius.

Ponzi next surfaced in Boston around 1917, when he met an Italian girl he married in 1919. Her name has appeared as Rose Guecco, but that is said to be a misspelling. Her name may actually have been Grecco. Ponzi took over her father's produce business and within a short time ran it into bankruptcy.

His next venture was the *Trader's Guide*, a loose-leaf publication Ponzi hoped to circulate among importers. He planned to secure the names of 200,000 overseas businessmen and mail the binder to half of them (initially) at no charge. Every six months he would mail inserts that contained advertisements along with new reading material. He anticipated that his targeted audience would keep the *Guide* as a permanent reference book, updated periodically with the inserts. He planned to sell three pages of advertising for each page of text.

Ponzi spent his days trying to raise funds to launch the publication, which would have been one of his more legitimate ventures, when he received an inquiry from overseas enclosing an international reply coupon to pay the postage for Ponzi's response. That transaction gave Ponzi the germ of the idea for the scheme that finally gave him the fame and fortune he craved. He abandoned all thoughts of the *Trader's Guide* and embarked upon his grand venture.

An organization known as the Universal Postal Union issued the international reply coupons to enable a correspondent to prepay the postage for a reply. Immigrants to the United States often included them in their letters home to help their old-country recipients, who often could not afford to pay postage. But all member nations of the Union offered the coupons for sale and redemption, at permanent exchange rates unaffected by currency fluctuations.

Ponzi realized he could send a dollar to Italy, have it exchanged for 20 lire at the going rate, and purchase 66 coupons. Each coupon would buy five U.S. 5-cent stamps, worth a total of $3.30. He understood he could not usually duplicate the 230 percent profit of the U.S.-Italian exchange, but the principle would work in any country in which the currency had depreciated relative to the United States.

The problem of converting the profit in stamps into cash remained, but Ponzi only gave that cursory thought. As he did not actually plan to deal in the coupons or stamps, only to convince others that he was doing so, he merely needed to provide a plausible explanation to potential investors.

Ponzi scheduled a series of public presentations to recruit profit-hungry investors to the scheme, which involved raising start-up capital for a Securities Exchange Company to perform the service of accomplishing the exchanges. An extraordinarily glib man, he could talk until his audience grew so confused that people could not focus on the problem or admit they did not understand what he was talking about. Sometimes when investiga-

tors came around in an effort to unmask a certain swindle, he had the police begging him to take their money before they left. His explanation of the postal exchange worked at least that well. Modest beginnings—five- and ten-dollar bills from friends in the Italian community—soon turned into a stream of investors, lured by Ponzi's promise of 40 percent interest on a 90-day loan to the company. He would pay the interest on the 90-day notes within 45 days and convince the happy investors to reenlist for another 45 days at 50 percent, enabling them to profit to the tune of 125 percent in 90 days.

For the next eight months Ponzi's scheme continued to grow at phenomenal rates. By the end of May 1920 he took in around $200,000 a day. He had become the talk of New England, and investors from Europe and South America tried to get in on his gold mine. Most of the initial investors had come from the ranks of workers, but soon millionaires literally stood in line along with street sweepers, waiting to put their money into Ponzi's hands. The only common denominators were greed and a desire to be part of the excitement that surrounded Ponzi and his venture. At one point, when a crowd cheered Ponzi and called him "the greatest Italian of them all," Ponzi replied that Columbus and Marconi were greater because Columbus discovered America and Marconi discovered the wireless. The crowd reportedly answered, "But you discovered money!"

Despite all the attention, not until the summer of 1920 did any word of Ponzi's operation make it into print. On June 9 a small article appeared in the *Boston Post*, but it did not even mention Ponzi by name. In July, the courts served him with a million-dollar lawsuit. Far from discouraging investors, however, the publicity brought in almost $450,000 the day after the story broke.

The lawsuit story also aroused the curiosity of the *Post's* acting publisher, Richard Grozier, who laid the groundwork for the paper's investigation of Ponzi. Eventually that led both to Ponzi's downfall and to a Pulitzer Prize for the newspaper, despite the fact that many of the reporters for the paper also invested and believed in Ponzi's scheme.

Meanwhile Ponzi had opened branch offices of the Securities Exchange Company and had started to diversify. He owned part of the Hanover Trust Company and talked about purchasing more banks as well as movie theaters and steamship lines. He badly needed to find some other major ven-

Ponzi on his way to Italy after his 1934 deportation from the United States (courtesy of the Boston University Journalism Library)

ture before the walls caved in. Although he took in phenomenal amounts of money, every dollar invested with him left him further in debt.

At that point Ponzi hired a publicity agent, William McMasters, who soon realized that Ponzi's operation could hardly be legitimate, and, largely to protect himself, urged Ponzi to give an interview to the *Post* and to answer questions for the district attorney.

An article then appeared in the *Post* that quoted Charles Barron, who had discovered that the amount of international reply coupons redeemed each day over the past several months averaged only $8.00. On the other hand, the article also quoted a local judge who vouched for Ponzi. Within hours of the appearance of that article the line of investors stretched for blocks, kept under control by six mounted policemen. That day Ponzi took in $2 million.

However, a U.S. district attorney decided that Ponzi's activities warranted an investigation and convinced Ponzi to discontinue taking in money pend-

ing a look into his books. He allowed Ponzi to continue paying off notes for a week. The investigation was complicated by the fact that Ponzi kept his records in a chronological card-file list. Federal and state auditors failed to come within a half million dollars of each others' estimates. Still, it became clear that Ponzi had no intention of using the massive capital funds he was generating to create a full-fledged postal exchange company. The final blow came on August 2, when the *Post* carried the headline, "Ponzi Hopelessly Insolvent." The article, written by McMasters, Ponzi's own publicity agent, concluded that Ponzi had fallen more than $2 million into debt even if he paid no interest on his outstanding notes. With interest the indebtedness increased to more than $4.5 million.

Ponzi and his attorney concocted a plan whereby Ponzi pled guilty to using the mail to defraud. A federal court sentenced him to five years in prison. His celebrity status there irritated state officials, who began prosecution on the state charges. His attorneys fought those efforts to little avail. The U.S. Supreme Court rejected their claim that Ponzi was strictly under federal jurisdiction. However, his subsequent trial resulted in a verdict of not guilty when the jury deadlocked.

In 1924 Ponzi was released from prison after serving three and a half years of his five-year sentence. Later that year the state brought him to trial on additional charges, and once again the jury deadlocked. A third state trial in 1925, however, resulted in a guilty verdict on larceny charges. Ponzi was sentenced to serve seven to nine years in the Massachusetts State Prison.

While out on bail awaiting his appeal, Ponzi attempted to raise money through a Florida land swindle. Convicted of fraud after an investigation showed that he had peddled swamp land, he received another year in jail. Ponzi jumped bail and fled to Texas, where he took a job on an Italian freighter. He never made it to Italy, as authorities captured him in New Orleans and returned him to Massachusetts to serve his sentence.

In 1931 the final bankruptcy report on the Securities Exchange Company was filed. It showed Ponzi's assets as $1,331,703.11 and his liabilities as $3,986,179.77.

Ponzi, released from prison on February 14, 1934, faced deportation to Italy within a year. He spent the next two years in Rome working as a bookkeeper and later as a salesman and working on his memoir, *The Rise of Mr. Ponzi* (1937). His wife, whom he had left in Boston, divorced him. Ponzi became very bitter and threatened to expose important people in a second book, to be titled, "The Boston Merry-Go-Round." He called a press conference in Rome and told reporters, "I'm going to pieces. I'm going to hell, and I'm going to take a lot of people with me. . . . And I'm making careful plans to make a surprise appearance in the United States when I'm least expected." Nothing came of the book, the threats, or the return to the United States.

In 1939 Ponzi's fortunes took a brief turn for the better through his connections with the Italian Fascists. Italian Air Force colonel Attileo Biseo, Benito Mussolini's personal pilot, was Ponzi's second cousin. Biseo offered Ponzi a position in Rio de Janeiro as business manager of LATI, an airline operating between Brazil and Italy.

That phase of Ponzi's career was short-lived, however, as investigations showed that LATI smuggled spies, strategic minerals, escaped military figures, and microfilm to the Axis. After the United States entered World War II, Brazilian authorities cut off gasoline supplies for the airline, and by the close of 1941 Ponzi's business affairs again struggled.

After that Ponzi had a succession of business failures and low-paying jobs until 1948, when his health began to fail. He died in the charity ward of a Brazilian hospital on January 15, 1949.

Shortly before his death Ponzi bragged that he had attempted to defraud the USSR of $2 million by falsely promising to smuggle gold into Russia while leaving the money in Western European banks. Scheming to the end, he said, "What a joke on the Communists that would have been."

Publication:
The Rise of Mr. Ponzi (New York & Rome: Published by the author, 1937).

References:
Donald H. Dunn, *Ponzi!* (New York: McGraw-Hill, 1975);

"The Rise of Mr. Ponzi," *New Yorker* (May 8, 1937): 18-22;

"Take My Money," *Time*, 53 (January 31, 1949): 21.

Postal Savings Banks

by James Smallwood

University of Texas at Tyler

The desire of reformers to transform the nation's banking system can be traced back at least as far as the Populist movement of the late nineteenth century. Led by such figures as "Sockless" Jerry Simpson and Mary Elizabeth Pease, early Populists called for either nationalization or strong government regulation of the banking industry. Although the Populist movement waned after the defeat of William Jennings Bryan in 1896, the Progressives who followed kept the idea of regulation alive—regulation designed especially to protect small depositors. Leading Progressives, however, would not support nationalization of the system, nor would a majority lobby for strict regulation; rather, they supported the creation of a system that would, in a sense, become a forerunner of the modern federal deposit insurance programs.

Although many bankers cried "socialism," in 1910 Congress passed, with President William Howard Taft's approval, an act creating the Postal Savings System. The system proved beneficial to small investors who remained suspicious of large private banks because of periodic depressions, recessions, and panics, such as those that swept the country in 1893 and 1907. Under the act the government authorized select post offices to receive deposits and to pay 2 percent interest on the accounts. The U.S. Treasury kept an amount equal to 5 percent of the postal deposits as a reserve. The Treasury could then redeposit the funds in existing national or state banks at an interest rate of at least 2 1/4 percent. Alternately, the fund's trustees could invest up to 30 percent of the deposits in government bonds. Further, on the president's order, all the moneys in the system could be converted to government bonds.

Although the Progressives achieved their goal, the Postal Savings System grew slowly, and it remained a minor factor in the national economy, leaving the banking industry virtually untouched. As late as September 1929, when the public held more than $3.8 billion in currency and commercial banks held more than $42.5 billion in deposits, postal deposits amounted to only $160 million. However, as the Great Depression ran its course from 1929 to 1941, and banks by the thousands closed their doors, small depositors lost faith in the private banking industry; postal deposits increased eightfold by December 1933. Still, by the end of 1940 postal deposits amounted to only $1.3 billion. Commercial banks and mutual savings banks dwarfed the postal deposit base.

With the success of the New Deal's Federal Deposit Insurance Corporation and Federal Savings and Loan Insurance Corporation, postal savings deposits slowly declined in the post-World War II era. By June 1960 postal deposits of $800 million stood

at a 28-year low. Continuing decline influenced Congress in 1967 to abolish the program: it had lived past its time.

Although the success the Progressives envisioned always evaded the Postal Savings System, it served a purpose. It reassured a distrusting public—especially during the recessions of 1912 to 1914 and 1919 to 1920 and during the early phase of the Great Depression—that banking was worthwhile. Congress did not abolish the program until it no longer seemed needed.

References:

Paolo E. Coletta, *The Presidency of William Howard Taft* (Lawrence: University of Kansas Press, 1973);

Milton Friedman and Anna J. Schwartz, *A Monetary History of the United States, 1867-1960* (Princeton: Princeton University Press, 1963);

William E. Leuchtenburg, *Franklin D. Roosevelt and the New Deal* (New York: Harper & Row, 1963);

Arthur S. Link, *Woodrow Wilson and the Progressive Era* (New York: Harper & Row, 1954);

Paul Studenki and Herman F. Krooss, *Financial History of the United States* (New York: McGraw-Hill, 1963).

William Proxmire

(November 11, 1915 -   )

by Scott W. Fischer

University of Virginia

CAREER: Student clerk, J. P. Morgan & Company (1940-1941); U.S. Army Counterintelligence Corps (1941-1946); reporter and political analyst, *Madison Capital Times* (1949); editor, *Union Labor News* (1949-1950); Wisconsin state assembly (1951-1953); vice-president, Brooks Implement Company (1951-1953); president, Artcraft Press Company (1953-1957), U.S. Senator, Wisconsin (1957-1989).

Edward William Proxmire, maverick Democratic senator who fought against government waste and for consumer protection in the banking industry, was born on November 11, 1915, in the northern Chicago suburb of Lake Forest, Illinois, the second of three children of Dr. Theodore S. and Adele (Flanagan) Proxmire. Dr. Proxmire, a staunch conservative Republican, was a surgeon and chief of staff at a local hospital and the founder of a

nearby tuberculosis sanitarium. At age six the future senator began using his middle name in honor of cowboy film star William S. Hart. In 1934 he graduated from the Hill Preparatory School in Pottstown, Pennsylvania, and four years later, in 1938, he graduated with a bachelor's degree in English from Yale College where he also boxed and played football.

After Yale, Proxmire entered Harvard Business School and earned an M.B.A., cum laude, in 1940. After six months as a student clerk with the New York investment firm of J. P. Morgan & Company, he joined the U.S. Army in March 1941 to serve in the Counterintelligence Corps. He spent his entire military service during World War II in the United States, stationed primarily in the Chicago area. Before his discharge in January 1946 he had risen from the rank of private to First Lieutenant.

William Proxmire

Proxmire returned to J. P. Morgan for a brief stint but soon went back to Harvard to pursue a graduate degree in public administration while serving as a teaching fellow. Completing all doctoral requirements except for the dissertation, he graduated with a master's degree in public administration in 1948. While at Harvard he decided to become a Democrat, because "Democrats came up with all the answers, while the Republicans always seemed to give explanations that nothing ought to be done, and the system would take care of itself." Proxmire's father later lamented, "I didn't raise my boy to be a Democrat. Harvard's where it happened." During that period Proxmire also decided to pursue a career in politics and began a search for a job at a medium-sized newspaper as a political writer. After researching states where party conditions offered good prospects for newcomers, he settled on Wisconsin, not very far from his native metropolitan Chicago. In April 1949 the liberal *Madison Capital Times* hired him as a reporter and political analyst but fired him less than a year later after personal conflicts with the paper's publisher and his efforts to unionize the paper's staff. He next became the editor of the *Union Labor News*, the local publication of the American Federation of Labor (AFL) in Madison. The job also included the hosting duties on "Labor Sounds Off," the AFL's weekly local radio program, which provided Proxmire with a public speaking platform.

During the later 1940s the Wisconsin Democratic party was not very strong and had few statewide officeholders. Proxmire quickly gained notoriety within the party and is credited with helping revitalize it during the 1950s. He participated in the activities of a group of liberal Democrats based in Madison and loosely affiliated with the journal the *Progressive*, the *Capital Times*, and the University of Wisconsin. Although several members of the group ran for offices across the state and were beaten badly, they came to dominate statewide politics after 1957.

In February 1950 Proxmire announced his candidacy for the Wisconsin state assembly. Using tactics that marked his subsequent campaigns, such as daily canvassing door-to-door and outside factory gates, Proxmire tried to make personal contact with as many voters as possible. Later, after he had become a senator, pundits said that it was almost impossible to enter a Green Bay Packers' football game without shaking Proxmire's hand. His persistence paid off, and he won an upset victory in the general election.

As a state representative Proxmire earned a reputation as a gadfly, a characterization that remained with him throughout his political career. He unsuccessfully proposed bills to restrain lobbyists, limit campaign spending, close tax loopholes, and protect consumers in utility rate hearings. When no Democrat wanted to challenge popular Republican governor Walter J. Kohler, Proxmire risked his assembly seat to run for the governorship in 1952. For a first-term state legislator to seek the governorship was unheard of, but he won the nomination that year and again in 1954 and 1956. He lost all three elections, although only narrowly in 1954. During his campaigns Proxmire took risks that only a few others willingly made, explicitly criticizing the smear tactics of Wisconsin's controversial Republican senator, Joseph R. McCarthy. While campaigning he supported his family as vice-president of the Brooks Implement Company, in which he had also owned an interest since 1951. In 1953 he sold his interest in Brooks to purchase half interest and serve as president for the Artcraft Press Company, a Waterloo, Wisconsin, printing company.

After three consecutive gubernatorial losses Proxmire's political career appeared over. Friends advised him to sit out for at least ten years and resign himself to the presidency of Artcraft. But the situation changed when Senator McCarthy died on May 2, 1957. Proxmire immediately tossed his hat into the ring. Easily defeating a Milwaukee congressman for the Democratic nomination, he once again faced Walter Kohler, who had won the Republican nomination after a divisive campaign. When Kohler attacked Proxmire as a "three-time loser," Proxmire responded, "My opponent doesn't know what it is to lose. I do. And I'll welcome the support of voters who do. I'll take the losers. I'll take the debtors. I'll take those who've lost in love, or baseball, or in business. I'll take the Milwaukee Braves." Surprising most observers, Proxmire won by a 56 to 41 percent margin over Kohler, and the election prevented a 48 to 48 tie that would have allowed the Republicans to organize the Senate. Because McCarthy's term was scheduled to expire the next year, Proxmire immediately faced a reelection campaign. In 1958, a big year for the Democrats na-

tionally, he won his first full term with 57 percent of the vote.

Once in office Proxmire again earned the reputation as a maverick and gadfly. After Senate majority leader Lyndon B. Johnson refused to appoint him to the Finance Committee, Proxmire attacked Johnson and House Speaker Sam Rayburn for their dictatorial control of Congress; colleagues referred to one such 1959 speech as "Proxmire's Farewell Address." He also earned the reputation as a populist, opposing issues and nominees that he feared would allow private interests, especially oil companies, to benefit at public expense. During that period, he also became a master of the filibuster. On one occasion he held the floor for more than 34 hours, one of the longest filibusters on record, to protest President John F. Kennedy's nomination of Texas oilman Lawrence O'Connor to the Federal Power Commission.

Proxmire also opposed Kennedy on five major issues decided by margins of five votes or less during 1961 and 1962. That resistance helped lower his popularity rating. In 1964 a methodologically questionable poll conducted by *Pageant* magazine asked journalists and members of Congress to rank congressmen and senators. The journalists ranked Proxmire as fourth lowest among all senators. Proxmire won reelection in Lyndon Johnson's landslide presidential victory, but with only 53 percent of the vote, and he believed that the poll had cost him at least 200,000 votes. After that he claimed he was more "pragmatic" and never won with anything less than 64 percent of the vote.

Proxmire gradually gained seniority on the Appropriations Committee and on the Banking, Housing, and Urban Affairs Committee. In 1968 he became one of two alternating chairmen of the Joint Economic Committee, a combined House and Senate body that reviewed the president's annual economic report. He also led its Federal Procurement Subcommittee on economy in government (the name of which he changed first to Economy in Government Subcommittee, and then later to Subcommittee on Priorities and Economy in Government). Those positions gave him more political leverage and public attention. He became known as a champion of the individual consumer and a critic of government spending. Proxmire authored several laws regulating the credit card industry, most of which the industry opposed.

In 1968 the Consumer Credit Protection Act (better known as the Truth-in-Lending Act) required financial institutions and companies offering credit cards to inform prospective buyers of finance charges in writing and in their advertising; the act was designed to allow consumers to shop for the best deal and to know if the lender was illegally taking advantage of them. The act also restricted the garnishment of wages. Two years later, in 1970, the Proxmire-sponsored Fair Credit Reporting Act granted individuals the right to review and correct personal files maintained by credit reporting agencies. When consumers are rejected for credit, insurance, or employment purposes, they must be informed about which credit agency issued the report. Credit agencies must also disclose all information in their files and correct any inaccuracies. All personal information must be kept confidential and can only be used for legitimate purposes. Proxmire also sponsored the Credit Card Act, which restricted unsolicited mailings of credit cards and placed a limit on the personal liability for stolen credit cards used illegally.

Although he took liberal positions on most issues, Proxmire sounded like a conservative when it came to government spending. Classifying himself as a "thrifty liberal," Proxmire stated, "When the big spending has been for the military, space, and highway and public works programs—all darlings of the conservatives, liberals have their pork barrels too. These must be examined critically." Many government agencies were embarrassed by his investigations into wasteful government spending. In 1969 Proxmire's Subcommittee on Priorities and Economy in Government discovered a $2 billion cost overrun in the production of the C-5A cargo plane. The subcommittee's report, entitled *The Economics of Military Procurement*, led to the adoption of new uniform accounting practices that allowed the government to estimate the costs of defense programs with more accuracy and mandated weapons production status reports showing cost overrun amounts. Proxmire's own book, *Report from Wasteland: America's Military-Industrial Complex* (1970), reiterated the warnings of President Dwight D. Eisenhower's farewell address that close relationships between the military and defense contractors posed a threat to the Treasury.

Almost all government departments and programs received Proxmire's attention. He successfully led the protracted fight against the construction of the Supersonic Transport (SST) airplane designed to compete with the British-French Concorde, which Congress rejected in 1971. Proxmire also thought that unmanned space exploration was safer and more cost efficient than manned missions, but Congress, also in 1971, rejected his proposals to cancel the space shuttle program. On the other hand, he battled against the Trident submarine program, which proved quite cost effective.

Proxmire also attacked numerous examples of subsidies and bailouts of private industries that would fail if left to market forces. Opposing Washington State's Democratic senators Henry Jackson and Warren Magnuson, he came within one vote of preventing the 1971 federal subsidization of nearly bankrupt Lockheed Aircraft Corporation, based in Seattle. He also opposed the federal purchase of ailing northeastern railroads to create the Conrail Corporation. Proxmire initially opposed the federal bailouts of New York City in 1975 and Chrysler Corporation in 1979, but he voted for them after obtaining conditions imposing strict cost efficiency measures and budget cutbacks. Although he normally opposed subsidies and bailouts, he consistently supported dairy price supports, opposition to which would have been tantamount to political suicide in Wisconsin. He justified the dairy subsidies by arguing that price supports were the only thing protecting dairy farmers from corporate takeovers.

Proxmire's 1972 book, *Uncle Sam—The Last of the Bigtime Spenders*, described examples of what he considered wasteful pork-barrel spending in government; however, a practice he began in 1975 attracted more consistent notoriety. He awarded a monthly "Golden Fleece Award" to government programs he felt best exemplified wasteful spending. Although some commentators criticized the awards as a publicity stunt, Senate Majority Leader Robert Byrd commented that the awards eventually became "as much a part of the Senate as quorum calls and filibusters." Golden Fleece recipients included a University of Virginia doctoral candidate who won a government grant to study bullfighting in Spain, the Army for spending $6,000 to study the best way to purchase Worcestershire sauce, and the Agriculture Department for a study of how fast the average American family prepares breakfast. Many academics criticized Proxmire for oversimplifying their research, and one researcher sued him for libel after he criticized a government-funded study about why monkeys clench their jaws.

Proxmire eventually settled out of court for $10,000 after the Supreme Court rejected his contention that senatorial press releases and statements were exempt from normal libel laws.

Proxmire also practiced economy measures in operating his Senate office and reelection campaigns. His office operated with much less personnel and one-third less funding than permitted under Senate rules. He always refused contributions from political action committees and after 1974 refused all contributions. His 1976 and 1982 campaigns each cost less than $200, most of which went for filing costs and the stationery and postage needed to return contributions.

In 1975 Proxmire assumed the chairmanship of the Banking, Housing, and Urban Affairs Committee. Because of his longtime efforts to regulate the credit industry, the national banking establishment expressed apprehension about such a prospect, and many businessmen and corporations attempted to prevent the series of committee switches that made Proxmire chairman by contributing large sums to the reelection campaign of Arkansas senator J. William Fulbright.

Their fears proved unfounded, and most of the banking community supported the major piece of legislation that came out of the Banking Committee during Proxmire's first stint as chairman. After a decade of advocacy by Proxmire, Congress passed the Depository Institutions Deregulation and Monetary Control Act in 1980, one of the most ambitious banking deregulation bills ever passed. The act gradually lifted the ceilings on interest rates for bank and savings accounts, allowed federally insured financial institutions to offer interest-bearing checking accounts, gave savings and loans new consumer lending powers, and required all depositing agencies to maintain reserves at levels mandated by the Federal Reserve Board.

When the Republicans gained control of the Senate in the 1980 election, Proxmire lost his chairmanship but became the ranking minority member of the Appropriations Committee. The new Banking chairman, Jake Garn, advocated further deregulation in banking, but Proxmire, still serving on the committee, held off and generally agreed with industry leaders that banks required different treatment from other financial institutions. He especially distrusted permitting nonbank financial institutions to purchase banks and provide traditional banking services, fearing that further deregulation would allow large banks and corporations such as Sears, Roebuck and American Express to drive smaller banks out of business.

Although Congress passed a major banking bill in 1982, conflicts between the Republican Senate and the Democratic House prevented the passage of any further major bills until the Democrats regained the Senate in the 1986 elections. Proxmire had been in line for the chairmanship of the Appropriations Committee, a position which would have better enabled him to uncover wasteful spending, but several senators, resenting Proxmire's continual opposition to congressional pay raises, perquisites and tax breaks, convinced John Stennis of Mississippi to switch from the ranking position on another committee to become the ranking member on Appropriations. Due to that move and changes in Senate membership, Proxmire was the only Democrat restored to his prior chairmanship.

The new composition of the Senate allowed Congress to pass a major banking bill, the Competitive Equality Banking Act of 1987, especially after Proxmire, along with House Banking Chairman Fernand St Germain, broke a congressional stalemate and successfully negotiated with the White House to prevent a veto by President Ronald Reagan. Congress intended parts of the bill to help the ailing savings and loan industry, which had been plagued with failing institutions due to faulty investment and management practices; the bill provided $10.8 billion to help rescue the Federal Savings and Loan Insurance Corporation, the federal corporation that insures individual savings deposits up to $100,000, funding that would eventually be paid back by the industry. Another section of the bill outlawed the further establishment of "non-bank banks," a loophole in federal law that allowed institutions to escape certain banking regulations by taking deposits or writing loans but not both. Proxmire's refusal to drop that provision delayed the passage of a major banking bill in 1986. The bill also contained provisions aimed at individual consumers. Banks had to make deposits available to their customers within two days for checks written on local banks and five days for out-of-town checks.

Upon the passage of the 1987 banking bill Proxmire stated that it was only the first installment of a total revision of the federal regulatory structure of financial institutions. Shortly thereafter, in a step that seemed somewhat out of character, he proposed the outright repeal of the Great Depression-era Glass-Steagall Act—the 1934 law that had instituted stiff regulation to separate the banking and securities industries in order to prevent corrupt self-dealing. Banks would have been granted securities powers. Although Jake Garn had suggested the repeal of Glass-Steagall during his tenure as Banking chairman, Proxmire had opposed the idea until colleagues convinced him in 1987 that regulatory actions had significantly removed many of the barriers between commercial and investment banks. In order to protect depositors from increased risks, the bill would have allowed banks to affiliate with securities firms through bank holding companies and also would have placed new capital requirements on banks and limited the financial and personnel connections between banks and their affiliates. Proxmire had hoped that the bill would give him a final triumph before he retired, but jurisdictional disputes between several House committees during the 1988 session delayed consideration, and the 100th Congress adjourned before both chambers could agree on an acceptable package.

Besides banking and business legislation, Proxmire was noted for several other interests. He led the successful effort that opposed Republican Minority Leader Everett Dirkson's efforts to overturn the Supreme Court's 1964 "one man one vote" decision, which mandated that the states each base their legislative districts on equal population and that each national congressional district also be of equal population.

Two Proxmire practices became daily traditions in the Senate. Proxmire prided himself that he never missed a roll call vote from 1966 until his retirement. Also in 1966, he began a 20-year campaign that resulted in what Proxmire considered the legacy of his Senate career. He opened each daily Senate session since that time with a speech advocating U.S. ratification of the international genocide treaty, giving more than 3,000 speeches in all. Many conservatives had opposed ratification because of fears of a possible loss of American sovereignty to an international body, but the Senate finally ratified the treaty in February 1986. The treaty changed the U.S. criminal code to include penalties for genocide, defined as acting with the intent to destroy, in whole or part, national, ethnic, racial, or religious groups.

On the personal side, Proxmire was an ardent proponent of physical fitness. After early morning exercise sessions he daily jogged the five miles from his home to his office. His diet consisted of high-protein breakfasts and light lunches. In 1973 he authored *You Can Do It! Senator Proxmire's Exercise, Diet, and Relaxation Plan.* On one occasion his colleagues used his fitness regimen to respond to his efforts to reduce congressional operating costs. After he unsuccessfully opposed the construction of the Hart Senate Office Building, he convinced the Senate to eliminate funds for a gym in the new building; the Senate amended the provision to close the existing gym that he used to shower and change clothes after his morning runs.

Proxmire's personal life has occasionally suffered at the expense of his political career. He married Elsie Borden Rockefeller, a grand-niece of John D. Rockefeller, Sr., in September 1946. They had two children, Theodore (Ted) and Elsie (Cici). After Proxmire had entered politics, his wife could not deal with his 19-hour workdays and filed for a divorce, granted in February 1955. On December 1, 1956, a month after his third gubernatorial loss, Proxmire married Ellen Hodges Sawall, the executive secretary of the Wisconsin Democratic party, who was also divorced with two children. Together Proxmire and his second wife had two children, William Wayne, who died the day after he was born in July 1958, and Douglas Clark, named after Democratic senators Paul Douglas of Illinois and Joseph Clark of Pennsylvania. Proxmire and his second wife temporarily separated during the early 1970s but announced in 1975 that they had reconciled.

On the 30th anniversary of his first Senate election, Proxmire announced in August 1987 that he would not seek another term. When he retired in 1989 at the age of seventy-three, he was third in seniority behind John Stennis, who also did not seek reelection in 1988, and Strom Thurmond. He announced that he would remain in Washington and write and deliver speeches on economic issues. He also vowed to keep issuing the Golden Fleece Awards.

Publications:

Can Small Business Survive? (Chicago: Regnery, 1964);

Report from Wasteland: America's Military-Industrial Complex (New York: Praeger, 1970);

Uncle Sam—the Last of the Bigtime Spenders (New York: Simon & Schuster, 1972);

Town Hall Meeting on Domestic Affairs: Can Congress Control Spending? (Washington, D.C.: American Enterprise Institute, 1973);

You Can Do It! Senator Proxmire's Exercise, Diet, and Relaxation Plan (New York: Simon & Schuster, 1973);
The Fleecing of America (Boston: Houghton Mifflin, 1980).

References:
Ellen Proxmire, *One Foot in Washington: The Perilous*

Life of a Senator's Wife (Washington, D.C.: Luce, 1964);
Jay G. Sykes, *Proxmire* (Washington, D.C.: Luce, 1972).

Reconstruction Finance Corporation

by Gary M. Pecquet

Southwest Texas State University

The Reconstruction Finance Corporation (RFC) was a federal credit agency that helped finance many of the New Deal programs of the 1930s. It also helped channel resources to direct the war effort during World War II. Similar in organization to the War Finance Corporation of 1918 to 1929, the RFC grew in scope and function during its first two decades until the Eisenhower administration finally dissolved it in 1954. Several other federal credit corporations have survived the RFC, including the Federal National Mortgage Administration, the Export-Import Bank, and the Small Business Administration.

After the stock market crash of 1929 many firms and individuals went bankrupt. The Smoot-Hawley tariff of June 1930 aggravated the situation by setting off an international wave of protectionism. American farmers who previously exported about half of their produce found themselves without markets for their crops. Prices of farm commodities plummeted, and farmers suffered dearly. In the midst of the crisis financial institutions also failed. Bank runs, monetary contraction, and price deflation ensued.

In the fall of 1931 President Herbert Hoover proposed the formation of a private corporation to restore confidence in the credit markets. He summoned the aid of the Federal Reserve chairman Eugene Meyer to secure the "cooperation" of private bankers, who established a National Credit Corporation. Chairman Meyer considered that plan inadequate. Hoover intended to threaten bankers with the possibility of a new War Finance Corporation to secure their unofficial cooperation. He was foiled, however, when a bankers' convention unanimously favored the WFC resurrection. In December

1931 Hoover formally proposed the reestablishment of the War Finance Corporation. He hoped, "It may not be necessary to use such an instrumentality very extensively. The very existence of such a bulwark will strengthen confidence."

Federal Reserve chairman Meyer, who had served as the director of the War Finance Corporation, helped draft the legislation for the new agency. The Reconstruction Finance Corporation came into existence on January 22, 1932. Its organization closely resembled the old WFC. The treasury contributed $500 million in operating capital, and the original law permitted the corporation to borrow another $1.5 billion. That limit was increased to $3.3 billion in July 1932.

Seven directors appointed by the president and approved by the Senate governed the RFC. All seven directors served simultaneous two-year terms and no more than four of the seven could claim membership of the same political party. The Federal Reserve chairman, the secretary of the Treasury, and the farm loan commissioner initially acted as ex-officio members of the RFC directorate. Meyer, as Fed chairman, became the first RFC chairman. He helped organize the corporation until a July 1932 amendment eliminated the Fed chairman and farm loan commissioner as ex-officio members of the directorate. In 1938 the ex-officio position of the Treasury secretary was eliminated along with another post, reducing the directorate to five members.

The RFC obtained financing from the sale of capital stock to the Treasury and the sale of the assets on terminated programs. It also reinvested its own interest receipts and borrowed heavily from the Treasury. During its lifetime the RFC borrowed $51.3 billion from the public. Administrative prob-

Reconstruction Finance Corporation counsel James L. Dougherty (left) swearing in the original RFC board in February 1932: Ogden L. Mills, Paul Bestor, Harvey Couch, Charles G. Dawes, Jesse H. Jones, and Eugene Meyer (courtesy of International News Services)

lems often arose because the goals and powers of the RFC often overlapped with other federal agencies. "Another administrative weakness," according to economist James M. Bickley, "was that the requirements for obtaining an RFC loan became so loose and vague that subjective case-by-case decisions were often made. The probability of obtaining a loan often depended upon political contacts, and unfortunately some credit may have been granted as compensation for political support."

President Franklin D. Roosevelt appointed Jesse Jones, a conservative Democrat, chairman of the RFC in 1933. Jones served as chairman until 1939, when he received the new post of Federal Loan Director, which oversaw the RFC and other lending agencies. Jones continued as the top administrator of government credit until he retired in 1945. Emil Schram (1939-1941) and Charles B. Henderson (1941-1947) filled his old post as RFC chairman. It was under Jones's tenure, however, that Congress greatly extended the scope and functions of the RFC.

Initially the RFC could lend money only to insolvent banks to assist in their reorganization. Later it could provide funds to any bank upon the recommendation of the Treasury. Still later the loan function was expanded to encompass practically all financial institutions, including insurance compa-

nies, agricultural lending agencies, and mortgage companies.

The original RFC Act organized several Regional Agricultural Credit corporations. The RFC could channel money through those federal agencies to help farmers in distressed regions. In 1933 the RFC was authorized to finance joint-stock land banks. Congress created the Commodity Credit Corporation in 1936 through which the RFC could finance farmers. That same year the RFC started to finance the Rural Electrification Administration. In 1941 the RFC obtained the power to advance credit to tenant farmers so they could acquire land.

During 1932-1934 Congress amended the RFC Act to enable the corporation to finance home mortgages. In 1935 the RFC could subscribe the capital stock in mortgage loan companies. The RFC subsequently established the RFC Mortgage Company and the Federal National Mortgage Association (FNMA). The RFC Mortgage Company lent $660,901 between 1935 and 1947, and FNMA financed more than $3 billion worth of home loans between 1938 and 1950.

In 1934 Congress gave the RFC permission to make business loans, provided that the firms could not obtain credit at the prevailing rate, and were adequately secured. The maximum term of such loans was five years and the maximum amount was

$500,000 per firm. In 1935 the collateral restriction was relaxed to read, "So secured as to assume repayment," and the maximum term of the loan increased to ten years. By 1938 the risk clause was weakened still further to read, "Of such sound value, or so secured as to reasonably assure retirement or repayment," and in 1940 the maturity deadline was extended to 15 years.

The Emergency Relief and Construction Act of July 1932 authorized the RFC to lend $300 million to distressed states. Those loans were to be repaid at 3 percent interest by 1937. In 1934, however, the loans turned into gifts. Legislation during 1933 authorized another set of loans to states and cities, including $1.5 billion in "self-liquidating" loans and another $322 million in other loans, not necessarily self-liquidating.

Additional loans went to support exports. Before Washington officially recognized the government of the Soviet Union in 1933, the RFC advanced a $4 million loan to the Soviet government to assist a Soviet trading company in the purchase of surplus cotton. The Export-Import Bank (a subsidiary of the RFC) was organized amidst negotiations with the Soviet government. Those talks broke down over the settlement of Russian debts contracted before the Revolution. The bank, nonetheless, entered into operations and lent more than $500 million between 1934 and 1945, mostly to Latin American countries.

Thus the RFC made loans to virtually every sector of the economy, and it also advanced disaster relief to flood victims and support to railroads. The RFC did refrain from making certain loans. Jones included oil drilling, the automobile industry, churches, newspapers, and radio stations on his "no" list. He considered the oil and automobile industries profitable enough to obtain private financing. Moreover, the nature of oil drilling is such that if someone was advanced money to begin drilling, his neighbors would have immediately applied for a similar loan, and the RFC could not have rightly refused to advance the funds. For similar reasons a loan to one church would require the RFC to lend equitably to every denomination. Jones refrained from lending to newspapers and radio stations for fear of being accused of influencing their editorial policies.

During World War II the primary duty of the RFC was to help shift resources toward the defense industries. More than 80 percent of the RFC's funds went to defense-related industries. Congress created many RFC subsidiaries, including the Defense Plant Corporation, the Defense Supplies Corporation, the Rubber Development Corporation, the Metals Reserve Corporation, the War Damage Corporation, and the United States Commercial Company.

The largest of those subsidiaries, the Defense Plant Corporation, alone helped construct 2,300 war plants costing about $9.2 billion. Jesse Jones wrote, "In the beginning most of our industrialists were rather cautious about having their companies undertake war work. They did not want to invest a lot of their own funds in equipment to manufacture things they believed would not be in demand after the shooting ceased." The government had to negotiate with the major industrialists. Jones had a great respect for A. V. Davis of the Aluminum Company of America (ALCOA), with whom he negotiated to secure his assistance in designing and operating new aluminum plants for the government. They struck an involved deal that promised a 15 percent return to ALCOA. Other businessmen, such as Henry Kaiser, willingly produced anything and everything as long as the government advanced the money.

The remaining subsidiaries performed other wartime duties. The Defense Supplies Corporation, for example, expended $9.26 billion. Jones called that corporation his "catch all, go-anywhere, do-anything organization." Among many functions, it stockpiled wool, silk, and rougher fabrics; purchased quinine; and subsidized industrial alcohol and foodstuffs. The Rubber Development Corporation produced synthetic rubber, and the Metals Reserve Corporation stockpiled strategic metals. The War Damage Corporation provided insurance against losses caused by enemy attack. The purpose of the United States Commercial Company was to deny strategic resources to the enemy by purchasing them at losses, often from neutral countries.

During the postwar years the RFC continued to function until the first Republican administration. During 1953 Congress passed the Small Business Administration (SBA) Act. The new SBA took over business loans formerly made by the RFC. Other subsidiaries of the RFC, including the FNMA and the Export-Import Bank, emerged as independent agencies. The parent organization, the old RFC, lost supporters. Leading politicians and former RFC friends argued for the abolition of the corporation. Those figures included Jones, former president Hoover, Senator Harry F. Byrd, and Federal Reserve chairman Marriner S. Eccles. They all declared that the restoration of prosperity rendered the RFC unnecessary. The market could allocate credit more efficiently.

The SBA act of July 30, 1953, officially terminated the RFC, and the Corporation formally closed its doors on June 30, 1954. By 1957 almost all the remaining loans of the RFC were liquidated. Since then, occasional calls have surfaced for another resurrection of the RFC to aid distressed sectors of the economy, such as the steel industry in the 1980s. Recent attempts to revive the RFC have met heavy opposition by economists who favor market allocation over government direction in credit markets.

References:

James M. Bickley, "An Evaluation of the Reconstruction Finance Corporation, with Implications for Current Capital Needs of the Steel Industry," in *New Tools for Economic Development: The Enterprise Zone, Development Bank, and RFC*, edited by George Steinlieb and David Listokin (Piscataway, N.J.: Rutgers University Press, 1981);

Arthur T. Denzau and Clifford Hardin, *A National Development Bank: Ghost of the RFC Past* (St. Louis, Mo.: Washington University Center for the Study of American Business, 1984);

Robert Higgs, *Crisis and Leviathan: Critical Episodes in the Growth of American Government* (Oxford & New York: Oxford University Press, 1987);

Jesse Jones and Edward Angly, *Fifty Billion Dollars: My Thirteen Years with the RFC (1932-1945)* (New York: Macmillan, 1951);

James Stuart Olson, *Herbert Hoover and the Reconstruction Finance Corporation (1931-1933)* (Ames: Iowa State University Press, 1977);

Hans F. Sennholz, "The Great Depression," *Freeman*, 38 (March 1988): 90-96;

Paul Studenski and Herman E. Krooss, *Financial History of the United States: Fiscal, Monetary, Banking, and Tariff, Including Financial Administration and State and Local Finance*, second edition (New York: McGraw-Hill, 1963).

Reserves (*see* Deposits, Reserves, and Fractional Reserve Banking)

State Banks (*see* National Banks and State Banks)

Henry S. Reuss

(February 22, 1912 -   )

by Robert D. Auerbach

University of California, Riverside

CAREER: Assistant corporation counsel, Milwaukee County, Wisconsin (1939-1940); assistant general counsel, U.S. Office of Price Administration (1941-1943, 1946-1949); U.S. Army (1943-1945); chief of the price control branch, Office of Military Government, Occupied Germany (1945); deputy general counsel, Marshall Plan (1949); member, Milwaukee School Board (1953-1955); U.S. representative, Wisconsin (1955-1983).

Henry S. Reuss was a primary force behind the development and passage of the Depository Institutions Deregulation and Monetary Control Act (DIDMCA) of 1980, the most important banking bill passed by the U.S. Congress since the New Deal. Earlier Reuss developed and promoted the Federal Reserve Reform Act of 1977, which opened the regional Reserve Banks to the employment of women and minorities. That act also served as a catalyst for opening the private banking industry to those previously excluded groups. Colleagues considered Reuss, a leading proponent of the Kennedy administration's Peace Corps, one of the leading liberals in Congress and a strongly partisan Democrat, but his accomplishments are difficult to categorize. An intellectual who loved scholarly discussion of policy issues, Reuss's eagerness to embrace new ideas was not easily distracted by parochial matters

Henry S. Reuss (ABA Banking Journal, September 1980)

such as the need for campaign money or the need to satisfy "special interests."

Reuss was born on February 22, 1912, in Milwaukee, Wisconsin, and received the first 12 years of his education in that city. He was the grandson of a German immigrant who had become a successful banker. He graduated from Cornell University in 1933 and from Harvard Law School in 1936. From 1939 to 1940 he served as assistant corporation counsel for Milwaukee County. In 1941 he went to Washington, D.C., to take a position as assistant general counsel in the U.S. Office of Price Administration. In 1942 he married Margaret Magrath, later an economics professor.

Reuss entered the U.S. Army in 1943 as a private and then won a commission as a second lieutenant in the infantry. He won the Bronze Star for service in the Rhine and Bronze Battle Stars for service in Normandy and Central Germany. In 1945 he served as chief of the price control branch of the Office of Military Government in Occupied Germany. Back in the States he served again as assistant general counsel of the Office of Price Administration from 1946 to 1949, taking time out to run for mayor of the city of Milwaukee in 1948. Then, as deputy general counsel for the Marshall Plan, he helped administer American aid to Europe in Paris in 1949.

After the Marshall Plan service, Reuss returned to Milwaukee again and began in earnest a career in politics. He found it difficult in the beginning, running unsuccessfully for state attorney general in 1950. In 1952 he mounted a challenge to Republican senator Joseph McCarthy, the bellicose anticommunist, but lost in the Democratic primary. Still, he showed courage during that campaign by accusing McCarthy of conflict of interest in connection with the bankruptcy of the Lustron Corporation. Reuss charged that McCarthy had received $10,000 from that housing firm in 1948 while he held the vice-chairmanship of a Senate subcommittee dealing with housing.

Reuss finally found success in politics in 1953, winning a two-year term on the Milwaukee School Board. In 1954 he ran for a seat in the U.S. House of Representatives and won, defeating a McCarthy ally, incumbent Charles J. Kersten. Although Reuss garnered only 52 percent of the vote in the victory, he won reelection every two years until his retirement in 1983 by margins of usually more than 70 percent. Moreover, he managed to win without incurring large campaign expenditures.

Reuss quickly emerged as a leading proponent of liberal ideology and policy in the House. He wrote in 1959 that he considered "the most distinctive feature" of the prototypical liberal to be "that he has no particular body of doctrine." For Reuss liberalism was the adherence to such concepts as the "concern for the welfare of the individual," an idea for which conservatives of his time no doubt expressed support. Also not particularly liberal was Reuss's belief that "government need not be a doer, but it must at least be a catalyst for action by others." His subsequent actions indicated that he interpreted that dictum more broadly than his conservative colleagues.

A visit to Cambodia inspired Reuss to develop the idea of a Peace Corps. In January 1960 he introduced an amendment to the Mutual Security Act calling for a study of the feasibility of implementing a youth corps to give technical and other developmental assistance in foreign nations at soldiers' pay. Early in 1961 he fashioned the plan for the corps, which passed Congress on March 1.

Reuss also developed an interest in economic issues. To the delight of many of his constituents and of the labor unions, which often gave him their highest congressional rating, Reuss berated large banks for charging overly high interest rates. He favored meetings of domestic and international industry, labor, and governmental leaders to create policy and solve problems. In 1966 he called for a study to develop new urban mass-transit systems emphasizing safety, speed, planning, and modern technology. He supported credit controls and sponsored the Credit Control Act of 1969. He supported public-works programs, calling for a $3.2 billion program in 1982 to create 600,000 jobs to repair bridges, roads, and mass-transit systems.

After the House changed its rules for selecting committee chairmen in 1975, sixty-two-year-old Reuss won the chairmanship of the Banking, Finance, and Urban Affairs Committee, ousting the eighty-two-year-old Wright Patman of Texas. Although observers considered both liberals, Reuss had an image as dignified, intellectual, and modern while Patman seemed a throwback to an earlier age. House Democrats thought Reuss could provide more vigorous leadership. The new chairman later commented on the reasons he challenged Patman: "In 1975, I'd been there for 20 years and I was still in the four place on the Banking Committee. I knew if I just waited around, by the time I got to be chairman, if ever, I would have developed watermelon seeds between the ears."

As chairman of the Banking Committee, Reuss proved instrumental in the passage of several pieces of legislation affecting the financial community. The GAO (General Accounting Office) Audit Bill, passed in 1976, made the Federal Reserve Board audit, except for its monetary policy activities, made subject to congressional scrutiny. The next year, in response to the cancellation of a New York Federal Reserve Bank loan to the Franklin National Bank by a Reserve member who was also a member of a law firm that represented a bank in competition with Franklin, Reuss sponsored the Federal Reserve Reform Act of 1977, which extended conflict of interest laws to the Fed. The act also required the Federal Reserve to appoint more women and minorities to regional Reserve directorships. Before its passage only four women and three minority persons held positions among 108 Federal Reserve directors.

Reuss was a legislative leader in the passage of the Depository Institutions Deregulation and Monetary Control (DIDMCA) Act of 1980. That act authorized the payment of interest on consumer checking accounts, a gradual lifting of the interest rates banks and savings and loans could charge, the

expansion of savings and loan lending powers, and the extension of Federal Reserve requirements to all depository institutions. The DIDMCA has received some blame for causing the savings and loan crisis of the later 1980s, but it was primarily a response to the easy-money policies of the Federal Reserve in the 1960s and 1970s. As inflation and interest rates rose, a substantial shift of assets from banks to money-market funds occurred. The fact that the money-market funds deposited their assets back into the banks only succeeded in concentrating assets in the larger banking centers in the country. Member banks of the Fed found it in their interest to leave so they could earn interest on their full portfolio of assets. The ensuing reduction in the number of banks covered by Fed reserve requirements (550 left in 1978 alone), coupled by the expansion on the state level (starting in New England and New York) of the services savings and loans were permitted to offer, forced Congress to act to make rules of competition uniform.

Obtaining the support of financial trade associations and the support of federal regulators for major bank reform proved difficult. With the exception of G. William Miller, chairman of the Federal Reserve from 1978 to 1979, the Jimmy Carter administration offered little help. The press generally remained silent because of low public interest in seemingly arcane banking matters. House-Senate conferees delayed passage of the bill until they could agree on checking-interest provisions strongly sponsored by Senator William Proxmire of Wisconsin. Finally, however, the bill passed both houses, and President Carter signed it into law in March 1981. The passage of the DIDMCA represented a great victory for Reuss after years of struggle.

By that time, however, Reuss had experienced heart surgery and a change of position in Congress. In December 1980 he left the Banking Committee abruptly to assume the chairmanship of the Joint Economic Committee. In that more public but less concentrated role, Reuss continued to serve in Congress until he retired in 1982.

A lifelong nature enthusiast, Reuss sponsored several bills designed to conserve and preserve the environment. He played a prominent role, for example, in the development of a nature trail winding through his native state. After retirement Reuss served as cochairman of the National Commission to Preserve Low-Income Housing, as chairman of the Wisconsin Energy Task Force, as president of the Wisconsin Housing Partnership, as a director of the Enterprise Foundation, and as a member of several other public service committees. He has received honorary degrees from the University of Wisconsin, Marquette University, and other institutions of higher learning.

Publications:
Critical Decade (New York: McGraw-Hill, 1964);

Revenue Sharing (New York: Praeger, 1970);
To Save Our Cities: What Needs to be Done (Washington, D.C.: Public Affairs Press, 1977);
On the Trail of the Ice Age (Milwaukee: Ice Age Park and Trail Foundation, 1981).

References:
Robert D. Auerbach, *Money, Banking, and Financial Markets* (New York: Macmillan, 1988);
Martin Tolchin, "Rep. Reuss: Looking Back on 28 Years in the House." *New York Times*, December 7, 1982.

Joseph Sartori

(December 25, 1858 - October 6, 1946)

by Lynne Pierson Doti

Chapman College

CAREER: Attorney and land speculator (1879-1887); cashier, First National Bank of Monrovia (1887-1889); cashier (1889-1894), president, Security-First National Bank of Los Angeles [Security Savings Bank to 1912, Security Trust and Savings Bank to 1929] (1895-1934); bond salesman (1894-1895).

Joseph Francis Sartori was born in Cedar Falls, Iowa, on Christmas Day in 1858 to German immigrants. His father, an apprentice stonecutter in Baden-Baden, left for the United States in 1852 after the parents of a woman he wished to marry rejected his prospects. After five years as a bricklayer in New Jersey he had produced an income sufficient enough to win the patient lady, Theresa Wangler. Shortly after their 1857 marriage in New Jersey they established a home in Cedar Falls.

Sartori enjoyed a childhood as the only son of doting parents. A second son drowned as a toddler. Joe was an avid athlete who particularly enjoyed swimming, skating, and baseball, but when it came to work he insisted he was suited only for mental endeavors. Only a wiry five feet, five inches tall as an adult, "Little Joe" saucily blamed his father, who "didn't make him big enough" for work that required muscle.

The boy did not lack energy and ambition, however. When he was eleven a railroad hired him to sell newspapers, snacks, and sundry items on the trains running from Cedar Falls to the end of the line. At a time when many grown men earned less than $30 a month, Sartori brought in $100 and

Joseph Sartori

earned free room and board on overnight stays by recommending a hotel to the train's passengers. But when another young worker was killed when he jumped off a moving train, Sartori's mother halted his career as a "train butcher" and put him back in school.

At age fifteen Sartori started attending Cornell College in Mount Vernon, Iowa. He loved the academic aspects of college, but the school's many rules chafed the independent young man. During his second year a lecture by a naval officer inspired him to apply to the Annapolis academy. He excelled in the mental sections of the entrance exam and squeaked by in the physical. After he had qualified as a candidate, he presented the idea of attending to his parents. They were appalled at the image of their son as a naval officer. Realizing his will had only become stronger with age, they offered him an alternative–a European education. So, at age seventeen, Sartori, along with his cousin Anton and a friend named John Markely, set out for Germany.

The trip turned into a tour. The three boys first stopped in Cincinnati to visit relatives. The Centennial Exhibition in Philadelphia was the next stop, but Sartori was more impressed with Independence Hall than with any of the special exhibits. In mid July the three traveled to New York and booked passage for Europe on the U.S.S. *Idaho*–steerage class, since second class was full. They spent the voyage eating, taking in the sights of the ocean, singing in the evenings, and debating the merits of American society with European passengers. They reached London on July 30.

On August 3 the boys reached Baden-Baden and Sartori's grandfather Wangler. Sartori's parents had strengthened family ties with a visit home when Sartori was small, and many of the relatives remembered him. He spent August improving his German and taking advanced piano lessons. He spent his spare time wandering over the rural land of the neighborhood and dreaming of a career in music. One issue facing him was the choice of a university. His grandfather wanted him to attend the University of Strasbourg, but Sartori had become acquainted with Hermann E. von Holst, a professor at Freiburg who had an American wife, and he wanted to attend university there.

Sartori began university life at Strasbourg, but after only a few weeks left for Freiburg. There he joined a dueling society and spent many evenings at the opera. A close friend, a young duke, presented him with a large bulldog when the friend had to leave for home to rethink an unwise affair with a local girl. Sartori's own disgrace soon followed. He spent freely (borrowing from his grandfather), perfected his dueling, and became enamored of an opera singer. The news traveled home to Cedar Falls. An angry letter soon arrived, with money for passage home included. Sartori's European education was over after one year.

After his return home Sartori reentered Cornell College. By spring 1876 he had received good academic reports, organized social events, played baseball, practiced public speaking, and worked on a new school paper. Having sampled heady freedom in Europe, he chafed under the restrictions of life in a small Iowa college town and persistently petitioned the authorities to bend the rules for him. Operating an off-campus business required the express permission of the faculty, and Sartori's file contained many requests to leave for sleigh, buggy, and horseback rides with W. S. Bemis and Misses Crandell and Crippen.

Sartori's character was not well formed until long after his college years, but many of his student essays express interesting ideas. He enthusiastically favored material progress, citing, for example, the improved standard of living that resulted from mechanization in farming. On the subject of personal values he once wrote, "Labor, industry and honesty are the grand sources whence come happiness, wealth and character." He also wrote an essay that warned of the dangers of extravagance, although his own spending habits continued to exasperate his thrifty father. Indeed, young Sartori celebrated his graduation by purchasing a new horse and buggy so that he and his cousin Anton could make the appropriate entrance for their homecoming to Cedar Falls.

Sartori had long before settled on his career path, and he spent the summer after graduation on final preparations for law school at the University of Michigan. He learned shorthand and began reading. The Michigan law school was known for its rigorous requirements, but Sartori still found time for social pursuits and baseball. He and his roommate, Harry M. Daugherty, later attorney general in President Warren G. Harding's cabinet, developed a mutually satisfying study arrangement. Sartori took all the class lectures in shorthand, then read them aloud to Daugherty in the evening, refining them as he read. They reread notes before tests. Daugherty learned as much as he felt necessary from the arrangement, and Sartori learned to communicate clearly. Daugherty contributed to their social activities, particularly in the important realm of protecting his still diminutive friend from the town toughs, who periodically harassed the college boys.

After completing law school in 1879 Sartori joined the law firm of Conner & Shaw in Denison, Iowa, specializing in land titles. One murder trial had convinced him his path would not be into criminal law. "Well, the man got life imprisonment," he said of the trial, "though no doubt he should have hanged." In addition to the title research that took him throughout northwestern Iowa and southwestern Minnesota, his growing feel for the land allowed him to purchase lots for profitable resale. After eight months as an assistant attorney he moved to Le Mars, Iowa, and opened his own offices in partnership with I. S. Struble. When Struble left to take a seat in the U.S. Congress, he asked Sartori to maintain the practice. Feeling the scope of the work would be too much for him, Sartori declined and arranged to join the law office of Peter Rishel. Eventually Rishel, Sartori, and Struble combined to form a new firm based in Denison, Iowa.

One summer, Sartori's life took a dramatic turn. He saw a lovely girl walking down the streets of Denison and fell in love. The girl was the daughter of his law partner Rishel. A teacher in Cambridge, Illinois, she had just joined her father during her summer break. Joseph Sartori and Margaret Rishel were married on July 3, 1885. The marriage stimulated Sartori's thinking about his future. Denison was a nice town, but Sartori's ambitions had outgrown the place. The money he had earned on land deals provided a certain independence, so the couple embarked on an 18-month honeymoon to find their future home. They visited Chicago, St. Louis, Kansas City, St. Paul, Denver, Spokane, Seattle, Portland, San Francisco, San Jose, and Los Angeles before settling upon Kansas City as the most promising area. Sartori rented law offices above the First National Bank.

Sartori's fame and fortune were not to come in Kansas City, however. Two of his old friends from Le Mars, John Brossart and John Wilde, resided in Los Angeles and had shown him the sleepy, widely spaced towns of Southern California. They telegraphed him to say the area had awakened from its slumber into the frantic activity of a land boom. Sartori hurried to his waiting friends in Monrovia, west of Los Angeles along the Santa Fe railroad line. No doubt an investment in Monrovia would have been profitable; Monrovia was probably the most successful boomtown of the growing

San Gabriel Valley, but Sartori preferred to act independently. He discovered a 56-acre ranch suitable for subdivision only a few miles away and bought an option for $150. A few days later he sold his option for $8,500. He promptly sent a telegram to San Jose, where Margaret had lingered over a visit with friends. His wire read, "This place is good enough for me. Come down."

In partnership with Brossart and Wilde, Sartori bought land, laid out subdivisions, and sold the lots, often by the popular technique of throwing a picnic for prospective buyers who rode the train out from Los Angeles to spend the day in revelry. Another development company once attracted 1,000 people to such a party and sold 160 lots in a day.

One could hardly fail in the land business in 1886-1887, unless lack of ready funds posed a problem. The traditional solution to such a problem involved starting a bank, and Sartori came to that realization some time in early 1887. When he heard that others had applied for a national charter for such an endeavor, he contacted Representative Struble by telegraph to preempt the name "The First National Bank of Monrovia."

Sartori's bank opened on July 2, 1887, with G. W. Perkins as president and Sartori making the day-to-day management decisions as cashier. He rented the first location but immediately started a permanent building at the southwest corner of Myrtle and Orange avenues in Monrovia. Sartori stayed in the position of cashier until the real estate boom ended in 1888. Even though the boom ended, and many people, including Sartori, still held unsalable land, the bank survived.

Sartori left Monrovia to start another bank in Los Angeles. In January 1889, the Board of Directors of the Security Savings Bank and Trust Company first met. F. N. Myers was elected president, and Sartori was made cashier. (Also among the original board members was Isaias Hellman, founder of Farmers and Merchants Bank of Los Angeles and later president of Nevada National Bank in San Francisco.) The bank had a capital of $200,000 on paper, but only $29,000 was actually paid before opening. Sartori himself had contributed $10,000 of that cash, which he had borrowed from Hellman with his stock in the new bank as collateral.

The bank had its first location in a former storeroom on South Main Street. An investment of $3,500 was required for the bank furniture, fixtures, and safe. A few days before its opening,

Sartori visited a nearby stationery store to buy his bookkeeping materials. There he made the acquaintance of a young clerk, Maurice Hellman, a relative of Isaias. Maurice later joined the bank's staff and rose with the growing institution to be a director.

The bank's initial days were quiet. On the first day only four depositors with total deposits of $1,365 came in the bank. One of those depositors, whose extended visits to the 13 saloons on the block may have befuddled him, deposited $490 on the first day but returned on the second to demand its return, thus substantially decreasing the bank's assets. At the end of the first week, the bank had $9,100.25 on deposit in 17 accounts, but about $4,500 of that belonged to Myers and Sartori. Only two of the three employees were usually on the premises, Sartori and William Shores, a black man with the title of janitor who also carried messages and presented checks for cash at the Farmers and Merchants Bank, which processed them through the Los Angeles Clearinghouse. Margaret occasionally helped with bookkeeping and correspondence, especially when Sartori worked evenings to catch up.

Fortunately, the new bank witnessed steady growth. On December 31, 1889, it reported 490 accounts, deposits of $154,006.33, and a profit of $4,249.99. It added new employees in 1890. Tracy Hall, a young boy, was employed as messenger, and W. D. Longyear was added as bookkeeper; both stayed to become vice-presidents. The bank passed $1 million in deposits in 1897.

The Sartoris adjusted well to Southern California life. They supported the opera, kept a horse for weekend buggy rides, and occasionally joined the bicycle parties that were so popular in the mild climate. Sartori fished the streams running from the local foothills in the winter and took a launch to sea to fish when the streams ran dry in summer. He and his friends took longer trips to camp in nearby mountains with abundant trout and deer and an inspiring view. Margaret joined social clubs and founded the Friday Morning Club for local women with an interest in bettering the community.

Trouble developed in 1893. Time has obscured the details, but Sartori and Myers disagreed about the running of the bank. Other directors split into the two camps, and the election of officers for the year 1893 resulted in Myers's ouster. In the following year the battle continued, with each side trying to gain control of the stockholders' votes. Sartori depended heavily on his friends and felt confi-

Sartori, circa 1913

dent that his group would remain in control, but he was voted off the board at the 1894 election. One of Sartori's friends had sold his stock to Myers.

Sartori was left with no job, and a large portfolio of unsalable stock to complement his illiquid land holdings. He also owed the bank $25,000. To repair his finances he became active in a partnership he had formed with Maurice Hellman to market bonds. Most of Southern California's train systems, schools, water supplies, electric and gas companies, and many private businesses were financed with money raised in the East, and Sartori traveled to sell those bonds. He was quite successful at that endeavor and enjoyed the opportunities to visit his family and friends in Iowa and Illinois, but his letters to Margaret reveal that the separations from his wife were painful and the rigors of travel tiring.

Therefore, when in January 1895, Security restored Sartori to power as president, he must have felt some relief. In addition to the Hellmans, he had gained the support of Jackson Graves, a Los Angeles lawyer who ran the Farmers and Merchants Bank after I. W. Hellman went to San Francisco. The support of those friends also proved helpful in weathering the financial panic that hit the city early in 1895. While other banks in town closed to avoid hasty withdrawals, Security, a savings bank, simply invoked a provision that allowed it to require 30-days' notice before funds could be withdrawn.

With Sartori firmly entrenched as president of the bank, renamed Security Savings Bank in 1896, his family settled even more permanently into the community. Margaret supervised the building of a home on West 28th street, served on the executive committee for the General Federation of Women's Clubs for their biennial session in Los Angeles, and became a regent of the University of California. Joseph added a new hobby to his list. In 1897 two Englishmen visiting Southern California introduced Los Angeles resident Ed Tufts to the game of golf. Tufts was immediately enthusiastic, and brought his friends, including Sartori, together to form "The Los Angeles Golf Club." They carved a nine-hole course from 16 rented acres of clay at the corner of Pico and Alvarado, using oiled sand for the greens. The color green appeared on other parts of the course only during the winter rains, but the sport thrived. Golf fever grabbed Sartori's group and spread so rapidly that Tufts and Sartori invited representatives of the various clubs to Security Bank for the inaugural meeting of the Southern California Golf Association on July 29, 1899. Sartori prepared the constitution and bylaws for that group and later served the association as president, secretary, and chairman of the handicap committee. He also remained active in the Los Angeles Golf Club and helped finance the purchase of a 107-acre site for the first 18-hole course west of Chicago, and the club built the course in 1899. That course also suffered from an abundance of clay and was soon overrun by the growing city; so in 1905 Sartori obtained an option on 320 acres some distance west of the city, setting up a company to buy the land for the use of the club, called the Los Angeles Country Club. Tufts and Sartori laid out the course, and golfers continued to enjoy the location even in 1989.

Sartori's ideas on banking proved just as farsighted. He led the bank to new locations as the business center of the city shifted and the bank grew in size. In 1904 he started to expand by purchasing other Los Angeles banks. The Main Street Savings Bank was the first acquisition, on January 11, 1904, and he acquired two more institutions by

1907. Those purchases brought more deposits and allowed the capital to increase to $500,000.

Expansion temporarily halted, however, during a difficult period in the lives of the Sartoris and the nation. Margaret Sartori developed an eye infection and had to travel to New York to get medical attention. At the same time Sartori engaged in the construction of a new bank at Fifth and Main Streets, which required a great deal of his personal oversight. Also, starting in New York and spreading westward began one of the worst financial panics in the nation's history. The Panic of 1907 started with the failure of the Knickerbocker Trust Company of New York, one of the largest institutions of its type. The stock market collapsed, and in three months business nearly came to a standstill. Only four banks closed in California while 132 failed nationwide, but the recession really hit the West Coast in 1908. In that year California state examiners closed 16 state banks, and another seven banks closed voluntarily.

The most lasting effect of that panic was the reexamination of state and national banking laws. In California a legislative committee met with bankers to draft a comprehensive banking code. A subcommittee of bankers was formed, consisting of J. M. Henderson, Sacramento Bank; Irving Moulton, Bank of California; Elliot McAllister, Decker & Jewett Bank of Marysville; J. Y. Eccleston, Oakland Bank of Savings; Lovell White, San Francisco Bank of Savings; and Sartori. In his usual lawyer's style, Sartori prepared for the meetings by acquiring copies of the banking codes of several other states and drafting versions suitable for California. The California state legislature promptly adopted the statutes suggested by the committee of bankers, and they became law July 1, 1909.

Two of the most important provisions of the new law, in Sartori's view, involved the authorization of branch banking, and the concept of departmental banking, where the assets of trust departments, savings banks, and commercial banks were required to be entirely separated. While Sartori followed that practice, he regarded it as particularly dangerous when other banks did not. Later changes in the laws made the separation even more complete.

Still, the changes in the laws gave Sartori new ideas for expansion. He bolstered the trust area of his institution and planned to enter the commercial banking area. He also started building a branching system that developed into the state's second largest behind A. P. Giannini's Bank of Italy (later Bank of America). During 1912 Equitable Savings Bank and Southern Trust Company were acquired, the name of the company was changed to Security Trust and Savings Bank, and the Equitable building constituted the first branch of the bank. In 1913 Security acquired Central National Bank and changed the name to Security National Bank, although that was kept separated from the other institutions until 1920. Again, events interrupted Sartori's plans for expansion of the bank; during World War I, his oil company, Central Oil, grew rapidly, and he served as a member of the capital issues committee for the twelfth district of the Federal Reserve System. He also served as president of the Savings Bank Division and chairman of the Currency Commission of the American Bankers Association.

But Sartori's expansion plans continued after the war. In 1919 he purchased the Hollywood National Bank and the Citizens Savings Bank of Hollywood and combined them into the "Hollywood Branch" of Security, and in 1920 he opened another branch in Los Angeles. However, he had reservations regarding the future of branch banking. He had contributed funds to a study of branch banking in Great Britain and Canada conducted by H. Parker Willis and Benjamin Beckhart, both banking professors, and others. That study reported that branch banking was preferable in many respects to the single office banks that were the norm in the United States. By lending in a variety of geographic areas, there was less risk that a large percentage of a bank's loans would fail to be repaid. Sartori, though convinced, still remained cautious. He feared that all of the larger banks would enter into branching too quickly, creating excessive competition. He also had some sensitivity to the fears of small-town bankers, who feared the larger banks entering their market and offering loans at lower interest or in other ways reducing their profits. Sartori therefore supported the state superintendent's de novo rule, which forced banks that wanted to enter a new market to buy an existing bank in town before erecting a new office.

Sartori's cautious approach quickly put him at odds with California's most prominent banker, A. P. Giannini. Giannini had also studied the branching issue and had developed a different vision: if branch banking was good, then more branching was better. He aggressively expanded his San Fran-

cisco Bank toward the goal of creating an international branch banking network. Giannini's expansion brought his banks to Los Angeles as early as 1913, when the Giannini-controlled Bank of Italy purchased four banks in Los Angeles. It took nearly a decade for the Bank of Italy to gain support in the area, and by then Sartori, deep in his own expansion, may not have noticed that change in circumstances. Security bought seven banks in 1921, some of which had previously acquired branches, seven more banks in 1922, eleven in 1923, and thirteen in 1924. By 1925 the bank had $253 million in resources. In 1927, when Security Trust and Savings Bank had 50 branches, Giannini stepped too close to Sartori's realm.

Opposed in his ambitious branching plans by state and national regulators, Giannini had coyly used several names for his various banks. When he decided to bring the Bank of Italy into the Federal Reserve System, he retained some flexibility by consolidating several banks into a new state bank. Since three of the banks used to form that new Bakersfield-based bank had the word "security" in their title, Giannini named his new bank "Security Bank and Trust Company." He used that new name as he acquired more banks south of the Tehachapi Mountains. When that bank bid for a La Habra bank located about 30 miles from Los Angeles, Sartori became exercised and demanded that the superintendent of Banks prohibit the use of the word "security" in rival banks. The superintendent complied. Giannini fought back, peevishly pointing out that he had bought and paid for the name three times and asking the Supreme Court to overrule a lower-court decision in Sartori's favor. Sartori also sought support outside California by writing letters to 28,000 bank presidents, accusing Giannini of infringing on the reputation Sartori had so carefully built. Finally, Giannini's associates convinced him the fight was too expensive. He changed the name of the bank to Bank of America of California, establishing recognition for a name that, in 1930, was adopted when Giannini consolidated his system as the state's largest bank.

The expansion of Sartori's bank reached a climax on March 1929. The steady acquisition of branches had made Security the best-known savings institution in the Los Angeles area, with branches stretching from Hollywood to Monrovia to Long Beach. To move into commercial lending, the bank merged with Los Angeles-First National Trust and

Savings Bank with branches covering from San Luis Obispo and Fresno to the Imperial Valley. Sartori brought the combined bank under national charter with the name Security-First National Bank of Los Angeles. That, briefly, ranked as the second largest bank in California (the Bank of Italy was the largest, and a merger in progress soon created American Trust, which took the position of second), and the eighth largest in the United States.

Sartori had reached an age when many people think of retirement. The market crash of 1929, which he predicted, and the rapidly changing conditions under which bankers operated in the Roosevelt years, presented challenges suited to younger men. Sartori had always maintained many interests besides the bank. He was instrumental in numerous business deals, including the founding of the Biltmore Hotel, the Southern Branch of the University of California (Now U.C.L.A.), building a new City Hall, and the subway terminal building. For leisure he visited the theater for plays and opera and played bridge. He also traveled to Europe nearly every year. In 1920 he had discovered the fisherman's dream: Mammoth Lakes. On the steeply rising eastern side of the Sierra Nevada mountains, the melting snow creates beautiful waterfalls that fill a succession of sparkling lakes and streams. Sartori and several friends bought 160 acres where they built cabins and indulged their taste for trout

for several weeks each summer. The willingness of those men to drive 12 hours to reach their spot of heaven attests to the attraction of the place.

In 1934 Sartori relinquished his presidency to George M. Wallace. Wallace came to Security as a messenger boy in 1901, when he was fifteen years old. As the bank grew he grew with it. His ties became even stronger when he married Juliette Boileau, one of several young people in whom the Sartoris took an interest.

Margaret Sartori died on May 2, 1937, of heart disease, in the hospital she supported as a board member. Joseph Sartori remained in the house she had built on 28th Street. A relative, Ruth Rishel, came to supervise the care of the house, and Sartori lived out his years in a quiet, modest life-style, gradually limiting his socializing to old friends. He died on October 6, 1946, leaving a powerful financial institution and a lifetime of public works.

References:

Ira Cross, *Financing an Empire: History of Banking in California* (Chicago: Clarke, 1927);

Marquis James and Bessie R. James, *Biography of a Bank: The Story of Bank of America, N.T. & S.A.* (New York: Harper & Row, 1954);

John Russell McCarthy, *Joseph Francis Sartori, 1858-1946* (Los Angeles: Ward Ritchie, 1948).

The Savings and Loan Crisis

by Anthony Chan

University of Dayton

With interest rates stable in the 1950s and early 1960s, Savings and Loans (S&Ls) found that making money could almost be taken for granted, especially because of the regulated interest rates imposed by the federal government. However, when interest rates rose above the regulated rates, the industry experienced great misfortunes, as depositors withdrew their funds and invested them directly into treasury bills, money market mutual funds, and the like. This process, often referred to as "disintermediation," occurred in 1966, 1969, 1974, and during the early 1980s.

To combat the problem, regulators in 1973 permitted S&Ls to offer Jumbo CDs, which paid higher rates on deposits of $100,000 or larger. In 1978 they lowered that amount by approving a money market certificate account that accepted deposits as low as $10,000 and offered rates tied to the treasury bill rate. Nonetheless, the government continued to regulate the general level of interest rates S&Ls could pay until 1980, when it gradually proceeded to deregulate the industry. More specifically, the Depository Institutions Deregulation and Monetary Control Act of 1980 deregulated both the interest rates S&Ls could charge on their loans

Federal Deposit Insurance Corporation chairman William M. Isaac and Federal Home Loan Bank Board chairman Edwin J. Gray in 1983, when they were unsuccessfully attempting to halt abuses of their agencies' deposit insurance funds (AP/Wide World Photos)

and those it paid to attract deposits. That act also permitted S&Ls to venture into other financial services, such as consumer loans, credit cards, checking, and investments in commercial paper and corporate bonds.

That seemed to ameliorate the disintermediation problem. However, once S&Ls could pay as much interest as they wanted, they had to search for loans that also generated higher rates of return. As simple theory predicted, generally only the riskier types of loans tended to generate higher rates of return. And, in 1982, the Garn-St Germain Act went much further and greatly expanded the powers of S&Ls by allowing them to pursue more aggressively many of the investments permitted under the 1980 act. That act also granted S&L institutions additional powers. The net result was that by 1982, S&Ls had obtained authority to behave more and more like banks. Unfortunately, however, the newly granted powers failed to raise the profitability of the S&L industry.

The Savings and Loan industry lost between $11 and $12 billion between 1981 and 1982. The main culprit was that the S&Ls generally made long-term fixed-rate loans and financed them with short-term deposits. That meant the high interest rates of the early 1980s caused the S&Ls to experience an explosion in their interest rate expenses they paid on deposits while their mortgage earning assets did not generate higher revenues because those interest rates were contractually fixed. To address that problem, in 1981 the government permitted S&Ls to offer adjustable rate mortgages that charged adjustable interest rates as a way of avoiding massive losses during periods of escalating interest rates. One major shortcoming of that solution was that it was not retroactive, which meant that the bulk of the 30-year mortgage loans held by S&Ls still continued to be of a fixed-rate nature throughout the 1980s. Therefore, although the remedy proved quite worthwhile, the beneficial effects lay many years down the road.

Fixed-rate mortgages also caused institutions to lose money during periods of rapidly rising or falling interest rates. That occurred because 30-year fixed-rate mortgages are generally financed with short-term deposits subject to short-term repricing. Thus, during periods of rising interest rates, mortgage holders held on to their relatively low interest rate mortgages while the institution had to incur losses as it paid higher prices to continue to hold the loans. On the other hand, during periods of falling interest rates, S&Ls failed to reap the fruits of a more favorable spread between their cost of funds and the earnings on mortgage loans, because mortgage holders tended to refinance their debt at lower interest rates. As a result the business of originating fixed-rate mortgages financed through short-term deposits was generally profitable only during periods of stable interest rates.

However, due to a combination of lower rates and favorable regulatory developments, S&Ls enjoyed a modest recovery between 1983 and 1985. Unfortunately, the recovery was short-lived, as S&Ls experienced a reversal from 1986 to 1988. Ironically, one major culprit was an increase in the provisions required to protect against the losses on many of the assets accumulated during the 1983-1985 period. The second damaging factor was the heavy decline in earnings that S&Ls reported from their service activities.

Thus, by 1989 the S&L industry faced a crisis, as the institutions set up to deal with the problems found themselves overmatched by the staggering losses incurred by hundreds of S&Ls. The Federal Savings and Loan Insurance Corporation (FSLIC), which was designed to insure against depositors' losses, closed its doors with an $87 billion capital deficit after accumulating losses of approximately $100 billion from 1984 to 1989. Legislation replaced the FSLIC fund with the Savings Association Insurance Fund (SAIF) and placed it under the administration of the Federal Deposit Insurance Corporation (FDIC).

Texas alone had more than 90 insolvent S&Ls, most of them already taken over by the federal government, and California had 25. Hundreds more stood little chance of meeting the capital requirements established by the bailout bill. Proponents of government bailouts argued that when the United States created the FSLIC in the 1930s, the government made a commitment to the industry and to depositors. Therefore, they argued, the nation had

a moral obligation to rectify the problems in the industry, especially insofar as they affected the security of insured depositors. A related view suggested that in the best of all possible worlds all externalities should be internalized, or, in simple terms, all the beneficiaries should pay. In the case of S&Ls the groups of beneficiaries tended to overlap each other. For example, a few of those who stood to gain from a healthier industry included the federal government, other healthy banks and S&Ls, and ultimately the taxpayers.

Opponents of that view pointed to the massive evidence of fraud in the industry, which had resulted in billions of dollars of losses, and argued that the government had limited commitments to depositors and should therefore simply pay off its insurance obligations and abandon the industry before the problems became even more unmanageable. Alternatively, that view suggested that the parties who caused the problems in the industry should also be responsible for the cleanup costs. Unfortunately, many of the individuals who abused the newly granted powers of the S&Ls and lost money no longer were in a position to finance the bailout of the industry.

Another important question arose: should an S&L industry even exist in light of the enormous costs of bailing it out without any guarantee of eventual success? The marketplace has provided a partial answer already. In 1960 some 6,000 S&Ls operated, but by 1990 that figure had shriveled to less than 3,000. The percentage of mortgages originated by S&Ls stood at 46 percent in 1970, but the growth of other financial institutions in the mortgage area caused the figure to drop to only 28 percent. S&Ls experienced a sharp drop in the level of mortgage-related investments held as a percentage of their total portfolio, as many institutions scrambled to diversify. The market rendered its verdict and strongly hinted that the traditional type of S&L that existed 20 years ago has become a dinosaur.

However, many S&L supporters maintained that since S&Ls received favorable tax treatment, they could offer lower mortgage rates, which promoted greater levels of home ownership. Moreover, they argued that the industry should continue to be subsidized because the laws that have been enacted during the last several decades clearly demonstrate that home ownership remains an important national priority in the United States.

Frightened depositors outside Cincinnati's Molitor Savings and Loan Association waiting to claim their savings after the failure of a neighboring Cincinnati S&L, March 1985 (courtesy of David Kohl)

During the mid to late 1980s S&Ls used many of their newly granted powers but still continued to register staggering losses. For example, during the first six months of 1989 the industry reported losses that were close to $8 billion. All indications suggested that the trend would continue into the immediate future. To deal with the problem Congress enacted the Financial Institutions Reform, Recovery, and Enforcement Act (FIRREA) in 1989. That legislation provided $50 billion to shut the institutions that regulators deemed insolvent, $40 billion to pay for the rescues undertaken in 1988, $33 billion to cover future failures of savings institutions and $43 billion in interest payments. The major disappointment with that legislation was that Congress designed it to handle no more than 500 ailing institutions. However, the S&L industry which had already dwindled from 6,000 S&Ls in 1960 to 2,934 in 1989, also suffered from approximately 1,000 S&Ls that faced immediate insolvency or had severe weaknesses.

Additionally, Congress made overly optimistic assumptions when formulating its legislation. For example, the bill expected declining interest rates over the 1990s to keep the financing costs of the bill quite low, a healthy growth in S&L deposits to generate substantial insurance premiums from the industry and aid in the bailout, and no further deterioration in the S&L industry. Most industry observers, such as the Congressional Budget Office and the Government Accounting Office (GAO), rejected those assumptions. In fact, the latter industry observers predicted that the eventual cost of the cleanup would require tens of billions more than the amount allocated in the legislation, 75 percent of which is taxpayer money. In 1989 the Office of Management and Budget (OMB) estimated that the total cost of the cleanup would be approximately $257 billion. That figure would cover the FSLIC's obligations; pay interest on the bonds issued by the new government financing entity, named the Resolution Trust Corporation (RTC); and pay administrative expenses. Unfortunately, the situation continued to deteriorate, and by April 1990 the GAO reported that it had increased the OMB computation by some $68 billion under a least-cost scenario. That meant that the GAO anticipated even higher expenditure demands.

The government also established new rules raising the core capital of S&Ls to 3 percent. Core capital consists of common equity, noncumulative perpetual preferred stock, and minority interests in consolidated subsidiaries minus most intangibles except purchased mortgage servicing rights and qualifying supervisory goodwill. Supervisory goodwill is the amount in excess of tangible net worth that can be paid for a troubled S&L. The government also set a new minimum of 1.5 percent for the tangible-capital-to-assets ratio. Tangible capital consists of core capital minus supervisory goodwill and all other intangibles except for qualifying purchased mortgage servicing rights. And by 1995 supervisory goodwill will be phased out completely.

By 1989, 46 percent of Texas S&Ls and 45 percent of California S&Ls considered solvent still had to raise more capital. However, the uncertain future faced by the industry prevented the stock markets from supporting institutions in their quest for accumulating greater amounts of capital. Recent legislation also increased the percentage of assets devoted to housing required (for S&Ls) to pass the qualified thrift lender test to qualify for tax benefits and low-interest advances from the Federal Home Loan Bank. In a similar vein, S&Ls were required to divest themselves of many of their junk bond holdings over a transition period. Those two developments were quite ominous in the short run as S&Ls have had to move away from higher yielding assets in the former case and also liquidate their junk bond holdings at significant losses in light of existing market conditions. However, in the long run, the survivors may exhibit more conservatism and possess less risky assets, and therefore bear less risk to the government insurance funds.

References:

James Ring Adams, *The Big Fix: Inside the S&L Scandal* (New York: Wiley, 1990);

C. A. Bowsher, "Resolving the Savings and Loan Crisis: Billions More and Additional Reforms Needed," *Mimeo* (April 6, 1990);

J. A. Cacy, "Thrifts in the Troubled 1980s: In the Nation and the District," *Economic Review*, 74 (December 1989): 3-24;

Anthony Chan and C. R. Chen, "The Link Between Monetary Policy and Savings and Loans," *Journal of Applied Business Research* (1988);

L. J. White, "The Problems of the FSLIC: A Policy Maker's View," *Mimeo* (July 1989): 1-46.

James J. Saxon

(April 13, 1914 - January 28, 1980)

by Robert Craig West

Federal Reserve Bank of Kansas City

CAREER: Various positions, U.S. Department of the Treasury (1937-1952); attorney, First National Bank of Chicago (1956-1961); director, secretary, counsel, First Capital Corporation (1961); U.S. comptroller of the currency (1961-1966); cochairman, American Fletcher National Bank (1966-1968); private legal practice 1968-1980).

James Joseph Saxon, U.S. comptroller of the currency under presidents John F. Kennedy and Lyndon B. Johnson, was born on April 13, 1914, in Cleveland, Ohio. He graduated from St. Johns College in Toledo in 1936 and studied business and fi-

Editor's note: the views expressed here are those of the author and not neccessarily those of the Federal Reserve Bank of Kansas City.

nance at Catholic University in 1937 and 1938. He received a law degree from Georgetown University in 1950.

Saxon held a variety of positions in the public and private sectors before he assumed the position for which he is best remembered—comptroller of the currency. While enrolled at Catholic University, he joined the Treasury Department as chief securities analyst for the Examination and Insolvent Divisions of the Comptroller's Office. Between 1938 and 1942 he served in various capacities for the Treasury Department, including with the Stabilization Fund, Foreign Funds control, and as treasury attaché to the U.S. high commissioner to the Philippine Islands. During the early months of World War II he acted as Treasury adviser to General Douglas MacArthur.

Saxon returned to the Treasury in Washington in 1942 and accepted the post of financial attaché to the U.S. Embassy in Sweden. He returned to the States in 1945 and served as economist and special assistant to the director of the Division of Monetary Research. His assignments included work on the National Advisory Council, the International Monetary Fund, and the World Bank. In 1947 he became assistant to the secretary of the Treasury. He also served as adviser to the U.S. governor of the World Bank and the International Monetary Fund.

In 1950, after completing his law degree, Saxon joined the Office of the General Counsel of the Treasury Department as a special assistant. He remained with the Treasury Department until 1956, when he accepted a position with the First National Bank of Chicago. In 1961 he moved to First Capital Corporation of Chicago as director, secretary, and counsel.

In November 1961 President Kennedy nominated Saxon to be comptroller of the currency. At the age of forty-seven Saxon had behind him a distinguished career in public service and the private sector. But he is chiefly remembered for his activities as comptroller. He was a controversial and aggressive advocate for the nation's banking system and for national banks in particular. During his five-year tenure he transformed both the national banking system and the operation of the Comptroller's Office. Perhaps most important, Saxon's years as comptroller mark the beginning of the continuing debate over expanded powers and competition in banking.

Saxon's impact as comptroller was concentrated in three areas: increased chartering and branching activity, expanded powers for national banks, and reform of the Comptroller's Office. His years as comptroller were also characterized by interagency disputes, particularly with the Justice Department and the Federal Reserve System.

Saxon realized that the support of bankers was important for the success of his program. Early in 1962 he asked the national banks for their views on desirable changes in law, regulation, and policy. He also appointed an advisory committee to study the responses provided by the banks and to make recommendations for change. The committee's report, entitled *National Banks and the Future* became the blueprint for much of the policy formulated during the Saxon years.

Almost immediately upon assuming office Saxon made it clear that he would support an increase in the number of national banks. He believed that competition in the banking sector was necessary and desirable. Without competition the banking system could not respond to the economy's needs. Accordingly, he actively encouraged expansion of the system during his first three years in office.

From 1962 through 1965 the number of de novo national bank charters granted was considerably higher than under previous comptrollers. The number of branches, which had seen considerable growth since the war, continued to rise. Even though Saxon encouraged applications, the comptroller's policy was to approve new banks and branches only where a strong case could be made for their success. However, a series of national bank failures in the mid 1960s brought Saxon's chartering policies into question. After 1964 the number of new banks approved per year declined sharply.

De Novo Banks and Branches

Year	Banks	Branches
1961	26	580
1962	65	480
1963	164	674
1964	205	782
1965	78	587

A significant portion of the new banks chartered during that period came in states that did not allow branching. Similarly, many of the new branches went into smaller towns and cities that may have lacked adequate banking services. The comptroller's report for 1965-1966 argued that the expansion of banking offices since 1961 had served the public interest. Banking resources had increased in areas where they were deficient, and the banking environment was more competitive.

Saxon also made it clear that he supported an extension of the powers of commercial banks. In the comptroller's view competition from other types of financial institutions had become a problem for commercial banks. He believed that the restrictions placed on banking activity during the Depression were no longer consistent with the financial environment. They primarily gave favorable treatment to nonbank financial institutions.

James J. Saxon (AP/Wide World Photos)

In the comptroller's report for 1963 Saxon provided a clear statement of his philosophy regarding the constraints placed on banking. He argued for a balance between safety and soundness and scope for initiative and innovation. Saxon believed in the principle that "any unique form of bank regulation which is not essential to the preservation of the solvency and liquidity of the banking system must be regarded as a harmful impediment upon the capacity of banks to meet the public requirements they are designed to serve."

Few of the regulatory changes proposed by the comptroller during Saxon's term became law. The Federal Reserve System opposed removing the restrictions on commercial bank activity, and the system had enough influence to block most of his efforts at legislative change. However, the broad powers granted to the comptroller allowed Saxon to achieve limited success through changes in administrative rules.

Saxon liberalized both lending limits and the types of loans made by national banks. His rulings on real estate lending enhanced the competitive position of national banks compared with nonbank intermediaries. Saxon also allowed national banks to expand their investments in state and local govern-

ment securities. He enlarged the lease-financing powers of national banks and granted them the power to issue insurance related to their banking activities. Some of the comptroller's rulings aimed at reform of the corporate practices of national banks. Saxon wanted to bring them into closer conformity with modern corporations.

Despite his belief in the desirability of competition and innovation, Saxon also strongly believed in effective supervision of banking activities. He enlarged the comptroller's field examination staff and through improved training increased its professionalism. He reorganized the comptroller's office, decentralizing the supervisory and examination functions and introducing modern management techniques.

Saxon increased the comptroller's legal staff, perhaps in anticipation of the response to his policies on chartering and mergers. As the first comptroller to stress basic research—he appointed an economist to his personal staff—in 1962 he created a department of banking and economic research. The department conducted economic studies and published a journal, *National Banking Review*. That journal was unusual in that it did not become a mouthpiece for the Comptroller's Office. It often carried articles that did not agree with official policy. The *Review* was one of the first publications to focus academic research on banking topics.

Throughout his term Saxon's aggressive support of the activities of national banks brought him into conflict with state regulators. Saxon publicly supported the nation's dual banking system, which divided authority over banking between federal and state agencies. However, he also stressed the healthy aspects of competition between the two segments.

Saxon also had sharp disagreements with other federal agencies. He had a particularly low regard for the Justice Department's role in banking. Saxon's problems with the Justice Department grew out of his desire to modernize the banking industry and increase competition. Under Saxon the Comptroller's Office supported many bank mergers on the grounds of economies of scale and scope. As a rule the Justice Department opposed mergers, particularly those involving larger institutions, as anticompetitive.

The disagreement between the two agencies was complicated by a murky legal environment. The Bank Merger Act of 1960 granted direct administrative control over bank mergers to the banking authorities. The act established standards by which mergers should be evaluated. However, the statute did not explicitly exclude bank mergers from antitrust law. The Justice Department usually ignored the 1960 act and used antitrust laws to bring suit against mergers approved by the comptroller.

Congress amended the 1960 act in 1966 to impose a single set of standards for all agencies to use in judging mergers. However, the act also gave the Justice Department the power to block a merger by beginning an action against it. The comptroller's *Annual Report* for 1965-1966 concluded that "decisions made by this Office in light of 104 years of experience are presently subject to interference by a department of the Government with no experience in bank regulation and a patent inability to perceive the nature of competition in banking and ascertain the relevant banking markets."

Whatever his feelings about the Justice Department, Saxon's chief adversary remained the Federal Reserve System. Given the comptroller's vision of the banking system, conflict with the Federal Reserve was not surprising. The Fed's policies derived from the central bank's responsibility for monetary stability. That responsibility caused the system to give more weight to sound, conservative banking than to competition. As a result, the Federal Reserve often opposed Saxon's goal of increased competition and innovation in the banking system.

Saxon believed that the banking system had to change for banking to keep pace with the rest of the economy. In his view, an outmoded set of restrictions hampered banking's role as the provider of credit and financial services. The Federal Reserve saw restrictions as necessary to insure against a recurrence of the troubles of the 1930s.

The Federal Reserve's influence and prestige were enormous. On most occasions the Federal Reserve could forestall legislative change. Saxon accomplished some of his goals through administrative actions, but the fundamental legal structure of banking remained static.

That confrontation continued through the 1980s. In a sense Saxon set the tone for succeeding comptrollers, who for the most part have kept up the pressure for change. Since Saxon's time comptrollers have usually advocated increased competition and liberalized banking powers. The Federal Reserve, though still a conservative force, has given its sanction to many of the changes Saxon advocated in the 1960s.

Saxon's appointment as comptroller had a permanent impact. The Comptroller's Office has become the advocate of change in banking. Succeeding comptrollers have advocated expanded powers, increased competition, and many other changes consistent with Saxon's vision of the role of the banking system. Saxon did not live to see the passage of the Depository Institutions Deregulation and Monetary Control Act of 1980 or the changes that have occurred since its passage. However, his actions as comptroller helped shape the debate and begin the journey.

After Saxon left the Comptroller's Office in 1966 he took a position as cochairman of the American Fletcher National Bank. He held that position until 1968. Failing health limited his professional activities during the last years of his life. Saxon died on January 28, 1980.

References:

Annual Report 1965-1966, The Comptroller of the Currency (Washington, D.C.: U.S. Government Printing Office, 1966);

The Banking Structure in Evolution, A Response to Public Demand, 102nd Annual Report of the Comptroller of the Currency (Washington, D.C.: U.S. Government Printing Office, 1965);

100th Annual Report of the Comptroller of the Currency (Washington, D.C.: U.S. Government Printing Office, 1963);

Ross M. Robertson, *The Comptroller and Bank Supervision* (Washington, D.C.: U.S. Government Printing Office, 1968);

Years of Reform, A Prelude to Progress, 101st Annual Report of the Comptroller of the Currency (Washington, D.C.: U.S. Government Printing Office, 1964).

Security Affiliates of Commercial Banks

by John Landry

Brown University

Between 1908 and the Great Depression many national commercial banks set up affiliates to deal in securities. Although commercial banks had other ways of participating in investments, security affiliates were the main vehicle that allowed banks to claim more than half of the growing market in securities by the late 1920s. After the stock market crash in 1929, public distrust of investment banking and charges that the affiliates had engaged in unethical practices led to congressional investigations and ultimately to a separation of commercial and investment banking. Some banks liquidated their security affiliates, while others spun them off into independent investment houses.

The National Banking Act of 1864 effectively forbade commercial banks from holding common stock, since such stock was not evidence of debt. Banks were allowed to invest in bonds, but they confined themselves for many years to the traditional practice of supplying short-term credit for goods in the process of manufacture and distribution. As the market for corporate securities grew at the turn of the century, however, banks began to participate in indirect ways: by purchasing bonds for inclusion in their own asset portfolios, by granting call loans to brokers, and by extending credit with securities as collateral.

In order to manage that indirect activity better, the large New York banks increasingly allied themselves with private investment banking houses. In 1908 one of those banks, First National, went on to organize its own investment banking subsidiary, the First Securities Company, to acquire securities that the parent bank was barred by law from holding. The National City Bank followed suit three years later with the National City Company.

Those and other banks used their security affiliates as full-fledged investment houses after World War I. The federal government, needing enormous loans for the war, allowed commercial banks to distribute securities during the campaigns for Liberty Bonds. The campaigns were a great success, and they interested both many commercial banks and the general public in securities for the first time. At the same time, the larger industrial firms shifted their method of financing from commercial loans to internal financing and issues of securities. In order to maintain their level of business and also to retain their customers, commercial banks newly experienced in handling securities looked to meet the increasing demand for investment banking. At first most banks merely set up or expanded their bond departments, but by 1929 the flood of new stock issues had prompted many of the commercial banks in large cities to set up one or more security affiliates. In 1931, the peak year, 114 national banks had such affiliates, while 123 others, mostly small ones, conducted investment business in their bond departments.

The banks modeled their security affiliates on the trust subsidiaries most banks had set up years earlier in response to competition from trust companies. The latter, with the advantage of resources from the trusts that commercial banks were forbidden from holding, had begun to expand and make commercial loans. By setting up independent trust companies that they controlled, commercial banks circumvented the prohibition on accepting trusts. Banks did the same with security affiliates, forming them under the general laws of incorporation. Not only could affiliates deal in and underwrite stocks, but they could also underwrite bonds, an activity forbidden in theory, if not in practice, to bank bond departments until the law was changed in 1927.

Banks maintained control over their legally separate affiliates in three main ways. Most commonly, they gave their own stockholders a pro rata interest in the stock of the affiliates. Some banks instead carried the stock of their affiliates on their own books as an investment, while others set up a holding company to own both the bank and the investment company. Despite the legal separation, affiliates could easily offer investment services to their parent banks' customers. Banks and affiliates usually operated out of the same office or building and together advertised their services.

The arrangement benefited both firms. Banks used the specialized research staffs of their affiliates to manage their own portfolios better and to give advice on investments to their depositors. Affiliates used their access to banks' resources and customers to develop greater networks of sales and underwriting, with smaller commissions, than many private investment houses could manage. Those same complementarities, however, led to a potential for abuse that doomed the system once the boom in the securities market ended.

The sharp decline in securities prices beginning in 1929, so soon after many banks had set up security affiliates, spurred a series of congressional hearings. The investigations revealed a variety of fraud and profiteering in the affiliates' activities. Most of the abuses had occurred in private investment houses as well, but many had arisen from the special position of affiliates. At first congressional leaders planned only to regulate the affiliates, but a flood of letters from disgruntled customers of affiliates persuaded Senator Carter Glass and others to propose prohibiting security affiliates altogether. The federal administration and many banking groups at first opposed the Glass bill in 1932, but another banking crisis in early 1933 discredited banking generally and weakened all opposition. Some prominent banks in early 1933 decided voluntarily to separate themselves from their affiliates. The prohibition soon passed as part of the Glass-Steagall Act in June 1933.

Politicians worried about two kinds of problems arising from the system of security affiliates. First, banks with affiliates could be drawn into conflicts of interest in serving their customers. In giving investment advice to their commercial depositors, they would be tempted to promote the securities offered by their affiliates. Second, because securities proved inherently more risky and illiquid than commercial loans, the penetration of investment services

into commercial banking jeopardized the soundness of the banking system. A bank might be tempted to rescue a failing affiliate, either by buying up unsuccessful securities issues or by making doubtful loans to the public in order to encourage the buying of those securities. Even if the parent bank did not risk its own stability by aiding its affiliate, the failure of an affiliate might undermine confidence in the parent bank, and by extension in the banking system overall.

A study of national banks with and without affiliates nevertheless shows statistically that the presence of an affiliate did not increase the probability of bank failure in 1931, the year when the largest number of banks with securities operations failed. Affiliates would have endangered banks the most if they were in trouble at times when their parent banks were also in weak positions, but drops in affiliates' earnings do not appear to have coincided regularly with declines in the earnings of their banks. Affiliates generally did not borrow from or draw a great deal on bank capital, nor did they reduce much of the liquidity of their parents, partly because they usually accounted for only about ten percent of the combined capital, with none greater than 28 percent in 1930. As for the first problem, whether banks persuaded their depositors to accept unsound securities, no comprehensive studies have been made.

By setting up security affiliates, commercial banks used their advantages in resources to draw away a good deal of the growing securities business from private investment houses. Those same advantages, coupled with the late spread of the practice, appear to have made the affiliates into a convenient target for securities customers and congressmen irate over the manifestly troubled financial sector in the early 1930s.

References:

W. Nelson Peach, *The Security Affiliates of National Banks* (Baltimore: Johns Hopkins University Press, 1941);

Eugene Nelson White, "Before the Glass-Steagall Act: An Analysis of the Investment Banking Activities of National Banks," *Explorations in Economic History*, 23 (Fall 1986): 33-55.

Securities and Futures Markets

As the New York Stock Exchange and other exchanges grew more sophisticated, traders recognized a fundamental fact: anything that has a price today will have a price in the future, although perhaps not nearly the same price. Traders realized that they could not only trade in securities at then-current prices, but could trade in those same securities at some future date automatically. Among the mechanisms they used to do that, puts and calls allowed traders to put in an order to buy a security when it reached a specified price or sell the stock when it similarly reached a specified price. Brokers called out those orders automatically without the need for further consultation with the buyer or seller. Theories that major "players" in the Great Crash of 1929 were wiped out were revised considerably when scholars discovered that the speculators often had call orders on their securities.

Another mechanism for dealing in the future development of a security, a warrant, allows a trader to exercise an option to buy stock in the future at a specified price. Warrants thus serve as an inducement to get traders to invest in securities that carry more risk.

In 1987 the stock market experienced a sharp drop—the worst since the Great Crash—which many observers blamed on still another phenomenon: program trading. With the advent of computers, money managers for large corporations started to offer stocks much like mutual funds, based on an index, such as the Dow Jones index. The stock automatically reflected portfolio shifts to keep up with the index. However, because a slight difference in price existed between the actual stocks and the indexes, an opportunity for arbitrage occurred. (Arbitrage is the act of taking advantage in price differentials in securities or money.) Still other computer programs appeared to make up the differences between the indexes and the actual stocks. Once several of the computer programs started to sell automatically, human investors, seeing the price fall, would themselves begin selling, further perpetuating the decline. In reality, however, most econo-mists have found few ill effects from program trading: the worst criticisms come from brokers, who generally receive fewer fees because the computers make the trades, and who also argue that smaller investors, who lack the large computers, are left out. Program trading represented a very sophisticated, automated version of puts and calls. However, it could trigger huge swings in volume before humans could react. Consequently, as a result of the 1987 crash, whenever a security drops 75 points in a single day, all program trading is halted automatically until the Exchange reopens.

The most automated form of securities trading, Instinet Corporation, based in England, allowed customers to purchase computer terminals permitting them to buy and sell stocks automatically, completely bypassing brokers. Although as of 1990 the system was available only to institutional customers, it demonstrates the fact that relatively soon the financial futures markets will be connected to home- or office-based computers.

Other stock futures packages have appeared, most of them similar in principle to the commodities futures that comprise the majority of futures activity. Agricultural goods and precious metals comprise the bulk of commodities futures. Both involve considerable speculation because of uncertainties associated with farming and mining, and with the fact that the future prices of coffee, sugar, gold, or platinum depend heavily on events in foreign countries, where the commodities are produced. Traders wanting to speculate on the price of, say, oranges (as in the popular movie "Trading Places") know that they must in essence gamble on future weather patterns, potential insect invasions, or the impact of foreign competition. Traders involved in metals must make reasonable guesses about mine conditions, labor markets, and the stability of foreign governments. The Chicago Board of Exchange arose specifically to handle the volume of commodities trading. In the 1980s, the Chicago Exchange came under intense investigation by the Securities and Exchange Commission for alleged violations.

See also:

Commodity Financing, Charles E. Merrill, Michael Milken, Charles E. Mitchell, New York Stock Exchange.

—Editor

Security Measures in Banks

People put their money in banks because it is convenient to do so and because they can earn interest on what they deposit. But no bank can pay enough interest to offset the perception that a depositor's money is unsafe. Consequently, bankers have had to find ways to convince depositors that their money is secure, both from the vagaries of business and, more obviously, from theft and natural disaster.

Until the appearance of deposit insurance during the New Deal, the first line of bank security was the banker himself. Quite often the very appearance of the banker signified financial success and economic security (at one time, a large girth was an essential). Many bankers established themselves in other businesses before they entered banking, providing a way for customers to look at their track records. When a businessman did enter banking, his own wealth and reputation stood behind his bank.

The second line of defense was physical: safes, vaults, barred teller windows, and even the bank buildings themselves. Especially in frontier areas, those projections were crucial. The building and the land it stood on constituted a major asset for every bank. Once a bank achieved a certain degree of success, it constructed a new building. In the early twentieth century those buildings frequently resembled huge and imposing temples and were clearly intended to signal that the banks were safe and secure.

Even when small-town banks lacked giant buildings—and in small towns even the most austere bank building often represented the most imposing structure around—virtually every institution had a first-rate safe or vault. If a bank was backed by another building to create a double wall, the built-in vault usually stood against that wall, behind the teller cages, in full view of the customers. Otherwise, architects usually placed the vault on a side inner wall, again in view of the customers. Typically the vault remained open during business hours and when closed at night would automatically open the next morning. The vaults held not only cash but jewelry, art, important papers, and any other valuables a customer cared to deposit. Of the many vault-making companies, Diebold emerged as the best known. That company's product endured the ultimate test when the contents of 700 safes emerged unharmed from the Chicago fire of 1871.

If a bank could not afford a vault, it had a freestanding safe. Early ball safes were constructed of very heavy iron balls to contain the cash and iron boxes welded on top for papers. Explosives might blow the ball from the box, but it remained a daunting task for a would-be robber to pick up the iron monster and make an escape. Meanwhile, the robber would have to deal with the shotguns tellers often kept behind the cage (George Wingfield passed out shotguns to all of the banks in his chain well into the 1920s).

The safes and vaults of the early banks established a remarkable record of safety from theft. Even in the frontier West, notwithstanding the television-induced fantasies accepted by many, virtually no bank robberies occurred before the 1920s. Why an obvious stranger would gallop into a town in front of the sidearm-carrying citizenry and attempt to hold up a bank in broad daylight is a question television westerns do not answer. Before the turn of the century, records show only a single robbery in Nogales, Arizona, in 1899 and a failed holdup by Butch Cassidy in Denver. Most brigands struck at the weaker link, the transport system—stagecoach and train—that got the money to the bank.

What did a banker do if he had not yet received his safe? Most would-be bankers hid their cash—under a bed, in a trunk, in a woodpile. Others employed guards. One Oklahoma banker put rattlesnakes in his strongbox. Usually a pistol sufficed.

Ironically, after the advent of several state deposit insurance schemes in the early 1900s and after the creation of the Federal Reserve System, both of which were intended to provide better overall confidence—and, one would think, better safety and security—the worst rash of robberies in American history occurred. Bonnie Parker and Clyde Barrow got the headlines, but hundreds of their cohorts "hit" banks with astonishing frequency and success, given the previous legacy of failure. The wave of robberies took place mostly in daylight, when the vaults stood open. The critical new factor was the automobile, which made a successful getaway possible. Barrow once wrote the Ford Motor Company about the utility of its vehicles: "I have drove Fords exclusively when I could get away with one."

In the 1920s bankers also tried the private sector to provide security. Many took out insurance on their assets, but rates soon rose to such alarming levels that bankers in states such as South Dakota and Minnesota, where many robberies had occurred, turned to state bankers' associations. Often the associations themselves hired private detective agencies to provide routine security and to investigate robberies. One Arizona banker tried a tear-gas gun system triggered by the tellers. In one of its first uses it misfired, gassing an unhappy employee.

The robbery wave, which lasted until about 1935, also took place during the brief period when the coordination of law enforcement had not reached a degree of sophistication equal to that of the criminal. But patrolmen learned to work together, using their radios to maneuver to potential escape routes. Also, alarm systems in the banks started coming into common use. In the 1940s some banks installed bulletproof glass, and pneumatic tubes for drive-in transactions appeared in 1946. In 1965 exploding dye packs made their first appearance. The packs marked money so that the thief could not use it without identifying himself. The earliest dye packs used timers, but more mod-

ern variations allowed tellers to set off the explosions with a radio signal. Still later, automatic triggering beams at the bank doors set off the packs. "Marked" money provided another, more clandestine way for law enforcement officials to trace criminals after a robbery.

By the 1960s, however, despite the thorough efforts of bankers and law enforcement officials alike, bank robbery revived as a profitable profession, perhaps as a consequence of the increased economic dislocation of urban individuals. The rise in the robbery rate led to the congressional passage of the Bank Security Act of 1968. The act required the appropriate federal regulatory agencies to require banks to appoint security officers, to publish security guides, and to train personnel to respond properly in the event of a robbery attempt. It also dictated strength and dimensional requirements for vaults and proposed the installation of cameras (either hard-copy film cameras or closed-circuit television cameras) to monitor all lobby and drive-through activities. It took a decade for the effects of the act to make themselves felt, and robbery rates did not turn downward until the late 1970s.

The advent of Automatic Teller Machines (ATMs), which by 1990 totaled 82,000 units, brought a new type of threat—the computer criminal. Banks found themselves developing ever more elaborate codes to secure money in ATMs from would-be "lottery winners." Still, well into the 1980s persistent or lucky button pushers managed to relieve an ATM of its contents from time to time. Moreover, violent crime associated with ATMs increased, occurring once every 3.5 million transactions, usually at walkup ATMs after customers received their cash. But the use of computers in banking operations has also given hacking embezzlers the entry they need into a bank's electronic tills. In the modern era bank security officers have to be as facile with computers as old-timers had to be with their Colts. The emerging system of electronic telephone transfers promises only to increase the challenge to computer security officers.

—Editor

Security Pacific National Bank

by Lynne Pierson Doti

Chapman College

The sixth-largest bank in the United States as of 1989, with $50 billion in resources, Pacific National Bank had a modest beginning as Security Savings Bank and Trust Company. When the bank opened in 1889, $200,000 in capital had been subscribed, but only $29,000 had been actually paid.

Of the original capital, Joseph Sartori, the bank's founder, paid $10,000. Sartori came to Monrovia, California, in 1887, leaving a career in law and real estate in Iowa to pursue the land boom in Southern California. He did well in land speculation but decided to open a bank and serve as its legal adviser. The First National Bank of Monrovia resulted from this intention. The bank weathered the end of the land boom, and Sartori retained his title of cashier when he moved to Los Angeles in 1888 to start Security Savings Bank.

The $10,000 Sartori contributed to the capital subscription was borrowed from the Farmers and Merchants Bank of Los Angeles. That bank's president, Isaias W. Hellman, a Los Angeles banker since 1868, served on Security's board for many years and guided the bank even after his formal connection with it ended. Hellman had organized Farmers and Merchants Bank in 1871 with former governor of California, John Downey, who had merged his private bank with the newly formed institution. Security acquired Farmers and Merchants Bank in 1956.

There were three paid employees when Security Savings Bank and Trust Company opened. The president, F. N. Myers, received $125 per month; the cashier, Sartori, received the same; and the janitor, William H. Shores, earned $30 a month for his highly varied duties.

As Shores opened the doors the first morning, a customer immediately entered and deposited $500. Sartori and Shores must have been pleased by this prompt response to their opening, and one can picture their attempts to retain that optimism

as the day passed quietly. They closed the day's books with three deposits totaling $1,365. Sartori later recalled the modest first days: "At the end of the first week's business we had opened seventeen accounts with total deposits of $9100.25, of which amount some $4500 had been deposited by the President and the Cashier. Where the first President and I got all this money I can't remember, because at that time we were both land and town-lot poor, all balled-up with debts, and practically busted!"

William Shores stayed with Security until his death, serving 30 years. Two other early employees stayed with the bank for long periods. Tracy Hall came to the bank in 1890 as an unpaid errand boy, recommended to Sartori by the boy's mother to "get him off the streets." He and W. D. Longyear, the bank's first bookkeeper, who also arrived in 1890, worked at Security more than 50 years each and became vice-presidents and directors.

The election of officers for 1893 started a struggle for control after Sartori and the bank's first president disagreed on policy. Sartori's friend, T. L. Duque, was elected to replace Myers as president, but the next year's election resulted in Myers's control and Sartori's ouster.

Sartori suffered more than deep disappointment and embarrassment at losing his position. He had depended on his salary (then $300 a month) to offset the difficulty of an illiquid collection of assets. To maintain his now prominent social position he turned to his partnership with Maurice Hellman. Hellman, a cousin of Isaias Hellman, had first come to know Sartori when the former, then a clerk in a stationery store, had assisted Sartori in the selection of account books for the new bank. Hellman was, by 1893, selling municipal bonds and other securities. Sartori actively participated in that business, traveling throughout the country to place the securities.

In the next annual election, Sartori, Hellman and Jackson Graves, Los Angeles attorney and banker, purchased additional stock to regain control of Security. Sartori was appointed president by the board, Maurice Hellman continued as vice-president, and W. D. Longyear served as cashier and secretary.

The office of the bank was relocated several times in the early years, reflecting the shifts in the city's business center. In 1896 the first move occurred, from 148 South Main Street to the northeast corner of Main and Second. The directors of the institution concurrently changed the name to Security Savings Bank. After eight years the bank moved into a new eight-story building constructed by Herman Hellman. This Hellman, a former president of Farmers and Merchants Bank, also was the brother of Isaias Hellman. In only two years the bank's extraordinary growth brought the need for another move. Sartori secured space in a new building at the southeast corner of Fifth and Spring Streets.

The outfitting of the bank's newest quarters occupied Sartori's time through most of the year 1907, and he preserved many of his activities in letters to his wife, who had sought medical treatment in New York. The bids for the light fixtures, Sartori wrote her, ranged from $13,000 to $24,000! The choice of a decorating scheme gave Sartori particular anxiety, but the heating and ventilation system proved a source of real pride. The bank occupied its new quarters on December 14, 1907, and remained there for half a century.

The rapid growth that precipitated the move came partly through the 1905 acquisition of Main Street Savings Bank, whose president and largest stockholder was Sartori's old ally T. L. Duque, and the acquisition of Los Angeles Savings Bank the same year. With those mergers, the deposits in Security Bank totaled more than $12 million. Late in 1907 Sartori purchased stock in Southern California Savings Bank. Owners of the remaining stock agreed to a merger. Security moved Charles H. Toll and John H. Griffin, Southern California employees, to executive positions, where they became prominent.

After Isaias Hellman moved to San Francisco to take the presidency of Wells Fargo Nevada National Bank, Sartori reigned as Los Angeles's most prominent banker. The panic and bank runs of 1907 disturbed his attitude more than his bank,

and, as a result, Sartori actively pushed for banking reform. The state banking law that passed in California in 1909 was heavily laced with passages developed by Sartori.

One of the provisions of the law allowed banks to engage in savings, commercial, and trust activities simultaneously, though with separate departments. Consequently, Sartori merged the previously acquired Southern Trust Company with the bank and changed the names to Security Trust and Savings Bank in 1912. Other acquisitions in that period included Equitable Savings Bank in 1912 and Central National Bank in 1913. The Central National Bank was renamed Security National Bank and remained independent to secure the name "Security" under both state and national charters.

At that time an intense rivalry developed between Security Bank and the Bank of Italy (later known as Bank of America). Sartori believed that locally established banks best served communities. A. P. Giannini, founder of the Bank of Italy, just as intensely favored the strength and benefits of a geographically dispersed system of branch banking. The invasion of Los Angeles by the rapidly expanding Bank of Italy brought their philosophies to the financial battlefield. Giannini's branches met with notably less success in Los Angeles than they had in other cities. The effort of maintaining those branches, so distant from San Francisco headquarters, exhausted Giannini and caused division among the Bank of Italy's directors. Nevertheless, by 1915 the Bank of Italy was firmly established in Los Angeles.

Sartori commissioned a study on branch banking in 1920, and subsequent to the commission's favorable report he, too, developed a system of branches in Southern California. Sartori's view of branching still differed substantially from Giannini's, and he found that the newly appointed state superintendent of banks, Charles Stern, leaned toward his view. Stern believed in "zonal banking," which in California meant San Francisco banks could establish branches in Northern California only in the southernmost portion of the northern section of the state. Stern curtailed the competition between the Bank of Italy and Security by denying all of Bank of Italy's requests to open new branches when those new branches were located south of the Tehachapi Mountains. The Federal Reserve System also supported the concept of banking zones and ruled that member banks were permitted branches only in home cities and contiguous territory.

The restriction on branch banking forced Giannini into an elaborate structure of ownership. At one point Giannini controlled five separate banks and two holding companies. By locating the headquarters of a holding company and a bank in Los Angeles, the branching restrictions were met while Giannini easily acquired extra branches in Southern California. When Giannini chose the name "Security Bank and Trust Company" for his newly consolidated state banking system, Joseph Sartori did not take it as a compliment. He sued over the name "Security," and the issue went to court in 1928. Giannini capitulated about a year later. He renamed the state bank, with its many branches, Bank of America. When the legal climate changed and Giannini combined his banking empire into a single corporate entity in 1930, he continued to use that name.

In 1920 the Security Bank and Trust Company joined the Federal Reserve System. The assets of Security had climbed to nearly $100 million and the bank had achieved the position of second largest in the state. In 1929 Security merged with Los Angeles First National Bank and adopted a national charter. First National brought 94 branches into the combination, spread throughout Southern California. The combined assets of the new Security-First National Bank totaled $600 million, making it the nation's eighth largest bank.

Joseph Sartori continued to manage Security-First National as its president until 1934, when at age seventy-three he relinquished the job to George Wallace. Sartori's influence at the bank remained strong until his death in 1955.

The stimulus of World War II and postwar growth in the California economy caused most of the larger California banks to expand, and Security-First National was no exception. In the decade of the 1950s it acquired 12 banks. Lloyd Austin implemented several major mergers during his presidency and term as chief executive, from 1957 to 1967. Mergers with Farmers and Merchants Bank of Los Angeles, Security Trust of San Diego, and Security Trust and Savings of San Diego took place during that era. A merger with Pacific National of San Francisco in 1968 gave Security a base for expansion in Northern California. The name of the bank was changed to Security Pacific National Bank to gain from the merger partner's reputation and to distin-

guish California's Security from the many other institutions using that word in their title. Security added to its northern system the Bank of Sacramento, purchased in 1970, and nearby Mother Lode Bank, Placerville, in 1975.

Frederick Larkin, president from 1961 and chief executive after 1967, emphasized a teamwork approach to management and spearheaded the modernization of the bank. Security Pacific Corporation was set up as a holding company in 1971 to allow the acquisition of businesses the bank could not enter directly. Under that arrangement, the bank purchased several finance and mortgage banks. The Northern California base was relocated in a new 45-story building in San Francisco's Embarcadero district, and the administrative center of the bank was moved to a new, architecturally dramatic 55-story building in the financial district of Los Angeles. The bank installed an impressive computer system in that building to process checks. Also during the 1970s, the bank expanded into the international market. Security Pacific Overseas Investment Corporation acquired a controlling interest in Bank of Canton, Hong Kong. As of 1989 Security was represented in 30 of the world's major cities. The bank's consumer finance operations also became successful internationally.

Richard J. Flamson III, who had played an active role in both of those areas as president of the bank, succeeded Larkin as chief executive of Security Pacific Corporation after Larkin retired in 1979. Flamson spent his entire banking career at Security. A native of Los Angeles, he graduated in 1951 from Claremont McKenna (then Claremont Men's) College with a degree in economics and business administration. Described by peers as brilliant and charismatic, he brought the bank to increased prominence in the difficult decade of the 1980s by anticipating the easing of restrictions on banks and using advanced technology to cut costs.

When it seemed the Glass-Steagall Act might be modified to allow banks into the brokerage business, Security Pacific Corporation purchased several brokerage firms. As interstate banking became inevitable, Security bought bank holding companies in Arizona, Oregon, Nevada, and Washington. Some of those banks changed their names to Security Pacific, anticipating the time when they could fully merge with the California bank.

Flamson continued in 1989 as chairman and chief executive of the corporation, heading up a team of nearly 23,000 employees. At the end of 1986 assets of the bank exceeded $47 billion, making it California's second largest bank.

References:

Robert G. Cleland and Francis B. Putnam, *Isaias W. Hellman and the Farmers and Merchants Bank of Los Angeles* (San Marino, Cal.: Huntington Library, 1965);

Ira B. Cross, *Financing an Empire: History of Banking in California* (Chicago: Clarke, 1927);

John Russell McCarthy, *Joseph Francis Sartori, 1858-1946* (Los Angeles: Ward Ritchie, 1948).

Muriel Siebert

(September 12, 1932 -)

by Mary F. Cordato

Garden City, New York

CAREER: Securities analyst, Bache & Company (1954-1957); analyst, Aviation Advisory Service (1957-1958); securities analyst and portfolio manager, Utilities and Industries Management Corporation (1958); senior securities analyst, Shields & Company (1958-1960); partner, Stearns & Company (1960-1961); partner, Finkle & Company (1962-1965); partner, Brimberg & Company (1965-1967); chairman and president, Muriel Siebert & Company, Incorporated (1968-1977, 1983-); superintendent of banks, New York (1977-1982).

Muriel Siebert, business executive, first female member of the New York Stock Exchange, and former New York State official, was born on September 12, 1932, in Cleveland, Ohio. She was one of two children, the daughter of Irwin and Margaret Eunice (Roseman) Siebert. During her early years, blond-haired, green-eyed Muriel, known as Mickey to her friends, lived comfortably. Her father, a dentist in Cleveland, died when Muriel was sixteen years old, and that misfortune had an important impact on her career decisions. Although she enrolled in college at Case Western Reserve University, practical financial considerations led her to drop out in 1954, a few credits short of an accounting degree. Shortly afterward she moved to New York. She came there with only $500, a beat-up Studebaker, and the drive to succeed. She literally had never been away from home before, but had found the Big Apple exciting during an earlier visit there.

Siebert encountered her first professional disappointment not long after her New York arrival. She had applied for a position with the United Nations but did not receive it because she did not speak

Muriel Siebert

three languages. "That was probably a blessing," she recalls, "because by now I would probably be chief messenger girl with a bad case of fallen arches."

A few months later, in November 1954, Siebert entered the securities industry. Banking, finance, and accounting courses had always interested her at Case Western, although she had often been the only woman in the class. After Merrill

Lynch rejected her for another position because she did not have a degree, she informed the next prospect, Bache & Company, that she did have a degree. Bache hired her as a research trainee at $65 a week, a salary considered low even for 1950s standards.

Siebert quickly learned that Wall Street was hardly prepared for her or for any female professional at the time. At Bache, the firm's transportation specialist assigned to her what he considered a dud, the airlines industry. The more experienced securities analysts, nearly all men, specialized in railroad and shipping stocks, and most experts in the early 1950s could see no real future in the airlines. Of course, when the aerospace and jet aviation fields started to flourish in the late 1950s, Siebert stood exactly in the right place at the right time. In September 1957 she resigned from Bache and went to work as an analyst for Selig Altshul, an aviation consultant with Aviation Advisory Service. In April 1958 she joined Utilities and Industries Management Corporation as a security analyst and portfolio manager.

Meanwhile, Siebert continued to experience sexual discrimination. While on one interview, a prospective employer informed her that women could not travel out of town to represent their firms on business. Men generally received higher compensation for their work than their female counterparts did, a factor that pushed Muriel to switch jobs frequently. Finding positions was not always an easy task for a woman, however. In 1958, when Siebert applied for a senior level spot, she wrote to 150 firms, and "no one answered," she noted. "Then the New York Society of Security Analysts sent out my résumé with my initial instead of my first name." She secured a position in November 1958 as a senior analyst with Shields & Company.

During her early days at Shields, Siebert's work consisted mainly of analysis. In 1959, however, she received her first commission order from an investment company as a reward for a research idea. That opened her eyes to the wider, more profitable vista of trading. By 1960 she had developed a reputation on Wall Street for conducting profit-making securities research and secured orders from her institutional customers. Her commissions amounted to $150,000 a year. Throughout the 1960s she moved to general partnerships with Stearns & Company, Finkle & Company, and Brimberg & Company, all members of the New York Stock Exchange. By 1967 she averaged $500,000 a year in commissions.

At about that time Jerry Tsai, a colleague from Bache, suggested to Siebert that she purchase a seat on the New York Stock Exchange (NYSE). The idea was an unusual one. Although two women had been admitted to the American Exchange in 1965, the NYSE had remained an all-male enclave throughout its entire 175-year history. Not one of its 1,366 seats had ever been held by a woman. Many considered the trading floor, with its clublike atmosphere and rough male humor, too risqué for women. However, no formal rules for excluding women existed. According to the exchange's constitution, the only requirements were that a person be older than twenty-one, a U. S. citizen, professionally competent, and wealthy enough to finance the seat.

Nevertheless, Siebert remained skeptical, and it took six months for her to decide. She worried that owning a seat on the NYSE would affect her relationships with clients, especially when they discovered her affluence. She worked with leading financial institutions around the nation, including banks and mutual funds, but most of the portfolio managers with whom she dealt directly made $25,000 to $30,000 annual salaries. "I wondered how they would react when they found that they were paying me commissions in a year that [collectively] were maybe two or three times what they were earning," she confided.

The idea of membership fascinated Siebert, however, and in December 1967 she filed her application with the NYSE. The Board of Governors recognized her as a candidate of outstanding potential, with sizable financial assets, a proven track record in the securities industry, and demonstrated competence. It approved her request for membership on December 28, 1967. On that date she paid $445,000 to purchase her seat, thus becoming, at the age of thirty-five, the first female member to join the Big Board.

As an individual member, Siebert avoided fanfare by refusing to conduct trading on the floor. In December 1967 she set up her own brokerage firm, Muriel Siebert & Company, at 120 Broadway, a few doors away from the NYSE. Another firm, Stern, Lauer & Company, handled her floor transactions. "I knew that people were watching," she confided to one interviewer. "I wanted to prove that a woman would buy a seat not for publicity, but for business reasons."

The response to Siebert's Big Board membership varied. Most people "were actually very proud," she exclaimed; "The people at the Exchange were grand." The reaction of one brokerage house partner, who preferred to remain anonymous, was typical: "I couldn't care less if a woman bought a seat. God bless America. I think it's great." However, the more conservative members in the financial community remained skeptical. "On the day I got my seat," she wrote, "one of the governors of the Exchange asked me, 'How many more are there behind you?' like I was leading a parade."

The movement Siebert led was not of women into the NYSE (she remained the only woman member for more than nine years) but of brokerage firms into discount trading. When she established her company in December 1967, she did so as an individual member. She conducted research for institutions, including buying and selling analysis. By the early 1970s she recognized the need to change the course of her business. Finding it more difficult to justify the cost of research, she gradually began to execute stock orders only. In 1975 a change in Securities Exchange Commission legislation proved quite profitable for Siebert. The regulations for charging fixed rates on market transactions were dropped on May 1, and commissions became fully negotiable. On that date Muriel Siebert & Company became a discount service and completely deactivated its research branch. Her firm was the first to announce (in ads picturing herself cutting a $100 bill in half) that it would offer small investors discounts of up to 50 percent less than other brokerage houses. According to Siebert, "I knew that a change this drastic would open doors to opportunities for someone and I decided to take the plunge and open the door. We became a discount broker, which means that the only thing we really offered was the execution of orders; no research, no advice." By the late 1970s, her company had become one of the leaders in the field.

Not everyone was pleased with Siebert's shift into commission cutting, however. Some non-discount brokers of the Wall Street establishment, in fact, expressed anger over it. One firm, Stearn & Company, which had cleared the Siebert company's transactions, cut her off in July 1975 under circumstances never fully disclosed. She brushed off the incident: "When you take a stand on something, a lot of people aren't going to like you. Of course, firms that didn't like me then now say I had foresight."

In April 1977 Siebert, a Republican, was appointed by Democratic governor Hugh Carey to the post of superintendent of banks of New York State. In order to avoid a conflict of interest, she placed her firm in a blind trust and accepted the offer immediately. "When you get a chance to become a regulator of something that is that important and that vital, you don't say to the governor, 'Come back two years from next Tuesday,'" she noted. At the time, the Banking Department regulated about $500 billion in assets and had jurisdiction over 103 savings banks, 104 commercial banks, and New York branches of 139 foreign banks. Siebert, the first woman to hold the position, remained superintendent for five years.

In one of the first problems she encountered as bank superintendent Siebert had to deal with the financially troubled New York City Municipal Credit Union (MCU). The MCU, chartered in 1919, held deposits of more than $120 million and consisted of 112,000 members. In April 1977 a controller had been hired by the MCU to straighten out mismanaged accounts, but management split over his recommendations. In August, Siebert assigned state agents to supervise the MCU's daily operations. They found that internal reforms were impossible under a divided directorship. Further examination disclosed increased loan delinquencies and little progress on collecting those loans. By late October rumors of insolvency and lack of confidence in management led to a run on the fund by members. On November 3, 1977, in a move to protect depositors, Siebert ordered a temporary state takeover of the MCU. Within six months, under her supervision, the credit union elected a new board of directors, resumed normal operations, and saw its credibility restored.

During her term as bank superintendent, Siebert often took unpopular stands, invoking criticism from several sources. In one instance she openly challenged Governor Carey over the question of foreign takeovers of New York financial institutions. The controversy centered on the Buffalo-based Marine Midland Bank, 13th largest banking company in America with assets of more than $15 billion. In 1978 the British-owned Hongkong and Shanghai Banking Corporation moved to acquire 51 percent of Marine Midland's outstanding shares. Carey supported the acquisition, seeing it as a way to boost New York's ailing economy and to help solve Marine's financial problems, which were plentiful at the time. Siebert, however, opposed the takeover. In a 48-page document prepared in May 1979 she questioned whether the Hongkong and Shanghai Bank had "the attributes needed for management of Marine Midland." She feared that a merger would not cater to the public interest of the Upstate New York community, where Marine held a dominant market position. She also argued that the strong influence of a foreign government over the Hongkong and Shanghai Bank could lead to investment policies in its own country that conflicted with policies of the New York banking system. Finally, she insisted that foreign banks did not face the same stringent disclosure requirements as their American counterparts, thus creating doubts about the soundness of such banks. When she asked the Hongkong and Shanghai for detailed information on its operations, the bank refused and held up the merger. In June 1979 the Marine Midland Bank proposed to switch from a state to a national charter in order to avoid Siebert's resistance. In 1980, under the new arrangement, the merger of the two banks was approved by the U.S. comptroller of the currency.

One of the most pressing problems confronting Siebert as bank superintendent was the battered condition of New York State savings institutions. She expressed concern over thrift industry losses that by the early 1980s were mounting at unprecedented rates. (New York savings banks lost $372 million in the third quarter of 1981, 23 percent greater than the record level of the second quarter.) Many savings banks, she contended, suffered from operating losses for the first time since their formation because of a flight of deposits into higher yielding investments. In November 1981 Siebert called for federal support. At a news conference she urged a presidential committee "to consider the future of the nation's thrift industry." She warned that several savings banks would collapse or be forced to merge, and unless the government could help the troubled industry, serious consequences would follow, including the loss of an important source of housing finance.

The real test for Siebert came with the near collapse of the Greenwich Savings Bank. In October 1981 observers realized that the Greenwich would not survive without assistance. It paid depositors increasingly high rates of interest at a time when most of its income came from old, low-yielding mortgages, and losses mounted. A collapse of the Greenwich potentially signaled a loss of confidence in other savings institutions as well. Thus Siebert searched for a strong merger partner. In November she found that partner, in the Metropolitan Savings Bank of New York. Acting quickly, she engineered a plan to present to the Federal Deposit Insurance Corporation (FDIC). The FDIC responded with $185 million to the Metropolitan to help finance the merger.

Throughout the late 1970s and early 1980s Siebert continued to negotiate mergers of ailing savings banks into stronger institutions. Those included, among others, the mergers of the Citizens Savings and Loan into the Astoria Federal Savings (February 1979) and the New York Bank for Savings into the Buffalo Savings Bank (April 1982). In Fall 1987 she lobbied for state legislation that made such mergers easier, including a bill permitting commercial banks to purchase thrift institutions.

In May 1982, at the age of fifty, Siebert resigned her post as banking superintendent and sought the Republican nomination for U.S. senator. She campaigned on the basis that she was a "woman who means business and who had succeeded in a tough man's world." She referred to her experience in state service and her 22 years of work on Wall Street as excellent preparation for the Senate seat. Throughout the primary campaign she called herself "very conservative fiscally" and "quite liberal in terms of people and human rights." Although a Republican, she differed with President Ronald Reagan over the size of the federal budget and believed that the government needed to cut the deficit as a prelude to reduced interest rates and an economic recovery. She proposed defense spending cuts and tax increases as potential solutions for lowering the deficit. She also challenged Reagan's social policies by supporting a woman's right to abortion (including government financed abortions for poorer women) and an equal rights amendment to the U.S. constitution. In September 1982 Siebert lost the nomination to Brooklyn assemblywoman Florence Sullivan, but she did not let the matter rest. In November she threatened legal action against the Conservative party, charging it with unfair campaign practices.

A bull market and the desire to expand her firm brought Siebert back to Wall Street in 1983, six years after leaving it. During her absence she had left the control of her company in the hands of others who lacked her expertise. The discount brokerage business had boomed at Siebert's expense. Her company had lost its position in the industry. Firms that were half its size when she had left had grown to many times its size when she came back. She sought to regain lost ground, and after two hard years of reorganization, Muriel Siebert & Company was well on the road to recovery. In May 1983 she opened a branch in the First Women's Bank of New York. In May 1985 she acquired the near-bankrupt discount brokerage firms of Bevill, Bresler & Schulman, Incorporated, and Parr Securities, thus adding several thousand accounts to her firm.

Throughout her career Siebert has given generously of her time and resources to various causes. She has been a guest lecturer at several colleges and universities and has served as a trustee of Manhattan College and as board overseer of the New York University School of Business. She has actively served on other boards and committees, including the New York State Economic Development Board, the Women's Advancement Committee of the Economic Development Administration (NYC), the Executive Committee of the Greater New York Area Council of the Boy Scouts of America, the United Way of New York City, the Executive Committee for the World Banking Congress, the Citizens Budget Committee, the Columbus Quintennial Foundation of New York, and the Business Committee of the Metropolitan Museum of Art. She has also received the following awards: the Spirit of Achievement Award, Albert Einstein College of Medicine (1977); the Women's Equity Action League Award (1978); the Outstanding Contributions to Equal Opportunity for Women Award, Business Council of United Nations Decade for Women (1979); the Silver Beaver Award, Boy Scouts of America (1981); the National Organization for Women Legal Defense and Educational Fund Award (1981); the Elizabeth Cutter Morrow Award, Young Women's Christian Association (1983); and the Emily Roebling Award, National Women's Hall of Fame (1984).

Siebert has involved herself with the advancement of women, especially educated women. "I think it's a crime for a girl to go to college for four years," she writes, "then suddenly be expected to stop thinking. It's a waste of creativity." Siebert sponsors women in the arts (she has contributed substantially to the National Museum of Women in the Arts), has helped pay tuition bills, and has shared her professional experiences with various women's groups throughout the country.

Siebert has been described by colleagues and friends as "very giving, very generous," despite the "very tough and businesslike image" she sometimes projects. According to one employee, people can call on her with problems, whether physical or emotional. She often cosigns loans for her workers and has helped them make important career decisions. She attributes her warmheartedness to her midwestern roots and early family upbringing. "I try to explain to people about the niceness and the hopefulness," she confided in an interview with reporter Mary Rowland. "There's a solidness in midwestern people."

Siebert, who has never married, has come a long way since her early days in Cleveland. One of the first female superachievers of Wall Street, as of 1990 she lived extremely well. She required a full-time secretary to handle a wide variety of tasks, both private and business. Over the years she developed flamboyant tastes for expensive cars and vacations, flashy clothes (she dislikes women who wear navy blue pinstripe suits or "uniforms" and prefers prints and brighter colors), fine restaurants, and solo plane flying. She resided at the exclusive River House in Manhattan and in a condominium in posh East Hampton, New York. She counts tennis, bridge, and concerts among her favorite pastimes. Siebert took pride in her achievements, which she earned by hard work, perseverance, and a can-do-anything attitude. According to writer Aileen Jacobson, "She is proud that she has enough money 'on the side' so that she would never have to work again if she did not want to." As of 1990, however, she devoted her energies to her discount brokerage firm, where she was chairman and president.

References:

Josh Barbanel, "G.O.P. Senate Hopefuls in a Race for Recognition," *New York Times*, September 13, 1982, p. B3;

Robert A. Bennett, "Bigger Losses in 3rd Quarter Upsets Albany," *New York Times*, November 10, 1981, D1, D15;

"Big Board Accepts Woman as Member," *New York Times*, December 29, 1967, p. 35;

Valerie Bohigian, *Ladybucks* (New York: Dodd, Mead, 1987), pp. 66-67, 220;

"First New York Exchange Seat For Woman Sought by Analyst," *New York Times*, December 9, 1967, p.1;

Patricia Harrison, *America's New Women Entrepreneurs: Tips, Tactics, and Techniques of Women Achievers In Business* (Washington, D.C.: Acropolis, 1986), pp. 183-186;

Aileen Jacobson, *Women In Charge: Dilemmas of Women In Authority* (New York: Van Nostrand Reinhold, 1985, pp. 206-213;

"Long and Painful Record of Little Progress in a Man's World: the Personal Views of Eight Women Who Succeeded In It," *Life Magazine*, 69 (September 4, 1970): 18-21;

Frank Lynn, "Muriel Siebert Joins G.O.P. Race for U.S. Senator," *New York Times*, May 26, 1982, p. B2;

Lynn, "3 Meet for First Debate In G.O.P. Senate Race," *New York Times*, July 22, 1982, p. B1;

Richard J. Meslin, "Miss Siebert Said to Bar Midland Bid," *New York Times*, May 12, 1979, pp. 27, 29;

"Miss Siebert to Oversee New York State Banks," *New York Times*, June 8, 1977, p. D12;

"Miss Siebert's Search," *Wall Street Journal*, May 30, 1979, p. 24;

"Muriel Siebert Acquires Bevill, Bresler & Schulman," *Wall Street Journal*, May 13, 1985, p. 7;

"Muriel Siebert & Co. Buys Accounts of Parr Securities," *Wall Street Journal*, May 15, 1985, p. 18;

"New York State Is Taking Over Municipal Credit Union," *New York Times*, November 3, 1977, p. B4;

Mary Rowland, "Rebel of Wall Street," *Working Woman* (April 1986): 64-65;

Julie Salamon, "Feisty Regulator: Muriel Siebert's Style In Overseeing Banks Is Hardly Banker's Gray. Brash New York Supervisor Fights to Rescue Thrifts," *Wall Street Journal*, December 18, 1981, pp. 1, 18;

Leonard Sloane, *The Anatomy of the Floor: The Trillion-dollar Market at the New York Stock Exchange* (Garden City, N.Y.: Doubleday, 1980), pp. 163-168;

Cindy Stivers, "Banks' Banker: New York's Siebert," *Working Woman* (November 1978): 23-24;

"The Flap Over Marine Midland," *Business Week*, no. 2589(June 11, 1979): 102-103;

Vartanig G. Vartan, "First Woman to Join the Big Board Finds 'Grand' Reception," *New York Times*, January 1, 1968, pp. 23-24.

Fernand St Germain

(January 9, 1928-)

by Robert D. Auerbach

University of California, Riverside

CAREER: U.S. Army (1949-1952); state representative, Rhode Island (1953-1961); U.S. representative, Rhode Island (1961-1988).

Fernand St Germain spent most of his adult life as a legislator. A lifelong Democrat, after a stint in the Rhode Island statehouse he won election to the U.S. House of Representatives in 1960. He served for ten years as chairman of the House Financial Institutions Subcommittee and then succeeded Henry Reuss as chairman of the parent Banking, Finance, and Urban Affairs Committee in 1981. On the Banking Committee he proved instrumental in the passage of several pieces of legislation, including the Federal Institutions Regulatory Act of 1978, which tightened rules on insider borrowing at depository institutions. That law also authorized the creation of a Central Liquidity Facility that made federal credit available to the credit union industry. St Germain also played a prominent role in the passage of the Depository Institu-

tions Deregulation and Monetary Control Act of 1980 and cosponsored with Senator Jake Garn the Garn-St Germain Act of 1982, which liberalized the investment policies of savings and loan institutions. He lost his reelection bid in 1988 as a result of a House Ethics Committee and U.S. Justice Department investigation of his relationship with members of the industry he had been entrusted to regulate. Neither body ever leveled formal charges against him.

St Germain was born on January 9, 1928, in Blackstone, Rhode Island. His father worked as a foreman in a dye plant. He graduated from Providence College in 1948 and enlisted in the U.S. Army for a three-year term as a medic in 1949. He graduated from Boston University Law School in 1955 after attending at night and working in a garment factory by day. He won election to the Rhode Island state legislature in 1953 in a campaign against alleged corruption in office. On his first day at the statehouse a doorkeeper mistook him for a

Fernand St Germain

page and asked him to "run down and get me a cup of coffee." He served ably, however, and vaulted to national service at the age of thirty-two in the election that brought John F. Kennedy to the White House.

As chairman of the Financial Institutions Subcommittee, in 1978 St Germain engineered the passage of the Financial Institutions Regulatory Act, aimed partly at the type of insider bank lending allegedly practiced by Bert Lance, President Jimmy Carter's director of the U.S. Office of Management and Budget. Lance allegedly made overdrafts from a bank in which he and members of his family owned stock and allegedly obtained loans from a bank that had received substantial deposits from a bank in which Lance served as an officer. The act also established an institution known as the Central Liquidity Facility to make federal credit available to the credit union industry.

St Germain also worked behind the scenes for the passage of the Depository Institutions Deregulation and Monetary Control Act (DIDMCA) of 1980, which authorized the payment of interest on checking accounts, a gradual lifting of the interest rates banks and savings and loans could charge, the expansion of savings and loan lending powers, the increase of federal deposit insurance coverage from $40,000 to $100,000 per depositor, and the extension of Federal Reserve reserve requirements to all depository institutions.

After Henry Reuss of Wisconsin announced his intent to leave the Banking Committee chair in 1980, St Germain won election to the post. He quickly turned the committee to the developing problems in the savings and loan industry. Insiders knew that the industry faced serious trouble. They found themselves in a profits squeeze as interest rates on new money rose while their incomes remained constant. With Federal Reserve chairman Paul Volcker and Richard T. Pratt, chairman of the Federal Home Loan Bank Board, St Germain came to support an emergency bailout of the industry "to administer a program of direct capital assistance for home mortgage lending institutions whose net worth slips below two percent of assets." After President Ronald Reagan promised to veto the $7.5 billion proposal, St Germain reworked it and made it a part of a larger piece of savings and loan legislation, the Garn-St Germain Act. The act also gave federal depository institutions permission to buy out state depository institutions that had sunk into financial trouble. That provision set the stage for competition between states to remove regulations barring out-of-state competition in the form of interstate mergers. The act also removed interest rate ceilings on certain types of consumer deposits, accelerating interest rate deregulation begun under the DIDMCA of 1980.

Largely because of the great increase in net worth St Germain experienced during his legislative career, the House Ethics Committee began an investigation of his finances in 1986. The committee cleared St Germain of allegations that he had personally benefited from no-money-down loans in a series of transactions that took place in 1972 and 1973 and that his office had improperly influenced federal banking regulators, but it did disclose that St Germain had failed to report properly his assets on financial disclosure forms, undervaluing his personal accounts by some $1.5 million. The House took no action against the congressman, but the publicity he received as a result of the episode, combined with new allegations of misconduct that came just before the 1988 election, convinced Rhode Island voters to send him home.

References:

Robert D. Auerbach, *Money, Banking, and Financial Markets* (New York: McGraw-Hill, 1988);

Brooks Jackson, *Honest Graft: Big Money and the American Process* (New York: Knopf, 1988);

Howard Kurtz, "Draft Report Clears St Germain on Influence-Abuse Allegations," *Washington Post*, April 12, 1987, p. 12.

Benjamin Strong

(December 22, 1872 - October 16, 1928)

by Anna J. Schwartz

National Bureau of Economic Research

CAREER: Clerk, Jesup, Paton & Company (1891); manager of British clients' investments, Cuyler, Morgan & Company (1891-1900); assistant secretary (1901-1903), secretary, Atlantic Trust Company (1904); secretary, (1904-1909), vice-president (1910-1913), president, Bankers Trust Company (1914); governor, Federal Reserve Bank of New York (1914-1928).

Benjamin Strong (courtesy of the Federal Reserve Bank of New York)

Benjamin Strong, the dominant figure in the Federal Reserve System from its start in 1914 until his death in 1928, was born on December 22, 1872, in Fishkill-on-Hudson, New York. In a family of five children of Benjamin Strong and Adeline Torrey Schenck, he grew up in Montclair, New Jersey, where they had moved after the elder Strong had become manager of the private fortune and philanthropies of Morris Ketchum Jesup. Earlier the father held a job as superintendent of the Hudson division of the New York Central Railroad. Strong's mother was the daughter of a prominent Presbyterian minister who was pastor of the Princeton First Presbyterian Church, the denomination with which her son also became affiliated.

In 1891 Strong graduated from the Montclair High School, but instead of entering Princeton as two of his brothers had he took a job in New York as clerk at Jesup, Paton & Company, private bankers. The firm later became known as John Paton & Company and later still as Cuyler, Morgan & Company. During the nine years that Strong worked for the firm, he represented British and Scottish clients who were investors in land improvement and irrigation companies in California and were large landholders in Nebraska, the Dakotas, Iowa, Georgia, and Kentucky.

At least a year and a half before he resigned from the firm, Strong investigated the possibility of working for a trust company. Trust companies, which had managed mainly personal trusts, by the end of the nineteenth century eagerly acquired corporate trust business. In addition to performing fiduciary functions, trust companies had also developed a commercial banking business. Strong proposed to his prospective employer at a trust company that opportunities existed in attracting interbank deposits from trust companies located outside New York. At the end of 1900 he resigned from Cuyler, Morgan & Company and in 1901 took the position of assistant secretary of the Atlantic Trust Company.

Strong's role in assisting in the merger of the Atlantic Trust Company with the Metropolitan Trust Company in 1903 won him the position of secretary of the larger institution in 1904.

Standing six feet three inches in height, Strong was a gregarious man with many interests and a talent for forming friendships. In 1895 he married Margaret LeBoutillier and settled in Plainfield, New Jersey. In 1898 they moved to Englewood, where their neighbors were Henry P. Davison and Thomas W. Lamont, who figured in an important way in Strong's future. He became active in the community's civic affairs and in 1900 became treasurer of the Englewood Hospital, of which Davison was president. Strong's marriage ended tragically with the suicide of his wife in 1905, leaving four young children, two sons and two daughters. The death of the older of his two daughters the following year added to the tragedy. In 1907 Strong married Katherine Converse, with whom he had two children. She was the daughter of Edmund C. Converse, the president of the Bankers Trust Company, where Strong had started to work in April 1904.

Davison, then vice-president of a leading New York national bank, offered Strong the job at Bankers Trust—his brainchild—which a group of commercial banks organized in 1903. Since national banks and most state-chartered banks were not permitted to conduct trust business, they were in the anomalous position of directing their customers to existing trust companies, which competed with them for commercial banking business. Bankers Trust Company, a commercial bankers' trust company, solved the problem. It proved an immediate success.

When Strong became secretary of Bankers Trust, he replaced Thomas W. Lamont, who became vice-president. The board of directors of Bankers Trust included executives of the principal New York and out-of-town commercial banks and of several investment banks, including J. P. Morgan & Company. That group of men was familiar with current developments in the banking and trust business. Of particular concern was the position of trust companies that were not members of the New York Clearing House because they were unwilling to be subject to its regulations. Members, however, could clear for nonmembers, so the trust companies with lower reserve requirements than those imposed on commercial banks suffered no penalty from nonmembership provided a member was willing to clear for them. The New York State superintendent

of banks was responsible for legislation in 1906 that required trust companies to keep a reserve of either 15 or 10 percent against aggregate deposits depending on the size of the city of their location. One-third of the reserves could be kept in bank balances. Those requirements were less stringent than those on commercial banks. Bankers Trust, like other banks and trust companies in New York, held the reserves of many other institutions.

For Strong the position at Bankers Trust offered a learning experience that was topped by his exposure to developments during the panic of 1907. The panic occurred when a widespread demand by depositors for immediate conversion of their deposits into currency spread from one bank to other solvent banks because of a loss of confidence in the banking system. A panic can be halted and confidence in the system restored by a demonstration that an ample supply of currency is available to satisfy all depositor demands.

In 1907 the first direct signs of trouble occurred during the week of October 14, when five banks that were members of the New York Clearing House and three outside banks required assistance. A group of Clearing House banks responded, and they seemed to have restored order by Monday, October 21, when the Knickerbocker Trust Company, the third largest trust company in New York, began to experience unfavorable clearing-house balances as a result of connections with the banks initially in trouble. The Bank of Commerce notified the New York Clearing House that it would no longer clear checks for the Knickerbocker. A run on the company the next day brought J. P. Morgan in as chief of staff to deal with the situation.

As one of his generals Morgan summoned Davison, who in turn arranged for Benjamin Strong to make an examination of Knickerbocker's assets. Strong reported to Davison that the company was not solvent, and Knickerbocker closed. On October 23 a run started on the Trust Company of America, the second largest trust company in the city. Strong went in with a force of examiners to examine the Trust Company of America's affairs. This time he reported to Morgan that the company was solvent, its surplus nearly wiped out but its capital not much impaired. Morgan's response was: "This, then, is the place to stop the trouble."

A loan to the Trust Company of America was immediately arranged, but ten days later it was apparent that even that money was not enough to save it. Strong returned to the Trust Company's office with his force of examiners to see whether the Trust Company had sufficient collateral to justify another loan. Strong was convinced that there was, but Morgan insisted that the trust company presidents who met with him agree to match the size of the loan he offered. They finally agreed, but the action failed to quell the panic. Strong himself delivered a bundle of cash to the Trust Company to enable it to open for business, but still more institutions found their currency holdings in danger of depletion. Belatedly, the New York Clearing House issued loan certificates to enable banks to conserve cash by paying balances due other banks with those certificates and simultaneously restricted the convertibility of deposits into currency. Countrywide restriction followed. In 1907 the right actions were taken too late to be effective in heading off panic.

Strong's experience during the panic of that year, in which the end of restriction of payments to depositors was not fully achieved until the beginning of January 1908, colored his thinking about the banking and monetary system for the rest of his life. He saw clearly that to prevent a financial panic in the future by depending on a chief of staff such as Morgan and cooperative actions by leading bankers hardly constituted a satisfactory strategy. The system required fundamental restructuring.

When Lamont resigned as vice-president at the end of 1909—he left to become vice-president of the First National Bank from which Davison had resigned to become a member of J. P. Morgan & Company—Strong succeeded him. Bankers Trust prospered in the next few years, absorbing the Mercantile Trust Company in 1911 and the Manhattan Trust Company in 1912 to emerge as the second largest trust company in the country. Since Converse delegated to him the operation of the company, Strong, though nominally vice-president, in fact became the ranking officer. When the former retired in January 1914, Strong acquired the title to match the responsibilities he discharged daily. He also served on the boards of directors of a dozen corporations and two other trust companies and was a trustee of a savings bank. Throughout his life, Strong contributed to the support of the Englewood Hospital and of Princeton University, which awarded him an honorary Doctor of Laws degree in 1918.

It took the dramatic experience of the panic of 1907 to make some measure of banking reform politically imperative. Bankers had to find a means to provide for an attempt by the public to change the form of money it held from deposits to currency without initially draining bank reserves. That drain in turn would force banks operating with fractional reserves to contract their outstanding liabilities by a multiple of the loss in reserves. The result would be a reduction in the total amount of money available to be held. An interim solution, the Aldrich-Vreeland Act, approved May 30, 1908, provided for the issuance of an emergency currency by groups of banks, on the basis of usual banking assets, with penalty provisions to force retirement after the emergency.

One clause of the Aldrich-Vreeland Act provided for the appointment of a National Monetary Commission consisting of nine senators and nine representatives. The chairman was Senator Nelson W. Aldrich, the vice-chairman Representative Edward B. Vreeland. The commission conducted hearings and arranged for a large number of special studies.

Strong actively participated in the preliminary discussions for banking reform. In November 1910 Davison organized a group of experienced bankers to travel with Senator Aldrich to the Jekyll Island Club off the southeastern corner of Georgia to spend a week together to hammer out a plan. Among those Davison asked to go were Paul M. Warburg; Frank Arthur Vanderlip, president of National City Bank; A. P. Andrew, then an assistant secretary of the Treasury; and Strong. Those men drafted a bill known as the Aldrich Plan, providing for a National Reserve Association—a single central bank. Because Aldrich fell ill, Vanderlip and Strong traveled to Washington from Georgia to prepare a report to accompany the plan that Aldrich could use in introducing it to Congress. Sailing on Aldrich's yacht in August 1911, Strong and several other bankers discussed the plan with the senator. In November 1911 Strong spoke in favor of the plan at the American Bankers Association convention and actively solicited bankers' support.

To Strong's disappointment Congress defeated the plan in 1912. The National Monetary Commission, appointed by a Republican Congress, had a Republican as its chairman. A Democratic majority along with Woodrow Wilson won the elections in November 1912 on a platform that contained a statement opposing the Aldrich Plan. Bills offered by the Democrats in 1913 were meticulously analyzed by Strong. One bill by Senator Robert Latham Owen and another by Representative Carter Glass impressed Strong as carelessly drawn and objectionable in their provisions. With Davison and Vanderlip he prepared a substitute bill that Senator Theodore Burton presented to no avail. In letters to congressmen he criticized the bills before them and proposed amendments. Strong worked on a speech by Senator Burton that criticized the Democratic bills as did also his colleague at Bankers Trust, Fred I. Kent, an expert on foreign exchange. Senator Elihu Root in a speech that warned of inflationary effects of the bills used arguments developed by Strong.

Strong objected to the Glass bill on five grounds: (1) twelve Reserve Banks was an excessive number; (2) he deplored appointment of politicians rather than bankers as Reserve Board members; (3) the issuance of Federal Reserve notes as government as well as Reserve Bank obligations portended a return to greenbackism and fiat money; (4) the bill, by failing to meet the views of bankers, would lead to the withdrawal of national banks from the system and not attract state banks and trust companies; (5) the bill neglected protection of national banks against losses as the result of retirement of national bank notes.

Despite his vigorous disapproval of the Owen-Glass bill, Strong reconciled himself to making the best of it, since some version of it appeared sure to pass. Once enacted, on December 23, 1913, he urged bankers to cooperate to make the new system a success. Nevertheless, given his preference for a central bank and his opposition to the government's backing of Federal Reserve notes, in the summer of 1914 he initially declined to be considered for the position of governor of the Federal Reserve Bank of New York, partly because his father-in-law vigorously opposed Strong's move to a semigovernment job with no financial future. Strong, however, changed his mind at the urging of Davison and Warburg. Four members of the newly elected board of directors of the New York Reserve Bank visited him on September 22, 1914, and asked whether he would give serious consideration to the position if the directors offered it to him. His only conditions were that the directors be unanimous and harbor no doubts in making the offer. On October 5, at the first formal meeting of the directors, they elected Strong governor and thereupon joined the meeting.

Strong later concluded that government backing of Federal Reserve notes did not constitute the de-

fect he originally asserted it did. He still retained his preference for a central bank but acknowledged that in the United States it would be subject to political attack. A real central bank, in his view, would have its base in New York and would find itself the target of hostile groups in the nation.

One reason Strong initially expressed reluctance to leave Bankers Trust in the summer of 1914 was the disruption of financial markets upon the outbreak of war in Europe. He had returned from a trip there only a few days earlier and had to confront the problems facing not only his bank but other financial institutions as well. Bankers Trust had to make foreign payments on its own account and for its depositors at a time when warring nations had cut off U.S. exports, the stock exchanges in America and abroad closed down, prices of commodities that collateralized loans tumbled, and depositors and correspondents had large demands for cash. By resorting to clearing house loan certificates and the issue of Aldrich-Vreeland emergency currency, the banks averted panic. Bankers Trust, however, had a special problem. It acted as issuing and paying agent for the American Bankers Association travelers checks that many Americans stranded in Europe needed cashed to obtain local currencies. Kent, who managed travelers checks for Bankers Trust, then happened to be in London and took charge of the problem. Strong had to find the funds to remit to Kent. He went to Washington on August 3, and after discussions with representatives of many government agencies and with Congressional approval they arranged to send a warship with $7.5 million in gold, two-thirds provided by bankers, one-third by the government, to Britain to relieve the plight of Americans abroad. That done, Strong saw that Kent was available to do some business for the company. He advised Kent to try to interest foreign banks in opening accounts with Bankers Trust.

In September 1914 Strong participated as an active member of the Gold Fund Committee, which had been organized at the initiative of the Treasury and the Federal Reserve Board (sworn in on August 10). The committee had a mandate to determine how to deal with U.S. short-term debts to Europe. Strong persuaded leaders of clearinghouses to subscribe $108 million in gold to the fund, to be drawn on as needed by those owing sums abroad. Only $10 million was actually exported, and the

Strong in Simla, Northern India (courtesy of the Federal Reserve Bank of New York)

very existence of the fund served to reduce demands for payment in foreign currencies or gold.

By 1915 the U.S. international position had changed dramatically. New York replaced London as the chief center for foreign deposits. The demand for American goods by neutrals and belligerents alike created an excess of exports over imports financed by gold inflows, the sale of American securities owned by foreigners, a reduction of short-term loans foreigners owed to Americans, and increased borrowing by foreigners in U.S. financial markets.

The board of directors had originally set the opening of the new Reserve Bank for early 1915, but on October 26, 1914, Secretary of the Treasury William McAdoo decided that because of the war in Europe it required an earlier opening. He fixed November 16, 1914, as the date for it to begin operations. Organizing the bank on such short order tested Strong's administrative skill, a test he met with distinction. Renting offices, assembling a staff, arranging for the custody of gold the member banks transferred in payment of the first installment of the Reserve Bank's capital, establishing reciprocal accounts with the other Reserve Banks and providing for interbank settlements, creating machin-

ery for check collection, determining the eligibility of paper for rediscount, organizing the issue of Federal Reserve notes—all Strong accomplished.

Thanks to his ability and intellectual force, Strong quickly emerged as the chief executive officer of the New York Reserve Bank. Member banks elected a majority of the board of directors, but the chairman, a Class C director, was the Federal Reserve agent who represented the Federal Reserve Board at the Reserve Bank. At other Reserve Banks a contest developed between the governor and the chairman for control, but in New York there was no contest: Strong was in charge. That position enhanced Strong's leadership of the governors, who also did not want their hands tied by the Federal Reserve agent and the board.

Strong also actively created cooperative arrangements among the individual Reserve Banks, principally through the Governors Conference that met shortly after they opened for business. He was elected chairman of the Executive Committee and of all meetings of the Governors Conference held before he became ill in mid 1916. At the meetings the governors criticized actions by the Federal Reserve Board, in particular their proposal of discount rate changes when the Federal Reserve Act clearly reserved that right to the Reserve Banks. In response the board decreed that the meetings should be called at the initiative of the board, limited to topics approved by the board, and to abolish the Executive Committee. The Governors Conference was discontinued in 1917 for the duration of the war and lost its effectiveness once Strong no longer attended.

One problem that arose among the Reserve Banks a few weeks after their opening resulted from their purchases and sales of municipal warrants, acceptances, and, in connection with the retirement of some national bank notes, sales of longer-term government securities. As early as March 1915 Strong advised the other Reserve Banks that New York would execute their orders but they could buy or sell on their own accounts. By late 1916 he proposed to discontinue purchases and sales for own accounts and that a committee of governors should operate for the system as a whole—a proposal that was not adopted until 1922.

In his speeches in 1915 Strong reflected on adjustments that the United States would undergo after the war when "international transactions in such volume or sequence as we cannot now forecast will begin promptly to cause the return flow of some part" of the gold the belligerents had shipped to America. He remained sanguine that the Federal Reserve Banks, "which can convert bank assets of a liquid character, such as commercial paper, into credit or currency at notice," would preclude an episode of panic like that of 1907.

At an early stage in his incumbency at the New York Federal Reserve Bank, Strong sought to enlarge his understanding of the operation of the central banks of other countries. In that connection he made the first of many trips to Europe in February 1916, remaining abroad until mid April. He spent most of the time in Paris and London, where he studied their financial systems, war finance and central bank techniques, and the operation of money markets and commercial banks. At the Bank of France on February 24 he met the governor and other officers and discussed establishing an account to handle foreign business of the Reserve Banks and a counterpart account for the Bank of France at the U.S. institutions, without reaching a definite agreement. In London on March 14 he met Lord Cunliffe, the governor of the Bank of England, and, four days later, Montagu Norman, then an assist-

ant to the deputy governor, with whom he later formed a close personal and professional friendship. Strong summarized the discussions the two had in a memorandum jointly prepared by him and Bank of England representatives.

The 11 points covered by the memorandum Strong brought back in April included provisions for the Federal Reserve Bank of New York to establish an account with the Bank of England that the other Reserve Banks might elect to join, for the Bank of England's account to be in the form of earmarked gold—since the Reserve Banks could receive deposits only from member banks and the U.S. government—and for the Bank of England to purchase sterling bills for the Federal Reserve Bank of New York on request. The memorandum also referred to the hope that a similar understanding with the Bank of France might be reached.

Soon after his return home Strong met with the Federal Reserve Board to inform them of what he had accomplished abroad. He also reported to the governors of the other Reserve Banks, who agreed to share the expenses of his trip. He wished to move ahead with the plan for foreign agencies and met again on May 16 with the Federal Reserve Board and McAdoo, but his hopes for personal involvement in completing the arrangements suffered a crushing blow early in June by the diagnosis that he was a victim of tuberculosis of the lungs. On being ordered to spend a year in Colorado to arrest the progress of the disease, he offered to resign from the bank, but the directors instead gave him a year's leave of absence. Strong's family life was also shattered that year when his wife left him, taking their two daughters with her.

Although absent from the New York Reserve Bank, to keep in touch Strong maintained an active correspondence with Robert H. Treman—a director who was appointed deputy governor—directors of the bank, and others in the system. He also used the time of his enforced rest to read financial histories of government operations in wartime, including British financial conduct of the Napoleonic Wars, the Crimean War, and the Boer War, as well as U.S. financial conduct of the Civil War. He formed definite ideas about the proper management of a wartime economy: to expand productive effort, divert as much as needed to war output by repressing consumption; to pay the cost of war, rely largely on taxes; to borrow, do so at short maturities, or if longer ones, make them callable at par in five or

Strong, January 1919 (courtesy of the Federal Reserve Bank of New York)

ten years and taxable. He opposed Federal Reserve direct purchase of government bonds as well as their sale to the banks. He emphasized the importance of bond sales to the public out of increased savings and short-term borrowing from the banks.

Strong had his wish to see the New York Reserve Bank's arrangement with the Bank of England granted on August 29, 1916, when the Federal Reserve Board approved it with the proviso that no operations would be undertaken before the end of the war without authorization. The State Department ruled that such an agency did not impugn U.S. neutrality. In February 1917 the board also approved agency relations between the New York Reserve Bank and the Bank of France. Thus Strong was responsible for anticipating the important role the Federal Reserve System was destined to play—at a time when its international operations were limited—during the 1920s in international financial arrangements.

At the end of 1916, in fact, Strong grew discouraged about the limited domestic impact of the Federal Reserve System. During the period of U.S. neutrality before April 6, 1917, monetary expansion essentially resulted from the gold inflow from

Europe. The Federal Reserve had the power to create the monetary base and to put it in the hands of the public or the banks by rediscounting paper or by purchasing bonds or other financial assets. It had no power to reduce the monetary base. It had no bonds or other assets to sell to accumulate funds, and it had no authority to issue its own securities or to borrow on the open market. It could have refrained from creating any additional base money, accumulating in the vaults of the Reserve Banks the gold and other lawful money transferred to them as reserves by member banks, acquiring no earning assets, and financing their expenditures solely by assessments on member banks. The Reserve Banks understandably expressed reluctance to follow so ascetic a policy. They wanted to acquire portfolios and use the income to free themselves of assessments on member banks. Discount rates were lowered from 6 percent in 1914 to 3 percent at the end of 1916, but even at those rates the amount of paper offered for rediscount was small. The Reserve Banks therefore purchased bills and acceptances, U.S. government securities, and municipal warrants, contributing a minor though not negligible amount to monetary expansion.

Demands on the Reserve Banks increased markedly on U.S. entry into the war, a development that Strong hailed while still in Colorado. He proposed to return immediately to New York, but Paul Warburg urged him to avoid foolhardiness. Strong, nevertheless, came back for two weeks in May but then reverted to Colorado for continued rest, delaying his final return until early in June.

Though the government raised taxes, ordinary receipts fell far short of government expenditures during the period of active warfare and continued to do so after the Armistice in November 1918 and through the remainder of fiscal 1919. The government financed large fiscal deficits by explicit borrowing and by money creation. The Federal Reserve became the bond-selling window of the Treasury. Although the government printed no greenbacks, it achieved the same result by more indirect methods using Federal Reserve notes and Federal Reserve deposits. During the period of neutrality a gold inflow mainly produced the increase in the monetary base; in the period of warfare the increase took the form primarily of an increase in Federal Reserve credit outstanding. Discounting bills secured by government war obligations provided the main source of that increase. Member banks made loans to their customers, who used them to purchase government securities, and banks in need of reserves in turn rediscounted at a Federal Reserve Bank the customer loans or their own collateral notes secured by government war obligations. Strong found U.S. war finance not far out of line with his views.

One change the war period introduced was the Reserve Banks' acquisition of fiscal agency functions, a change Strong particularly sought in order to increase the usefulness of the banks, to augment their gold reserves by the transfer of the government's deposits, and to improve the procedure for redeeming Treasury currency. Previously the secretary of the Treasury appeared reluctant to entrust to the Reserve Banks the functions exercised by the Independent Treasury and to relinquish the interest on deposits that commercial banks paid, although the Federal Reserve Act authorized him to appoint the banks as the government's fiscal agents.

Faced with the need to place the first Liberty Loan on May 3, 1917, the secretary advised each Reserve Bank of its appointment as fiscal agent and directed each of them to set up a Liberty Loan Committee, with the governor as chairman. Committees—largely of bankers—to sell bonds were appointed in every city and town. The work of the Reserve Banks enormously increased due to the transactions related to war financing, requiring both enlargement of the number of employees and office space. They had responsibility for disbursements and receipts and for overseeing the sales organizations for Liberty and Victory bonds, including the delivery of interim certificates and the permanent bonds to the purchasers.

The wartime changes greatly enhanced the position of the New York Reserve Bank and of Strong as its head. The bank, located in the central money market, sold half of the bond issues, transacted most of the Treasury's foreign exchange dealings, distributed payments to foreign countries and to suppliers of war goods to them, and bought most acceptances. Strong found himself occupied with the financing of successive issues of the Treasury's obligations, speaking eloquently to bankers, mass meetings, and patriotic citizens groups in support of the bond sales.

The end of the war brought an immediate termination of orders for munitions and much confusion about both the immediate and longer-range future. Prices and output declined briefly, but, beginning in March 1919, prices started to rise at a more rapid pace than during the period of active war, and an intense boom got under way, marked by rapid accumulation of inventories and commodity speculation. The monetary base rose despite the net outflow of gold after the lifting of the embargo in June 1919. A continued rise in Federal Reserve credit outstanding, mainly through increased rediscounting, partly through purchase of government securities and of bankers' acceptances originating in the main from foreign trade transactions, more than offset the outflow. The rediscount rate at the Federal Reserve Bank of New York, which had been raised in December 1917 to 3 1/2 percent and in April 1918 to 4 percent, was kept unchanged until November 1919. Those rates hovered decidedly below market rates. Throughout the period member banks operated entirely on borrowed reserves: from September 1918 through July 1921 the outstanding volume of bills discounted by Federal Reserve Banks exceeded member bank reserve balances.

The Reserve Board was aware that discount rates were below current market rates throughout 1919, and that the discrepancy contributed to monetary expansion, and that monetary expansion contributed to inflation, yet it restricted itself to moral suasion, urging banks to discriminate between "essential and non-essential credits." Federal Reserve inaction stemmed not, as in the earlier period of U.S. neutrality, from the absence of technical power to control monetary expansion. On the one hand, a gold outflow rather than inflow existed; on the other, the Federal Reserve system had acquired a substantial portfolio. By raising discount rates and selling securities on the open market, the system clearly stood in a position to keep down the growth of the stock of money to any desired rate. Nor was the reason, at least after the spring of 1919, Treasury deficit financing. Rather it facilitated Treasury funding of the floating debt and involved an unwillingness to see a decline in the price of government bonds. Commercial banks still held on their own account substantial amounts of the Victory Loan, floated from April 25 to May 10, 1919, and had extensive loans to their customers on those securities.

In early 1919 Strong's health forced him to take a three-month leave. He spent most of it at Lake George, using the time to write voluminous letters to officials in Washington and to Montagu Norman. He was concerned with the need to arrest inflation but was not prepared at the time to recom-

Strong with his son, Benjamin Strong, Jr., in Myanoshita, Japan (courtesy of the Federal Reserve Bank of New York)

mend discount rate increases. By April 3 he had returned to the city, presiding over a luncheon meeting with bankers at which Carter Glass, author of the Federal Reserve Act and successor to McAdoo as secretary of the Treasury, spoke. Strong's introductory remarks were not critical of the Treasury.

On behalf of the New York Reserve Bank, on July 12 Strong sailed to Europe, remaining there until September. He proposed to gather information on European conditions, to discuss operation of the agreement between the bank and the Bank of England, and to see about the bank's purchase of gold from the Reichsbank, at the Treasury Department's request, to furnish food to Germany. He had numerous discussions with central bankers and relief workers and grew convinced of the desirability of the early settlement of war debts and the urgency of U.S. help for Europe. Those views had little influence on U.S. foreign policy decisions. While in Europe he expressed an interest in promoting "a better understanding between the managements of the various important central banks of issue," but no concrete results followed.

Even abroad Strong kept in touch with domestic developments, but once he returned from Europe he started to argue the case for higher discount rates. At issue were two questions: (1) Was it possible for the Federal Reserve Board to restrain the growth of credit outstanding by the exercise of moral suasion that would deter member banks from borrowing for speculative purposes, without raising discount rates? (2) If some rise in discount rates was essential, was it possible to restrain speculative borrowing and at the same time maintain a preferential rate for "legitimate" borrowing—which in 1919-1920 consisted of paper secured by Treasury obligations? To both of those questions Strong answered in the negative.

Secretary of the Treasury Glass, on the other hand, knew with certainty that the Federal Reserve could discriminate against "undesirable" credit uses without rate increases. In addition, before mid January 1920 both he and Assistant Secretary Russell C. Leffingwell regarded any plan to tighten the money market as an intolerable interference with their program of Treasury financing. Despite poor health, which shortly forced Strong to take a leave of absence for all of 1920, Strong undertook to oppose the Treasury, though neither the Federal Reserve Board nor most governors of other Reserve Banks wanted to support him. Strong appeared harried and frustrated and at times tactical retreats obscured his strength of purpose in driving for higher rates.

At a Governors Conference on October 28, 1919, Strong argued that the rate on 15-day paper secured by Treasury certificates should be raised from 4 to 4 3/4, not 4 1/4 percent, as proposed in a schedule drawn up after discussions between Secretary Glass, ex-officio chairman of the board, Assistant Secretary Leffingwell, Governor Harding of the Federal Reserve Board, and Governor Strong. In view of Treasury opposition, however, Strong announced that he would advise his directors to fix a rate of 4 1/4 percent. Under the schedule the rate on 90-day paper secured by Liberty bonds was to be raised to 4 3/4 percent. After the meeting Glass in private conversation denounced the proposed increase. Two days later, as recounted in the diary of Charles S. Hamlin (held in the Library of Congress), Strong telephoned from New York "that his directors feared a 4 3/4 percent rate would depress Liberty bonds to 90 and might cause a panic." Strong said he wanted to reconsider the rate. In Washington on October 31, Strong said "he would have to insist on rate advances, that the reputation of the New York Bank was at stake." Ultimately, the rate schedule that went into effect on November 4 at New York raised to 4 1/4 percent the rate on 15-day paper secured by 4 1/4 percent Treasury certificates, and to 4 1/2 percent the rate on 15- and 90-day paper secured by Liberty bonds. The schedule raised the rate on commercial paper maturing within 15 days, including member banks' collateral notes secured by such paper, from 4 to 4 3/4 percent; the rate on 15- to 90-day commercial paper remained at 4 3/4 percent.

On November 13 Strong told the Federal Reserve Board "that last August, when Treasury revenues began to equal expenditures, rates should have been put up, whatever the result on Treasury operations. . . . He said he had loyally carried out Treasury and Board policy of control other than by raising rates and would see this particular crisis through, but after this he would resign rather than continue such a policy." The Boston and New York Federal Reserve Banks proposed further rate increases on November 24, which the board rejected because of Treasury opposition.

A few weeks later, as a result of an improvement in its position, the Treasury withdrew its unqualified opposition to a rate increase, and the Federal Reserve Board so informed the Reserve Banks. On December 12, 1919, the New York Bank raised the rate on 15-day paper secured by Treasury certificates to 4 1/2 percent, and on 15- and 90-day paper secured by Liberty bonds to 4 3/4 percent. Certain New York Reserve Bank directors were reported to have "said they were whipped into agreeing to" the increase by Strong. On December 30, after Strong went on leave to recover his health, New York raised the former rate to 4 3/4 percent, with the result that all discounts by the bank achieved a uniform rate, an objective Strong had sought.

Despite Strong's vigorous fight to raise discount rates, he apparently began to have some doubts, even while in the middle of the battle, about whether the time for such action might not already have passed. On November 29 Strong "said it would *not* do to increase rates now—should have been done long ago—to do it now would be to bring on a crisis."

Federal Reserve policy during 1919 gave rise to much controversy. The continued expansion in Federal Reserve credit outstanding during the year plus the gold outflow after the lifting of the embargo combined to produce a rapid decline in the reserve ratio of the Federal Reserve System. The declining reserves finally rendered some action imperative. The Board of Governors had the power to suspend the legal reserve requirements, but it could hardly have justified doing so when the declining reserves so clearly had resulted from internal inflation fed by Federal Reserve credit creation. In consequence, at long last it permitted the Reserve Banks to raise discount rates—first, as already noted, in November and December 1919, to a level of 4 3/4 percent at most Reserve Banks, then in late January or early February to a uniform level of 6 percent at all Reserve Banks. The second rise, one and one-fourth percentage points at most banks, represented the sharpest single rise in the entire history of the system.

Surprisingly, in view of its earlier role, the Treasury suggested the sharp discount rate increase to 6 percent that the New York Bank adopted on January 22, despite misgivings of the executive committee, as did also the Boston and Philadelphia Reserve Banks.

For reasons of health, Strong took a leave from the Reserve Bank of New York for 13 months beginning mid December 1919. During a trip around the world, he did not keep in close touch with New York Reserve Bank officials. In view of Strong's belief in November 1919 that an increase in rates had been delayed beyond the point when it could be imposed without precipitating a crisis, it seems likely that he would not have agreed to the steep rise in January 1920 had he then been at the helm.

The rise in discount rates in January came not only too late but also was probably too steep. Just as it took time for the higher discount rate to affect member banks, so it must have taken time for the higher open market rates and the higher rates charged by banks to affect commercial and other borrowers. It seems likely that had the system maintained the January rates, they alone would have produced a decline in the stock of money before very long. A further rise in rates rendered the result certain. On June 1, 1920, New York raised the rediscount rate to 7 percent, and most other Reserve Banks either did the same or adopted other measures involving higher rates. It represented the highest rate imposed by the system before 1974. Concern over the Reserve System's own reserve position apparently dominated discount policy. Despite the collapse in prices in the final months of 1920, the discount rate fell to 6 1/2 percent at the New York Bank only in May 1921, when the system's reserve ratio had climbed 16 percentage points above the minimum requirement. That was 16 months after the cyclical peak and only 2 months before the cyclical trough. Four additional reductions in the balance of 1921 brought the rate down to 4 1/2 percent in November.

Strong resumed active control of the New York Reserve Bank in mid January 1921. He had been in London in December 1920 shortly before returning home and, based on discussions with bankers there, had cabled the bank that he favored a reduction in rates. In response, the officers cabled their opposition to a reduction at that time. Strong took that position when he objected to reducing rates in the spring of 1921. He wanted to wait until wage rates fell lower. He noted that deposits had fallen moderately, wholesale prices precipitously, but wages had hardly shown any effects.

Lower discount rates would force up wholesale prices, and prices and wages would be stabilized at too high a level. Strong proposed waiting to reduce discount rates until the "curve of wages, deposits and prices, wholesale and retail, were more nearly together—on a much lower basis."

Some confusion existed in Strong's understanding of Walter Bagehot's rule that central banks should lend freely at a high rate of interest in brief periods of panic. Apparently Strong believed in 1921, which was a period of deep cyclical contraction, not a brief period of panic, that he had merely applied Bagehot's rule. When the New York Reserve Bank agreed to reduce the discount rate on commercial paper to 6 1/2 percent May 4, 1921, in response to pressure from the board, Strong wrote to Montagu Norman that he found it against accepted central banking principles.

The collapse of prices of farm products and agricultural land in 1920-1921 prompted the comptroller of the currency at the time—John Skelton Williams—to accuse the Federal Reserve System of having engineered the decline and the Reserve Bank of New York of mismanagement. In Williams's view a disproportionate amount of the bank's loans accommodated New York banks at the expense of country banks and farmers. He also alleged that the New York Reserve Bank had made no effort to halt illegal practices by a large national bank in New York. In the summer of 1921 the Joint Congressional Commission of Agricultural Inquiry held hearings to investigate the charges. Governor Harding of the Federal Reserve Board and Governor Strong testified. Harding's defense of the system did not acknowledge that contractionary actions in 1919 rather than later in 1920 could have moderated the run-up in prices and the subsequent debacle. When his term of office expired, he was not reappointed.

Strong's testimony, on the other hand, was a tour de force. In three days of hearings between August 2 and 11, he replied to Williams and then proceeded to give a full account of the policies of the New York Reserve Bank both during and after the war. Strong was frank and straightforward. He refuted the charge that actions to deflate the economy provided evidence of wrongdoing, citing widespread support for monetary tightening, including statements by Williams himself. He showed that New York banks had borrowed to enable interior banks to withdraw funds, and that smaller loans to the New York institutions would have raised interest rates and shifted the demand for funds to other districts. With respect to the allegedly illegal practices of a New York national bank, Strong countered that the investigation had not confirmed the charge, and, moreover, the comptroller had the responsibility to examine national banks; yet his office had not conducted even the minimum number of examinations the law specified, and the Reserve Bank in any event had not received reports of the condition of the bank in question.

Strong contrasted the contrary events that would have occurred before the establishment of the Federal Reserve with the availability of funds for legitimate uses in 1920-1921 and the absence of financial panic under the system's aegis. He regarded the deflation as an ordeal that had to be endured. Both here and abroad observers acclaimed Strong's performance at the hearings as vindication for himself and for his views on monetary policy. By 1924, however, in a much milder recession than that of 1920-1921, Strong had changed his mind about the need to endure deflation.

The Federal Reserve System in 1921 had been guided by traditional gold standard rules: contract in the face of a decline in the gold reserve ratio, expand in response to a rise in the gold reserve ratio. The realization grew after that episode that the rules were inapplicable in a world where only the United States maintained gold payments. Strong's round-the-world trip in 1920 had impressed on him the need to restore monetary stability in countries that had left the gold standard during the war. However, the flow of gold from those countries to the United States in 1921-1922 threatened monetary stability in America if the authorities responded with expansionary actions. As a solution, Strong sought to vary earning assets of the Federal Reserve in inverse relation to gold holdings. His objectives were stable domestic economic activity, stable prices, and world monetary reconstruction.

To achieve the first objective of stable domestic economic activity required first the development of an understanding by Strong and others in the Federal Reserve System of the uses of open market operations. Open market purchases were initially regarded as a means to obtain earnings for the Reserve Banks. The banks individually bought government securities without apparent concern for the influence of those purchases on the money market. Their uncoordinated operations disturbed the government securities market. At the Governors Confer-

ence on May 2, 1922, Strong reported the Treasury's dismay. Under his leadership the Reserve Banks organized in that month a committee of five governors from eastern Reserve Banks to execute joint purchases and sales and to avoid conflicts with Treasury plans for new issues or acquisitions for its investment accounts. No one suggested that the committee determine monetary policy. It met for the first time at the New York Bank on May 16 and elected Strong as permanent chairman. Although the centralization of open market operations ultimately led to a recognition of the bearing of purchases and sales on monetary policy, it did not happen immediately.

At the next meeting of the Governors Conference on October 10, Strong proposed that the committee assume the duty of recommending investment policy to the Reserve Banks, but the governors balked at adopting considerations other than earnings needs. So matters stood in mid February 1923, when Strong took a six-month leave of absence to cope with tuberculosis of the throat that left him voiceless and in pain. He stayed in Colorado until October, maintaining contact by correspondence.

In the spring of 1923 the Open Market Investment Committee for the Federal Reserve System, appointed by the board with the same five members, superceded the Reserve Banks' committee. Future operations were placed under the general supervision of the board, a decision that earned Strong's anger. He objected to a political body assuming control of open market policy. In fact, however, during his lifetime Strong rather than board members dominated open market operations. Moreover, the board's letter to the Reserve Banks on establishing the Open Market Investment Committee explicitly defined the need for open market purchases to be "governed with primary regard to the accommodation of commerce and business, and to the effect of such purchases or sales on the general credit situation." It thus deemphasized earnings and focused on the larger purposes of the operations.

The Governors Conference on November 12, 1923, less than a month after Strong's return from Colorado, when he was still limited in ability to speak, recorded a major step forward in Federal Reserve understanding of what it could accomplish. The report of the Open Market Investment Committee, which was read for him, proposed open market purchases to counter a business slowdown. In the year from November 1923, the Reserve System's holdings of government securities increased by $500 million, most of the increase taking place in the seven months from February to September 1924. The recession that began in May 1923 reached a trough in July 1924, and the synchronism between Federal Reserve action and the movement of business during the episode played an important role in convincing observers both within and outside the system of the potency of its powers. By 1925 the Federal Reserve had also learned to use open market operations to offset undesired effects of gold movements, Treasury payments to and withdrawals from the market, as well as currency flows to and from banks.

A second objective of Federal Reserve policy that Strong came to regard as achievable was price stability. In a speech to the American Farm Bureau Federation in Chicago on December 13, 1922, he noted that by providing a supply of money and credit that would lead neither to inflationary nor deflationary pressures, the Federal Reserve could promote price level stability, leaving relative prices free to change. Yet he adamantly maintained that the Federal Reserve should not be subject to legislation requiring it to stabilize the price level. He argued that the Federal Reserve could control credit, but prices responded to other forces as well.

In so arguing, he seemed to neglect his own distinction between absolute and relative price change. To Strong, assigning responsibility for a stable price level to the Federal Reserve had an undemocratic tinge, oddly enough on the ground that a small group of men would fix prices. In 1926 Representative James B. Strong of Kansas introduced a bill to amend the Federal Reserve Act to direct the Federal Reserve to stabilize commodity prices. Governor Strong testified at hearings before the House Committee on Banking and Currency in opposition to the bill. He argued that once the gold standard was restored price stabilization would result automatically, making legislation to do so unnecessary.

At those hearings Strong also reviewed the open market purchases of 1923-1924 and the credit arrangement with the Bank of England that enabled it to return to the gold standard in 1925. That introduced the third objective Strong set for the Federal Reserve System: promoting world monetary reconstruction in the postwar world. As early as 1916, when he initiated the establishment of correspondent relations with the Bank of England and the

Bank of France, Strong saw the advantages of cooperative arrangements with the central banks of Europe. In cooperation with them or newly established central banks after the war, he saw the possibility of re-creating a world in which currencies would again be convertible and international financial relations would revert to their peacetime character.

Strong took the lead in international financial negotiations in the postwar period, individually representing the Federal Reserve System, although always with the knowledge and approval of the other governors and the Federal Reserve Board as well as the administration. The cooperation between central banks that developed, usually at Strong's initiative, stood in marked contrast to the tension that existed in international political relations. When World War I ended, the United States emerged as a creditor country embroiled in a controversy with its wartime allies, who were reluctant to repay the borrowings expended in a common struggle. It had no tradition of participation in European affairs. Against that background Strong's personal friendships, particularly with Montagu Norman, governor of the Bank of England from 1920 to 1944, and with the heads of other central banks, fostered his interest in international reconstruction. He regarded that goal as a contribution to the welfare of the European countries and of the United States. The restoration of gold standards would halt the flow of gold to America, reduce inflationary pressures, and eliminate discretionary management of the money supply. At the same time recovery abroad and exchange rate stability would stimulate the demand for U.S. exports and promote international lending.

Before reconstruction was possible, Strong believed that the parties had to reach a settlement concerning German reparations and interallied war debts. With respect to the latter, he favored a limited moratorium, hoping that it would temper existing bitter feelings. As for reparations, the end of the German hyperinflation in November 1923 and the adoption of the Dawes Plan in September 1924 set the stage for the larger purpose Strong had in mind. The plan required a series of annual German payments, stabilization of the German currency in terms of gold, and the flotation of the Dawes Loan in the United States and other countries, part of which was to be used to provide gold reserves to the Reichsbank.

Strong at his desk (courtesy of the Federal Reserve Bank of New York)

Early in 1924, before the public announcement of the Dawes Plan, Owen D. Young, a director of the New York Reserve Bank and the first agent general for reparations under the plan, asked Strong to collaborate with Norman in reviewing the provision to establish a new German central bank of issue. After sailing to Europe a month later, Strong met with Norman. They found the plan ingenious and gave their approval.

Shortly after his mid-May return to the United States, Strong sent Secretary of the Treasury Andrew Mellon a long letter with his recommendations for European stabilization and separately advocated a domestic easy-money policy to combat recessionary conditions and simultaneously encourage subscriptions to the Dawes Loan.

In planning international stabilization, several principles guided Strong. For one, he knew that stabilization could not be achieved on a wholesale basis. It had to be arranged on a country-by-country basis, when initial conditions for success—balanced fiscal budgets, balanced international trade accounts, noninflationary monetary conditions, a responsible central bank of issue holding adequate gold reserves—were in place. Under those conditions

a nation was entitled to financial assistance. Central banks would then offer to extend foreign credits to the central bank—never the government—of such a nation. The government of a stabilizing country could, however, borrow in capital markets abroad, if necessary, using part of the proceeds to retire its short-term debt in the central bank's portfolio. It would thus reduce its domestic debt and increase its foreign exchange reserves. Both Norman and Strong played pivotal roles under those arrangements, since each in his own capital market could determine whether a foreign loan should be approved and whether the Bank of England and the Federal Reserve would participate in a loan to the central bank that wanted to return to the gold standard.

Although Strong emphasized a second principle in planning international stabilization, that formal international conferences of central bankers were pernicious, he did not oppose informal conferences. He based his negative assessment of formal conferences on the judgment that many central banks, as creatures of their governments, had their policies dictated by political interests rather than by monetary considerations only. He also declined to put himself in the position of representing the only institution at such a meeting with lending capacity where the would-be borrowers could outvote him. Finally, he held that, since the United States had not joined the League of Nations, it was improper for Federal Reserve officials to attend a conference of world central banks that might adopt a program that public opinion would judge as not in the interest of the country.

The success of the flotation of the Dawes Loan in October 1924 in New York and eight other European centers meant that reparations temporarily did not constitute a disturbing factor in international affairs. Economic recovery in Germany followed. Its stabilized currency had a firmer foundation than in the immediate posthyperinflation period. Capital outflows from the United States in the wake of the 1924 U.S. recession buoyed the European exchanges. Norman and Strong found the time propitious in the spring of 1925 to achieve the next major step in their program of international monetary reconstruction, namely, restoring sterling to its prewar parity with gold.

Before England returned to the gold standard in April 1925, except for the United States and a few other countries no gold standard world existed.

Upon England's return other countries fell in line, so that by early 1926 nearly three dozen countries had linked their currencies to gold.

For sterling to be viable at its prewar parity, Strong and Norman agreed that British prices had to be in line with U.S. prices, interest rates in New York had to be lower than in London, and a settlement had to be reached on British war debts to the United States. Although Strong thought the terms of payment of the debts set in early 1923 unwise, he advised Norman to accept them as preferable to continued uncertainty about the outcome. Restoration of the gold standard, however, could not be contemplated so long as the issue of German reparations disturbed foreign exchange markets. Once that question appeared to have been settled, it became possible to address the relation between economic conditions in this country and Britain.

The wartime and postwar rise in prices in Britain had exceeded the rise in the United States. The subsequent fall in prices in Britain was not as great as the U.S. price fall. Of one thing Strong was certain: a domestic price rise to close the gap, induced either by gold imports or expansionary monetary policy, was not desirable. A domestic policy of price stability was in the best interest of both countries. The question, however, remained of how to achieve the downward adjustment of British prices. Was it necessary to do so before restoring sterling to par or would the restoration itself readjust relative U.S. and U.K. price levels? In the upshot, Britain returned to gold before the downward adjustment of its price level had been completed.

By mid 1924 economic conditions in both Britain and the United States reached a favorable enough state to establish the desired interest rate relationships in the two countries. The interest-rate differential was intended to shift long-term foreign borrowing from London to New York, a change that was achieved.

After having established the conditions for reintroducing the gold standard in Britain, Strong next had on his agenda the provision of credits to the Bank of England and the British government. He proposed a credit of $200 million by the Federal Reserve to the Bank of England. In January 1925 the directors of the New York Reserve Bank heard the proposal, then the Open Market Investment Committee, and finally the full Federal Reserve Board, members of which had attended earlier meetings in New York with a British delegation. Arranging a

credit for the British government by J. P. Morgan delayed the final decision to resume until April 28, 1925. In fact, neither the Bank of England nor the British government drew on the Federal Reserve credit and the Morgan credit during the two years they were in effect.

When Strong sailed to Europe, accompanied by his oldest daughter, on June 26, 1925, Britain apparently had successfully returned to gold. Short-term balances and gold flowed to London, strengthening the sterling exchange rate. On visits to the capitals of western European countries that had recently resumed, Strong grew concerned that gold inflows would lead them to ease credit conditions. At the same time news from home suggested that credit conditions needed tightening. On his return to the United States in mid September, he found rising speculation in the stock market and commodities. An increase in the discount rate at the New York Reserve Bank, taken on January 8, 1926, would compel the Bank of England to raise its rate also, as it did on December 3, 1925, in anticipation of the increase here. The United Kingdom faced the dilemma that domestic conditions required monetary ease whereas maintaining the tie of sterling to gold at its prewar parity required monetary tightness. Strong faced the dilemma that his response to domestic needs here hampered Norman, whom he wanted to help.

While in Europe, Strong discussed with Belgian officials steps to stabilize Belgium's franc, and negotiations for credits from foreign central banks and a loan to the government continued through the rest of 1925 until mid March 1926, when the stabilization effort collapsed. Strong returned to Europe at the end of April 1926 and resumed the effort to link the Belgian franc to gold. Because he fell ill in September 1926 and had to return home, an associate of Strong's at the New York Reserve Bank completed the negotiations on behalf of the Belgian stabilization.

Strong's trip to Europe came in response to an appeal from Norman that he testify before the Royal Commission on Indian Currency and Finance on a proposal to establish a gold standard in India, providing convertibility of the rupee into gold coins. Strong and Norman believed that the proposal ran contrary to the interests of India and of monetary reconstruction in the rest of the world. The testimony on four days in May by Strong, two U.S.

academics, and two Federal Reserve associates who accompanied him, helped defeat the proposal.

Secretary of the Treasury Mellon had assured Strong in advance that it was appropriate for him to testify, but some members of the Federal Reserve Board after the fact refused to allow the board to reimburse his expenses. Mellon ordered the expenses charged to the Treasury's fiscal account. An earlier clash with Adolph Miller, a board member, had occurred at the Governors Conference in mid March. Miller objected to open market operations, arguing that changes in member bank borrowing offset them and therefore had no effect on credit conditions, and that instead the Reserve Banks should limit provision of credit to rediscounting bills that member banks submitted. Backbiting by the board was a trial that Strong had to bear.

During the rest of the time Strong spent in Europe in 1926, he met with officials in France, Italy, and Poland to discuss steps needed for stabilization of their currencies. Ill when he returned home in September, an attack of influenza and pneumonia in October worsened his condition. Only by mid February 1927 did he regain enough strength to write letters, and not until the end of April did he return to the bank.

The issues that confronted international monetary authorities in 1927 developed from the effects on Britain and the United States of inflows of foreign balances into Germany and France. Borrowing abroad accounted for the German inflows. The actions of the Poincaré government in July 1926 to deal with the chronic French budget deficit and the uncertainty about the exchange rate of the franc on stabilization stimulated the capital flows to France. The franc was stabilized de facto vis-a-vis the dollar in December 1926 at about 4 cents. Private purchases of francs soared, based on the belief that the currency would be revalued upwards following the announcement that France had repaid a loan from the Bank of England in a lump sum in April 1927. For the French authorities the inflows came from the London and Berlin money markets, and the solution was to raise interest rates in those markets.

Strong knew of the tensions between the French and the Germans and British and expressed concern that those currents would undermine the gold standard in both Germany and Britain. Moreover, further tightening to curb stock market speculation might be in order in New York, leading to gold inflows that would further endanger the gold re-

serves of countries abroad. He concluded that an informal meeting of central bankers would be helpful. At his invitation, Norman, Hjalmar Schacht of the Reichsbank, and Rist of the Bank of France met with him on Long Island from July 1 to 6 at the home of Ogden Mills, under secretary of the Treasury. The next day they attended a lunch as guests of the Federal Reserve Board in Washington. Treasury officials also attended.

The conference essentially arranged that New York would ease in order to remove the pressure on London and Berlin to tighten and that central bank demand for gold would be met in New York rather than in London. The Federal Reserve reduced the buying rate on bankers' acceptances one-quarter of one percentage point from July to August 1927, and bill holdings rose by $200 million; the Reserve Banks reduced the discount rate from 4 to 3 1/2 percent between July and September 1927; and they made open market purchases of government securities totaling $340 million between early July and the middle of November 1927. The rise in Federal Reserve credit partly offset a gold outflow from the United States, as the Bank of France and the Reichsbank shifted their gold purchases from London to New York.

The easing of monetary policy in 1927 occasioned much subsequent criticism in light of the bull market in stocks that had then started to gather steam and its collapse in October 1929. For Strong the policy served two purposes: overcoming slack business conditions, despite his concern about speculation in the stock market; and helping to strengthen European exchange rates. By the end of 1927 he judged the outcome of the Long Island central bankers' conference a success: recession in the United States reached a trough in November 1927 and European exchange rates strengthened.

Strong left for Europe on December 2, 1927, to continue efforts to stabilize the currencies of Italy, Poland, and Romania. On earlier visits to Europe he had met with Italian and Polish officials and familiarized himself with their financial and economic conditions. On the present occasion, working with Norman and representatives of the Bank of Italy, Strong participated in the negotiations to stabilize the Italian lira at 5.26 cents, 27 percent of its prewar gold value. A group of 13 central banks joined with the Federal Reserve and the Bank of England to grant $75 million in credit to the Bank of Italy. They also concluded arrangements for credits from investments bankers. On December 22 stabilization became official. Strong had no illusions that under Mussolini the Bank of Italy would be independent of political influence.

Strong's introduction to the Bank of Poland dated from December 1924. Established as part of a monetary reform in May 1924, when the zloty was valued in gold at 19.3 cents, equal to the 1914 franc, the Bank of Poland sought correspondent relations with the Federal Reserve Bank of New York. The Federal Reserve Board approved in February 1925. When the Polish balance of payments turned adverse in August, the Bank of Poland obtained a $10.5 million credit from the Reserve Bank of New York against a gold deposit in the Bank of England but, despite the loan, the zloty depreciated in exchange markets.

In December 1925 the Polish minister to the United States approached Secretary Mellon about arranging a loan to the government to stabilize the zloty. Mellon advised him to see Strong. The minister adamantly stated that Poland sought U.S. assistance only, not that of England or the League of Nations. Stalemate followed in 1926, with no agreement on alternative plans and in any event a halt in negotiations following the Pilsudski coup d'état. In February 1927, while Strong recuperated in Biltmore, North Carolina, different parties interested in the Polish situation visited him, including the private bankers who had floated Polish loans, a successor banking firm, Polish and French representatives–the Bank of France had become interested–and Norman.

Too ill to undertake a trip to Europe, in early March Strong sent George Harrison, who later succeeded him as governor of the New York Reserve Bank, with detailed instructions about whom to see, in which order, and the points to make to each. In the end the Bank of Poland submitted a stabilization plan to Strong with a request for a central bank credit. Strong orchestrated participation by 14 central banks in the credit. In Norman's view the central bank credit was based on negotiations of private bankers rather than the reverse.

The stabilization decree, fixing the zloty at 11.22 cents in a gold exchange standard, was announced on October 13, 1927. The Polish government's borrowing arrangements with private bankers followed. In that stabilization the Bank of England played no leading part, and Strong and Norman had conflicting views on how to proceed.

Strong's efforts to divorce central banks from political rivalries came up short.

The political overtones in the case of the stabilization of the Romanian leu proved even more blatant than in the Polish case. In 1926 the leu was worth less than half a cent compared to its 1914 parity of 19.3 cents. In December 1927 the government proposed to negotiate a loan with American private bankers and then ask the Bank of France to provide central bank credits without involving the League of Nations. Norman and the governor of the Bank of France each wrote to Strong soliciting his help. Strong told the New York Bank directors that he knew too little about conditions in Romania to take the initiative, and he wished to avoid political controversies. Norman, however, insisted that Romania apply to the League for assistance and not follow the Polish example. Strong, however, agreed to accept a plan for stabilizing the leu presented to him by Bank of France officials in March 1928 but refused to act as a joint initiator of the plan. He proceeded to obtain approval in principle on April 4 by the Federal Reserve Board for a credit of $10 million to be granted by the New York Bank to the National Bank of Romania.

Strong had returned home from London in late December 1927 in ill health. Until his death he was rarely at the bank, although he kept in touch with its affairs. The tubercular condition of his left lung had reappeared. In addition he developed a bad case of shingles that afflicted his head and one side of his face. In weakened condition, he sailed for Cherbourg on May 12, 1928, hoping to reconcile the hostile governors of the Bank of England and the Bank of France and to help protect the gold reserves of the former.

Strong's final meeting with Norman ended in a dispute. Norman could not forgive Strong's alignment with the Bank of France. Strong, on the other hand, believed that he had only tried to preserve central bank cooperation. On June 6 he wrote a note of apology to Norman for the heated tone of his exchanges.

From Cherbourg, Strong went to Paris for discussions at the Bank of France, but he made little progress in smoothing relations between its officials and Norman. The completion of the stabilization of the leu was not achieved until after Strong's death.

While still in Europe in July 1928, Strong received advice from his doctors that he would have to stop working. Home in early August, he tendered his resignation to the directors of the New York Reserve Bank, but they asked him to defer it to the end of the year. Death came before he reached that date. After an apparently successful operation on October 6 for an abscess in his abdomen, he died on October 16, the morning after a hemorrhage.

Strong's death left the Federal Reserve System without a leader. The goals of a stable price level, stable economic conditions, central bank cooperation, and a revitalized gold standard that he had achieved collapsed in the succeeding years. One of his associates at the New York Reserve Bank wrote in 1940 that if Strong could "have had twelve months more of vigorous health, we might have ended the depression in 1930, and with this the long drawn out world crisis that so profoundly affected the ensuing political developments."

Publication:

Interpretations of Federal Reserve Policy in the Speeches and Writings of Benjamin Strong, edited by W. Randolph Burgess (New York & London: Harper, 1930).

References:

Lester V. Chandler, *Benjamin Strong, Central Banker* (Washington, D.C.: Brookings, 1958);

Stephen V. O. Clarke, *Central Bank Cooperation, 1924-31* (New York: Federal Reserve Bank of New York, 1967);

Milton Friedman and Anna J. Schwartz, *A Monetary History of the United States, 1867-1960* (Princeton: Princeton University Press, 1963);

Thomas W. Lamont, *Henry P. Davison: The Record of a Useful Life* (New York: Harper, 1933);

Carl Snyder, *Capitalism the Creator* (New York: Macmillan, 1940);

Frank A. Vanderlip and Boyden Sparkes, *From Farm Boy to Financier* (New York: Appleton-Century, 1935).

Papers:

The Benjamin Strong Papers are housed at the Central Records and Archives Division of the Federal Reserve Bank of New York. The collection includes an unpublished biography of Strong written by his older son. In addition, the diary of Charles S. Hamlin, one of the members of the original Federal Reserve Board, in the Hamlin Papers at the Manuscript Division of the Library of Congress, and the George Leslie Harrison Papers on the Federal Reserve System at the Columbia University Library Manuscript Division contain material pertaining to Strong.

SunTrust Banks

by Larry Schweikart

University of Dayton

SunTrust Banks, Incorporated, headquartered in Atlanta, Georgia, commenced operation as a regional bank holding company on July 1, 1985, the effective date of reciprocal interstate banking laws in Florida and Georgia. SunTrust was created by the combination of two major bank holding companies—SunBanks, Incorporated, based in Orlando, Florida, and Trust Company of Georgia, based in Atlanta. At the time it was the largest banking merger in U.S. history. In December 1986 SunTrust acquired Third National Corporation, the second largest bank holding company in Tennessee, based in Nashville.

As of 1989, through its three principal subsidiary holding companies in its three-state area, SunTrust owned and operated 53 full-service commercial banks with more than 600 banking loca-

tions and 20,000 employees. Banks in the three states continue to operate with the same names and identifications in use prior to their becoming parts of the SunTrust organization.

Trust Company of Georgia traces its origin to the Commercial Traveler's Savings Bank, formed in Atlanta in 1891 as one of 22 relatively small banks serving that city. SunBanks got its start in 1934 as the First National Bank of Orlando. Third National was organized in Nashville in 1927.

The three holding companies are well established within their respective states, providing corporate and retail banking and specialized financial services. Nonbank subsidiaries include SunTrust Mortgage, Incorporated, which has a mortgage servicing portfolio of $3.5 billion; SunTrust Securities, Incorporated, offering discount brokerage services;

James B. Williams, president and chief executive officer of SunTrust Banks from 1990 (photograph by Gittings; courtesy of SunTrust Banks, Inc.)

SunTrust Service Corporation, providing internal data processing and support; and SunTrust Data Systems, Incorporated, which handles data processing services for correspondent financial institutions throughout the Southeast.

Based on total assets of more than $27 billion, SunTrust ranks among the 25 largest U.S. banking companies. Its stock is listed on the New York Stock Exchange and traded under the symbol "STI." In terms of the 1988 market value of its 130 million outstanding shares of common stock, SunTrust was among the top ten U.S. banking companies. The company operates the largest trust and investment management business of any bank in each of its three states and in the Southeast as a whole.

One of SunTrust's unique assets is ownership of more than 6 million shares of common stock of the Coca-Cola Company. The stock was acquired by Trust Company in 1919 in lieu of a commission for the bank's role in underwriting the first-ever public offering of shares of Coca-Cola. Each 1919 share has multiplied 576 times through stock splits and dividends. SunTrust carries its Coca-Cola stock at its original value of $110,000, although the recent market value is well in excess of $200 million. That value represents unbooked capital and helps make SunTrust one of the most strongly capitalized banking businesses in the country. The only written copy of the formula for Coca-Cola is locked in a safe deposit box in the vault of the Atlanta bank.

SunBanks was instrumental in putting together the purchase of extensive Florida orange grove land for the site of Walt Disney World, one of the nation's most popular tourist attractions. Since its inception, SunBanks has served as the official bank of the "Magic Kingdom." In Tennessee, Third National counts Opryland U.S.A. among its important customer relationships. SunTrust thus represents one of the most powerful regional bank holding companies in the United States.

Transamerica Corporation

by Lynne Pierson Doti

Chapman College

Transamerica Corporation, started as a bank holding company in 1928, quickly diversified into other financial businesses, then sold its banks in 1958. Its primary business then became insurance, although diversification was important to the company at various times.

The company grew from the Bank of Italy, started in San Francisco by A. P. Giannini in 1904. In the early years especially, Giannini focused on providing banking services to individuals and smaller businesses. Also a champion of branch banking, Giannini opened his first branch in 1907. After 1915 he rapidly added new offices and acquired other banks to create a large, statewide branch banking network.

As he blanketed the state, Giannini widened his plans to branch, acquiring the East River National Bank of New York in 1919 as a first step toward nationwide branching. He then set out to buy other New York banks, a plan that culminated in the 1928 purchase of the venerable and respected Bank of America. The expansion alarmed other bankers, and when regulators blocked his attempts to consolidate his banks into one branch system, Giannini discovered the flexibility afforded by a holding company. The Bancitaly Corporation, part owner of Bank of Italy, and all of the $850 million in outstanding shares of Bank of Italy stock were exchanged for shares in the newly formed Transamerica Corporation.

By the end of 1929, Transamerica was a diversified holding company with $68 million in annual income from banking, securities trading, mortgages, agricultural and livestock loans, investments in Pacific National Fire Insurance Company, real estate, and a metals manufacturer. Transamerica also had control of a string of California state-chartered banks in addition to the Bank of Italy's nationally chartered branch system. In 1930 Giannini moved to gain the diversification advantages of branching

A. P. Giannini, chairman of Transamerica Corporation from 1929 to 1930 and from 1931 to 1949, the year of his death (courtesy of BankAmerica Archives)

by merging the state branch network into the Bank of Italy, changing the name to Bank of America, National Trust and Security Association (N.T. & S.A.). That move formed the nation's fourth largest bank.

The year was important to Transamerica also because Giannini purchased Occidental Life Insurance Corporation, a $25 million company that eventually established the ultimate direction of Transamerica. A. P. Giannini tried retirement that year after 26 years in banking. He named Elisa Walker his replacement as chairman of the Transamerica board, hoping Walker's East Coast connections would help smooth the way to a nationwide branching system. A. P.'s son Mario was made president. While at first sympathetic with A. P.'s goals, the deepening Depression led Walker to return to more traditional views. Instead of continuing to work toward a nationwide branching system, Walker proposed selling banks to gain liquidity. Although his health was poor, A. P.'s outrage led him into a fierce battle to regain control. With Mario's help, he solicited the stockholders' support and regained his position as chairman in 1931.

With A. P. Giannini back in power, Transamerica cut expenses and worked hard to loan in the face of little demand. It also continued to buy banks in California, Nevada and Oregon, saving many from failure. A new company moved into the area of real estate development as the banks collected a portfolio of foreclosed farms that were difficult to sell.

Regulators continued to oppose the expansion of Transamerica's branch banking system. To diffuse the opposition, Transamerica reduced its holdings in Bank of America to 42 percent in July 1937. In spite of that, by the end of the decade Secretary of the Treasury Henry Morgenthau had developed an intense distaste for Giannini's master plan. The first regulatory attack against the financial giant came from the Securities and Exchange Commission (SEC), which charged Transamerica with filing false and misleading disclosure forms. In April 1939, Transamerica was also charged with misrepresentation for a stock purchase plan. The IRS also attacked the company, although that case went to court and was settled in favor of Transamerica.

In the 1930s and 1940s A. P. Giannini had purchased about 200 small banks and combined them into 46 banking companies, with the intention of merging them with the voracious Bank of America. Until bank regulators would permit the acquisitions, Giannini parked the banks in Transamerica, where they coexisted with the Bank of America and numerous other companies, including insurance companies, tuna packers, tobacco growers, and an airline.

World War II produced radical changes in the American economy, and Transamerica shifted its focus to match. One change was the federal government's vast need for funding. Banks responded quickly. By 1946, 92 percent of banks' investments were government bonds. Transamerica helped the war production effort by moving into manufacturing. General Metals, owned since 1928, began producing ship castings. Sales for the company grew

from \$2.3 million to \$12 million. Transamerica acquired Enterprise Engine and Foundry Company, Aerco Company, and Adel Precision Parts, then provided them with funding to move into manufacturing aircraft parts.

The insurance business experienced expansion also, because as consumer goods became unavailable, people channeled their extra income into savings and insurance. Other parts of Transamerica slowed their activity. Land development was impossible and unnecessary when all building was war-related. Automobile insurance and financing became equally superfluous.

The war's distractions soon lessened, but that did not dismiss Henry Morganthau's attempt to reduce the strength of Transamerica. The California State Banking Department was the next instrument used to block Bank of America's expansion. When the war provided a need for banks in new areas, the state delayed and then rejected Bank of America's requests to provide the branches. In one celebrated situation, the Bank of America countered a denied branching request by setting up a new bank, in which Transamerica purchased shares in defiance of an agreement with the Federal Reserve Board. The case went to the Supreme Court, which refused to hear it.

While Transamerica's problems with regulators escalated, the war ended with many of the people who had come west for military or defense jobs making their permanent homes there. The economy boomed, especially in California. Transamerica responded with moves into mortgage credit and building. To allow freedom to grow to meet the needs of the economy, they divested more of the shares held in the Bank of America, bringing Transamerica holdings down to 23 percent. Transamerica officers hoped in vain that the divestiture would reduce the attacks on the holding company. Instead, the Federal Reserve Board charged that those holdings, when combined with ownership of other banks in Arizona, California, Oregon, Nevada, and Washington, constituted a monopoly of western banking. The case generated national attention and continued for five years. While Transamerica was ultimately cleared, the direction of the company and national banking law changed because of it.

A. P. Giannini died in 1949 after naming James F. Cavagnaro chairman of the Transamerica board. Mario Giannini, then president of Transamerica, passed away in 1952. In 1953 Frank

Belgrano, Jr., took on the leadership of the holding company. Belgrano was the son and namesake of one of A. P.'s closest associates and had followed his father into a banking career. Left as head of the newly structured company, he was to lead the company on its new path.

Two new insurance companies had joined Transamerica by 1950: Manufacturers Casualty and Paramount Fire Insurance Company. Both were multiple-line companies writing all types of insurance except life and title, and they provided an excellent complement to previously purchased Pacific National Insurance. In 1952 Transamerica rounded out its insurance line further with the acquisition of Automotive Insurance Company to cover high-risk cases.

Although he was president of Pacific National from 1930 to 1944, Belgrano was at heart a banker. Once the suit was settled, Transamerica began to rebuild its banking empire. Between 1953 and 1956, the company grew to 226 branches in 11 western states, then again it was halted. The Bank Holding Company Act of 1956 made bank holding companies subject to the same restrictions on crossing state lines that individual banks endured. The same law forbade the holding of other businesses by a holding company that owned more than one bank. That provision, unlike the prohibition on interstate banks, was retroactive. Transamerica chose to retain maximum flexibility by selling its remaining banks. A new company, Firstamerica Corporation, was formed under Delaware law and its stock distributed to Transamerica shareholders by 1958.

While arrangements for the stock transfer progressed, Firstamerica executives were arranging a merger with Frank King of California Bank, a Los Angeles-based bank. That merger would bring experienced top management to the new system, now composed of 322 offices, and make Firstamerica the fourth-largest bank holding company in the country. Unfortunately, as arrangements for the merger were nearly complete, the Justice Department objected. While the new combination would give the Bank of America some strong competition, the Justice Department was more concerned about the situation in small communities, where all the banks would be controlled by Firstamerica. Firstamerica went ahead and bought stock in California Bank and made Frank King president of the holding company. He negotiated a settlement that carved off $500 million in assets to create a new retail bank

called First Western. That bank was sold to Greatamerica Corporation and then resold several more times, finally losing its name when it was sold to Lloyds Bank of California. The other bank, consisting of California Bank and the remaining California offices of Transamerica's First Western Bank, was renamed United California Bank (UCB), and the holding company for UCB and the banks outside California was renamed Western Bancorporation. That system became First Interstate Bancorporation in 1980.

Transamerica emerged as a major insurance holding company with the $11.5 million from the sale of bank stock and $2.3 million from selling other unrelated businesses. Belgrano set out to become the major player in the new league. One of the first acquisitions was Phoenix Title and Trust Company, the largest company of its type in Arizona. Next, Belgrano began arrangements to acquire American Surety Company of New York. Just one day after that merger was complete, Belgrano suffered a fatal heart attack.

In accordance with the new direction of the company, the president of Occidental Life, Horace Brower, was selected as the new president. Brower, a longtime associate of the Gianninis, had begun at Bank of America in 1921, while it was still Bank of Italy, and was known for his skill at redeeming the value of real estate. Mario Giannini had moved him to Occidental to repair the Depression's damage to the real estate portfolio there, and his success in that endeavor brought him to the presidency in 1951. Close to retirement by 1959, Brower managed both the Transamerica and the Occidental presidencies for a year, then brought in John Beckett as president of Transamerica.

Beckett worked to unify the company and to improve its overall profitability. Occidental Life was doing well, but General Metals, Pacific National Fire Insurance, and American Surety were all struggling with industry-wide problems. Capital Company held four large tracts of land for development, which were slow to bring returns.

To unify the holding company, Beckett arranged the first Transamerica Management Conference, designed a logo, and launched a modest advertising campaign. Once dependent on high dividends to sell stock, presentations were now made to the investment community. A plan suggested selective expansion as a cure for low earnings. One of the first major acquisitions was the purchase of Pacific Finance. In addition to its good earnings record, the purchase brought an old company back into the Transamerica fold and supplemented its operations with retail and wholesale auto financing, personal loans, and some insurance businesses. To pay the $80 million acquisition bill, Transamerica exchanged newly issued convertible stock. In addition to Pacific Finance, in 1961 and 1962 Transamerica acquired the remaining shares of Phoenix Title and Trust, Surety Title and Trust, and trust companies in California and Colorado. America Surety was tightened up, combined with Pacific National's Surety division, and moved to Los Angeles in 1962. In 1963 Pacific National changed its name to Transamerica Insurance Company.

General Metals was obviously an odd possession for a company increasingly known for financial operations, but management decided to keep it when the opportunity came to merge with De Laval Turbine. To tie the company together further, Capital changed its name to Transamerica Development Company. Several other title companies were acquired in the next decade, along with a mortgage company and a mortgage bank. After five years, Transamerica had unified the corporation. Earnings were up in several areas, and Occidental completed a switch to electronic data processing. Beckett identified two major new areas of expansion: leisure and educational services. While several other acquisitions occurred, the major new area of expansion in the 1960s was in the purchase of United Artists, which produced and distributed movies and music. That was soon supplemented with Liberty Records. Further expansion into leisure industries came with the purchase of Trans International Airlines, then Budget Rent a Car. The move into education came with the Foreign Study League, which offered American high school students the opportunity to study abroad.

A handsome new logo was unveiled in 1968, but the company achieved even more public recognition with the construction of an exciting new headquarters building in San Francisco in 1972. At first controversial because of an unusual design and be-cause it brought high-rise development closer to the city's most historic area, the pyramid-shaped structure has become one of the world's most easily identified landmarks.

The decade of the 1970s, with its alternating inflation and recession, was difficult for Transamerica and indeed for most companies. While revenues reached an all-time high in 1974, high oil prices caused first-ever losses to the airline, and a series of disastrous storms ravaged the earnings of the casualty companies. Those companies recovered in 1975, and other Transamerica companies brought the parent into a better situation that year. Further improvement in most areas marked the end of the decade. Positioning the company to be less sensitive to changes in interest rates and oil price fluctuations proved useful when both rose again in 1980-1981.

The decade of the 1980s brought further refinement of the holding company's direction. The manufacturing sector was spun off to Transamerica shareholders, and Budget Rent a Car, the airline, and United Artists were also sold, leaving Transamerica Corporation holding companies in the area of finance and insurance. In finance, the companies operate in consumer lending, commercial lending, leasing, and real estate services. In insurance, the corporation provides life insurance, property and casualty insurance, insurance brokerage, and asset management. John Beckett remained on the board of directors until 1990, although his executive vice-president, James Harvey, was made president of the corporation in 1981 and chairman of the board in 1983. Harvey turned the presidency over to Frank Herringer in 1986, continuing the well-ordered succession that has characterized the company.

References:

Daniel C. Kibble, *Their Bank-Our Bank; The Quality Bank: A History of First Interstate Bank of California* (Costa Mesa, Cal.: First Interstate Bank of California Professional Publications, 1981);

George H. Koster, *The Transamerica Story: 50 Years of Service and Looking Forward* (San Francisco: Transamerica Corporation, 1978).

Trust Companies and Trust Departments

Nineteenth-century trust companies managed property and the estates of wealthy individuals, holding the estates for final sale or, in the case of a trust beneficiary who still lived, for regular disbursement. The companies charged a fee for such services, but more important, they had access to the extensive funds in their care as a source of investment and lending. Thus they soon came to assume banking duties as well, although some states, such as New York, passed laws prohibiting trust companies from engaging in banking activities.

A New York company, Farmers' Loan and Trust Company (incorporated as Farmers' Insurance and Loan Company in 1922), was the nation's first company to engage in trust activities, but the first company chartered exclusively as a trust company was another New York City company, the United States Trust Company, which received a charter in 1853. That charter provided a model for New York's subsequent trust charters.

By mid century trust companies had already wedged themselves into banking businesses, and by the 1870s they emerged as important competitors to banks. In 1913 more than 1,800 trust companies conducted operations, and by that time they differed little from banks. In 1929 trust companies reached their all-time high of 18 percent of the total assets of American financial intermediaries.

In the 1920s trust companies provided an avenue by which banks engaged in the securities boom known as the Great Bull Market. Some 380 banks engaged in the securities business, most of them through security affiliates or trust companies. Bank-ers Trust, Equity Trust, Guaranty Trust, and Union Trust were among the most prominent securities affiliates. In 1933 Congress separated commercial banking from investment banking with the Glass-Steagall Act, largely out of the mistaken belief that investment in securities had weakened the commercial banks and made them vulnerable after the crash. Recent evidence, in fact, suggests that the banks with security affiliates actually performed better than those banks that lacked an affiliate.

Banks recovered many of the trust activities after World War II. The federal government over the years expanded its list of the activities permissible under the law. Bank holding companies held a variety of businesses, including trusts, mortgage companies, equipment leasing, and computer companies. In the early 1990s, discussions of removing the barriers separating investment banking from commercial banking gathered steam. Because nonbank firms, such as Merrill Lynch and Sears, Roebuck (now just Sears), could offer almost any service, banks rightfully complained about unfair competition. Meanwhile, commercial banks have continued to maintain their trust departments to handle those estate-administration activities permitted by law.

See also:

Bank Holding Company Act of 1956, Commercial Banks and Investment Banks, Glass-Steagall Act, Security Affiliates of Commercial Banks, Transamerica Corporation.

—Editor

Truth in Lending Act

As part of the Consumer Protection Act, in 1969 Congress passed the Truth in Lending Act. The act required the full explanation by lenders of all terms of consumer credit transactions. It also prohibited advertising goods and services not equally available to all borrowers and required the advertising of either all terms of a credit offering or none of them. Finally, it required that if the length of a repayment period exceeded four payments, then the purchase agreement had to indicate clearly, in conspicuous print, that the cost of the credit was included in the price indicated for the goods or services. As a result of the act's passage, consumers found themselves awash in information on their credit card statements, much of it in legalese. Nevertheless, consumers could determine the total repayment cost of a loan or insist that the lender explain the terms.

—Editor

Paul A. Volcker

(September 5, 1927-)

by Thomas F. Cargill

University of Nevada at Reno

CAREER: Economist and special assistant (1952-1957), president, Federal Reserve Bank of New York (1975-1979); financial economist (1957-1962), vice-president, Chase Manhattan Bank (1965-1968); director, Office of Financial Analysis (1962-1965); under secretary for monetary affairs, U.S. Department of the Treasury (1969-1974); senior fellow, Woodrow Wilson School of Public and International Affairs, Princeton University (1974-1975); chairman, Board of Governors, Federal Reserve System (1979-1987); chairman, National Commission on the Public Service (1987-).

Paul A. Volcker devoted almost 30 years to serving the public and private sectors in the interrelated areas of international finance and public monetary policy. After his retirement from full-time duty he continued his commitment to service as chairman of the National Commission on the Public Service—a privately sponsored body formed to study problems arising from the recruitment, training, and employment of public-service employees.

Paul A. Volcker (courtesy of Paul A. Volcker)

While Volcker played an important public role

in the 1970s as under secretary for monetary affairs at the U.S. Department of the Treasury and as president of the Federal Reserve Bank of New York, his appointment by President Jimmy Carter in August 1979 to chair the Federal Reserve Board of Governors made Volcker one of the most influential economic policymakers in recent history. He emerged from public obscurity to assume the leadership of the Federal Reserve at a time of great financial, economic, and political instability in the United States.

Two important caveats need to be taken into account to survey Volcker's public contribution. First, few direct links between individuals and specific policy actions exist. Policy formulation and execution are complex processes involving many individuals and, often, uncontrollable external forces. Volcker's conservative, free-market orientation consistently reinforced this passive rather than reactive view of public policy. He considered himself simply a part of a process, and his greatest contribution often rested in his ability to recognize forces for change, to accommodate those forces, and to convince others of the need for change. Second, only a few years have elapsed since Volcker's end to active government policy-making, and considerable debate remains both about the economic problems of the 1970s and 1980s as well as Volcker's specific role in shaping Federal Reserve policy.

Volcker first exerted a powerful policy influence as U.S. Treasury under secretary for monetary affairs during the breakdown of the Bretton Woods exchange rate system in 1973. The Bretton Woods exchange rate system, established by the Allies in June 1944, was designed to establish the postwar international financial system on a fixed exchange rate regime, widely considered the most suitable framework for the encouragement of international trade and global economic growth. By the mid 1960s the system had come under increased pressure. One of the most severe problems originated from the heavy responsibility placed on the U.S. dollar, which served as the basic international currency, requiring the United States frequently to place external above internal considerations in order to maintain international faith in the value of the dollar. Specifically, the United States at times was required to reduce the pace of domestic economic activity in order to maintain the value of the dollar.

The system started to unravel in the early 1970s. After several attempts at repair failed, it be-

came apparent that the new environment required a more flexible system. As under secretary of the Treasury for monetary affairs, Volcker was the principal U.S. negotiator in developing and installing the new international monetary system. The new system was based on the principle of flexible exchange rates, in which market forces played an important role, but at the same time central banks intervened on occasion to stabilize exchange rates if necessary.

Volcker did not initiate the flexible exchange rate proposal; rather, events imposed that framework on the world financial system. Volcker's skill as chief U.S. negotiator definitely smoothed the transition toward a more flexible exchange rate regime, and in that regard Volcker earned high marks and established himself among world central bankers as objective, balanced, and politically astute. He further enhanced that reputation when he became president of the Federal Reserve Bank of New York in 1975—the bank that had traditionally served as a focal point for international policy issues. Volcker's reputation played an important role in both his less than enthusiastic appointment by President Carter as chairman of the Board of Governors of the Federal Reserve in 1979 and his ability to shape Federal Reserve policy in the first half of the 1980s.

Unstable economic performance characterized the decade of the 1970s, and by 1979 the U.S. economy was in serious trouble. Inflation had reached double-digit levels; interest rates stood at an all-time high; the value of the dollar was falling in foreign exchange markets; the loss of U.S. competitiveness in world trade was reflected by trade balance deficits; gold prices reached levels that even the "gold bugs" never anticipated; and growing instability characterized the financial system. That instability alarmed almost everyone, and in 1979 and 1980 federal regulatory authorities expressed serious concern that a major financial breakdown similar to the collapse during the Great Depression was possible. The fact that the United States had just "celebrated" the 50th anniversary of the start of the Great Depression did not go unnoticed, and that further heightened concern about whether "it" could happen again.

Thrift institutions in particular experienced problems, as depositors withdrew funds and invested in higher-yielding money market instruments, though depositors also withdrew bank deposits and invested in money markets. The disintermediation of funds from depository institutions

Volcker being sworn in as Federal Reserve chairman, 1979. President Jimmy Carter looks on (courtesy of the Carter Library).

to the direct money markets occurred because federal government deposit rate ceilings on saving and time deposits (Regulation Q) remained considerably less than interest rates that could be earned in the open money market. The disintermediation process threatened the viability of banks and thrift institutions and sharply reduced the availability of consumer and mortgage credit. In fact, disintermediation grew so intense on several occasions (1966, 1969, 1974-1975, 1979-1980) that the periods were referred to as "credit crunch" periods because consumer and mortgage credit was available only at high interest rates as funds had been disintermediated to the money markets.

Observers generally agreed that the Federal Reserve contributed in an important way to those unstable conditions because of its failure to maintain price stability. Inflationary monetary growth rates starting in the mid 1960s led to high interest rates, as market participants incorporated anticipations of future inflation into nominal interest rates. Regulation Q ceilings, however, never permitted interest rates on deposits at banks and other institutions to increase. While Regulation Q ceilings could have

been raised significantly to reflect high market interest rates in the open money and capital markets, they were raised only marginally for fear that thrift institutions would be unable to operate with high deposit rates given that they held the majority of their assets as fixed-interest-rate residential mortgages. Thus, the failure to achieve price stability rendered Regulation Q ceilings binding, which in turn generated the disruptive disintermediation process that eventually threatened the stability of the entire financial system by the end of the 1970s.

The failures of the Federal Reserve to achieve a noninflationary monetary policy were increasingly recognized by the late 1970s, even to some degree within the Federal Reserve itself. By that time, however, the situation had reached crisis proportions and required major structural changes in both the financial system and the conduct of monetary policy.

The times demanded strong leadership. Volcker had the skills and the reputation to assume that leadership role. He was respected by the financial community, both domestically and abroad, as a conservative central banker who considered price stability as a major central bank responsibility. President Carter appointed Volcker chairman of the Board of Governors in August 1979; however, that appointment was not the outcome of careful presidential consideration and a desire to select the most qualified individual. The Carter administration faced a political crisis, and the economy faced a financial crisis. Volcker had already played an important part in the monetary policy process since his appointment as president of the Federal Reserve Bank of New York in 1975. As bank president he was a permanent member of the Federal Open Market Committee (FOMC) and had been elected vice-chairman of the FOMC shortly after assuming the position of bank president.

The FOMC consists of 12 members, seven of whom comprise the Board of Governors, one of whom is the president of the Federal Reserve Bank of New York, and four of whom are chosen on a rotating basis among the other 11 Federal Reserve banks. The chairman of the Board of Governors serves as chairman of the FOMC. The power of the FOMC resides in its ability to increase and decrease bank reserves by purchasing and selling U.S. government securities on behalf of the Federal Reserve. Those actions are referred to as open market operations and have come to represent the most powerful and flexible instrument of monetary policy in the United States.

As chairman of the Board of Governors, however, Volcker assumed the most prominent and visible position in the Federal Reserve. He influenced the board's decisions on discount rate policy, reserve requirement policy, bank regulation, open market operations, and, as chairman of the FOMC (which is dominated by the Board of Governors), he influenced the most important instrument of monetary policy—open market operations. In addition, Volcker assumed the position of spokesman for the Federal Reserve System at a time when Congress and federal regulatory agencies considered major changes in the structure of the financial system.

The Federal Reserve received increasing criticism for inflationary monetary growth in the 1970s, and much of that criticism focused on the Federal Reserve's operating strategy of targeting interest rates (more specifically, the federal funds rate) at levels that necessarily generated inflationary monetary growth. As a result of congressional pressure the Federal Reserve had been required since 1975 to establish and announce money supply growth rate targets for each year; however, the actual mone-

Volcker delivering a semiannual report of the Federal Reserve to Congress in 1982 (courtesy of the Federal Reserve Board)

tary growth rate exceeded the targets most of the time, while the Federal Reserve consistently achieved its interest rate target. The basic problem was that the interest rate target needed to be raised, but the Federal Reserve, for a variety of reasons, proved unable or unwilling to raise the rate.

The Federal Reserve responded to the criticism by claiming that the growth of new forms of money in the 1970s and its declining membership base reduced its ability to control the money supply. While those arguments possessed some merit, the overwhelming weight of professional opinion viewed the Federal Reserve as making a conscious decision, at least until 1978, to focus on interest rates irrespective of the behavior of the money supply. Many critics also questioned the independence of the Federal Reserve and saw its inflationary monetary policy as an effort to gain favor with the administration and Congress.

In any event, fundamental changes were required in the conduct of monetary policy by the time Volcker assumed the chair of the Board of Governors, and such changes were not long in coming. In November 1979 the Federal Reserve publicly announced an end to targeting the interest rate within a narrow band, and henceforth it focused on the money supply in an effort to break the inflationary psychology of the country. In addition, the Federal Reserve publicly announced that it had failed to achieve price stability in the past because of insufficient attention to the money supply and that price stability would in the future be a primary objective of Federal Reserve policy. It was obvious that a tight monetary policy was in the making.

Those bold moves promised to restore the credibility of the Federal Reserve and set the stage for a restrictive monetary policy that threatened to impose a severe but short recession on the economy.

Much discussion in 1979 and 1980 ensued about whether the Federal Reserve under the leadership of Volcker had finally accepted the monetarist position of steady, noninflationary monetary growth. Events have shown that this view was inaccurate. The Federal Reserve could have maintained the interest-rate-focused policy and reduced money supply growth by raising the targeted interest rate; however, by announcing a new money-supply-focused policy, the Federal Reserve could temper public criticism that it was raising interest rates by claiming that it now focused on money rather than interest rates. By late 1982 observers noted that the Federal Reserve had shifted away from a money-focused policy and by 1987 had returned to an interest-rate-focused policy not much different than the one followed in the 1970s, but with one major distinction. The Federal Reserve appeared more concerned about inflation and the need to raise interest rates early in the process to prevent inflation from getting out of hand.

The public perception that Volcker and the Federal Reserve adopted a monetarist approach has been grossly overstated and misinterpreted. While price stability ultimately involves controlling the money supply, that can be accomplished by procedures not much different from those followed by the Federal Reserve in the 1970s. One only has to read a Volcker speech given at a 1976 joint meeting of the American Economic Association and the American Finance Association to see that he did not embrace a monetarist approach. In that speech Volcker expressed the traditional central banker attitude toward targeting the money supply—in an un-

certain world, monetary targeting cannot be the primary guide to the conduct of monetary policy.

In any event, little doubt remains that a restrictive monetary policy constituted the best path. Under Volcker's leadership the Federal Reserve imposed very tight monetary policy conditions that were followed by a severe but short recession in 1981-1982. The inflation rate over those years fell from 13.5 percent in 1980 to 1.9 percent in 1986.

That represented the major contribution of Volcker: the return of Federal Reserve policy to the primary responsibility of a central bank—price stability. The Federal Reserve's new emphasis on monetary targeting and Volcker's role in that regard have been overstated. In the final analysis, those are issues best relegated to the technical strategies that can best achieve price stability.

Federal Reserve credibility had sunk to a low in the late 1970s. The failure to achieve price stability in the 1970s generated intense criticism from academics and Congress. Federal Reserve arguments that money either was not the primary determinant of the inflation rate or that monetary control was difficult to achieve were largely rejected by the critics. A widely held view surfaced that a more consistent noninflationary monetary growth path had resulted from Federal Reserve unwillingness rather than ability. Congressional efforts in the form of the 1975 Concurrent Resolution 133 and the 1978 Full Employment and Balanced Growth Act failed to reduce the inflationary bias of the Federal Reserve in the second half of the 1970s. In fact, inflation accelerated sharply after 1978.

Experts increasingly recognized that the failure to achieve price stability was not solely due to technical issues about interest rates versus monetary aggregates or stability of the demand and supply functions for money. Ample evidence suggested that the Federal Reserve under the chairmanships of Arthur F. Burns and G. William Miller on several occasions had overly focused on the political implications of monetary policy rather than the effects easy monetary policy had on the inflation rate.

A clear example of politicization was illustrated by the behavior of the Federal Reserve shortly after Carter's election in 1976. Burns wanted to remain chairman of the Board of Governors—a position he had held since 1969. Burns had one more year to serve in his then-current four-year term, and, in an effort to gain favor with the new administration, he played a role

Volcker conferring with President Ronald Reagan at the White House, 1983 (photograph by Bill Fitzpatrick; courtesy of the White House)

in inducing an easier Federal Reserve policy. The discount rate was lowered, and money supply growth increased. The effort failed because President Carter appointed Miller to replace Burns in early 1978. Serious consequences resulted from this politicization of monetary policy. Not only did the expansionary policy contribute to inflation, it further reduced the credibility of the Federal Reserve as an independent agency of government that had the primary purpose of providing price stability. The Miller appointment did not enhance the reputation of the Federal Reserve, since Miller's short tenure as chairman (about 17 months) was characterized as less than satisfactory both outside and within the Federal Reserve.

Central bank credibility is fragile. It can easily be lost, and once lost takes considerable time to be regained. In that regard Volcker played a major role in restoring Federal Reserve credibility. Not only did the Federal Reserve show strong resolve to bring inflation under control by a restrictive monetary policy, he further enhanced credibility when he proposed this action during the time of a presiden-

tial election and when he publicly admitted the past failures of the Federal Reserve to control inflation.

But the financial problems of the U.S. economy required more than a return to noninflationary monetary policy. The regulatory parameters that had been inherited from the Great Depression, such as Regulation Q, deposit ceilings, and a variety of portfolio restrictions on the uses and sources of funds by depository institutions limited competition, reduced efficiency, and rendered the financial system unstable.

Volcker and the Federal Reserve were major forces for financial restructuring and along with other regulatory authorities convinced Congress of the need for fundamental changes in the financial system. Congress initiated these changes in the March 1980 Depository Institutions Deregulation and Monetary Control Act and extended them in the October 1982 Garn-St Germain Act.

Volcker and the Federal Reserve argued that a restructured financial system was necessary to achieve a more efficient and stable flow of funds from lenders to borrowers, but, more important, a restructured financial system would improve the ability of the Federal Reserve to control the money supply. Thus, the 1980 act was as much concerned with issues of monetary control as it was with deregulating the financial system.

The Federal Reserve's position only partly stemmed from concern for monetary control. It's conversion to a monetarist strategy was less than complete. The Federal Reserve focused on monetary control issues for another reason—its declining membership base. Less than half of the banks in the United States were members of the Federal Reserve and thus subject to Federal Reserve reserve requirements; however, they held approximately 75 percent of total bank deposits. A gradual erosion in membership had occurred during the postwar period, and it accelerated in the 1970s. Banks increasingly withdrew from the Federal Reserve system to operate under less restrictive reserve requirements imposed at the state level. It had always expressed concern about its membership base, arguing that it needed a stable and large membership for effective monetary policy. The Federal Reserve wanted to require all banks to become official members; however, the dual system of financial regulation acted as an effective political constraint.

The crisis conditions of 1979 rendered Congress more willing to deal with the membership issue, even though it conflicted with the dual system to aid the Federal Reserve's effort to stabilize the economy. At the same time, the Federal Reserve itself grew increasingly alarmed about its shrinking membership base when many banks indicated their intention in 1979 to withdraw from the system.

Thus, the maintenance and extension of regulatory power offered an additional perspective to the Federal Reserve's arguments on the need to restructure the financial system, at least in terms of reserve requirements. In any event, the 1980 act essentially made all federally insured depository institutions (banks, thrifts, and credit unions) de facto members of the Federal Reserve. Any depository institution operating with federal deposit insurance henceforth had to meet reserve requirements imposed by the Federal Reserve. The extension of Federal Reserve reserve requirements to other depository institutions can be defended on many points, and it did make some improvements in monetary control; however, Volcker and the Federal Reserve responded as much to regulatory self-interest as they did to a need to achieve noninflationary money supply growth.

Volcker also had an influence on the Fed's role as lender of last resort. The central bank performs two important functions: the provision of noninflationary monetary growth to support the natural growth path of the economy, and the provision of liquidity at discrete points in time to limit contagion in the financial system. The second refers to the lender of last resort function of the central bank.

Financial systems naturally evolve toward structures that incorporate fiat or fiduciary money supply mechanisms in the form of fractional reserves. Reserve or base money is only a fraction of outstanding deposit money. Fractional reserve systems are more flexible and efficient than systems that have no fiat foundation; however, they can experience instability on occasion. The failure of one or several banks may induce depositors to withdraw their funds from healthy institutions and thereby cause their failure, since they hold only a fractional reserve. Thus, the failure of one or a few banks could generate a general run on banks and thereby contaminate otherwise healthy institutions.

Central banks play an important role in preventing contagion by serving as lenders of last resort because they have the ability to create and destroy reserves. The Federal Reserve accomplishes the lender of last resort function through the discount window, since it can direct discounted funds to the affected institutions. The Federal Reserve recognized this critical role after learning from mistakes made during the Great Depression, when it failed to lend effectively from 1930 through 1933.

Volcker stressed that aspect of central banking and regarded it, along with price stability, as a fundamental central bank responsibility. However, Volcker was involved in two lender of last resort operations that were questionable at best.

In January 1980 the Hunt brothers of Texas manipulated the silver market to more than $50 per ounce with funds supplied largely by banks. The silver market then began a massive decline to almost $10 per ounce by the end of March. As a result, the value of the bank loans that had supported the price increase declined along with the price of silver. As part of their strategy, the Hunt brothers had invested heavily in silver futures, anticipating a price increase that did not materialize, and they stood on the verge of defaulting when their payments fell due. A default by the Hunt brothers would have reduced silver prices even more and further reduced the value of the bank loans that had supported the speculative rise of silver.

Volcker became aware of the threat to the silver market and was concerned that its collapse might spread to other financial markets, especially via a collapse in the value of the silver bank loans. The Federal Reserve did not directly lend to the Hunt brothers or to the banks that had loans outstanding; rather, Volcker persuaded a group of large banks to provide a private bailout to the brothers. As a result, the brothers received a $1.1 billion loan from 13 banks to avoid defaulting on their silver contracts.

The second questionable lender of last resort action involved Continental Illinois Bank of Chicago. Continental, at the time one of the 10 largest banks in the United States, experienced a run of large certificates of deposit in 1984, and for all practical purposes ceased to be economically viable. Considerable support existed for the "too-big-to-fail" view among federal regulatory authorities. Volcker, the comptroller of the currency, and the chairman of the Federal Deposit Insurance Corporation arranged a federal bailout. Continental Illinois was ultimately provided more than $8 billion in funds through the discount window of the Federal Reserve.

The two lender of last resort actions were criticized both in terms of whether the Federal Reserve should have so actively involved itself and also what signals those actions provided to the financial community in terms of how far the government would go to prevent market discipline. Given the financial problems of the thrift industry in the second half of the 1980s the actions of the Federal Reserve in those two instances were, at a minimum, questionable. They did not represent high points of public policy, either for the Federal Reserve or for Volcker.

Volcker also faced the problem of external imbalances. The U.S. current account and trade balance with the rest of the world showed large deficit positions in the 1980s. The external deficit is closely related to the federal budget deficit, which also increased in an absolute sense (but not in proportion to GNP) during the Reagan presidency. While the specific channels of relationship between the two deficits are not clearly understood, there is no doubt about the basic cause of the U.S. current account and trade deficit. The large federal government deficit combined with a low household

savings rate necessarily meant that the United States consumed more than it produced domestically. The difference must be imported from abroad, thus contributing to the trade deficit, and the funds to support the spending must be borrowed from abroad, contributing to the current account deficit, or net capital inflow.

The Federal Reserve has little impact on federal deficits and the household savings rate; however, Volcker as spokesman for the Federal Reserve frequently took the opportunity to encourage Congress to deal with the basic causes of the external imbalances. For example, in testimony before Congress on February 7, 1984, Volcker remarked, "We simply can't have it both ways—on the one hand, look abroad for increasing help in financing the credits related to our budget deficit, our housing, and our investment and, on the other hand, expect to narrow the growing gap in our trade accounts."

Those views were not popular with the Reagan administration or Congress, both of which found it far more convenient to point the finger to other causes, such as the trade and macroeconomic policies of Japan. Volcker deserves considerable credit for frequently and publicly pointing out the conflicts between internal and external imbalances.

Volcker's conviction that the Federal Reserve's major responsibility was to achieve a credible price stabilization policy brought an end to his chairmanship. Criticisms of the federal deficit and unwillingness to blame the external deficit on the Japanese did not endear Volcker to the Reagan administration. In fact, Reagan seemed less than enthusiastic about reappointing Volcker as chairman in 1983. The Reagan administration did, however, change the direction of the board by appointing supply-siders when board openings appeared. The new members felt that the Federal Reserve should concern itself more with ensuring that money supply did not constrain economic growth and felt that since the price level had been stabilized, the Federal Reserve could be less concerned with price stability, at least for the time being. After 1985 Volcker found himself in the minority, and in 1986 he was overruled in his effort to maintain the discount rate rather than lower it. In 1987 Volcker argued for tighter monetary policy and again was overruled. At that point it became obvious that Volcker's leadership position had lapsed, and it was only a matter of time before he left. He resigned his chairmanship in August 1987, and the new chairman, Alan Greenspan, assumed the leadership role of the Federal Reserve.

Volcker played important roles in restructuring the financial system and implementing the lender of last resort responsibility of the Federal Reserve. But the Federal Reserve's efforts to extend reserve requirements were at least as much related to its effort to maintain and enhance regulatory power as they were to achieving more effective monetary control. More serious, the direct involvement of the Federal Reserve to support and arrange a private bailout for speculators and to provide multi-billion-dollar loans to a large bank to avoid bankruptcy cannot be positively viewed.

References:

Thomas F. Cargill and Gillian Garcia, *Financial Reform in the 1980s* (Stanford, Cal.: Hoover Institution, 1985);

Garcia and Elizabeth Plautz, *The Federal Reserve: Lender of Last Resort* (Cambridge, Mass.: Ballinger, 1988);

William Greider, *Secrets of the Temple: How the Federal Reserve Runs Wall Street* (New York: Simon & Schuster, 1987);

William R. Neikirk, *Volcker: Portrait of the Money Man* (New York: Congdon & Weed, 1987).

Maggie L. Walker

(July 15, 1867 - December 15, 1934)

by John M. Coski

Museum of the Confederacy

CAREER: Right Worthy Grand Secretary-Treasurer of the Independent Order of St. Luke (1899-1934); president, St. Luke Bank and Trust Company [St. Luke Penny Savings Bank to 1923] (1903-1930); chairman, Consolidated Bank and Trust Company (1930-1934); founder and president, Richmond Council of Colored Women (1912-?).

Maggie Lena Walker is best known as the first female bank president in the United States. A black woman whose business career arose from her leadership of a black fraternal order, Walker never achieved national celebrity. She was, however, a legendary figure in her native Richmond, Virginia. And, as the moving force behind a successful black mutual benefit association and the founder of the oldest surviving black-owned bank, Walker looms large in the early history of black business and finance. Underlying her activities was a clear vision of racial solidarity and self-help typical of black economic thought in the half century after emancipation.

Born in Richmond on July 15, 1867, two years after the close of the Civil War, Walker lived her entire life in the former Confederate citadel. Her mother, Elizabeth Draper, was a servant in the home of eccentric Richmond unionist Elizabeth Van Lew. Draper later married Van Lew's mulatto butler, William Mitchell, whose name Maggie assumed, but evidence suggests that her natural father was a white northern newspaperman, Ecles Cuthbert. She graduated from Richmond's Armstrong Normal School in 1883 and taught for three years at the Lancaster elementary school that she had attended as a child. During those same years she took accounting classes and became an agent for the Women's Union, a local insurance company. Her teaching career and other activities ended abruptly in 1886 when she married Armstead Walker, son of a prominent black brick mason and contractor.

A woman of extreme energy and purpose, Maggie Walker chafed at her youthful retirement to the role of homemaker. She later cautioned young people against "hasty marriage" and devoted her life to finding productive roles for black women. "I felt like a spendthrift," Walker later recalled of her idle years. "I knew I had the energy to do a lot of things for my people that needed doing, and I felt I ought to be about it in some way. Yet I didn't know what I could do or where to begin. I was restless and wanted work that was of some account."

She found her outlet through the Independent Order of St. Luke, the organization that became her lifework. She joined the order on her fourteenth birthday in 1881 and held a succession of local offices in the 1880s and 1890s. She led a

Maggie L. Walker (courtesy of the National Park Service)

drive to create a Juvenile Department within the order to encourage thrift among children and build up the order's membership rolls. Walker was elected Right Worthy Grand Secretary-Treasurer, the order's most powerful position, in 1899, in the midst of a financial and organizational crisis. She held that post until her death.

The Independent Order of St. Luke was one of the many black fraternal orders and mutual benefit associations that provided the foundation of black finance and insurance in the half century after the Civil War. St. Luke was founded in Baltimore in 1867 as a self-help agency for black women. Under the leadership of Walker's predecessor, William M. T. Forrester, the order expanded to include men and moved the Right Worthy Grand (executive) Council to Richmond, a city that one historian dubbed the "alma mater" of black fraternal orders in the United States. St. Luke also followed the lead of the most progressive order, the United Order of True Reformers (also headquartered in Richmond) in providing members with insurance policies that paid small sickness and death benefits, not merely burial expenses. By 1887 St. Luke had more than 2,000 members in 100 local "subordinate councils" scattered throughout the East.

Membership had fallen by more than half, the treasury was nearly empty, and the order was plagued by incessant feuds between the executive and subordinate councils when Walker assumed the reins from Forrester in 1899. Walker brought to the job a blend of forceful leadership and inspirational vision, realism, and religiosity that soon made her a messianic figure within the order and among Richmond's black community. Thereafter the order marked two birth years: 1867, its founding date, and 1899, "the year of the resurrection of the Independent Order of St. Luke."

Maggie Walker's paramount objective was to make the order an instrument for the progress of the race and especially for black women. She first sought to strengthen the order itself, denouncing the "rebellious spirit" among some of the subordinate councils, recommending the purge of dissidents, and even suspending temporarily one council that refused to pay a new compulsory endowment levy. Using the Biblical imagery in which she and the order were steeped, Walker urged members to drive the "black sheep" out of the fold, to "bind our tares together and burn them" with "the fires of condemnation, and the silent contempt of all honorable, loyal St. Luke." The order, she argued, could no longer be "an old-fashioned society," but must be progressive and efficient to survive the competition of a "commercial age." She convinced the order to modernize its administration and bookkeeping practices. Believing that any organization must either grow or die, she pressed for continual expansion; by 1912 the order had almost 700 subordinate councils and more than 16,000 members concentrated in Virginia, West Virginia, Washington, D.C., Pennsylvania, and New York.

In order to fulfill the mission that Walker envisaged for it, the Independent Order of St. Luke had to develop into more than just a mutual benefit association. Consistent with the ideals articulated by both Booker T. Washington and his black critics, Walker believed that blacks should learn the skills and habits of economic independence. Emulating the ambitious program of the True Reformers, Walker unveiled in 1901 a master plan for diversification that included a newspaper, a factory and store, and a savings bank. A weekly newspaper, the *St. Luke Herald*, began publication in 1902. While a factory to produce men's clothing never materialized, a store, the St. Luke Emporium, opened in 1905.

The Saint Luke Penny Savings Bank (changed in 1923 to the St. Luke Bank and Trust Company) proved to be the most enduring monument to Maggie Walker. Chartered by the Commonwealth of Virginia, the bank opened its doors on November 2, 1903. While falling far short of the target for first-day deposits, the bank met with undeniable success. Like its model, the True Reformers Bank (founded in 1888), the Saint Luke Penny Savings Bank was primarily a safety vault for its parent order and a source of capital for its other ventures. The bank's board of directors stipulated that it sell no more than one-quarter of its stock to persons not belonging to St. Luke.

The October 1910 collapse of the True Reformers Bank and related enterprises threatened the stability of the St. Luke bank and its relationship with the order. That event not only felled the giant of the black financial world, but·it also prompted Virginia authorities to look more closely than ever at black financial institutions.

In the wake of revelations of corruption and unwise investments by the True Reformers Bank, the Virginia State Corporation Commission enacted regulations to restrict the activities of fraternal orders. The regulations compelled the Order of St. Luke to sever its formal link with the Saint Luke Penny Savings Bank, which became an independent corporation. The SCC also frustrated Walker's plans to use the order's funds as capital for business diversification by pressuring the bank to avoid the kind of investments that contributed to the True Reformers collapse and invest instead in approved bonds. The laws nevertheless forced only superficial changes in the administration of the bank: Walker continued as bank president and the order still owned the majority of the bank's stock and deposited its funds with the bank.

Even before 1910 Walker saw the proliferation of state laws to regulate banks and insurance companies as a campaign against black business. Who were the regulators after? she asked. "They are after the Negro Banks which have come into existence in Richmond, Hampton, Norfolk, Newport News, and all over the southland. The white man doesn't intend to wait until the Negro becomes a financial giant, he intends to attack him and fetter him now, while he is an infant in his swaddling clothes, helpless in his cradle."

This perceived attack on black business, along with the white insistence on racial segregation, provided powerful support for Walker's plea for racial solidarity. Within the Order of St. Luke, Walker raised the spectre of state hostility to promote unity, modern business methods, and the establishment of an Emergency Fund from which to finance the state-mandated insurance reserves. "The bank book tells the tale," she pointedly reminded delegates to the order's 1907 convention.

The heart of Walker's economic philosophy was that blacks must patronize black stores and institutions. While ethnic groups supported their own people, Walker noted in 1905, "the Negro is so wedded to those who oppress him that he carries to their bank every dollar he can get his hands upon and then goes back the next day and pays the white man to lend him his own money. It makes my heart ache! Will our eyes never open?" She was especially bitter at the social-climbing black elite who only patronized white stores, and at the mass of unenlightened black men who turned their backs on the St. Luke institutions because they were run by women. It was to the tragic failure of black economic solidarity that Walker attributed the dissolution of the St. Luke Emporium in November 1911.

While the Order of St. Luke and the St. Luke Bank were the most important expressions of Walker's vision, she devoted herself to other black organizations. She actively participated in the National Association for the Advancement of Colored People, Booker T. Washington's National Negro Business League, and the National Urban League.

Her most passionate concern remained the condition of the black woman, whom she often described as the most "helpless" and the most "circumscribed and hemmed in" creature on earth. In 1912 she founded the Richmond Council of Colored Women, which affiliated with the National Council of Colored Women. The liberation of black women from their restrictive roles, Walker believed, was essential for the progress of the race. A fundamental objective of the Independent Order of St. Luke and of the St. Luke bank was to provide useful employment for black women and to prove to black men that the liberation of their wives and daughters was essential for racial progress.

Walker also carried her vision and her activism into the political arena. Alienated by the so-

Walker toward the end of her career (courtesy of the National Park Service)

called "lily white" Virginia Republican party's neglect of black interests, Virginia blacks sponsored a "lily black" ticket in the 1921 state elections. Walker was nominated for state superintendent of public instruction on a ticket headed by editor and banker John Mitchell, Jr. Walker stumped for the ticket and fought against the legal barriers and obstructionist tactics that restricted black voting. Not unexpectedly, the ticket polled only 5,000 votes. Walker's political career ended.

Walker's busy public life was complicated by a tragic personal life. She fractured her kneecap in a 1907 fall. The increasingly debilitating injury left her a virtual paraplegic by 1928 and confined her to a wheelchair in her final years. In a bizarre incident at her family's home in 1915, her son Russell accidentally shot and killed her husband. Although a jury acquitted Russell in his trial for murder, enemies within the order exploited the publicity in a futile effort to force Walker from power. The most devastating result of the episode was the alcoholic dissipation and back-alley death in 1923 of her son Russell, who had before 1915 provided valuable assistance to his mother in modernizing the administration of St. Luke.

The personal tragedies took their toll on a spirit already tried by a life of championing difficult causes. She wrote in her diary of sleepless nights spent wrestling with her "inner thoughts." Anxieties over the alcoholism of her surviving son, Melvin, and indecision over her own future intruded on the considerable burdens of her position. "I am so unfit for it all. Strength, Oh God!" she lamented in February 1925.

Despite this inner torment and her quasi paralysis, Walker continued her energetic leadership of the order and of the bank. She traveled constantly to visit subordinate councils throughout the eastern United States and had her home, office, and automobiles modified to accommodate her wheelchair. Membership in St. Luke exceeded 100,000 in 1925, but 1933 found Walker appealing for the recruitment of 5,000 more adult and 5,000 juvenile members to compensate for declining revenues. She also reiterated her appeal to all members to patronize their bank and delivered an "urgent request" to adopt unanimously her recommendations for weathering the financial crisis of the Depression.

Financial pressures antedating the 1929 stock market crash compelled the merger of the St. Luke bank with two other black-owned Richmond banks in 1930-1931. The two-staged merger created the Consolidated Bank and Trust Company under the leadership of the St. Luke bank, the strongest of the three. Walker surrendered the presidency of the new bank but served as chairman of the board until her death. The consolidation allowed the new bank to be one of the few black-owned banks to survive the crisis of 1933. The Consolidated Bank and Trust Company broke free from the restrictive "savings vault" policies to become a full-fledged commercial bank by the late 1950s.

Maggie Walker died of diabetic gangrene on December 15, 1934. Her home in Richmond's historically black Jackson Ward became a National Historic Site in 1978, a shrine to her intellectual and spiritual influence. The Consolidated Bank and Trust Company survived as a monument to her business acumen. In contrast, Walker's successors never transformed the Independent Order of St. Luke into a full-fledged modern insurance business; it entered a long period of decline after World War II and went into receivership in 1987-1988.

The survival of the bank and the demise of the order in itself symbolized the maturation of black finance in Maggie Walker's lifetime. Fraternal orders such as the Independent Order of St. Luke were the first black insurance and financial institutions. Although religious and ritualistic in their origins, those fraternal orders provided the organizational foundations for bona fide banks and insurance agencies. Maggie Walker exemplified the generation of black leaders at once steeped in the original ideals of the fraternal orders and committed to building them into viable modern financial institutions.

Publication:

Historical Report of the R.W.G. Council, I.O. Saint Luke 1867-1917 (Richmond: Everett Waddy, 1917).

References:

Sally Chandler, "Maggie Lena Walker," thesis, Virginia Commonwealth University, 1975;

Wendell P. Dabney, *Maggie L. Walker and the I.O. of Saint Luke: The Woman and Her Work* (Cincinnati: Dabney, 1927);

Jesse E. Fleming, "A History of Consolidated Bank and Trust Company: A Minority Bank," thesis, Stonier Graduate School of Banking, Rutgers University, 1972;

Lily H. Hammond, *Race And The South: Two Studies, 1914-1922* (New York: Arno, 1972);

Abram L. Harris, *The Negro As Capitalist: A Study of Banking and Business Among American Negroes* (Philadelphia: American Academy of Political and Social Sciences, 1936);

Charles Willis Simmons, "Maggie Lena Walker and the Consolidated Bank and Trust Company," *Negro History Bulletin* (February-March 1975): 345-349.

Archives:

The papers of Maggie L. Walker are housed at the Maggie L. Walker National Historic Site in Richmond, Virginia. The collection includes Walker's diaries and some of her correspondence, a bound volume of mimeographed speeches entitled "Addresses of Maggie L. Walker," and some records of the Independent Order of St. Luke dating primarily since 1934.

Paul M. Warburg

(August 10, 1868 - January 24, 1932)

by Benjamin J. Klebaner

City College, CUNY

CAREER: Partner, M. M. Warburg & Company (1895-1914); partner, Kuhn, Loeb & Company (1902-1914); member (1914-1916), vice-governor, Federal Reserve Board of Governors (1916-1918); chairman, International Acceptance Bank (1921-1932).

Paul Moritz Warburg, international banker, outstanding spokesman for banking reform in the United States, and early leader of the Federal Reserve System, was born on August 10, 1868, in Hamburg, Germany, the son of Moritz M. and Charlotte Esther Oppenheim Warburg. Warburg's father represented the 11th generation of a banking family that traced its ancestry to Simon of Cassel, a pawnbroker and money dealer granted permission to reside in the Westphalian town of Warburg in 1559. His descendants subsequently took the name of the town as their family name. In 1798 Moses Marcus Warburg and his brother Gerson opened the firm of M. M. Warburg & Company in Ham-

burg. The firm operated under the designation "money changers" until 1868, when it changed its title to "bankers." Moritz, son of Moses, succeeded to the business.

In 1886 Paul Warburg graduated from the Realgymnasium in Hamburg and was exempted from military service because of an injured arm. He spent two years with Simon Haver, a Hamburg importer and exporter, entering M. M. Warburg & Company in 1888. The company sent him to London in 1889, where he familiarized himself with British banking methods at Samuel Montagu & Company. In 1891 his apprenticeship continued at the Paris agency, Banque Russie pour Le Commerce Etranger. His training mainly involved dealing with the huge sums governments held in foreign countries as reserves. In 1892 his father sent him on a trip to India, China, and Japan.

Three of Warburg's four brothers pursued banking careers. The oldest, Aby, was the exception. He became a scholar in the humanities and

Paul M. Warburg

amassed a great library, the Warburg Institute, which he moved to London in 1934. Max, the second brother, became a partner in 1893 and, later, head of M. M. Warburg & Company. He remained in Hamburg until the Nazis made it impossible. Paul Warburg became a partner in the family business in 1895. Felix, born in 1871, married Jacob Schiff's daughter Frieda soon after joining Kuhn, Loeb & Company in New York in 1894. That cemented the tie between the Hamburg and the Wall Street bank. Fritz, the youngest brother, remained with Max in Hamburg.

Paul Warburg stood as best man at Felix's wedding in March 1895. The maid of honor was Nina Jenny Loeb, the daughter of Kuhn, Loeb's founder. Warburg married her in October 1895; the fashionable wedding took place in Red Bank, New Jersey. He and his bride returned to Hamburg. In 1901 Warburg was made a freeman of Hamburg and became the first Jewish person elected to the lower house of the Hamburg assembly. Until he moved to New York in 1902, his brother Max discussed every business decision involving M. M. Warburg & Company with him.

The two brothers placed a German treasury bond issue of 80 million marks in the United States in 1900 and participated in a loan to Japan in 1905 at the invitation of Kuhn, Loeb. Already a leading Hamburg dealer in commercial bills and foreign currencies, the Warburg bank increased its activity in government loans. The bank's balance sheet grew from 30 million marks in 1895 to 127 million in 1914. The years 1900 to 1914 "were the years of the most happy and harmonious development of the firm," Fritz Warburg stated in retrospect. Paul Warburg continued as a partner in the family bank until August 7, 1914.

Family reasons led to Warburg's coming to New York in 1902: Nina's parents, very old and ailing, wanted her nearby. Warburg, however, doubted that he would stay in America. At first the family spent half the year in New York and half in Hamburg but soon only summered abroad.

Shortly after Warburg's arrival in New York, his brother-in-law, James Loeb, decided to retire from business. Warburg became a partner in Kuhn, Loeb. That firm, established 35 years earlier by two German-Jewish immigrants, Warburg's father-in-law, Solomon Loeb, and the latter's brother-in-law, Abraham Kuhn, sold railroad and U.S. treasury bonds in America and Germany. It added industrial issues in 1900. Under Jacob Schiff, who became head in 1885, Kuhn, Loeb & Company grew to be second in importance to J. P. Morgan & Company among American investment houses.

The years Warburg spent with Kuhn, Loeb gave him more worry than satisfaction. He amassed a considerable fortune as a partner. J. P. Morgan, the Jupiter of Wall Street, listed him as number two among six "coming financiers of the country." Schiff considered Warburg's resignation from Kuhn, Loeb to join the Federal Reserve Board in 1914 "a great deprivation" to the firm and the family.

After only three weeks in the United States, Warburg wrote a pamphlet on the evils of the system of decentralized cash reserves. He put it in a desk drawer for five years, as he did not wish "to write about a country that I had just learned to know," he explained to the House Banking and Currency Committee in January 1913. In 1907 he brought the 1902 manuscript up-to-date with a few changes, and it appeared in the *New York Times* Annual Financial Review on January 6, 1907, as "Defects and Needs of Our Banking System." Professor Edwin R. A. Seligman, Columbia University economist who had gathered a small group of bankers and economists in the fall of 1906 to discuss banking issues, had encouraged its publication.

On November 12, 1907, soon after the panic of that year, Seligman invited Warburg to present "A Plan for a Modified Central Bank" before Columbia University's Academy of Political Science. Warburg spoke there again on February 3, 1908, on "American and European Banking Methods and Bank Legislation Compared," in a lecture series devoted to the currency problem.

Warburg felt that he had "a mission to perform," as he told the Senate Banking and Currency Committee in 1914. His work for monetary reform had a great deal to do with his decision to stay in the United States. He perceived "a distinct duty" that he thought he could fulfill. Consequently, he took out his first papers for citizenship in 1908.

Schiff introduced Senator Nelson A. Aldrich to Warburg in the fall of 1907, when the senator came to Kuhn, Loeb to inquire about German banking legislation. About a year later the influential Republican leader revealed to an elated Warburg that he had come around to the view that the United States not only should but could have a central bank.

At the end of November 1910 Aldrich gathered five men on Jekyll Island, Georgia, purportedly to hunt ducks. Three other New York bankers attended the highly secret meeting: Henry P. Davison of J. P. Morgan, Frank A. Vanderlip of National City Bank, and Charles Norton of First National Bank. Warburg was "the ablest banking mind of the group," according to Professor J. Lawrence Laughlin, the University of Chicago economist. Out of their discussions came the first draft of the Aldrich bill for a central bank, which was presented before a gathering of businessmen on January 16, 1911.

Warburg expressed his delight at the bill, as the main principles of the Aldrich plan were "so much akin to the ones I had preached so long and so often." The plan called for centralizing bank reserves and making them available in times of need, rendering commercial paper a quick asset, and providing for "conservatively elastic" bank note issues.

Warburg energetically enlisted support for the Aldrich bill. In January 1911 the National Board of Trade's monetary conference adopted resolutions offered by the Chamber of Commerce of the State of New York under his leadership. The conference ap-

pointed him chairman of a steering committee to organize a "businessmen's monetary reform League in support of a central bank." On June 8, 1911, the nonpartisan National Citizens' League for the Promotion of a Sound Banking System was established in Chicago. The league campaigned vigorously for reform "on the general principles of the Aldrich plan," but, to Warburg's dismay, did not endorse it specifically. He was the most active member of the New York branch.

Meanwhile, in November 1911, Warburg assured the American Bankers Association, which gave its approval, that Aldrich's National Reserve Association would take the American monetary system out of Wall Street. On February 19, 1912, as chairman of the subcommittee on banking reform of the Republican Club of the City of New York, he secured the club's endorsement of the general principles of the Aldrich Plan. B. C. Forbes later reported a remark in financial circles that "what was good in the Aldrich bill was Warburg's, and what was bad was the work of Aldrich and his colleagues."

The Aldrich bill contained technical clauses taken from Warburg's United Reserve Bank plan of March 1910, which later appeared in the Federal Reserve Act. Warburg insisted that the Glass-Owen measure that became law incorporated "the most important parts" of the Aldrich bill. The two bills, contrary to Democratic senator Carter Glass's claim, were "surprisingly akin" in principles, purposes, and processes. Warburg emphasized the Federal Reserve System carried into effect "the basic idea of the original plan" and devoted some 330 pages of his volume on the history of the system to reprinting parallel passages. Republican Warburg eagerly wanted the system to be "the child and ward of both parties." He also sought to have Aldrich's "important contributions" recognized.

From the beginning of his campaign for a central bank in January 1907, Warburg stressed reform of reserves and liquidity arrangements over bank note elasticity, which had long occupied center stage in public discussions. The ideal solution—"though, perhaps, we may not live to see it"—was a central bank "ready at all times to rediscount the legitimate paper of the general banks." Without a central bank the "horrible crisis" of 1907 would recur, he told the American Economic Association at the end of 1908. His plan for a United Reserve Bank called for a central institution to rediscount paper maturing in 28 days without requiring a guarantee of the member bank, or maturing up to 90 days if it carried its guarantee. In July 1910 the Merchants Association of New York endorsed his plan and printed 30,000 copies of the paper published by the Academy of Political Science. In a talk before the academy that November he avoided using the term "central bank" because it implied greater powers than his "central reservoir," which would not be able to engage in a general banking business.

In the fall of 1913 Warburg made frequent trips to Washington in the hope of removing some of the objectionable features in the Glass-Owen bill. He agreed with Aldrich's critics that it would not be practicable to have a uniform discount rate throughout the country and that the Republican bill should have specified the reserves kept with the National Reserve Association. He counted nine of his suggestions in the final act that amended Glass bill provisions. Among them were a reduction in the maximum number of reserve banks, authority for state bank membership, a reduction in the required reserve amounts, a lengthening to 36 months the period in which commercial banks could transfer reserves to the reserve banks, a requirement that no interest on U.S. government deposits be charged, and a limitation of dividend payments on Federal Reserve Bank stock to six percent. At his suggestion, too, under the Glass-Owen bill a bank could rediscount and access the system's clearing arrangements only through its own reserve district bank.

Though he had opposed several features—especially the provision making Federal Reserve notes an obligation of the U.S. government—he was satisfied that the act was sound in its fundamentals. He hailed what the new law held in store: the gradual elimination of the bond-secured currency, scattered reserves, immobilized commercial paper, and pyramiding of call loans. "I have had the success which comes to few people of starting an idea . . . and it has assumed some tangible form."

Warburg disclaimed originating "any new banking principle." Rather, he had sought to adapt tried and tested European principles to American conditions. Seligman insisted that "in its fundamental features the Federal Reserve Act is the work of Mr. Warburg more than of any other man in the country." No one had labored harder for the cause, in speeches, articles, and letters to influential citizens. As Warburg wrote to Woodrow Wilson's aide and confidant, Colonel Edward M. House, in the summer of 1913, "I have preached the gospel of reform on the lines now adopted at a time when Messrs. Owen and Glass had not yet begun to study the alphabet of banking."

On December 24, 1913, the day after Wilson signed the Federal Reserve Act into law, Glass asked Warburg to consider the possibility of an appointment as a member of the Federal Reserve Board. As a U.S. citizen naturalized only three years earlier, a Wall Street banker, and Jewish, Warburg did not expect such a prestigious nomination; any one of those factors would have sufficed to disqualify him, he believed. A day after the president asked Warburg to serve, House wrote to Wilson: "I never saw anyone so appreciative. . . . His eyes were moist when he told me how grateful he was to you for having thus honored him, and he promised to give the best that was in him to the service." The financial and business community hailed Wilson's choice, but progressive Republicans and radical Democrats could not forgive his Wall Street connection. When Warburg's nomination was forwarded on June 15, 1914, the Senate singled him out for a hearing. Glass understood Warburg's disgust "at the sort of opposition you have encountered," but argued that "it would be a tremendous mistake to surrender to such demagogism."

As Warburg had not sought the office, he deemed a hearing humiliating. Wilson tried to convince him otherwise. When war broke out, Warburg agreed to put aside his feelings and appeared before the Senate Committee on Banking and Currency. Senator Joseph L. Bristow of Kansas grilled him for a day and a half, on August 1 and 3, 1914, seeking his comments on specific Kuhn, Loeb transactions. Warburg politely stood his ground, refusing to pass judgment or provide details on his partners' business activities but freely answering all questions regarding his own views and background. He would go on the board "to represent the country and the future of the country." He offered to make the financial sacrifice because he thought "there is a wonderful opportunity for bringing a great piece of constructive work into successful operation." Many called him quixotic for agreeing to a position paying only $12,000 a year. As a Kuhn, Loeb partner, the press variously estimated his earnings as 20 to 40 times that.

Bristow spoke for four hours against Warburg in committee executive session and continued his assault on the Senate floor for four hours as his colleagues listened in silence. A 38-to-11 vote confirmed him for a four-year term.

The five members of the first Federal Reserve Board took the oath of office on August 10, 1914. Wilson's choices met with general approval. Financial leaders expressed relief at the Warburg nomination: "A guarantee that sanity, skill and common-sense will govern," B. C. Forbes reported. The other member with the banking experience called for in the law was William P. G. Harding, former head of the largest Alabama bank, the First National of Birmingham. Secretary of the Treasury William Gibbs McAdoo and Comptroller of the Currency John Skelton Williams served ex officio. McAdoo had favored Warburg's appointment, and thought the Wall Street viewpoint should be represented on the board.

Disharmony characterized the board almost from the outset. The anti-Treasury faction consisted of Warburg, economist Adolph C. Miller, and Frederick A. Delano, a railway executive. The three feared that McAdoo intended to turn the board into an auxiliary of the Treasury Department. They even opposed locating their offices in the historic Treasury Building adjacent to the White House, even though the act authorized that. Harding remained neutral and held the balance of power.

President Wilson named Charles S. Hamlin, a Boston attorney who served as assistant secretary of the Treasury in the second Grover Cleveland presidential administration, the first governor of the Federal Reserve Board. Hamlin suspected Warburg of having little sympathy with common people; he believed that Warburg and Harding planned to use the board as a representative of the banks: the public would have to be satisfied with what was good for the banks. Hamlin viewed both bankers as "reactionaries to the last." "Warburg is evidently willing to cripple the whole system to please Member Banks," he noted in his diary for November 5, 1915. A few days later he recorded a conversation with Laughlin, who considered Warburg "absolutely unfit" for the board. The Chicago professor claimed that Warburg had secured confirmation "by use of money" and that "the New York people have retained lobbyists and had even put spies in his office."

Governor Hamlin created further dissatisfaction with his policy of having every board member serve on committees that considered each proposal carefully, and then went over them in the board as a whole. What H. Parker Willis (secretary of the board) called a "cabal" unhappy with Hamlin's management urged Wilson to adopt the principle of automatic rotation of the top two posts and to appoint Warburg governor. McAdoo thought that it would not do to appoint a pro-German to head the system. In mid July 1916 he told Hamlin that Warburg "is nearly crazy in his desire to be Governor." After two years, on August 10, 1916, Wilson replaced Hamlin with Harding and named Warburg to Delano's place as vice-governor. Both were reappointed a year later. McAdoo congratulated Warburg "on this new evidence of the President's confidence."

Fresh from his four years on the board, Warburg shared his experience in a talk on February 6, 1919, to the Chamber of Commerce of the State of New York: "I conceived it as my first duty to see to it that the law was equally enforced to offer the fairest possible deal to all." He deemed "the opportunity for constructive work" to be "the real privilege" and most fascinating aspect of the job: "creating and offering new facilities, to provide a wider . . . and safer basis for banking operations, to place a new and stronger substructure under the vast banking machine without ever arresting its going at top speed, to modify its operation without disrupting its organization."

Glass referred to Warburg as "the greatest international banker in America" at the American Bankers Association convention in October 1914. McAdoo deemed his command of international finance to be useful and in certain respects invaluable. Warburg's knowledge of foreign exchange proved essential in the early days of World War I. In September 1914 some of the major American banks formed a $100 million foreign exchange pool to assist the movement of a record cotton crop.

Until 1914, Warburg lived emotionally on both sides of the Atlantic. Kaiser Wilhelm II had awarded him the Order of the Crown of the Second Class in May 1913. The German ambassador to the United States, Johann von Bernstorff, called Warburg a highly esteemed financial adviser to Germany. As long as the United States trod a neutral path, Warburg felt a bond toward his native land, where his favorite brother Max emerged as a leading figure during the war.

Sir Cecil Spring Rice, British ambassador in Washington, argued that German-Jewish influence was very great in America. He wrote to Sir Valentine Cherol in November 1914 that Warburg was "*the* man" on the reserve board: "He practically controls the financial power of the Administration." Rice told Sir Edward Grey, the foreign minister, that since Morgan's death on March 31, 1913, "the Jewish banks are supreme," and had forced Warburg's appointment on McAdoo. The secretary of the Treasury justifiably called Rice "a prize conveyor of misinformation."

On April 2, 1915, the Federal Reserve Board adopted Regulation J for bankers' acceptances. Warburg and Miller ("the Prussianized members of the Board," Comptroller Williams called them) succeeded in having restrictions inserted that made a large proportion of acceptances based on munitions exports ineligible for rediscount at the Federal Reserve Banks. McAdoo suspected the two of deliberately seeking to embarrass the administration and wanted the restrictions removed. Five days later, on August 26, 1915, Wilson approved lowering the bars to loans to belligerents. After hearing from Hamlin, House assured Wilson that Warburg and Miller had not allowed their sympathies to influence their actions in the slightest.

In November 1915, Hamlin's diary records Warburg's bitterness toward the administration because of munitions exports. He accused Warburg of seeking to embarrass the administration for pro-German purposes. "I have fought to protect the Federal Reserve System from a political assault by Warburg," he recorded for December 20, 1915.

In November 1916, Davison came to the board to announce a Morgan plan to offer $100 million in British treasury bills maturing in less than a year. Warburg registered his concern that, as those securities were unlikely to be self-liquidating, that would mean "a lockup of the funds of our banks." The Federal Reserve Board cautioned member banks on November 5, 1916: "The Board . . . does not regard it in the interest of the country at this time that they invest in foreign treasury bills of this character." "Warburg is in 7th Heaven . . . he is so prejudiced against the Allies that he will go to almost any extreme to injure them," Hamlin recorded. Morgan wired London that the incident represented "the most serious financial development" in the United States since the war began. He interpreted the release as Warburg's handiwork to advance Germany's peace propaganda. Morgan believed that Warburg dominated the board and was

very bitter about it, Hamlin reported. In January 1917, Harding disabused Morgan of the notion.

In fact, Wilson had initiated the board's statement. He was concerned that the British securities would interfere with the ability of the American government to borrow from American banks, should that be necessary, the Senate Special Committee on Investigation of the Munitions Industry concluded in 1936.

When the United States broke off diplomatic relations with Germany in February 1917, Warburg told Harding that America could not have done less. He favored Germany as against Britain, but he would be as loyal to the United States as a native American. In May 1918 he wrote to Wilson: "I waited ten years before determining upon my action, and I did not swear that 'I absolutely and entirely renounce and abjure all allegiance and fidelity to any foreign potentate, and particularly to Wilhelm II, Emperor of Germany,' etc., until I was quite certain that I was willing and anxious to cast my lot unqualifiedly and without reserve with the country of my adoption and to defend its aims and its ideals."

Warburg marched in the forefront of those advocating the unity of the Americas. He participated in the first Pan-American Financial Conference called by McAdoo in 1915 to study the problems created by the European war. The outgrowth of that Washington meeting, the International High Commission (subsequently called the Inter-American High Commission), worked for uniformity in the commercial and fiscal laws of Latin America. On his 1916 trip to the Buenos Aires meeting of the group (Warburg and McAdoo were the only Federal Reserve Board members to go), he was gratified to see branches of U.S. banks in Latin America: "We had at last become an integral part of the world's banking machinery." The Federal Reserve Act had authorized foreign branches for the first time.

In April 1916 the Federal Reserve subcommittee headed by Warburg recommended that those American nations in a position to extend capital and credit "eliminate all obstacles . . . which might prevent their banks from extending their activities abroad." In 1917 and 1918, Warburg again served as a member of the U.S. section of the International High Commission.

Over the years Warburg persisted in arguing for a small number of Reserve Banks. The soundness of the system depended entirely on the number; he thought even five too many, as he wrote in a 1913 memorandum. With 12, important money centers would not develop outside New York, and liquid assets would remain concentrated in stock exchange loans. The Glass-Owen proposal for 12 Reserve Banks "will prove a failure," he predicted in the *North American Review* in November 1913: that large number would destroy prospects for "a reliable and strong discount market," weaken the nation's reserve power, and sacrifice "a strong and efficient foreign exchange and gold policy."

As a member of another board committee, in October 1915 Warburg redrew the reserve districts, proposing to turn the Reserve Banks in Atlanta, Dallas, Kansas City, and Minneapolis into branches. Those four had less than 20 percent of the capital of the 12 combined. Four appointive members approved the plan, while Hamlin joined his friends McAdoo and Williams in opposition. The plan collapsed when the attorney-general concluded that the board's power did not include redistricting.

Because of excessive decentralization, the Federal Reserve Board took on administrative functions that, Warburg believed, were difficult for officials remote from the local scene to handle. A strong board was needed to induce the cooperation required to overcome the inherent weaknesses of the excessively fragmented districts.

After leaving the board, Warburg continued to argue for merging the districts. The organizing committee that set up 12 had responded to local pressures instead of including "such a diversity of interests and such a volume of banking and private capital that the total reserve within the district will be adequate for its financial needs in all but times of special emergency, or of very heavy seasonal demands." Moreover, "smaller reserve districts make for smaller men." Had the districts been stronger financially and more diversified economically, they would not have raised discount rates so soon in 1920 in order to protect their reserves. Warburg contended that the Federal Reserve Act had carried decentralization too far but did not succeed in having the law changed.

Warburg proudly noted his role in persuading several of the Federal Reserve System's "best servants to enter . . . the ranks at great personal sacrifices." The greatest of those, Benjamin Strong, had first declined to leave Bankers Trust Company, which he headed, because of concern for his clients

and his reservations about the Federal Reserve Act. But eventually Henry Davison and Warburg prevailed. Just before October 5, 1914, when Strong was officially elected governor of the Federal Reserve Bank of New York, Warburg wrote to ask him "to . . . frame the by-laws so as to give yourself sufficient power as Governor, but bear in mind at the same time that there are many other banks where we want to be careful not to have the Governor run away from the Federal Reserve Agent and the Board, so there must be some flexibility in this respect."

Warburg insisted that open market operations could not be left to the separate discretion of the 12 Reserve Banks. The system needed a "joint and definite plan of action" embracing all of the banks to enable it to act as a stabilizing force. Warburg insisted that "Earning capacity must never be considered the test of the efficiency of Federal reserve banks. *Personally, I should have felt heartily ashamed had all our banks, considering the circumstances under which they began operations, earned their dividends in the past year.*" Critics took the italicized sentence, which came from a talk given to the bankers of Minneapolis and St. Paul in October 1915, out of context. Glass thought Warburg opposed open market operations, when in fact he feared inflation. Some board members eagerly wanted the new Reserve Banks to show earnings; the comptroller of the currency proudly noted that in his native state the Federal Reserve Bank of Richmond had earned a dividend. To avoid such pressures Warburg prepared to recommend a reduction in paid-in capital, and insisted that at times reserve funds might have to sit idle.

Warburg viewed himself to be "the outstanding champion of open market operations," often in the minority on the board. In his opinion acceptances were "the most desirable securities for the purpose," but the undeveloped state of those obligations in the early years of the system forced the Reserve Banks to deal in government securities. Until the acceptance market had thoroughly developed, the Federal Reserve System would not operate safely and efficiently all the time, he explained. The volume of member bank acceptances increased from $266,000 in November 1915 to $244 million in August 1918.

Warburg hailed the opening of the Federal Reserve Banks on November 16, 1914, as "the foundation of our financial emancipation." Theretofore

American businesses financed their overseas trade in London, Paris, or Berlin. The war gave New York an opportunity to develop the market for Latin America as well as for U.S. merchants. "The present constellation," Warburg wrote Strong on September 8, 1915, "[is] a rare opportunity which will never return of establishing our dollar acceptance in the world market." Warburg anxiously wished for America to play the role of international banker previously in European hands. He urged the board not to restrict acceptances to "safe lines." From the outset he stressed that "acceptance business was destined to become a most important factor in our system."

The use of acceptances in America's financial structure occurred largely due to Warburg's leadership. As he had long advocated, the 1913 act authorized member bank involvement in bankers' acceptances for foreign trade purposes. He told the board in March 1915 that bankers' acceptances would bring about "real fluidity of credit and . . . serve as an equalizer of money rates all over the country." A September 1916 amendment extending their power to bills for domestic trade represented another victory for Warburg. The Fed's credit facilities thereby became more accessible.

Warburg also labored—in vain, as it turned out—to have Federal Reserve notes count as part of the reserves legally required of member banks. In the Senate bill, under Willis's tutelage, the House conferees removed the provision as inflationary. Warburg considered the matter so essential that in August 1914 he proposed to delay opening the Reserve Banks until Congress amended the act. In October he anticipated (quite incorrectly, as it turned out) that circumstances would force them to close quickly.

Warburg continued his campaign with a memorandum to his board colleagues in December 1915 arguing that the Reserve Banks "will not find their ultimate and proper place" until Federal Reserve notes could count toward member bank reserves. An extensive letter of February 1916 explained that until Congress amended the law, "the System will be lacking in safety, and the country will not be able to derive the fullest measure of benefit from it."

Warburg's concern to overcome "the dwarfed and limping system" created by the 1913 act related to the system's gold position. He convinced a board majority to use every device to concentrate the nation's gold in the vaults of the reserve banks. He also urged member banks to keep only the amount of gold they needed and deposit the remainder in the Reserve Banks. He told the American Bankers Association convention in September 1916 that by keeping gold in bank and business tills, the country had robbed itself of "its legitimate opportunity of growth, of helping itself, and of helping the world." The Federal Reserve Banks constituted the best places for gold and gold certificates.

Warburg hailed the amendments of June 21, 1917, requiring member banks to keep *all* legal reserve balances at their district banks. That federal reserve notes did not count in the legal reserve no longer mattered. The Reserve Banks would gain some $200 million in gold. Further, the amendments permitted Reserve Banks to issue Federal Reserve notes directly against gold collateral, as Warburg had long advocated. The 1917 amendments, he believed, enabled the system to mobilize the nation's gold and meet the unprecedented demands of war finance. Thanks to the 1917 legislation, the system enjoyed unparalleled gold strength.

In the fall of 1917, Warburg proposed to follow the European example of passing on wartime securities issues to assure that such issues would serve the public interest. At McAdoo's invitation the board reviewed proposals submitted by businesses and local governments. With Warburg in the chair, 46 meetings were held to review 361 applications from January 12 to mid May 1918. The new issues sought approval for an amount of $219.8 million, but the committee approved only $154.1 million. When the board found the purpose acceptable, the applicant received notification that the bond issue was "not incompatible with the interests of the United States." Public offerings had to include the statement that approval was unrelated to "merits, security, or legality in any respect."

The War Finance Corporation Act of April 5, 1918, which gave the approval committee legal standing, continued its voluntary approach, relying on patriotism for cooperation. By then, only three of the seven committee members came from the Reserve Board, and the president appointed all seven, subject to Senate confirmation.

Senator Owen succeeded in his goal of keeping Warburg out of the picture because of his German brothers. Hamlin was made chairman. Warburg was furious at not being named. Soon after the Armistice, the committee disbanded—a mistake, in Warburg's opinion. Warburg also bore a large responsibility for shaping the concept of the War Finance Corporation (WFC), with Governor Harding the only Reserve Board member to serve as a WFC director. Funded by the Treasury to make long-term loans otherwise unavailable, the WFC continued to make new loans until 1924, and the government used it to relieve postwar agricultural distress.

In 1917 Warburg advised McAdoo to borrow more than $2 billion in the Treasury's first wartime loan ("Liberty Loan"), whereas other financiers thought $1 billion a more likely limit. The secretary of the Treasury succeeded with a $2 billion loan. On numerous occasions, Warburg accepted invitations to speak in connection with loan drives. In April 1918 he told his audience, "Save and subscribe to save our country—that must be our slogan." Americans had "a national and humane duty" to save wherever they could, because saving furthered the war effort and helped avoid inflation. On April 15, 1919, Warburg called upon the clergy of Baltimore to "impress upon the masses the true and deep meaning of thrift," in connection with the Liberty Loan drive. Thrift offered the "fundamental remedy for our economic ills."

Warburg, "deeply and genuinely interested" in his work on the board, wrote to Wilson on May 27, 1918, that he considered it only "half done." His term was due to expire on August 9, 1918. The letter pointed out that his renomination might exacerbate the animosity to Americans of German descent and subject the board to relentless attack. Hamlin thought the "equivocal letter" a great mistake, as otherwise the president would have found it difficult not to reappoint him. Schiff thought the letter read as if it left Wilson with no choice. Wilson delayed a reply until August 9: "I read between the lines . . . that you will yourself feel more at ease if you are free to serve in other ways."

Hamlin recorded that Warburg was "evidently bitterly disappointed": he thought that if nominated, he would be confirmed. Many said Warburg carried a particularly bitter feeling for Senator Owen. The *Nation* considered it to the "lasting discredit" of Wilson that he consented to Warburg's withdrawal, attributing it to jealousy of certain highly placed men more than to the German connection.

Warburg resumed his social and business involvements with the Old World after he left the Fed-

Letter from President Woodrow Wilson requesting Warburg's services on the Federal Reserve Board (Paul M. Warburg, The Federal Reserve System: Its Origins and Growth, *1930)*

eral Reserve Board. He made his first postwar trip in the summer of 1919. That October he accepted an invitation to participate in a seven-member Amsterdam economic conference. Together with John Maynard Keynes, he formulated a memorandum later signed by leading Europeans and Americans, including William Howard Taft, Herbert Hoover, Andrew Mellon, and J. P. Morgan, Jr. They issued a call for all countries to assist one another to provide long-term foreign credits to restore production and to keep diplomacy and international trade free from government restrictions.

Warburg deemed uncertain exchange rates and depreciating currencies a curse. In February 1920 he argued against tinkering with foreign exchanges before halting inflation. He saw the world heading to economic and social disaster. Only "individual effort and hard work" could save the situation.

Regarding gold policy, Warburg had correctly foreseen in November 1916 that the concentration of gold in central bank reserves would continue after the war. In December 1918 he recommended a policy of gradual deflation and continued concentration of gold, so as to make it available to settle international balances and serve as the basis for an elastic currency. Trade and economic growth would suffer, he told the Pan-American Financial Conference in January 1920, until the world reestablished stable exchange rates via a gold standard.

In a January 1922 talk Warburg revealed that each of the three visits he had made to Europe since the Armistice had left him "in a more depressed state of mind." As a consequence of nationalism and petty party politics, "the first three postwar years had been marked by waste and misery." Governments showed no awareness of the dire consequences of huge armament outlays, unbalanced budgets, inflationary financing, and impossible reparations demands.

In 1921 the directors of the Federal Reserve Bank of New York selected Warburg to represent the second district on the Federal Advisory Council (FAC). He was elected vice-president of the FAC in 1921, 1922, and 1923 and president in 1924 and 1925. The FAC, composed of one banker from each of the 12 Federal Reserve districts, was made part of the system at the suggestion of Wilson, who had disappointed the bankers by not giving them control of the Federal Reserve Board. McAdoo viewed the FAC as "a helpful adjunct to the Board," but it never became a significant element in the system and did not have any notable effect on it.

In May 1921, Warburg was one of four FAC members who stated that the board did not operate under any moral obligation to continue the wartime arrangement of quoting a lower rediscount rate for Treasury-bond-secured collateral than for other types. Warburg also served on a special committee to seek the reappointment of Federal Reserve governor William Harding, whose term expired in August 1922. He met several times with President Warren Harding to caution him that failure to reappoint William Harding might inflict irreparable harm to the system. The governor had served his country faithfully and courageously, Warburg insisted. The president refused to heed the advice and named Daniel R. Crissinger, a hometown Ohio crony who had little banking experience and none in international finance.

Political interference with the Federal Reserve System proved a matter of great anxiety to Warburg over the years. In November 1923 the FAC expressed its concern over the appointment of the Class C directors, the government-appointed directors to the Reserve Banks. Political pressure on the board regarding them was "apt to injure the System and to undermine its high standards."

Warburg never ceased thinking about the Federal Reserve System, expressing his views in speeches and letters. A few days after leaving the board he told the New York Times that the system constituted "our chief line of financial defense. At present it appears impregnable." Privately, Warburg wrote to Delano on July 30, 1919, "I have a strong feeling as if the Board is gradually slipping back and losing prestige. . . . Of course [t]hey cannot assert an independent policy until government borrowing is well out of the way; but even granting that, . . . they might have shown some punch." In January 1922 in a Boston talk he expressed regret that the board had not emancipated itself sooner from Treasury dominion, but he also acknowledged the great difficulty of attempting it. At the same time he denounced "malicious slander" spread by politicians and demagogues about the system's administration. He recalled the system's vital wartime services and claimed it had been "of almost equal benefit" to the country "in liquidating the War's aftermath. Without that protection by the System, the country would have become the prey of the worst panic it ever witnessed."

As of the spring of 1927, Warburg thought that the system "has been functioning admirably and . . . has surpassed all expectations." Federal Reserve policy in 1927 was appropriate: lowering the rediscount rate to arrest the gold flow to the United States and "to give the rest of the world the fullest advantage of our affluence insofar as possible without detriment to our own interests." However, on March 7, 1929, he openly deplored the system's loss of control over the American money market. The Fed had taken "a position of world leadership" in lowering rediscount rates during the 1927 recession but lost the leadership within a year by not raising rates in the face of a stock market run riot. Rediscount rates—"grotesquely impotent and out of line"—threatened the regular business of the country because speculation absorbed so much credit. He cautioned that "if orgies of unrestrained speculation are permitted to spread too far, however, the ultimate collapse is certain not only to affect the speculators themselves, but also to bring about a general depression involving the entire country." The market value of 90 leading stocks had nearly doubled in just two years, "an accretion, in the majority of cases, quite unrelated to respective increases in plant, property or earning power."

London hailed his call for federal reserve leadership and severe comments on speculation. A *New York Times* editorial praised his statement as "a breath of fresh air." In the stock market, a brief reaction ensued, followed by a surge to record highs in the next six months.

On March 8, 1929, Warburg wrote to Secretary of the Treasury Andrew Mellon that the Federal Reserve System as then organized and functioning "is neither safe nor efficient." He recommended that government make the board and the Reserve Banks cooperative organs. A few weeks later he warned Hamlin that "a Federal Reserve System that wants to create sunshine all the time is a most dangerous institution." Hamlin replied that deflating the stock market by raising discount rates would lead to a worse deflation than in 1920.

In April 1930 the Macmillan Company published Warburg's *The Federal Reserve System: Its Origin and Growth* in 1,750 pages. The appearance of Glass's version of Federal Reserve history, *An Adventure in Constructive Finance*, prompted Warburg to pick up the project he had contemplated eight years earlier. He had written the first draft of volume 1 early in 1927 and completed most of it in the spring of 1928. He devoted volume 1 to his recollections of the origins of the system and included many letters and memoranda. The first part of volume 2 contained a reprint of his earlier *Essays in Banking Reform in the United States*, with an additional paper of April 1908 inadvertently omitted in the *Essays*. The second part consisted of a selection of articles and addresses from the time he joined the Board in 1914 to 1924.

Warburg continued to push the use of acceptances after leaving the Board. From 1919 to 1923 he served as a leader of the American Acceptance Council, first as chairman of the executive committee and then as president. At its organizational meeting in January 1919 he hailed the future of acceptances in the United States as "extremely bright." He viewed the council as supplementing the Fed's work in the area, serving as a link between the system and the business and banking communities. In 1920 he insisted that "a wide market must be our aim." "American acceptance banking," he wrote early in 1922, "has now grown to full manhood." He hailed the May 1922 liberalization of the board's 1915 acceptance regulation. A *Harvard*

Business Review article in April 1923 urged major banks to increase their acceptance activity. Warburg insisted that "only through a country-wide free use" of prime bankers acceptances could there be "genuine fluidity of money and credit of the highest type." That also enhanced the effectiveness of the Fed, he argued.

He got the Federal Advisory Council to recommend in May 1924 that the Federal Reserve Board give the most liberal interpretation of the act with respect to acceptances. British competition at the time threatened to monopolize the field.

In the spring of 1927 Warburg deplored the fact that bankers' acceptances were not the main link between the system and the commercial banks; the open market rate for acceptances had not gained "an adequate influence over the money market." However, he satisfied himself by 1929 that America had permanently established its position as an acceptance banker. But the United States had not developed "an adequate amount of two-named paper," he complained in February 1931. His hope of market centers all over the country failed to develop. Most of the activity centered in New York and San Francisco as late as the 1970s.

Another disappointment involved the growing amount of call loans in the 1920s. Warburg insisted that the accumulation of the nation's idle money in stock exchange loans posed a dangerous weakness of the banking machinery. The Federal Reserve Act had not emancipated the United States from all loans as a reservoir of surplus funds. He deeply regretted that important discount markets had not developed away from Wall Street and that funds were more concentrated on the Stock Exchange than before 1913.

Characteristically, Warburg did not limit himself to preaching the virtues of acceptances. In the spring of 1919 he began to contemplate a new type of institution in New York that would promote and finance overseas trade. It would secure for the dollar acceptance a leading position in world markets and free American traders from dependence on foreign credits. The International Acceptance Bank (IAB) received a New York charter and a special license from the Federal Reserve Board in April 1921. Leading European banks that had been correspondents of the Warburg bank in Hamburg became shareholders, as did such major American banks as the First National Bank of Boston, First National Bank of Chicago, Cleveland Trust Company,

Wells Fargo Nevada National Bank of San Francisco, First National Bank of Los Angeles, First National Bank of St. Louis, Corn Exchange Bank of New York, New York Trust Company, and Kuhn, Loeb. Total capital of IAB's American bank shareholders came to $276 million, and its foreign bank holders (including the London Rothschilds) pitched in another $271 million. IAB took only foreign deposits, and actively financed American exports and imports, trade between foreign countries, and warehoused staples. The IAB took over the foreign credit business of a New York subsidiary of the First National of Boston as well as the foreign exchange department of Huth & Company on Wall Street. The fifty-three-year-old Warburg was chairman; his son James was vice-president and secretary.

IAB met with success from the start. In the early years, troubled conditions overseas induced a policy of caution. IAB drew on the advice and participation of its foreign shareholding banks. To reduce risk it distributed credits over many commodities and countries. The IAB opened with a staff of some 35; by December 1923 there were 187, and six years later, 302. Average annual net earnings hovered around $1 million in 1922 and 1923, $1.8 million in 1924 and 1925, and more than $2.1 million in 1926, 1927, and 1928.

In 1930 the daily average amount of IAB's acceptances outstanding totaled $90 million, compared with $71 million in 1929, $40 million in 1926, and $19 million in 1922. It extended credits to some 36 countries on more than 32 commodities in the late 1920s. Acceptance commissions declined from around 2 percent in 1925 and 1926 to 1.43 percent in 1927 and 1.25 percent in 1928. Warburg deplored that "unfortunate development." Commissions had fallen to a level "hardly in keeping with good banking practice and a conservative appreciation of the risks involved in acceptance banking." Meanwhile, Warburg might have derived satisfaction from the growing volume of acceptances. The U.S. total reached $820 million in 1924 and peaked at $1,732 million in 1929. Acceptances overtook commercial paper volume by September 1926 and had grown almost three times as great by 1929.

In March 1926, IAB organized the International Acceptance Securities and Trust Company (renamed International Acceptance Trust Company in January 1928) to round out its activities. The next month that subsidiary handled its first public issue,

$5 million of notes of the city of Hamburg. By 1928 it had originated 22 issues totaling $300 million and had participated in a large number of selling syndicates as well.

Near the end of World War I, Warburg rejoiced that "a democratic Germany has come at last and it has come to stay." He wrote to House on October 17, 1918, that "the chastening defeat will bring about a healthy rejuvenation." A major motive in establishing the IAB was to provide a conduit for the family bank in Hamburg, to aid in reconstruction of Germany. IAB's most intimate relationship was with M. M. Warburg & Company. Its American connection enabled it to recover its standing. In 1923 it helped set up the Hamburger Bank, the first German institution granted a dollar credit by the IAB. Warburg participated in the discussions for stabilizing the mark after the 1923 hyperinflation, and in reparations negotiations. That resulted in the IAB being named American agent of the Reichsbank and its newly created subsidiary, Gold Discount Bank, and brought the Warburgs into close contact with Dr. Hjalmar Schacht.

In 1924 IAB played an important role, together with several other institutions, in organizing the American and Continental Corporation. It sought to tide over some German industries with intermediate-term credits not available elsewhere.

IAB's capital reached more than $21 million in less than eight years. While Warburg expressed pride in IAB's pioneering role and profitability for several years, he contemplated the need to diversify, to move beyond IAB's heavy involvement in foreign lending. After exploring several possibilities, on March 7, 1929, IAB merged its shares with those of the Manhattan Company, the holding company that owned the venerable Bank of Manhattan Company, founded a year after the family bank in Hamburg. As an alternative to merger, IAB Trust Company would have had to develop domestic business aggressively, while Manhattan Bank would have had to enlarge greatly its recent foreign department and to move into security distribution. The combination reflected the tendency to vertical integration then prevailing in banking as in business, as well as the then irresistible trend toward "departmental banking," as Warburg called it.

The two organizations complemented each other admirably, in Warburg's view, to form a "happy union." By combining, they eliminated duplication and enhanced efficiency by concentrating domestic activities in the Manhattan Bank and foreign in IAB. Warburg was named associate chairman of the Manhattan Company. On March 9, 1929, the company formed a new entity, International Manhattan Company, Inc., to handle securities distribution for the two banks. It operated successfully, but the bank discontinued it in December 1931, at a time when other banks also moved to drop their securities affiliates.

IAB links with the Hamburg family bank were reinforced with the establishment of Warburg & Company Amsterdam in 1929. The Dutch firm represented the two as well as International Manhattan Company. Exuberant Max Warburg's firm borrowed heavily in the United States, especially from IAB. Max ignored Paul's advice to retrench.

In just a few days in late December 1930, in the wake of the collapse of Austria's largest bank and investor concerns about Central European economies, the Hamburg bank faced calls to repay 80 percent of its foreign deposits and half of its domestic deposits. Paul and Felix Warburg came to its rescue in New York. They considered the rapid success of IAB to be largely due to the good will developed by the ancestral bank in Hamburg. Paul wrote to his son on June 16, 1931: "What good does money do us if we lose our good name and desert those we love—even though they acted like idiots." Concerning Max, he wrote, "I love him dearly and pity him from the bottom of my heart." Over half of Paul's already severely shrunken fortune went to the Hamburg rescue.

The sixty-one-year-old Warburg became chairman of the board of Manhattan Company on December 10, 1929. He occupied the position until his death. Total capital of the Manhattan Company soared from $45 million at the end of 1928 to $139 million a year later. It declined to $83.5 million by the end of 1931 as controlled institutions wrote down their value. The Manhattan Company greatly benefited from Warburg's "long experience and connection with large and important financial interests" here and abroad, a memorial resolution noted.

Warburg's business career and his writings reflected an ongoing interest in international economic and financial relations and the U.S. role therein. One reason for his advocacy of thoroughgoing reform was his desire to see the United States become the world's financial center. Until reorganization of the Federal Reserve system, he told the American Bankers Association convention in 1911, America could not be on a par with European nations as a center of international finance. In 1916 he foresaw that "it is an absolute necessity for the United States to take a very important share in financing the world." In a May 1919 talk to the Bond Club of New York he suggested that investment trusts might be the vehicle to develop a market for foreign securities in order "to keep American exports moving and the world's balance sheet reasonably square." In January 1930 he (wrongly) expected that, following the ratification of the Young plan of reparations, the United States would soon again occupy the role of world banker that it had held in the mid 1920s, by reopening its markets for long-term foreign issues. In June 1931 he hailed the Hoover moratorium on international debts as possibly marking the turning point in the economic disorganization threatening the world. In fact, however, the nations continued to march toward the abyss.

Overall, Warburg had developed the reputation of a pessimist. "Here comes old Gloomy Gus! " someone is said to have shouted as Warburg entered the Century Country Club in 1928. He agreed with his son's description of him as "a sad optimist."

In less than a dozen years after his arrival in New York, Warburg became involved in many philanthropic organizations. By 1914 he was vice-president of the American Association for Labor Legislation, the Academy of Political Science, and the Chamber of Commerce of the State of New York. He served as treasurer of the Institute of Musical Art founded by his brother-in-law, James Loeb (which became the Juilliard School in 1927), the New York Foundation, the National Employment Exchange, the Solomon and Betty Loeb Home for Convalescents, and the New York Child Labor Committee. He sat on the boards of the National Child Labor Committee (of which he was a charter member), New York School of Philanthropy, the Community Organization Society, the Mt. Sinai Hospital in New York, and the New York Knapp Memorial Eye Hospital. When appointed a Federal Reserve member in 1914, he resigned from all of his trusteeships and directorships.

After leaving the Federal Reserve Board, Warburg resumed his various interests. His associations at the time of death included the boards of Tuskegee Institute, Juilliard, Dropsie College for Hebrew and Cognate Learning in Philadelphia, Institute of Economics (after 1927, the Brookings Institution) in Washington, New York Foundation, and the National Child Labor Committee. He devoted himself to the Henry Street Settlement and its founder, Lillian Wald, and was a director of the Council on Foreign Relations from the beginning. In April 1929, he was named a councillor of the National Industrial Conference Board (together with Calvin Coolidge).

Among his outside business board directorships were the Farmers Loan and Trust Company in New York, First National Bank in Boston, Baltimore & Ohio Railroad, Union Pacific Railroad, Western Union, American I.G. Chemical Corporation, and Agfa Ansco. From 1920 until his death he remained on the Economic Policy Commission of the American Bankers Association, and served as its vice-chairman and chairman. He belonged to the Chamber of Commerce of the United States, the Chamber of Commerce of the State of New York, the Merchants Association of New York, the Economic Club, and many social clubs.

Warburg worked for the strengthening of cultural relations between his native and adopted countries in education and the arts. Toward that end he was a founder-member of the Carl Schurz Memorial Foundation and served as its treasurer from May 1930 until his death. He made donations to the library in Hamburg founded by his family, to the college hall at Heidelberg University known as the American House, and to the Academy of Political Science in Berlin.

Warburg received several honorary degrees. In June 1919, New York University awarded him the Doctor of Commercial Science degree. In July 1926, Heidelberg recognized his work in international banking and finance with a Doctor of Political Science degree. In April 1931, Occidental College honored him with a Doctor of Law degree for his work in the financial and economic development of the United States.

Like his father before him, Warburg had the pleasure of watching his son's progress. James Warburg joined the IAB at its formation, and rose from vice-president of the IAB in January 1929 to president of the International Manhattan Company in March 1929, vice-chairman of IAB in January 1930, and IAB president in December 1931. Eleven days after his father's death, the Manhattan Company named James vice-chairman.

The Paul Warburg of 1914, "given to smiling and causing smiles" as B. C. Forbes reported, had changed. Mental depression and lassitude, probably due to Max's letting him down, according to James, rather than to the great monetary loss involved, marked his last months.

After several weeks in a coma, Warburg died on January 24, 1932. His close friend Dr. Cyrus Adler, president of the Jewish Theological Seminary and of Dropsie, officiated at the funeral attended only by family members. At the time of his death, bankers estimated the size of Warburg's estate to be anywhere from $50 million to $150 million. When it was settled in 1937, it turned out to be just more than $2.5 million. After Warburg's wife, Nina, died, the estate was to go to their son and daughter, who had already received almost $3 million in shares from Warburg in 1922. The will also instructed his family to make charitable donations in accordance with his known wishes and views. Nina Warburg died January 21, 1946. Her will provided for a Paul M. Warburg professorship at Harvard's Graduate School of Business in recognition of Warburg's lifelong interest in central banking.

Until the end Warburg continued to concern himself with the present and future of the system he had helped to establish. He had devoted the best part of his life to a solution of America's banking problems, he wrote in January 1930. He might have drawn satisfaction from such praise as Sir Ernst Cassel's. The eminent financier wrote from London on September 18, 1918: "Your name will always be associated with the formation and successful working of the greatest banking institution of the world." Warburg chose as his motto *in serviendo consumor* (to serve the consumer). His career reflected a recognition of the obligations that wealth brought. Villiard praised his "unsurpassable example of public service."

Publications:

The Discount System in Europe (Washington, D.C.: U.S. Government Printing Office, 1910);

The Federal Reserve System: Its Origin and Growth, 2 volumes (New York: Macmillan, 1930).

References:

David Farrer, *The Warburgs* (New York: Stein & Day, 1975);

Harold Kellock, "Warburg, the Revolutionist," *Century*, 90 (May 1915): 79-86;

Edward Rosenbaum and Ari Sherman, *M. M. Warburg & Company 1798-1938* (New York: Holmes & Meier, 1979);

James P. Warburg, *The Long Road Home* (Garden City, N.Y.: Doubleday, 1964).

Archives:
The papers of Paul M. Warburg are at Yale University Library.

Clark A. Warburton

(January 27, 1896 - September 18, 1979)

by John B. Davis

Marquette University

CAREER: U.S. Army (1917-1919); lecturer, University of Allahabad, India (1921-1924); instructor, Rice Institute [later Rice University] (1925-1928); associate professor, Emory University (1929-1932); member, Brookings Institution (1932-1934); researcher, chief administrator, Banking and Business Section, Division of Research and Statistics, Federal Deposit Insurance Corporation (1934-1966).

Clark Abram Warburton, economist, educator, and public administrator, was the author of more than 50 scholarly articles concerning the nature of fiscal and monetary policy in the United States. His practical experience came from working for more than three decades in the Federal Deposit Insurance Corporation, where he developed his life-long interest in the relationship of banking and monetary policy to business fluctuations. Beginning in the Great Depression of the 1930s, Warburton entered into a study of the role of the money supply in episodes of depression and inflation. That ultimately led him to conclude that monetary authorities in the United States had consistently failed to provide sufficient stability, at an appropriate rate of growth, in the supply of money available to the nation's people and its business enterprises. In those conclusions, Warburton was later credited for pioneering the Quantity Theory of Money and cited as a forerunner of the economist Milton Friedman.

Warburton was born in Shady Cove in upstate New York on January 27, 1896, the son of Melvin Eugene Warburton, a clergyman, and Florence Vough Warburton. He originally enrolled at Houghton College in Houghton, New York, in 1915, but with the U.S. entry into World War I he left school in 1917 to join the American Expeditionary Forces. After serving two years in France from 1918 to 1919, Warburton returned to the United States to attend Cornell University in Ithaca, New York, where he received his B.A. in 1921.

Warburton took his first academic position as a lecturer in economics at the University of Allahabad in Allahabad, India, where he taught until 1924. In his final two years in India he served as the managing editor of the *Indian Journal of Economics* and thus obtained an acquaintance with the standards and practices of scholarly publishing. He returned to the United States in 1925 to take a position as an instructor in economics at Rice Institute (later known as Rice University) in Houston, Texas, and he remained at Rice until 1928, when he received an M.A. from Cornell. He married Amber Arthun on July 5, 1929, and accepted a position as associate professor of economics at Emory University in Atlanta, Georgia. In 1932 Warburton received his Ph.D. from Columbia University. His dissertation, *The Economic Results of Prohibition*, was published by Columbia University Press that same year.

Warburton did not return to academia but instead elected to devote his time and efforts to economic and financial research. He took a position in 1932 as a member of the research staff at the nonprofit Brookings Institution in Washington, D.C. There he was among the first economists to work on the newly conceived national income accounts, which summed total annual economic activity. In 1934 Warburton left the Brookings Institution to join the recently established Federal Deposit Insurance Corporation (FDIC). As a result of the bank failures and national financial panic of the early 1930s, the FDIC had been created by a provision of the Glass-Steagall Act of June 1933 to guarantee small deposits in the banking system. Banks paid the cost of the insurance in the form of a fee based on the size of their deposits. Thus, first as a researcher and then later as chief of the Banking and Business Section of the Division of Research and Statistics, Warburton acquired firsthand knowledge of commercial banking operations in a fashion never before enjoyed by students of the American financial system. He remained at the FDIC until he retired from government service in 1966.

Upon retirement Warburton briefly was made a visiting professor of economics at the University of California at Davis through the efforts of Professor Thomas Mayer. In poor health, which prevented him from assuming a full teaching load, he conducted small weekly seminars for a few students investigating economic history (notably Thomas F. Cargill). Though he had often encountered frustration from an economics profession less concerned with monetary phenomena than with Keynesian expenditure concepts, Warburton lived to see his ideas gain broad acceptance among an emerging monetarist school of economics. He died at eighty-three on September 18, 1979, in Fairfax, Virginia.

Along with Carl Snyder, Lionel Edie, Lauchlin Currie, James Angell, and Arthur Marget, Warburton was recognized by 1989 as one of the pioneering voices of monetarism—the doctrine stating that changes in the quantity of money are the dominant independent determinant of cyclical changes in economic activity. His special talent involved empirical investigation into the relationship between money and economic activity, and it was on that basis that he anticipated many of the conclusions of later monetarists. However, despite his painstakingly careful examination of economic data, and because he did his most extensive publishing during the height of the Keynesian revolution in the 1940s and 1950s, his work went largely unappreciated until the 1960s, when, through the leadership of Friedman, monetarism received attention from large numbers of economists. Warburton's professional recognition was thus belated, and the full nature of his contribution to an understanding of monetary phenomena has accordingly only begun to gain the notice it will likely receive in future years.

Warburton first developed his understanding of the relationship between the quantity of money in the economy and economic activity as a result of research carried out at the FDIC in the 1930s to determine the required insurance premium for bank deposits. He initially had to develop a reasonably detailed analysis of the regional distribution of bank failures and deposit contractions over the period from 1930 to 1935. He also needed to carry out a thorough evaluation of Federal Reserve operations during the same period. The results of those studies transformed Warburton's views. Despite his earlier adherence to a real theory of the business cycle, whereby investment and production decisions accounted for economic fluctuations, Warburton came to believe that money and monetary policy played the fundamental role in determining the level of economic activity.

Warburton accordingly went on to challenge Keynesianism, which was dominant at the time not so much in terms of its logical consistency as in terms of its empirical relevance. By the early 1940s, after having comprehensively examined the annual tabulations of bank deposits from 1920 to 1935 from country to country, he had concluded that money quantity was indisputably the central factor in the Great Depression downturn. By the late 1940s and early 1950s he felt confident in blaming the Federal Reserve and "an erratic money supply as the chief originating factor in business recessions and not merely an intensifying force in the case of severe depressions." Indeed, his 1951 paper, "The Misplaced Emphasis in Contemporary Business Fluctuations Theory"—perhaps his best known and often considered his single most important contribution to economic thought—argued against the view of Keynes and his followers that an imbalance in the savings-investment relationship alone provided a sufficient explanation of business fluctuations, precisely because of a conviction that the historical record placed the chief blame for business fluctuations on the discretionary monetary policy of the Federal Reserve.

Warburton's work has influenced present-day monetarists in many respects. Most important, in the course of his writings he developed an empirically useful version of the Quantity Theory of Money, distinguishing between the long-run or equilibrium version of the theory and the short-run or disequilibrium version. Adapting Irving Fisher's Equation of Exchange, which related an economy's volume of money and velocity to output and prices, Warburton tested the relationship between money and prices across key periods in American economic history. In addition, he also provided evidence that the lag in the effect of monetary policy was both long and variable, which led him to conclude that a discretionary monetary policy was undependable and that the most appropriate strategy for the monetary authority to pursue was that of a steady growth in the money supply. Finally, Warburton also argued that because the Keynesians had misjudged the role of the Federal Reserve in the Great Depression by emphasizing the use of interest rates as a guide to monetary policy, they were insufficiently sensitive to the potentially inflationary effects of deficit fiscal policies.

In 1953 Warburton abruptly suspended his studies and his professional activities, apparently because of pressure exerted by the Department of the Treasury after the Eisenhower administration came into office to restrict independent research by individuals at the FDIC. He resumed his research after 1962, when he was briefly employed by the House Banking and Currency Committee. The development of new interest in monetary theory among professional economists, combined with the recognition by the early 1960s that many economists had neglected the seriousness of the problem of inflation, likely stimulated the continuation of his work.

By the early 1960s economic historians had begun to draw attention to Warburton's work. In the preface to their monumental *A Monetary History of the United States, 1867-1960* (1963), Friedman and Anna J. Schwartz acknowledged Warburton's anticipation of many of their ideas concerning the history of monetary policy and the quantity theory of money as well as his early monetarist interpretation of the Great Depression. More recently, Cargill has brought Warburton to the attention of historians of economic thought, generating debates over the respective contributions of the forerunners of contemporary monetarism. Finally, in 1966 the Johns Hopkins Press collected and published many of Warburton's more important post-World War II papers as *Depression, Inflation, and Monetary Policy, 1945-1953*.

That Warburton failed to have a significant impact upon his colleagues during his most active years as an economist can best be explained by his intellectual isolation in the immediate postwar period. Keynesian economics was dominant in the period from the end of the war until the early 1960s, and Warburton found himself devoting more space to arguing against the Keynesian focus than to presenting the results of his own research. Further, Warburton's absence from academia left him without the resources and connections available to economists in universities.

Nonetheless, Warburton's talent as an empirically minded economist has guaranteed him a place in the history of economic thought. With the relatively recent emergence of sophisticated econometric tools, Warburton's conclusions have gained increased plausibility. Many economists now regard money quantity as an important variable in the economy, and few believe any longer that increases in output and employment can occur unattended by inflation.

Selected Publications:

"The Misplaced Emphasis in Contemporary Business Fluctuation Theory," in *Readings in Monetary Theory* (Philadelphia: Blackiston, 1951);

Depression, Inflation, and Monetary Policy: Selected Papers, 1945-1953 (Baltimore: Johns Hopkins University Press, 1966).

References:

Michael D. Bordo and Anna J. Schwartz, "Clark Warburton: Pioneer Monetarist," *Journal of Monetary Economics*, 5 (1979): 43-65;

Thomas F. Cargill, "Clark Warburton and the Development of Monetarism since the Great Depression," *History of Political Economy*, 11 (Fall 1979): 425-449;

Cargill, "A Tribute to Clark Warburton, 1896-1979," *Journal of Money, Credit, and Banking*, 13 (February 1981): 89-93;

Milton Friedman and Schwartz, *A Monetary History of the United States, 1867-1960*. (Princeton: Princeton University Press, 1963).

War Finance Corporation

by Gary M. Pecquet

Southwest Texas State University

The War Finance Corporation (WFC) was a federally owned and operated credit agency established during World War I to provide government credit to essential wartime industries. It subsequently provided financial loan assistance to export industries and distressed farmers. It was liquidated from 1925 to 1929 but was resurrected in 1932 under the name Reconstruction Finance Corporation.

During the brief involvement of the United States in World War I, Congress created several new regulatory agencies and public corporations. The intellectual leadership of the Progressive Era opposed laissez-faire government and consistently looked toward new laws and institutions to solve the problems of society. The wartime emergency served as a catalyst for the creation of agencies including the War Industries Board, the Shipping Board, the Emergency Relief Corporation, the Food and Fuel Administration, the Housing Corporation, the Grain Corporation, and the National War Labor Board. Those agencies established a wartime command economy in which the government regulated prices and wages, promoted unions, and enforced the standardization of certain products. War contracts were made on a cost-plus basis rather than through competitive bidding.

The practices of the war agencies produced market distortions that spilled over into the credit markets. Certain industries, considered essential to war mobilization (such as lumber, coal mining, public utilities, and certain manufacturers), simply could not raise funds on the private capital markets. Treasury Secretary William Gibbs McAdoo recommended the establishment of a government lending agency to remedy the problem. On April 5, 1918, Congress created the War Finance Corporation to achieve that aim, and on May 20 (less than six months before the armistice) the WFC began operations.

Eugene Meyer, chairman of the War Finance Corporation from 1918 until the suspension of the corporation's operations in 1920 and from its restoration in 1921 until its final dissolution in 1929 (courtesy of Underwood & Underwood)

The WFC was organized along lines similar to other temporary public corporations. The Treasury purchased $500 million worth of stock to supply it with its operating funds. Although the government empowered the corporation to lend directly to firms, ordinarily it was supposed to lend to the financial institutions that served the critical industries.

The WFC could also purchase government securities to stabilize interest rates. Before the war J. P. Morgan & Company privately attended to that task, and much later the Federal Reserve System provided stability to the government bond markets through its Federal Open Market Committee (the early Fed did not coordinate its dealings in government securities, however).

Eugene Meyer, a prewar associate of Bernard Baruch, became the first director of the WFC. During the war the WFC lent $71 million to a variety of concerns, including public utilities, power plants, mining and chemical companies, railroads, and banking institutions. After the wartime mission ended, Director Meyer sought to preserve the corporation by adopting a new "rescue mission." In March 1919 Congress authorized the WFC to finance American exports, thereby assisting the industries that were particularly distressed during the restoration of peacetime trading patterns.

The 1919 law soon expired, and Meyer resigned his position in 1920, but he pleaded before congressional committees for the restoration of the WFC. Congress responded by directing the secretary of the Treasury to refund the WFC once more, this time to finance export loans. President Woodrow Wilson vetoed the measure, but Congress overrode the veto. On March 14, 1921, the Senate reconfirmed Meyer as director of the WFC. Between 1921 and 1924 Congress enlisted the WFC in a new relief mission—to provide assistance to distressed farmers. Farm prices had fallen substantially below their wartime levels. Moreover, the agricultural sector lagged behind the manufacturing industries throughout the 1920s.

In January 1925 the WFC actually entered liquidation. It continued to phase out its operations until its final demise in 1929. Throughout its active life it lent $300 million to war industries, $100 million to help finance exports, and another $300 million to support distressed farmers. During that time the WFC seemed to die several times. Its apparent final demise in 1929 proved to be another false alarm. That year marked the beginning of the Great Depression.

The Great Depression led to another relief mission, which required the revival of the WFC. In an October 4, 1931, meeting, bankers unanimously demanded the reestablishment of the corporation to stabilize the economy. President Herbert Hoover initially preferred to establish a private credit corporation to achieve the same end, but in November 1931 he accepted the advice of the bankers and asked Meyer once again to revive the WFC. Meyer drafted new legislation, which Congress adopted in January 1932. The new organization had a similar structure and many of the same personnel as the old WFC. Its name was changed, however, to the Reconstruction Finance Corporation (RFC).

Economist Robert Higgs noted how closely the RFC was patterned after the old WFC. Section 6 of the RFC Act merely revised a portion of the WFC Act by inserting the words "Reconstruction Finance Corporation" where "War Finance Corporation" had been. The new RFC continued the same missions as the WFC and greatly expanded their scope. The RFC also added many new functions during the New Deal and World War II. It remained in operation until 1954.

References:

Robert Higgs, *Crisis and Leviathan: Critical Episodes in the Growth of American Government* (Oxford & New York: Oxford University Press, 1987);

James Stuart Olson, *Herbert Hoover and the Reconstruction Finance Corporation, 1931-1933* (Ames: Iowa State University Press, 1977);

Leonard Peikoff, *The Ominous Parallels: The End of Freedom in America* (New York: Stein & Day, 1982);

Paul Studenski and Herman E. Krooss, *Financial History of the United States: Fiscal, Monetary, Banking, and Tariff, Including Financial Administration and State and Local Finance*, second edition (New York: McGraw-Hill, 1963).

Western Banker

by Robert J. Chandler

Wells Fargo Bank

The *Western Banker*, founded in San Francisco in 1908, is the oldest banking journal in the West. It documents changes in nearly a century of western finance. Originally titled *Coast Banker*, the monthly became the *Western Banker* in 1951. It is exceptionally useful for the period from 1908 to 1930.

Founder and editor George Porter Edwards was a lifelong publicist. Born in 1868 into a family living in Dunkirk, New York, he attended schools in Buffalo and became sports editor of the *New York Sun*. In 1900 he began a financial journal in Cleveland, Ohio, started another in 1902 in Pittsburgh, Pennsylvania, and in 1906 moved to California. The Panic of 1907 unsettled the financial world, closing some state and private banks but no national banks. Out of the turmoil came California's progressive Bank Act of 1909 and two publications. The law replaced the weak Bank Commission with a strong superintendent and permitted departmental banking and branch offices. The first publication was Edwards's *Coast Banker*, which appeared in October 1908. In 1909 H. D. Walker brought out the second, *Walker's Manual of California Securities and Directory of Directors*. It, too, remains in publication.

Edwards called for a "public awakening" to change a "wrong attitude," mostly negative, toward banks and corporations. "The *Coast Banker* is published solely for the purpose of disseminating banking news among bankers," began Edwards, "and to give owners of money and prospective investors correct information concerning securities of corporations that are either primarily Pacific Coast corporations or are dealt in freely on the Coast." He emphasized that "The *Coast Banker* will stand first, last, and for all time for the interests of the Pacific Coast states." In September 1911 he refined his philosophy. The journal sought "to boost the Pacific coast and slope as a whole and to boost the

men and institutions who are making that territory the great empire it is."

At first, Edwards had a narrow geographic vision. In October 1908 he wrote, "The territory which it serves directly is Alaska, Arizona, California, Idaho, Montana, Oregon, Washington, Territory of New Mexico, and the Mexican Province of Lower California." In practice, the *Banker* said little about Mexico, but by 1913 also regularly covered Colorado, Hawaii, Nevada, Utah, and Wyoming.

Its increasing size indicated that the *Coast Banker* flourished. Its first issue consisted of only 32 pages, but by the end of 1908 the magazine had grown to 56. In January 1913 it had 96 pages, and though the number fluctuated from issue to issue, it kept that size until 1930. Leading bankers regularly wrote on topics of concern, such as the creation of a central bank, which became the Federal Reserve System, or described helpful banking practices. Local news, reported state-by-state but centered primarily on California, was full, and a section on "Bank and Office Utilities" reviewed the most up-to-date equipment available. The monthly was not blind to changes in the bank work force. In December 1915 it introduced a section called "Women in the Banking World." "All over California," declared columnist Olive F. Vore, "woman has taken her place in the banking world." For bankers' conventions Edwards produced lengthier issues, often incorporating geographical descriptions.

The *Coast Banker* stressed history, bank architecture, and advertising to promote two of Edwards's primary themes: bank strength and publicity. In October 1909 the journal started a series on California banking history by Leroy Armstrong and J. O. Denny. In 1916 the *Coast Banker* published the articles in book form, the still-useful *Financial California*. To make the point, Frederick L. Lipman of Wells Fargo Bank wrote the "Value of History to the Banker" in March 1913. The journal also featured laudatory biographies of important financiers such as James D. Phelan (July 1914) and Harry T. Scott (February 1915).

"To be a tenant of a first-class magnificent building adds immeasurably to one's moral assets," asserted the *Banker* in January 1909. The journal regularly described exterior and interior bank architecture in articles such as "Modern Interior Bank Buildings" (March 1910) and "Bank Office Buildings" (September 1911) as well as in advertisements, and it often featured the work of architect William H. Weeks. Photo essays of prominent banks such as the Wells Fargo Nevada National Bank (October 1908, August 1911), Anglo & London Paris National Bank (May 1910), Donohoe, Kelly Banking Company and the Bank of California (July 1914), D. O. Mills & Company of Sacramento (June 1911), Ladd & Tilton of Portland, Oregon (March 1911), Dexter Horton National Bank of Seattle, Washington (July 1911), and Walker Brothers of Salt Lake City, Utah (March 1913) commonly filled the journal's pages.

Edwards particularly advocated bank advertising. Most advertisements had a black-bordered tombstone look. "The fact is," wrote James K. Lynch of the First National Bank of San Francisco, a regular contributor, "that in any community those who use banks are but a small minority." In August 1910 he wished to increase that percentage through advertising. Publisher Edwards had to combat a fear among many bankers, he noted in January 1909, that their "standing in the eyes of the people will suffer if they advertise." Many thought advertising was undignified. "If we were to advertise that we had a bigger capital and surplus than any other bank," explained a banker in the October 1909 issue, "such a statement would contain a covert assumption that other banks were not so good as ours. Such action would not be right or in good taste." Beginning in October 1911 the *Coast Banker* had a regular advertising section edited by C. E. Auracher, founder and editor of the *Bank Advertiser*.

In the mid 1920s the *Coast Banker*, "devoted to the business interests of the Pacific Coast, paying particular attention to banking, corporations, securities, real estate, and insurance," was full of the changes in the California banking world. It captured the controversy between state and national banks, unit and branch banks, and the emergence

of the three largest California banks as of 1990, BankAmerica, Security Pacific, and Wells Fargo. "Books for Financiers" appeared as a regular column, while window displays provided a popular form of promotion. Added to earlier advertisements for Todd check protectographs and various Burroughs machines used to speed checks in transit were descriptions of safety paper, night depository safes, metered mail, air mail, and airplanes.

The Great Depression brought retrenchment in content, length, and quality. Most articles appeared unsigned, and the *Coast Banker* ran about 50 pages monthly. Edwards, though, still retained his "faith in the future of the West." He would fight the Depression, he wrote in February 1933, through what he called "printed salesmanship"; that is, positive "publicity and advertising" for business. By the late 1930s the monthly had rebounded to around 80 pages. In July 1941 Edwards died at seventy-three years of age. He had ignored many conflicts in the *Banker*, said a friend summing up his career, since "the management of a bank" remained the most important element needed to achieve his goal of a "constantly sounder and more serviceable banking structure" for the nation.

Harry Lutgens, the new owner, and his family would change the journal's name and run it for 40 years. Born in 1893 in San Francisco, Lutgens enjoyed a career split between journalism and public service. He began as a newspaperman. Following an apprenticeship in San Francisco, he published two small Sonoma County papers before producing the *San Rafael Independent* between 1926 and 1937. From 1923 to 1927 he served as private secretary to the conservative Republican governor Friend W. Richardson, who from 1934 to 1939 was the California superintendent of banks. During that time Lutgens was a member of various state boards, and when he bought the *Coast Banker* he was secretary of the California Press Association. Richardson was president, and in 1947 Lutgens took charge. From 1955 to 1961 he gained banking experience as a director of the Bank of San Rafael and its affiliated First National Bank in San Rafael.

War rationing dropped the journal's size to about 50 pages, and the new *Coast Banker* naturally had shorter articles than under Edwards. Its advertisements revealed great changes in graphics and themes since 1908. In 1948 Lutgens began the *Western Bank Directory*. It covered 11 western states, presenting date of establishment, bank officers, year-end figures, and other statistics for each listed institution. Three years later Lutgens changed the name of the monthly banking journal to reflect what the publication had been in fact since its founding, *Western Banker*.

In the mid 1960s *Western Banker* was the "Financial Journal of the Nation's Fastest Growing Banking Field." It covered topics such as check routing through MICR (Magnetic Ink Character Recognition), a telecredit network for check verification; and the introduction of credit cards and scenic checks. A section on "Bank Charges in the Twelfth Federal Reserve District" recorded new banks and branch offices, while the focus of the news notes stayed on California.

Harry Lutgens died in October 1968, but his widow, Helen, son-in-law Thomas M. Gannon, daughter Peggy L. Gannon, and John L. Gannon

ran *Western Banker* until January 1985. In the late 1970s the journal published about 50 pages per month, but in 1983 that dropped to 30. It often ran topical issues, such as on bank security (January 1978 and January 1982) and bank buildings (November 1978 and November 1982). A "What's New" section described innovative equipment.

In February 1985 the Gannons retained the *Western Bank Directory*, but sold the *Western Banker* to Gregory B. Saffell, a publisher for 15 years in Tiburon, California. On the journal's cover he announced it was "Serving Financial Institution Management." Among other changes, a section on "Bank Changes" noted the opening and closing of banks and branches across the United States. After four years R. Daniel Harris, Jr., took over "The Voice of the Western Financial Community."

Harry Dexter White

(October 9, 1892 - August 16, 1948)

by Larry G. Gerber

Auburn University

CAREER: Professor of Economics, Lawrence College (1932-1934); economic analyst (1934-1936), assistant director, Division of Research and Statistics (1936-1938), director, Division of Monetary Research, U.S. Department of the Treasury (1938-1945); assistant secretary of the Treasury (1945-1946); U.S. executive director, International Monetary Fund (1946-1947).

Harry Dexter White was a leading adviser to Secretary of the Treasury Henry Morgenthau, Jr., during the Great Depression and World War II. The principal architect of the Bretton Woods agreements that led to the establishment of the International Monetary Fund and World Bank, he also played a role in drawing up the Morgenthau Plan for the deindustrialization of postwar Germany. Just before his death he became the subject of highly publicized charges that he had been involved in a Communist spy ring during his service in the Treasury Department.

White was born in Boston on October 9, 1892. His parents, Sarah and Jacob White, were Lith-

uanian Jews who had come to the United States less than a decade before his birth. After graduating from a Boston public high school at the age of sixteen, White spent two years working in the family hardware business. In 1911 he enrolled at the Massachusetts Agricultural College (now the University of Massachusetts at Amherst), but he left school the following year to return to the family business. Immediately after the outbreak of World War I, White enlisted in the army and gained a commission as a first lieutenant. Although he was subsequently sent to France, he saw no action during the war.

In 1918 White married Anne Terry, a woman of Russian Jewish origin who later became a well-known children's writer. When White returned home after the war, he resolved to leave the family business. After running an orphanage and then serving as the director of a settlement house in New York, he decided, at almost the age of thirty, to pursue an academic career.

White entered Columbia University in 1922. The next year he transferred to Stanford University where he majored in economics and earned a bache-

Harry Dexter White (Wide World Photos)

lor's degree in 1924. He established an excellent record as a student at Stanford, winning election to Phi Beta Kappa and going on to earn a master's degree in 1925. That same year he returned to Massachusetts to study economics at Harvard University under the direction of Frank W. Taussig. White was awarded a doctorate in 1930 after writing a prize-winning dissertation that was published in 1933 under the title, *The French International Accounts, 1880-1913*. While working on his doctorate he taught economics at Harvard, receiving annual appointments from 1926 to 1932. During that time, he and his wife had two daughters, Joan and Ruth.

Unable to gain a permanent appointment at Harvard, White accepted a position in 1932 as an assistant professor of economics at Lawrence College in Appleton, Wisconsin. He quickly won promotion to full professor. However, when Jacob Viner, a University of Chicago economist then doing research for the Treasury Department, invited White to come to Washington in the summer of 1934 to help him prepare a comprehensive study of monetary and banking policy, White eagerly accepted the opportunity. Although the assignment with the government was intended to last only for the summer, White ended up remaining in Washington for the next 13 years.

In October 1934 White joined the Treasury Department as an economic analyst. The following year the department sent him to England to explore the possibility of reaching an agreement with the British government to stabilize exchange rates. The preliminary discussions he had at that time with British experts, including John Maynard Keynes, helped pave the way for the signing of the Tripartite Agreement in 1936. The resulting accord with the British and the French represented an attempt to avoid competitive devaluations. No fixed exchange rates were agreed to, but the governments involved committed themselves to utilize their own stabilization funds to help maintain orderly markets for the currencies of each signatory to the agreement.

Although many perceived White as irascible and overly ambitious, his keen intellect and willingness to put in long hours of work greatly impressed Treasury Secretary Morgenthau. By 1936 White had become a member of Morgenthau's inner circle of advisers. His primary responsibilities over the next decade related to international monetary problems, but within the Treasury, White also emerged as one of the most forceful advocates of a Keynesian approach to dealing with the Great Depression, an approach that Morgenthau himself never fully understood or supported.

From an early date, though, White and Morgenthau agreed that the United States needed to take concrete action to demonstrate American opposition to the rise of totalitarian aggression. In 1936 White played a key role in negotiating a silver purchase arrangement with China that was intended to bolster China's economy at a time of increasing pressure from Japan. After the Japanese initiated hostilities with China in 1937, White actively supported the U.S. decision to extend credits to China as a form of American aid. Before the outbreak of war in Europe he called for economic sanctions against Hitler's Germany and a new "arrangement" with the Soviet Union, including the provision of a $250 million loan to the Soviets, as a further means of deterring German expansionism.

As tensions between the United States and Japan mounted, White, in May 1941, drafted for Secretary Morgenthau a program of new initiatives that was intended not only to avert the possibility of war between the United States and Japan but also to isolate Germany. White recommended extending to the Japanese a $3 billion loan, recognizing their dominant role in Manchuria, and offering a 20-year nonaggression pact (including a withdrawal of American naval forces from the Pacific) in exchange for a Japanese military withdrawal from China and the rest of Southeast Asia and an agreement by the Japanese to lease to the United States for a period of three years up to one-half their naval vessels and aircraft. White also proposed offering the Soviet Union a $500 million credit if the Soviets agreed to halt their trade with Germany and to sign a mutual assistance pact with the United States. In November, White prepared an updated version of the plan as a last-ditch effort to avoid war with Japan so that the United States might concentrate on the threat posed by Nazi Germany. Morgenthau actually forwarded White's memo to President Franklin D. Roosevelt and to Secretary of State Cordell Hull just weeks before the Japanese attack on Pearl Harbor.

The day after Pearl Harbor, Morgenthau announced to his Treasury Department staff that White would henceforth "be in charge of all foreign affairs for me." During the course of the war White often represented the Treasury on interdepartmental and inter-Allied committees created to deal with various financial and economic matters. One of White's main wartime responsibilities was supervising American aid to the Chinese to help them stabilize the value of their currency—aid that White ultimately came to believe was useless because of the corruption and inefficiency of the Chinese government. White was influential as well in helping to determine Allied policies relating to the issuance of currency in occupied and liberated territory. In addition, he played an important role in drafting the "Morgenthau Plan" for postwar Germany.

In the summer of 1944, Morgenthau directed White to prepare a plan for partitioning and deindustrializing postwar Germany so as "to make Germany so impotent" that she would not again be able to "forge the tools of war." Like Morgenthau, White believed that a policy of weakening Germany would eliminate a major threat to peace and, at the same time, enhance the chances for postwar cooperation between the United States and the Soviet Union. White, however, favored less extreme measures than did Morgenthau. When he worked on the first draft of the Morgenthau Plan, White tried unsuccessfully to moderate his superior's desire to dismantle all industry in the Ruhr, even to the point of flooding the region's coal mines, by suggest-

ing that the Allies make the Ruhr an international zone out of which they could take reparations for a period of 20 years. White argued that the coal resources of the Ruhr would be especially needed to alleviate postwar shortages throughout Western Europe. Morgenthau was adamant, however, and White and other Treasury officials loyally carried out the wishes of their boss in drafting the final version of the plan.

In its final form, the Morgenthau Plan called for partitioning a somewhat truncated Germany into three separate states and dismantling virtually all of Germany's industrial base. Because the Soviet Union would not have access to ongoing reparations out of current production if the Morgenthau Plan were adopted, both Morgenthau and White supported a substantial American postwar loan to the Soviets to aid them in their efforts at reconstruction. Although Franklin Roosevelt at first seemed favorably inclined toward the Morgenthau Plan, continuing opposition from the War and State Departments, and Harry Truman's later hostility to Morgenthau's ideas, ultimately killed the plan.

Without question, White's most important wartime assignment involved developing plans for a postwar restructuring of the international monetary system. Within a week after Pearl Harbor, Morgenthau, who had little expertise in the area himself, asked White to prepare a memo on the establishment of an inter-Allied stabilization fund that built on, but went far beyond, the Tripartite Agreement of 1936. By early 1942, White had completed the draft of a comprehensive plan to prevent "the disruption of foreign exchanges and the collapse of the monetary and credit systems; to assure the restoration of foreign trade; and to supply the huge volume of capital that will be needed virtually throughout the world for reconstruction, for relief, and for economic recovery." White and Morgenthau both sought to establish a system of multilateral trade that would encompass the entire world in order to prevent a return to the global depression and economic warfare of the 1930s.

What soon came to be known as the "White Plan" called for the creation of both a "United Nations Stabilization Fund" with $5 billion in assets and a "Bank for Reconstruction" with a capitalization of $10 billion. By providing short-term access to foreign currencies, White designed the stabilization fund to allow member nations to deal with temporary balance of payments problems without having to resort to exchange restrictions or competitive devaluations. In return, member nations had to surrender a certain degree of control over their own domestic financial policies, since, as White later explained, the proposed fund was based on the principle that "international problems are an international responsibility to be met through international cooperation." The size of a member nation's contribution to the stabilization fund determined that nation's voting strength in the new organization, as well as the amount of foreign currency it purchased from the fund. The United States, with a projected quota of $2 billion, would clearly play the dominant role in the fund, especially since only the dollar would be convertible to gold (at $35 an ounce).

Although White gave more attention to the proposed stabilization fund than to the accompanying plan for an international bank, the bank he initially envisioned would not only have guaranteed loans made by private investors for purposes of reconstruction, but also would have the power to make loans on its own and to issue currency. In later refinements of the plan for a world bank, White saw loans for long-term economic development projects as at least as important as purely transitional loans to aid in reconstruction.

While White developed an American plan for restructuring the postwar international monetary system, John Maynard Keynes devised a comparable plan on behalf of the British government. The so-called "Keynes Plan" was, in several respects, even more ambitious and innovative than the White Plan. It also obviously reflected the somewhat different interests of an economically weakened Britain in the postwar world. Keynes proposed creating an "International Clearing Union" that, unlike the stabilization fund of the White Plan, had no fixed quotas for contributions and drawing rights. In fact, the Clearing Union would have no actual gold or currency reserves of its own. It provided member nations with significant overdraft rights in the temporary settlement of international accounts by means of a purely technical bookkeeping system based on a new unit of value, the "bancor," which was not to be tied to gold. Keynes intended the Clearing Union to authorize overdrafts amounting to a total of $26 billion, with overdraft rights related to the share of world trade a member nation had prior to the war. In comparison to the White Plan, the Keynes Plan called for an international monetary system far more expansive and an international mone-tary authority far less intrusive in supervising the domestic policies of its member nations.

White and Keynes served as the principals in two years of bilateral negotiations between the United States and Britain that prepared the way for the convening, in July 1944, of a United Nations conference on international monetary affairs at Bretton Woods, New Hampshire. That conference, at which White and Keynes were the dominant figures, produced the final agreement for the establishment of the International Monetary Fund (IMF) and the International Bank for Reconstruction and Development (World Bank). The Bretton Woods agreements represented something of a compromise between the original White and Keynes plans, but they clearly fell more in line with White's initial proposals.

The IMF had resources worth $8.8 billion, with the United States supplying roughly one-third the total. In order to reduce liquidity problems as an obstacle to trade White and the American delegation officially headed by Morgenthau had accepted a fund larger than the White Plan had at first envisioned. However, Keynes's conception of a Clearing Union with overdraft facilities for its members was rejected (only to be resurrected in modified form more than 20 years later with the creation of Special Drawing Rights). The Bretton Woods agreements did not give the IMF as clear-cut an oversight role with regard to member nations' domestic policies as White had hoped, but neither did the IMF allow its members to draw automatically on their quotas as Keynes had suggested. Similarly, White had wanted to require any nation wishing to devalue its currency to seek IMF approval in advance, but he made a partial concession to Keynes when he agreed that member nations need not seek IMF approval for devaluations of less than 10 percent. In another important concession to the British, White willingly accepted a "scarce-currency clause" in the Bretton Woods agreements. With that clause the United States acknowledged that creditor nations might have to bear some of the responsibility for reducing trade imbalances by allowing members of the IMF to discriminate against the exports of nations with trade surpluses.

The World Bank that emerged from Bretton Woods was far less ambitious than the international institution White originally envisioned. Although the bank was capitalized at $10 billion, it was not given the power to issue currency, and its lending authority was severely restricted.

Throughout the planning stages for the IMF and World Bank, White hoped for the Soviet Union's participation in the new world financial system. White recognized that the IMF was only of limited use to the Soviets because of their system of state-trading, but he thought that Soviet involvement in the IMF and World Bank could be a harbinger of postwar cooperation between the Soviets and the West. The Soviets did send a delegation to Bretton Woods, and White and Morgenthau's willingness to accede to their demands for a larger than originally proposed IMF quota helped convince the Soviets to sign the Bretton Woods agreements in 1944. In the months to come White also advocated a bilateral American loan of $10 billion to the Soviet Union because he remained convinced that "the major task" of American foreign policy in the immediate postwar period was "to devise means whereby continued peace and friendly relations can be assured between the United States and Russia." The subsequent development of Cold War tensions, however, as well as the Soviets' persisting reservations about involvement in international institutions designed principally for market economies, kept the Soviet Union from ultimately participating in either the IMF or the World Bank when those institutions started operations after the war.

The signing of the Bretton Woods agreements in 1944 did not result automatically in the organization of the IMF and the World Bank. In both the United States and Britain, legislative bodies had to ratify the agreements. White assumed a highly visible role in the administration's efforts to gain congressional approval for the new institutions, defending them against charges that they would operate primarily in favor of debtor nations and be inflationary in their impact. Against White's wishes, however, the Truman administration made some concessions about the international character of the IMF in order to win congressional approval of the agreements. While White had envisioned the IMF as managed by technical experts who would adopt a truly international perspective, Congress insisted on making the American director subject to the political oversight of a Cabinet-level committee chaired by the secretary of the Treasury. With that and some other modifications, Congress ratified the Bretton Woods agreements in the summer of 1945.

On January 23, 1946, President Truman nominated White to be the first American executive director of the IMF. In May 1946, at its first organizational meeting in Savannah, Georgia, the IMF agreed to establish its permanent headquarters in Washington, thereby symbolizing the influence of the American government over the new institution. The IMF, however, proved largely ineffective during White's year of service as an executive director. It became apparent that White had greatly underestimated the difficulties that most nations were to face in the postwar transition period. During the winter of 1945-1946 he had mistakenly argued that the British exaggerated their need for a $3.75 billion American loan, even though British participation in the Bretton Woods institutions came to depend on American approval of such a loan. Because of the severity of the worldwide dollar shortage, most nations continued to find exchange restrictions and bilateral trade agreements necessary in 1946 and 1947. Subsequently, the Marshall Plan, which adopted a regional rather than global approach to economic recovery, superseded the IMF and World Bank in importance. Only years later did the IMF operate in a manner somewhat akin to White's original design.

Shortly before White assumed his position with the IMF, the Federal Bureau of Investigation (FBI) had begun an investigation into charges by former Communist Elizabeth Bentley that White had long been involved in a Soviet spy ring. The charges against White, however, did not became public until July 31, 1948, when Bentley testified before the House Un-American Activities Committee. Although Bentley never produced any documentary evidence to support her charges against White and acknowledged that she had never personally met him, she claimed that between 1941 and 1944 she had served as a courier for a Soviet espionage network that included several Treasury Department officials, and that White, though not himself a member of the Communist party, had been a source of sensitive information.

Another former Communist, Whittaker Chambers, partially corroborated Bentley's testimony in his appearance before the same House investigating committee on August 3, 1948. Chambers did not at that time directly accuse White of espionage, but he claimed that he was personally acquainted with White and had firsthand knowledge that White had been a "fellow traveller" since as early as 1935.

Chambers stated, in fact, that he had first expressed his concerns about White to the FBI in 1943.

White, who had moved to New York to become a financial consultant following his departure from the IMF in 1947, requested the opportunity to appear before the House Un-American Activities Committee in order to refute the charges against him. When White made his dramatic appearance before the committee on August 13, 1948, he was still recovering from a severe heart attack he had suffered the previous September. He categorically denied ever having been a Communist or ever having been involved in espionage or any other disloyal act, and proclaimed: "My creed is the American creed." Almost immediately after returning to his summer home near Fitzwilliam, New Hampshire, White experienced another heart attack and died on August 16, 1948.

Three months after White's death, Chambers contradicted his own earlier testimony and for the first time explicitly claimed in a statement to the FBI that White had been involved in espionage. Moreover, he produced some documentary evidence to substantiate the accusation in the form of notes, dated January 1938 and in White's own handwriting, which dealt with Treasury Department affairs. Chambers maintained that White had given the notes to him ten years earlier to pass on to the Soviets. Although Representative Richard M. Nixon first made the charges public in a speech on the House floor in 1950, they again appeared in the headlines in 1953 when Dwight D. Eisenhower's attorney general, Herbert Brownell, accused Harry Truman of having appointed White executive director of the IMF after having been presented with conclusive evidence of White's involvement in Soviet espionage.

The validity of the charges against White remains a matter of controversy. White's biographer, David Rees, does not find the evidence against White to be conclusive, given the many discrepancies in the stories of both Bentley and Chambers, but he does, in the end, find the evidence for the charges to be credible. On the other hand, Athan Theoharis, one of the leading authorities on the FBI and anticommunism during this period, finds it most suspicious that Chambers did not produce any concrete evidence against White until after White had died and that Chambers himself had become embroiled publicly in the Alger Hiss controversy.

An irony exists in the fact that White, who was accused of having been a Communist agent, was also instrumental in creating the IMF and World Bank, institutions that many see as symbols of American efforts to extend capitalism throughout the world. White himself, though, might well have been disappointed that the Bretton Woods system he helped to create did not prove more successful in fostering a single world economic community.

Publications:

The French International Accounts, 1880-1913 (Cambridge, Mass.: Harvard University Press, 1933);

"Postwar Currency Stabilization," *American Economic Review*, 33 (March 1943): 382-387;

"The Monetary Fund: Some Criticisms Examined," *Foreign Affairs*, 23 (January 1945): 195-210;

"The International Monetary Fund: The First Year," *Annals of the American Academy of Political and Social Science*, 252 (July 1947): 21-29.

References:

John Morton Blum, *From the Morgenthau Diaries*, 3 volumes (Boston: Houghton Mifflin, 1959-1967);

David Rees, *Harry Dexter White: A Study in Paradox* (New York: Coward, McCann & Geohegan, 1973);

Athan Theoharis, "Unanswered Questions: Chambers, Nixon, the FBI, and the Hiss Case," in *Beyond the Hiss Case: The FBI, Congress, and the Cold War* (Philadelphia: Temple University Press, 1982);

Charles L. Whipple, "The Life and Death of Harry Dexter White," *Boston Globe*, beginning November 15, 1953, 12 parts;

Nathan I. White, *Harry Dexter White: Loyal American* (Waban, Mass.: Bessie [White] Bloom, 1956).

Archives:

The Harry Dexter White Papers are housed at Princeton University Library. A smaller collection of materials taken from White's home in 1953 and 1955 was published by the U.S. Government Printing Office in 1956 as *Interlocking Subversion in Government Departments*.

George Wingfield

(August 16, 1876 - December 25, 1959)

by C. Elizabeth Raymond

University of Nevada at Reno

CAREER: Vice-president (1906-1909), president, Goldfield Consolidated Mines Company (1909-1959); president, Reno National Bank [Nixon National Bank to 1915] (1912-1935); president, Reno Securities Company (1915-1955); president, Getchell Mines, Incorporated (1936-1959).

George Wingfield was the central economic and political figure in the state of Nevada from 1906 until the collapse of his empire in 1935. Among those who made mining fortunes in Nevada, he was unique in that he remained in the state with his money. Sometimes tagged the "king of Nevada" in the popular press, Wingfield invested in major hotels in Reno, in ranches and mines, and in a chain of 12 banks that effectively dominated the state's economy until its failure in 1932.

Born on August 16, 1876, into a Methodist family near Fort Smith, Arkansas, Wingfield moved as a young child to Lake County, Oregon. There, in isolated sagebrush country, his father operated a cattle ranch, and Wingfield was educated through the eighth grade in Lakeview. Reportedly an "incorrigible boy" with erratic school attendance, he left home at an early age to work as a cowhand and a gambler. Seeking wider scope for his talents, he moved permanently to Nevada in 1896, residing in the railroad town of Winnemucca, the traditional railhead for cattle drives from southeastern Oregon. By 1898 he had moved east to the small copper mining camp of Golconda, Nevada, where he operated the California Saloon, raced horses, scouted likely copper prospects, and gambled. His customary game was faro, although he was also a skilled poker player. Of medium height and undistinguished appearance, Wingfield was most often described as tough, taciturn, and poker-faced.

When the silver mining boom in Tonopah created excitement in 1901, Wingfield sold his Golconda property and moved to the new central

George Wingfield (courtesy of the Nevada Historical Society)

Nevada camp. At first he relied on his gambling skills for economic support, running a faro game at the famous Tonopah Club Saloon. Evidently skilled at his chosen trade, he made enough money as a gambling concessionaire to buy into partnership in the successful club. He also invested significantly in other Tonopah real estate, including houses and business buildings as well as saloons and hotels.

Meanwhile, beginning in 1902, Wingfield acted as a representative for Winnemucca banker George S. Nixon, then the state agent for the powerful Southern Pacific Railroad and soon to become, in 1905, a Republican U.S. senator. Never formalized legally, the partnership of Nixon & Wingfield was destined to become a major force in the spectacular central Nevada mining boom that began in 1904 in Goldfield, 30 miles south of Tonopah. Even before that, however, the partners invested in common ventures, buying and trading mining stocks and lending money to prospectors and businessmen. By 1904, as the new gold mining boomtown at Goldfield started to attract attention, Nixon & Wingfield already owned mining claims and real estate there. In 1905 Nixon and Wingfield invested together in banks for the new communities: the Nye and Ormsby County Bank in Tonopah, and John S. Cook & Company in Goldfield. About that time Nixon, who was Wingfield's senior by 16 years, counseled his partner to give up gambling and concentrate exclusively on their joint business affairs. Evidently Wingfield took his partner's advice. While he remained a skilled card player, he never again relied on gambling to earn his living.

By 1906 Nixon & Wingfield had its own letterhead stationery and offices in the Nixon Block in Goldfield. In that year the partners arranged Goldfield's most important mining transaction, when they combined six of the camp's richest individual mining companies into a single corporate giant, the Goldfield Consolidated Mines Company, capitalized at $50 million. They achieved that consolidation with the aid of substantial eastern capital, to which Nixon's connections as a banker and U.S. senator gave him access. Among the investors in Goldfield Consolidated were Bernard Baruch, William H. Crocker, and Henry Clay Frick. The resulting company avoided dissipating its profits in legal disputes about ownership of the rich Goldfield veins and became instead phenomenally successful, paying handsome dividends to its stockholders through 1913.

As vice-president and effectively chief executive officer of the new company, Wingfield became one of the wealthiest men in Nevada, with a fortune estimated at the time to be between $25 million and $30 million. He continued to manage the joint business interests of Nixon & Wingfield, surrounding himself with a talented staff of accountants, attorneys, bankers, and engineers to look after his affairs. From those men he expected and received hard work and absolute loyalty.

Wingfield is also credited with almost singlehandedly facing down the notorious Industrial Workers of the World (IWW) union during its strike against the Goldfield mine operators in 1906-1907. During that quarrel—which was triggered by measures taken by the mine operators to prevent the miners' common practice of stealing particularly valuable "high grade" ore—Wingfield's life was publicly threatened, and he ventured out only with guns and bodyguards. Ultimately, Wingfield and Nixon orchestrated a request from Governor John Sparks that federal troops be sent to Goldfield to restore order. Although a subsequent congressional investigation harshly criticized that blatant manipulation of federal police power when no emergency existed, the troops effectively stopped the strike. Using all the resources at their disposal, including private detectives to infiltrate union ranks and subsidized newspaper coverage, Wingfield and his mine superintendent eventually broke the power of the IWW in Goldfield. The incident left Wingfield vehemently opposed to socialist labor organizations for the remainder of his life.

In 1908 Wingfield signaled his social arrival as a dignified multimillionaire investor by his marriage to a San Francisco banker's daughter, Maude Azile Murdoch. In 1909 Nixon and Wingfield amicably dissolved their partnership and split their holdings. Wingfield took Goldfield Consolidated and John S. Cook & Company, while Nixon retained the real estate and the network of other banks the partnership had developed.

After his society marriage, Wingfield moved to Reno in 1909. The town remained his center of operations for 50 years, until his death in 1959. During most of that time it was the largest town and the political power center of Nevada. Most observers also generally acknowledged it as Wingfield's dominion, especially after the death of Senator Nixon in 1912. The latter event brought Wingfield into the national limelight when Republican governor Tasker Oddie offered him an appointment to fill Nixon's seat. He refused the Senate seat on the grounds that he could do more for the state "at present" by remaining in Nevada to take care of his business interests rather than going to Washington.

In the national press Wingfield instantly became "the Cowboy Who Refused a Toga," but his reasons for doing so were sound and shrewd. Always an intensely private man, he did not want to risk focusing public attention on his past, which in-

Fourth of July 1907 drilling contest in Goldfield, site of Wingfield and partner George S. Nixon's Nevada gold mining operation, incorporated in 1906 (courtesy of the Nevada State Historical Society)

cluded certain embarrassing souvenirs of a wild youth, among them an unsuccessful, but scurrilous suit for divorce brought by an alleged common-law wife in Tonopah in 1906. Never happy for long outside his adopted state, he also genuinely disliked the prospect of moving to Washington. Most important, he recognized that he was no politician. Reserved and not at all charismatic, he was more comfortable as a private businessman than as a public figure. Instinctively, he assumed the role of power behind the throne. He played that role comfortably and enthusiastically for the next 20 years, until the Depression-caused failure of his banking chain in 1932 led to his personal bankruptcy in 1935.

Nixon's death provided the opportunity for him to develop as a kingmaker, since Wingfield immediately assumed the mantle of financial leadership in Nevada's Republican party. Wingfield also purchased from Nixon's estate all of the banking interests they had formerly owned together. Building on that base, he went on to establish or buy other banks, which effectively operated as a chain. The new purchases included the Carson Valley Bank, the Churchill County Bank, the First National Bank of Winnemucca, the Henderson Banking Company, John S. Cook & Company, Reno National Bank,

Riverside Bank, the Bank of Sparks, the Tonopah Banking Corporation, United Nevada Bank, Virginia City Bank, and Wells State Bank. By 1932 his 12 banks controlled more than half the total deposits and perhaps 80 percent to 85 percent of the loans outstanding in the state.

In addition, Wingfield's Reno Securities Company owned the city's two largest hotels: the Golden, which he purchased in 1915, and the plush Riverside, a popular resort for Reno's fashionable divorcées, which he built in 1927. Always passionate about horses, in 1914 he founded the Nevada Stock Farm, which raised thoroughbred horses that raced throughout the country. Wingfield also had an interest in ranching companies in Nevada and California, and in a pioneer rice-growing effort in Butte County, California, the Sutter Butte Canal Company. He founded and operated Nevada's only bonding company, the Nevada Surety and Bonding Company, from 1924 to 1943. Although he lived in a relatively unassuming home in Reno, he had considerable real estate holdings in the city. Giving modestly to virtually every charity that approached him, Wingfield took seriously the responsibilities incumbent upon him as the wealthiest man in Nevada.

His fortune, and the prominence that it brought in a small state that was chronically short of resources, placed George Wingfield in a position of undeniable power, which he did not hesitate to use. Through a network of attorneys and associates he lobbied energetically on behalf of issues such as the residency requirements for divorce, which affected his business interests. As Republican National Committeeman for Nevada from 1920 to 1932, he is alleged to have directed a notorious and efficient bipartisan political machine under which the political parties orchestrated control of the state in order to ensure the election of one Republican and one Democratic U.S. senator. By that means, Nevada always assured itself of political clout in Washington, no matter which party was in power, and both political parties remained equally sympathetic to the prevailing economic interests of the state.

One of the most controversial incidents associated with Wingfield's political domination of the state was the infamous Cole-Malley case, triggered in 1927 by the $500,000 defalcation of the state treasurer and controller along with the cashier of Wingfield's Carson City bank. Despite the fact that his cashier had knowingly issued bogus cashier's checks and that he was personally responsible in the amount of $75,000 as bondsman for the state officials involved, Wingfield engineered a compromise in the 1928 special legislative session called to deal with the problem, whereby he paid only 30 percent of the state's losses ($154,986 out of $516,322). Newspapers railed about the injustice of a settlement that required from Wingfield less than half of the total loss sustained by the state. However, as Wingfield had pointed out in a letter to the legislature, he had the option of simply liquidating the bank, taking a loss on the $45,000 he had invested there, plus the $75,000 due from him as bondsman, and leaving the state liable for the remainder. From his perspective, then, the $155,000 that he did pay already constituted $35,000 more than he owed, and his actions ought to have been regarded as those of a public-spirited citizen.

In any event, Wingfield's political power dissipated in November 1932, when his chain of banks failed to reopen after an emergency bank holiday declared by the acting governor. Depression conditions in Nevada had combined with a severe drought to reduce drastically the value of sheep and cattle outfits to which the Wingfield banks had made large loans. In 1932 the chain lost $3.5 mil-

lion through defaults. As the losses mounted, the Wingfield banks sought relief from the Reconstruction Finance Corporation (RFC), which loaned them $5.17 million in 1932. By late October, when Wingfield requested further loans from the RFC, the banks no longer had sufficient collateral to secure them, and the RFC denied the requests. When Nevada's bank holiday ended on November 12, 1932, the Wingfield banks remained closed, with devastating consequences for the state. Even the state government temporarily suspended its operations.

During the following two years, Wingfield fought desperately to reorganize the banks. He proposed a plan to combine the assets and operate the banks as a chain, even obtaining the necessary changes in legislation from an unfriendly Nevada legislature in 1933. Substantial opposition to the plan emerged, however, due to local resentment of Wingfield's alleged mismanagement, and the legislature defeated it in late 1933. With the banks in receivership, Wingfield's personal assets were also jeopardized. In addition to his director's liability, he also was personally liable for the losses of the two national banks in his chain and had borrowed money against the two Reno hotels while trying to stave off the bank collapse. As a result, on November 30, 1935, the former multimillionaire filed a petition for personal bankruptcy.

Bankruptcy did not leave him destitute, however. His house had been a wedding gift to his second wife, Roxy Thoma Wingfield, whom he married in 1930 after divorcing Maude Murdoch in 1929. The Reno Securities Company was in the hands of Crocker First National Bank, which had foreclosed in order to protect the loans it had made on the property. The bank retained Wingfield as a salaried manager to operate the hotels on its behalf. Having placed some stocks and real estate in trust for his two children, Jean and George, Jr., Wingfield also remained president of Goldfield Consolidated, which paid a salary sufficient to allow him to continue operating his office.

Although he never regained his political power, Wingfield staged a remarkable economic recovery in the next few years. In 1936 a longtime friend, Noble H. Getchell, sought Wingfield's help to attract investors to a promising gold mining prospect outside Golconda, Nevada. Wingfield contacted Bernard Baruch, who remained a close friend from the early days in Goldfield. Baruch arranged to bring in the Newmont Mining Corporation to help finance the mine, which proved to be extraordinarily profitable. Wingfield and Getchell each received a one-third interest in the resulting company, Getchell Mines, Incorporated.

When gold production was curtailed during World War II, the Getchell simply switched to producing tungsten, a highly demanded strategic defense mineral. The profits continued unabated. In 1944 those profits combined with the wartime crowding of the Reno hotels to pay off the outstanding loans of the Reno Securities Company, which the Crocker Bank had offered Wingfield the chance to repurchase. The latter company was finally sold in 1955.

In his final years, then, Wingfield returned to his first loves: mining and horses. He continued to give personal oversight to the affairs of Goldfield Consolidated and Getchell Mines. Although the Nevada Stock Farm had vanished in the bankruptcy proceedings, he established a new breeding operation for quarter horses, at Spanish Springs Ranch, north of Reno. There he hunted game birds, stocked fishing ponds, and raised Labrador retrievers, which he gave as gifts to many friends and local residents.

In 1957 Wingfield was awarded the honorary degree of doctor of mining economics by the University of Nevada, the sole public recognition of his tremendous influence on his adopted state of Nevada.

Although his fortune was originally based on mining, he had consistently promoted economic diversification by his own example. His policy of investing primarily in Nevada promoted the establishment of industries less precarious than mining, including the embryonic tourism industry that developed first from easily available divorce, and, after 1931, from legalized gambling. At George Wingfield's death from a stroke on December 25, 1959, the newspaper obituaries were lengthy and candid, both about his contributions and his considerable power in the state of Nevada. As the obituaries pointed out, Wingfield had left his stamp indelibly upon a desert state where few others had lingered long enough to be similarly influential.

References:

Jerome E. Edwards, *Pat McCarren: Political Boss of Nevada* (Reno: University of Nevada Press, 1982);

Clel Georgetta, *Golden Fleece in Nevada* (Reno: Venture, 1972);

Gilman M. Ostrander, *Nevada: The Great Rotten Borough, 1859–1964* (New York: Knopf, 1966);

C. Elizabeth Raymond, "George Wingfield's Political Machine: A Study in Political Reputation," *Nevada Historical Society Quarterly*, 32 (Summer 1989);

Raymond, *A Guide to the George Wingfield Papers* (Reno: Nevada Historical Society, 1988).

Archives:

An extensive collection of the business and personal papers of George Wingfield is at the Nevada Historical Society in Reno.

Women in Banking: Early Years

by Sara Alpern

Texas A&M University

Men dominated the banking and financial industry in the nineteenth century, but more and more women entered the profession in the early decades of the twentieth century. Opportunities for female advancement in banking came as a result of several factors: the social dislocation produced by World War I, the advent of national woman suffrage, the creation of women's departments in banks, and the increased availability of courses in banking open to women at colleges and at the American Institute of Banking. Early on, midwestern banks occasionally produced high-ranking female officers, including presidents. In addition, in 1903 Maggie Lena Walker initiated the St. Luke Penny Savings bank in Richmond, Virginia, and served as its president until 1930, when the institution merged with two other black-owned Richmond banks to become the Consolidated Bank and Trust Company. Walker served as chairman of Consolidated until her death in 1934. In Tennessee from 1919 to 1926, Mrs. F. J. Runyon served as president of the First Woman's Bank of Clarksville, a bank organized

Virginia D. H. Furman, a banker at New York's Co-lumbia Trust Company from 1915, a director of that bank's woman's department from 1919, and president of the Association of Bank Women from 1921 to 1923

and managed entirely by women. Other banks employed women informally, as early as the late nineteenth century, and only later gave them formal titles. Margaret Cassidy worked at the Washington Savings Institute of Lowell, Massachusetts, from 1894 but did not receive the title of assistant treasurer until 1921.

While gaining the vote in 1920 was symbolically important in that it signified that women had achieved some status in the political arena and gave many career-minded women a greater sense of self-confidence, World War I yielded concrete benefits for professional women. During the war women joined the work force to take the places of the men fighting in Europe. Some of these women found positions in banking. Women also volunteered their services in the Liberty Loan drives and the thrift campaigns. Sometimes women asked for help from female bankers. For example, a women's committee formed in New York City to aid in the war effort turned to Virginia D. H. Furman, an official of the

Columbia Trust Company since 1915, for help in obtaining war bonds.

In 1919 Furman's bank inaugurated a women's department, and she became assistant secretary in charge of it. With more women in the work force earning paychecks to deposit, and some with money to invest, Columbia Trust thought a department managed for women by a woman would attract female customers. The idea spread to several other New York banks and then to banks in other parts of the country as New York City departments served as the training ground for women across the nation. For example, Edna Howard traveled to New York to observe women's departments there, then returned to Chicago and established a women's department at Northern Trust Company. The departments opened accounts, gave financial advice and even advice beyond strictly financial matters, and transacted the usual bank business. Some departments even helped their female clients plan their household budgets. Under women's department manager Anne Seward, beginning in the 1920s the Hamilton National Bank of New York offered female clients a clubroom facility in which they could keep business appointments of their own or rest during the business day.

Not all women supported the idea of women's departments in banks. Some, such as Mrs. Edward Dexter Knight of San Francisco, launched careers in banking through women's department work, but others, such as Adele H. Kirby of Plainfield, New Jersey, took the conventional route. In the 1920s Knight organized a women's department in A. P. Giannini's Bank of Italy. Kirby started at the Plainfield Trust Company as a stenographer in 1907 and worked her way up to administrative positions. Until 1920 the bank listed her on employee rosters using only her initials, concealing her gender. During the 1920s many argued that women no longer needed the advantage of special bank departments to work their financial dealings. But only during the Great Depression did most of the women's departments dissolve, more because of the necessity of austerity measures in strained banks than because of progressive attitudes among bankers.

As a consequence of the increasingly prominent female role in banking, several bank women's organizations formed in the early twentieth century. A Women's Bankers Association existed in Texas as early as 1912. In 1921 Virginia Furman and five other women who had recently started working in

New York City banks met to discuss how they could make themselves more valuable to their banks and to other women who wanted to enter the profession. They decided to form a national women's banking association called the Association of Bank Women (ABW), pledging to "uphold the dignity and integrity of women associated with or employed by banks." Furman became the association's first president, serving in that capacity from 1921 to 1923. Female executive bank employees with regular contact with bank customers qualified for ABW membership.

During the ABW's first year the group held monthly meetings at member banks. Within a year the New York City-centered group of 16 members had grown to a national organization of 59 members from 18 states and 28 cities. Letters from out-of-town members were read at the monthly meetings. The first ABW general convention was held in Atlantic City, New Jersey, in September 1923, coinciding with the convention of the American Bankers Association. After that convention the ABW inaugurated publication of its own journal, the *ABW News*, which became known as *The Woman Banker* in 1939, the *National Association of Bank Women Journal* in 1970, and *Executive Financial Woman* in 1985.

In 1923 the ABW divided its membership into six districts and gave each district a vice-president. In later years the association also supported the formation of local chapters. During the 1920s, through its Public Education Committee, the ABW gave attention to vocational counseling to encourage more women to enter the profession. A Publicity Committee created in 1930 also sought to increase membership. The association established a national office in New York City in 1949. That headquarters moved to Chicago in 1970.

In its early years the ABW concentrated on making women more valuable to their male-dominated institutions. Beginning in 1930 the association began to recognize the special needs of female bank executives and their increasing role in the profession. The organization announced new purposes: "To bring together women executives engaged in the profession of banking for mutual exchange of ideas and experiences in order that practical benefits may be derived therefrom," and to "promote the interests of its members and to forward the interests of all women in the banking profession." The

name of the organization changed to National Association of Bank Women (NABW) in 1954.

While the empowerment of women in the banking profession has remained the fundamental purpose of the NABW, the 27,000 members as of 1989 include men who agree with that goal. The organization has continued to maintain statistical data on female bank executives, conducting surveys intermittently from 1925, with more regularity since 1941. The modern NABW has also become more involved in public affairs. Members of the association have testified before congressional committees. The organization continues to amass data on issues relevant to members and to working people in general. For example, in 1988 the NABW conducted a study of the child care needs of parents working in financial institutions.

Several women achieved special prominence in the banking and financial industry in the early years of the twentieth century. Among them were the founders of the NABW: Virginia Furman, Nathalie Laimbeer, Jean Ried, Mina Bruère, Key Cammack, and Clara Porter. Aside from her work as the first administrator of a bank women's department and her service from 1921 to 1923 as the first president of the Association of Bank Women, Virginia Furman, born in New York in 1861, worked in other women's organizations, including as chairman of the Women's Liberty Loan Committee in the Second Federal Reserve District and as a member of the finance committee of the Women's City Club of New York.

Nathalie Schenck Laimbeer, born in New York in 1883, worked as the manager of the Bureau of Home Economics of the New York Edison Company before joining the U.S. Mortgage and Trust Company in 1919. In 1920 she became manager of both the women's department and the business department of that bank. Six months later she won promotion to the position of assistant secretary. In 1925 she became the first female assistant cashier at National City Bank, where she also headed the women's department. She served as vice-president of the ABW from 1921 to 1923 and as president from 1923 to 1926.

Jean Arnot Reid, born in Brooklyn in 1882, worked as an artist, specializing in miniatures. She joined Bankers Trust Company after she served as a director of a Red Cross hospital unit during World War I. At Bankers Trust she managed the women's department and later became a bank treasurer. She served as treasurer of the ABW from 1921 to 1923 and edited the *ABW News* from 1924 to 1926. She won election as ABW president in 1926 and served in that office until 1928. Under her leadership the organization established a finance committee.

Mina M. Bruère was born in St. Charles, Missouri. She became a singer, then director and later executive secretary of the Choral Symphony Society of St. Louis. Then she joined the staff of the Charity Organization Society to investigate agencies asking for public contributions. In 1913 she became a secretary at National City Bank, then moved to Central Union Trust Company to manage that institution's women's department in 1921. She wrote the constitution and bylaws of the ABW, served as the association's first secretary, and was its president from 1928 to 1930.

Key Cammack, born in 1893, specialized in budgets. She served as an assistant secretary of the New York Trust Company, an organization that did not open a women's department, but maintained a reading room for women. Cammack served as the NABW program chairman from 1921 to 1923. Arranging speakers for monthly meetings, she started with the fiery feminist, Anne Martin, an unsuccessful candidate for the Nevada senate, who spoke on female solidarity. The next year Cammack featured many distinguished speakers, including university professors and bank experts and the well-known muckraking author Ida Tarbell.

Cammack became the first editor of the *ABW News*.

Clara F. Porter, born in Pittsburgh, Pennsylvania, in 1884, taught school briefly in Montclair, New Jersey, sold Liberty Bonds during World War I, and then worked for five years at the New York Edison Company as editor for the company publication. In 1920 she took a job as assistant secretary with the Guaranty Trust Company. She argued against establishing a women's department at that bank with the statement, "We believe that there is no sex in business." While Porter attended several formative meetings of the NABW, she resigned from the organization in 1921 without ever holding office. She served as the first president of the Business and Professional Women's League of New York, and is remembered as New York's first bond saleswoman.

Reference:
Genevieve N. Gildersleeve, *Women in Banking: A History of the National Association of Bank Women* (Washington, D.C.: Public Affairs Press, 1959).

Archives:
Material on the history of women in banking is housed at the headquarters of the National Association of Bank Women in Chicago. Additional material can be found in the papers of the Bureau of Vocational Information and the Women's Educational and Industrial Center at Schlesinger Library, Cambridge, Massachusetts.

World Bank (*see* Bretton Woods Conference, the International Monetary Fund, and the World Bank)

Walter B. Wriston

(August 3, 1919 -)

by Gregory S. Hunter

Long Island University

CAREER: Junior foreign service officer, U.S. Department of State (1942); U.S. Army (1942-1946); junior inspector, Comptroller's Department (1946-1949), National Division (1949-1950), assistant cashier (1950-1952), assistant vice-president (1952-1954), vice-president (1954-1958), senior vice-president (1958-1960), executive vice-president (1960-1967), president (1967-1970), chairman and chief executive officer, Citibank [First National City Bank to 1976] (1970-1984); president (1968-1970), chairman and chief executive officer, Citicorp [First National City Corporation to 1976] (1970-1984).

Walter Bigelow Wriston, called by Milton Friedman one of the most important American bankers of the twentieth century, was the driving force behind Citibank's expansion over the past quarter century. Wriston molded Citibank into a truly national and international presence. He also led the entire banking world into a period of technological change symbolized by today's omnipresent automatic teller machines (ATMs). Moreover, with Wriston as its forceful spokesperson, Citibank became the recognized leader of the international banking community, and, more specifically, Wriston emerged as the industry spokesman.

Walter Wriston was born on August 3, 1919, in Middletown, Connecticut. His father, Henry Merritt Wriston, a college history professor, later served as president of Brown University and adviser to President Dwight D. Eisenhower. His mother, Ruth Colton (Bigelow) Wriston, taught chemistry. Wriston's parents were of English and Irish descent.

In 1925 Henry Wriston received his first appointment to an administrative post, as president of Lawrence College. The Wriston family, therefore, moved to Appleton, Wisconsin, that year. Young Walter was raised in a strict Methodist household. On Sundays he was forbidden to smoke, drink, lis-

Walter B. Wriston (courtesy of Citibank)

ten to the radio, or go to the movies. To get to school he regularly walked several miles, even in subzero weather. He actively participated in the Boy Scouts, achieving the rank of Eagle Scout at age fifteen. In 1937 he graduated from Appleton High School, having particularly distinguished himself in debating.

Wriston enrolled at Wesleyan University the following fall. Initially a chemistry major, he eventually changed his major to history. While at Wesleyan he edited the college newspaper and won the Parker Prize for public speaking. After graduation he studied French at the Ecole Française, one of the summer language schools at Middlebury College in Vermont. He then enrolled in the Fletcher School of International Law and Diplomacy at Tufts University, completing his master's degree in 1942.

With his M.A. in hand, Wriston joined the State Department as a junior foreign service officer. His primary responsibility involved negotiating the exchange of Japanese interned in the United States for Americans held prisoner by the Japanese. Wriston was drafted into the U.S. Army in 1942, spending part of his tour commanding a Signal Corps center on Cebu in the Philippines. He received his discharge in April 1946 with the rank of second lieutenant.

Wriston returned to the United States planning to resume his career with the State Department. The unexpected death of his mother, however, led him to look for work in New York City in order to live near his father. The tight postwar job market forced him to settle for an entry-level position in banking, a vocation he considered the height of dullness. He joined the First National City Bank in June 1946 as a junior inspector in the Comptroller's Department, and pledged to leave the job in a year if it proved as boring as he expected. Wriston's one-year tenure ultimately turned into thirty-eight years.

In 1949 Wriston joined the bank's National Division, where he experienced rapid promotion. He became assistant cashier in 1950, assistant vice-president in 1952, and vice-president in 1954. Wriston came to the attention of George S. Moore, who had the assignment of expanding First National City's international presence. Even though Wriston had no foreign banking experience, Moore chose Wriston as his assistant on the basis of a written evaluation that touted Wriston as the most brilliant person ever to work at the bank. Wriston's initial assignment was running the European district. After 1956 Wriston advanced quickly in international operations. The bank promoted him to senior vice-president in 1958, head of the overseas division in 1959, and executive vice-president in 1960.

International banking had long comprised one of First National's strongest areas. Beginning with the largest international branch system of any American bank, First National expanded its network, entering new countries and adding branches in countries where it already had a presence. Within each branch the bank offered a wide range of financial services. It thereby intended to expand the local customer base and extend the services available to U.S. multinational corporations. At the time, Wriston described the program of the division as follows: "The plan in the Overseas Division was first to put a Citibank branch in every commercially important country in the world. The second phase was to begin to tap the local deposit market by putting satellite branches or mini-branches in a country. The third phase was to export retail services and know-how from New York. All of these phases ran concurrently and sometimes overlapped."

In addition to expanding the Overseas Division, Moore and Wriston radically revamped the personnel involved. They had inherited an international branch system that had become complacent and stagnant: the overseas staff had aged, and it suffered from low morale. Moore and Wriston breathed new life into the structure by bringing in officers from other divisions who had an interest in becoming agents of change. They also added approximately 50 recruits per year from the nation's leading universities and business schools.

Existing managers and supervisors were not exempt from the changes. By the end of 1959, the bank had changed two-thirds of the division's supervisors, either due to retirement or a call to return to New York. Moore and Wriston attempted to deepen the sense of team spirit among the managers by holding an annual meeting of senior officers from all branches. While that seemed like an obvious step, no one had ever done it at the bank before. Moore and Wriston also implemented decentralized decision-making in the international area. Although the reins were loose, New York retained control over major strategies and decisions. Those and other changes transformed the Overseas Division from a place of managerial exile into a much-coveted stepping stone for career advancement. When Wriston took over sole direction of the international operation, he had a very simple philosophy of branch expansion: put the bank—or an extension of it—everywhere a reasonable chance of profitability existed. Such broad expansion would diversify the bank's portfolio and permit it to make money where its competitors could not.

Europe was one area that received Wriston's attention. In 1959 First National had branches only in London and Paris, plus a representative office in Frankfurt. Europe was ripe with opportunity, due to the formation of the European Economic Community (EEC) in 1957 and the restoration of currency convertibility in 1959. Under Wriston's leadership, by 1965 the bank had at least one branch in each of the major European countries.

Even more dramatic branch expansion occurred in the rest of the world. The bank moved aggressively in the Middle East, Asia, and Latin America. By 1967, when Wriston was promoted to the bank's presidency, First National had 148 direct foreign branches in 42 countries. In addition, 93 offices of bank subsidiaries or affiliates operated in 21 countries. Those totals placed the bank far ahead of Chase Manhattan and the Bank of America, its nearest U.S. competitors.

During those years at the Overseas Division, Wriston also exhibited his talent for creativity and his vision of the future of banking. In 1961 Wriston and another First National City executive developed a new and revolutionary financial instrument, the negotiable certificate of deposit, or CD. First National offered the certificates to corporations in denominations of $100,000 or more at interest rates 1.25 percent to 1.75 percent above normal passbook rates. That permitted corporations to maximize their return on the large amounts of surplus capital they had available from time to time. CDs became an immediate success, with other banks soon following First National's lead.

The certificate of deposit, in the generic sense of a time deposit agreement between a bank and a large customer, was hardly new in 1961. Such certificates had appeared on bank balance sheets before the turn of the century. What was new was effective *negotiability*. Traditionally, deposit certificates had been nonnegotiable by their terms or by custom, and in practice they were not marketable— there was no secondary market for transforming an illiquid investment into one the investor could quickly turn into cash. To succeed, the new CD had to have an efficient secondary market, since it would compete for investor funds against the well-organized markets for Treasury securities and commercial paper.

In order to realize the CD's potential, Wriston persuaded the Discount Corporation of New York, a dealer in government securities, to start a secondary market in CDs. The Discount Corporation was willing, provided the bank supported the venture with an unsecured loan of $10 million. The bank broke its rule of not making unsecured loans to brokers, and the market for CDs was born.

Because the CD so changed the way banks generated funds, it also changed the way banks themselves had to operate. In the past, banks primarily served customers in a relatively protected geographical region. Within those regions, banks provided a bundle of financial services in exchange for deposits on which the bank paid less than a competitive rate. Once banks had to compete for deposits, however, they became more like other businesses: profits depended more on cost-conscious management, imaginative product development, and aggressive marketing. Wriston played a key role in the bank's adjustment to these new realities.

When Moore left the presidency of First National in 1967, the directors chose Wriston to succeed him. A few years later, Moore was quoted as saying, "Walter frightens me." Moore expressed a feeling that Wriston's daring aroused in many others as well. That sense of innovation flowed from a confidence in his own judgment, often in the face of widespread criticism and temporary setbacks.

As Wriston assumed First National's presidency, the bank faced many challenges. Business had become global, and so had finance. As the industrializing countries of Latin America and the Far East exerted their economic power, the United States no longer could completely dominate the world economy. The emergence of domestic inflation and the consequent weakening of the dollar as the undisputed world currency compounded the situation. As a result, a more pluralistic economic world, more volatile financial markets, and more competitors for First National City emerged. To take full advantage of the opportunities afforded by the changing economic environment, the bank had to broaden its geographical scope, customer base, and product line.

Two obstacles, however, stood in the bank's way. One was the sheer size of the institution. The bank had grown from 15,000 employees in 1955 to more than 27,000 in 1967. As the bank grew, management found it more difficult to coordinate diverse activities, identify and develop managerial talent, and even handle the mountains of back office paperwork. Clearly the bank needed a major reorganization.

The second obstacle, the regulatory environment then present in the United States, limited the bank's ability to adapt quickly to the changing and highly competitive economic situation. Despite such innovations as the certificate of deposit and the Eurodollar, structurally the U.S. banking system remained much the same as it had been since the Great Depression.

One of the hallmarks of Wriston's tenure as president was a constant probing and stretching of the limits of federal regulations. He viewed himself and the bank as "agents of change," and he later noted that "agents of change are rarely welcome." Wriston illustrated this with a folksy story:

> At the very beginning of the world, when Adam and Eve were driven from the Garden of Eden for disobedience and told that they must earn their bread henceforth by the sweat of their brows, Adam consoled Eve by saying: "We live in an age of transition." For them change was both rapid and drastic.... All history since has been dominated by change.... Despite protestations that innovation is welcome, mankind in general and sovereign authority and bureaucracies in particular resist change to the bitter end.... Everywhere change is popular in concept but unfortunate in practice.

In his first year as First National president, Wriston indeed became an internal agent of change: he initiated a major study leading to a massive corporate reorganization. As Wriston recalled later, he wanted "to completely reorganize this thing so that we're faced off against the marketplace and get generally in the twentieth century."

Wriston contracted with McKinsey and Company, a leading management consulting firm, to study the bank's organization. Toward the end of 1967 the McKinsey team presented a preliminary report that asked two major questions: "1. Is Citibank organized soundly–and for optimum profits–against the separate markets that it serves? 2. Is Citibank organized to provide sufficient top-management direction to its evolution as a financial conglomerate?" The consultants answered "no" to both questions.

The bank's structure at this time resembled the structure it had in the 1920s: geography provided the basis for most organizational decisions. The National Division, which handled corporate accounts outside of New York City, was organized regionally. The Metropolitan Division managed the bank's branches (both individual and corporate accounts) in the Greater New York City area. The Overseas Division handled international branches and accounts. Finally, three product or functional divisions completed the organization: the Trust Division, the Bond Department, and the Operations Division (back office support).

After an additional year of study, the consultants recommended a new structure effective on January 1, 1969. The new structure was based upon customer group or industry rather than geography. It divided the bank into seven major areas: personal banking (families and neighborhood businesses); commercial banking (medium-sized businesses); corporate banking (national and multinational businesses, governments); international banking (overseas operations); investment management (complete range of financial services to major institutions and wealthy individuals); the Money Market Division (formerly the Bond Department); and the Operating Group (the old Operating Division).

In another important structural change, the 1968 formation of the First National City Corporation provided a holding company that took over ownership of the bank. Although smaller banks previously had established holding companies, First National was the first of the large banks to implement that structure. Within a few months seven of the nation's ten biggest banks followed First National's lead and established holding companies. Upon the founding of First National City Corporation, Wriston became its first president.

The background for the decision to establish a holding company showed the inner workings of the bank's top management. In June of 1967, before he became president, Wriston received a memorandum that detailed a structural loophole in banking laws. The memorandum pointed out that the Bank Holding Company Act of 1956 applied only to holding companies that owned "two or more" banks. The same applied to the New York Holding Company law. The memorandum concluded that a holding company owning a single bank–a one-bank holding company–would not be subject to those laws. Furthermore, since the holding company was not a bank (it only would *control* the bank), the holding company could engage in activities beyond the bank's own charter. And all of that could take place without the approval of the Federal Reserve Board.

The federal government quickly recognized the large loophole the bank had discovered. In 1970 Congress made changes to the Bank Holding Company Act that restricted the businesses bank holding companies could enter. Nonetheless, the use of a holding company remained crucial to

Wriston's plans. Establishing separate subsidiaries of the holding company permitted First National to engage in a broad range of financial services forbidden to banks. In particular, it could engage in some activities, such as consumer finance, free from the geographical restrictions imposed on bank branches. The holding company also put the bank in a position to benefit from interstate banking, which people in the industry expected to be approved at any time. (The federal government has not authorized true interstate banking as of this writing.)

Under the Citicorp umbrella, Wriston expanded into several areas prohibited to banks. The corporation ventured into data processing, mortgage banking, real estate development, consumer credit, and commercial leasing. As an indication of the seriousness of his efforts, by 1973 Citicorp's leasing operation had an international scope and clearly was the largest in the world.

When Moore retired on May 1, 1970, Wriston succeeded him as chairman of both Citibank and Citicorp. Wriston also became chief executive officer of both organizations, titles Moore never held. Wriston remained in those positions until his retirement in 1984.

As chairman and chief executive officer, Wriston continued to innovate. Perhaps his biggest accomplishment was the development and installation of Citibank's $50 million electronic banking system. Today's ubiquitous automatic teller machines, or ATMs, obscure the revolutionary nature of Citibank's efforts. Modern Americans take for granted twenty-four-hour-a-day access to cash and financial services. But just a decade ago, few people accepted the idea of machines handling personal banking transactions. Not only did Citibank install a functioning network, but its extensive advertising made the concept of electronic banking not just palatable but essential. Citibank's efforts in the area of ATMs put it temporarily far ahead of its West Coast rival, the Bank of America. Indeed, Citibank attempted to put two of the machines at every business location, an undertaking that at first proved extremely costly.

Throughout his career, Wriston supported technological innovation and used it as a key wedge into new businesses. He also practiced what he preached, and leading-edge technology spread rapidly throughout the bank. At Citibank headquar-

ters, for example, robots even moved through the corridors, stopping at each desk to deliver mail.

But new technologies, computers in particular, always were more than toys: they served two deeper purposes. First, in order for Wriston's decentralized decision-making to be successful, top management needed sophisticated tools for monitoring worldwide performance. Improved systems of management information, therefore, provided necessary complements to decentralization. Second, in the increasingly competitive world of modern finance, a crucial need existed to control the overhead costs commonly associated with the "back office" support function.

Citibank had not always met with success, however, with its previous automation efforts, especially in the back office. It took many years of frustration to learn that applying the computer effectively required major changes in procedures and work flows. It was not enough to try to do conventional banking as usual, only faster. For computers to be effective, the entire back office operation would need to be studied and revamped.

When Wriston inherited the problem of automating the back office, morale had sunk to low levels. After a disappointing experience installing new computers in 1962, George Moore turned to an outside consulting firm for advice. The consultants followed the traditional efficiency-expert approach of establishing task standards and eliminating redundant positions. The consultants concluded that the bank could reduce operations personnel at the Head Office and the branches by 33 percent and still accomplish the same work, without raising average salaries. In order to realize those savings, however, the consultants insisted on having the power to identify "redundant" personnel and to have them discharged without question. Moore agreed to that condition over the objections of the bank's director of personnel. Giving the consultants that authority had disastrous results: morale declined, turnover increased, and a strong threat of unionization developed. In 1966 the bank canceled the reorganization and terminated the agreement with the consulting firm.

In 1969 Wriston addressed the problem by forming a task force under the leadership of John S. Reed. This group avoided the traditional pitfall of trying to apply computers to existing operating functions and work flows. Rather, the group redefined functions and reshaped work flows in a way that realized the computer's cost-reducing potential. While it took years to implement changes fully, the new way of thinking instituted by Wriston and Reed made long-term success possible.

Price increases by the Organization of Petroleum Exporting Countries (OPEC) in the early 1970s presented the bank with other new challenges. At first the inflation generated by the oil price rise seemed to pose the greatest threat, reaching previously unseen heights in the United States of 10 percent to 12 percent and bordering on hyperinflation. Citibank could adjust its interest rates to maintain its profit levels, but it could do little about the impact on the American (and Western European) economy as a whole. Recession and stagflation set in, and American productivity fell. At the same time, the OPEC countries took $80 billion a year out of the world economy, the equivalent of 10 percent of the world's exports. Kuwait and Saudi Arabia added some $37 billion a year to their accounts. Most of that transfer of wealth came in the form of American trade deficit dollars that flooded overseas into the Eurodollar market.

The Eurodollar had originated in 1949 when the People's Republic of China, concerned about the possibility that American presidential administrations might block the dollars it earned by freezing them in U.S. banks, started to place its dollars in a Soviet-owned Paris bank, with a cable address: "Eurobank." Soon, dozens of virtually unregulated banks in Europe held hordes of dollars, essentially creating a black market for currency. By the 1970s, the money earned by the OPEC countries—"Petrodollars"—flowed into the same unregulated European money market to mix with the Eurodollars. Early in the 1960s the Kennedy administration, then, later, European governments, tried but failed to establish controls over Eurodollars. Instead, as Wriston observed, the entire Eurodollar system was "fathered by controls," with the expected natural development that money sought out its own value and levels. As British historian Paul Johnson explained it, the Eurocurrency market was "a kind of black market world financial system. Freed of government interference, it was able to make the maximum use of the new electronic communications devices which became available in the 1960s and 1970s." Wriston pointedly noted that "mankind now has a completely integrated international financial and information marketplace, capable of moving money and ideas to any place on this planet within minutes."

Those two forces—inflation brought on by OPEC price increases, and the Eurodollar/Petrodollar market—seemingly combined to pose a danger in that from 1974 to 1977 the Arab countries held one-half of the world's liquidity. Concerns arose in the United States that, due to American support for Israel, the Arabs might use their "money weapon" by suddenly withdrawing billions of dollars from the banking system, throwing American banks into chaos. Wriston, however, remained calm: "If Exxon pays Saudi Arabia $50 billion, all that happens is that we debit Exxon and credit Saudi Arabia. The balance-sheet of Citibank remains the same. And if [the Saudis] say they don't like American banks, [and] they'll put [their deposits] in *Credit Suisse*, all we do is charge Saudi Arabia and credit *Credit Suisse*: our balance sheet remains the same. So when people run around waiting for the sky to fall there isn't any way that money can leave the system. It's a closed circuit."

Better from Citibank's point of view, the bank suddenly found itself with billions of petrodollars to lend and few domestic borrowers. Thus, American banks shipped most of it out to "the bottomless pit of needs in the developing nations," in Johnson's words. Ironically, while the OPEC countries had not expressed any interest in aiding underdeveloped countries—indeed, the petroleum price increase was directly responsible for the downturn in the developing countries' economies and thus contributed to massive malnutrition and disease-related death—they had no choice. They could either make direct aid transfers or put their money in banks that loaned it with or without their consent: their lack of control baffled them.

Citibank and other major American banks immediately targeted foreign borrowers who begged for money, the developing countries. It proved an ironic policy for Wriston, who years later had his name withdrawn from consideration for a position in the Reagan administration because of those loans, which by then had been rolled over several times, each time without any of the principal paid. At the time, however, Citibank's policies seemed wise. Given the increasing price of oil, Mexico and Venezuela in particular seemed good risks, and Wriston defended the loans vigorously.

Not all of Wriston's innovations met with success. In some cases, federal regulators concerned about the growing power of the institution forced the bank to change course. In 1980, for example, Citicorp tested the limits of interstate banking laws by offering a broad range of financial and banking-type services under the aegis of a credit card in the Washington and Baltimore areas. Called the "Choice Card," it combined traditional credit card services with quasi-banking functions. Citicorp's paying of 8.45 percent interest on money "prepaid" into Choice credit card accounts proved particularly irksome to the Federal Reserve. To some bankers, that seemed very close to accepting out-of-state deposits, an activity strictly forbidden under the McFadden Act of 1927.

In other cases, changing economic circumstances led to failures where the bank once experienced successes. In the mid 1970s, Citibank concluded that its future growth lay in consumer banking. At that time other major institutions, such as Bankers Trust, had withdrawn from consumer banking because of its expense: it traditionally yielded low margins, and remained at the mercy of capricious interest rates. Though New York's usury law capped interest on consumer loans at 12 percent, Citibank executives expressed little concern about shrinking margins because they expected interest rates to drop. In characteristic fashion, Citibank plunged into the consumer market with both feet, increasing its consumer loan portfolio from $4.2 billion in 1974 to $14.7 billion in 1980. But soaring interest rates cut Citibank's spread and also its profits. As a result, in 1980 Citibank lost $150 million on its consumer operation (a development that afflicted other large banks as well).

Another area where initial success later turned to problems involved the aforementioned loans to developing countries. Wriston had forcefully advocated lending money to "Third World" countries and committed sizable Citibank assets, again, which the bank had available through the petrodollar deposits, to the effort. For many years those seemed prudent investments; however, beginning with Mexico's failure to keep up with payments on its foreign loans in 1982, the "international debt crisis" threatened to undermine the banking system. In fact, much of the lending proved absolutely useless: in Indonesia, one official pocketed $80 million of that country's total borrowing of $6 billion. Zaire borrowed $3 billion with little hope of repayment.

Despite the problems, Wriston continued to insist that large-scale lending to developing nations was in the best interest of all concerned. Amid the fears of a Mexican default, in fact, Wriston wrote an article for the op-ed page of the *New York Times* in September 1982. Concerns over default were exaggerated, Wriston maintained, because "there are few recorded instances in history of governments–any government–actually getting out of debt." Countries do not "go bankrupt," he asserted, they just keep rolling over their debts. "When problems arise, they are problems of liquidity, not insolvency."

After his retirement, Wriston reflected further on the problem of international loans: "The worry beads labeled 'loans to less developed countries' have been rubbed bare, and needlessly so. Some of the rhetoric of concern flows from various forums of Third World gatherings, some from scholarly studies, and a lot from the pages of our daily newspapers. It is produced by people with short memories or near vision who see only problems. In the course of my banking career, I've lent money to France, Britain, Italy, and about every country in Latin America, and at the time each borrowed it was in bad shape, otherwise none would have had to borrow. All those loans were repaid in time. That experience is not unique."

Wriston went on to remind his readers that the United States, too, once was a "less developed country." Only with the help of foreign investors did the United States achieve its potential. "The most productive role our commercial banks can play in the prospective world environment," he concluded, "is to keep the conduits [for money and credit] open and to play our traditional role of reminding all who will listen that there are no magic solutions to problems brought on by bad monetary and fiscal policies. These problems can be cured only by a return to sound policies. These policies take time to work, and while the banks can help supply that time, only political will can put the proper programs in place. Those programs do not make headlines, but they have worked in the past and will work in the future."

Indeed, the major problem in most of the debtor countries was that they still maintained strict controls on their economies, thus choking any potential growth. Nevertheless, Wriston the prudent businessman presided over a policy that set aside ever-increasing loan-loss reserves.

Throughout the 1970s, Citibank was also criticized for its domestic actions. The Ralph Nader Study Group, for example, conducted a lengthy investigation of the bank and issued a highly critical 406-page report entitled *Citibank*. Among other things, the report charged that Citibank invested trust funds to its own advantage, failed to disclose interest rate charges on checking accounts, favored corporate customers over individual borrowers, and paid its clerical workers unlivable wages. Citibank prepared a detailed response to the Nader charges and published it in 1974 under the title *Citibank, Nader and the Facts*. Wriston wrote an introduction to the volume attacking the Nader group for its "reckless misuse of facts." He continued, "But what disturbs us most about this book is the [Nader] study group's irresponsible and multiplied use of the 'presumption of guilt' technique whereby it states its own unsubstantiated suspicions of alleged Citibank wrongdoing and then calls on us to prove otherwise. This is like asking a man to prove that he has never kicked his dog."

Citibank also received criticism during the New York City financial crisis of the late 1970s. As head of the city's biggest bank, Wriston naturally was criticized by those people who believed that the banks were partly to blame for New York's problems. According to the critics, Citibank took too hard a line with the city before lending money. In exchange for additional financial assistance during the time of crisis, Citibank led the way in demanding stricter budget controls by the city. Wriston responded to the critics by stating that Citibank aimed its efforts at keeping the city solvent during a time of near bankruptcy. Several years later Wriston commented on New York's crisis: "Bad economic policies can ruin any economy over time. We have all seen in our lifetime countries destroyed by inflation. Recently we saw the City of New York almost go down, but we also saw it pull itself back to economic health by the novel economic device known as balancing the budget. Today . . . New York City enjoys an investment-grade rating on its bonds and access to the market. There was no bold breakthrough. It was simple Benjamin Franklin economics [spend less than you receive]."

Beyond preaching fiscal soundness, Wriston played a personal role in resolving the city's problems. Working with Jack Bigel, a financial consultant to the municipal labor unions, Wriston forged a coalition between bankers and the unions, two perennially hostile groups. The coalition and the cooperation it fostered helped avert the city's bankruptcy.

Wriston's role in the New York City financial crisis reaffirmed his role as statesman as well as banker. His peers considered him to be an intellectual, almost a "banker-philosopher." During the 1970s and 1980s, Wriston emerged as one of the leading champions of the free enterprise system and a spokesperson for the traditional American values of hard work, ambition, and achievement. He often served as an adviser to President Ronald Reagan and even headed the President's Economic Policy Advisory Board. Reagan and Wriston shared similar views on most economic matters, with Wriston quoted as saying: "I was and am a big supporter of attacking budgetary problems on the spending side. I was and am a supporter of moderate and steady monetary growth. I was and am a supporter of decontrol of oil prices and the deregulation of industries." A few years later, Wriston explained this further: "In my country, the free market and the bureaucracy furnish models of one system that works and one that doesn't. There is no mystery about it. The free market works because thousands of participants vigorously pursue what they believe to be their own self interest, and thus rational bargains are struck between buyers and sellers. The [bureaucratic] model doesn't work because it attempts to substitute centralized policy judgment for the distributive wisdom of the marketplace. If all that did were to fail, the damage would be contained. But in most instances of this kind, the real casualty is individual liberty, the loss of a little bit more of our freedom of choice."

As Wriston's mandatory retirement approached in 1984, there was widespread speculation about who would succeed him as head of Citibank. The leading candidates were John Reed, the man who had led the bank's expansion in consumer operations and electronic banking; Thomas Theobald, the head of the bank's biggest profit centers, the departments devoted to corporate clients and governments; and Hans Angermueller, a lawyer rather than a banker, who was in charge of legal, regulatory, and external affairs. Rather than naming a successor early, a year before his retirement Wriston promoted all three men to vice-chairman and gave them identical salaries and bonuses totaling $560,842. Wriston made it clear that the bank probably, though not necessarily, would choose his successor from their ranks.

The nature of the succession process provided just one example of the tough, competitive atmosphere Wriston fostered at Citicorp. He built a management system that gave supervisors a great deal of autonomy—Wriston once referred to it as a "meritocracy." Along with the autonomy, however, came a great deal of pressure on managers to produce quick results. Those achieving quick results received rapid promotions; those who failed to achieve results were expected to look for work elsewhere. Management intended that supercharged environment to identify and nurture Citicorp "superstars."

The bank conducted its nurturing, however, in a very formal way. Citicorp's senior executives kept careful watch over a group called its Corporate Property—75 managers identified early as having top leadership potential. Locked away on the executive floor stood a large board featuring photographs and biographies of the current elect. Those 75 managers were watched carefully and moved regularly from job to job in order to give them maximum experience and exposure. As long as the 75 lived up to expectations, they remained on the board and before the watchful eyes of senior management.

The entrepreneurial philosophy and aggressive attitude did help Citicorp to grow. Its assets soared from $26 billion in 1970, when Wriston became chairman, to $151 billion in 1984. Its net income in that final year was $890 million. In terms of profitability, Wriston early in his career set a public goal of increasing profits by 15 percent per year. While early in his tenure the bank met that goal, between 1976 and 1981 earning rose by only about 8 percent per year, barely enough to keep up with inflation.

At the time of Wriston's retirement on August 31, 1984, Citicorp's empire consisted of 71,000 employees in 41 states and 91 countries, all linked by one of the most sophisticated and expensive communications networks in the world. Wriston ultimately selected John Reed, forty-five years old at the time, to succeed him as chairman. William E. Simon, a former Citicorp director, attributed the selection to Reed's vision as much as to his banking acumen: "I think it was his absolute brilliance, coupled with his willingness to take a risk and be way ahead of the power curve in terms of getting Citi into the future" that made the difference. Or as Wriston summarized his own management philosophy, "I think the most important thing is to take a chance on people. Somebody took a hell of a chance on me."

Wriston's retirement—"achieving statutory senility," as he called it—led to major changes in his life. He quipped to one reporter: "When you retire from Citibank, you go from who's who to who's that." Wriston made the decision to stay aloof from the bank's day-to-day operations, in order to give Reed the freedom to manage the bank his own way. "The deal is that anytime he thinks my perspective might be useful, I'm here," said Wriston. "But I won't pick up the phone. I will never intrude unasked." Wriston, in fact, set up his postretirement office in the Citicorp Center, across the street from Citicorp's headquarters at 399 Park Avenue.

Wriston's hands-off attitude with the bank did not mean, however, that he was ready to take it easy. "The issue is: If you have your health, something I've been blessed with, what do you do with the rest of your life?" Wriston was not about to follow some people and "get the golf clubs and sit on a beach."

In his first year after retirement, Wriston was a director of eight corporations, including J. C. Penney, General Electric, Pfizer, and Pan American. Wriston also was an unpaid consultant to the State Department, chairman of the President's Economic Policy Advisory Board, and a frequent lecturer and speaker. In addition, he continued his charitable activities, assisting numerous nonprofit organizations with their fund-raising efforts.

Wriston also continued his extensive publication efforts. In a 1988 issue of *Foreign Affairs*, he displayed his deep grasp of the changes that had occurred in the world of finance. His article, "Technology and Sovereignty," perceptively noted the fundamental changes in money and finance brought about by new technology. Arguing along the lines of economic theorist George Gilder, whom he quoted frequently, Wriston maintained that "the relative importance of intellectual capital invested in software and systems will increase in relation to the capital invested in physical plants and equipment." Equally important, "traditional accounting systems designed for an earlier age no longer reflect what is really happening, either in business or economics." Pointing to the information revolution that had changed the global economy and political and business institutions, Wriston observed that information technology made it possible for politicians to bypass traditional political structures and appeal directly to mass populations. The result was eroding control by governments over the "management of institutions and how citizens live and work." Nation states could no longer mandate the value of their currency: information screens displayed the value of any currency worldwide, 24 hours a day, to millions of locations. As Wriston concluded, "The entire globe is linked electronically, with no place to hide." The effect of that technology on government fiscal and monetary policies had proved "more draconian than the gold exchange standard and a great deal faster."

After his retirement, insiders often mentioned Wriston as a candidate for a high-level governmental appointment, a process he likened to "being hung out on the line to flap around and dry." Despite the drawbacks, in several interviews Wriston seemed to relish the idea of government service. He specifically referred to W. Averell Harriman and John J. McCloy, two bankers who also made important contributions in government.

Wriston had been mentioned as a leading candidate in 1980 to be President Reagan's Treasury secretary, a position ultimately given to Donald T. Regan. He later insisted that President Reagan never offered him the job, though both presidents Nixon and Ford did offer him the Treasury position. As Wriston told the story: "I agonized about it and elected to keep the job I had. History is not written in the subjunctive mood, my professors used to say. Whether I could have made a contribution on the other side, nobody knows. I'm not a fellow who plays what-if. You play the cards the world deals you. That's it."

In 1985 Wriston's name was again floated as a trial balloon for the position of U.S. trade representative. Reagan administration officials, however, soon came to fear difficult Senate confirmation hearings. They expected Wriston to receive a great deal of criticism about Citicorp's extensive loans to developing countries during the 1970s, which erupted as a world debt crisis in 1982. Wriston apparently withdrew his name from consideration when he learned of the expected Senate problems.

The irony of Wriston's withdrawal showed the highly partisan nature of the "trade deficit" question and the weakness of the criticisms aimed at the administration over it. Loans to developing countries in the 1970s and early 1980s, when the nation frequently had a favorable balance of trade, appeared on the *asset* side of the ledger. They added $100 billion to the American balance of trade. Yet only when the banks finally determined on their

own that the developing nations would never repay their loans—despite Wriston's public positions to the contrary—did they put aside loan loss reserves, write off the existing loans, and refuse to make new loans. When that happened, the $100 billion or so that had shown on the asset side of the ledger came off. Suddenly, the United States had a "trade deficit." Suddenly it was a "debtor nation."

Yet the actual position of the economy relative to overall trade, when measured in real recoverable values, had not changed at all, and indeed one could argue that carrying worthless debts as an asset for almost a decade invalidated the very statistics upon which critics built their case. Was the United States actually any worse off than if American banks added back $100 billion in loans to Brazil or Nigeria to "balance the trade deficit"? Was the United States better off in the stagflating 1970s with a trade surplus? Certainly no one thought so when the situation was viewed in those terms. The basic admission that the loans would not be repaid removed roughly $100 billion from the U.S. balance of trade—almost exactly the size of the "deficit." If anything, the lending by Citibank and the other large banks only concealed the nature of the international trade picture.

Shortly after Wriston retired, Citibank had recognized the problem before any other bank, and only after it set aside large loan loss reserves (and saw its stock soar as the market reacted) did other large banks put aside larger loss reserves. Thus, whatever Wriston had preached, the bank followed a much more realistic policy.

One of Wriston's retirement projects involved preparing a collection of essays for publication by Harper & Row in 1986. The book, *Risk and Other Four-Letter Words*, featured edited versions of Wriston's speeches, many delivered during the height of various public controversies. The major theme of Wriston's book is that risk is a normal part of living, a fact recognized by the Founding Fathers as well as numerous entrepreneurs and politicians since then. According to Wriston, "All of life is the management of risk, not its elimination. We can have too much exercise, or too little; too much food, or too little; too much medical attention, or too little; take too much risk with our investments, or too little. Increased disclosure may help reduce ignorance-induced risk but can never protect against the natural risks inherent in decision making." Or, he wrote elsewhere in the book, "The society that promises no risks, and whose leaders use the word 'risk' only as a pejorative, may be able to protect life, but there will be no liberty, and very little pursuit of happiness. . . . In short, uncertainty is the opportunity to make the world a better place."

Wriston's retirement also gave him more time to devote to family matters. In 1966 his first wife, Barbara Brengle Wriston, died. She and Wriston had one child, a daughter named Catherine. In 1968 Wriston married his second wife, Kathryn Ann Dineen, an associate at Shearman Sterling, Citibank's primary law firm. The second Mrs. Wriston, 20 years her husband's junior, also served as a director of several corporations and on numerous panels in the law and accounting professions. The couple spent a great deal of time at a country home, a Connecticut tree farm, where, in Wriston's words, he acted as "carpenter, electrician, plumber, backhoe operator, front-end loader operator, and chain saw operator—you name it." Wriston stayed in shape by playing tennis regularly. During the 1977 New York City blackout, he thought nothing of walking down 23 flights of stairs in his apartment building, hiking to corporate headquarters, and then climbing 15 flights to his office.

Perhaps that incident, better than any other,

aptly summarizes Wriston's personal and professional life. Never one to let the world pass him by, he aggressively faced all challenges in pursuit of his goal of making Citibank the premier financial institution in the world. Both Wriston and Citibank chose to lead rather than follow, expand rather than contract, and innovate rather than stagnate. The combination of a visionary individual with a powerful institution left the world of finance forever changed.

Publications:

Risk and Other Four-Letter Words (New York: Harper & Row, 1986);
"Technology and Sovereignty," *Foreign Affairs* (Winter 1988).

References:

Citibank, Nader and the Facts (New York: First National City Bank, 1974);
Harold van B. Cleveland and Thomas F. Huertas, *Citibank, 1812-1970* (Cambridge, Mass.: Harvard University Press, 1985);
Paul Johnson, *Modern Times: A History of the World from the Twenties to the Eighties* (New York: Harper & Row, 1980).

Owen D. Young

(October 27, 1874 - July 11, 1962)

by Stephen A. Schuker

Brandeis University

CAREER: Attorney (1896-1907), partner, Tyler & Young, Boston (1907-1912); vice-president and general counsel (1913-1922), chairman, General Electric Company (1922-1939, 1942-1944); founder and chairman (1919-1929), director and chairman of the executive committee, Radio Corporation of America (1930-1933); Class B (industry) director (1923-1927), Class C (public) director (1927-1940), deputy chairman (1927-1938), chairman, Federal Reserve Bank of New York (1938-1940); delegate, Reparations Commission (1924); acting agent-general, Dawes Plan (1924); chairman, Young Committee (1929).

Owen D. Young, a patent and utilities attorney, served as chairman of the General Electric Com-

pany between the two world wars and founded the Radio Corporation of America in 1919. One of the most widely admired Americans of his era, he won particular recognition as the prototype of the modern industrial leader who emphasized amicable labor relations and service to the public as much as the "bottom line." Young figured as the most influential member of successive international committees that investigated German reparations in 1924 and 1929. As deputy chairman of the New York Federal Reserve Bank, he assumed considerable responsibility for the open-market operations that stopped the spiral of monetary deflation during the Great Depression.

Owen D. Young, the only surviving child of Jacob Smith Young and Ida Brandow, was born on

Owen D. Young

October 27, 1874, in Van Hornesville, a small up-state hamlet in the vicinity of Cooperstown, New York. The paternal family, originally named Jung, migrated from the German Palatinate to the Mohawk country around the middle of the eighteenth century; the maternal family arrived shortly after the American Revolution from the Netherlands. Smith and Ida Young ran an 80-acre farm that belonged to the paternal grandfather on the well-watered, rolling hills along the Otsquago Creek. The family made a fairly satisfactory living producing dairy products, hops, fruit, and vegetables, but only by dint of unremitting toil. The elder Youngs had waited eighteen years for a child, and young Owen, always a sunny personality, became the apple of their eye. He was recognized early in the area's "little red schoolhouse" as a promising student and sent on to the East Springfield Academy. A windfall profit on the hops crop in 1890 enabled his parents to send him to St. Lawrence University, a small college in Canton, New York. St. Lawrence was associated with the theologically liberal Universalist religion and offered a degree of intellectual freedom rare among church-related institutions of the period.

St. Lawrence had a formative influence on Young, and he remained intensely loyal to the college all his life. He became a trustee, then chairman of the board, and not only provided his own generous benefactions but persuaded many friends in the business community to make contributions as well. At St. Lawrence, Young courted Josephine Sheldon Edmonds, an intellectually gifted and financially comfortable fellow student from Southbridge, Massachusetts, whom he married in June 1898. The couple had five children (all later distinguished in their own right) and re-created the close and gentle family life of Owen's own home; they remained intensely devoted to each other until Josephine's premature death from heart disease in 1935.

After receiving his A.B. degree in 1894, Young aimed to go on to the Harvard Law School, but he was refused admission because he lacked the funds to attend without working part-time. Undaunted, Young used his Universalist church connections to obtain a scholarship from the fledgling Boston University Law School. Although he sometimes ran short of food and other necessities, Young was determined to "get on." He worked indefatigably. "There isn't much frosting about Owen," his future mother-in-law remarked, "but he is a true gentleman, with the best kind of breeding that comes from the heart, and that is the noblest, best kind after all." Young ranked at the top of his class when he obtained the LL.B. in 1896 and was asked to remain as a part-time instructor. (He declined the offer of the law school deanship seven years later.) He also became a clerk in the corporate and real estate law offices of Charles Tyler in Boston, where he proved so valuable that he doubled his salary within six months.

Despite his modest beginnings, Young's star rose unusually rapidly in the socially stratified Boston legal fraternity. He had enjoyed an untroubled relationship with his father. He related easily to older men. Tyler became his enthusiastic patron and made him a full partner in 1907. In the first decade of the century Boston still figured as a major center of railroad corporate headquarters. Young became a specialist in railroad reorganization—later known as merger and acquisition work—and developed the knack of compromising apparently irreconcilable positions. This talent for bringing people together in harmonious negotiation would stand Young in good stead throughout his life. He shortly progressed from railroad cases to public-utilities law.

His firm became the lead counsel for Stone & Webster, an engineering company that specialized in building and managing electric street railways and public utilities—a hot growth industry of the period. Young emerged as a recognized authority on public utility law and testified frequently in favor of the sort of regulation that would safeguard consumers' rights as well as preserve the ability of utility companies to provide satisfactory service. He had earlier concentrated on personal advancement and devoted little thought to politics, but his utility work inspired his interest in municipal reform and moved him to the left. Although never a radical, he remained throughout most of his life a reform Democrat with a lively interest (uncommon among top corporate executives of the era) in the problems of the common man.

Young's work in the utilities field brought him to the attention of Charles Coffin, president of the General Electric (GE) Company. In a form of backward vertical integration, GE—the leading firm in the field—supplied generators and other electrotechnical goods to power and light companies in return for part of their stock. Electric Bond and Share, a GE subsidiary formed to hold those equity positions, had thereby become a major force in the utilities industry. Coffin needed a strong vice-president and general counsel with sufficient flexibility to handle a wide variety of problems in the burgeoning fields of patent and regulatory law. Young had gotten bored with what he deemed the "mediaeval" character of general practice, and at the end of 1912 he agreed to join General Electric in New York.

GE then held almost a quarter of the national market for electrical goods. But it faced difficulties in expanding market share beyond that because it had accepted a 1911 consent decree under the Sherman Antitrust Act regarding patents and pricing procedures for the production and marketing of the incandescent lamp. Young subscribed to the form of Progressivism championed by Woodrow Wilson and Louis Brandeis rather than that of Theodore Roosevelt. In principle he favored strict limits on business combination and the enforcement of competition, in part by the elimination of tariff protection, rather than the acceptance of publicly useful trusts. Yet he also wished to show that a major corporation need not be inefficient or antisocial, and he sought to shape GE policy so that the firm could prosper, not merely within the letter, but also

within the spirit, of the law. Despite complaints from radicals about the "power trust," it made good economic sense for Electric Bond and Share and other utility holding companies to acquire at least minority interests in the power plants that provided a major market for capital goods in the highly cyclical electrotechnical industry. Young insisted that the GE legal department guard against abuses by developing a yardstick for fair competition and the full disclosure of all such investments. He did not oppose the Clayton Antitrust Act of 1914 and expressed willingness to live with an ably manned Federal Trade Commission. He opposed the notion that public utility commissions should guarantee a set profit rate for all utilities, even if badly managed, and urged only that rates be set high enough so that efficiently run franchises could justify further capital investment.

Despite a difficult regulatory climate, GE experienced a boom in revenues and profits during World War I. Spurred on by overseas orders and the demands of American defense, the firm developed a host of new products, including turbine generators, other ship-propulsion equipment, and radio. Young helped solve the problems of corporate prosperity, including several patent disputes and the demands of labor for a larger share of the pie. Largely owing to Young's influence, GE stood among the minority of progressive employers that embraced enlightened labor policies and accepted the union shop. Young helped to settle a strike at GE's Lynn, Massachusetts, plant in 1919 by perceiving that the workers sought a voice in labor conditions there as well as higher wages. At industrial conferences convened by the federal government in 1919 and 1920, Young elaborated his vision of labor-management cooperation on a national level. He spoke out for collective bargaining and employee representation on corporate boards.

In 1919 Young, under the prodding of the U.S. Navy, helped to found the Radio Corporation of America. Four years earlier GE had acquired the patent to the Alexanderson alternator, a device for generating high-frequency radio waves. The navy had quickly grasped the military importance of long-distance wireless transmission, and during the war it had seized all shortwave radio stations and directed the manufacturing companies to ignore patent restrictions for the duration. In April 1919, as GE prepared to resume normal commercial relations and to license its Alexanderson alternator to

Young (left) with Charles G. Dawes and Henry M. Robinson in New York after concluding the Dawes reparations agreement in April 1924 (courtesy of Keystone View Company, Inc.)

the British Marconi Wireless Telegraph Company, the navy intervened again to block transfer of the new technology. The British already controlled all ocean cable traffic, and, if they gained access to the Alexanderson alternator, U.S. officials feared they would monopolize international communications. Admiral William Bullard, director of naval communications, acting with the approval of Assistant Secretary Franklin D. Roosevelt, made a patriotic appeal to GE to form an American-owned radio operating company with sufficient capital to compete head-to-head with Marconi around the world. Bullard offered government patent cooperation. He made it clear that President Wilson himself, for strategic and economic reasons, thought it vital to prevent British dominance of Western Hemisphere communications.

In the fall of 1919, after arduous negotiations, the Radio Corporation of America came into being, and Young assumed the post of chairman. In a complicated deal, RCA became the exclusive American agent for marketing GE radio equipment; British Marconi's American subsidiary sold its U.S. stations and other assets in return for valuable patents and cross-licensing concessions and for a generous di-

vision of the world into radio zones; and the navy placed a representative on the RCA board to protect the national interest. After several more years of jockeying the U.S. government had to abandon its objective of an all-American shortwave monopoly in the Western Hemisphere but in turn managed to defeat a British-sponsored scheme for government allocation of international radio rights.

Young took great pride in the development of broadcasting and believed that radio could serve as a force for enlightenment of the citizenry at home and for peace and understanding abroad. Under his leadership GE made agreements with Westinghouse Electric and the American Telephone & Telegraph (AT&T) Western Electric Division in 1920-1921 that brought a strong capital infusion for RCA and the right to use advanced vacuum-tube technology. Broadcasting developed into a booming business. Five years later one-fifth of American households had already purchased radio receivers. In 1926, Young and his protégé David Sarnoff created the National Broadcasting Company, the first chain of radio operating stations, to meet the growing demand for radio entertainment. Young acknowledged that the American system of competitive private broadcasting would result in fewer cultural programs than were supplied by the government broadcast monopolies of Europe, but he considered the tradeoff worthwhile in order to avoid state censorship and control. Under Young's leadership in the later 1920s, RCA scientists pushed at the frontiers of knowledge in the record business, talking pictures, radio facsimile, and other new technologies.

Paradoxically, at the end of the 1920s the government turned against the radio patent pool that it had appealed to GE just a decade before to create. In 1924 the Federal Trade Commission filed suit against RCA for violation of antitrust laws, but after several years of intermittent harassment it dropped the action in 1928. In May 1930 the attorney general revived the suit and charged the "radio group" (RCA, GE, Westinghouse, and AT&T) with constituting a patent monopoly. RCA officials privately blamed President Hoover and spoke darkly of "an act of betrayal in high places, . . . prompted . . . by jealousy and fear." As the Depression deepened, Washington politicians found it easier to attack the "radio trust" and other business groups than to design an effective countercyclical policy. The secretary of commerce admitted privately to Young that the case had a large political component, but the government persisted nevertheless. By November 1932, RCA, which had sustained tremendous business losses, could no longer afford the costs of litigation. The radio group accepted a harsh consent decree that forced GE and Westinghouse to dispose of their RCA holdings. Young, to his disappointment, had to resign as chairman.

In May 1922, Charles Coffin and the other top leaders of General Electric retired. Young, long the heir apparent, became chairman of the board, and Gerard Swope took over as president. The two men, who complemented each other perfectly, ran GE together until the end of 1939. Young, the smooth-talking diplomat and negotiator, set general policy and represented the firm to the public, while Swope, the precise and hard-driving engineer, managed internal operations.

Young and Swope provided a new type of industrial leadership that attracted wide popular admiration and set a model for the progressive business community. They articulated their philosophy frequently at business schools and in other public forums, contending that the separation of ownership from control in the modern corporation imposed fresh responsibilities on management. In the new environment, Young argued, managers should regard themselves as the "trustees of an enterprise in which capital and labor cooperate." He and Swope believed that they could foster higher productivity and improve profitability by providing not merely a living wage but what they felicitously described as a "cultural wage." They pioneered in the use of employee stock options and savings programs, pension and medical plans, disability insurance, and home ownership loans. Of course, it helped that the electrical industry enjoyed a high rate of technical innovation in the 1920s, with many products at the most profitable points in their product cycles. Not coincidentally, the favorable publicity generated by the firm's enlightened labor policies also helped to counteract radical attacks on GE and its subsidiary, Electric Bond and Share, as components of a sinister "power trust."

Meanwhile, Young and Swope redesigned the firm's strategy to emphasize forward rather than backward integration. Selling generators for power plants was at best a cyclical and risky business. In late 1924, Young and Swope spun off GE's utility holdings and determined instead to expand the production and marketing of household consumer goods. In the following years they also diversified geographically by purchasing shares in European electrical firms and concluding cross-licensing agreements. The new strategy did not proceed fast enough to avoid sharp losses when the American capital goods market collapsed completely during the Depression. In the long run, however, it produced a firm better suited to withstand the vicissitudes of the domestic business cycle. When Young retired on the eve of World War II, electrical appliances and other consumer products accounted for half of GE's total output.

In December 1923, Young was tapped by Secretary of State Charles Evans Hughes to serve as the second American delegate on an Expert Committee established in Paris to investigate German reparations. Young had no prior experience in international diplomacy, but his service at the National Industrial Conference in 1919-1920 and on other government boards had won him much esteem in Washington. While he had never left North America before 1921 and spoke no foreign languages, he had negotiated successfully with the British on wireless issues and with executives in the German electrical industry on patent exchanges. Thus he already had many contacts in the European business world.

Hughes and his administration colleagues also sought to give American representation on the Expert Committee a bipartisan cast. Young, a lifelong Democrat who had no connection with "Wall Street" except for brief service as an outside director of the Federal Reserve Bank of New York, fit the bill admirably.

Reparations had become the most prickly issue of international politics in the years after World War I. The statesmen at the Paris Peace Conference of 1919 had not reached a consensus on how much Germany should pay to compensate the Allies for the wartime destruction caused by the armies of the Reich. They had set up a Reparations Commission to assess the damages and determine reconstruction costs. After two years of ongoing dispute the commission reported in May 1921, and the Allies coerced Germany into accepting the so-called London Schedule of Payments. This schedule set the theoretical bill at a stratospheric $33 billion in order to appease the Allied public but limited Germany's practical obligations to $12.5 billion. The annual payments would consume approximately 5.4 percent of German national income. The government in Berlin probably could have paid with some strain, but did not want to do so. It allowed a hyperinflation to take place rather than impose taxation that would have facilitated a transfer of the indemnity. Reparations came to be the focus of the struggle between France and Germany for economic dominance in Europe, just as the controversy concerning European payments of war debts to the United States became a proxy for Anglo-American rivalry over leadership in world finance. American policymakers did not want to entangle themselves directly in the squabble over reparations, but they felt that, so long as the dispute remained unresolved, European economic reconstruction could not proceed and therefore American trade would suffer.

At the end of 1922, Secretary Hughes had tried to break the deadlock by proposing that an independent committee of businessmen reexamine German capacity to pay. The Hughes initiative came too late to stave off a Franco-Belgian occupation of the Ruhr, and a test of strength between the two sides ensued. By the autumn of 1923, however, passive resistance in the Ruhr had failed, while the effort to coerce Germany had imposed perilous strain on the French currency and tax system. Hughes revived his idea, and this time all parties to

the reparation dispute accepted.

The Expert Committee appointed by the Reparations Commission (the U.S. government pretended for political reasons not to be officially involved) was charged with considering ways to balance the German budget and to stabilize the German currency. It had no official mandate to revise the London Schedule but in practice could recommend a schedule of annual payments that would fix the level of reparations until the passage of time made a definitive settlement possible. Young's senior colleague, the Chicago banker Charles G. Dawes, assumed the chairmanship of the committee that came to bear his name. But Dawes had no patience for detail. He envisaged his task as keeping good relations among committee members and representing the group to the general public. It fell largely to Young (along with a British colleague, Sir Josiah Stamp) to oversee the investigation of the German economy and banking system and to shape the intricate negotiations among committee members that resulted in a unanimous report.

After three months of arduous work in Paris and Berlin, the Dawes Committee in April 1924 proposed a new schedule of annuities that would start out modestly and gradually increase to $625 million in 1929 (about 3.1 percent of German national income at the time). The committee sought to solve the controversy over German ability to pay by creating the office of agent-general in Berlin to oversee the workings of the scheme. It established a multilateral Transfer Committee to assume responsibility for converting German marks into foreign currency. It also elaborated guidelines for a new German central bank and set the stage for alignment of the Deutsche mark on the gold-based American dollar. All the European countries had some private objections to the package. British Treasury officials, stung by the preference for the dollar over sterling, referred to it privately as the Americans' "beastly plan," and the Germans immediately laid plans to demand another inquiry once a decent interval had elapsed. But under the circumstances none of the European countries could afford to voice their objections publicly. As Young candidly observed some months later, "The committee followed the best commercial and financial practice by having its goods sold before they were manufactured. In the language of the advertiser a 'consumer demand' was built up for the Dawes Report before anybody

Young (standing) giving advice on banking legislation to Senators Charles Townsend of Michigan and Carter Glass of Virginia, 1935 (courtesy of Harris & Ewing)

knew what it was to be and before a line of it had been put on paper."

J. P. Morgan & Company, the Wall Street bankers who would have to make the loan to Germany that would render the plan operational, still nourished strong objections. The Morgan partners considered the burdens on Germany excessive and the safeguards against another Ruhr occupation insufficiently categorical. "Now that Dawes and Owen have discovered the simple formula of making bread without flour," the leading analyst at Morgan wrote with heavy sarcasm, "the wonder is that no one thought of it before." While Dawes returned to the United States and plunged into a campaign for the vice-presidency, Young carried the principal burden of bringing the bankers around. At the London Conference of July-August 1924 he labored behind the scenes to work out a broadbased political settlement and to elaborate the institutional arrangements that would permit the Dawes Plan apparatus to function smoothly. Young also agreed to serve as interim agent-general to put the plan into operation. J. P. Morgan and Thomas Lamont, the bankers who had faced off against Young in London, initially suspected that the GE

chairman harbored the ambition to remain in Germany as a sort of economic dictator. The newspapers joked about "Owen the First." For a time tempers ran high. But Young persuaded Morgan that he sought merely to offer a temporary public service, and eventually former undersecretary of the Treasury S. Parker Gilbert, a candidate acceptable to Morgans, assumed the post of agent-general.

During the next four years European economies recovered smartly from the devastation of war. Americans invested so much money in Germany as to dwarf reparation outpayments, and the capital flow ran toward the Reich rather than the other way. But Young always thought investment in Germany a risky proposition, and his contacts with the oleaginous Hjalmar Schacht, president of the Reichsbank, led him to anticipate trouble sooner rather than later. In 1928 Young cooperated with Agent-General Gilbert in devising plans for a new committee that would fix reparations definitively before the Germans had a chance to default. Gilbert, Young, Secretary of the Treasury Andrew Mellon, and other parties to the scheme hoped to arrange a simultaneous write-down of reparations and the out-year annuities of European war debts to the United

Young (center) concluding the revised German war reparations schedule with Reichsbank president Hjalmar Schacht (left) and Banque de France official Emile Moreau, June 1929

States. However, the election of the highly nationalistic Herbert Hoover to the presidency in November 1928 made the latter idea infeasible. And though German foreign minister Gustav Stresemann had seemed to agree ahead of time to a standard German annuity of about $500 million a year, he could not control Schacht. When a new Expert Committee began its deliberations under the chairmanship of Young in February 1929, the prospects for an arrangement that all countries could endorse with enthusiasm seemed slight.

The negotiations of the Young Committee proved grueling and occasionally ugly. The figleaf of an investigation into German capacity to pay that had promoted good fellowship on the Dawes Committee almost totally disappeared. Schacht and his German colleagues insisted that they could not strike a deal at all without reacquiring the Polish Corridor and overseas colonies. The British and the Continental Allies engaged in an unedifying quarrel about how to apportion the diminished spoils. Wash-

ington, meanwhile, continued to snipe at the American delegates, whom it suspected of readiness to accept an implicit reduction of debts owing to the United States. Caught in the cross fire, Young sought to remain an "honest broker" and to preach the gospel that "any settlement was infinitely better than no settlement." Although the committee threatened numerous times to break up in disarray, it finally staggered toward agreement in June 1929. The Young Plan reduced immediate German obligations to just more than $400 million per year (around 2.1 percent of national income) and promulgated a 59-year schedule of payments. It provided for the withdrawal of the agent-general and other mechanisms for supervising the German economy; instead it placed responsibility for transfer squarely on the Reich. By separating the annuity into unconditional and conditional parts, with the latter matching Allied obligations to the United States, it established an unofficial link between reparations and war debts.

The most constructive feature of the Young Plan involved creation of a Bank for International Settlements (BIS) in Basel to facilitate reparation payments and counterdeflationary tendencies under the gold-exchange standard. Young and his expert advisers from the New York Federal Reserve Bank hoped that the acrimony over reparations would fade over time, and that the BIS would foster lasting cooperation among central bankers. The Young Plan went into effect, and the BIS began operation in the spring of 1930, but neither fulfilled its progenitors' hopes. While the Young Plan annuity almost certainly fell within German capacity to pay, the deepening Depression upset the political calculations upon which Young had relied. Hoover and his undersecretary of the Treasury bitterly resented the implicit link between reparations and debts. "The boys over there," they complained, "put it all over ours." Neither the Hoover administration nor Whitehall exhibited much enthusiasm for the BIS, which they regarded as a French-dominated institution. The Nazis and the Nationalists attacked the Young Plan as a form of "slavery" in the 1930 German Reichstag elections, and the Berlin government laid plans to repudiate it as soon as it decently could. In June 1931 Hoover proposed a one-year moratorium on reparation and debt payments without resort to the postponement procedures specified by the Young Plan, and by the time the moratorium expired the Allies had agreed to put an end to reparations altogether.

Despite his uneasy relations with Hoover, Young stood at the apex of his prestige in the early 1930s. Radicals did not like his attempt to obscure the purported realities of class conflict (Felix Frankfurter once described him as a "genial cuttlefish"), but moderate reformers by the same token appreciated his pragmatic approach to economic problems. As deputy chairman of the New York Federal Reserve Bank, Young played a central role in promoting open-market operations on a massive scale in the spring of 1932. At a time when economists still debated whether the purchase of government securities would produce the desired effect of increasing commercial bank liquidity, Young urged his colleagues to try the experiment. By July 1932 open-market operations had brought the monetary deflation in the United States to an end. Young spoke out also for self-liquidating public works to counteract the fall in output and employment, and in 1932 headed the Banking and Industrial Committees set up under the authority of the Fed to promote mortgage relief, housing construction, aid to railroads, and investments to stabilize bond and commodities markets.

Young was touted in many circles, especially in the John Raskob-Jouett Shouse wing of the Democratic party, which wished to head off Franklin Roosevelt for the presidential nomination in 1932. In other circumstances Young might have proven susceptible to a draft. In 1931-1932, however, his personal life fell apart. His mother died and his wife suffered a heart attack and became a chronic invalid. At the same time, although it remained a secret from everyone but his friend Gerard Swope, Young essentially went bankrupt. A congenital optimist for whom things had always gone well, Young purchased $1.8 million of GE and RCA stock on margin just before the 1929 stock market crash. Expecting a turnaround, he continued to buy more as the market steadily declined in 1930-1931. By the time he liquidated his holdings in desperation in the summer of 1931, he had a negative net worth of $2 million. Young reduced his standard of living and disposed of his precious collection of rare books, but he insisted on keeping the charitable pledges that he had made in easier times. In an old-fashioned display of fidelity to his word, he continued his contributions to St. Lawrence, the international relations school at The Johns Hopkins Univer-

sity, and the village of Van Hornesville. Young did not emerge fully from debtor status until 1950.

Young supported Roosevelt for president in 1932 as the lesser of evils. There was some talk of making him secretary of state. But Young believed the squire of Hyde Park too lightweight to deal effectively with the problems of the international economy, and for his part Roosevelt shunned a close association with a representative of the public utility industry. Young tried to suspend judgment on the National Recovery Administration (with which his partner Swope was associated as head of its Business Advisory Board), and he actively supported other early New Deal measures. He felt that business had failed to discipline itself and that under the circumstances no way existed to avoid increased public control of the economy. But Roosevelt's policies in the Second New Deal progressively alienated him. He opposed the Banking Act of 1935, which centralized control of monetary affairs at the Federal Reserve Board and undermined the prerogatives of the regional reserve banks. He decried the Holding Company Act of 1935. Although he worked to bring about an amicable compromise between the utilities and the government, he became disillusioned when it turned out that the Securities and Exchange Commission had prepared a legal suit against Electric Bond and Share while he was in the next room negotiating in good faith. "It was not only in dealing with other governments," he remarked in a disabused mood, "that the New Deal was ruling out the ordinary decencies." Young did not oppose development of the Tennessee Valley Authority as a "yardstick" for measuring utility rates, but he came to suspect that the administration had a demagogic political agenda and would not deal fairly with the power companies under any circumstances. While Young took part in discussions with Adolf Berle, Rexford Tugwell, and John L. Lewis to explore the possibilities of tripartite business-labor-government cooperation to counter the economic downturn of 1937-1938, Roosevelt showed little personal interest in the "politics of productivity." Increasingly, Young began to suspect that at bottom Roosevelt preferred perpetual class warfare to economic recovery. Feeling out of place in Washington, he retreated to GE offices and the lecture circuit.

Young and Swope both retired at GE at the end of 1939, but, when their successors were called to Washington for war-related duties, they returned to harness temporarily in 1942-1944. During the war Young became what he called a "handyman" who shouldered various second-echelon defense advisory tasks; he took particular interest in the problems of industrial training for youth. In 1946 Governor Thomas Dewey appointed Young the head of a Temporary Commission on the Need for a State University. Young's formative experience at St. Lawrence led him to prefer many small campuses to one large one, and the commission report reflecting that preference formed the blueprint for the State University of New York. In 1947, Young worked under Averell Harriman on the President's Commission for Foreign Aid and helped to implement the Marshall Plan. In 1948-1949 he served with Herbert Hoover's Commission on the Organization of the Executive Branch of the Government, and had the satisfaction of a belated reconciliation with his erstwhile nemesis from Young Plan days.

Young had always maintained that old men should know when to let the reins of power slacken, and he greatly enjoyed retirement. After the death of his first wife, he made a happy second marriage in 1937. In later years he spent much of his time at his spouse's citrus grove in St. Augustine, Florida, and with his grandchildren in Van Hornesville. He referred to himself as a "rocking chair consultant" and sat for an interview on beginning life at sixty-five. He died of abdominal cancer on July 11, 1962.

Publications:

Address at The Johns Hopkins University, February 23rd, 1925 (New York: New York Committee for the Endowment of the Walter Hines Page School of International Relations, 1925);

Address, National Electric Light Association, 53rd Annual Convention, June 19, 1930 (San Francisco, 1930);

Address to Graduates, St. Lawrence University (Saratoga Springs, N.Y., 1931);

St. Lawrence Summer School Commencement Address (New York, 1931);

Higher Courage, being an address delivered at the commencement exercises of the University of Notre Dame, June 5, 1932 (New York: Dutton, 1932).

References:

Hugh G. J. Aitken, *Syntony and Spark: The Origins of Radio* (New York: Wiley, 1976);

Denise Artaud, *La question des dettes interalliées et la reconstruction de l'Europe (1917-1929)*, 2 volumes (Lille & Paris: Librairie Honoré Champion, 1978);

Erik Barnouw, *A History of Broadcasting in the United States*, volume 1: *A Tower in Babel* (New York: Oxford University Press, 1966);

John M. Carroll, "Owen D. Young and German Reparations: The Diplomacy of an Enlightened Businessman," in *U.S. Diplomats in Europe: America's Search for Peace, 1919-1941*, edited by Kenneth Paul Jones (Santa Barbara, Cal.: ABC Clio, 1980);

Josephine Young Case and Everett Needham Case, *Owen D. Young and American Enterprise* (Boston: Godine, 1982);

Stephen V. O. Clarke, *Central Bank Cooperation, 1924-1931* (New York: Federal Reserve Bank of New York, 1967);

Frank Costigliola, *Awkward Dominion: American Political, Economic, and Cultural Relations with Europe, 1919-1933* (Ithaca: N.Y.: Cornell University Press, 1984);

Roberta A. Dayer, *Bankers and Diplomats in China, 1917-1925: The Anglo-American Relationship* (London: Cass, 1981);

Frank Freidel, *Franklin D. Roosevelt: Launching the New Deal* (Boston: Little Brown, 1973);

Ellis Hawley, *The New Deal and the Problem of Monopoly* (Princeton: Princeton University Press, 1966);

Wolfgang J. Helbich, *Die Reparationen in dar Ära Brüning: zur Bedeutung des Young-Plans für die deutsche Politik 1930 bis 1932* (Berlin: Colloquium Verlag, 1962);

Michael J. Hogan, *Informal Entente: The Private Structure of Cooperation in Anglo-American Economic Diplomacy, 1918-1928* (Columbia: University of Missouri Press, 1977);

Brady Alexander Hughes, "Owen D. Young and American Foreign Policy, 1919-1929," dissertation, University of Wisconsin, 1969;

Jon Jacobson, *Locarno Diplomacy: Germany and the West, 1925-1929* (Princeton: Princeton University Press, 1972);

Melvyn P. Leffler, *The Elusive Quest: America's Pursuit of European Stability and French Security, 1919-1933* (Chapel Hill: University of North Carolina Press, 1979);

Werner Link, *Die amerikanische Stabilisierungspolitik in Deutschland 1921-1932* (Düsseldorf: Droste Verlag, 1970);

David Loth, *Swope of GE* (New York: Simon & Schuster, 1958);

Kim McQuaid, "Competition, Cartelization, and the Corporate Ethic: GE during the New Deal Era, 1933-1940," *American Journal of Economics and Sociology*, 36 (November 4, 1977): 417-428;

McQuaid, "Corporate Liberalism in the American Business Community, 1920-1940," *Business History Review*, 52 (Autumn 1978): 342-368;

McQuaid, "Young, Swope, and GE's 'New Capitalism': A Study in Corporate Liberalism, 1920-1933," *American Journal of Economics and Sociology*, 36 (November 1, 1977): 323-334;

Proctor Reid, "Private and Public Regimes: International Cartelization in the Electrical Equipment Industry in an Era of Hegemonic Change, 1919-1939," dissertation, School of Advanced International Studies, Johns Hopkins University, 1988;

Stephen A. Schuker, "American Foreign Policy and the Young Plan, 1929," in *Konstellationen internationaler Politik 1924-1932*, edited by Gustav Schmidt (Bochum: N. Brockmeyer, 1983), pp. 122-130;

Schuker, *American "Reparations" to Germany, 1919-33: Implications for the Third-World Debt Crisis* (Princeton: Princeton Studies in International Finance, 1988);

Schucker, *The End of French Predominance in Europe: The Financial Crisis of 1924 and the Adoption of the Dawes Plan* (Chapel Hill: University of North Carolina Press, 1976);

Lola L. Szladits, *Owen D. Young, Book Collector* (New York: Reading Books for the New York Public Library, 1974);

Ida M. Tarbell, *Owen D. Young: A New Type of Industrial Leader* (New York: Macmillan, 1932);

Eckhard Wandel, *Die Bedeutung der USA für das deutsche Reparationsproblem 1924-1929* (Tübingen: J. C. B. Mohr, 1971).

Archives:

The Owen D. Young Papers, one of the most important collections for business and diplomatic history of the interwar era, are located in the Owen D. Young Library, St. Lawrence University, Canton, New York. Other collections containing significant amounts of Young material include the Stuart Crocker Papers, Library of Congress; Federal Reserve Bank of New York; George Harrison Papers, Columbia University; Thomas W. Lamont Papers, Harvard Business School; and the David Sarnoff Research Center Archives, Princeton, N.J. Young's collection of rare books was acquired for the Berg Collection of the New York Public Library.

Contributors

Sara Alpern–*Texas A&M University*
Leonard J. Arrington–*Utah State University*
Robert D. Auerbach–*University of California, Riverside*
David T. Beito–*University of Nevada, Las Vegas*
Michael D. Bordo–*Rutgers University*
W. Elliot Brownlee–*University of California, Santa Barbara*
Walter L. Buenger–*Texas A&M University*
Thomas F. Cargill–*University of Nevada at Reno*
Anthony Chan–*University of Dayton*
Robert J. Chandler–*Wells Fargo Bank*
Mary F. Cordato–*Garden City, New York*
John M. Coski–*Museum of the Confederacy*
John B. Davis–*Marquette University*
Peter De Trolio III–*University of Dayton*
Lynne Pierson Doti–*Chapman College*
Scott W. Fischer–*University of Virginia*
Douglas Fisher–*North Carolina State University*
David M. Fitzsimons–*University of Michigan*
Larry G. Gerber–*Auburn University*
Marcia Grodsky–*University of Pittsburgh*
Thomas F. Huertas–*Citibank NA*
Gregory S. Hunter–*Long Island University*
Rebecca Strand Johnson–*Loyola University of Chicago*
Alec B. Kirby–*George Washington University*
Benjamin J. Klebaner–*City College, CUNY*
Barry Koling–*Marine Midland Banks*
Michael F. Konig–*Westfield State College*
Diane B. Kunz–*Yale University*
John Landry–*Brown University*
John Majewski–*University of California, Los Angeles*
Tiarr Martin–*University of Dayton*
Martha May–*Bowdoin College*
William C. McNeil–*Barnard College, Columbia University*
Douglas K. Pearce–*North Carolina State University*
Gary M. Pecquet–*Southwest Texas State University*
Edwin J. Perkins–*University of Southern California*
Barry Provorse–*Documentary Book Publishers*
Olin S. Pugh–*University of South Carolina*
C. Elizabeth Raymond–*University of Nevada at Reno*
Stephen A. Schuker–*Brandeis University*
Anna J. Schwartz–*National Bureau of Economic Research*
Larry Schweikart–*University of Dayton*
James Smallwood–*University of Texas at Tyler*
Thomas G. Smith–*Nichols College*
Richard H. Timberlake–*University of Georgia*
Marc A. Weiss–*Columbia University*

Contributors

Robert Craig West–*Federal Reserve Bank of Kansas City*
Steven Wheeler–*New York Stock Exchange Archives*
Eugene N. White–*Rutgers University*
Jeffrey Williams–*Stanford University*

Index

The following index includes names of people, corporations, organizations, laws, and technologies. It also includes key terms such as *automatic teller machines, branch banking,* etc.

A page number in *italic* indicates the first page of an entry devoted to the subject. *Illus.* indicates a picture of the subject.

Index